KISS TOMORROW GOODBYE
The Barbara Payton Story

Kiss Tomorrow Goodbye
The Barbara Payton Story

Second Edition

by
John O'Dowd

BearManor Media
2015

Kiss Tomorrow Goodbye, The Barbara Payton Story
Second Edition

©2015 John O'Dowd

ALL RIGHTS RESERVED.

No part of this book may be reproduced in any form or by any means, electronic, mechanical, digital, photocopying, or recording, except for inclusion of a review, without permission in writing from the publisher.

Published in the USA by:

BEARMANORMEDIA
P.O. BOX 71426
ALBANY, GEORGIA 31708
www.BearManorMedia.com

ISBN-10: 1-59393-443-2

ISBN-13: 978-1-59393-443-9

TABLE OF CONTENTS

Acknowledgements vii
Foreword ix

CHAPTER ONE	*Where Dreams Die*	1
CHAPTER TWO	*Roots*	5
CHAPTER THREE	*Running with the Wind*	23
CHAPTER FOUR	*Reaching for a Dream*	31
CHAPTER FIVE	*Like a Mustang on the Loose*	53
CHAPTER SIX	*Dark Clouds on the Horizon*	75
CHAPTER SEVEN	*World by the Tail*	85
CHAPTER EIGHT	*Fast Times in Hollywood*	103
CHAPTER NINE	*Candlelight and Champagne*	119
CHAPTER TEN	*Front and Center*	145
CHAPTER ELEVEN	*Head Over Halo*	159
CHAPTER TWELVE	*Cowboy in a Bathing Suit*	181
CHAPTER THIRTEEN	*Love's Jealous Rage*	197
CHAPTER FOURTEEN	*Damage Control, Hollywood Style*	217
CHAPTER FIFTEEN	*A Nightclub Spit-Spat*	229
CHAPTER SIXTEEN	*All the Wrong Moves*	237
CHAPTER SEVENTEEN	*Boozin' and Brawlin'*	243
CHAPTER EIGHTEEN	*Over-Exposed*	257
CHAPTER NINETEEN	*Bad Blonde*	279
CHAPTER TWENTY	*Riot on Sunset Strip*	293
CHAPTER TWENTY-ONE	*Hot Love Hits Tank Towns*	305
CHAPTER TWENTY-TWO	*Back in the Arms of Trouble*	319

CHAPTER TWENTY-THREE	*High Times and Heartaches*	327
CHAPTER TWENTY-FOUR	*Fur Coats and…Heroin?*	345
CHAPTER TWENTY-FIVE	*The End of a Career*	353
CHAPTER TWENTY-SIX	*Wild Nights, Wasted Days*	359
CHAPTER TWENTY-SEVEN	*Down Mexico Way*	369
CHAPTER TWENTY-EIGHT	*Busted!*	375
CHAPTER TWENTY-NINE	*The Greatest Loss of All*	385
CHAPTER THIRTY	*Battle-Scarred*	397
CHAPTER THIRTY-ONE	*Going for Broke*	407
CHAPTER THIRTY-TWO	*Drifting*	415
CHAPTER THIRTY-THREE	*With the Best of Intentions*	423
CHAPTER THIRTY-FOUR	*Hanging on to Nothing*	437
CHAPTER THIRTY-FIVE	*Drowning in Memories*	455
CHAPTER THIRTY-SIX	*The Road to Hell*	461
CHAPTER THIRTY-SEVEN	*Lost in the Fog*	475
CHAPTER THIRTY-EIGHT	*I Am Not Ashamed!*	479
CHAPTER THIRTY-NINE	*Trapped in the House of the Rising Sun*	495
CHAPTER FORTY	*Down in Dreamtown*	509
CHAPTER FORTY-ONE	*Detour to Death*	517
CHAPTER FORTY-TWO	*Death of a Prince…Death of a Pauper*	527
CHAPTER FORTY-THREE	*The Darkest Hour*	535
CHAPTER FORTY-FOUR	*Crossing the Bridge of Sighs*	553
CHAPTER FORTY-FIVE	*Memories of a Life Lost*	561
CHAPTER FORTY-SIX	*And Life Goes On*	581
	Epilogue	591
	Notes	593
	Selected Bibliography	601
	Index	607

ACKNOWLEDGEMENTS

I wish to thank: The Lord, Jesus Christ, for His many blessings in my life; Saint Anthony and Saint Francis, for being my guardian angels and most loyal mentors; my beloved parents, Tot and Bette O'Dowd (who taught me that kindness, gratitude and compassion are, by far, the greatest human traits of all, and whose exemplary character and unconditional love I continue to miss), and the O'Dowd, Manella and Bock families for giving me wonderful roots for which I am forever grateful; a special thanks to Steve Bock, the greatest friend I have ever known; to my sisters, Kathy O'Dowd Allen (and her family) and Peggy O'Dowd; to my beloved companion animals over the years: Baby and Rusty, Beau-Beau and El Gato, Licorice, Whiskers, and the unforgettable Susie Wong; to my friends (in alphabetical order): Donna Bushey Galella, Kathy Matta, Barbara Michaelson, the late Lois Schreiner, Janine Torsiello, Ron and Gina Ur (and family), and to all my other friends (you know who you are, and I appreciate you); to John Lee Payton and Jan Zollinger Redfield, whose warmth, friendship, encouragement and deep generosity of spirit got me through the many rough spots; to Tony Provas, Frank Redfield, the late Colonel John Payton, Barbara Payton Miller, Karen Payton, Leslie Redfield, Walter Burr, Tom Neal, Jr., Jana Payton-Lackey and Tina Ballard, for their trust in me in documenting the lives of their loved ones; to the beautiful Lane Bradbury, Pat Daisy, Diane Jordan, Yvette Vickers, Conny Van Dyke, Sami Jo Cole, Jody Miller, Sally Todd and Lindsay Bloom; a special thanks to screenwriter Linda Boroff for her expert editing of the second printing of this book, and for her stunning and powerful work on the Barbara Payton film script; to producers Ira Besserman and Barrett Stuart for believing in the merits of Barbara's story; to Webmaster Lynn Powell Dougherty of www.LynnPDesign.com, for her terrific book cover design and her management of the Barbara Payton Web site: www.hollywoodstarletbarbarapayton.com; to Beverly Washburn, Unita Akins, Mike Farmer, Stacy Harris, Bob Kramer, Jennifer Anne McMullen, Eileen Grimes, Douglas Mason, the late Stephen Daddario, Kent Adamson, Barbara Buffington, Kevan MacDonald, Dagmar Meyer-Historische Fahrkultur, Josie Coccia, Shannon Kennedy Onasis-Ore, Andy Martello, Jake Hinkson, Ann Meyer, Mike Barnum, Lee Martin, Steve Thompson, Dolores Heitman, Gary Weickart, Ralph Berger and Carolyn W.; and to Lisa Burks, Robert Easton, Mark Moran and Mark Sceurman at WEIRD NJ Magazine, David Alexander Nahmod, Roger Galloway, David Murcott, Maximillien de Lafayette, Michael Adams, Ron Green, John W. Thomas, Paul Ybarra, Guy Savage, Joe Mannetti, Lawrence Fultz, Jr., Estrellita C. Alonzo, Jery Tillotson, Phil Hall, Wheez Von Klaw, Nicole Chang, Jeremy Cullen, Stanley J. Neu, Jennifer E. Williams, Jim Lutes, Andre Soares, Norma Ames, Brian Taggart, Don Lemmon, Joseph Peterson, Steve Hayes, Mickey Knox, Stone Wallace, David Drake, Robert Rotter, Kirk Crivello, Larry Kleno, Julie Sanges, Joe Lesnick, Donna Martell, Richard Fleischer, A.C. Lyles, Bob Lippert, Jr., Cheryl Christie, Laura Wagner, Lee Wiseman, the late Alan Betrock, Michael Stein, Joe Kane, Michael J. Weldon, Beverly McColloch, Jonathan at Michael Ochs Archives, Berniece Johnson, Steve Sullivan, Coco Olson, Liz Smith, Dr. Joyce Brothers, Randal Barrack, Robert Polito, Bill "Red" Hilser, Norma "Knockers" Dodson, the late John Rayborn, Bob Rains, Millie Peterson, Mete Sarabi, Nick Bougas, Pat O'Connor, Jeff Rankin, Dace Taube, Carolyn Cole, Richard Workman, Peter Canavese, Steve Richards, Dan Leissner, the late Tim Choate, Peter Steelquist; to all of Barbara's devoted fans and friends; and lastly, a special thanks to a lot of editors and publishers who told me that a book on Barbara Payton would never be published, and to Ben Ohmart at BearManor Media, a fair and patient man (and, unlike many others, a true professional) who believed in Barbara and me, and gave me the chance when I needed it most.

This book is dedicated to all of society's lost, forgotten and disenfranchised—with the hope that they will find lasting peace in their lives, and a realization of all their dreams, somewhere down the road.

And, of course, to Barbara: Your suffering was as great as your beauty. Thank you for sticking by me and seeing me through this project. I hope this is the book you needed me to write for you.

Foreword

It has been over 50 years since I have seen my mother, Barbara Payton. For a few minutes one afternoon when I was nine years old, she swept me into her arms, and we held onto one another as if for life itself. Then she was gone.

Much has been written about her, most of it to sell magazines or books, little of it true. Yet, it is undeniably true my mother led a life that was bound to raise eyebrows and heartbeats. Equally, it was inevitable that her life caused and still causes lip-smacking glee among the professionally indignant and self-righteous. So many mistakes, so many bad choices.

She is no embarrassment to me. My mother was a strong woman, full of life, and she lived it on a different plane from the rest of the world. Then, Barbara Payton was an easy target for that special brand of puritanical hypocrisy typical of the times. Today, she would be right at home among those who live out on the very edge of life, and likely would be celebrated for it, rather than condemned. My mother was outrageously easy, and impossibly complex.

For me, of course, she was simply my mother. She was happiness, play, laughter and dance. She was shopping and parties and nights on the town. She was my safe harbor, my loving hugs and sweet kisses, my companion and my friend. She was, and of course she still is, loved and loving. With her I felt safe, and sure. Without her, I was lost and very much alone for many years.

I have resisted any books or movies about my mother because they always had only one raison d'etre: Trash sells. The ghoulish necrophilia of those who have used her since her death, as many did when she was alive, disgusted me all through the years, and it still does today.

Then, I met John O'Dowd. I've watched this book come together, virtually sentence by sentence, as he tried to tell her life story without fawning or flinching. It has often been an agony for him, and certainly reading it has been painful for me. Yet, it does what she could not. It takes all the shattered bits and puts them together to reflect a life lived fully, for better or worse. John does not render judgment. He neither condemns nor celebrates her. He simply offers fact, speculation, memory and context from prodigious research and personal interviews.

Readers of *Kiss Tomorrow Goodbye* are left to do the work of coming to grips with the complexity of Barbara Payton themselves. It is my hope that they will find that some of it resonates in their lives. If, occasionally, they find themselves on common ground, then, perhaps, at the end they will feel compassion for this wondrous woman. Perhaps they will even feel respect for the mysteries of her life. If so, I will be content.

– John Lee Payton

In the ever-burgeoning constellation of fallen Hollywood stars, hangs one faded and forgotten nova that, for a brief moment in the 1950s, lit up the Sunset Strip and the motion picture soundstage alike. A relatively obscure actress of estimable talent and even greater potential, the gorgeous and sexy Barbara Payton had an impressive start in motion pictures and was poised at the very brink of film stardom when a series of turbulent events in her life derailed her career and sent her plummeting into oblivion. Like Marilyn Monroe, a stunning blonde, and the possessor of a shimmering and incandescent beauty, Barbara (unlike Monroe) flashed but briefly across the Hollywood landscape. From the outset, a blazing fireball burning out-of- control, she quickly flamed out, and then crumbled to earth in a pile of ash.

During the course of a short life packed with more bedlam than most could ever imagine, she rubbed shoulders with many of Hollywood's elite (including Bob Hope, Gary Cooper and Gregory Peck) and with several of its artistic geniuses (among them, master glamour photographer Andre de Dienes and film-noir icon Edgar G. Ulmer), as well as with a host of other, far less desirable creatures; many of whom led lives so dangerous, they could have been characters lifted from the pages of James Ellroy's *L.A. Confidential*.

Indeed, much of Barbara Payton's story—from her restless, small-town upbringing and her inevitable exodus to Hollywood, to her final slide into an obscurity far worse than her humble beginnings—reads like a cheap and tawdry paperback come-to-life. Hers is perhaps the ultimate cautionary tale; an almost stereotypical story of a gutsy and self-assured young girl from the Midwest who hit Hollywood in the late 1940s, equipped with little more than a suitcase full of dreams, a ravenous hunger for fame, and a devastating beauty, only to see each one of her dreams destroyed by a disastrous private life that led her straight through the gates of Hell. Barbara's ill-fated career shot across the motion picture stratosphere in record-time, only to collapse in a devastating free-fall from which she would never recover.

A rowdy and unrestrained iconoclast trapped in an outwardly staid period in American culture, Barbara has come to symbolize the dark and sordid side of postwar Hollywood. If Mickey Spillane and James Ellroy had ever collaborated on the quintessential bad-girl character, the offspring of their literary union might well have been a creation similar to the tough and intrepid Barbara Payton. A quick-thinking, wild and reckless knockout who lived her life as if there were no tomorrow—such were the qualities rather joyously displayed by this compelling and archetypal figure. In an era where conventionalism was the mandatory order of the day, she shamelessly defied society's taboos and restrictions, and was seemingly impervious to any criticism of her freewheeling lifestyle.

And yet, beneath the hard-partying, expletive-spouting, Bad Girl veneer, there was more, much more, to Barbara. Throughout her life, in fact, she routinely displayed such paradoxical behavior that it often confused and confounded those who knew her best. A loving and fiercely devoted mother to her son, she was often mercurial and less than loyal to the husbands and the many lovers in her life. Outwardly cocksure and brazen, she hid below that flashy facade a painful self-doubt and an almost childlike need to please others—a recipe that for Barbara would only spell disaster. Described differently by various individuals who knew her as "a witless, mean-spirited, man-chasing floozy," and "the most objectionable person you'd ever want to meet," to "a kind, warm and wholesome girl whose greatest fault was her almost total naiveté," the unsophisticated Minnesota country girl-turned-Hollywood seductress was nothing if not a true enigma. In the words of her loyal barrister, Milton Golden, "She

Hollywood's Sunset Boulevard: the place of Barbara's lost dreams. Courtesy of University of Southern California Library/Dept. of Special Collections/L.A. Examiner Collection

was as much at home doing needlepoint or upholstering a couch as she was cutting a rug in a Hollywood nightclub."

The true tragedy of Barbara's life is that she was never able to meld the wildly vacillating and contradictory elements of her persona into a life she could manage. As she ventured further down a misguided path, deep into the tangled jungles of a sex-and-sin-drenched Hollywood, whatever small-town virtues she possessed, disappeared in a winding maze of men, booze and notoriety. In the end, her beautiful blue eyes, once the mirror of a vast array of riches Hollywood bestows on but a chosen few, would reflect only the tortured memories of a million shattered dreams.

Chapter One:
Where Dreams Die

At first, the sanitation workers thought it was a bag of trash. Only when the two men got a closer look did they realize that what they had thought was a pile of garbage scattered beside the dumpster they had come to empty, was instead the body of a woman lying on her side. The location was a vacant parking lot hidden behind a group of stores on Sunset Boulevard and Fairfax Avenue, in the heart of Hollywood. The dumpster, and two others nearby, faced Fairfax, servicing a Thrifty Drugstore, an A&P supermarket and The Brush Wave Beauty Shop. Although Los Angeles is known for its temperate climate, at 5:30 a.m. in February, the chilly air can often hover somewhere near the 45-degree mark. Despite this, the woman was clad only in a thin, cotton shift and a pair of flip-flops. With the smudge of dried blood caked thickly around her nose and upper lip, she appeared at first glance to be dead.

Standing over her, the garbage men could see the mass of angry bruises and welts that covered her arms and legs—like purple inkblots, vivid, even in the subdued light of dawn. The woman's dirty-blonde hair, with two inches of dark roots showing, was bunched in knots atop her head, like some tangled bee's nest gone awry. So battered was her appearance that it made it almost impossible to determine what she looked like underneath all the layers of dried blood and grime. One of the men later said that the sight of her crumpled body lying on the pavement made it seem as if she had been "dumped out of the sky." When at last they noticed that she was still breathing, the two workers rushed to get help.

Later that morning, word spread quickly down Sunset Boulevard and all across town that the woman the men had found was none other than Barbara Payton, a former movie star and tabloid queen, and a longtime denizen of Hollywood's Skid Row. Those who remembered the name were not surprised, for despite the fact that her film career had ended 12 years earlier, in a blaze of sordid scandal and poisonous publicity, Barbara had never really left Hollywood, at least not for long.

From the late 1950s, right up until her death in 1967, she had remained a conspicuous presence in town, not as a film player or as a celebrity, but as an in-your-face reminder of how life in Hollywood, for some, can go so terribly, terribly wrong. In spite of facing insurmountable odds that would, in time, destroy her, Barbara couldn't bear to turn away from the place of her lingering hopes and dreams, and thus see them die forever. So she stayed there for years, hoping for another chance at Hollywood's brass ring. But instead of finding cheering crowds and klieg lights awaiting her, Barbara would find only the deafening silence of a town that no longer cared.

When Barbara Payton was found lying beside the garbage dumpster in February 1967, she had spent much of the last decade of her life in a self-imposed prison that spanned a 20-to-25-block radius of Hollywood—an area roughly the size of New York City's Central Park. Hidden somewhere in all the gloss and tinsel, Barbara figured, were the remnants of who she used to be and what she once had, and if she looked hard enough, surely she could reclaim all that she had lost. But, by the time she landed unconscious in that Sunset Boulevard parking lot, Barbara had long since bypassed the gloss and the tinsel, and had instead found herself laid to waste and stranded on a sad, lonely road of physical, mental and emotional ruin. That she had managed to survive the previous ten years of her life had amazed those who knew her and the unrelenting hell she had endured.

Barbara Payton's many attempts to embrace the mythical dream of Hollywood delivered her instead to its darkest and ugliest corners. Few others have fallen from its most coveted opulence to its deepest squalor in such rapid and complete fashion, and fewer still, with the absolute determination Barbara possessed, to completely destroy her life. When taking into consideration the many enemies she made during her 20 years in The Land of Lost Dreams, it is somehow ironic that she would be found lying beside a trash bin, for Barbara truly had been chewed up by the Hollywood machine, and then spit out like so much garbage. Her meteoric plunge from the pinnacle of movieland infamy into the deepest bowels of L.A.'s back streets and alleys had brought her to where she was now: lying alone in a contorted heap beneath a mound of rotting trash.

In the gray dawn of that February morning in 1967, Barbara Payton was fast approaching her final exit. The path that led her to this place of such utter solitude and inner desolation had begun 39 years earlier, in a small, Midwestern town: 2,000 miles, and a thousand lifetimes, away.

CHAPTER TWO:
Roots

There is an old saying that "Minnesota's way of life seems permanently positioned in the middle of the American dream." If this is true, it has proved especially so for the hardworking citizens of Cloquet, located west of Duluth on the banks of the St. Louis River. One of the state's leading lumber towns, Cloquet had its official beginnings in July 1857 when a group of men built the first saw mill in the area and started The Knife Falls Lumber Company. Originally home to members of the Sioux and Chippewa tribes, Cloquet, from the French word *Claquet*, meaning "sound of the mill," soon attracted a large contingent of immigrants from Western Europe, who found the dense and verdant hillsides to be reminiscent of their beloved homeland. Over the next several decades, both the town's population and its many lumber mills prospered, and by the early 1900s Cloquet's residents numbered a healthy 7,000.

Despite its auspicious beginnings, the dream almost died for the people of Cloquet when the town was entirely destroyed by a forest fire on October 12, 1918. What had started out as a clear and breezy Indian summer morning, ended in a seething holocaust when brush fires, stoked by 75 mile-per-hour winds, enveloped the town and left it in ruins. Smouldering peat bogs and passing trains sent sparks into the dry countryside and were eventually blamed for starting the conflagration that was actually 50 to 100 forest fires merged into one. Although only five lives were lost in its flames, the physical damage to the town was devastating.

While a catastrophic event like the Fire of 1918 might have crushed the collective spirit of a townspeople of less feisty mettle, Cloquet's citizen's were a robust lot, and immediately banded together in the fire's aftermath to rebuild their lives, literally, from the ground up. This determined, blue-collar work ethic, fueled by dreams of a better life, created a town of tough and irrepressible survivors. Home to about 11,000 in 2006, the close-knit community known as Tree City, U.S.A., stays rooted in a strong and unwavering Midwestern mind-set of solid conservative principles that continues to flourish despite the changing social and economic times.

By 1918, Weyerhauser Timber had replaced The Knife Falls Lumber Company as the most successful forestry business in Cloquet and was responsible for providing hundreds of jobs for its residents. One of them was Erwin Lee Redfield, who began working for Weyerhauser in his early teens, as an apprentice to his father, Frank, an independent building contractor who had a long-standing agreement with Weyerhauser to build lumber camps in the area.

Born May 27, 1863 in Elva, Wisconsin, Frank L. Redfield was the son of Warren and Harriet Redfield, both former residents of Cloquet. During the Civil War, Warren had served as a musician in the First Minnesota Volunteer Infantry and later worked as a blacksmith in both Minnesota and Wisconsin. Although Warren and Harriet lived in Elva for several years, their son Frank came to Cloquet as a young man in 1885, and married the former Mabel Ann McNitt on August 26, 1887. Soon afterward, Frank and Mabel moved 230 miles south to the town of Albert Lea, Minnesota, where their four children, Fay, Frank Jr. (a.k.a. Tim), Murel and Erwin were born.

Shortly after Erwin's birth in 1899, the couple moved their family back to Cloquet, where Frank began working as a contractor. Further details of the Redfield family's early years in Elva, Albert Lea and Cloquet remain sketchy, according to Erwin's son (also named Frank), who says, "We know our ancestors on the Redfield side are of English descent, but the family journal and most of Cloquet's town records burnt up in the fire of 1918, and with them, unfortunately, went a lot of our history."

Despite the loss of these documents, and a distinct mulishness among many of the family's current members to discuss any of their relatives, living or deceased, it is known that the Redfields were one of Cloquet's oldest and more prominent families. The elder Frank Redfield was a longtime member of the local Masonic Lodge and had also served as the town's postmaster for several years. In addition, he and his family enjoyed both a business and personal association with Rudolph Weyerhauser and his sons that had proved quite rewarding.

Frank was friendly with the Weyerhauser boys and found a staunch supporter in Rudolph, who nurtured Frank's goals of purchasing some of the area's prized property of Red Norway Pine to build new homes for the town's residents. The Weyerhausers successfully managed a tree nursery dubbed "The Experimental Forest," and Frank hoped to develop a similar business in time. Over the next few years, he banked much of what he earned at his company and eventually bought several acres of timberland for harvesting lumber that government engineers would then transport across the country by railroad.

Following the 1918 fire and the loss of much of this property, Frank received a large claim settlement from the state for the land that had been destroyed. He continued working as a building contractor and was responsible for rebuilding much of Cloquet's business and residential sections. A strong believer in diversifying his interests, he later operated a cabinet molding mill behind his house on Chestnut Street.

Frank's son, Erwin Lee, was said to be a headstrong and rebellious youngster who often incited his father's anger with his defiant behavior. Erwin's grandson, Leslie (Les) Redfield, recalls one such story, related to him by his grandfather: "Grandpa Lee told me that he sometimes carried a shotgun to school so he could shoot at ducks and geese on his way home. One day he used an entire box of 25 shells and brought home 22 quail. Lee said his father wound up giving him a real 'whuppin' for wasting all those shells on such small birds."

As a child, Erwin Lee developed a severe and embarrassing speech impediment that would plague him for the rest of his life. "He had a very fast and choppy way of speaking," explains Les, "like he wanted to get everything out at once. I have often wondered if this was a by-product of his difficult childhood." Les's theory gains further credence when one considers that Frank L. Redfield was, by all accounts, a stern and unyielding disciplinarian who demanded that everyone in his dominion toe the line, or risk expulsion. Perhaps as a result of being raised in this kind of environment, "Lee was not a warm and fuzzy kind of person," adds Les.

By the early 1920s, Erwin Lee (now nicknamed "Flip" by family and friends) had grown into a tall and strapping young man and was courting Mabel Irene Todahl, a lovely Norwegian girl whose parents, Ida and Knute, had migrated from Norway to Canada and then to Little Falls, Minnesota, where Mabel was born in 1905. She was one of six siblings, the others being Dora, Selvin, Mildred, Daniel and Eleanor. Later, the Todahls moved northeast to Cloquet, where Knute Todahl secured a position as an operating engineer at Weyerhauser. He eventually bought some land and built a house for his family on Spring Lake Road. It was beneath the towering pines of this cold, rustic Eden of wind and fire that Flip and Mabel met, and were later married.

Shortly after their wedding, Flip left his job at Weyerhauser Timber, and he and Mabel opened a combination ice cream parlor and small restaurant on the corner of Avenue C and Arch Street, in the busier west end of town. The building was owned by Frank L. Redfield, and included a small, two-bedroom apartment above the restaurant in which Flip and Mabel resided. Within the walls of these humble quarters, their daughter, Barbara Lee, entered the world on November 16, 1927, followed a few years later, on April 19, 1931, by a son, Frank Leslie III (named after Flip's father and older brother).

Barbara Luokkala, a relative whose mother was a first cousin of the Redfield children, says she remembers hearing what an extraordinarily beautiful baby Barbara Lee was, "…with hair so blonde it was almost snow-white, and the deepest, most beautiful blue eyes. I heard that Mabel, in particular, was completely bowled over by Barbara's beauty. She was said to adore her, right from the start."

Beautiful baby Barbara Lee Redfield. Even as a small child, Barbara had a kinship with the camera. Courtesy of Jan Redfield

One of Cloquet's two most famous daughters (actress Jessica Lange being the other). Courtesy of Jan Redfield

To those who knew her best, Mabel Todahl Redfield will forever be remembered as a kind and warmhearted lady whose love for her family was always unwavering and without provision. When Flip first met her, Mabel had a quiet and dignified air about her, born not of a wealthy upbringing, but of a strict religious background, with strong ties to the Norwegian Lutheran Church. This was in striking contrast to Flip, who was a freethinking hellion, known in their small town, along with his older sister Fay, as "The Redfield Rebels." As hard as he worked at his apprentice position at Weyerhauser Timber, Flip Redfield liked to smoke and drink a lot, too. His marriage to a lady as refined as Mabel was said to have caught both of their families off guard.

Frank and Barbara Lee Redfield (c. 1932). Courtesy of Star Tribune

Flip's father, family patriarch Frank L. Redfield, allegedly condemned the union at first, mostly due to Mabel's Norwegian heritage. Never one to mince words, Frank made it known that he would have preferred for his son to have married either an English or a German girl instead. In time, however, he and the rest of the Redfields grew not only to accept Mabel, but to consider her, in many ways, the pillar and peacemaker of the family.

Over the next forty years, the latter role was one she would be called upon to play countless times, for the marriage of Flip and Mabel carried with it internal struggles so staggering, their entire family unit would not survive them intact.

By all outward appearances, Barbara Lee Redfield's early years in Minnesota were carefree, if unremarkable. From ages six to eleven, she attended the Leach Elementary School on Park Avenue, where her first- and second-grade teacher, Aile Kovisto (who died in May 2004 at age 99) remembered her two years earlier with surprising alacrity. "She was an excellent and well-behaved student," said Kovisto. "Barbara was an outgoing youngster who was well-liked by everyone at Leach."

A true child of the North Country, Barbara spent most of her summer days bicycling beside the crystalline lakes and lush fields that surrounded the area, usually accompanied by her best friends, Corliss Davis and Beverly Cash. To many of the town's residents, the trio was known as the Three Musketeers, although their circle often included two other neighborhood girls, Rosemary Kennedy and Mary Cox.

During the winter months, the group went tobogganing and ice skating at nearby Pinehurst Park, and skied in the hills above the Cloquet water tower. Like many children in the Depression years, Barbara managed to find enjoyment in life's simple pleasures. She liked pulling taffy, according to longtime Cloquet historian Joseph Peterson, who recalls that she and her friends were frequently seen engaging in this pastime inside the Redfield's ice cream parlor.

Each Sunday, the family attended services at Our Saviour's Norwegian Lutheran Church on Carlton Avenue, a religious organization with which the Todahls were long affiliated. Due to the elder Frank Redfield's ubiquitous presence in town, even his relatives by marriage enjoyed a certain prestige as one of Cloquet's better known (if decidedly middle-class) families.

Barbara seemed nestled in a warm and fuzzy cocoon of slow-motion days bathed in sepia. On the surface, at least, it appeared to be an idyllic life for the little girl.

"I especially loved the winters," Barbara later wrote of her childhood in Cloquet. "The cold, crisp Minnesota winters, with a blue-black sky at night, and a billion stars you could reach up and grab by the handful. I think I made a wish on every one of those stars."

Reared in a typical, small-town manner, and one that practically demanded domestic aptitude in all female family members, Barbara took an early interest in cooking and became quite good at it by her preteen years. It was a skill she learned from her mother, a marvelous cook. Barbara would later relish the opportunity to whip up lavish, gourmet meals for her various beaux, husbands and friends.

Longtime Cloquet resident Mildred Golden, a contemporary of Barbara's, often babysat for the Redfield children and recalls, "Barbara's culinary specialty was a delicious casserole recipe she invented, in which she used three different kinds of Campbell's soup. She was a very pretty, bright and sweet young girl."

Nine-year old Barbara in 1936. Courtesy of Jan Redfield

A photo depicting the All-American ambiance of Cloquet. Courtesy of Carlton County Historical Society

Mabel passed along her expert talent in sewing to Barbara, as well. Marjorie Melby Russell, whose mother Dora was Mabel's younger sister, says, "My Aunt Mabel was an excellent seamstress. She could look at a dress in a store, buy the fabric and then go home and sew an exact replica of the garment." There is no question that Mabel was a dedicated homemaker who had found a more-than-receptive student in her daughter.

In addition to the more conventional skills of cooking and sewing, Barbara also showed an interest in areas generally thought in those days to be less traditional for females. Surrounded by a father and a grandfather who were both adept at carpentry and construction, Barbara learned the art of refinishing furniture at a relatively young age, a talent that impressed their neighbors and certainly set her apart from her friends. In her later teens, other practical skills would follow, including house painting and wallpapering. Home improvement, in fact, quickly became an area in which the youthful Barbara excelled. Upon closer inspection of her life, it can be argued that these were ways for an attention-starved daughter to win the acceptance of a father who was said to often be taciturn and emotionally distant.

While Flip and Mabel Redfield had passed along some of their unique qualities and talents to their children, their various eccentricities and personal problems had made them, over time, the targets of a lot of small-town gossip. According to Barbara Luokkala, Flip seemed to lose money as easily as he acquired it. "They often struggled, financially," says Luokkala. "They never lacked for money; they just had a problem keeping it. It was also common knowledge in town that both Flip and Mabel had a bit of an alcohol problem. They apparently became somewhat odd when they drank, and I don't know how well that went over in a place as small and staid as Cloquet."

Barbara's first cousin, Richard Kuitu, has a less equivocal opinion of his aunt and uncle's behavior, gleaned from past family discussions as well as from his own childhood observations. "Lee [Flip] and Mabel were horrendous, if functioning, alcoholics," he asserts. "Throughout their adult lives, and especially when they were between jobs, they would often start drinking by ten in the morning and continue drinking all day long, until well after midnight. I remember hearing that they would start out very happy and docile, but by early afternoon, the fighting would begin. Lee had a vicious temper when he drank. He would sometimes beat Mabel, and I'm certain that Barbara and Frank witnessed this often as children."

These days, a recalcitrant Frank Redfield refuses either to deny or affirm these allegations, however, Mary Kuitu Nunley, Richard's older sister, holds similar memories of turbulence in the Redfield home: "My uncle Lee was a very cold and quiet person until he started drinking. Then he gradually became boisterous, and finally, extremely obstinate, especially with my aunt. The alcohol seemed to let loose something terrible inside him, and before long he'd be off and running. Aunt Mabel was usually very mild-mannered, but when she was drinking a lot too, she would really come out of herself, and then there was no telling what would happen. It often got physical. And yet, Mabel always stood by him. She lived for Lee."

Mabel was, by far, a much more open person, and more outwardly loving and accessible than Lee. People who knew her in her later years use the same words to describe her as those who knew her as a young woman: kind, warmhearted, decent; devoted to her family. These seemed to be her truest and most intrinsic qualities, and why she would later choose to cloud and compromise them with alcohol remains a mystery. Unfortunately, nothing is known today about the drinking habits of either of Flip's and Mabel's parents, but considering both Barbara's and Frank's future struggles with alcoholism, a hereditary predisposition to the disease obviously cannot be discounted.

Unlike his wife, who enjoyed socializing with her family and friends, Flip was normally more solitary and work-driven, and would often lose himself for hours in various household projects. When set free by liquor, he was especially creative and built things; mostly offbeat things that seemed to serve no useful or obvious purpose. For instance, he once built a life-size spiral staircase made of balsa wood and airplane glue, which led to the upper reaches of the living room wall. "It didn't have a center post to support it," says Barbara's brother, Frank. "People said it couldn't be done and he wanted to prove them wrong. You could say Dad was a bit of a visionary."

"Uncle Lee was a real craftsman in carpentry," says Marjorie Melby Russell. "There wasn't anything he couldn't build, or fix."

"The man was a master tool and die maker, a genius in carpentry, and a talented machinist," echoes Richard Kuitu. "In his own way, he was actually quite brilliant."

When not under the influence, the most prominent characteristic Flip displayed was a kind of austere forbearance that discouraged the expression of any emotion deemed undue or inappropriate. This was an era in American society where difficult questions were often left unasked, and the family dynamic within the Redfield household proved no different.

It was also an era of secrets, and lies. A time when feelings and problems were routinely submerged and then squashed before they could surface and possibly cause public embarrassment. It was in this emotionally-barren environment that Flip had created for his family that Barbara would learn the vital importance of denying uncomfortable truths, and of always keeping one's pain at arms' length, no matter what the cost.

In 1938, when Barbara was 11, Flip Redfield heeded his older sister Fay's advice and decided to leave Cloquet to try his professional luck elsewhere. Disinherited by her father due to her fiercely independent nature, Fay (born August 27, 1894) had taught disabled children for a while in Kansas City, before meeting an oil tycoon from Fort Worth named George Calvert, who soon hired her to be his secretary.

Calvert was born to affluence, as part of the family that founded the famous Calvert Whiskey business in Maryland, but he would make an even greater fortune in the 1930s as a wildcatter in the oil-rich prairies of west Texas. During this time, he and two local Texans, A.J. Broderick and Mike Healy, became business partners, buying oil rights and acquiring various land holdings in Fort Worth and Odessa. Although George Calvert was married to a woman from his home state of Maryland, his wife refused to move to Texas, and Fay eventually became his mistress and full-time companion. In deference to that era's societal restrictions, he and Fay lived apart in Fort Worth, in side-by-side apartments, even though it was common knowledge to all who knew them that they were lovers. Calvert and Fay had a similar living arrangement in Odessa, and the couple went back and forth between the two cities often. Assuring her brother that the money in west Texas was "flowing like water," Fay persuaded Flip to move to Odessa.

"She told him there was a real need for tourist courts in the area and suggested that he utilize his construction skills and build one," says Frank Redfield. "My father felt that there was no future for our family in Cloquet, and he wanted to see if things might be better for us in Odessa. So, he left my mother and my Aunt Eleanor in charge of the family restaurant in Cloquet, and he headed west."

Berniece Johnson, a longtime resident of Texas, knew the Redfields for years, and in fact shared similar roots in Minnesota. Oscar Johnson, her future father-in-law, and Fred Haish, both friends of the Redfields, had moved to Odessa in 1927 from Carlton, Minnesota, a small town five miles southeast of Cloquet. Berniece's family followed in 1936, and she remembers the area as a kind of "rough and rowdy new frontier."

In those days, there were no paved streets in Odessa, and kerosene lamps were used in homes right up until 1938, when the first electric line was run through town. One rooming house had the only indoor shower for miles: a pipe over an old clawfoot tub. "The owners of the rooming house charged a quarter per shower," laughs Berniece.

Upon arriving in Odessa, Johnson's father bought some property in the middle of town to build a house. It took him three months to complete the job, and during that time, the family lived outside in a tent. "By the mid-1930s, there was a major influx of people in Odessa and housing became a top priority," Berniece explains. "I remember one of my brothers saying that you didn't dare turn over a cardboard box, as there would likely be someone living under it—which was true." Soon, former Minnesotan Oscar Johnson built two motels in Odessa that were always fully occupied, and this news further encouraged Flip's dreams.

By now, Flip realized that he was in the same boat as Fay. Neither was in line for their father's inheritance, and both of them knew it. Their mother, Mabel Ann, had died in 1923, and their older brother, Tim, was clearly the favored child. Frank had made it known early on that his business and land holdings would be left to Tim alone. "Tim never drove a nail in his life," says Barbara's brother, "but, unlike Dad, he had gone to college, and had thus earned my grandfather's respect. My father's wild nature worked against him with his Dad, and they often locked horns."

As for Fay, she, too, had always challenged her father's authority. An early archetype of the gutsy, freethinking feminist, she chain-smoked, talked tough, and for reasons not known, wore only the color blue. "She was sweet," says one source, "but she also let you know at once whether she liked you, or not. And if she didn't, oh boy, she could tear your head off."

Fay Redfield liked Frank and Barbara, however, and was said to be someone that Barbara, in particular, admired, and even emulated. The fact that Barbara would later lead a similarly unconventional lifestyle lends further weight to this claim.

The tough-talking, chain-smoking Fay Redfield, at one of several winning oil wells that George Calvert invested in for her. Courtesy of Jan Redfield

Fay, Mabel and Barbara Lee Redfield (c. 1937). Courtesy of John Lee Payton

As a child, Barbara reportedly spent several weeks each summer with Fay and George Calvert in Fort Worth. Barbara was so comfortable with them, she referred to Calvert as "Uncle George." A relative of hers insists that he always treated the little girl as one of his own, showering her with presents and spoiling her. According to this relative, Barbara was said to have "put up a fuss" each time she had to go back to Cloquet.

Unlike her more spirited siblings, the Redfields' younger sister, Murel, was a quiet and refined person who had left the family fold only briefly, at 18, to attend a music conservatory in Pasadena. For years, a picture hung in the Redfield's family home in Cloquet, showing Murel and some of her fellow female students riding in a horse-drawn carriage in the city's very first Rose Bowl parade.

A placid woman known for the lavish gifts she gave her relatives at Christmas, Murel lived a mostly cloistered existence with her father in Cloquet. "My grandfather was a stern patriarch, and he always kept my Aunt Murel under his thumb," explains Frank. "So much, in fact, that she never married, or even left home. But everyone in the family loved her. Barbara and I were close to Aunt Murel—we were all close to her.

"My grandfather, Frank L. Redfield, was one hell of a taskmaster, and he never gave any of the Redfields a free ride. You really had to toe the line with him, as Uncle Tim and Aunt Murel always did, or else he would cut you off like nothin' flat."

Explaining Flip's decision to leave Minnesota, Frank says, "My father couldn't get the type of job he wanted in Cloquet. He wanted to be in the construction business, and like everyone else in the family, he felt controlled and overshadowed by my grandfather. So, Dad took my Aunt Fay's advice and drove down to Odessa to check out the opportunities there."

Located in the semi-arid plains of the Permian Basin, midway between Fort Worth and El Paso, the town of Odessa was founded in the late 1880s when the Texas and Pacific Railway extended its route to the outer reaches of the state's south plains region. The discovery of oil in 1926 led to Odessa's incorporation on April 5, 1927, and changed it from a ranching Mecca into a town that was more industry-driven. As a result, by 1935 the population was a respectable 4,000; ten years later, that number had ballooned to 30,000. In the ensuing years, the city's reputation continued to thrive as one of the world's most important oil technology centers—a position it still holds today. In Odessa, Flip Redfield hoped to find a place big enough to harness his youthful dreams of financial success and total independence from his father.

Soon after his arrival in town, Flip, who by now preferred to be known by his middle name, Lee, began searching around for an affordable piece of property on which to build a business. By this time, Fay had received a monetary windfall through some wise investments that her boyfriend, George Calvert, had orchestrated for her. As a result, she was living extremely well.

"My Aunt Fay had previously invested some of the money she earned in Kansas City into the NYC stock market," says Frank Redfield. "She turned a big profit, and then Calvert suggested she take $1,000 of that money and invest it in one of his oil wells in Odessa. She did, and it turned out to be a gusher. From that point on, Aunt Fay was able to live off the $30,000 annual interest she made on the deal. In those days, that was some bucks."

Berniece Johnson recalls that Calvert and Fay took great pleasure in parading their wealth. "After a while, the two of them were really rolling in clover. To illustrate their economic condition, at one point they hired a young black man named Royce McCollums to chauffeur them all around town. They really lived the high life, and that greatly impressed a lot of the locals, including Lee and Mabel."

Fay's good fortune inspired Lee to finally put into action his dream of building and managing a traveler's court. Always the closest of siblings, when he told Fay of his plans, she lent him $25,000. He put up another

$25,000, and they bought some property the size of a city block on 2nd Street, one mile outside of town. "My father built the Antlers Court, which consisted of 20 cabins and an office," says Frank. "Upon completing it, he arranged for my mother, Barbara and me to join him."

In 1939, the rest of Lee Redfield's family moved from Cloquet to Odessa and settled into a house on 3rd Street, just behind the court, at which time Mabel commenced overseeing the motel's housekeeping duties.

"Our mother was a hard worker," Frank recalls. "To show you what I mean, I remember one time when Barbara and I walked into the house, and Mom was on her hands and knees, scrubbing the kitchen floor. It was summer, and hot as hell; she was literally sweating buckets. I had never seen anyone sweat that much before. I was around ten, and Barbara was 14 or so. We decided to walk down to the liquor store in town and buy Mom a soda. The problem was, we only had a nickel, and a soda cost ten cents. So we asked a black porter named Lonny, who worked at the motel, if he would lend us a nickel, and he did. Barbara and I walked several blocks to the liquor store, and when we got there we decided that mother would probably appreciate a beer more than a soda, so we used the dime and bought her a bottle of beer. We walked home and found Mom still down on her hands and knees, washing the floor. When she looked up and saw what we had done for her, she burst into tears, hugging and kissing us. You would have thought we had handed her a million bucks. For some reason, I've never forgotten that."

With a father who often worked fifteen hours a day, seven days a week, Frank and Barbara grew up feeling much closer to Mabel, who was both affectionate and supportive. In contrast, Lee's often-curt manner of communicating with his children only increased the distance between them.

"Dad wasn't around much, and when he was, he didn't know how to relate to us very well," adds Frank. "He may have taken me duck hunting a few times in Odessa, but as a rule, we didn't do many father-and-son-type things together.

"He was definitely a man of few words. He was the same with Barbara and our mother. My father was moody, I guess you could say. And he yelled at Barbara a lot. Mom was pretty much in charge of our upbringing. She was a wonderful parent. In later years, her drinking got way out of hand, but even then, she was always a decent and loving woman."

Lee did his best to avoid becoming involved in any personal problems that Barbara or Frank encountered, preferring that Mabel handle those

As a youngster, Barbara was often the target of her father's anger. Courtesy of John Lee Payton

matters alone. "Dad always believed you should take care of things the way you saw fit. As a result, we had to learn to handle a lot by ourselves. His favorite saying was, 'We don't cry over spilled milk, we just mop it up.' Dad wasn't a warm person, not by any means. But our mother was. Always."

Berniece Johnson remembers Lee as a serious workaholic, who, at times, had a slightly oblique way of looking at things. She recalls that a heavy rain once caused the doors to the rooms of the Redfields' motel to swell, making them impossible to close. "Lee took all the doors off their hinges, laid them out on sawhorses, and went down the line with a power saw. With great gusto, he told my father-in-law, Oscar: 'Mass production is the only way to fix anything.'"

Another time, the drive-shaft fell out of Lee's '41 Dodge. Oscar asked Lee if he ever lubricated the engine, to which Lee replied, "No, never. It's cheaper that way."

"They added up the cost of lubrication," says Berniece, "and balanced it against the price of the repair, and Lee was right. It was cheaper not to lube. Lee had a totally different way of looking at things, but sometimes, he was right on the money."

While Lee jumped from one skewed observation to the next, Mabel stood on the sidelines in a mostly mellow haze, planted firmly in the strange world her husband had fashioned for them. She spent a lot of time drinking, as well as cooking meals for her family and friends, recalls

A dour looking Barbara poses with the family dog (c. late 1930s). Courtesy of John Lee Payton

Berniece, although Oscar Johnson and his wife always tried to avoid eating with them.

"On one of the few occasions they did go to dinner at the Redfields," Berniece says, "Mabel, while drunk, made a cake with fresh grated coconut as one of the ingredients, and then told Oscar, 'God knows how many fingernails I lost in there.'"

Another time, the Johnsons were visiting the Redfields when they spotted Barbara sitting on the kitchen floor, stirring a bowl of cake batter. "The family cat was down there, too, rubbing around the sides of the bowl and dipping its dirty tail into the batter. It was a very off-the-wall environment."

Like the Sycamore clan in the Frank Capra film classic, *You Can't Take It With You*, the Redfields bounced around in their own topsy-turvy world—where anything could happen, and usually did. Against this chaotic backdrop of heavy drinking and odd behavior, Frank and Barbara Redfield grew up wild—and fast.

Chapter Three:
Running with the Wind

The Antlers Court proved a popular tourist stop for wartime travelers, providing the Redfields with a steady income for nearly nine years. "During the war, Dad was hamstrung by having to charge three dollars a night for a room, due to price controls," says Frank, "but even so, we made out all right." The Antlers was a respectable establishment, he stresses, unlike other local motels, which catered more to the ramblers and fly-by-nights who hit town in search of their own piece of the pie. "For a long time, the Antlers was the nicest motel in these parts," recalls Berniece Johnson.

"In those days, everything was progressing very fast in Odessa," explains Frank. "It was a boomtown that just rocked all day long. There was one place about half a mile away from our court, called the Blue Top Motel, that was a real hot-runnin' joint. My father always called it the Hot Pillow Motel, because its main clientele consisted of good lookin' guys in Army uniforms and their teenage 'dates.' Whenever the servicemen from Midland Air Force Base rolled through town, I don't think there was a single virgin that was left untouched."

To further illustrate Odessa's raucous environment in the 1940s, Frank recalls that the Blue Top Motel had huge loudspeakers in its parking lot that played "ear splittin', hillbilly music," morning, noon and night. "It was so loud we could hear it plain as day inside our house, even with the windows closed. I'm telling you, with all that hooting and hollering and country bop playing all the time, the place was just nonstop action." The Ace of Clubs nightclub, owned by the Bargesser family, opened in 1939, and was another rocking joint. Much like the Blue Top Motel, it often played host to the soldiers stationed at the nearby Pyote, Marfa and Midland Air Force Bases.

On weekends, Lee and Mabel usually patronized either the Ace of Clubs, or the bar at the bowling alley across the street from their motel, where, Frank says, "They went for a couple of beers and some laughs. While they were gone, Barbara and I watched out for ourselves and stayed out of trouble. Well, for the most part, anyway."

During the week, Lee and Mabel often fortified themselves with cold Cokes from the office soda machine—which they would lace with rum from a bottle they kept stashed under the counter.

Frank and Barbara's cousin, Richard Kuitu, has his own take on the younger Redfields' upbringing: "I was told by relatives that Barbara and Frank basically raised themselves," he offers. "According to the family, Lee and Mabel were usually too drunk to keep an eye on them. As aunts and uncles go, they were always wonderful to me, but apparently they were terrible parents to Barbara and Frank.

"There is an old saying in Texas: 'Midland is where you go to raise a family; Odessa is where you go to raise hell.' Lee and Mabel took that saying to heart, believe me. But I gotta hand it to them—although their drinking was excessive, they somehow always managed to run their business and remain solvent."

In 1947, after nearly ten years in operation, Lee and Mabel sold the Antlers Court and most of its property, saving one-third of the lot on U.S. Highway 80 to build a second business they named the Cypress Court (later changed to the Deluxe Court). They continued to live in the house in the back of the property until 1952 when, Frank says, "They sold the entire court for $100,000 and a '51 Mercury, and then headed for California."

Like the town's Desert Sage, Barbara Redfield's beauty burst into full flower under the west Texas skies, and by the time she entered Odessa Junior High, she was a stunning sight to behold. Cloquet resident Mildred Golden saw her often over the years, when Mabel and the children returned to their hometown every summer to visit family. She remembers, "Barbara's eyes were a striking shade of crystal-blue and her hair had darkened over time to a natural brunette color. She had a gorgeous figure and complexion. Even as a young girl, Barbara turned heads wherever she went."

Mabel's early obsession with her daughter's beauty had only intensified over the years, and now, as Barbara was heading into adolescence, Mabel was taking every opportunity to show her off around town. As a result, much of the attention Barbara received (especially from some of Odessa's middle-aged gentlemen) seemed somewhat awkward and even improper.

"Even at 11 and 12 years old, Barbara got a lot of catcalls and lustful stares from older men," says one of the Redfields' neighbors (who wishes to remain anonymous). "Barbara would blush at first over all that lip-smacking and winking, but then she got used to it and just smiled."

Being paraded around dressed and made up older than her years, with the "lip-smacking" attention it drew to her, had to be profoundly confusing for Barbara, who probably didn't know how to deal with it at first and had likely turned to her mother for guidance. Although the inappropriate attention Barbara was receiving was obvious to everyone else, much of it seemed lost on Mabel, who perhaps saw in Barbara the promise of overcoming the confines of her own ordinary existence, and thus chose to ignore the overtures. "Aunt Mabel absolutely worshiped Barbara," claims Richard Kuitu. "She always sang her praises, loud and strong, to whomever would listen. Barbara always got a lot of attention because of how she looked, and I think that from a very early age she saw that it gave her a kind of power over people."

It was during this period that Lee seemed to disconnect further from his daughter, becoming even more cold and intolerant. Though it isn't certain today, Barbara's burgeoning sexuality, and Mabel's encouragement of it, may have played a part in this separation. As Barbara would later tell Leo Guild, a gossip columnist for *Variety* who was the ghostwriter of her 1963 memoir, *I Am Not Ashamed*: "I think the day my father realized I was a real, feminine girl—I was about 12 or 13—he became afraid of me. He didn't know how to be a father to an all-female kind of girl, and he just wanted to strike out the whole mess. I suppose the responsibility was frightening to him."

While much of Barbara's autobiography was highly fictitious, this particular observation seems plausible. There's no question today that there was a definite breaking point somewhere in Barbara's relationship with her father that grieved her deeply; a breach of trust and security between them that she would spend the entire rest of her life trying to mend. If there was a single, life-changing catalyst for their emotional estrangement, it isn't known; however, pundits familiar with Barbara's story have long conjectured that there may have been an "inappropriate" relationship at some point between father and daughter. With her surviving family members understandably loath to even entertain this theory—and with no real evidence of such an incident, or incidents, ever occurring—it is a speculation that nonetheless gains credence when one looks at the entire scope of Barbara's life (including her endless, and ultimately fruitless, quest to win Lee's acceptance). One has the feeling that a force both powerful and primitive drove Barbara to the many dark encounters in her life, and it very well may have been rooted in the longings of a little girl who had somehow, along the way, lost her father forever.

Her murky relationship with her father aside, Barbara really began to experience her strong (and seemingly effortless) influence on the opposite sex when she reached her adolescence. Years later, she would recall an incident that occurred when she was twelve, when a famous actor appeared at a war bond rally in Odessa. A star-struck Barbara claimed she got to see the celebrity only after negotiating with an older boy to sneak her into the auditorium. He wanted to put both of his hands under her blouse and "cop a feel" in exchange for the ticket, but Barbara would only allow him to "rest" one hand between her legs. Barbara, however, had gotten her way, and the lesson stuck: Bargain for what you want, then play the game and win. It was the first in a long series of tradeoffs that would greatly alter the course of her life.

Accompanying Barbara's beauty and eagerness to please was a devil-may-care restlessness shared by her younger brother. Beverly McColloch of Odessa dated Frank in junior high school and retains vivid memories of their courtship. "Like his parents and older sister, Frank was a real hell-raiser who smoked and drank a little, too. I remember his nickname in school was Rod. Although he had quite a wild reputation in town, he was always a perfect gentleman with me. Oh, he was a lot of fun."

Today, Frank smiles when told of Beverly's comments. "Yes, that description of me is pretty accurate," he says. "I was a lot like Barbara in that we were both footloose and itching to get out of Odessa so we could see the world. We must have gotten that desire from our father, who seemed fueled by his wanderlust. I guess I was, too, because I wound up quitting high school after the 10th grade to join the Navy."

The 5'4", dark-blonde, blue-eyed Barbara developed an eye-catching figure in her early teens and entered Odessa High School as the object of many of her male classmates' fantasies—something of a small-town goddess. According to a future Universal Studios biography, Barbara excelled in English and History and continued her early interest in sports by dabbling in swimming and gymnastics.

"I recall her being a cheerleader for one year and being on the tumbling team, too, for a while," says Frank, while their cousin, Mary Nunley, offers, "Barbara also did a lot of ceramics in high school, and

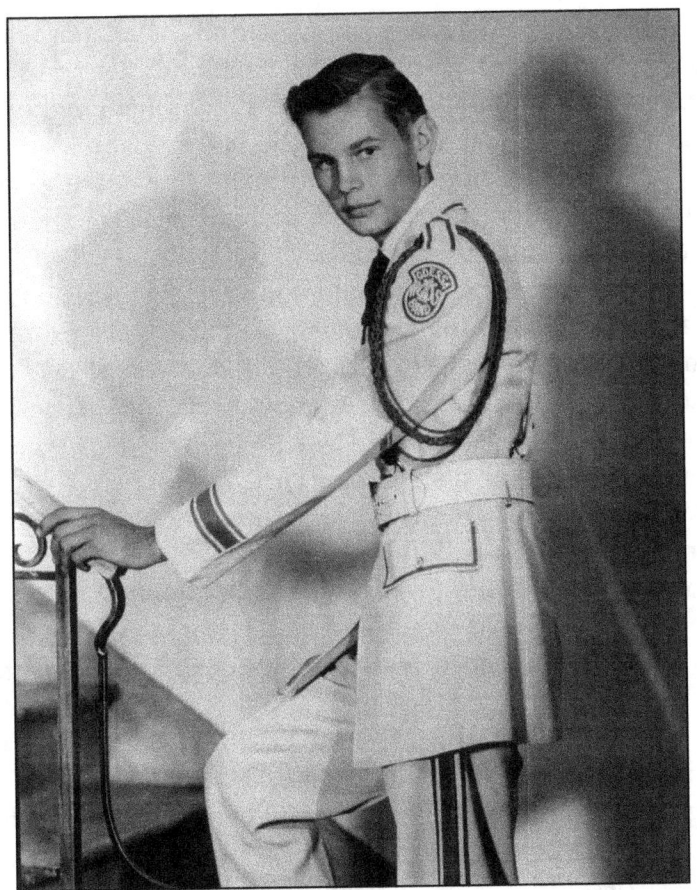

Barbara's brother Frank in his Odessa High School band uniform (c. mid-1940s). Courtesy of Beverly Moore McColloch

she was very good at it, too. I still have a ceramic piece she made for me all those years ago. Barbara always had an artistic side, and a talent for creating beautiful objects from scratch."

As a counterpoint to her innate wholesomeness in high school, Barbara picked up a noticeably ballsy quality to her character which soon became a kind of ever-primed, built-in defense mechanism. Perhaps she felt that if she kept people off balance by her rough and hard-edged facade they would never be tempted to abuse the very real vulnerability that was just below the surface. However, while this tantalizing blend of sweetness and bravado proved a potent (and extremely appealing) mix, it would also become an unwieldy weapon for Barbara—and the source of many future heartaches.

Beneath her new, tough-talking persona, Barbara remained an impressionable teenager, easily seduced by all the attention she received in high school. She would later write that she lost her virginity at age 15, to a schoolmate's 45-year-old father, who had sexual relations with her in a dry bathtub in his home while the unknowing guests at his surprise birthday party celebrated downstairs. Barbara never reported what was, without question, statutory rape.

Today, one can imagine the profound effect this act had on Barbara's fragile adolescent soul. Although she would publicly refer to the incident only once, in a brief passage in her memoir, Barbara's alleged rape surely influenced her subsequent attitudes about men. Indeed, one can argue that her future sexual habits carried with them an element of subconscious revenge against the older man (or men) who robbed her of her innocence; revenge she would play out in her life, time and again, with countless partners. It is clear that with this one fateful act, a huge part of Barbara's world turned dark—and still—and was forever changed.

Racing like a prairie wind into her adulthood, in November 1943, 16-year-old Barbara eloped with her high-school sweetheart, William Hodge. Frank Redfield and the Kuitus all admit they remember very little about Hodge, or the marriage. "I was 12 at the time and obviously not too concerned with that sort of thing," says Frank. "But I do recall he was a good-looking kid. Quite honestly, there's really not too much to say about it. He got into Barbara's pants and then they ran off to Lubbock and got married. My parents were not pleased, and they had the marriage annulled after about a week."

The late Leslie Snyder, who worked in Hollywood for many years as a personal assistant to gossip columnist Louella Parsons, was a friend of Barbara's in the 1950s. She later said that Barbara once told her that her father had beaten her after she had eloped with Hodge. Snyder shared this information with her best friend, Charlene Golden, the wife of Barbara's longtime attorney, Milton Golden. "Barbara's father had threatened the boy, too, and told him that if he ever came around her again, he'd kill him," said Charlene.

Frank Redfield claims he has no knowledge of any of this, which given the volatile situation and his young age at the time, is certainly understandable. However, he is also quick to add that he personally believes that Barbara did not put up much of a fight when her parents forced her to have the marriage annulled: "At that point in her life, she knew that being married was not for her, so I'm sure she went along with my parents' orders to end it. I think she eloped with that boy more for a lark than for anything else. Once the novelty of it was gone, she didn't care about it anymore. She was like that. Barbara was a healthy, red-blooded girl, but she was also a free spirit. She always did exactly as she pleased, consequences be damned."

This was further evidenced a few months later when the teenager decided she had enough of high school and quit at the end of her junior year. Neither Lee nor Mabel seemed too concerned, Frank remembers, as "they had gotten along okay without a lot of schooling, and they felt that Barbara (and I) would, too."

Barbara's wild nature really seemed to kick into high gear following her exile from school. "She was a fast chick, hot to trot, as they said back then," wrote journalist Tom Johnson in his November 1987 *Fallen Star* article on Barbara in *Los Angeles Magazine*. "...[Barbara was] always way ahead of everyone. She never did seem to be able to decide on anything and stick with her decision."

An unidentified woman from Odessa, who was a neighbor of the Redfields, told Berniece Johnson that, "Barbara was always much older than we were, even though we were the same age." Johnson adds, "There were rumors back then of two other quickie marriages for Barbara—following the one to William Hodge—that her parents also had annulled. One of these marriages was said to be to a shoe salesman that Barbara had met while shopping. He supposedly sold her some shoes, and then asked her to marry him. She agreed, and off they went."

Once again, Frank Redfield is unsure of the veracity of this information. "I don't know about any other marriages or annulments for her in high school," he says vaguely, "nor do any of our relatives. But I wouldn't be surprised if it's true. Barbara wasn't the least bit bashful. She didn't give a rap what you thought about her, and she had a real sassy attitude at times.

"To give you an example of what she was like as a young girl, I do remember one instance when I overheard her talking to a teenaged boy in the living room of our house. I was nine or ten, so Barbara was about 14. I was hiding in the stairwell, spying on them, when I heard Barbara say to him, 'I'll trade sex with you, outside, in the sticker patch.' The kid she was with was a little bit shy and started stammering, and then Barbara grew much more aggressive and said, 'Oh, come on, brother, give it up. I'll show you mine if you show me yours.'

"I don't remember what happened after that," adds Frank, "but I guess they went outside to the sticker patch."

Barbara's sexual precociousness is further illustrated by the following revelation by Berniece Johnson: "I remember hearing one day that Lee had told Barbara, who was 14 or 15 at the time, that she shouldn't run around the motel in just her bra and panties when (an unidentified boarder) was there. Barbara just laughed and said, 'Oh, daddy, it doesn't bother him. I already found out he doesn't like girls.'"

"Things just always seemed so off-kilter in that house," adds Berniece. Indeed, with two hard-drinking parents, and very few—if any—rules in place, Barbara and Frank were basically free to run amok.

Barbara's lack of boundaries, and her failure in setting and enforcing limits, speaks volumes on how her life had been altered by the inappropriate propositions of her childhood and adolescence. The sexual violations that had taken place—and all indications are that these were not isolated, or rare, incidents—had resulted in some serious self-worth issues for her. Although often concealed behind her headstrong and sometimes profane exterior, this loss of self-worth had apparently made it difficult, if not impossible, for her to ever say "no."

Perhaps in the dark tangle of the family's "sticker patch," Barbara had lost a lot more than her innocence.

A teenage photo of Barbara in Odessa, Texas.
From the Author's Collection

Chapter Four:
Reaching for a Dream

During World War II, Mabel often invited soldiers from the nearby Midland Army Air Force Base to the Redfield home for informal dances. The mixers provided a carefree couple of hours for soldiers and civilians alike; a welcome respite from the stark wartime atmosphere that had draped much of the world in darkness. With her buoyant personality and wholesome looks, Barbara was a popular presence at these gatherings and turned more than a few heads. However, none of them turned hers like the man she would meet late one night at Odessa's Ace of Clubs bar.

In 1944, 22-year-old Air Force pilot John Payton had recently been assigned to the Midland Air Base after flying forty combat missions in North Africa in 1943. Tall, handsome and with enough inherent confidence to place him just this side of cocky, Payton apparently cut a dashing figure in his uniform when Barbara first saw him at the bar. She later confided to her friends that she was immediately attracted to him, and had deliberately orchestrated their meeting. The attraction was mutual, said Payton, who added that the couple "quickly became really good dance and party partners who truly enjoyed each other's company." It was the start of a relationship that, while complex and far from trouble-free, John Payton held dear to his heart until his passing in May 2006.

Born January 29, 1922 in Nebraska, John (a.k.a. "Jack") Payton and his younger siblings, Donald, Robert and Barbara, enjoyed an upper-middle-class upbringing in suburban Omaha. Their mother, the former Mamie Burns, owned a nationally-renowned antiques business while their father, John, Sr., had a successful thirty-year career with the A&P Company as a troubleshooter for its chain of grocery stores. As the position required him to be available at different locations (sometimes for many months at a stretch), the family moved nearly a dozen times over the years, with homes in Indiana, Illinois, Iowa, Wisconsin and several other states.

Though first and foremost a devoted wife and mother, Mamie Payton was also an enterprising woman who decided to open an antiques store in Omaha after the family moved there from Milwaukee. What is especially interesting about this venture is that she reportedly funded it

Air Force pilot John Payton met Barbara at an Odessa, Texas nightclub, and was immediately attracted to her. Courtesy of John Lee Payton

herself, without any financial assistance from her husband. Over time, Mamie became a recognized expert on antique glassware and watched her business thrive for many years, until Alzheimer's Disease claimed her health in the 1970s.

Following his high school graduation in 1940, John and Mamie's son, John, Jr., attended the Midland Army Air Force Base training school for bombardier cadets, and by the time he met Barbara, he was already a highly-decorated WWII combat flier. In just four years, he had gone from flying combat missions overseas to training new pilots, and had quickly climbed the ranks at Midland to attain his current status as Captain.

A few months prior to his death at 84, John Payton described his and Barbara's meeting with deliberate brevity: "When I was stationed at Midland Air Base, that section of Texas was designated a dry, no booze county. Nearby, in a wet county, was Odessa—complete with frantic-action nightclubs featuring drinking, dancing, and many pretty girls. All this was very compatible with a wartime serviceman's goals of obtaining a little R & R.

"During the spring of 1944, while in Odessa, I became acquainted with the Queen of the Ball—and far and away, the very best—Barbara Lee Redfield. She was audacious and beautiful and strutted through life with her head held high, and I was instantly smitten. A real warmth developed between us; a warmth that whenever we were together, whether married or divorced, never—repeat, never—changed."

"Jack was an upright, All-American guy," remembers Frank Redfield. "His family was, financially speaking, quite comfortable, and they were really nice people. Jack was a terrific guy, and he was crazy about Barbara."

Despite dating Barbara exclusively for the next several months, John Payton apparently still had doubts about forsaking his bachelor status, so in early 1945, he accepted a new assignment at Selman Field in Monroe, Louisiana, and left without telling her. "I wasn't comfortable with goodbyes," he said, "so I didn't announce my departure to her. I suppose I was feeling a little bit gun-shy about marriage, but I soon found out that wasn't going to fly with Barbara."

Indeed. When John arrived at Selman Field, he was told that there were no quarters available on base, so he took a room at a local hotel. Several days later, John got the shock of his life. On returning to his hotel room, he discovered a wedding gown hanging on the closet door. Though Barbara was nowhere to be found, it was clear that she had followed him to Louisiana, and her intentions were obvious.

John Payton, Barbara Redfield and an unidentified friend at Odessa's Silver Dollar Bar. Courtesy of Arlene Shaner.

"After I found the wedding gown (and caught my breath), I went downstairs and was pleased and surprised to find a smiling Barbara waiting for me in the lobby. As soon as I saw her again, I realized how much I loved her and we were married on February 10, 1945."

Lee and Mabel Redfield were said to have breathed a huge sigh of relief when Barbara and John were wed. Unlike Barbara's first husband, a mere schoolboy (and apparently a wild one, at that), John was a steady, stable man with a good head on his shoulders, and a guaranteed future with the Air Force. If nothing else, Barbara's parents were probably hoping that John would be able to harness her unbridled energy more than they ever could. Lee, in particular, who had always seen Barbara as "a major headache and a huge thorn in his side," as one relative claims, could only be relieved that he would no longer have to witness the sometimes difficult situations she often found herself in (not that he ever did much to help her out of them).

After their wedding, John and Barbara moved into the barracks at the Air Base and he immediately went back to work. As he was unable to obtain a military leave, the couple was forced to postpone their honeymoon until that June, at which point John received a discharge from his duties. He and Barbara then spent several months in Rock Island, Illinois, where his parents were living at the time.

Barbara and John Payton's wedding photo. Courtesy of Jan Redfield

John's younger sister, Barbara Payton Miller, remembers the newlyweds moving into the family home. "My brother loved coming home on leave and surprising all of us, so his staying in close contact with our parents and me was not unusual for him. My first impression of Barbara was that of a happy, talented, beautiful, charming and unpretentious person who was great fun to be with. She used to play Monopoly with my friend and me, and she tried very hard (unsuccessfully, I might add) to teach me to tap dance. During the time my brother and Barbara lived with us, John took a production line job at a local manufacturing plant, and Barbara got a job at the Rock Island Arsenal. John didn't get off work until after midnight, and Barbara always fixed him a full dinner when he got home. She was a person of no specific age, in my mind. When she lived with us, Barbara could be just another one of the kids playing Monopoly—and yet ten minutes later, she'd be wearing a great looking suit, hat, gloves and high heels, looking like a million dollars.

"I must say, Barbara was not like any of the other brides or housewives I knew in Rock Island, Illinois. It was obvious that she was destined for a career, perhaps in modeling or dancing. Maybe she thought so, too, as it wasn't very long before they decided to move out west."

In 1945, John decided to take advantage of the GI Bill, which provided monetary assistance to young veterans wishing to further their education, and he enrolled at USC in Los Angeles. The government bill also allowed funds for housing, so the couple rented an apartment on Figueroa Boulevard, close to the USC campus, where John attended accounting classes, and Barbara threw herself into cooking and housecleaning.

While John studied, Barbara washed clothes and scrubbed floors, but she soon grew tired of what she felt was a very menial existence. "She was bored stiff," says Frank. "In 1946, when I was 15, my parents allowed me to take the train from Odessa to L.A. to visit Barbara and Jack, and I stayed with them for two weeks. One morning after breakfast, I remember Barb saying to me, 'How long does it take me to clean this little apartment? An hour? And then what? Aside from shopping for groceries at the market, I've got nothing else to do for the rest of the week.' Barbara was happy with Jack, it wasn't that. But, she felt confined."

For a while, Barbara tried to busy herself at home with several do-it-yourself projects. Frank remembers her refinishing and painting two bookcases and even painting some rooms in the apartment. "I recall a few home improvement/self-help books lying around, and seeing Barbara with her nose in them. My sister was a good designer, with a good eye for color, but she always lacked patience. In everything she did."

Apparently, it was during the first few months of her marriage that Barbara first expressed a desire to be a fashion model and/or actress. Frank contends that she had shown no interest in either profession while growing up. "I don't remember Barbara ever saying as a child or young girl that she wanted to be in the movies," he says. "She didn't have fan magazines or photos of celebrities lying around the house. From the time she was a little girl, Barb always just wanted to be a housewife and a mother.

"That's not to say she didn't like going to the movies. She did, and of course, Jimmy Cagney [her future co-star] was always her favorite actor. She liked him, she said, 'cause he was tough.'"

At some point, Barbara's striking good looks, and the constant attention they brought her from nearly everyone around, had caused the teenager to have a sudden revelation about modeling, at least enough for her to give it a try.

In early 1946, Barbara paid a local business, Gerald-Leonard Photography, to take some pictures of her around town in a variety of outfits. The photos were seen by a Hollywood dress designer named Saba of California, a company that was so impressed with Barbara, it immediately signed her to a contract, and then hired her to model a new line of their clothing called Sue Mason Juniors.

Barbara officially began her modeling career in March 1946, and over the next six months she appeared in dozens of clothing and product advertisements for the magazines *California Stylist*, *Charm*, *Junior Bazaar* and *The Californian*. Not yet 19 and still a brunette, Barbara bore only the slightest resemblance to the sexy, platinum-blonde movie star she would eventually become.

John Payton claimed that he had little issue with his wife's newfound passion for modeling. "I was busy with school, and even though Barbara was working a lot, she had remained a good housewife and an excellent cook. Things were fine between us, and then they got even better that spring when we received some very good news from her doctor."

Barbara's excitement over her flourishing modeling career was only momentarily dampened when she discovered in May that she was pregnant. As she had set her sights by now on eventually breaking into motion pictures, at first Barbara had mixed feelings about her pregnancy,

Fledgling model Barbara Payton at 18. Courtesy of Jan Redfield

but they were soon replaced with the kind of strong maternal instincts her own mother had. Barbara continued modeling for Saba of California until the early part of September, after which her condition became apparent and made posing for any future Junior Miss ads impossible.

With a child on the way, John and Barbara decided they needed a bigger place to live than their tiny apartment near the USC campus, so in

October 1946 they migrated a few miles east, to the town of Compton. The couple moved into a small, government-subsidized tract house at 1244 East 150th Street, in one of those spanking-new, suburban communities that were so prevalent after the war. "It was a nice neighborhood," says Frank, "populated by several other new families just starting out." Their

*Barbara modeled for L.A.'s Gerald-Leonard Photography in 1946.
Courtesy of John Lee Payton*

Montage of Barbara's early modeling shots. Courtesy of John Lee Payton.

relocation to Compton delighted Barbara as it brought her just fifteen miles outside Hollywood, the town she now believed held her destiny.

In 1946, Tina Ballard was a 19-year-old housewife and part-time model living in Lynwood, California, about halfway between Compton and Hollywood. She first met Barbara when the latter began working for Saba of California, and from their first introduction, the girls immediately clicked and grew to be close friends. In fact, next to Barbara's future sister-in-law, Jan, Tina was probably Barbara's best friend during her early years in Compton, and they remained close friends throughout Barbara's film career and into the 1960s.

"My late husband Dave and I were crazy about Barbara," says Tina. "Dave's line of work took him out of town a lot, and as a result I spent many weekends with Barbara in Compton. Barb and Jack were a happy couple—fun, beautiful together and very much in love—and they were so excited to be having a baby.

"I don't think I've ever met another person as outwardly self-confident as Barbara. She had this wonderful, wide-open quality to her personality, like she wanted to experience everything (and all at once). She was bubbly and very outspoken, but she was always careful about not hurting your feelings. She was unique. Barbara had a delightfully naughty side to her that reminded me of a little mischief maker, but it was somehow innocent. She always had this glint in her eyes like she was up to something, and she usually was. Barbara was naive and naughty and sweet, and just a pleasure to be around. I have never met anyone else, certainly not another woman, who was quite like Barbara.

"As for Jack, well, he was larger-than-life. Very good-looking, very confident. He wasn't what I would call conceited, but he was extremely sure of himself. And with good reason—he had accomplished quite a lot in his career, even by that time. I mean, the man was a real, honest to goodness, Air Force hero with several successful combat missions under his belt. Believe me, that impressed all of us (Barbara, especially). I think a man had to be strong and assertive if he wanted to be around Barbara because she was like that herself. She really came on like gangbusters at times, you know? And Jack was mad about her."

Tina remembers Barbara looking forward to giving birth to her child, and eventually, to getting back into modeling full-time. "She liked being married to Jack and was so happy to be carrying his child, too, but like many other women, she also enjoyed the attention she received from other men. Barbara was a beautiful girl and she photographed well, so she figured why not pursue it [modeling]. Besides, the money she made came in handy as she and Jack were really just starting out at the time.

"I'm not certain if Barbara had already decided by this time that she wanted to be an actress, but I know she definitely wanted to be out front, and noticed. I think she had already made up her mind that she wasn't going to let her dreams of being famous die, just because she was married and pregnant; she would just pursue it [modeling] again after she had her baby."

Following their move to Compton, Barbara and John maintained the stereotypical lifestyle of young, postwar newlyweds expecting their first child. It was apparently a blissful time for the couple, and as the weeks passed, the bond between them and their unborn child seemed to only grow stronger. John nicknamed Barbara "Queenie" and regarded her as just that—a queen; his queen, a woman he not only loved, but revered. Almost as soon as she learned that she was pregnant, Barbara bought several scrapbooks and photo albums that she would later fill with both written entries and snapshots. She also put a lot of effort into readying a nursery for the baby, and even wallpapered the room herself. As the event drew closer, she received a visit from Mabel, who came to Compton to help Barbara and her girlfriend Tina prepare for the baby's arrival.

After much anticipation, Barbara and John welcomed a son, John Lee, into the world on Friday, February 14, 1947, at L.A.'s Doctors Hospital. Weighing eight pounds and 13 ounces and measuring 20 inches at birth, the brown-haired, blue-eyed boy was described by Barbara in the photo album's initial entry as having a "perfectly shaped head, and [being] simply precious. He is the best Valentine's Day gift I've ever had!"

Over the next several months, Barbara literally went on to record every waking (and non-waking) moment of the new infant's life. Her devotion to her son was obvious, proven by the following entries from John Lee's baby album:

> Johnny had his picture taken on his first birthday (one week that is), February 21, 1947. He went for a drive when he was two weeks old and also visited the doctor. He was all dressed up and looked just precious!

Further into the album, she writes:

> October 8, 1947… Our baby is extremely handsome like his father (so Father Payton declares)!

Johnny stands while holding on to things with his hands. He is very healthy, and cute!

And, a few pages later:

Johnny is beginning to walk! He is holding on to things and shaking them so. He loves to kiss and don't think we don't! How cute can you get?

Johnny's first words today were: "Thank you… Da-Da… Ma-Ma… Kitty." He loves to pucker his sweet mouth and say, "Ohhhhh…" So precious!

Clearly, Barbara was enamored of her baby son and lavished as much love and attention on him as any mother could. While the amount of attention she gave him would admittedly waver over the years, the love never did. "From the moment he was born, Barb loved Johnny with all that she had," says Tina Ballard. "I would even go so far as to say she never

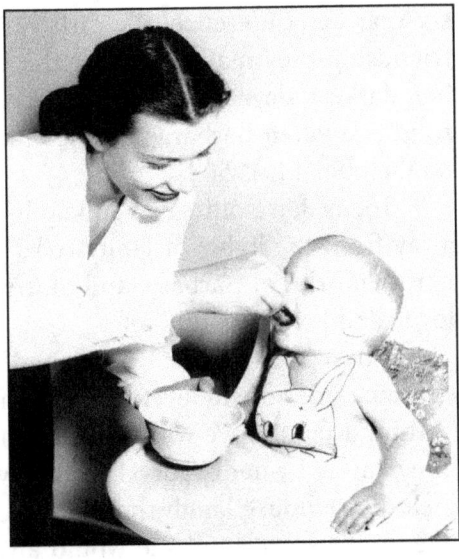

LEFT: Barbara's beloved son John Lee Payton. Courtesy of John Lee Payton/ RIGHT: Barbara and John Lee at their home in Compton, CA. Courtesy of John Lee Payton

loved another human being more than she did her son."

"No doubt about it, she was amazing with Johnny," said John Payton in 2006. "In Compton, Barbara was totally committed to our son's well-being." In many ways, their relationship was the most satisfying Barbara would ever experience.

That it would also be so short-lived was a cruel irony that would become her life's harshest punishment.

Dorothy and John Allen Zollinger were among the young married couples residing in Compton at the time who befriended John and Barbara following their son's birth. John (also known as "Al") Zollinger worked in construction, building homes in Diamond Bar and throughout the San Gabriel Valley, while Dorothy was the quintessential 1940s housewife, forgoing a career outside the home to manage the household and raise the couple's two children, Janice and Ron. The Zollingers lived on South Central Avenue, just around the corner from the Paytons, and both Dorothy and 14-year-old Janice enjoyed spending much of their spare time with Barbara and John Lee. They often accompanied the pair on their afternoon strolls through the neighborhood, where they would listen to Barbara's nonstop declarations that she was going to break into the movies. Barbara took a sisterly interest in Janice, and despite their six-year age difference, the girls quickly became close friends. It was a friendship they maintained for the balance of Barbara's life, even during her darkest days in the 1960s. The bond between them was further solidified when Barbara's brother Frank married Janice a few years later, on October 14, 1950.

Today, Jan Zollinger Redfield lives in a modest Midwestern town, far away from the lights of Hollywood and its upscale suburbs, if not from her memories of Barbara, and of the many years when she was her most loyal, and loving, confidante.

"She was the sister I never had," says Jan, who still uses her former surname of Redfield, even though she and Frank were divorced in 1968. "I think I fell in love with Barbara the first time I met her. Besides being blown away by her beauty, I really loved her sense of humor. She had this great barrelhouse laugh that seemed to come up from her toes. Barbara liked to tease me, and she would always keep at it until she had us both in stitches. She wasn't mean-spirited, though, nor did she ever make fun of anyone, or deliberately hurt a person's feelings. She had a tremendous, fun-loving spirit, and she always made sure that everyone around her had a good time when they were with her. Barbara and I went through a lot together."

Though she couldn't possibly know it in 1946, Jan would see Barbara through some of the very best times of her life—as well as the worst.

When John Lee was about six months old, Jan began watching him for Barbara, so that she could resume her modeling career. "I was the first one to baby-sit for Johnny," says Jan, "but as I got older and began dating, it interfered with my social life, so my mother Dorothy took over."

Sometime during this period, Barbara began inviting several local teenage girls to the house for company. The gatherings eventually evolved from strictly social visits to informal makeup classes, where Barbara would demonstrate proper grooming habits to her friends and give them beauty tips she had learned through modeling.

Though barely in her teens, Jan attended these informal "classes" too. She remembers: "Barbara taught us all how to dress properly and how to do our makeup with a light touch, for that natural look. Barb herself never wore a lot of makeup. Trust me, she was so beautiful she didn't need it.

"Barbara showed us all the correct way to walk and sit, and even the proper way to get in and out of a car. We were all so impressed with her that I asked the principal of our high school if Barb could come out to the school one afternoon and address a girls assembly. He agreed, and Barb, who always loved to be the center of attention, jumped at the opportunity."

On the day of her speech, Barbara arrived at Compton High School wearing a stylish black dress with long sleeves, her mother's pearl necklace, and a wide-brimmed black hat. "She was absolutely gorgeous," says Jan. "Barb made a tremendous impression that day. It wasn't too long after that when she began doing print ads for Max Factor, and that's when her modeling career in Hollywood really started to pick up."

After quitting high school, Barbara's brother Frank had enlisted in the Navy and at the time of John Lee's birth, he was stationed in Long Beach at the Terminal Island Naval Base. Several months later, during one of his military leaves, he met Jan at a local roller-skating rink. Amazingly, neither of them knew that she and her family were babysitting Frank's nephew.

"Even though I first met Frank at the skating rink," Jan says, "it was nearly a year later when I saw him again. It was the funniest thing. One day I recognized his skates hanging on a hook at Barbara's house, and that's how I found out that he was her brother. The next time I saw him at the skating rink I told him that my mother was taking care of Johnny, and it was a big surprise for all of us."

Jan, who was raised in a close-knit and ultraconservative family, admits to initially being attracted to Frank's rough-and-tumble ways, and soon noticed that he also shared much of his sister's fearlessness and irreverence. "Both Barbara and Frank had a real bravado about them that was very appealing to me. I never felt I had that quality myself, so I really liked being around them." Frank and Jan dated exclusively for two years before their marriage in October 1950.

As she watched her brother and her best friend grow closer, Barbara found herself pulling away, emotionally, from her husband. Although there is no question that she still cared about him, Barbara's dreams of getting into show business had, over time, become far too big to contain, and John had become an unexpected obstacle to Barbara's realizing that dream. While Jan and some of her other friends were amused by Barbara's almost daily insistence that she was going to be a movie star, John had

Barbara's best friend Jan Zollinger and her husband, Barbara's younger brother Frank Redfield, on their wedding day in October 1950. Courtesy of Jan Redfield

gradually begun to seethe over his wife's obsession with the idea, and kept hoping she would outgrow it.

"All that Hollywood jazz was not for Jack," says Frank. "He was his own man and he didn't want any part of that. For himself, or for Barbara."

Undeterred by both John's disapproval of her career goals, and by her responsibilities at home with a new baby, Barbara continued making day trips into Hollywood to see if she could obtain some further contacts in the modeling field. She eventually connected with the right people, and in September 1947, Barbara signed a one-year contract with agent Stratford Corbett of the Rita La Roy Agency on Wilshire Boulevard.

Born in Paris, France in 1907, Rita La Roy was a former movie actress specializing in small, showgirl parts, and had opened the modeling agency after her film career ended in the early 1940s. As a La Roy model, Barbara immediately resumed her print work, most notably in a series of car catalogue ads for the 1948 Studebaker Champion.

"Barbara did a lot of those Studebaker ads with another Rita La Roy model named June Bright," says Jan Redfield. "They became good friends, and after a while, my mother and I began collecting all the newspaper and magazine ads they appeared in together. We pasted them in a huge scrapbook that I kept for many years. Unfortunately, though, it was lost several years ago by a very careless family member, and now it's gone forever."

In October, just a short month after signing with Rita La Roy, Barbara and June Bright were sent by the agency to audition for famed costume designer Don Loper, who was putting together a variety production at Slapsy Maxie's nightclub on Beverly Boulevard in Hollywood. Both girls apparently passed their auditions with flying colors, and on October 16, they were hired by the nightclub's president, Sy Devore, to appear with six other starlets and burlesque comics Benny Fields and Henny Youngman in a baggy-pants comedy revue.

Barbara's American Guild of Variety Artists (AGVA) employment contract for the job stipulated that she was to be part of a ten-member ensemble for two performances daily, between the hours of 8:00 p.m. and 2:00 a.m., six days per week, for a period of eight weeks, "for which the employer agrees to pay the artist the sum of one hundred dollars weekly." The contract also stated that Barbara was to pay 10% commission to the Rita La Roy Agency, "immediately preceding the final performance of each work day or week."

Minneapolis Star news clipping of Barbara during her modeling days in Hollywood. Courtesy of John Lee Payton

Barbara went blonde for the first time in this 1948 Studebaker ad. Courtesy of Jan Redfield

The job (and its quite handsome salary for a 20-year-old girl in 1947) must have thrilled Barbara, as it placed her smack in the middle of one of Hollywood's most popular nightspots, one that was frequented by some of the industry's biggest stars.

"Things went well for Barbara and me in 1947, and for the early part of 1948, mainly due to the Zollingers, who were wonderful," said John Payton in 2006. "They gave Johnny loving care while I was in school, and Barbara's interest in modeling escalated."

But while she was making positive strides in her modeling career, Barbara's increasing fascination with the nightlife she had tasted during her late-night job at Slapsy Maxie's had driven a wedge between her and John that had finally pushed their marriage apart.

Just prior to his death, John Payton would only say, "Barbara and I really started drifting apart in mid-1948, mostly due to her huge interest in show business, which contrasted greatly with our prior life together in Compton."

Finally, after nearly three-and-a-half years of marriage, Barbara and John separated on July 4. "One day, she up and moved to Hollywood," he said sadly, "and I lost her."

Past that, John Payton refused to comment further on a relationship he had always viewed as a private and inviolate treasure.

Following their separation, Barbara rented a small, second-floor apartment on Hollywood Boulevard, just west of La Brea Avenue. As she had already proved to be an excellent and caring mother, John agreed to allow Barbara to keep John Lee with her at her new home. No doubt helping this decision was the knowledge that the Zollingers lived nearby and were always available to take care of Johnny if Barbara, for some reason, couldn't.

Eventually, Dorothy and Al Zollinger became kind of surrogate parents to Barbara's son, and he went on to spend a good part of his youth in their care. "When Barbara and John separated that summer," says Jan, "she brought Johnny to my mother and father, and he stayed with them, sometimes for days or weeks at a time, for many years afterward."

Little is known today about Barbara's exact activities between July and December 1948 other than she continued modeling for Rita La Roy while working very briefly as a carhop at the famous California landmark, Stan's Drive-In, on the corner of Sunset Boulevard and Highland Avenue. Obviously, she continued making further inroads in Hollywood, and with her marriage to John now over (at least unofficially), this included dating other men, as well.

Footloose and single for the first time in nearly four years, Barbara began frequenting many of the bars and nightclubs that dotted the town's glistening Sunset Strip, and it wasn't long before she had amassed quite a following of friends and admirers. With a tendency to spend her money a bit too lavishly ("In those years, Barb never had two nickels to rub together," says her brother), Barbara was often strapped for cash, so in the fall of 1948 she took in a roommate, a purported "aspiring actress" named Marie Allison, to help her with the bills. Allison, of whom little is known today (other than she was later married to the famous jazz drummer Buddy Rich), was said to run with a fast crowd of Hollywood clubgoers and hoods, including a particularly slimy young swell by the name of Don Cougar, who quickly took a liking to Barbara. A brawny, 27-year-old movie extra, Cougar was also a known drug user and part-time dealer, who had business ties to some high-level L.A. mobsters, including the west coast's infamous Sica Brothers. At some point between late 1948 and early 1949, he and Barbara began dating, albeit casually, and it was an association that would soon bring her the first of many unfortunate headlines.

One of Barbara's early modeling shots in Hollywood. Courtesy of L.A. Public Library/ Herald Examiner Collection

Reaching For a Dream • 51

As a small child, John Lee lived with Barbara in Hollywood.
Courtesy of Jan Redfield

On her own for the first time in her life, Barbara had taken a wrong turn right out of the gate, and in keeping company with the likes of Don Cougar, had landed in some pretty muddy water. Yet, as was so often the case with her, Lady Luck gave Barbara a second chance, with a golden opportunity that seemed to come from clear out of the blue.

William Goetz, the production chief at Universal-International Studios, had first seen Barbara when she was part of the variety revue at Slapsy Maxie's nightclub, and had been impressed at the time with both her beauty and her onstage poise. Although Goetz hadn't approached Barbara then to join Universal as an actress, when he saw some of her later modeling work (and reportedly, her standout presence on the Hollywood club scene), his interest in her was renewed, and in spite of Barbara's total lack of acting experience, Goetz signed her to the studio in

January 1949. Needless to say, the star struck 21-year-old was elated with her good fortune.

"It all seemed to happen so fast for Barbara," says Jan Redfield. "Everything fell into place right away for her. It was actually pretty amazing."

With a starting salary of $100 per week, Barbara was placed in Universal's contract stable of stock-players, which in 1949 included Rock Hudson, Tony Curtis, Shelley Winters, Jeff Chandler, Donna Martell, Howard Duff, James Best, Peggy Dow, and several other promising young neophytes. Over the next six months, Barbara (now a very attractive strawberry-blonde) posed for countless publicity photos for U-I's portrait photographer, Ray Jones. Along with her fellow greenhorns, she also studied with the well-respected Sophie Rosenstein, the studio's resident acting coach. A whole world of opportunity had presented itself to Barbara, and she went after her exciting new career with everything she had.

CHAPTER FIVE:
Like a Mustang on the Loose

Barbara's first film roles at Universal came in two Western musical shorts starring Country-and-Western bandleader Tex Williams: *Silver Butte* (released in July 1949) and *Pecos Pistol* (released the following October). In both features, Barbara's screen time as Williams' leading lady took a back seat to the action and musical scenes, and was restricted to a few sporadic appearances of brief duration.

Beginning in 1948, Universal producer/director Will Cowan churned out twenty-eight of these half-hour shorts—seventeen of them starring Tex Williams and his longtime band members, Smoky Rogers and Deuce Spriggens—as co-features to the studio's full-length Westerns. Partial remakes of several earlier Universal B's starring the likes of screen cowboys Johnny Mack Brown, Bob Baker and Kirby Grant, the shorts were heavily laden with stock footage from those films, and were, at best, extremely minor productions. Though well-received by the Saturday matinee crowd, these mini "featurettes" were eventually deemed not profitable by the studio, and were discontinued in 1950.

Silver Butte and *Pecos Pistol* remain extremely obscure films, according to Western film historian Boyd Magers, who says, "For some reason, copies of those two Tex Williams shorts with Barbara continue to elude most collectors. As a result, they remain unseen by many modern-day fans of the genre, including me." Indeed, all that seems left of these films today is a limited series of long-forgotten production stills, several of which feature a shapely and smiling Barbara, looking clear-eyed and eager to take on whatever came next.

Universal seemed intent on grooming its new acquisition slowly, and in March 1949, it handed Barbara a bit part in a Robert Montgomery/Ann Blyth comedy, *Once More, My Darling* (a.k.a. *Come Be My Love*, and

Barbara Payton and Tex Williams in the U-I western short, **Silver Butte.**
Courtesy of Universal Pictures

filmed after *Pecos Pistol*, but released one month earlier, in September 1949).

Montgomery also directed the high-energy farce that found him playing Collier Laing, a middle-aged actor and lawyer, who is hired by the military to romance zany debutante Marita Connell (Blyth). Though the latter's former boyfriend, an alleged dealer in Nazi jewelry, is Montgomery's principal quarry, the tables are turned when he finds himself being pursued by the love-hungry Blyth, eventually eloping with her to Las Vegas.

Tex Williams, Smokey Rogers and Barbara in a scene from **Silver** *Butte.*
Courtesy of Universal Pictures

Lauded in some circles for its witty dialog and brisk pace, *Once More, My Darling* was a pleasant enough production, although Barbara's tiny role, as a pert nightclub photographer, limited her once again to a fleeting blip on the screen.

The lovely Donna Martell (*Abbott and Costello Meet the Killer, Boris Karloff*), a frequent television guest star on several Western series episodes in the 1950s and '60s, and a U-I contract player for two years, befriended Barbara in 1949. The former actress recalls a breathtakingly beautiful young woman who was both unpretentious and accessible. "I first met Barbara right after she was signed to the studio, when they brought her into our acting class to meet the rest of the contract players. She was sweet, and an absolutely lovely girl. We got to know each other pretty well and I considered her to be a good friend. Barbara was much more forward than I was, but I liked that about her. She didn't seem afraid of anything, really."

When Barbara was first signed to Universal, she didn't own a car, but Donna did, and often gave her rides to, and from, work.

Barbara as she appeared in the U-I western short, Pecos Pistol.
Courtesy of Universal Pictures

"After a while, she started bringing little John Lee to the studio. He was a darling, blond boy, I guess about two or three years old. At the time, I was still living at home with my parents, and my mother would often invite Barbara and John Lee over for dinner. Mom was crazy about him, as we all were. He was a gorgeous child."

Barbara had grown very close to her son (whom she called "Johnny") and loved showing him around the studio lot. "She would even bring him with her to Sophie Rosenstein's acting class," says Donna, "which really bothered Miss Rosenstein. In fact, it made her furious. But Barbara didn't seem to care. And she didn't fight back, either. Barbara had this uncanny way of mentally blocking-out peoples' anger with her, almost like she didn't notice, or it didn't exist. It really was something to behold."

Donna remembers the rapid transformation that took place in Barbara shortly after she was signed to the studio. "Barbara hadn't been there for very long, and she was really struggling financially. Remember, a lot of us at the studio were only making about $100 a week. Barbara didn't have very much, as far as clothing or jewelry, but one day she came to work really dressed to the nines. I remember saying to her, 'Oh, Barbara, you look so beautiful, honey. Where did you get that outfit?' And she said, 'Georgie gave it to me.' I later found out from the others, 'Georgie' was the actor, and notorious lady-killer, George Raft. He must have been very fond of Barbara because the clothes and jewelry he bought her were just stunning."

Robert Montgomery, Barbara and Ann Blyth in a scene from the U-I comedy, **Once More, My Darling**. *Courtesy of Universal Pictures*

Fellow U-I contract player Donna Martell, a friend of Barbara's in the late 1940s. Courtesy of Donna Martell

While many of his business colleagues were largely devoid of integrity (gangsters Benjamin "Bugsy" Siegel and Owney Madden were said to be close associates of his), George Raft was a well-liked man in Hollywood whose generosity was legendary. Jan Redfield recalls that

Barbara had first met him at Slapsy Maxie's, the nightclub where she had performed a year earlier. "George spotted her there one night and asked her out. He seemed to really like Barbara. I remember being with her in her apartment one evening when she received a huge bouquet of red roses, a case of champagne, and several boxes of black silk stockings, all presents from George Raft. She was ecstatic."

With her gorgeous looks and brazen manner, Barbara was just the type of woman Raft found enticing. Although married for many years to former dancer Grayce Mulrooney, he had always seen other women on the side (most notably, actress Betty Grable), and in 1949 Barbara was merely the latest of Raft's many passing diversions. By all accounts, their affair, if one can call it that, was not exclusive, and lasted a few months, at most.

Donna Martell recalls that Universal wasn't really utilizing Barbara's talents at the time, outside of occasional publicity tours and photo sittings in the stills gallery. "I'm not sure why, either, because I know she wanted to work, and she was certainly well liked around the lot. Barbara would frequently go into the casting office and tell them that she wanted to work more and do lots of pictures, like me. By that time, I had already done a few of those Tex Williams musicals, and she had, too. But, while I went on to do the Abbott and Costello film, the studio didn't seem to have anything else lined up for Barbara." [1]

Donna remembers posing for several national magazine layouts with her friend in 1949, and fondly recalls the day they were inducted into the American Legion as "Honorary Colonels" (along with fellow U-I players Piper Laurie, Peggie Castle, Ann Pearce and Peggy Dow). "We received a lot of publicity for that. Our group picture was in all the papers and Barbara got such a kick out of it. I remember she mailed a whole bunch of those clippings back home to Minnesota and Texas, where she had relatives."

Although Donna insists her fellow acting novice was quite naive and innocent at the time, a more realistic guess is that the small-town girl from Cloquet had already fallen under Hollywood's intoxicating spell, where the lure of the finer things in life proved a most inviting temptation. Donna later lost touch with Barbara after their respective contracts with Universal Studios lapsed, but says, "I thought of Barbara often over the years and wished we could have stayed in touch. She was sweet and friendly, and just a wonderful, down-to-earth girl." [2]

As her short-term affair with ladies' man George Raft suggests, Barbara was impatient, and anxious to make her mark in Hollywood. Admittedly more fun-loving than ambitious, she quickly resumed her nightly assault on the Sunset Strip and reveled in its all-out drinking and partying scene. In those days, plush, happening nightclubs like Ciro's, Mocambo and the Trocadero were a hedonist's delight, and the glitz and glamour of their surroundings washed over the young starlet like the foamy California surf.

From her first appearance on the Strip in late 1948, Barbara was an instant success in the all-important area of networking, helped by the fact that she had an outgoing and bold personality coupled with devastatingly good looks.

Reminiscing about the young Barbara, legendary film producer A.C. Lyles remembers meeting her for the first time at Ciro's. "When I first saw her, I was naturally struck by how lovely Barbara was," he says. "I thought she had the most beautiful eyes. The best way I can describe them is that they were both sexy and innocent." A.C. also recalls her gregarious manner and how she moved around the club with total confidence. "I think she came over and introduced herself to me. I don't believe there was a shy bone in Barbara's body. She seemed to make friends very easily. Whenever I saw her in any of the restaurants or clubs on the Strip, she was always surrounded by a lot of people, both men and women."

A.C. recalls dining with Joan Crawford one night at Ciro's, just a few weeks after he met Barbara. He says that Crawford, who didn't know Barbara at the time, seemed spellbound by her beauty when Barbara came over to their table to say hello to A.C. "After I introduced them and Barbara left, Joan turned to me and said, 'That is a very lovely, very sweet girl. Who is she? Where is she from? If her acting is as good as her looks, she is going to be big in this town.'

"Trust me, Joan Crawford rarely complimented another female. She was notoriously jealous of most women, and usually very tough on them, too. But she really thought Barbara was something else."

Although she was initially impressed with Barbara, Crawford would be singing a far less pleasant tune about her before long.

In addition to Don Cougar and George Raft, Barbara dated a whole slew of available—and not so-available—men during her first several months in town. Although she was still legally married to John, it was reported in 1949 that she was seen around Hollywood with slick, Chicago

A 1949 publicity still of Barbara in Palm Springs, CA. Courtesy of USC/Dept. of Special Collections/L.A. Examiner Collection

camera manufacturer Ted Briskin (then married to movie star Betty Hutton), wealthy L.A. paving contractor and lounge lizard Jerry Bialac, and stone-faced actors John Ireland and Ralph Meeker. Hollywood gossip columnists also wrote that Barbara was spotted "drinking and dining at

Ciro's" with the very-married, violent west coast mobster Mickey Cohen, and later announced her engagement to high-powered entertainment lawyer Greg Bautzer.

"I know that Barbara dated Greg," says Donna Martell, "but I'm not sure if it's true that he ever intended to marry her. Their affair began when Barbara was still at Universal and I know it lasted for several months until the studio dropped her. Greg was quite a ladies man in town, and I remember hearing that he was once engaged to both Lana Turner and Joan Crawford at the same time."

Apparently, Barbara also had a brief relationship with roguish, B-movie actor Robert Lowery, best known today as the second person to play Batman, in Columbia Pictures' 1949 *Batman and Robin* movie serial. In a March 2005 interview on the *Celluloid Dreams* radio program, actor John (a.k.a. Johnny) Duncan, who played Robin to Lowery's Batman, spoke to movie critic Peter Canavese about an incident that occurred one morning when Lowery invited his friend and co-worker over for breakfast.

"[Bob Lowery] loved the women," said Duncan. "He used to go with, oh, what's her name, Barbara—oh, he did a lot of starlets—he went with a lot of starlets. Barbara Payton is the name of the little girl.

"I'd come over one day to visit him on a Sunday morning, and we were gonna have breakfast together. Bob had just talked to me about an hour before. 'Get over here,' he said, 'we'll have some breakfast.' So I said, 'Okay.' And this is right after we made *Batman and Robin*. So I went over there and knocked on the door, and he hollers, 'Come on in!,' and here he's in bed with Barbara Payton, with crumbling cracker crumbs in his bed. I said, 'You've got to be crazy!'"

"Barbara was head over heels in love with Bob Lowery," claims her future husband, Tony Provas. "In her mind, it wasn't just a casual affair. She told me she was serious about him and that she would have married him if he had asked her. But apparently, he didn't feel the same way about her. To Bob Lowery, I suppose, Barbara was just another wide-eyed and willing starlet in his long line of conquests."

While Robert Lowery could be considered at the mid-to-lower end of the Hollywood food chain, billionaire industrialist and entertainment tycoon Howard Hughes was inarguably at the very top. And today there is a modicum of evidence suggesting that Barbara and Hughes may have, at the very least, crossed paths socially at some point in 1949. What happened beyond that, however, remains open to conjecture.

Though much of what he writes about Barbara in his 2005 Hughes bio, *Howard Hughes: Hell's Angel*, is unnecessarily crass and demeaning, author Darwin Porter rightly describes Barbara being introduced to Howard Hughes by her ex-boyfriend Greg Bautzer, who was also Hughes' attorney. Unfortunately, Porter goes on to paint Barbara in a singularly unflattering light, utilizing several alleged quotes from Hughes crony, mob figure and alleged pimp, Johnny Meyer, to bolster his apparent disdain for her.

Calling Barbara "Hollywood's biggest trollop," Meyer described her to Porter as a kind of man-eating piranha who latched onto Howard Hughes after he expressed an interest in her purported lack of sexual inhibitions. Today, however, her family and friends uniformly deny that anything substantial occurred between the pair other than a casual dalliance, and perhaps, even a job offer. Former Hollywood agent Philip Feldman agrees, telling author John Gilmore in his 2005 tome, *L.A. Despair*: "Rumors got around that Barbara was 'seeing' Howard Hughes, but there was little evidence other than her invasion of Hughes' party at Ciro's. I recall an occasion when they were at the same table—Barbara and Hughes. She'd no doubt invited herself to join them because John Ireland, the nervous actor she'd been dating a few times, sat chewing his fingernails while she hopped around the club like a rabbit."

Barbara's best friend, Jan Redfield, says, "The longstanding rumor of an affair between Barbara and Hughes is a big bunch of you-know-what. Barbara always gave me blow-by-blow descriptions of all the guys she dated, and all she ever said about Howard Hughes was that she met him a few times and that she thought he was sloppy (and strange)."

Tina Ballard, Barbara's closest confidante after Jan, echoes her sentiments. "I don't believe the story that Barbara ever dated Howard Hughes. In those years, he had all the women he wanted or needed, and Barbara's dance card was more than full. As everyone knows, Hughes was an odd and reclusive person, and that wouldn't have appealed to Barbara at all; billionaire, or not. Barbara was all about being seen, laughing the loudest, and having fun. She definitely met him, though, as she bragged about it later on. And I believe it *was* Greg Bautzer who introduced them. But as for Barbara actually seeing Hughes, off and on, for a couple of years, I doubt it."

Barbara's brother Frank has his own story to share regarding her supposed connection to Hughes. "I was told by my parents that Hughes had talked to Barbara a few times about starring in a kid's picture that was being made at his studio (RKO), called *Mighty Joe Young*. He evidently thought she was perfect for the part of the young girl in the film, but my parents said that Barbara had turned him down because she didn't want to be 'in some stupid movie where she would be carried around by a giant ape with her butt sticking out'. I guess she didn't know that a little film called *Bride of the Gorilla* was in her future." [3]

A stunning head shot of Barbara from 1949. Courtesy of Wisconsin Center for Film and Theater Research

*The sexy and super-confident Barbara Payton in 1949.
Courtesy of The Trinity Mirror*

Though the true extent of her relationship with Howard Hughes remains a topic shaded in gray, there is plenty of evidence to prove that Barbara's "dance card" during this time was not only full, but overflowing. Shortly after he met Barbara at Ciro's, A.C. Lyles recalls seeing her milling around the commissary at Paramount Studios, in apparent pursuit of yet another new boyfriend. "I know Barbara started out at Universal, but in those days I frequently saw her on the Paramount lot, as well. I believe she was interested in one of the studio chauffeurs at the time, as she would often join him there for lunch. Her fling with him was probably short-lived, though, because after a while she was hitting the clubs every night with a different date.

"She was an awfully restless girl."

Kicking up dust like a wild mustang on the loose, it's safe to say that Barbara was playing the entire field. Now in his late 80s, and with his fondness for her still evident, A.C. Lyles adds, "Dear Barbara never had an itch she didn't scratch."

In 1949, Barbara met a young man who would later become a good friend, as well as a beau, of sorts: 18-year-old British actor Ivan Hayes, who had recently arrived in Hollywood by way of Richmond, England. The strikingly handsome, blond and blue-eyed Hayes had landed in town that year with just eleven dollars in his pocket, but had quickly found shelter at the local YMCA and a job parking cars at Ciro's and the Mocambo. Although he would soon embark on a ten-year acting career in Hollywood (often billed as Steven Hayes)—first, as a contract player at 20th Century-Fox, where he had bit parts in *The Desert Fox: The Story of Rommel*, *Belles on Their Toes* and *Titanic*, and later as a freelance actor working at several other major studios in town—Hayes would enjoy greater success in the 1980s as a film and television writer and producer.

"I came to Hollywood as 'Ivan Hayes,'" he says, "but when I was signed to Fox in 1951, it was at the height of McCarthyism in this country, and it was suggested that I change my first name (which is Russian for John) so that people wouldn't think I was a Commie. I was friendly with a body builder named Steve Reeves [who would later play Hercules], so I took the name Steve because I thought it fit well with Hayes."

A highly colorful, oft-married raconteur who graduated from parking cars at Hollywood's most glamorous nightclubs, to doing bit parts in several films, to working as a night manager at the Sunset Strip's famous Googie's restaurant, to later fighting in Cuba's Castro Revolution, and even spending time as a soldier of fortune in the Belgian Congo in 1961, Steve Hayes has experienced a lot in his 75 years—and counts his affair with Barbara as one of his more interesting relationships.

"I first saw Barbara one Saturday night in 1949 when I was parking cars at Ciro's," he recalls. "She was with Greg Bautzer, a handsome lawyer-to-the-stars, who was also Hollywood's most eligible bachelor at the time. I had met Greg earlier through a mutual friend, the writer-director Preston Sturges, and after saying hello to me, he and Barbara waltzed into the club. Barbara was clinging to his arm and laughing, and besides thinking that she was an absolute knockout, I also thought she seemed full of fun."

Steve soon learned that Barbara had a good memory, because the next time he saw her, two weeks later, he was parking cars at Sturges's The

Actor Steve Hayes dated Barbara for a time in the late 1940s and early 50s. Courtesy of Steve Hayes

Blue Room (formerly The Players), a restaurant-bar on Sunset Boulevard, and Barbara had surprisingly remembered his name.

"She kidded me," he says, "asking me if I was trying to get rich by working all the clubs along the Strip. Preston, who had the quickest wit I've ever known, said something to her that inferred that she and I had dated before, and Barbara came back at him, saying, 'Are you kidding? I never date guys who are prettier than me.' Preston got a big kick out of that and never let me forget it, often needling me about my blue eyes, long eyelashes and blond curls, in front of others, but never in a nasty way. After a while, I got used to it and refused to get pissed, so he stopped doing it. Preston really liked Barbara's wry sense of humor, and he told me he thought she had a lot going for her."

Although they exchanged brief pleasantries that day, Steve and Barbara didn't formally meet until a few weeks later, at the Bel Air estate of wealthy film producer Bryan Foy (the son of vaudevillian Eddie Foy, of *Seven Little Foys* fame). At the time, Steve was dating Bryan's daughter, Mary Jane. When he picked her up to take her out to dinner at Mocambo ("Her dad's treat, because I sure as hell couldn't spring for it"), Barbara was at the house talking to Foy about starring in his next picture (Barbara's 1949 film noir, *Trapped*).

"Barbara cocked an eye at me as Mary Jane introduced us," recalls Steve, "but she had the smarts not to say she knew me in front of my date. But as Mary Jane kissed her dad goodnight, Babs winked at me and in an almost motherly, proud fashion, whispered: 'Bel Air. Coming up in the world, aren't we?'

"She had such an impish wit, I remember thinking that I wanted to get to know her better."

Steve Hayes eventually *would* get to know Barbara better—intimately, in fact—but in 1949 that opportunity was still a year off.

Shortly after their meeting, Steve remembers hearing that Barbara had become the latest conquest of weathered film star (and purported satyr) Errol Flynn, who by 1949 was fully submerged in his notorious lifestyle of round-the-clock debauchery.

"Barbara was seen a lot at Flynn's house, up in the hills above Mulholland Drive," says Steve. "Unfortunately, word was already getting around in town that she didn't seem to care about anything except getting laid and having a good time."

Jan Redfield says, "Barbara got caught up in that wild, Hollywood lifestyle pretty quickly, it's true, but that's because she was so full of life and just blown away by all the company she was keeping. She was standing in some pretty high cotton with all those big stars, and she just wanted to be liked and accepted by all of them. I guess Barb was willing to do whatever she had to do to be part of that crowd. Still, she probably would have been a lot better off if she hadn't gotten in with Errol Flynn. She probably stepped right off the cliff with that one."

Steve Hayes himself would later see Barbara at Errol Flynn's house, and it was the start of a brief, if memorable, liaison.

In March 1949, Barbara took a break from her Hollywood adventures to take part in a Universal publicity tour throughout northeast Texas. As Bob Rains, the former Assistant Head of Casting at U-I explains, "Barbara, along with several other contract players at the studio, sometimes accompanied Head of Casting, Bob Palmer, and me on national tours that U-I arranged to help publicize some of the studio's new pictures. Although they were often not in the pictures themselves, Barbara and the other contract players in the troupe would act in some skits we wrote for them to perform on stage in the theaters premiering the films. During her time at Universal, Barbara and I had gone on several of these tours together and we eventually became good friends."

It was on the tour's stopover in Dallas that Barbara met her next professional diversion, this time in the guise of 46-year-old married man Bob Hope. While staying at the city's Baker Hotel, Barbara bumped into an old friend from Odessa, a wealthy oil tycoon and playboy named Bob Neal, one afternoon in the hotel lobby. Like so many others, Neal found Barbara enchanting and invited her to accompany him to a cocktail party Hope was throwing that evening in his suite. It would be a meeting that would have far-reaching consequences for Barbara, none of them good.

When Bob Hope met Barbara, he was in the middle of his own publicity tour of twenty-one cities with the cast of his nationally broadcast radio show, and had stopped off in Dallas to compete in a charity golf tournament. In Arthur Marx's unauthorized biography of the actor, *The Secret Life of Bob Hope*, he writes, "…at their first meeting, there was immediate chemistry between Hope and Barbara." (Barbara verified this herself, in a 1956 interview with *Confidential* magazine, in which she brashly declared, "We only knew each other a few hours before we knew each other as well as a boy and girl ever can!")

Following their meeting, Barbara spent the night with Hope in his room and then left the next morning to keep a business appointment at the Shamrock Hotel in Houston. That evening, he allegedly joined her there to continue their escapades in a room registered under Barbara's name. Upon their return together to the west coast, Hope promptly set her up in a furnished, duplex Hollywood apartment at 2475 Cheremoya Avenue, complete with, in the words of *Confidential* magazine, "a king-size double bed that was the set for many rollicking good times...." [4]

Within days, Barbara had commenced following Hope around the country as he resumed his publicity tour, while completely ignoring her various professional commitments at Universal. According to Arthur Marx, in June the couple spent two weeks together at New York City's elegant Waldorf-Astoria, where they took adjoining suites with a connecting door. When Hope attended the premiere of his film *Sorrowful Jones* (co-starring Lucille Ball) at Broadway's Paramount Theater, Barbara stood nearby, on the arm of his agent/manager, and frequent beard, Louis Shurr. While in N.Y., Hope and Barbara dined together at such high-class West Side establishments as El Morocco, 21, and The Little Gypsy, but always with Louis Shurr and several other actors from Hope's entourage. Following their holiday in The Big Apple, the pair traveled to Washington, D.C., where Hope competed in a charity golf match while Barbara rooted for him, anonymously, from the sidelines.

For a while, it seemed that wherever Bob Hope's business brought him, Barbara went along to keep him company; so often, in fact, that Universal's Head of Talent, Rufus Le Maire, first warned her, and then canceled her contract. "Barbara was dropped from the studio on a morals charge," says Bob Rains. "Everyone there knew about her affair with Bob Hope, and how he was paying her way. That was pretty serious stuff back then."

In those days, a starlet's carrying on openly with a married man was verboten, if not for the married man (especially one as successful as Hope), then definitely for the starlet. Still, Barbara was strangely unruffled by the studio's rejection of her, and continued to act like Bob Hope's number one groupie.

"When Universal fired Barbara, she couldn't have cared less," recalls Donna Martell. "She wasn't mad or the least bit upset, which really puzzled me, because she always told me how much she wanted to be a movie star. But I think she was more interested in her personal life at the time, than in her career. Barbara was all over the map at that point and I don't think she really knew what she wanted."

Although Barbara and Bob Hope had a cozy thing going for the better part of the summer, it wasn't long before greed replaced lust, and the couple's idyllic arrangement turned ugly.

In between their cross-country jaunts, Barbara had taken to appearing unexpectedly on the set of Hope's latest movie, *Fancy Pants* (again co-starring Lucille Ball), where in front of the film's entire crew, and in a voice far above a whisper, she would ask him for money to help cover her living expenses. Much to her chagrin, Hope tried instead to placate her with less costly presents, including, in her own angry words, "a couple of lousy jars of cheap jam." A highly-insulted Barbara would later complain in a 1956 tabloid piece, "Boy, was he ever tight! I never got more than a hundred dollars out of him at a time."

Increasingly irate at having to compete not only with Hope's excessive ego and the ever-present clique of "yes-men" he surrounded himself with, but also with his obvious allegiance to his wife Dolores and their two children, Barbara's tough and self-preserving side surfaced. She began to needle him by constantly answering 'No' to almost everything he asked her. When he pressed her for an explanation, Barbara reportedly said, "You pay your people plenty just to say 'Yes' to you. At the rates I'm getting, I'm saying 'No!'"

When that tactic failed to elicit the desired response from him, Barbara retaliated by telling everyone she knew about their affair and, especially, about Hope's rather lackluster skills in bed. "He was the greatest that first night in Dallas, but once it became 'old hat' to him he was no longer such a tiger," she later told the tabloids. Already tired of Barbara's unpredictable nature and covetous ways, Hope was enraged by the aspersions she was now casting on his virility.

The death knell rang on the Bob Hope/Barbara Payton *affaire d'amour* in late August 1949, when an accident on the *Fancy Pants* set landed the actor in Hollywood's Presbyterian Hospital. During one scene, Lucille Ball's character was trying to teach him how to ride a horse by using a wooden barrel that had been electrically rigged to buck like a wild bronco. Within moments of mounting it, Hope was flung off the device and knocked unconscious. He wound up hospitalized for a week with some temporary paralysis and a mild concussion. During his recovery, Barbara made it a point to visit him every day—usually in the middle of the night, so she wouldn't be seen.

Not wanting him to think she was losing interest in their arrangement, Barbara prepared a gourmet meal one afternoon for Hope and had it delivered to his hospital room at dinnertime. A few hours later, she took a chance on his being alone and dropped by the hospital, expecting to hear words of praise for her cooking. Instead, she walked into his room to find her culinary gift untouched and Hope chowing down a three-course meal he had ordered from Romanoff's. As *Confidential* later wrote, "One word led to another, and, before it was over, they were shouting at each other over Bob's bed of pain." Barbara stormed out of Hope's room, and by all known reports, right out of their affair, as well.

When Barbara later threatened to tell Dolores Hope of her husband's infidelity, the actor had his advisors pay her off with a handsome sum, reportedly in the many thousands, with the stipulation that she keep quiet and disappear. With all bets now off, Barbara allegedly grabbed the cash and happily bowed out. She left their Cheremoya Avenue "love nest" and rented a new apartment on Hollywood Boulevard. She also supposedly went through all of Hope's hush money in a matter of months.

Although it appeared that Bob Hope was rid of Barbara, she wasn't exactly finished with him. Little did he know then that she would resurface in his life, seven years later, in a most embarrassing way.

"That whole thing with Bob Hope was an unfortunate experience," admits Jan Redfield, "but I think Barbara reacted that way because she knew she was being used. Barb was usually very loving and very giving, too, but she definitely had a tough side. She saw herself on the same playing field as any man, and if they mistreated her—well, she definitely wasn't going to take it lying down."

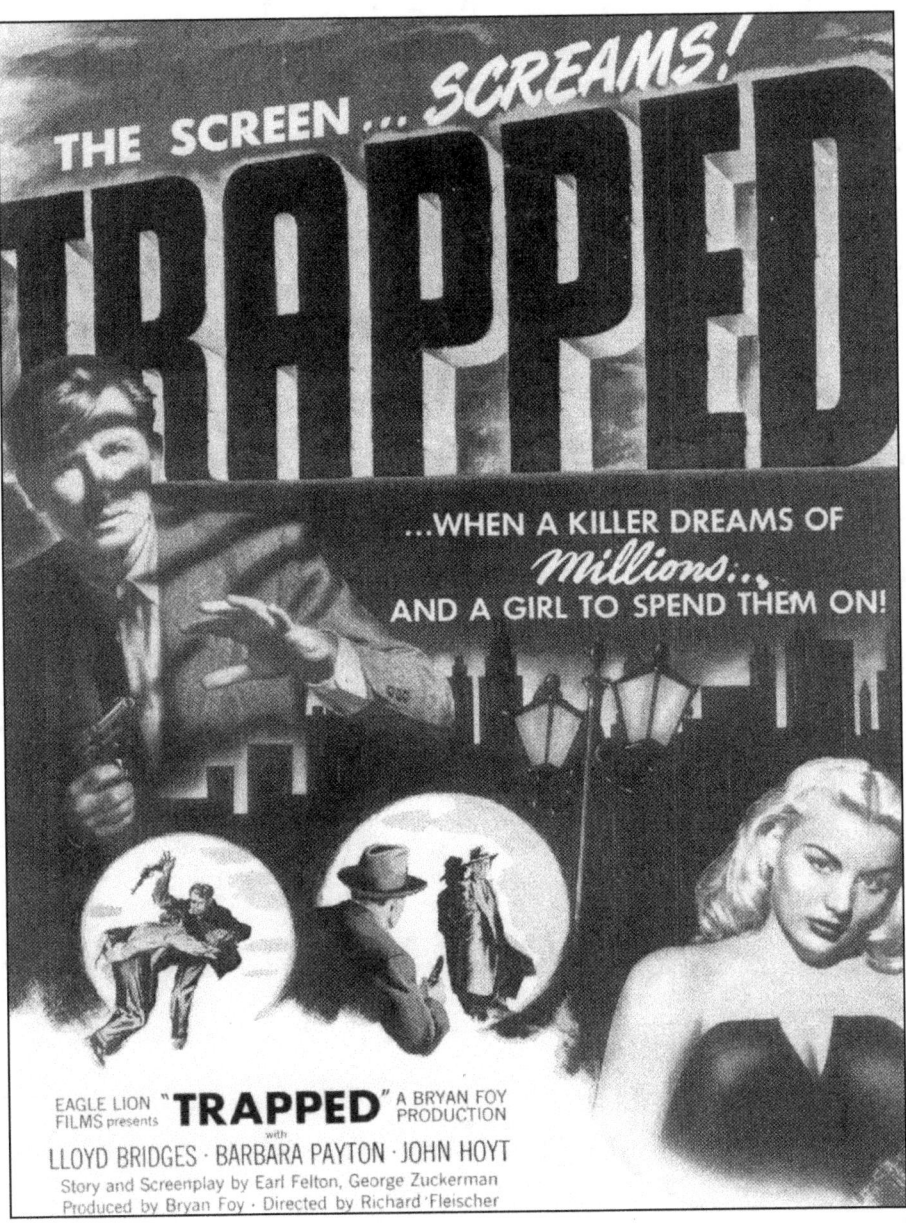

Ad matte for the 1949 film noir Trapped, *in which Barbara starred with Lloyd Bridges. From the Author's Collection*

CHAPTER SIX:
Dark Clouds on the Horizon

Barbara's pursuit of work, fun—and notoriety—in California was suddenly interrupted in 1949 when she received word that her mother had been diagnosed with breast cancer and would have to undergo a radical mastectomy. Barbara immediately flew home and arrived in Odessa soon after Mabel was admitted to the hospital.

"The doctors who performed the surgery on Mabel did a real hack job on her," remembers Jan. "I'm sure there was very little known about the procedure back then, and afterwards, Mabel developed several blood clots in her legs. In fact, she had to have another operation right after the mastectomy, just to get rid of them. All of us in the family were extremely worried, but Mabel eventually pulled through. She was still recuperating and confined to her bed when Frank and I visited her in Odessa the following year. That's when I saw her mastectomy scars, and they were pretty nasty."

Barbara spent several weeks in Odessa after her mother's surgery and did everything she could to help her with her recovery. "She cooked and cleaned and waited on her hand and foot," says Jan. "People can say what they will about her, but Barbara was a model daughter to Mabel. Always."

Naturally, while she was home, there were problems between Lee and Barbara—there were *always* problems between them—but Barbara managed to get through the visit without any major blowups. She returned to Hollywood only after she was convinced that her mother, who had always been her strongest advocate, was out of danger.

Somehow in the middle of all this bustle and chaos, Barbara continued to pursue her acting career. In the summer of 1949, just prior to her breakup with Bob Hope, she was cast as the female lead in a crime drama, *Trapped* (Eagle-Lion), directed by future film noir icon Richard Fleischer

(*The Narrow Margin*). After languishing for nearly a year in three small roles at Universal, it was an impressive opportunity for Barbara, and she was determined to make the most of it.

With her newly acquired status as a freelance actress, Barbara had moved from Universal, a mid-level movie studio that had been in existence for more than 35 years, to one that was in its earliest days of operation. In his 2005 article, *Charles McGraw: Tribute to A Bad Man*, for author Karen Burroughs Hannsberry's *The Dark Pages* newsletter, fellow author and film noir expert Alan K. Rode explains, "Eagle-Lion was formed by the absorption of the late (poverty row studio) PRC organization into a joint organization with producer J. Arthur Rank from England. [In its first years] it quickly garnered both publicity and cash for making economical, fast-paced crime films that looked good and made money."

Much like Barbara and the fledgling studio to which they had been assigned, in 1949 thirty-three-year-old Richard Fleischer was at the beginning of his film career, and several years away from the accolades he would later receive for his work. The son of famed animator and inventor Max Fleischer, who was responsible for bringing the Popeye comic strip to cartoon life in the mid-1930s, he began his directing career in 1944 with the RKO wartime short, *Memo for Joe*. He eventually moved on to helm several well-regarded crime films for the studio, including *Follow Me Quietly*, *Bodyguard* and *The Clay Pigeon*.

A few years before his death in March 2006, Richard Fleischer recalled that he and casting director Owen McClain chose Barbara over dozens of other actresses who were up for the role in *Trapped*, solely on the strength of her physical appearance. "Owen and I were going through stacks and stacks of head shots, trying to find the right girl for the part," he said. "We needed a girl who was visually stunning, and we both knew that head shots were usually retouched and were therefore very unreliable. Often the girl would look good in the photo and then disappoint you when you would call her in for a reading. When we came across Barbara's photo, we both looked at each other and I said, 'That's her. That's the girl. If she looks this good in person and she can act, she's in.' Well, when Barbara came out to the studio to read for us, believe me, we thought she was perfect. She looked every bit as good, if not better, as she did in the photo. To top it all off, Barbara gave us a very good reading, so we signed her. It was that easy; she was just what we were looking for."

A hard-working, 36-year-old Lloyd Bridges, by then steadily making his way up the Hollywood ranks via a chain of well-received "B" films, was Barbara's leading man in this tough, semi-documentary film noir that offered a gritty look into the violent L.A. underworld. The plot finds veteran character actor John Hoyt as John Downey, a U.S. Secret Service agent who manages to infiltrate a counterfeiting gang by arranging the getaway of Bridges' character, Tris Stewart, the former head of the ring

Publicity still of Barbara and Lloyd Bridges from Trapped.
From the Author's Collection

Barbara and co-star Lloyd Bridges in a publicity still for Trapped. *Courtesy of The Trinity Mirror*

Barbara looking beautiful in a head shot from Trapped. *Courtesy of Wisconsin Center for Film and Theater Research*

who's been serving time in Alcatraz. After Bridges escapes from the custody of a Treasury Agent who's been assigned to monitor his activities, he reunites with his sexy girlfriend, Meg Dixon, a.k.a. Laurie Fredericks (Barbara), a mini-skirted cigarette vendor at a local nightclub.

Masquerading as a small-time crook, Hoyt's character gains the trust of Fredericks, while Bridges hooks up with Jack Sylvester (played by James Todd), the demented owner of the ring's master plates, who plans on flooding the area with new counterfeit bills. Sylvester tells Bridges' character that he must raise $25,000 in order to work a deal with him for more counterfeit cash, so Bridges decides to rob the nightclub where Barbara works. Though the robbery is thwarted, Bridges is eventually captured and sent back to prison while the police close in on the rest of the gang. By now, Barbara has discovered Hoyt to be a government agent, and foolishly exposes his true identity to Todd, who reacts wildly with a spray of bullets. Hoyt survives the ambush, but Barbara's character is killed when she is gunned down in a car barn by Todd, whose subsequent attempt to escape in a railway tunnel leads to his death when he accidentally strikes the guide wires above a trolley car.

In her first starring role, Barbara looks gorgeous and performs well as a young woman whose ardent loyalty to her lover is matched only by her unmitigated greed. "Money, there's just never enough of it," she purrs in one scene, as she slowly massages Bridges' shoulders. Not the typical film noir femme fatale, her character seems much more devoted than duplicitous. She is willing to go along with her boyfriend's unlawful schemes so they can be together, with barely a thought to the possible consequences.

Barbara seemed to infuse some of her real-life characteristics of wide-eyed innocence mixed with a kind of reckless self-assurance into the role, which, of course, makes watching her performance in the film even more intriguing today.

An extremely affable, modest and soft-spoken gentleman, director Richard Fleischer remembered Barbara in the early-2000s, with great fondness: "We filmed *Trapped* in about thirty-five days and Barbara was very easy to work with during the entire shoot. She tried very hard to do a good job and always gave us her best. In those days, because of our very quick shooting schedules, directors rarely had the chance to rehearse with the actors; there just wasn't enough time. So, there were many nights when Barbara stayed after work to do line readings, either with me or with

'Bud' [Lloyd Bridges' nickname]. She never once complained about the overtime, she did whatever we asked her to do. She was a delightful girl."

Her strong sense of professionalism aside, there is some evidence that suggests that Barbara and Bridges indulged in a brief affair during the filming of *Trapped*. In her 1963 autobiography, Barbara briefly mentions a fling with her co-star in a film they completed in late 1949, a man whom she calls "the champion ruiner of girls in Hollywood", a man she refers to as "Bud."

In a 2001 interview with author Tom Weaver for *Monsters from the Vault* magazine, former actress Nan Peterson (*The Hideous Sun Demon*) verified Barbara's claim that Bridges was prone to stray from his marital bed. Peterson guest-starred twice on Bridges' 1950s TV series, *Sea Hunt*, and she told Weaver, "Lloyd Bridges was really a bad guy. After I did the second *Sea Hunt*, he was driving me home, and he made a pass at me! And he wanted me to go to bed with him. That really made me mad, especially since I had met his whole family—at a big Christmas party, I met his sons, the two boys, and his wife, and they were all very nice. He seemed like such a nice family man."

Lloyd Bridges, Barbara and John Hoyt in a scene from **Trapped**.
From the Author's Collection

Two unidentified players, John Hoyt and Barbara in a scene from Trapped. *Courtesy of Wisconsin Center for Film and Theater Research*

Family man (or not) Lloyd Bridges may have been the first of Barbara's co-stars—the first of many—to succumb to her charms. Richard Fleischer admitted that the young woman had a warmth and an approachability that made her almost irresistible to the opposite sex. "Besides being beautiful and charismatic," he said, "Barbara was a very earthy woman, a real regular gal. She liked a good, dirty joke just like anyone else, but I don't recall her using bad language herself. She was earthy without being vulgar. I liked her very much."

A hard-hitting, tightly-edited script by Earl Felton and George Zuckerman, along with Barbara's alluring presence, and several strong performances, helped make *Trapped* a moderate-sized box office hit in October 1949. The young actress received several favorable notices for her portrayal of the ill-fated nightclub cigarette girl, with *Film Daily*'s review of the picture noting, "With all of the necessary curves and attractiveness in abundance, Barbara Payton effectively renders the feminine portion of the script with looks and acting ability."

Acclaimed NYC stage director and writer David Drake, the star of one of off-Broadway's longest-running one-person shows, *The Night*

*22-year old Barbara at the height of her beauty and sex appeal.
Courtesy of Jan Redfield*

Larry Kramer Kissed Me, recently saw *Trapped* for the first time and agrees with the positive reviews that Barbara received at the time of its release: "Without question, Barbara displays a lot of raw, able talent in the film. I found it very telling that her best scene work was with Lloyd Bridges. She really knows how to play the act of seduction, not the phony 'Hollywood' indicating that so often passed as seduction in Barbara's era, but the real stuff. It is in the way she caresses Bridges' hair and shoulders. [It was] very real, very true. She clearly understood the who, what, where, when and why's of grasping and accepting and playing a character's intentions and actions in a script. This was a smart girl with solid acting instincts. Barbara was a natural."

Though often overshadowed by any number of similar films from that era, *Trapped* remains one of the better, if more obscure, examples of late '40s film noir, as well as a potent gauge of Barbara's strong potential as a performer.

While Barbara's acting career was off to a nice start, her increasingly lurid private life was becoming a constant distraction. On September 11, 1949, her name made the local newspapers when her sometime-boyfriend, Don Cougar, beat up Barbara's landlady when the woman refused to accept $30 as full payment for Barbara's rent of $112.50. Mrs. Anna Johnson, 57, whom Barbara called "Granny," filed a $15,000 assault-and-battery suit against Cougar after he hit her and knocked her down in the three a.m. dispute. In defense of Barbara, she *did* try to end the row by getting Mrs. Johnson away from Cougar and then hiding the injured woman in her apartment until the police arrived. (Anna Johnson would have to wait until October 1951 for the matter to be resolved, at which time she collected $3,500 in a judgment decided in her favor.)

According to a story in the *L.A. Mirror*, Don Cougar, who at times also went by the name of Don Junior, had been arrested earlier that year for possession of "190 sacks of marijuana." And that wasn't his first brush with the law, either. In 1941, he had been jailed in San Bernardino for drunk driving, and in 1945, while serving in the armed forces, Cougar went AWOL and was ordered to a rehabilitation center at Camp Bowie, Texas.

With his bullying ways and propensity for using strong-arm tactics, Don Cougar was just one of the many shady characters in Hollywood to whom a thrill-seeking Barbara had gravitated. [5] In her endless quest for excitement, Barbara was aligning herself with some of the biggest lowlifes in town. The effect this would have on both her career, and her life, would be devastating.

Chapter Seven:
World by the Tail

By early 1950, as a result of the good notices she received for her performance in *Trapped*, Barbara began fielding job offers from several major film studios. Most notably, perhaps, was when industry giant MGM screen tested her for the part of Angela, the sexy, 18-year-old mistress of crooked lawyer Louis Calhern, in director John Huston's masterpiece, *The Asphalt Jungle*. (Also tested were starlets Lola Albright, Joi Lansing, Claudia Barrett and model Georgia Holt, the mother of Cher.) Though she and the others lost the role to relative newcomer Marilyn Monroe, an extremely self-confident Barbara moved on and was subsequently offered an interview with Warner Bros. Casting was taking place for the female lead in James Cagney's latest crime drama, *Kiss Tomorrow Goodbye*, and Barbara was again tested; this time, with several Warner Bros. contract players. She later wrote that she found out about the movie's casting call from "a madam plying her trade in Glendale." Considering the caliber of people Barbara was associating with, this assertion isn't all that implausible.

Kiss Tomorrow Goodbye came one year after James Cagney's classic turn as psychopathic gangster Cody Jarrett in Warner Bros.' box office smash, *White Heat*, and it was the studio's hope that the film would repeat its forerunner's success. Though separated in direct succession by the lackluster Cagney/Doris Day musical *The West Point Story* in 1950, the two crime films nonetheless signified a welcome return to form for the actor, who had spent the previous few years feeling frustrated in his attempt to distance himself from his screen gangster persona.

By the early 1940s, Cagney was tired of playing generic hoodlum roles at Warner Bros. and wanted to tackle more diverse projects. His great success playing legendary song-and-dance man George M. Cohan in

1942's *Yankee Doodle Dandy* had earned him an Academy Award for Best Actor. With it came a desire to exert more control over his future cinematic efforts. In 1943, Cagney and his brother Bill (who had long served as Jimmy's manager) severed ties with Warner Bros., claiming the company had done some creative bookkeeping with his profit participation. The duo then formed an independent production company named William Cagney Productions. The company signed a distribution deal with United Artists to produce five films at a total budget of six million dollars.

Its actual output at UA, however, was a bit less prolific. As film historian Stone Wallace explains, "Between 1943 and 1948, William Cagney Productions made just three films: *Johnny Come Lately*, *Blood on the Sun* and William Saroyan's *The Time of Your Life*. Of the three, only one, *Blood on the Sun*, turned a modest profit."

Although he was enjoying the artistic freedom he had long desired, Cagney was disappointed at the lack of box office his company's films had generated. (*The Time of Your Life*, for instance, had lost over half a million dollars.) "Then," says Stone Wallace, "Jack L. Warner offered the Cagney brothers a sweetheart deal they couldn't refuse. If Jimmy would return to Warner Bros. to appear as the mother-obsessed criminal Cody Jarrett in *White Heat* (just the type of role and film Cagney was trying to avoid), Warners would give William Cagney Productions a co-distribution deal through which they could pay off their considerable losses."

White Heat, of course, turned out to be a big hit, and seeing the potential financial gain, William Cagney Productions purchased a similar property for Jimmy with *Kiss Tomorrow Goodbye*, while continuing to seek out projects that would further broaden his repertoire.

When Barbara was called to the Warner Bros. lot to audition for the leading female role in *Kiss Tomorrow Goodbye*, she hadn't expected too much to come of it. With the recent loss of the mistress part in *The Asphalt Jungle* still fresh on her mind, Barbara had resigned herself to the possibility that this job, too, would slip through her fingers.

She needn't have worried. Upon viewing her screen test, Bill Cagney, who would again be producing the film, was evidently so taken with Barbara's beauty and talent that he immediately gave her the part, and then signed her to a personal contract, to be shared equally with Jack Warner. In the winter of 1950, Warner Bros. and Cagney Productions hired Barbara at $5,000 a week—an exorbitant amount for a Hollywood newcomer. The studio then embarked on an intensive program designed

Barbara practicing her ballet moves at Warner Bros. Courtesy of Jerry Ohlinger's

to mold their new acquisition into one of the lot's top players. This involved the usual rituals of voice, acting, and dance lessons, ballet class, and the requisite glamour shots—the results of which quickly graced the pages of many of the country's leading newspapers and movie magazines.

Barbara in her role as official starter for the Los Angeles Junior Chamber of Commerce Scotch Trophy Race. Courtesy of L.A. Public Library/ Herald Examiner Collection

In an interview at the time with UPI reporter Patricia Clary, Barbara recounted a somewhat sanitized version of her normal daily activities: "I get up at nine o'clock so I can be at my dance class by ten. Then I rush over to the Beverly Hills Hotel for tennis lessons." Clary continued, "Sometimes she doesn't have time to change in between and appears on the courts in the unusual tennis costume of black leotards. In the afternoons Miss Payton travels out to the Will Rogers ranch where she rides horseback for the rest of the afternoon. Then she goes home and rests up to hit the nightclub circuit at night." Barbara explained, "The dancing, tennis and horseback riding are to keep me in shape. The nightclubbing is just for fun."

Warner Bros. leading lady Barbara Payton in 1950. Courtesy of Jerry Ohlinger's

A striking and moody shot of Barbara from 1950. Courtesy of Jerry Ohlinger's

Photographed by Warner Bros. studio photographer Bert Six in a wide variety of outfits and settings—from poolside and ballet barre to golf course and tennis court—the many portrait stills of Barbara from this time show her 34-23-37 figure in more than fine shape, with her vibrant beauty at its absolute peak.

Through the years, there has been much speculation that Barbara slept with William Cagney in order to get her contract at Warner Bros. One story that has circulated for decades (which Barbara herself rehashed in her 1963 memoir) is that she had arrived at her audition for *Kiss Tomorrow Goodbye* appearing hot and disheveled, and once behind producer Cagney's closed office door, proceeded to lift her skirt over her head and proclaim, "Shit! It's a hot fucking day."

What transpired that afternoon following Barbara's impromptu "flashing" episode is anybody's guess; however, the end result was a new contract with both Warner Bros. and William Cagney Productions.

Publicity still of Barbara at The Beverly Hills Country Club.
Courtesy of Jerry Ohlinger's

Ad matte for Barbara's best known film, the crime drama Kiss Tomorrow Goodbye. *From the Author's Collection*

A few years before her death in 2005, former Warner Bros. leading lady Virginia Mayo, who had sizzled on screen as James Cagney's sluttish wife Verna in *White Heat*, told writer Laura Wagner: "Barbara was notorious for going after men. Bill Cagney was absolutely crazy for her. Everyone at the studio knew they were having an affair."

By this time, it was pretty clear that Barbara had discovered the merits of the Hollywood casting-couch, and was indeed using it to get ahead. It hadn't taken her very long to figure out that sex equaled power in Hollywood, and since she wasn't particularly against sleeping with the men whom she thought might help her career, Barbara was making some powerful strides. The fact is, Barbara wanted, more than anything, to be a star, and she was determined to get there any way she could.

Sadly, whatever morals and Midwestern values that were taught to the ex-country girl during her formative years in Minnesota, had seemingly been long forgotten, and forever lost—much like her innocence.

Kiss Tomorrow Goodbye is a cynical, violent film in which Barbara renders what is inarguably her best and most memorable performance. She plays Cagney's moll, Holiday Carleton, a good-hearted, if somewhat gullible, blonde who goes bad through her association with a sadistic gangster, Ralph Cotter (Cagney).

Adapted from the Horace McCoy novel of the same name, the screenplay has convict Cagney escaping from a brutal prison farm with the help of another inmate's sister (played by Barbara), only to continue his criminal activities on the outside. As he plots the robbery of a local market's payroll, he shacks up with the trampy and naive Barbara, who, after being beaten by him with a rolled-up towel, quickly succumbs to his advances. Though it is known to the audience from the film's opening frames that her brother was shot and killed by Cagney, and not the authorities, Holiday is unaware of this and allows him to live with her in her apartment.

The plot thickens when two crooked cops (played by Ward Bond and Barton MacLane) attempt to shake down Cagney and his gang, only to be blackmailed themselves by Cagney's far more cunning, and blatantly mad character, Ralph Cotter. When Cotter dallies with a wealthy politician's daughter (Helena Carter), a hot-tempered Holiday responds by flinging a coffee pot at him, after which, the couple make love. Only after it is revealed to the impressionable woman that he is responsible for her brother's death, does she take her revenge by killing him.

Though Cagney is obviously the focal point of the show, the motion picture boasts a strong supporting cast of Warner Bros. contract players, including the aforementioned Bond, Carter, and MacLane, as well as

A scene still of James Cagney and Barbara from Kiss Tomorrow Goodbye. *Courtesy of Wisconsin Center for Film and Theater Research*

Rhys Williams, Steve Brodie, James Cagney and Barbara in a scene from Kiss Tomorrow Goodbye. *Courtesy of Wisconsin Center for Film and Theater Research*

Publicity still of Helena Carter, Cagney and Barbara from Kiss Tomorrow Goodbye. *From the Author's Collection*

Steve Brodie and John Litel, with an outstanding performance by Luther Adler as a crooked lawyer who is in cahoots with Cagney.

In a veritable sea of finely wrought characterizations, Barbara acquitted herself admirably in a very high-profile part, which brought her a great deal of public notice and media attention. In its review of the film, *The Hollywood Reporter* declared, "Barbara Payton, in the difficult role of a basically good girl who turns to evil in spite of herself, makes a vivid appearance. She manages the subtle transition with polished artistry."

A.C. Lyles recalls the hoopla surrounding Barbara's performance upon the film's release. "When the picture came out and I went to see it in the theater, I saw that all of those things that I heard about Barbara Payton were absolutely true. She was excellent in the part, totally believable. She really came off with a strong personality on the screen, and Barbara had

Cagney roughs up Barbara in a publicity shot from Kiss Tomorrow Goodbye.
From the Author's Collection

Steve Brodie, Luther Adler, Cagney, Barbara, Ward Bond and Barton MacLane in a scene from the tough crime thriller **Kiss** Tomorrow **Goodbye**.
Courtesy of Stephen M. Shearer

that elusive star quality, in spades. It seemed like the entire industry was talking about her."

Author Lisa Burks, who has spent years researching the life of Barbara's future husband, actor Franchot Tone, for the forthcoming biography *Urbane Rebel: The Franchot Tone Story*, also gives high marks to Barbara's acting in the film. "She really held her own against James Cagney," she says, "and it was a gutsy performance, particularly for a newcomer. Aside from her captivating beauty, Barbara had a lot of onscreen charisma."

Many of the film's reviews commented on Barbara's sexy looks, with *The New York Times* stating, "As the moll, a superbly curved young lady [named] Barbara Payton performs as though she's trying to spit a tooth—one of the few Mr. Cagney leaves her."

Premiering in New York City on August 4, 1950, *Kiss Tomorrow Goodbye* was a fairly sizable hit, despite being banned in several Midwestern states due to its excessive violence. In fact, the profits from the picture were so good they enabled William Cagney Productions to

Barbara in the climactic scene from **Kiss Tomorrow Goodbye**.
Courtesy of Larry Kleno

pay off the half-million-dollar bank loan it owed after *The Time of Your Life* tanked.

Barbara would later give a great deal of credit to James and William Cagney for her initial success in Hollywood. They took a chance on her while she was still an unknown commodity, and gave her career a perfectly respectable launch-off with her role in the film; a wonderfully generous opportunity that she never forgot.

"Barb was crazy about James Cagney," says Jan Redfield. "She talked about how great he was to work with and said she studied hard to do just the right thing at the right time, as she really wanted to please him.

"She also raved about his sister, Jeanne, who must have visited the set because Barb said she had some conversations with her and she thought she was a dynamite lady. Barbara didn't usually compliment other women, so Jeanne must have really impressed her."

As for the film's star, Barbara had idolized James Cagney ever since she saw him in person at a war bond rally in Odessa in 1943. Then just 16 years old, she had gotten to meet him that afternoon and never dreamed that six years later, she would be starring as his leading lady in a prestigious Hollywood film. "Working with James Cagney was magical," Barbara later wrote. "He gave me my big break. I would have done anything for him."

For his part, Cagney's recollections of Barbara were cordial, but much less impassioned. He once made the comment that, "Barbara was an actress of impressive, if limited skill." In his 1976 autobiography, he discusses the film they co-starred in, yet never once mentions Barbara by name. Her alleged affair with his brother might have had something to do with that. Said Virginia Mayo (to writer Laura Wagner), "I don't think Jimmy approved of that relationship, so it went nowhere."

As a result of her successful appearance in *Kiss Tomorrow Goodbye*, Universal-International Studios, which had unceremoniously dumped Barbara the previous year, sent word out that it wanted to borrow her from Warner Bros. and Cagney Productions to co-star in a new picture with Donald O'Connor that would be produced by Robert Arthur and directed by Arthur Lubin. [6] William Cagney had left the decision up to Barbara (who was, naturally, very skeptical of the offer) as to whether she would do the film or not, so she scheduled a meeting with Arthur and Lubin at Universal.

Bob Rains, U-I's Assistant Head of Casting who had befriended Barbara during their publicity tours for Universal in 1949, met her for lunch that day at the studio's Sun Room commissary, prior to her meeting with the other U-I executives. Rains got there before she did and, in his 2001 memoir, *Beneath the Hollywood Tinsel: The Human Side of Hollywood Stars*, he remembers Barbara's head-turning entrance: "Suddenly the noisy room became silent and motionless," he wrote. "Standing in the doorway, magnificently dressed and groomed, was [Barbara]. I stood up to go over to her but she saw me and headed my way before I could. Every eye in the room moved with her. Conversation only resumed when she sat down."

During Barbara's lunch with Bob Rains, several studio executives allegedly stopped by their table to flirt with her. Rains felt that they were obviously trying to woo Barbara into doing the Donald O'Connor film, and that she, in turn, had played right along with them like she was interested. First to arrive was William Goetz, head of production at U-I, who stopped by "just to say hello" on his way to the executive table. Next came Rufus Le Maire, Head of Talent at Universal, who gushed that "Barbara never looked more beautiful," and added that he hoped she would soon be back working at the studio. Even Ed Muhl, Vice President of Production, stopped by, as did Leo Spitz, Chairman of the Board, to congratulate Barbara on the success she had found at Warner Bros.

"Barbara was friendly and charming to each of them," Bob Rains wrote in *Beneath the Hollywood Tinsel*. "Even to Bob Palmer, Head of Casting, who had told her she was being dropped from the studio and why." Rains was amazed by Barbara's graciousness in the presence of a group of men who had once been her adversaries. He later told her that he didn't know how she was able to be so friendly to all of them when they had orchestrated her firing from the studio just a few months earlier. Barbara just laughed and told him that he hadn't spent all those hundreds of hours in acting class at Universal like she had.

As Barbara and Bob Rains proceeded with their lunch, it soon became clear to him that she never had any intentions to meet with Arthur Lubin and Bob Arthur regarding the O'Connor film. She had merely shown up to see if the people she had left behind at the studio were as phony as she had always believed them to be. And she had invited Rains, of whom she was very fond, so he could enjoy all these high-powered types practically groveling at her feet. "Barbara hated phonies," says Jan Redfield, "and she could always see right through them, too. She thought it was ridiculous to try to kiss-up to people, and, trust me, the only time she ever did it was to prove a point."

On her way out of the Universal commissary that day, Barbara used the telephone to tell Bob Arthur's secretary that she had a headache and that she was leaving the lot. Her strategy to have the last laugh worked—in fact, too well, perhaps. Barbara never worked at Universal Studios again. She walked away that day leaving the proverbial bridge, and perhaps even

Ad matte for Barbara's 1950 WB western, **Dallas.** *From the Author's Collection*

a few incensed executives, burning behind her.

Adding to Barbara's growing list of personal and professional victories during this time was Warner Bros.' announcement that it was rewarding her for the success of *Kiss Tomorrow Goodbye* with a then-unprecedented pay raise to $10,000 per week, the bulk of which was thought to come from William Cagney Productions. Already acquainted with the likes of Bob Hope, Errol Flynn and George Raft, as her star shone brighter, Barbara found herself mingling with even more members of Hollywood's A-List, and soon counted Lana Turner, Frank Sinatra and Ava Gardner among her latest celebrity friends. In keeping with her newfound induction into the jet set, Barbara loved to bet on the horses and became part of a high-rolling contingent of film players who were known to drop thousands of dollars in cash at L.A.'s Hollywood Park Racetrack.

Deeply immersed in the city's nightlife, in late 1950 Barbara was dubbed "New Queen of the Clubs" by *Hollywood Reporter* gossip columnist Harrison Carroll. Accompanying the accolade was the following blurb from one of his columns:

> The glittering clubs along the Sunset Strip have crowned a new queen—Warner Bros.'s blazing blonde bombshell, Barbara Payton, who is turning heads nightly as she winds her superb curves through all the hottest spots in town. Barbara is hoping to take a step up to A-list pictures, having moved to Warners after several years [sic] in Universal-International's stock player training program. The impression Barbara made on audiences in Warner Bros. *Kiss Tomorrow Goodbye* is almost as impressive as the one she's making on the local club scene.

Unlike most of the typical PR sludge of the era that masqueraded as news, Harrison Carroll's description of Barbara's high profile presence in town was dead-on. Indeed, the part-time actress and full-time party girl would often race home from a binge of club and bar-hopping to catch a few hours of sleep before showing up for work at Warner Bros., but Barbara never looked worse for the wear. Swimming in money, beauty and confidence, it seemed that the "blazing blonde bombshell" had the world by the tail—and Hollywood by the balls.

CHAPTER EIGHT:
Fast Times in Hollywood

Despite the strong showing she made in *Kiss Tomorrow Goodbye*, Barbara's next film appearance for Warner Bros. was in a small, supporting role in a routine Gary Cooper Western, titled *Dallas* (1950). Barbara worked solely under her Warner Bros. contract on the film as William Cagney Productions had no affiliation with the project. Somewhat enhanced by its rich, Technicolor cinematography, and a stirring Max Steiner musical score, the Stuart Heisler-directed film cast Cooper as Blayde Hollister, an ex-Confederate officer who poses as a U.S. Marshal in order to get the goods on the Marlow Gang, a group of thugs who are attempting to take control of Dallas. Hollister has switched identities with the true marshal (played by Leif Erickson), an ineffectual, Caspar-Milquetoast type who abhors guns and violence. Unbeknownst to Cooper, the Marlows (Steve Cochran, Zon Murray, and the brains of the outfit, Raymond Massey) are also responsible for torching his home during the Civil War, and are now plotting to steal the land holdings of the wealthy Robles family (headed by patriarch Antonio Moreno). Leading lady Ruth Roman is his upstanding daughter, Tonia, who is engaged to marry Erickson until she meets and falls in love with Cooper's character. Meanwhile, the none-too-bright Bryant Marlow (Cochran) is holed-up in a dirt floor shack with his nagging, indolent girlfriend (played by Barbara, looking luscious in Technicolor).

Although billed fifth in the credits, Barbara's role in the film, as the sexy and duplicitous shanty tramp, Flo, was, alas, little more than a glorified bit. Appearing suitably cheap and sultry in tons of gold jewelry, a low-cut corset, and with waist-length bedroom hair, Barbara has very little screen time in four small scenes, and disappears completely about halfway through the film. By the time the exciting climax rolls around

Gary Cooper, Steve Cochran and Barbara in a scene from Dallas.
From the Author's Collection

Steve Cochran and Barbara as Bryant Marlow and his tawdry girlfriend, Flo, in
Dallas. *From the Author's Collection*

(in which Cooper engages in a gun duel with Massey over Ruth Roman), Barbara's character is long gone.

Considering how undeveloped and minor her role was in *Dallas*, Barbara was really not to blame for adding so little to the finished product. Her part, in fact, could have easily been played by any one of the other starlets under contract to Warner Bros. at the time (Mari Aldon, Patrice Wymore, Lucille Norman, et al), with little discernible difference.

There is some speculation today that Barbara's role in *Dallas* was originally much larger and may have been cut down in size by either director Stuart Heisler, or by the studio's vice president, Jack L. Warner, himself. For instance, there is a scene in the film that has Barbara's character reading the riot act to Cochran while delivering a fairly lengthy piece of dialogue. Even though the scene clearly belonged to her, the cameras only shot the back of Barbara's head and didn't allow her even a single close-up, much less a two-shot with Cochran, where she would have at least been seen in profile.

It was strange for Stuart Heisler not to photograph Barbara's stunning looks—and fiery performance—in this scene, and her friend Steve Hayes considers the studio's possible reasons behind the decision: "Although she had made quite a good impression in the Cagney film, by this time Barbara was misbehaving a lot in her personal life, which very likely pissed off Jack Warner. Old 'JL' was a vindictive and controlling prick, and he may have ordered Barbara's part cut down as a form of punishment for her so-called, wild ways.

"Also, Barbara could have easily mouthed off at someone during the film. Stuart Heisler, say, or even Warner himself. Believe me, Babs had the mouth and the temperament to do it, too.

"Then again, it could also be that Warner simply wanted to build up Steve Cochran, whose entire contract belonged to the studio, at the expense of Barbara, whose contract was split between Warner Bros. and William Cagney.

"The why's, if's and wherefore's in any business are always convoluted, but you can bet on one thing: when she was on her way up, rather than on her way down, Barbara would not have had to put up with this treatment. The fact that she did, however, shows that she must have already known that she was on very shaky ground with Jack Warner. Because, otherwise, why not fight it? (And trust me, Barbara was always a fighter.)"

Ex-actor Bill Ramage, a future acquaintance of Barbara's, has a different take on the possible cause of her abbreviated role in the film.

"There are reasons for the kind of cutting used in Barbara's big scene with Cochran. I've watched the film several times and have taken careful notice of her body language in that scene.

"In short, I'll bet anything that Barbara was wired the day that the scene was shot. Barbara once told me that her weight was a lifelong problem for her and that as a result, she had to diet constantly. In order to stay thin, she often used amphetamines, and during the film's shoot Barbara may have been eating those cross-eyed bennies and dexies like they were popcorn.

"The normal procedure for filming goes like this: first, there is always a master shot. An example of this is what was ultimately used in the scene in question: where Barbara tears into Steve Cochran. Strangely, even with her lengthy monologue, there was no cutting away from Cochran for Barbara's reaction shots, close-ups or over-the-shoulder shots. (By the way, close-ups are always shot.) The assistant director usually reads the lines to the actor being filmed close up. Stars get their close-ups early in the day to look their best. It's possible that Barbara's blue eyes had photographed with very large pupils that day and perhaps Stuart Heisler felt it best not to show her close-ups.

"Having 'been there' (used diet pills) myself—years ago—I suspect that Barbara may have nibbled that day on an amphetamine or two. She was very feisty in that scene [and] full of energy. I wonder how long Barbara was on that junk?"

Jan Redfield says, "Barbara did take those green diet pills [Dexamyl] throughout the '50s. I remember her telling me that there was a doctor she knew when she worked at WB who gave them to her whenever she gained a few pounds. She told me that all the studio doctors in town handed them out to the actors like candy."

Taking into consideration Barbara's past (and continuing) alliance with both dope dealer Don Cougar and known drug user Errol Flynn—among other hardcore pill-poppers and partyers—the theory that she had begun using speed to help her lose weight is, indeed, plausible. Add to this, her fearlessness and her willingness to try whatever felt good, or different, and it's possible that Barbara had fallen right into the grip of a new and dangerous vice.

Although her tiny part and subsequent performance—if not her alleged drug use—may be less than noteworthy today, Barbara's presence on the set of *Dallas* evidently meant something to at least two of her co-

A candid shot of Steve Cochran and Barbara on the WB back lot during the filming of Dallas. *Courtesy of Wisconsin Center for Film and Theater Research*

stars, for it's been reported that she had sexual encounters with both Steve Cochran and Gary Cooper during the filming of the picture.

She and Cochran shared an affinity for the same extracurricular activities (drinking and sex), and allegedly indulged their passions in after-work dates and between scene "set-ups." It is also said that they later took their affair on the road during the film's promotional tour.

Steve Cochran and Barbara Payton attend a press reception for Dallas.
Courtesy of Kirk Crivello

A former scene-still photographer, who worked for another studio in the 1950s, knew Barbara socially and agreed to speak about her today, on the condition that his identity remains anonymous. "Barbara bragged to me once that she and Steve Cochran fooled around with each other when they were making *Dallas*," he says. "During breaks, they used to go behind the western sets on the WB ranch in Calabasas and grab a quickie. In those days, Barbara was very sexy and incredibly hot-looking. She was also ballsy beyond belief. She not only did whatever she wanted, she made sure she told you about it afterward. As for Steve Cochran, he was an extremely macho and good-looking guy, and one of the town's biggest

Cochran shows Barbara the fine art of using as lariat in this publicity still for **Dallas.**
Courtesy of BFI Stills, Posters and Designs

studs. He supposedly had one of the biggest *tools* in the business, too. Ha, you couldn't have kept those two apart if you tried. Both of them were horny little devils."

If Barbara was indeed carrying on as this man contends, Bill Ramage offers this as further proof of her possible use of amphetamines at the time. "Trust me, there was a reason they called them 'cross-eyed bennies.' They made people so horny, even the popular aphrodisiac Spanish Fly couldn't touch them. Barbara's already-active libido must have gone into overdrive on those buzzards. Someone with her lack of inhibitions would be absolutely out of control on speed."

Regardless of the actual cause of Barbara's escapades, candid photographs taken on location during the filming of *Dallas* certainly show an easy and playful relationship between her and Cochran. Several photos find the two embracing, while others show the pair on horseback or attempting to catch each other with a lariat.

As if her purported affair with Steve Cochran weren't enough of a distraction, Barbara and married man Gary Cooper were rumored to have had a short-lived romp as well, described by her set photographer friend as "…hot, dressing-room visits." Author Hector Arce revealed similar information in his book, *Gary Cooper: An Intimate Biography*, writing, "[Cooper] also had a brief fling with Barbara Payton, a supporting player in *Dallas*, in the midst of his affair with [actress] Patricia Neal."

Barbara's alleged affairs with both Gary Cooper and Steve Cochran, while conceivable, have never been fully substantiated, and since all the parties involved are deceased, it is doubtful if the full extent of either relationship will ever be known.

In her lifetime, Barbara never publicly addressed the Steve Cochran matter, and her sole comment on her association with Gary Cooper was issued several years later. When asked by the ghost writer of her autobiography, Leo Guild, if there had been an affair between her and Cooper, Barbara coyly responded, "It was a difficult time for both of us. Let's just say Gary and I were good friends."

Someone who apparently was *not* a good friend of Barbara's, though, was *Dallas*'s leading lady, Ruth Roman. The late Milo Anderson, who worked at WB for many years as a costume designer, once divulged to his friend Bill Ramage that the actress despised Barbara. "According to Milo," says Bill, "Ruth Roman was a bit nonplussed at how all the men on the film responded to Barbara, while they barely gave her a second look. Ruth

An on set candid of Steve Cochran, Barbara and Gary Cooper during the filming of Dallas. *Courtesy of WB Archives/USC*

hated Barbara's guts."

Tina Ballard verifies this. "In all the years that I knew her, Barbara never talked much about other actresses, or about any of her female co-stars. And I doubt if she was ever jealous of any of them, either. That was simply not a part of her nature. Barbara was never envious of other women. I do know, however, that she didn't like Ruth Roman. She told me once that she couldn't stand her, though she never explained why. [It was] just a clash of personalities, I guess."

One final note on Barbara's *Dallas* experience comes from the above-mentioned scene-still photographer, who recalls an amusing, if pathetic, homage to Barbara's increasingly trashy persona: "There was a story going around at the time that the crew on the *Dallas* set would celebrate the end of each day's filming by sending Barbara's petticoats up a flag pole, flying them over the Warner Bros. lot at half-staff. Barbara Payton was some piece of ass. A real raunchy broad."

Barbara's lewd shenanigans were certainly not the kind of activities a serious-minded professional would indulge in, and word continued to spread through town about Warner Bros.' resident good-time girl.

Her minuscule role and off-screen antics aside, *Dallas* was mediocre entertainment at best, and as a result, its influence on elevating Barbara's professional standing in Hollywood was slight.

Fledgling actor Steve Hayes, who had befriended Barbara the previous year, saw her again in 1950, the first time at a Hollywood nightclub with her sometime-boyfriend, L.A. "asphalt baron" Jerry Bialac. Today, Steve admits to disliking Bialac intensely, even though he barely knew him. "For years I saw him around The Corner (Sunset Boulevard and Crescent Heights), and I thought he was a smarmy bastard. I would imagine he saw himself as a mover and shaker—I heard he came from money—but I always had the feeling he was just pussyfooting around while trying to climb up Barbara's ass. Over the years, I saw him out with her a lot. Seems I also saw him hanging out sometimes with the King Brothers, who were these sleazy, slot-machine thugs-turned-film producers. Barbara later worked for the King Brothers in *Drums in the Deep South* and I'm sure she met them through that snake Jerry Bialac."

The next time Steve saw Barbara was at a celebrity gathering at Errol Flynn's Mulholland Drive estate. Steve had met Flynn through his current girlfriend, a beautiful actress and model from Amarillo, Texas, named Gloria Brower (who went by the alias of 'Brandy Wyne' in Hollywood, and whom Steve later married). Flynn had taken a liking to Steve and eventually offered to sponsor him so he could obtain a social security card and thereby work in films.

Steve and Brandy had been invited to attend a send-off party for Flynn, who was leaving for Gallup, New Mexico the following week, to begin shooting his Warner Bros. western, *Rocky Mountain*. Flynn hadn't yet married his third wife, actress Patrice Wymore (who would, incidentally, co-star with him in *Rocky Mountain*), and he was still seeing Barbara, among several other young starlets.

Barbara and her boyfriend, wealthy L.A. paving contractor Jerry Bialac, party at Hollywood's Mocambo nightclub. Courtesy of L.A. Public Library/ Herald Examiner Collection

Barbara had arrived at the party with Hollywood gossip columnist Sidney Skolsky, a non-driver who was notorious in town for always sponging rides from the very celebrities he wrote about. Skolsky had a tiny office above Schwab's Drugstore and later became a close confidante of Marilyn Monroe's. He and Barbara weren't especially close, though they both knew that being seen in public together had its benefits. It aroused both attention and conversation, which in Hollywood, is always a good thing.

As soon as Steve saw Barbara, he went up to her to say hello, and then reminded her of their prior meeting at Bryan Foy's house. "She remembered me right away and was very friendly," he recalls, "but I noticed immediately that she was also very drunk.

"My girlfriend, Brandy, couldn't stand Barbara. She felt she was prettier and more talented than Babs and she resented how Barbara was getting a lot of film work, even though all she seemed to care about was (in Brandy's words) 'getting drunk and fucking movie stars.'

A sexy publicity shot of Barbara from 1950. From the Author's Collection

"In order to keep peace with my girlfriend, Babs and I didn't really say too much to each other. From what I witnessed, I got the impression that she was still seeing Errol Flynn, although I'm sure it was an extremely casual relationship. What struck me most, I think, was seeing how smashed Barbara was. She was lit up like a Christmas tree and just this side of falling down. I was very surprised to see her that way, especially with Sidney Skolsky and half of Hollywood there to see it, too."

Steve bumped into Barbara again a short time later at the Chateau Marmont Hotel on Sunset Boulevard. Built in 1929, the secluded, castle-like hotel had become a haven over the years for celebrities seeking solitude, especially those who had a penchant for misbehaving in their private lives. It is best known, perhaps, as the place where comedian John Belushi died in 1982, after injecting a lethal "speedball" of heroin and cocaine.

Barbara in her patented, 1950s tough girl pose. From the Author's Collection

"In the 1950s," says Hayes, "the Chateau had the largest private swimming pool in Hollywood. I knew the day clerk there and he used to let me sneak in for a swim whenever I wanted. That's what I was doing when I saw Babs."

Following the party at Errol Flynn's home, but prior to seeing her at the Chateau Marmont, Steve had spotted Barbara a few times, from a distance, as she was sunbathing by the swimming pool at Hollywood's Garden of Allah Hotel.[7]

"She looked like a golden goddess," Steve recalls. "Those long, tanned legs, her slicked-back, platinum blonde hair, those full, delectable lips. She was scrumptious." Although he hadn't spoken to Barbara at the Garden of Allah, this time Steve made it a point to go over to talk to her. Steve was still dating actress Brandy Wyne, but admits he found Barbara thoroughly enticing.

"At the time, she was an intimate guest of someone who was staying at the hotel, though I don't know whom. I had heard rumors that it was Howard Hughes, but I have no way of knowing if that's true."

Barbara seemed happy to see Steve, and after a brief conversation, the couple left the pool and went back to her apartment where, with not a trace of hesitation, they made love.

"After our first encounter that night, I left her apartment," Steve says, "and although I would continue to spend occasional evenings with Barbara, we never saw each other exclusively, or acted any differently toward each other, either.

"What I thought was interesting about her was the emphasis that Barbara always put on how much I cared about her, wanted her, liked her (though she never once mentioned the word 'love'). For instance, after we would sleep together, Babs would always say, 'You do like me, don't you? You do care about me?' As if this was necessary and important to her. I said 'Yes' each time, because it was true. I did like Barbara and for some reason, maybe because I was young and immature myself, I cared about her, too."

There was an immediate kinship between Steve and Barbara, he insists, that they had both felt. Perhaps knowing that they had each come from far-off places ("other worlds," he says) was a common bond for the pair. Barbara told Steve that she admired the fact that he had left England with only thirty dollars in his pocket, and had survived.

"She said she was amazed that I had actually gotten into movies without having to 'spread my legs.' (I think she was probably thinking of the act in a female way.) I took that as meaning that she, obviously, hadn't."

Steve saw Barbara off-and-on for a while, but their relationship was never more than casual. Neither of them seemed interested in pursuing anything other than the physical side of their friendship, and besides, with both her career and her social life in high gear, Barbara had bigger fish to fry.

Meantime, Barbara was continuing to cause a commotion everywhere she went. One night in mid-1950, she entered a Charleston contest on the Sunset Strip, and not only walked away with first prize, but with a new admirer, as well. An International News Service story reported the events of that night in an article later published by many of the nation's newspapers:

> Barbara Peyton [sic], "the girl in green, with the chandelier earrings hanging to her shoulders" had everyone screaming for her to win the Charleston contest at the Mocambo, a week ago Monday night, and she did.
> Many people did not recognize her except to say that she looks like a cross between Jean Harlow and Carol Channing. She is certainly dressing in 1920 styles!
> Franchot Tone was one of the judges when she won the Charleston prize last Monday.

An ex-husband of Joan Crawford, and an accomplished stage and screen star since the 1930s, Franchot apparently was impressed that night with a lot more than Barbara's dancing. It was later said that their eyes locked across the nightclub's dance floor, and that with one glance at the flaxen-haired temptress, the stylish sophisticate, and inveterate connoisseur of female beauty, was instantly hooked.

Chapter Nine:
Candlelight and Champagne

Born February 27, 1905, in Niagara Falls, New York, Franchot Tone excelled in playing the debonair, tuxedo-suited aristocrat in his many film roles, which included an Academy Award-nominated performance in the classic 1935 picture *Mutiny on the Bounty*. By 1950, he had nearly 60 films to his credit and was one of the town's wealthiest and most respected stars. *Los Angeles Magazine* writer Tom Johnson, in his November 1987 *Fallen Star* article on Barbara's life, offers a description of the actor as astute and succinct as any: "Franchot Tone [was] a dapper man-about-town, the kind of guy who could make lighting a cigarette look like mankind's highest calling. He was safe, secure, successful, dignified, and everything a woman could ask for."

To a diehard (if not always discriminating) romantic like Barbara, getting to know this handsome movie star up-close was an opportunity too delicious to miss.

Their meeting, like a film scene lensed in soft-focus, and lit by the warm glow of candlelight and champagne, was storybook. Though it couldn't have had a more glamorous or promising start, the relationship of Franchot Tone and Barbara Payton would prove to be a life-altering disaster, for both of them.

Stanislas Pascal Franchot Tone was raised in an environment of fabulous wealth and prestige, as the second son of Dr. Frank J. Tone, a pioneer in the field of electrochemistry and former president of the Carborundum Company of America, and Gertrude Franchot Tone, of the socially and politically prominent Franchot family of upstate New York. A life of tremendous advantage had allowed Stanislas the best of educational opportunities, beginning at the fashionable Hill School in Pottstown, Pennsylvania, then at Cornell University (where the aspiring actor was President of the Drama Society and graduated Phi Beta Kappa), followed by a summer semester in Paris at the University of Rennes.

In 1927, Stanislas (who had taken his mother's maiden name, Franchot, as his first name) joined The McGarry Players, a theater stock company in Buffalo, before moving to New York City the following year, where he became affiliated with the New Playwrights Company in Greenwich Village. Tone's first role of any merit was as stage star Katharine Cornell's son in a 1929 production of *The Age of Innocence*. The classically handsome young actor then joined The Theater Guild in 1930, where he appeared in a series of plays, including *Red Dust*, *Hotel Universe* and *Green Grow the Lilacs* (an early incarnation of the famous musical *Oklahoma!*).

Franchot met the brilliant director and acting instructor Lee Strasberg around this time and became a ground-floor member of Strasberg's fledgling Group Theatre, where he performed in productions of *The House of Connelly* and *A Thousand Summers*. "Everything I know about acting I learned from Lee Strasberg," Franchot said in a 1966 *TV Guide* article. "At the Group, I learned Strasberg's variant on the Stanislavsky System. That's S-y-s-t-e-m, not Method. Method actors lack discipline. System actors are disciplined."

As his stage credits mounted and he became a known quantity on the east coast play circuit, Franchot began fielding offers for motion picture work. He accepted his first movie role in 1932, as co-star to Claudette Colbert in Paramount's *The Wiser Sex*, filmed at the company's Astoria, Long Island studio. He performed so well before the cameras, MGM in Hollywood offered him a five-year contract, which he accepted, albeit hesitantly.

Franchot was playing in the Group Theatre's production of *Success Story* at the time, and he had mixed feelings about leaving the highly creative circle of brilliant artists he had surrounded himself with for the uncertainties of a west coast film career. Having the attitude that Hollywood films were somewhat beneath a stage actor's dignity, Franchot thought it through, however, and soon realized he might be able to utilize his motion picture contract as a means of subsidizing the efforts of the Group Theatre. His initial plan was to work in Hollywood for a year, then return to New York City with a substantial amount of cash to keep the Group Theatre rolling.

At 28, Franchot relocated to California in 1933 and began work on his first MGM film, the somewhat awkwardly titled *Gabriel Over the*

White House. All told, he completed seven motion pictures for MGM that year, co-starring with his future wife, Joan Crawford, for the first time, in Howard Hawks' popular World War I drama, *Today We Live*. One of his finest enactments of his near-patented, rich playboy characterization was in *Dancing Lady*, in which he and Clark Gable were rivals for Crawford's affections. He was paired with Crawford for a third time in *Sadie McKee* (1934), before being loaned to Paramount for *The Lives of a Bengal Lancer*, a well-made historical adventure in which he and Gary Cooper starred.

Dapper leading man Franchot Tone in the 1930's. From the Author's Collection

*1930's MGM publicity shot of Joan Crawford and Franchot Tone.
Courtesy of Blackie Seymour/The Pentagram Library*

Following this noteworthy project, Franchot was given one of his most famous roles, as midshipman Roger Byam, the British gentleman who goes to sea, in the nautical adventure film, *Mutiny on the Bounty*. Although he lost out on his bid for an Oscar as best supporting actor,

Franchot's performance in *Mutiny* brought him a ton of film work, and ensured his place as one of Hollywood's most popular and promising actors. As a result, he temporarily put his theater objectives on hold and dove into his movie career. Tone was an architect hopelessly in love with Bette Davis in 1935's *Dangerous*, and appeared as a wealthy industrialist who commits suicide over Jean Harlow in that same year's *Reckless*.

His frequent co-star, Joan Crawford, whose impoverished family background was the direct antithesis of Franchot's almost regal upbringing, was somewhat surprised to find herself attracted to the erudite New York thespian she initially thought a snob. Tone was equally fascinated with Crawford's tough-minded manner, and on October 11, 1935, the couple was married in New Jersey.

In *Joan Crawford: A Biography* by Bob Thomas, the author relates that Crawford, divorced two years earlier from actor Douglas Fairbanks, Jr., had initially discouraged Franchot's pursuit of her, but had gradually succumbed to his intense devotion. Thomas writes, "He was charmingly insistent, lavishing on her not only flowers but also rare books and works of art. At night he built a fire in her den and read Ibsen, Shaw and Shakespeare to her while she hooked a rug."

Despite this rather idyllic picture of their relationship, the Tone/Crawford union was, in truth, an extremely rocky one that found Franchot often bristling at his wife's greater career success.

Attorney Milton Golden, who knew the actor for many years, may have said it best when he later wrote of their marriage, "It must be awfully hard for a born prince to become a mere consort to a queen raised from the chorus."

Rumors of Franchot's intense professional jealousy and alleged heavy drinking, physical arguments, and rampant unfaithfulness on both their parts culminated in the couple's divorce in April 1939. Although they were no longer husband and wife, Franchot Tone and Joan Crawford eventually resumed a comfortable civility with each other, and remained close friends for the remainder of his life.

After a staggering 29 motion pictures in six years, Franchot left MGM after *Fast and Furious* (1939), a Busby Berkeley-directed mystery/comedy, co-starring Ann Sothern. He returned to the New York stage, and to the Group Theater, to co-star with Sylvia Sidney in *The Gentle People*, a fine production that nonetheless, flopped. The following year, he received excellent notices in New York City for his role in Ernest Hemingway's *The

Universal Studios publicity still of Franchot from 1940. Courtesy of Blackie Seymour/ The Pentagram Library

Actress Ella Raines and Franchot, as they appeared in Universal Studios' Phantom Lady. *From the Author's Collection*

Fifth Column, and continued his Hollywood career in 1940, freelancing in a string of moderately enjoyable comedies and dramatic efforts for Universal, Columbia, Warner Brothers and Paramount Studios, the best of these being the war-themed *Five Graves to Cairo* (1943) and *The Hour Before the Dawn* (1944), and the moody film noir, *Phantom Lady* (1944).

Often relegated to second male leads for the remainder of his film career, Tone never quite managed to break out of the narrow mold

Franchot looking tough and dangerous in the 1949 Columbia Pictures B-film,
I Love Trouble. Courtesy of Columbia Pictures

Hollywood had cast him in from the outset, and thus never experienced the same level of superstardom enjoyed by such cinematic contemporaries as Cary Grant, Clark Gable and Spencer Tracy. His fellow actor and friend, the late Burgess Meredith, once offered the following theory as a possible reason for Franchot's second-tier status in films: "Franchot Tone is a gentleman by breeding and inclination," Meredith told *TV Guide* in January 1966. "He's always been a man's man, a hunter, a fisherman, and also a woman's man. He's an intellect, a man of charm, good looks, perception and enormous natural gifts as an actor, which alas, he hasn't always cherished or developed. Perhaps if Franchot had had a different temperament and less appetite for the good life. Ah, but who in this world has ever had a better time?"

Meredith's incisive proposition notwithstanding, the man who was said to be "blessed with a profile meant to adorn coins," carried on with an inherent flair, and worked constantly—in radio, on stage, and later, in television, as well as in more than 100 films. Not a bad legacy for someone who somehow just missed being a Hollywood superstar.

In 1941, Franchot, then 36, married 18-year-old, ex-Earl Carroll showgirl and Paramount starlet Jean Wallace (*Blaze of Noon*). The couple eventually had two sons, Pascal Franchot (a.k.a. "Pat," born in 1943) and Thomas Jefferson Tone (a.k.a. "Jeff," born in 1945). However, this marriage, too, proved stormy and problematic, and would not endure. The blonde-haired Wallace, whose facial appearance and provocative figure bore striking similarities to Barbara Payton's, would later go up against her lookalike nemesis in a highly-publicized court case. She also appeared to share Barbara's propensity for trouble.

By 1948, Jean's frequent domestic squabbles with Franchot led to an acrimonious breakup that found them wrangling over custody of their sons. During their divorce trial, Franchot accused his wife of committing adultery with several men, including Hollywood gigolo Johnny Stompanato, who would later gain posthumous notoriety when he was stabbed to death by 14-year-old Cheryl Crane (the daughter of his lover, Lana Turner). After a lengthy court battle that received widespread coverage in all the L.A. newspapers, Tone was given custody of their sons, Pat and Jeff.

Following the couple's split in 1949, a devastated Jean lost her emotional footing and began drinking heavily. On November 11, there were more unsavory headlines for the actress when she stabbed herself in the stomach with a 14-inch salami knife while staying at her mother's house in North Hollywood. *Mother Awakened by Screams in The Night; Wrests Knife From Daughter in Kitchen*, reported the *L.A. Times*, adding, in a bizarre postscript, "[Wallace's] mother received a small cut on one of her fingers in the ensuing scuffle." The self-inflicted attack was precipitated by

Barbara Payton look-alike Jean Wallace with her husband Franchot Tone in the mid 1940's. Courtesy of Blackie Seymour/The Pentagram Library

a telephone call from Franchot, in which he told his ex-wife that he had a date that night with another woman. Treated at Georgia Street Receiving Hospital and released, Jean later remarked to reporters, "It's no big deal, really. In fact, I did it just for laughs."

A little over one month later, on December 26, Jean was booked in Lincoln Heights Jail on a charge of drunk driving after she hit a parked car in downtown Los Angeles. Every newspaper in town saw fit to report that the troubled actress was "...clad only in a red coat, lace-trimmed panties and bedroom slippers" when the accident occurred, and that she had "...railed at the police officers, and then winked" when they questioned her about her scanty attire.

Fortunately, Jean Wallace's life calmed down and gained a much-needed equanimity when she married actor Cornel Wilde in 1951. The lurid headlines ceased and she went on to co-star with Wilde in several 1950s films, the best of these being the violent crime drama *The Big Combo* (Allied Artists, 1955).

Many years later, after reports of marital infidelity on both their parts: his with the wife of actor Richard Conte (his co-star in *The Big Combo*), and hers with hard-drinking actor Lawrence Tierney (of *Dillinger* fame), Cornel Wilde and Jean Wallace were divorced in 1973. Leukemia would end Wilde's life at 74 on October 16, 1989, while Wallace, 66, died just four months later, on February 14, 1990, of complications from an internal hemorrhage.

When Barbara Payton met Franchot Tone at Ciro's nightclub in early 1950, she was making fast tracks up and down Hollywood's Sunset Strip, while dating a multitude of men and enjoying her whirlwind lifestyle to the hilt. Publicity-wise, she scored a major accolade that spring when The Foreign Press Association deemed her "The Most Beautiful Girl in Pictures" and ran her photo in dozens of newspapers around the world.

During this time, fan mail for Barbara (much of it addressed, simply: Barbara Payton, c/o WB Studios, Hollywood, CA) began flooding in from all over the country and, according to her sister-in-law Jan Redfield, Barbara often answered a lot of the mail herself. "I sometimes helped her with it," says Jan, "but Barb always took a look at the really good letters and wrote back to those people herself. Barbara would hand me several shoeboxes full of her fan mail and a big stack of her head shots (which she would always autograph), and then she would say, in a joking voice, 'Now, Janice, get to work!' I always thought it was fun answering her mail, especially reading what some of the people had to say to her. She got a lot of questions about her life (like, did she ever want to get married again) and just silly little cards asking for souvenirs and dates, and things like that. But as much as Barbara enjoyed the attention (and believe me, she did), she only sent out photos, and sometimes, in rare instances, little handwritten notes, in return.

"For a while, Barbara was very conscientious about having me mail out those photos of her, but after her career picked up and she started traveling a lot more, it got to be too much. But believe it or not, I still have a lot of Barbara's fan mail from those two or three years [sic] she was at Warner Bros., tied up in the same blue ribbon she used, and in the same old shoeboxes she always kept them in, too. Even after she left the studio, she saved all those letters, and she would bring them with her wherever she moved. Then one day, she brought me the shoeboxes and asked me to keep the letters for her until she could come back to get them. This was in the bad years, after she had gotten into all that trouble. She never did come back for them.

"Every once in a while I sit at my kitchen table and reread some of Barbara's old fan mail. It's a nice reminder for me that she had quite a following (for a while, anyway). At one time, people really loved her."

As her ever-growing fan base proves, Barbara's star was undeniably on the rise, and in mid-1950, the *L.A. Times* reported that both MGM and 20th Century-Fox were trying to spirit her away from Warner Bros.. Meanwhile, the cool and cultivated Franchot seemed spellbound by his new girlfriend's raucous demeanor, just as he was in his prior relationships with rough-at-the-edges Joan Crawford, and with the feisty and hot-tempered Jean Wallace. This was much to the disapproval of his friends and colleagues, for although Barbara had been in Hollywood for just a little over two years, her bad reputation—in the industry's eyes, if not yet the public's—had seemingly already been set in stone. Franchot's associates, including ex-wife Crawford (who had been so impressed with Barbara at their initial meeting, but had changed her mind about her once she had learned of her lifestyle), did their best to dissuade the actor from consorting with the vampy starlet, with Crawford allegedly chastising him with the haughty, and rather laughable, warning, "If I were you, Mister, I'd leave that cheap little chippie alone. She has the morals of a common tart." As is so often the case when pointing fingers, a self-righteous Crawford evidently had forgotten about her own checkered past.

Despite the numerous warnings he was receiving about Barbara, Franchot seemed completely captivated by her. Initially pulled in by the sharp dichotomy between Barbara's wholesome looks and highly irreverent nature, he soon appeared to take an almost Pygmalion-like interest in her. It was a perfectly understandable reaction, for while Barbara often affected a worldly air, her general attitude about life (and people) bore more than a trace of her humble, Minnesota roots. Franchot, on the other hand, *was* worldly, and he was also keen enough to know that he had before him a woman who was not only impressed with both his professional and social status, but also one who would allow him to mold her, to a degree, into someone that would feel right at home in such a rarified setting.

Barbara's former flame, Steve Hayes, recalls seeing her one day when she was lunching at the MGM commissary with Franchot and Clark Gable, both of whom Steve knew slightly. "Babs seemed perfectly comfortable and at ease with these guys," he says, "like she was exactly where she belonged." On their way out, Barbara saw Steve and came over to him, with Franchot and Clark walking behind her. "Babs said, 'Hi,

Franchot, Barbara and Ciro's nightclub owner Herman Hover in 1950. Courtesy of L.A. Public Library/Herald Examiner Collection

Candlelight and Champagne • 131

Barbara and Franchot on a typical night out in 1950. Courtesy of Jan Redfield

where have you been? Haven't seen you around lately. I thought maybe you had gone back to jolly old England or something.'"

When Steve told her that he was doing some bit parts at the studio, Barbara was thrilled for him and gave him a big hug. "I really liked Babs. I honestly believe that underneath the ball-busting, party girl façade, she had a very sweet, almost 'motherly instinct' in her—rather like Monroe; although Marilyn also exuded a wonderful vulnerability that I personally never saw in Barbara.

"At any rate, it was good to see she was in such good company (with Franchot Tone and Clark Gable). Babs had a lot to offer the male gender that had absolutely nothing to do with sex. It had to do with her ability to really listen to a man and to speak intelligently, and it had to do with her making a person feel good when they were with her. Babs had all that."

Several weeks into their relationship, Franchot was still walking around in a kind of daze over Barbara and continued to court her with almost daily gifts of champagne, flowers and expensive jewelry. Barbara responded in kind by lovingly nicknaming him "Doc" and treated him to delicious, home-cooked meals at her Hollywood Boulevard apartment. Socially, they double-dated a lot with a married couple by the name of Kent and June Modglin, who were quite wealthy. "Barbara told me that

Kent Modglin had invented the world's first garbage disposal," says Jan Redfield. "Apparently, he and Franchot were friends from way back. Kent, June and Franchot were all close in age, so Barbara was definitely the baby of the group. June and Barbara got along well, and the four of them dined out a lot together."

"Franchot Tone was a very nice and extremely generous man," adds Jan. "We saw him several times at Barbara's apartment and he was a lovely person. Although I don't think I ever saw him without a drink in his hand, he was never out of line nor did I ever hear him raise his voice at Barbara—ever. His manners were always impeccable. Lee and Mabel both liked him and were impressed with how cultured he was. I know they were hoping that he would get Barbara to finally settle down and start behaving herself.

"Franchot wasn't that much younger than Lee (six years), and I think Barbara saw him as someone who would love her unconditionally and take care of her and support her—things that she didn't always get from her father."

Tone hit it off so well with Barbara's family that he even offered Frank and Jan jobs as caretakers of a hunting lodge his family owned on Muskoka Lake in Canada. "It was a great opportunity," says Jan, "but after giving it some thought, we turned it down. Frank and I were both very young at the time and neither of us had any background for that type of work. We would have been responsible for all the other people who worked at the lodge and we didn't think we could handle it. Also, the only way to and from the lodge was by seaplane and we would have been totally alone up there during the off-season, so we thanked Franchot but declined the offer. He understood.

"Franchot was a gentle human being, and Frank and I were always very comfortable around him. And he adored Barbara. He showered her with gifts, and she loved it."

In the summer of 1950, Franchot accompanied Barbara to Miami where she not only drew a sizable crowd of admirers at the world premiere ceremonies for *Kiss Tomorrow Goodbye*, but also received the Key to the City that night from the town's Mayor. Photos from the event show Franchot beaming at an obviously elated Barbara.

The late actor Gig Young, who would co-star with Franchot in the 1953 Broadway play *Oh, Men! Oh, Women!* , once said of his friend and co-worker, "Without being a fool about it, Franchot shares the limelight.

Franchot accompanies Barbara as she receives the Key to the City of Miami from the town's Mayor. Courtesy of RKO Pictures

He's an unselfish man, and when you say that an actor is unselfish—well, who's ever heard of an unselfish actor? But Franchot is."

Franchot's biographer, author Lisa Burks, wholeheartedly agrees: "The look on Franchot's face in those photos (where Barbara's receiving the Key to the City) says it all. It's like he's presenting her to the world, and very proud to do so. I think this says a lot about why he was drawn to Barbara. Besides her obvious beauty, I think Franchot was really impressed with her acting abilities, and his taking her to a premiere of her work was a big moment for both of them.

"Franchot had the desire to help young Hollywood hopefuls with his experience and his flair for mentoring, and Barbara was an ambitious and willing student. He encouraged her, as he encouraged all the women in his life. He saw her outward beauty but he also saw past it to her potential, both as an artist, and as a human being."

It was clear that Franchot saw a potential wife in Barbara, as well, and in October 1950 he announced their engagement at a swanky party held at the Stork Club in New York City. [8] Along with the news that

*Barbara and Franchot Tone at a NYC nightclub in 1950.
Courtesy of the Library of Congress*

they would be married the following September, Barbara's formal entree into high society found her wearing an expensive satin outfit and a pearl necklace given to her by Franchot, along with a gaudy, pasted-on face tattoo. Perhaps Franchot loved Barbara's playful, "give 'em all the finger" attitude, most of all.

Jan Redfield clearly remembers Barbara's penchant for wearing tattoos. "There was a period of time in the early '50s when she wore those things a lot. I remember little leprechauns and snakes, and a tattoo of a star that she sometimes wore, too. She would strut into those Hollywood nightclubs with all that wild stuff on her face and people's jaws would drop open. And she loved it. And then there was that huge charm bracelet she always wore on her wrist, with all those noisy baubles and bangles dangling from it. You could hear Barbara coming from a mile away with that thing. Knowing her as well as I did, I'm certain Barbara wore those face tattoos and that loud bracelet just to shake people up."

And shake people up, she did. Barbara loved all the press coverage her engagement to Franchot was generating and soaked it up like a sponge. "I'll never forget the night Franchot and I went to the opera," she later wrote. "I wore a mink stole he had given me and I was dripping ice. We marched into the opera house and it was like everyone had been struck silent. People stopped whatever they were doing and just stared at us. Man, we were really something."

Barbara's fetish for high fashion was witnessed by her girlfriend, Tina Ballard, who says she once took a picture of the big, walk-in closet in Barbara's bedroom and counted several expensive furs and at least 100 pairs of shoes. "When Barbara went shopping, if she saw something she liked, she would buy two or three of the exact same item, but in different colors. She had some lovely furs, including the full-length mink that Franchot bought her, and which she wore for many years afterward, even after they split up. Barbara also owned a gorgeous white fur stole that had long tails hanging off the edges. But she didn't like the tails, so she took them off and gave them to me. I still have them, too."

One time during this period Barbara and Franchot visited her brother and his wife at their home in North Long Beach. It was Frank's birthday, and Barbara showed up bearing an armful of gifts. "I'll never forget it," says Jan. "Barbara strutted in wearing a hot pink dyed fox stole over a sexy, low-cut pink dress, and she had also put several pink streaks in her hair. She looked like a 1950s version of a punk rocker. Trust me, it was very over-the-top. Barbara had bought Frank a complete wardrobe of tailored suits, in box after box, all done up in big, red bows. Needless to say, our neighbors got quite an eyeful."

Barbara's unceasing generosity extended far past her brother, to include her parents, sister-in-law, and friends, as well. For instance, she would routinely send big bouquets of fresh flowers to Mabel in Odessa, and often bought her expensive bed robes and nightgowns as well. "Barbara also sent Mabel lots of boxes of beautiful, personalized stationary," Jan recalls. "Barbara and her mother always wrote letters to each other, and I received letters from Mabel on that stationary, too.

"Christmas and birthdays were always important to Barb; everyone in the family always got something special from her. Once, she took my mother on a shopping spree and bought her a lovely two-piece navy-blue suit, a white blouse and a white hat with gloves, and then she took her to the shoe department and even bought her a pair of matching shoes. Barb dressed her up and Mom looked great, and I still have some pictures of the two of them together, smiling and looking very, very sharp."

Barbara also brought Jan big bags of clothes that she no longer wanted, some of which she had worn only once. "Barbara did this many times," says Jan, "as Frank and I were just starting out and she knew that we were on a very tight budget. And there were other times when she took one look at my plaid skirt, sweater and saddle shoes, and whisked me off upstairs to her closet. She would give me the choice of anything I wanted to wear, and then she would sit me down and put a little make-up on my face and put my long ponytail up in a 'do,' as she called it. Barbara always took real good care of me."

Tina Ballard agrees with Jan about Barbara's generosity. She says, "I remember Barbara and her ex-boyfriend, Don Cougar (with whom she had stayed friends), taking me to the Moulin Rouge in Hollywood one year for my birthday. It was a huge nightclub that put on these magnificent Las Vegas-styled floor shows, with all these flashy can-can dancers in beautiful, feathered costumes. I seem to remember that Barbara, rather than Don, paid for the whole night. She got us front-row seats right on the runway, and bought dinner and drinks for everyone around us. She even gave me an expensive ruby and pearl ring that night as a birthday gift.

"When Barbara was at Warner Bros., she commissioned an elderly lady from Mexico City to make a lot of her street clothes. Barbara would draw a picture or write down what she wanted and send it to this woman, who would then make a pattern for it and create the outfit from scratch. In fact, one of the dresses she made for her was the beautiful white chiffon gown with a matching cap that Barbara later wore in *Bride of the Gorilla*. Anyway, she paid this Mexican lady a lot of money to create some original outfits for me, too, and they were knockouts. Barbara bought this little old lady a new sewing machine once and sometimes she even sent her money for no particular reason, other than that the lady always made Barb look so beautiful.

"Speaking of which, Barbara lent me money, too. There was a time in the early '50s when my husband Dave and I hit a bump in the road and had trouble making ends meet, and Barbara was right there, offering to help us. 'How much do you need?' she'd say. 'Five hundred? A thousand?' And she gave it to us, too. No questions asked. Later on, when we tried to pay her back with a check, she refused to take it from us. By then she

A candid of Barbara at a Hollywood party in one of the original outfits made for her by an elderly dress designer in Mexico. Courtesy of Tina Ballard

was making money hand over fist at Warner Bros., and she said she didn't need it. If she cared about you and loved you, Barbara would stand on her head to see that you were happy and well taken care of.

"Barbara always believed in spreading the wealth around. What was hers, was yours. She had a heart of gold."

Even in the midst of her busy film career (and her equally busy social life), Barbara put a lot of effort into maintaining close ties to her brother and sister-in-law. Frank had enlisted in the Navy in the summer of 1948 and had been transferred from Long Beach to a destroyer in Portsmouth, Virginia, when Jan learned she was pregnant with their first child. During this period Barbara often made time to visit Jan at her parents' home in Compton (where she was living while Frank was away). "In those early years, she was always there for me," says Jan. "And when Barbara couldn't come, she would send Lee and Mabel, who were by then living in a beautiful Spanish-styled house overlooking the Naval base in San Diego. They took me out many times to buy me maternity clothes. I always got along extremely well with my in-laws. Like Barbara, they were generous to a fault."

Throughout Jan's pregnancy, Barbara would frequently invite her and Lee and Mabel over to her house for dinner. "Things would go well at first but then they would all start drinking and Barbara and Lee would always get into an argument over something," says Jan. "It was usually a battle of wills over who was right about some minor topic. The arguments got

A rare candid of Barbara, Franchot and an unidentified maitre d' at a Hollywood restaurant in 1950. Courtesy of Michael Ochs Archives/Venice, CA

Another rare candid, this one showing a tender moment between Franchot and Barbara. Courtesy of Michael Ochs Archives/Venice, CA

pretty bad sometimes, and their drinking was always behind it. Mabel would clam up and kind of shrink down in her chair, but Lee and Barbara would really go at it.

"I always felt that Barbara wanted to make her father love her the way that he loved Mabel, Frank and me (and later, our four children). But as far as Lee was concerned, Barbara couldn't do anything right. And those times when it was clear that she *had* done something right, Lee refused to acknowledge it. I know that always bothered Barbara. In fact, it devastated her. I have never been able to figure out why Lee had such a problem with Barbara."

One day Jan found (and read) a journal of Barbara's that she used mostly as an appointment book, although she had also scribbled down some personal thoughts in it. Much to Jan's surprise, many of these notations of Barbara's were secret prayers to her father, pleading with him to love her. "Barbara had written down things like, 'Oh, Daddy, please love me,'" recalls Jan. "Just page after page of, 'Daddy, please love me. Please, daddy, love me!' And then, on the next page, 'Daddy, why do you hate

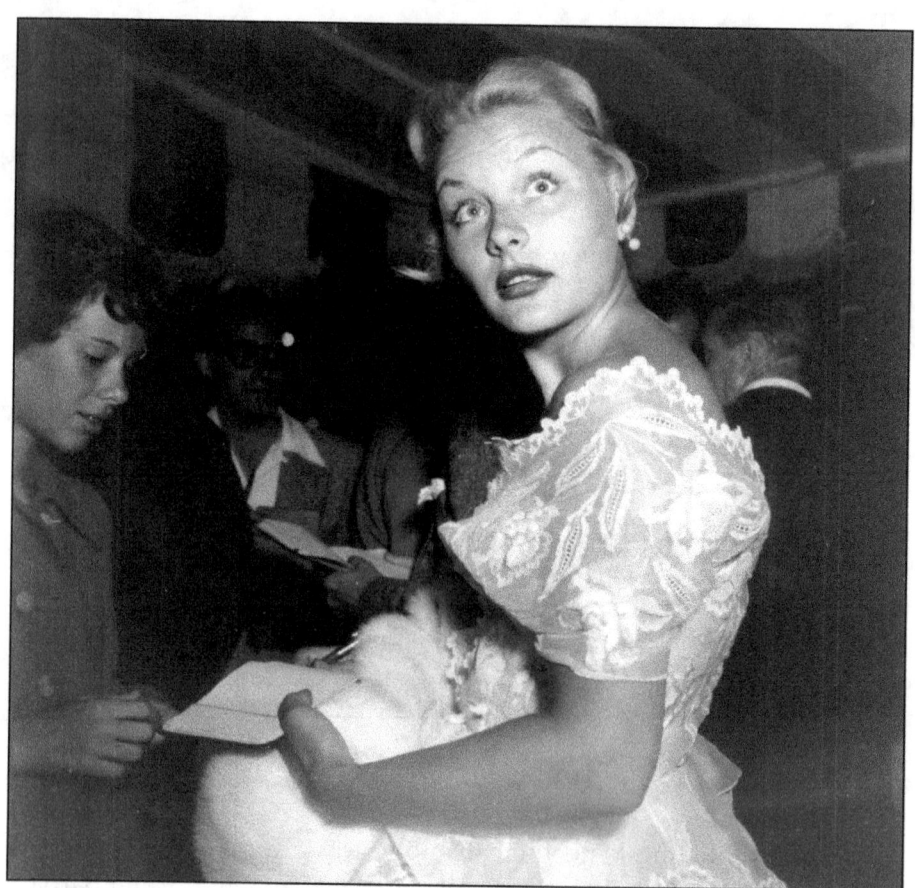

A little seen candid of Barbara signing autographs outside a Hollywood restaurant in 1950. Courtesy of Michael Ochs Archives/Venice, CA

me? Well, I hate you, too!' It broke my heart when I read that, but Barbara and I never talked about it. She also wrote some very cryptic things in that journal that I still don't understand. Weird-sounding stuff about being on fast-moving trains, and how she wanted to be cremated.

"Barbara gave me the journal many years later, along with several photo albums and a lot of other stuff that she wanted me to keep for her. But when Frank and I split up in 1968, he took most of the things she had given me and wound up losing all of them after he married his second wife. I feel especially bad that Barbara's journal was lost. I think it revealed a lot of the inner turmoil that Barb was dealing with in those years. Even though she was accomplishing a lot professionally, there was always an emptiness in her heart."

All these years later, Barbara's anguished pleas to her father in her journal remain ripe for contemplation. Were they merely the stream-of-consciousness thoughts of a neglected and wounded daughter who longed to receive the type of paternal nurturing she couldn't get from an unfeeling man? Or did they carry a much more ominous message? Did they hint at an inappropriate encounter, or were they just the plaintive words of a girl who never really felt her father's love?

The heartrending laments in Barbara's journal echo in silence today, and their motivation remains a mystery to everyone, perhaps, but the two people who are no longer here to explain them. Indeed, if anyone who knew Barbara, or Lee, can shed any light on the meaning of these words, they aren't saying.

Despite the serious personal problems she was experiencing with her father, things were continuing to move along nicely for Barbara on the work front. In September 1950, it was reported that she was to make her Broadway debut in producer S.N. Behrman's play, *Let Me Hear the Melody*, but the project was temporarily scrapped when the financing for it collapsed. (It was later produced in Philadelphia, without Barbara, in May 1951.) However, on September 12, Barbara did fly out to the east coast to co-star with Franchot in a summer stock production of another S. N. Behrman play, *The Second Man*. The Theater Guild had staged the original version of the play on Broadway in 1927.

Produced at New York's Somerset Theater by Franchot's friend and Group Theatre associate, Jean Dalrymple, *The Second Man* was a comedy about a social activist and novelist (Tone) who realizes that "the second man" in him is really an opportunist wise enough to turn to his wealthy mistress (Barbara) for the luxuries his other lifestyle has denied him. Former film star Margaret Lindsay (as Franchot's wife, Mrs. Kendall Frayne) and Broadway veteran Walter Brooke rounded out the four-character cast. The show's playbill described Barbara as "captivating" in the role of Monica Grey, a part which was later played by newcomer Cloris Leachman when Franchot reprised the production in June 1951.

The Second Man ran for one week as the Somerset Theater's final summer stock play of the season, and was the first of Barbara's two stage efforts (the second being *The Postman Always Rings Twice*, in 1953). Upon the show's completion, Franchot brought Barbara to the family homestead in Upstate New York, to meet his mother, Gertrude. (His father, Dr. Frank J. Tone, had died in 1944.) While it remains unclear what Gertrude Tone thought of Barbara following their introduction, Lisa Burks suggests it may have been somewhat of a strained meeting.

"Gertrude, as a general rule, was very possessive of Franchot and did not warm up to any of the women in his life," she says, "so at this point I assume that would have included Barbara."

Other Tone family members may have been more welcoming, adds Lisa. "Overall, it is my impression that Barbara was initially perceived by the rest of Franchot's family to be intelligent, beautiful, warm and friendly. I think that they truly liked her as a person, but, of course, their strongest loyalty would always be to Franchot and to *his* best interests."

Following their brief visit to Niagara Falls, the pair returned to the west coast in late September, only to find more trouble awaiting Barbara in L.A.

Despite her enviable alliance with such a respected member of the industry as Franchot Tone, Barbara's growing connection to the Hollywood underworld was again apparent on October 29 when she was called before a Federal Grand Jury as a defense witness in the perjury trial of a suspected murderer and dope addict named Stanley Adams. A so-called "jewelry salesman" whose face was known in every nightclub on the Sunset Strip, Adams, 38, a reputed member of the notorious Sica mob of organized crooks, and a close friend of both Barbara and her former boyfriend, Don Cougar, was accused of murdering Hollywood drug dealer, "Singing" Abe Davidian.

Adams and 15 others, including Davidian, had earlier been indicted as suspects in a million-dollar, statewide dope ring. Like a slam-bang scene from one of Warner Bros.' toughest crime films of the period, Davidian's arrest had followed a high-speed car chase that ended with the state police shooting out the tires of his sedan as he was transporting heroin from L.A. to Fresno. Hoping to be exonerated of the charges, Davidian informed Federal investigators of the ring's inside operations, but, on February 28, 1949, he died a grisly, stool pigeon's death when he was found shot in the head in the living room of his mother's home in Fresno.

On the first day of her two days of testimony, Barbara, reportedly "nervous to the point of hysteria," provided an alibi for Adams, testifying that he was with her in her apartment at the time of the killing. Looking beautiful with a new brunette hairstyle offset by her cool, blue eyes, Barbara was accompanied to the Federal building in Los Angeles by Franchot and the other witness for the defense, Don Cougar. The latter testified that he had also been present at Barbara's apartment on the night she entertained Adams. One can only wonder what the distinguished Franchot, who was the absolute epitome of good taste, thought of Barbara's involvement with such dangerous and unsavory characters.

Despite Barbara's and Don Cougar's best efforts on his behalf, Stanley Adams was ultimately found guilty of perjury, and was sentenced to four

A frightened looking Barbara appears before a Federal Grand Jury in the perjury trial of her friend, drug dealer Stanley Adams. Courtesy of L.A. Public Library/ Herald Examiner Collection

years in prison. Later that year, Cougar was busted a second time for possession of marijuana and served a one-year sentence in the county jail.

As a result of her participation in the Adams trial, Barbara received a plethora of unfavorable publicity, of which her boss, Jack Warner, took careful notice.

A wild and wide-eyed Barbara had skated blissfully onto thin ice, and it was already cracking beneath her.

Chapter Ten:
Front and Center

Six weeks after her appearance before the Federal Grand Jury, Barbara was slapped with a subpoena to appear as a witness in the ongoing custody fight between Franchot and his ex-wife, Jean Wallace. The former Mrs. Tone was seeking to regain custody of her two sons, of whom she had been granted partial visitation rights since the couple's August 1948 divorce.

On December 8, Jean testified in Santa Monica Superior Court that she "…had warned [Franchot] against association with Barbara Payton, because Barbara was mixed up with narcotics." Jean then pointed to Barbara in the courtroom and used her presence as the main reason why Franchot should not be allowed custody of the children. When asked by her attorney, S.S. Hahn, to explain why she felt this way, Jean Wallace simply replied, "Because Barbara is a well-known tramp." She went on to tell the court, "I told Franchot that I didn't want my sons around her. I said that I heard confidentially that she was mixed up in narcotics and was going to be called to court very soon (in the Stanley Adams matter). If Franchot is going to marry her, she's not a fit mother for our children." It was reported that Barbara sat in the courtroom and listened attentively to Jean's denouncement of her, but showed very little reaction. Nor did she once try to contest the allegations. Then again, she couldn't. After all, her name had not only been linked in the press with drug dealers and mobsters, she had also been called before a Federal Grand Jury to tell what she knew about a real-life murder. At this point, Barbara's character was pretty much fair game. Though she may have had the face of an angel, it was clear that Barbara was anything but innocent.

In his questioning of Franchot, S.S. Hahn managed to elicit a confession from him that he had seen Barbara naked "many times." When

Jean's attorney asked the court to acknowledge that Barbara was living a notorious life, it was reported that she "…raised her head proudly and smiled," as if she weren't the least bit embarrassed. Indeed, Barbara may have felt more than a little pleased that she was the focal point in what was, at the time, a turbulent and well-publicized spectacle that saw her name splashed front and center across the nation's newspapers. Alternating

Barbara was starting to appear in courtrooms as often as she appeared in films. Courtesy of USC/Dept. of Special Collections/L.A. Examiner Collection

between civil and contentious, the custody battle between Franchot Tone and Jean Wallace would continue into the following year, with Barbara's name often dragged into the proceedings, and always in a disparaging way.

A few weeks after the hearing, the December 11 edition of the *San Francisco Examiner* ran a story later circulated by the national wire

Barbara and Franchot attend the January 1951 world premiere of the Warner Bros. film, Operation Pacific. *Courtesy of AP/Wide World Photos*

services, that revealed how a group of Hollywood publicists had chosen seven movie starlets as "...the baby stars of 1950 most likely to succeed." The actresses mentioned in the article were Debbie Reynolds, Piper Laurie, Barbara Rush, Mala Powers, Barbara Bates, Mary Castle—and Barbara Payton.

"Not since the famous Wampas Baby Stars were chosen every year by movie publicity men more than a score of years ago, have the lads who toot

Barbara gazes intently at Franchot in this January 1951 photo.
From the Author's Collection

An evocative and telling shot of the equally tempestuous Barbara Payton and Franchot Tone. Courtesy of The Hulton Archive

the horns and hopefuls gone out on a limb and named their choices from the ranks of newly-born luminaries," wrote International News Service correspondent James Padgitt. With regard to Barbara, "the only blonde among the six," Padgitt wrote, "Big things are planned at Warner Bros. Studios for this luscious beauty." Evidently Barbara's recent court appearances hadn't adversely affected her still-rising star, or the benign image that the Warner Bros. publicity mill was trying desperately to craft for her, and the "Baby Stars" mention provided her with yet another impressive accolade.

On January 12, Barbara and Franchot seized even more publicity at the world premiere of a John Wayne/Patricia Neal war film for Warner Bros., titled *Operation Pacific.* Arriving in an Army jeep to a chorus of deafening screams from a crowd of autograph seekers, the duo was led up the red carpet by a hovering mass of strapping young servicemen,

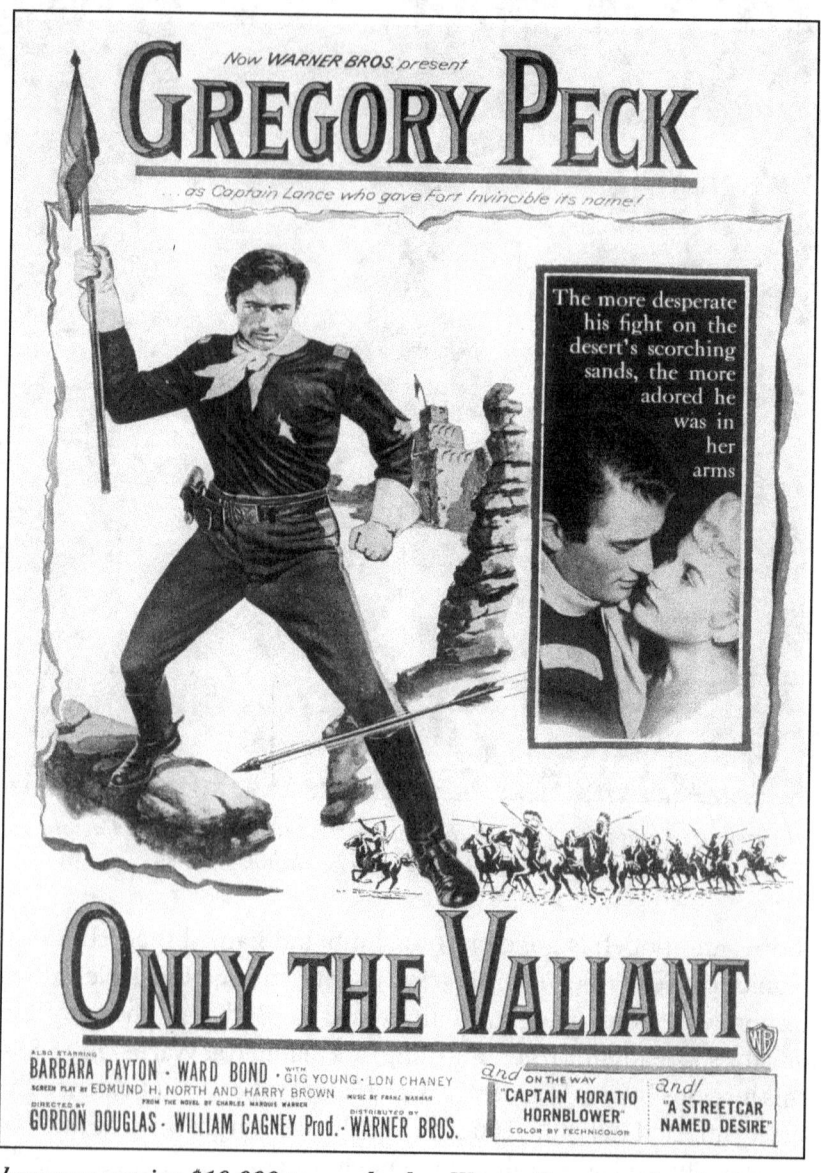

Barbara was earning $10,000 per week when Warner Bros. gave her the female lead in a Gregory Peck western, **Only The Valiant**. *From the Author's Collection*

while Barbara, who was dressed like a 1920s flapper, mugged wildly for the cameras.

Standing outside the Pantages Theater on Hollywood Boulevard before a throng of photographers, journalists and movie fans, the elegant pair—Barbara, looking resplendent in a new, $10,000 mink coat and dangling diamond earrings, and Franchot, natty and debonair as ever—seemed blissfully untouched by the critical (and legal) brickbats that had earlier been thrown their way. Amidst a sea of frenzied, bobbing heads uttering shouts of recognition and approval, clearly all the validation they needed was present in the crowd's cheers.

Judging by the response they got, Franchot and Barbara's celebrity status seemed safe to them, and permanent.

In mid-March, it was announced in the L.A. trade papers that Barbara would be starring in another crime film for William Cagney Productions titled *The Evil Eyeful*. The blurb noted that the picture was to be shot the following September and that Barbara was to receive top billing for the first time in her career. Not bad for someone who had been in Hollywood for all of two years.

Of the proposed film, Bill Cagney was quoted in the article as saying, "Barbara plays a doll who outsmarts the smartest racketeer to gain power." Though both the film's premise and Barbara's casting as its star makes for fertile fantasies today, the project, alas, never got off the ground. In fact, by September 1951, Barbara would be seeing her days as a leading lady at Warner Bros. and Cagney Productions quickly coming to an end.

Although *The Evil Eyeful* never came to pass, Barbara had the female lead in her third, and what was to be final, Warner Bros. film, *Only the Valiant*, a William Cagney production starring Gregory Peck (on loanout from David O. Selznick), and released on April 21, 1951. Lensed partially on location in the New Mexico desert, the starkly lit, black-and-white film deals with an Apache attack on a cavalry troop led by hard-nosed commanding officer Captain Richard Lance (Peck). Gig Young co-stars as Bill Holloway, an army lieutenant who harbors an unrequited love for Peck's fiancee, Cathy Eversham (Barbara), the soft-spoken daughter of a retired Army Captain. When Peck mistakenly assumes that Barbara is carrying on an affair with Young, he deliberately dispatches the young lieutenant into the desert on a suicide mission, resulting in Young's death. This act, viewed as unjust and heartless by Peck's detachment of assorted misfits, brings on their subsequent refusal to support his efforts to keep the warring Indians at bay.

Horror film icon Lon Chaney, far past his glory days at Universal Studios, and with over ten years of severe alcohol abuse etched indelibly on his face, provides potent background support in the film as a crazed trooper, one of many in Peck's band who despise him. Chaney's near-maniacal, wild-eyed performance is one of the few real standouts in the piece, which was also bolstered by a supporting cast of well-known character actors, including Neville Brand, Jeff Corey, Warner Anderson, Michael Ansara, and three supporting players from Barbara's *Kiss Tomorrow Goodbye*: Steve Brodie, Dan Riss and the great Ward Bond (once again superb, this time as the alcoholic Corporal Gilchrist).

Though second-billed, and featured prominently in the film's print ads and theatrical trailer, Barbara's scenes were few and fleeting in this undistinguished Western, commonly thought to be one of Gregory Peck's weakest films. While she was undoubtedly lovely, with her high cheekbones, expressive eyes and fulsome curves (the latter displayed prominently in a wide selection of skintight gowns), Barbara delivered a performance in the film that was incredibly lame, often appearing as if

Gregory Peck, Barbara and Gig Young as they appeared in Only The Valiant.
Courtesy of The Trinity Mirror

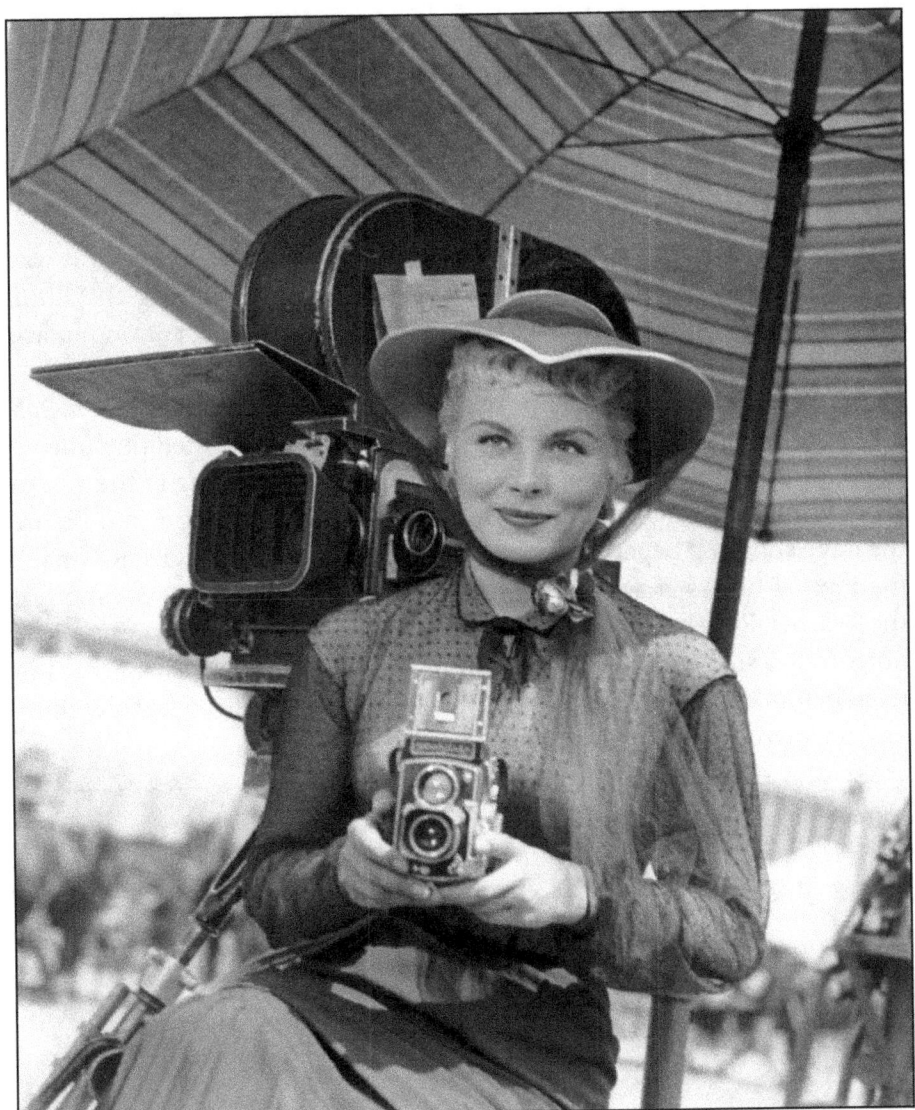

A rare, on set candid of Barbara during the filming of Only The Valiant. *Courtesy of Jan Redfield*

she were concentrating more on her boisterous personal life than on her acting.

Aside from her somewhat shaky emoting, it is possible that Barbara's role in *Only the Valiant*, much like her previous one in *Dallas*, had been drastically cut, as she later made the strange claim that she was the first actress ever to be barred from the set of a movie in which she had the leading female role. According to her 1963 memoir, *I Am Not Ashamed*, Barbara's presence in the film was evidently so unnerving to Peck, he had complained to director Gordon Douglas that he couldn't concentrate on his performance when she was around. If one is to believe Barbara's tale, Douglas responded by ordering her to stay off the Warner Bros. lot when her services weren't required. [9]

Peck's displeasure with Barbara was evidently short-lived, for it was later alleged that an affair took place between them during the film's production, an occurrence that was becoming increasingly commonplace for Barbara.

In a *Confidential* magazine article, *The Girl Who Made Peck a Bad Boy*, published a few years later, in April 1956, it was reported that during the filming of *Only the Valiant*, "...the two took to meeting at the studio early in the morning for rendezvous in Barbara's dressing room before the day's shooting began. They liked nothing better than their 'milkman's matinees'—unless it was their afternoons. Once, while on location at the Warner Ranch, they held up shooting for an entire afternoon. Peck borrowed a single horse from the studio corral and perched Barbara in front of him on the nag. With one hand on the reins and another clutching Payton, he rode off into the hills for a little action."

LEFT: *Barbara and Gregory Peck embrace in a publicity still for* Only The Valiant. *Courtesy of Wisconsin Center for Film and Theater Research* / RIGHT: *Barbara and Peck in the WB western,* Only The Valiant. *From the Author's Collection*

Peck and Barbara in a little seen publicity still for **Only The Valiant**.
Courtesy of Wisconsin Center for Film and Theater Research

While Tina Ballard recalls with some certainty that the two dated, she never saw Peck at Barbara's apartment, nor did she ever meet him. "I think they saw each other briefly; very briefly. In other words, it was strictly a casual thing. Barbara did mention him to me a time or two, and she said that she liked Greg because he reminded her a lot of [her ex-husband] Jack. They were both extremely handsome men."

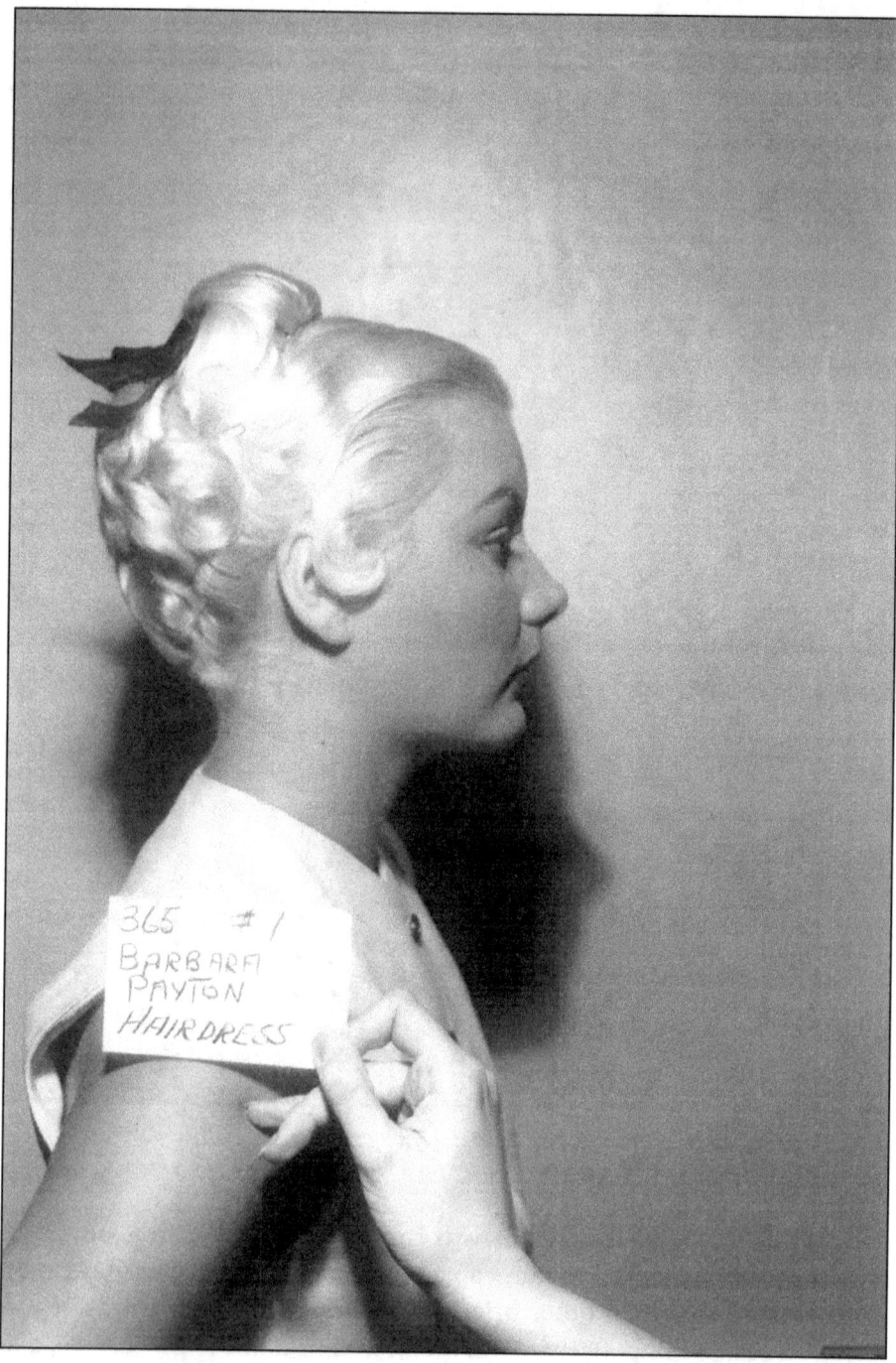

Barbara's wardrobe and hair test for her 1951 film, **Drums in the Deep South.**
Courtesy of Eddie Brandt's

Actress Virginia Mayo, who knew both Barbara and Peck from WB, confirmed Tina's assertion that the couple had dated. As Mayo once told her biographer, Laura Wagner, "I know he [Gregory Peck] had an affair with Barbara Payton. They were making a movie together at Warners at the time. Greg didn't care much for the movie, but she was in it and she set her sights on him. He was good looking and all, so you can't blame her, I guess. She invited him to her house one night, and that was it. His marriage was failing at the time, and he just didn't care."

With the passing of Gregory Peck in 2003, along with his decades-long stature as one of Hollywood's most irreproachable and untarnished stars, the true extent of his relationship with Barbara will likely remain unknown.

At the very least, Barbara was quoted as saying she had a wonderful time working with the actor. In an interview given to the *New York Morning Telegram* on April 17, 1951, Barbara raved, "Greg is a honey, and what a sense of humor! His next picture should be a comedy. He's really the end!"

Obviously, as her association with Gregory Peck proves, Barbara was keeping busy, professionally and otherwise. While up to now, Franchot Tone had been unaware of his fiancée's rambling ways—or perhaps, just unconcerned about them—that was all about to change.

Meanwhile, Barbara's serendipitous ride on the gravy train continued when Franchot announced plans to purchase a ranch for her in Pomona. Life was good—very good, indeed—for the woman Warner Bros. had begun promoting as "the white diamond with blue eyes."

Says Jan Redfield, "That was probably the happiest time in Barbara's career. She was really on her way up and everything seemed to be going her way. It's a shame her luck didn't last. She could have been a big star, you know?"

CHAPTER ELEVEN:
Head Over Halo

Following the release of *Only the Valiant* in April, Warner Bros. loaned Barbara out to the King Bros., an independent movie company, to co-star with former MGM actor (and Clark Gable lookalike) James Craig and Hollywood heartthrob Guy Madison in the RKO release, *Drums in The Deep South* (1951). Filmed on two massive soundstages at West Hollywood's Sam Goldwyn Studios, the medium-budgeted historical drama found Barbara cast as Kathy Summers, a pure-hearted and genteel Southern belle—a somewhat inventive casting decision that, given her wild, party girl image, must have caused a collective roar within the industry. Written by Philip Yordan and Sidney Harmon, and based on a story by Hollister Noble, the Civil War saga borrowed heavily from its forerunner, the timeless *Gone With the Wind*, in its overall tone, texture and ambience, but it fell far short of that classic film's excellence.

The plot concerns friends and West Point graduates Clay Clayburn (Craig) and Will Denning (Madison) finding themselves fighting for opposite sides in 1861 Georgia when General Sherman's troops commence an assault on the bloodstained Georgia landscape. Barbara's character is wed to a former classmate and friend of the duo, Braxton Summers (Craig Stevens), but pines for Confederate soldier Craig (her former beau), whom she helps by supplying him with information gathered from the enemy. While Craig and his troop of 20 soldiers keep Sherman's trains and supply wagons at bay from their camp atop a cave-laden mountain near Barbara's home, she indulges in espionage activities against the Union, carrying on like a Southern Mata Hari from the confines of her besieged plantation. Although her efforts are successful in helping Craig hold back the Union lines, the reunited lovers eventually meet a tragic, if heroic, end when they're blown off Devil's Mountain by a Yankee brigade led by Madison.

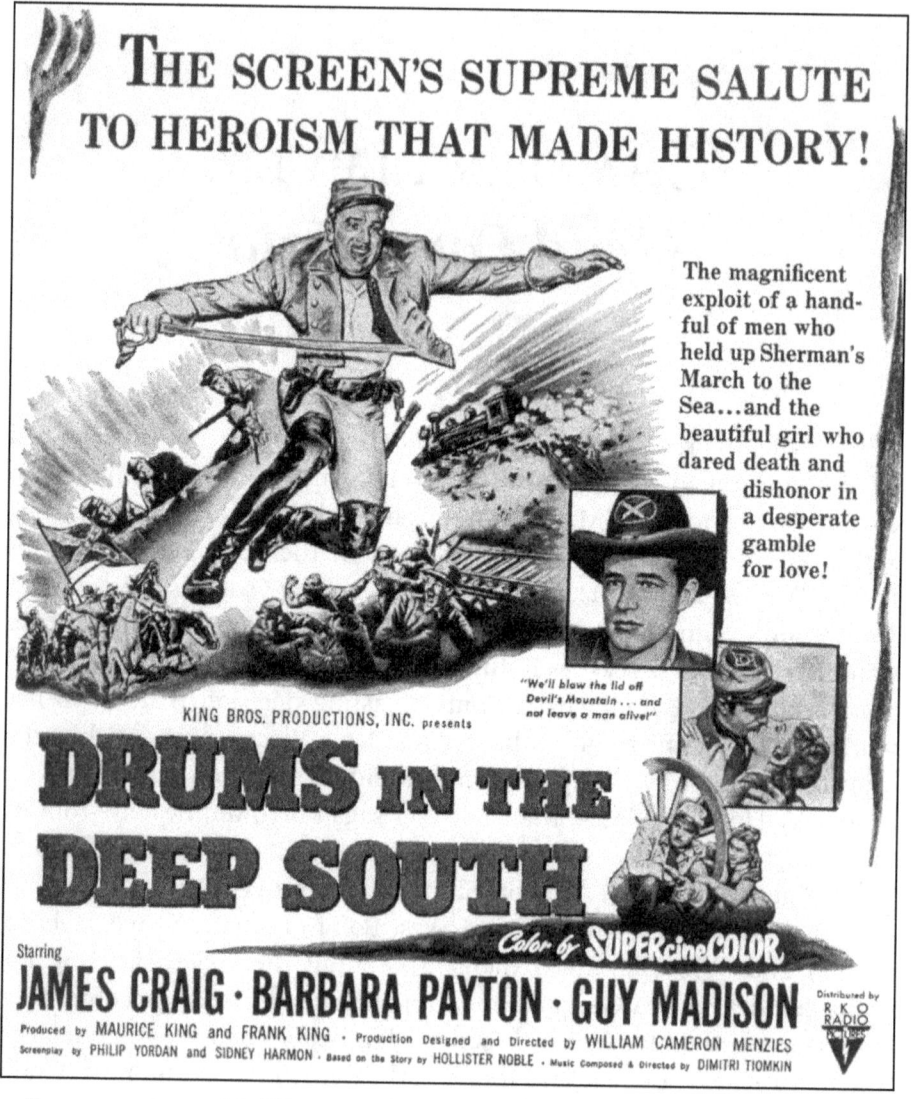

Rare newspaper ad for Drums in the Deep South. *From the Author's Collection*

Drums in the Deep South, filmed in Supercinecolor by noted Hollywood art director William Cameron Menzies, the set designer of Tara for *Gone With the Wind*, was a highly stylized production whose best features, perhaps, were its almost surreal, labyrinthian sets and Dimitri Tiomkin's robust musical score. Despite minimal promotion from RKO and mostly tepid reviews, the film did brisk business at the box office and was deemed a moderate success following its fall 1951 release.

Billed seventh in the credits of *Drums in the Deep South* was an apple-cheeked, 21-year-old actor from the Midwest named Robert Easton. Bob came to the King Bros. straight from MGM, where he had appeared in another Civil War drama, the infinitely better and much more highly regarded *The Red Badge of Courage*. A prolific character actor who specialized in gangly, slow-talking hillbilly roles, Bob Easton would go on to appear in nearly 80 films and more than 800 television shows, while carving out an outstanding ancillary career as Hollywood's leading dialectician and vocal coach.

Barbara and her co-star James Craig in a publicity still for **Drums in the Deep South.** *Courtesy of RKO Pictures*

Barbara's dramatic death scene (with James Craig) in Drums in the Deep South. *Courtesy of RKO Pictures*

Born Robert Easton Burke in Milwaukee, Wisconsin, he was blessed as a child with an intellectual prowess so impressive he was one of radio's original *Quiz Kids*, a show that featured some of the nation's youngest and best academic prodigies. Moving to San Antonio with his divorced mother in the 1940s, he later attended the University of Texas in Austin, where he took freshman, sophomore, junior and senior classes concurrently. Bob eventually moved to Hollywood in the late 1940s and began a film career that was, amazingly, still in progress in 2007. Beginning in the 1960s, he would take his talent in creating perfectly executed dialects and become the industry's most renowned voice coach, working with everyone from Sir Laurence Olivier and Sir John Gielgud to Robin Williams and Bette Midler. In March 2006, Bob Easton came forward to share his personal memories of Barbara and the film they did together:

"*Drums in the Deep South* was my sixth film (with billing) in Hollywood. I did *The Red Badge of Courage* right before it, which, of course, was a very successful film starring Audie Murphy and directed by John Huston. Having worked with a director like Huston, it was very apparent to me that *Drums* director, William Cameron Menzies, while a very nice man, was no John Huston. Given his artistic background, Menzies seemed more interested in the set design and in the look of the film than he did in the relationships of the characters."

Drums was one of the first films to use a new cost-efficient color process called Supercinecolor, which unfortunately gave the proceedings a somewhat flat and washed-out look. "The color used in the film was very poor," says Bob. "Supercinecolor was an experimental color process and the producers of the film, the King Bros., used it because they were extremely cheap. The sets, on the other hand, were very interesting. The mountaintop seen in the film was built on one soundstage and the huge maze of caverns was built on another. In fact, I think the entire budget was spent just on the sets.

"Frank and Maurice King were real characters, as was their brother, Herman (a.k.a. "Hymie"), who was also on the picture, as its technical advisor. Their real surname was Kazinsky, and they had made a lot of money in slot machines before deciding one day that they wanted to make movies. In fact, they were known around town as The Slot Machine Kings. I think it's fair to say that all three brothers were a bit on the shady side. They were very loud and crude and they didn't treat any of us on the film with respect; not even Barbara. On the other hand, their mother, Mrs. Kazinsky, used to come to the set a lot and she was a sweet lady. In fact, I used to look at her and wonder, 'How could you produce three horrible sons like this?' The third brother, Herman, was morbidly obese—grotesquely obese—and he treated Barbara very badly. One day my mother visited the set and Herman King bullied Barbara into giving up her chair so my mother could sit down. Then he ordered Barbara to sit on his lap. And she did. From then on, throughout the entire shoot, you'd hear him say, in that gruff, sleazy voice of his: 'Come on over here, baby, and sit on my lap.' And Barbara would go over and very dutifully sit on his lap, though she was clearly uncomfortable doing it. I felt so sorry for her. Barbara was a professional actress, hired to act, not to sit on some fat guy's lap. Trust me, the King Brothers were not nature's noblemen."

Former child actor Claude Jarman, Jr., who had given a touching performance a few years earlier in the family classic, *The Yearling*, was originally slated for the role of the young, Confederate soldier, Jerry, in *Drums in the Deep South*, but when he asked for too much money, Bob Easton got the part. "I loved working with Barbara. There was an incredible warmth and a likeableness about her that I noticed immediately. When I first met her, I remember we both talked about growing up in Texas—her in Odessa, and me in San Antonio. We had that in common, so we got along with each other right from the start. *Drums* was about a four-week shoot and I feel I got to know Barbara pretty well during that time. She had a friendly and cuddly quality to her personality and she was very beautiful. Those warm, sensitive eyes of hers, along with those gorgeous, full lips, made her extremely appealing. I'll never forget how in the morning she used to stand in front of an arc light in the studio, to warm up, because it was always so cold on the set. Most times when she did this, Barbara was wearing something flimsy and kind of diaphanous. One morning my mother came with me to the set and she said, 'Barbara is such a beautiful girl, and she's sweet, too, but it's a shame that she's so absent-minded.' I said, 'What do you mean?' And she said, 'Well, the poor thing forgot to put on her underwear.' And there was Barbara, warming herself in front of the arc light in her see-through outfit, with not a care in the world.

Barbara's beauty is admired by Craig Stevens, James Craig and Guy Madison in this scene from Drums in the Deep South. *Courtesy of RKO Pictures*

A rare candid of Barbara with six students from Savannah, Georgia's Armstrong College during her lengthy publicity tour of several Southern states, on behalf of her film, Drums in the Deep South. *Courtesy of Nick Bougas*

"Yes, she was totally uninhibited but it was never a sleazy thing; there was a wholesomeness about Barbara. A wholesome sexiness, you might say. Though I was 21 at the time, just three years younger than Barbara, I played an innocent and much younger boy in the film. Believe me, whenever she was around I had to work very hard to stay focused on my job."

Commenting on Barbara's work in the film, Bob says, "I thought she was wonderful. She definitely infused a lot of herself into that part. For instance, there's a scene in *Drums* where my character, Jerry, is trapped in a cave under some rocks, and she's desperately searching for me. Barbara played that scene with a very strong maternal instinct that, in my opinion, was very believable. It was a joy working with her. She was absolutely professional at all times and never caused any problems. Barbara was an intelligent woman and a talented actress. I liked her. I liked her a lot."

Despite Bob Easton's feelings to the contrary, Barbara's performance in *Drums*, much as it was in *Only the Valiant*, once again seemed inconsistent, alternating between restrained and believable to detached and tentative. Said *Variety* in its October 3 review of the film, "Miss Payton, a busty blonde, has the only femme role in the cast and she is none too convincing—either in the few romantic scenes *or* in her espionage activities." The distractions of Barbara's outside pursuits seemed to have gotten between the actress and her ability to deliver a good performance.

Apparently, there was a distraction on the set, as well; this one, in the guise of her hunky co-star, Guy Madison. As two of Hollywood's most aesthetically pleasing people, Barbara and Madison (then married to troubled ex-Paramount actress Gail Russell) had formed an easygoing bond of sorts during the film's shoot by trading stories of their various exploits (and conquests) in town. Their intimate conversations in Barbara's dressing room had soon led to their stopping off at Santa Monica Blvd.'s Formosa Cafe after work, for cocktails. One evening, after several rounds

Drums in the Deep South *co-star, actor Guy Madison, an alleged intimate partner of Barbara's during the filming of the picture. Courtesy of Jan Redfield*

of drinks, and one assumes, some serious flirting, the two headed back to Barbara's apartment for a little privacy.

Hollywood has always been a small, insular town, and by mid-1951 Franchot was probably wondering if all the gossip he was hearing about Barbara's character was true. Perhaps smelling trouble in the air, he placed her in a second-floor apartment at 7456 Hollywood Boulevard and then secretly dispatched an L.A. private detective named Fred Otash to put her under 12-hour surveillance.

On the night of Barbara's date with Madison, however, it was Franchot himself who was doing the spying, while hiding behind a church sign that was directly across the street from her home. As he watched his fiancée and her latest fling enter her apartment, Franchot intuitively knew something was amiss. In agony, he waited several minutes, then barged into the apartment and allegedly found the couple making love in Barbara's bed.

Franchot reportedly confronted Madison with the terse (but in retrospect, oddly restrained) comment, "I'm engaged to this girl and I'm going to marry her. Are you?" As a nude and scarlet-faced Guy Madison jumped out of bed to gather his clothes, he supposedly replied, "No, I can't. I'm already married."

Barbara's reaction to the havoc she had stirred up was said to be one of pure, unbridled bliss. Lying naked across the bed, she punched a pillow in victory, kicked her legs high in the air and burst out laughing. An almost demonic streak of sadism had found its way into her personality, and it was not only cruel, but totally uncharacteristic. Being caught in the act seemed to unleash a truculent side to Barbara that had never surfaced before. It was a side to her personality that was as puzzling, perhaps, as her need to undermine herself, literally, at every turn.

Franchot's ambush of Barbara and Guy Madison made it into the pages of *Confidential* magazine and brought the openly-promiscuous actress yet another round of bad press. With one embarrassing faux pas after another, Barbara was dismantling her career, and her future, step by step.

Warner Bros. production chief Jack L. Warner, incensed with Barbara for the adverse publicity she was getting, sought to punish her for her antics by assigning her a secondary role in a mawkish tearjerker for the studio called *Close to My Heart*. The story of a childless couple's attempts to adopt a newborn found abandoned at a police station, the film starred Ray Milland, as a businessman driven to find the baby's birth parents, and Gene Tierney, as his vulnerable wife who quickly grows attached to the infant. When it is revealed that the child's father is an accused murderer, Milland and Tierney are allowed to bring the baby home to raise as their own.

To show her how expendable she was to him, Warner had tossed Barbara the small role of Arlene in the film, which would have placed her fifth in the credits. Following her second-billed parts in the Cagney and Peck films, Barbara instantly recognized this gesture for what it was: a vindictive Jack Warner flexing his "boss muscles" by putting her in her place for her headstrong nature. Despite her flighty, playgirl persona, Barbara was still savvy enough about her career to know that a backwards step like this would soon find her doing bit parts in B-westerns again, so she refused the film. She and Warner apparently exchanged heated words over this, and he responded by immediately placing Barbara on suspension.

By 1951, thirty-two-year-old perennial starlet Mary Beth Hughes, whose career had flourished in the 1940s with her roles in some high-caliber films (*The Ox-Bow Incident*, *Orchestra Wives*, etc.), was down to doing supporting parts (*Passage West*) and blowsy bits (the neglectful mother in WB's *Young Man With a Horn*). When Barbara dropped out of *Close to My Heart*, Warners hired Hughes, another gorgeous blonde, to replace her. Unfortunately, however, the minuscule role did nothing for the ex-leading lady's fading career. Just a few years later, Mary Beth Hughes was spotted singing torch songs in an open-all-night bowling alley in Anaheim.

Of Barbara's boss and unforgiving adversary, her friend Steve Hayes says, "Jack L. Warner was a mean prick. Not as bad as Columbia's Harry Cohn (nobody was his equal), but J.L. always wanted to show everyone who was top dog.

"All those guys were ruthless bastards: Cohn, Warner, and Louis B. Mayer—all of them. They were nothing more than thugs in business suits. Jack Warner didn't like unruly actors or actresses, except, perhaps, Errol Flynn, whom no one could dislike for very long (as he was that charming). Warner actually punished Barbara on several occasions, but knowing her, and knowing how she never liked being told what to do, she likely always fought back."

"I don't remember Barbara telling us that the studio had suspended her," says Jan Redfield, "but if Mr. Warner had tried to give her a part she

Ad for Barbara's 1951 cult classic, Bride of the Gorilla. *From the Author's Collection*

didn't like, believe me, she would have let him know. Barbara always had plenty of chutzpah."

Barbara had indeed let Jack Warner know, and the bad blood this had created would do irreparable harm to her career. She didn't realize it at the time, but Barbara's days at WB were numbered.

A July 14, 1951 blurb in the *L.A. Times* reported that Barbara had been taken off the studio suspension list and that it had handed her over to independent producer Jack Broder for the jungle potboiler *Bride of the*

A sultry shot of Barbara from **Bride of the Gorilla.** *Courtesy of Wisconsin Center for Film and Theater Research*

Gorilla. Although it was meant to be yet another act of punishment, the loanout was actually an unintentional blessing as it would provide Barbara with the second of two films for which she will forever be known.

Shortly before his death in 2002, *Bride of the Gorilla*'s assistant producer, the late Herman Cohen, told author Tom Weaver in an interview, that Jack Broder and Jack L. Warner were card buddies at the Hollywood Athletic Club on Sunset Boulevard and that one day Warner had mentioned to Broder that he "had this cunt under contract, doing nothing, sitting on her ass." When Broder responded that he was looking for a sexy, young girl for the lead role in his new film project, Cohen alleged that Warner offered him Barbara: "Take her!" he said. "You can have her!" With all the class and diplomacy of a snake, he supposedly told Broder, "She's fuckin' everybody on the lot. I gotta get rid of that cunt!"

"Barbara was very unhappy about being loaned to do the film," Cohen told Tom Weaver. "Here she thought she was gonna be another Joan Crawford or Bette Davis, and she ends up doing *Bride of the Gorilla*."

Despite her anger at being banished once again from the classy Warner Bros. lot to a rented, old soundstage at Sam Goldwyn Studios, Barbara gave the job her best shot. "As much as she was pissed off at Warners, 'cause she knew they were gonna dump her," said Herman Cohen, "and that therefore *Bride of the Gorilla* was on her way to being dumped, she never let it interfere with her work. Deep down, Barbara was a lovely person, she was very sweet."

The Poverty Row company that Barbara had landed at that summer was the brainchild of two enterprising businessmen who had started the operation just a few years earlier. In 1948, film distributor Broder and his business partner Joseph Harris had secured the theatrical rights to the entire vault of Universal talkies from 1930 to 1946 and had reissued them under the Realart Pictures logo. That year, Universal had merged into Universal-International and, as Scott MacGillivray and Ted Okuda wrote in their June 1993 *Filmfax* article, *Play It Again, Jack! Remembering Realart, The Re-Releasing Company*, "Realart's acquisition of the film library was part of Universal's housecleaning process and a great stroke of luck for Broder and Harris." By their use of such innovative marketing tools as creating new titles for several of the films in the Universal collection, customizing double bills featuring pictures with similar themes, and designing full-color poster and lobby card displays that were both memorable and eye-catching, Broder and Harris managed to turn their reissue library into a fairly successful enterprise.

A rare, on set candid of Barbara and an unidentified man thought to be Bride of the Gorilla's *director Curt Siodmak. From The Borst Collection*

Jack Broder had branched out into film production in 1950 and issued a few minor programmers (*Kid Monk Baroni, Two-Dollar Bettor*, etc.) before producing what would later become his two best-known efforts: *Bela Lugosi Meets a Brooklyn Gorilla*, starring the eponymous actor and the short-lived comedy team of Duke Mitchell and Sammy Petrillo, and its forerunner, the campy, and thoroughly enjoyable, *Bride of the Gorilla*.

Broder had originally hired 24-year-old Herman Cohen as his executive assistant, but soon made the ex-Marine an assistant producer on both films. Cohen later recalled that German-born director Curt Siodmak had brought Broder a script he had written, titled *A Face in the Water*, which he intended to film as a serious, psychological thriller. Siodmak was the younger brother of the more famous Robert Siodmak, a director who had found success in Hollywood with such film noirs as Franchot Tone's *Phantom Lady* and Burt Lancaster's *The Killers*, although Curt had attained success himself in 1941 as the writer of Universal's classic horror film *The Wolf Man*.

With a title change from *A Face in the Water* to *Bride of the Gorilla*, it's quite likely that the version that was filmed and shown in theaters was far different from Curt Siodmak's original vision for the story, and was tailored to better satisfy Jack Broder's shameless love of the bottom line. Cheaply rendered and even unintentionally comical in spots, the film nonetheless featured a few good performances, including a surprisingly effective one from Barbara. She not only looked luscious, but, also for the first time in her career, won top billing over her male co-stars (Raymond Burr, Lon Chaney and Tom Conway).

Barbara and her co-star Raymond Burr, as they appeared in the campy horror film, Bride of the Gorilla. *From the Author's Collection*

The plot of *Bride of the Gorilla* cast Barbara as Dina, the lonely wife of a much older rubber plantation owner Klaas Van Gelder (Paul Cavanagh), a cold individual who runs both his business and his marriage with an iron fist. Whiling away the hours dancing beneath a slow-moving ceiling fan, an isolated Dina finds herself attracted to the surly plantation foreman, Barney Chavez (played with brooding menace by Burr), and the two start an affair. Later, Chavez argues with his boss while the two are alone in the garden, then nonchalantly watches as Van Gelder is bitten and killed by a poisonous snake.

Unbeknownst to Chavez, the incident is witnessed by Van Gelder's housekeeper, Al-long (Gisela Werbisek), a wizened and sinister native woman well-versed in the practice of voodoo. Out of loyalty to her deceased employer, the gypsy brews a potion from the bark of a mysterious "evil tree" and tricks Chavez into drinking it, thereby cursing him with a spell that has him come to believe he has the ability to turn into a gorilla.

Lon Chaney, in his second and final film appearance opposite Barbara, is handed a supporting role as the jungle-reared, Police Commissioner

A shadowy and ominous looking shot of Barbara just before her death scene in Bride of the Gorilla. *Courtesy of The Borst Collection*

A lurid publicity still of Barbara and friend, from **Bride of the Gorilla**.
Courtesy of The Borst Collection

Taro, a shrewd individual whose instincts tell him that Chavez is responsible for Klaas Van Gelder's death. He tries to convince the local doctor, Viet (played by a dissipated-looking Tom Conway), of Chavez' guilt, but Viet is more concerned with his own unrequited affection for Dina. When a series of brutal jungle murders erupts, it becomes clear that the metamorphosis of man-into-gorilla that we believed Barney Chavez had only imagined is indeed occurring, although no one besides Al-long knows that it's taking place.

The film's over-the-top finale finds Taro and Viet in hot pursuit of Chavez, who has reverted to his simian state and is stomping across the soundstage jungle with an unconscious Barbara lying supine in his arms. The final scene shows Taro and Viet unloading a volley of bullets into a mass of underbrush where the gorilla is hiding, killing it and (in an ambiguous last scene), presumably, Barbara's character, as well.

Now finding herself in far less prestigious surroundings than those she had known at Warner Bros., Barbara nonetheless delivers a good performance in *Bride of the Gorilla*, rising well above her many personal diversions and a less than stellar screenplay. Whatever the back lot thriller lacked in plot and production values, however, it more than made up for in its lurid and kitschy ambiance. Its poster art alone was worth the price of admission. "*A Blonde and a savage, alone in the jungle... Her clothes torn away, screaming in terror... Her marriage vows were more than fulfilled!*" screamed its title card, which also featured a photo of Barbara draped seductively in the ape's embrace. With one's tongue firmly planted in cheek, viewing the film today can be an entertaining experience, certainly worth sitting through its brief running time of just 64 minutes.

Aside from its obvious camp appeal, *Bride of the Gorilla* is probably most effective in showcasing a sizzling Barbara at the height of her sexiness. Author Andrew Dowdy attended a midnight showing of the movie upon its Halloween, 1951 release, and in his book, *The Films of the Fifties: The American State of Mind*, he recalls the undeniable power of Barbara's magnetism. First seen dancing alone in a tight, low-cut sarong and slinky espadrilles, the curvaceous Barbara smolders with a sexual intensity that is nothing less than riveting. "Barbara's appearance onscreen was greeted with instant verbal approval," Dowdy writes, "accompanied by whistling, stomping, and the ecstatic tribute of flying popcorn boxes, many of them sacrificed unemptied."

An understandable response for Barbara, who, at 24, was a mesmerizing beauty; fully displayed here with her long-legged, hourglass figure, sensuous mouth, provocative eyes and flawless skin. That her beauty would elicit such a vociferous reaction was proof enough that film audiences loved the sight of this new, blonde bombshell. Indeed, her appearance in *Bride of the Gorilla* proves that in 1951, Barbara Payton was, without question, a Grade-A knockout.

But one, evidently, that the film's producer thought needed a little "tweaking." "Jack Broder had Barbara wear falsies under her sarong and he also made her pad her bra for the film," reveals an amused Tina Ballard. "With a bra size of just 34B, Barbara always wished she was bigger on top, but she absolutely hated it when the studios made her pad her bra. She would say, 'I feel so phony,' and, of course, Barbara was anything but a

*A close-up of the beautiful and brash (but kindhearted) Barbara Payton.
Courtesy of Jerry Ohlinger's*

phony. Still, she really did look beautiful in that film. And I guess Jack Broder got the big-bosomed sexpot he wanted, too."

Hidden beneath her physical appeal was a quality even more attractive, insists her fourth husband, Tony Provas, even if it rarely surfaced. "Barbara was like a Catholic church with a blazing neon sign out front," he says emphatically. "Underneath her brash exterior, and try as she did not to show it, Barbara had a heart of pure gold."

To illustrate his point, Tony recalls a story that reveals the deep empathy Barbara often showed the underdog. He says that when Raymond Burr first auditioned for the role of Barney Chavez in *Bride of the Gorilla*, Jack Broder had almost immediately rejected him due to his hefty girth.

"Raymond, a hell of a good actor, read for the part beautifully," says Tony, "but Broder felt he was much too overweight to play the male lead, who was supposed to be a handsome stud. Ray promised to go on a crash diet and bring his weight down to an acceptable level in time to start shooting, but Broder didn't believe he could do it, so Ray lost the role." Tony claims that Burr sought help from Barbara, who had already been signed to do the film, telling her that he was desperate for work.

At the time, Burr was broke and in-between pictures, and thus in dire need of a job. "He really needed the work and Barbara felt sorry for him. She truly believed him when he said he could lose the excess weight in time to shoot the film. So, she told me she went to Jack Broder and demanded that he hire Raymond, or she would walk off the picture. Since Barbara was the only one in the film with star status at the time, as well as its main draw, Broder gave in."

Burr rented a room in a cheap, downtown Hollywood hotel, where he surrounded himself with several jugs of water, and managed to fast off the excess weight in one week's time.

"Ray confirmed this story to me many years later at a Hollywood party," adds Tony. "He said that he would always be grateful to Barbara for helping him out when he really needed a break.

"Barbara was the softest touch in Hollywood, and a very sentimental girl. I remember her telling me once that she had always identified with the title character in the Charles Tazewell children's tale, *The Littlest Angel*. It is the story of an adorable but unruly tot who dies and goes straight to Heaven, and then finds he just cannot stay out of trouble. He is rather awkward with his new wings; so much, in fact, that when he tries to fly, he tumbles 'Head Over Halo' instead.

"It's no wonder Barbara loved that character so much; she was just like him. A mischievous little angel with a tarnished halo and broken wings, but one with a glorious heart. That was the Barbara I knew. That was the real Barbara."

Tough guy actor Tom Neal, whose July, 1951 meeting with Barbara would change both their lives forever. From the Author's Collection

Chapter Twelve:
Cowboy in a Bathing Suit

In July, during the filming of *Bride of the Gorilla*, Franchot Tone traveled to New York City on business, leaving Barbara feeling restless, and, as her friend Tina Ballard contends, "A little bit lonely. I guess she couldn't bear the thought of being alone, even if it was only for a few days. Barbara had this constant need to please and to be noticed and wanted and desired. She craved affection. There was something about Barbara where she needed companionship—male companionship—at all times. I'm not condoning her behavior, I'm just trying to explain how her mind worked."

Franchot was gone just a few days when Barbara attended a Hollywood pool party at the Sunset Plaza Apartments, where she met a handsome and unemployed B-movie actor named Tom Neal. [10] According to an *Exposed* magazine article, Barbara spotted the muscular Neal on the pool's high-diving board, "…displaying his masculinity via a brief pair of bathing panties [sic]." She took one "lip-drying look," said the article, and later uttered a statement to the press that was not only unintentionally comical but also a dead-on display of her endearing, if rather quirky romanticism: "Honey, I took just one look at him and I absolutely flipped!" she gushed. "It was love at first sight. He looked so wonderful in his trunks I knew he was the only man in my life."

In leering detail, *Exposed* surmised, "The memory of whatever Tone resembled in his undies was blurred by strutting Tom's conspicuous bulges." [11] The passionate duo quickly started an affair, with *Time* magazine writing, "Neal spent the next month and a half lolling around Barbara's patio doing nip-ups with bar bells while Barbara gazed at him adoringly."

The object of Barbara Payton's adoring gazes was born Thomas Carroll Neal, Jr., on January 28, 1914 in Evanston, Illinois. The only son of wealthy banker Thomas Carroll Neal and the former Mayme Martin, Tom and his two older sisters, Mary Elizabeth (born 1906) and Dorothy Helen (born 1910), enjoyed a privileged upbringing at 1200 Judson Street, in one of Chicago's cushy outlying bedroom communities.

Mary Neal's son, Walter Delano Burr III, describes the elder Neals as having a kind of quiet and understated elegance. "Even before he sold all his bank stock in 1934, my grandfather was worth over one million dollars on paper," says Walter. "His best friend was accounting giant Arthur Andersen, who for many years came over to my grandparents' house for breakfast every Saturday morning, to talk about their various investment deals.

"My grandfather was very low-key about his good fortune, but then again, he was always very stoic, in general. He and my grandmother were not flashy types; they were just nice, decent people. Tom's father was a member of the Westmoreland Country Club and the family lived in a beautiful, ten-room house, but that's about as much 'flash' as they ever showed."

Tom received a prep school education at nearby Lake Forest Academy before entering Evanston High School in 1928. Upon his graduation, he enrolled at Northwestern University in Evanston, where he joined the Sigma Chi fraternity and majored in Mathematics. However, despite prior accounts that he graduated from Northwestern, Walter Burr reveals that Tom abandoned college life after just one year. Burr also negates the many articles through the years that paint Tom as an extremely athletic individual who excelled in several sports in college, most notably boxing.

"At five-foot, eight inches tall and 145 pounds, Tom was too small for football, and although he did some boxing, he definitely never won a Golden Gloves title," says Walter. "Tom's main interest never was in sports. It's true he began lifting weights in high school, but I think he did it mainly to attract girls. He was never what you would call 'a team player'. Tom's interests were always geared more toward acting, and women. Lots of women."

During his brief stint at Northwestern, Tom joined the Drama Club and won a few leading roles in some school plays, which Walter admits, "stroked Tom's very healthy ego. That was his first real taste of public adulation and he loved it." In the summer following his freshman year, and against his father's wishes, Tom left Evanston for nearby Chicago, where he worked briefly in summer stock.

He then migrated to New York City in the fall of 1933 and obtained small parts in several unsuccessful productions, including *If This Is Treason* (a trite anti-war melodrama which dealt with the [then] unlikely prospect of a U.S. war with Japan), *Spring Dance* (co-starring Jose Ferrer), and *Daughters of Atreus* (which featured Edmond O'Brien and Cornel Wilde, and closed after two weeks). While in New York, he met Inez Martin, described in one source as "a buxom ex-Follies girl with a deep southern accent." Despite a considerable age difference (Martin was nearly twice Tom's age), the couple began seeing each other and were engaged in 1935.

Coarse, loud and tawdry, Inez Martin was the former mistress of New York City mobster Arnold Rothstein, who had been mysteriously shot to death at the Park Central Hotel on November 4, 1928. Martin was the sole beneficiary of Rothstein's life insurance policy, which upon his passing, netted her over $150,000. Tom's father, a conservative and strait-laced man, was adamantly opposed to his son's impending marriage to the older and worldlier ex-showgirl, and counseled him on the matter. His gentle advice was apparently persuasive, as Tom eventually complied with his father's wishes and ended his relationship with Martin.

On the professional front, Tom appeared next in a road company production of *Brother Rat*. Tom had a small role in the play, which in his mind, was far beneath his capabilities and stature. In a *Hollywood Studio Magazine* article, titled *Tom Neal: A Tormented Life Marked by Violence and Tragedy*, Oscar A. Rimoldi writes, "Neal couldn't conform with seeing his name always in small print at the bottom of the cast." When *Brother Rat* reached Florida, Tom left the production in a snit and went to Fort Lauderdale, where his family had a winter home. Reportedly, he was working there as a lifeguard when a vacationing Metro-Goldwyn-Mayer studio talent scout noticed his good looks and great physique and, in a typical scenario of the day, shipped him off to Hollywood in 1936 for a screen test.

"When he first moved to California," says Walter Burr, "Tom rented a bachelor pad near the beach with about six other guys. Right away he got a job delivering bread at night for a local bakery, but he only did that for a few months before MGM signed him."

At 24, Tom was added to the studio's talent roster in 1938, with his first movie being *Out West with the Hardys*, an episode of the popular series of films starring Mickey Rooney. Tom had a small part as Aldrich Brown.

A rare candid of fledgling actor Tom Neal. Courtesy of Saul Goodman.

That same year, Tom auditioned for a part in Samuel Goldwyn's drama, *The Hurricane* and with great confidence, believed he had won the lead role of the Polynesian sailor Terangi. However, a physically similar Jon Hall was given the role instead, playing opposite Dorothy Lamour in what would be a smash box office hit that boasted some spectacular (pre-computer-generated) special effects. Tom was extremely angry over the loss, telling one reporter, "It was the perfect part for me. Losing it is a bitter pill to swallow."

Despite this reverse, Tom forged on, turning in a number of solid supporting performances in such films as *Another Thin Man* (a segment of the classic series starring William Powell and Myrna Loy), *Sky Murder* and *Andy Hardy Meets Debutante*.

The crime film *They All Came Out,* lensed in 1939 by the masterful horror and film noir director Jacques Tourneur, cast Tom in a lead role as a

Paul Cavanagh and Tom Neal in a scene from the 1939 MGM crime film, **Within the Law.** *From the Author's Collection*

tough gang member rehabilitated by both his stay in federal prison and the love of a gun moll (Rita Johnson). As a result of his fine work in this film, Tom was handed the male lead in another crime drama, *Within the Law*, co-starring Ruth Hussey. The fourth adaptation of a 1923 Bayard Veiller Broadway hit, the film, unlike its predecessor, was uninspired and only moderately successful, causing the actor to complain to studio head Louis B. Mayer about his dissatisfaction with the way MGM was handling his career.

Tom Neal as he appeared in the popular movie cliffhanger, **Jungle Girl.**
From the Author's Collection

"During this time, Tom was carrying on with both Joan Crawford and a studio executive's wife," claims Walter Burr, "and when Crawford learned he was two-timing her, she did her own complaining to Mayer, who wound up blasting Tom."

Angered by both the lackluster film roles being handed to him, as well as Mayer's lecturing him on behalf of a jilted Joan Crawford, Neal reportedly ranted at the tyrannical executive in front of several studio employees—a stupid move that would cost him dearly. An irate Mayer immediately retaliated by banishing Tom from the lot and releasing him from his contract after just one year.

With his massive self-confidence seemingly unscathed by the loss, Tom was determined to make it in Hollywood and over the next few years he went on to freelance at nearly every other film studio in town—from 20th Century-Fox and RKO to PRC and Republic (where he was the hero opposite Frances Gifford in the studio's memorable 1941 serial, *Jungle Girl*). One of his best performances was as a tough, John Garfield-type character in RKO's production of *The Courageous Dr. Christian*, an excellent installment of the popular series starring Danish actor Jean Hersholt.

Tom worked consistently throughout the '40s with small roles in A-movies (*The Flying Tigers, China Girl* and *Pride of the Yankees*), and starring parts in low-budget programmers (*One Thrilling Night, Klondike Kate*). At all times, however, he was merely swimming upstream, along with countless other mediocre actors whose faces and careers were all too often, completely interchangeable. Despite this obvious liability, Tom did manage to nail a few breaks.

Behind the Rising Sun, an RKO picture filmed in 1943, is, according to the Jay Robert Nash/Stanley Ralph Ross-edited *Motion Picture Guide*, "A slam-bang, flag-waving, anti-Japanese movie that was released at the nadir of World War II and served to rally moviegoers behind the War Bond effort." Tom starred as the son of an Asian publisher who is forced by his father to join the Japanese army, only to witness, firsthand, the various atrocities of war. The politically controversial Edward Dmytryk directed the film dubbed "the sleeper hit" of the year, and Tom received a great deal of national recognition for his role as Taro. Also starring in this highly exploitative action picture were Mexican actress Margo, J. Carrol Naish and Robert Ryan.

Despite the attention the film brought him, however, and some good reviews, Tom was soon back emoting in forgettable clinkers with titles

 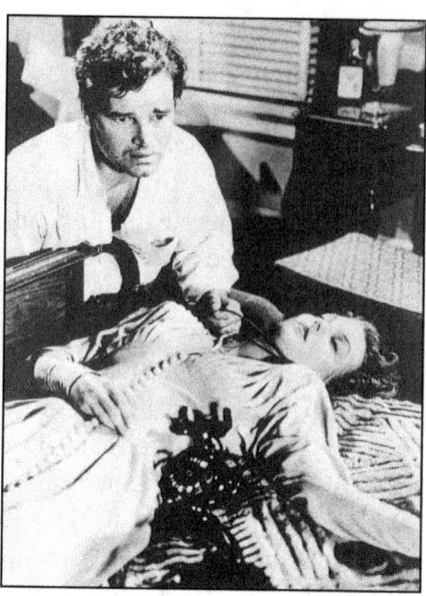

LEFT: Ann Savage and Tom Neal in the 1945 Columbia B-film, Klondike Kate. *Courtesy of Kirk Crivello / RIGHT: Tom Neal and Ann Savage in a scene from the film noir classic,* Detour. *From the Author's Collection*

like *She Has What It Takes*, *The Unwritten Code* and *Thoroughbreds*.

He had his second turn at portraying a Japanese soldier in the commercially popular, but critically panned, *First Yank into Tokyo* (RKO, 1945). As an American Air Force officer whose face is surgically altered to look Oriental so that he can help an atomic scientist escape from behind enemy lines, Tom received mostly mixed reviews for his performance. While the *Motion Picture Guide* wrote that "Neal does a fine job with an impossible role," the film has been widely lambasted through the years for its cartoonish, over-the-top plotline, and for Tom's somewhat broad interpretation of an Asian.

Tom followed *First Yank into Tokyo* with a film John Cocchi's *Second Feature* book calls "the very best film ever made by ('Poverty-Row' studio) PRC," the Edgar G. Ulmer-directed *Detour* (1945). The moody and atmospheric film, shot in just six days with a budget of $30,000, has been the object of much debate through the years: considered by some cinema historians to be a film noir classic; to others, little more than a claustrophobic and overrated bomb. As Wade Williams explains in a *Filmfax* magazine article from July 1988, "Media critics have labeled it as everything from cynical, to surreal, to perverse, to absurdist, to paranoid and nihilistic." [12]

Based on a 1938 Martin Goldsmith novel, *Detour* is recognized as a salient prototype in the film noir genre, beginning with Neal's lead character—a down-and-out antihero of the first order. As a hard-luck musician named Al Roberts, who, while traveling cross-country, becomes involved in an accidental murder, the actor expertly conveys the ordeal of an ill-fated loser who blindly follows a pre-destined path to an ominous outcome. In addition to the trouble-plagued Roberts character, the film features the most strident and venomous femme fatale in screen history, Vera (played in mordant style by B-movie actress Ann Savage). Told in flashback, and with its numbed voice-over setting a precedent in its use of the narrative device (which was widely used in subsequent film noir vehicles), *Detour* is an exercise in fatalism at its most bleak. Widely touted as such, its fan base is legion, and has placed Ulmer, its celebrated director, in a select and rarefied league of B-Film icons.

Detour arguably contains the definitive Tom Neal performance, and remains his best remembered film. The fact that his exemplary work in the picture would be overshadowed by future off-screen events in his life makes a classic line from its screenplay even more relevant: "No matter

Barbara Hale and Tom Neal in a scene from First Yank Into Tokyo.
From the Author's Collection

what you do, no matter where you turn, fate sticks out its foot to trip you."

Tom followed *Detour* with a celluloid mishap, *Club Havana* (PRC, 1945), which was a penny-pinching rip-off of the 1930s MGM classic, *Grand Hotel*. When it bombed at the box office, he continued his bumpy slide down the Hollywood career ladder in cheap, 60-minute trash like *The Hat Box Mystery* and *Train to Tombstone*. From the mid-1940s on, the man whom writer Oscar Rimoldi once described as, "always yearning to reach the top and yet not knowing how and when to start climbing," became a staple in these low-budget projects—and was actually quite prolific—appearing in 30 features between 1945 and 1953 alone, and amassing more than 70 film credits in all.

It is safe to say that Tom Neal had roughly the same amount of lasting success with the women in his life as he had in building a truly significant film career. In the years prior to his meeting Barbara, his name was linked to a bevy of Hollywood stars, starlets (and strippers), including Ava Gardner, Joan Crawford, Lana Turner, Lorraine Cugat (the wife of Cuban bandleader Xavier Cugat) and Dixie Dunbar. In the early 1940s he even flirted with American aristocracy for a time when he

Murray Alper, Paul Bryar, Tom Neal and Regis Toomey in the Monogram B-film, **Navy Bound.** *From the Author's Collection*

Tom Neal and his first wife, actress and nightclub singer Vicky Lane.
Courtesy of Walter Burr

was engaged to Gay Parkes, a member of the wealthy DuPont family of industrialists.

Married for five years to a little-known nightclub singer and film actress from Bel-Air, the stunning, Brooke Shields-lookalike Vicky Lane

(*Jungle Captive*), the couple bred and raised Dobermans together until she divorced him in 1949 following accusations of "mental cruelty and insane jealousy."

For several years, a hell-raising cohort of actors Errol Flynn and Mickey Rooney, and in every sense, a true man's man, Tom possessed a natural toughness that must have immediately aroused Barbara's already heightened sensibilities. (13)

A sexually charged Barbara had seemed to meet her male counterpart in the macho Tom Neal. With few restraints, and even less resistance, it's likely the couple was off-and-running just moments after they met that day at the Sunset Plaza swimming pool. Little did they know, however, of the disaster that loomed on the horizon—for both of them.

Industry rebels Tom Neal and Barbara Payton at a Hollywood restaurant in 1951. Courtesy of Jan Redfield

Within days of meeting Tom, Barbara was introducing him to her family and friends as her boyfriend, almost as if Franchot never existed. Her confidante Tina Ballard remembers visiting Barbara that July and suspecting that Tom had already moved in with her. "I noticed that his clothes and personal belongings were strewn all over the house and Barbara was just gaga over him. He had kind of a rough exterior but Tom was really a nice guy. And I could tell by the way he looked at Barbara that he was just crazy about her.

"I asked Barbara, 'What about Franchot?,' but she just waved her hand and said she would deal with it later."

Tom's nephew, Walter Burr (who would meet Barbara the following year), says he is fairly certain that Tom moved in with her pretty quickly. "With Barbara working at Warner Bros. and Tom freelancing at Lippert and Monogram, I'm sure she was doing a lot better financially than he was. I could definitely see my uncle shacking up with her right away, especially if she asked him. When given the chance, Tom played the

Tom and Barbara announce their engagement at a Hollywood nightclub, although she is still engaged to marry Franchot Tone. Courtesy of Jan Redfield

part of the 'resident stud' very well. He had no problem at all letting a lady foot most of the bills, especially since he was usually stone broke between films."

In the weeks following their meeting, Tom and Barbara were seen playing tennis at The Beverly Hills Hotel and dining together at Ciro's, and Hollywood's eagle-eyed scribes, naturally, took notice. Finally, on July 31, Barbara broke off her engagement to Franchot, and proposed to Tom, telling reporters, "Four minutes after we met, we decided to get married. Four minutes!" Neal later told *Newsweek*, "Barbara asked *me* to marry *her*. She was engaged to Tone when I met her, but she told me that she wanted me because he was too dull. She said I was exciting."

In her typically straightforward manner, Barbara breathlessly admitted to friends, "I look at him and I feel hot peppers go up my thighs! He's a beautiful hunk of man." In no time, Barbara was bragging to her friends about Tom's consummate finesse at lovemaking, and of his estimable physical endowments, only qualifying her rapture years later in her memoir, with the comment, "They talked about our wild sex life. It was really no wilder than anyone else's. It's just that he had a circus strongman's physique, and I had a great shape, too."

Tom's son, Patrick Thomas Neal (a former actor who goes by the name of Tom Neal, Jr.), remembers his father telling him some years later that "Barbara was very aggressive in the bedroom and had the sex drive of a man. Dad said she got off on playing games with men and that she could never get enough attention. She apparently drove the men in her life wild and took great pride in her lovemaking skills. He said she was almost like a wildcat in heat, and that she was always ready, willing and able to have sex at any time, anywhere."

Barbara's hot-blooded appetites had apparently found their match in a man whose awestruck son describes as "a total sex machine and completely irresistible to women." The couple reportedly expressed their mutual attraction in somewhat unique and unorthodox ways, with Barbara later admitting in her autobiography that they both loved cats so much, they would often bedeck themselves in fake whiskers and tails "… and play games which would eventually end up in love-making."

Herman Cohen also noticed this fascination with felines, and told author Tom Weaver in his book, *Attack of the Monster Movie Makers*, that "[Barbara] was a bit strange. She thought she was a cat, and always wanted to play cat with me, [too]."

Tom and Barbara apparently slid effortlessly into their cat-playing, lovemaking groove and were soon inseparable. In Weaver's book, Cohen recounts his memories of Barbara, and of the two men she was seeing: "During the making of *Bride* was the big *menage a trois* [sic] with Franchot Tone and Barbara Payton and Tom Neal. Barbara and I became good friends, and—well, what can I say? Even in those days, Barbara Payton, who was a gorgeous gal, was one step away from working Sunset Boulevard. I remember the gate calling one day to say that Tom Neal was there. And Franchot Tone was in Barbara's dressing room! So I had to keep the two of them from meeting."

It has also been inferred in a few sources that during the filming of *Bride of the Gorilla*, Barbara had a physical interlude with her aging co-star Tom Conway. At least twice, the depressed and alcoholic brother of George Sanders was seen exiting Barbara's dressing room, it was said, "in a much lighter mood." [14]

Evidently, Barbara had come to believe her main value, both in Hollywood and as a human being, was as a dispenser of sexual favors. Veteran celebrity interviewer Skip E. Lowe claims that she became increasingly known in town for her seemingly unequaled prowess in this area—a dubious accolade at best, but apparently an asset when one is trying to make friends in a town infamous for its carnal excess.

In his final interview with Tom Weaver, Herman Cohen confessed that he had his own sexual episode with Barbara: "Oh, Barbara gave me a great blow job when she first arrived [to do the film]. I was a young kid, I was scared stiff! She put whiskers over her eyebrows and on her lips. Drew them on. Barbara was a little crazy, but she was a hell of a lot of fun."

Far more important than the nature or expression of her sexual proclivities was a disturbing truth Barbara's behavior revealed. In her desire to step out-of-the-pack in a town deluged by an endless stream of beautiful young women seeking fame, Barbara was discarding her self-respect on every level. Though she couldn't possibly know it at the time, this total lack of self-regard would be the genesis of her downfall.

Barbara's tangled love life with Franchot Tone and Tom Neal would cause an explosive reaction on September 14, 1951. From the Author's Collection

Chapter Thirteen:
Love's Jealous Rage

When Franchot Tone returned from his business trip to New York in late August, Barbara abruptly changed her mind about Tom, and publicly stated that she would marry Franchot after all. Tom was already living with Barbara at her new apartment at 1803 Courtney Terrace (for which Franchot was paying the rent), and was undoubtedly puzzled by his paramour's fickle behavior. Driven by too much booze and her healthy libido, the ever-changing Barbara again renounced Franchot and took off for a Las Vegas weekend with Tom, with the couple stating that they would marry on Sept. 14, 1951, in San Francisco.

They returned to Los Angeles on September 10 and spent the next three days together, but on the morning of Sept. 13, Barbara borrowed Tom's car for a clandestine meeting with Franchot at the Beverly Hills Hotel. Tom waited all afternoon in Barbara's apartment for her to return from what she told him was "…an important business appointment." At 5:30, Barbara phoned her maid, Mamie, and asked that her mink coat and an overnight bag she always kept packed with some cosmetics and clothes be sent to the hotel. That evening, Barbara and Franchot freshened up (presumably, after a day of lovemaking) and hit several Sunset Strip nightclubs, both apparently forgetting that she was scheduled to marry another man in the morning. At Ciro's, they met their friends Kent and June Modglin for drinks, and took in stripper Lili St. Cyr's provocative bathtub performance, in which the ecdysiast writhed au natural in a see-through tub of bubbles.

While his bride-to-be and her lover cuddled and cooed in public, Tom Neal sat alone, in Barbara's apartment, and got smashed. By nightfall, he found that his patience with the whole absurd situation had evaporated. He called in some friends, including an ex-roommate of his named Jimmy

Barbara borrowed Tom's car on September 13 for a secret meeting with Franchot at the Beverly Hills Hotel. Courtesy of AP/Wide World Photos

Cross, Barbara's old boyfriend, paving contractor Jerry Bialac, and two unidentified women, and threw himself a raucous pity party.

At approximately 1:30 a.m., Franchot and Barbara drifted in on a cloud of martini fumes and laughter and were met by a houseful of people, including Tom, who was by now, furious. The trio, each of whom was feeling no pain, nonetheless attempted to discuss the dilemma at hand.

As her two suitors began clamoring for top spot in her heart, Barbara positioned herself directly between the men, which likely only worsened the situation. One can imagine the heady sense of power she felt as the dialogue between Franchot and Tom grew increasingly more combative. Their heated discussion quickly snowballed into a screaming match of bitter invectives, with Barbara cruelly kissing Franchot and urging him to "get rid of Tom." Franchot, with his ego pumped-up to the max by Barbara's clinging presence (and with an equally strong desire to impress her with his control of the situation), foolishly challenged the younger actor with an outright dare: "Let's settle this thing outside."

Barbara later commented in her memoir, "When he said that to Tom, it was like throwing a pebble at an elephant."

The threesome had moved to the front patio of Barbara's apartment when an adrenaline-powered Tom delivered a punch that—literally—sent his opponent airborne, knocking him a distance of twelve feet before

The front patio at Barbara's home was the scene of a brutal fist fight between Tom and Franchot. Courtesy of AP/Wide World Photos

slamming him into the ground. According to later news reports, Tom then pounced on Franchot, battering him in a brutal and bone-crunching assault.

Rail-thin and bird-like at 155 pounds, Franchot was twenty-five pounds lighter than his attacker, and crumpled like a blood-splattered rag doll as Tom inflicted one ham-fisted blow on him after another. At some point, Barbara threw herself into the fray and was given a black eye by Tom, whose wayward elbow clipped her face, sending her reeling unconscious into a rhododendron bush. (15)

A next-door neighbor of Barbara's named Judson O'Donnell claimed to have witnessed the fight from his bedroom window, drawn there, he said, "by the sounds of a woman shrieking hysterically." He would later say that Tom pummeled Franchot over thirty times, adding, "It was like watching a butcher slaughtering a steer. At first, I thought my refrigerator was on the fritz. It sounded like a prizefighter in a gym beating the bag. It was one of the bloodiest fights I've ever seen, and I've seen plenty—on that very lawn."

The altercation ended after ten minutes when Jimmy Cross interceded and managed to restrain Tom by tackling him to the ground. As the other party guests dispersed into the night, Cross telephoned for an ambulance and Franchot was rushed to California Lutheran Hospital.

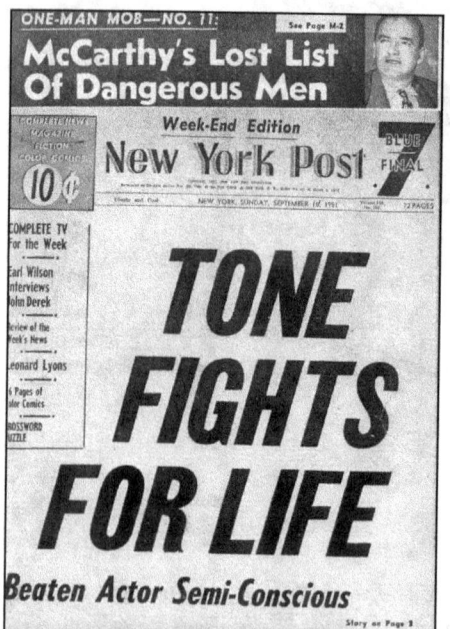

ABOVE: The Mirror *newspaper's headline of the brawl. From the Author's Collection*

LEFT: New York Post *cover from September 16, 1951. From the Author's Collection*

Later that morning the shocking news came over the newswire that Franchot was in grave condition with a cerebral concussion, a broken nose, a shattered left cheekbone and a fractured right upper jaw. He would remain unconscious and near-death for the next eighteen hours.

The incident, quickly dubbed "The Love Brawl" by reporters, made front-page headlines around the world. In bold letters, one newspaper's banner screamed, *"Tom Neal Knocks Out Tone in Love Fist Fight!,"* while another offered, *"Tone, Payton, Neal in Bloody, Pre-Dawn Love Duel!"* (Incredibly, in many of the country's newspapers, such history-making news as America's involvement in the political conflicts occurring in Korea was reported *beneath* the story of the brawl.) [16]

In 1951, Barbara's friend Steve Hayes was continuing to supplement his income from his freelance film career by moonlighting as a car jockey at Mocambo, The Players and Ciro's (the latter being the last nightclub that Barbara and Franchot had visited prior to the fight). As word of what happened quickly swept across Sunset Boulevard, a concerned Steve rushed over to Barbara's apartment to see if she needed his help.

"By the time I heard about it and got over there, though, everything was finished," he says, "although several of Barbara's neighbors were still outside their homes, gossiping about it. I got the feeling from what I was hearing that a lot of people there thought Babs was to blame for what had occurred."

They were not alone. According to Bob Easton, Barbara's co-star in *Drums in the Deep South*, "Following the fight, everyone in the industry was talking about it, and were offering their own opinions of what they think had happened. I believe the overall consensus was that Barbara's erratic behavior with Franchot and Tom had caused the whole thing. Knowing Barbara as I did, I wasn't entirely convinced of that myself but I'm sorry to say that most of the people I spoke to about it, did indeed, blame her."

Naturally, Hollywood's top gossip columnists, led by the infamously wicked and ultra-moralistic Louella Parsons and Hedda Hopper, had a field day dissecting the sordid tale in print. Hopper, especially, seemed to amuse herself as much as her readers with scathing entries like the following, which was picked up by the wire services and appeared in many of the country's top newspapers: "This little trixie is rolling in glamour and love like a big beautiful bee in a pot of amorous honey, getting boudoir and business all mixed up in an unbalanced hash. For months, Tone and Neal have been panting pop-eyed after pouty Payton's wriggling charms."

A Hollywood police detective investigates a broken window at the scene of the Tone/Neal brawl. Courtesy of L.A. Public Library/Herald Examiner Collection

Despite her outwardly tough demeanor, Barbara was always hypersensitive to any kind of criticism (due, no doubt, to her father's continual lambasting of her over the years), and she was deeply hurt by the poison now being hurled at her in Hollywood. It is said that Hopper, in particular, was brutal in her private comments about Barbara, and only slightly less harsh in her written attacks against her.

"Barbara once told me that Hedda Hopper was a cruel bitch," says Tina Ballard. "I remember Barb called her a 'self-righteous sow' (which I thought was so funny), and she said that Hopper loved crucifying people. Hedda really hated Barbara, and believe me, the feeling was mutual."

A detective inspects Tom Neal's barbells on the patio of Barbara's home at 1803 Courtney Terrace in West Hollywood. Courtesy of USC Library/Dept. of Special Collections/L.A. Examiner Collection

But Hopper wasn't Barbara's only enemy. Underneath the stark headline *Barbara's Nude Sun Bath with Neal Told in Beating Case*, Judson O'Donnell gave an eyebrow-raising interview to Louella Parsons where he expounded on his neighbor's somewhat unconventional personal habits. "I used to see Miss Payton in the patio [sic]. She was sunbathing in her—ahem—birthday suit. That is, she was nude, completely nude, above the waist. I don't exactly know about the rest of her. And Tom Neal would be beside her. He was exercising with his big bar bells. He was nude, too—above the waist, that is. But he wore trunks. I heard her say to him once, 'Oh, Tom, you have such big muscles!' I used to see him washing his socks and underwear there, too."

O'Donnell's eagerly delivered discourse was followed by similar offerings from other insiders who were familiar with the duo's affair. One after another, people were clamoring out of the woodwork with their own tales of lust about the stars-in-question. Nearly every story and anecdote painted Barbara in the worst light imaginable.

Immediately after news of the fight went out over the wire, hordes of newsmen and photographers converged at the hospital and stationed themselves in the hallway outside Franchot's room. The late Will Fowler, a veteran reporter for the *L.A. Herald Examiner*, recalled that upon their arrival, he and his fellow newsmen were officially told that they were on a "death watch."

Although he declined a request in 2003 to be interviewed for this project, due to serious health problems that would later claim his life, Fowler, in his 1991 book, *Reporters: Memoirs of A Young Newspaperman*, wrote: "The worry now was that a blood clot caused by the concussion might become lodged in Tone's brain and cause instant death, or at least, a stroke." He related that Hollywood homicide detective Sgt. Arnold Hubka, who had been assigned to the case, told him, "If Tone dies, we have enough on Neal all ready to drag him in on a murder charge."

Wearing sunglasses to hide her black eye, and clad provocatively in a skin-tight, white sun dress, Barbara tried to avoid the press by sneaking up an outside fire escape to the second floor of the hospital, only to blow her ruse when finding the door locked to Franchot's room. An order handed down by Franchot's attending physician, Dr. Lee Siegel, that the actor was not to have visitors (including Barbara) had apparently fallen on deaf ears. In a fit of anger and frustration, Barbara responded to being locked out by shouting and pounding on the door, sending hospital personnel running from all directions. For several minutes, Barbara turned the hospital floor

Tom Neal at police headquarters immediately following his beating of Franchot Tone. Courtesy of L.A. Public Library/Herald Examiner Collection

upside down with her tearful pleas, until the head nurse finally allowed her into his room.

It was a suitably mournful Barbara who kept vigil that night as Franchot underwent extensive plastic surgery for his injuries. Afterward, when reporters inquired about his prognosis, Dr. Siegel responded cryptically, "In a general way it's reasonably certain he'll look like Franchot Tone, but as for closeups, who knows?"

In her own well-intentioned, perhaps, (if slightly skewed) interpretation of Florence Nightingale, Barbara ministered to her beau the next day by sneaking in martinis in a thermos bottle. A heavily bandaged Franchot, with his entire head and face wrapped like a mummy, watched from his hospital bed as Barbara stood nearby, shaking-up a fresh batch of martinis for him. As the saying goes: Only in Hollywood.

Los Angeles Herald-Examiner staff writer James Bacon reported that he visited Franchot the morning after his plastic surgery. "He was wrapped in enough bandages to fill a Johnson and Johnson warehouse," said Bacon. "I was told that his face underneath looked like a piece of beefsteak that had been run over by a truck."

Wearing sunglasses to hide her black eye, Barbara is photographed en route to Franchot's hospital room. Courtesy of USC Library/Dept. of Special Collections/ L.A. Examiner Collection

A nurse glowers at Barbara and her ex-boyfriend Jerry Bialac as they leave Franchot's hospital room. Courtesy of USC Library/Dept. of Special Collections/ L.A. Examiner Collection

In the days following Franchot's surgery, a subterfuge-loving Barbara was often seen creeping around the hospital and slipping into his room at all hours of the day and night, sometimes accompanied by her old boyfriend, wealthy playboy Jerry Bialac. News photographers seemed to take great delight in snapping pictures of a startled and sexily clad Barbara as she shimmied her way along the fire escapes and alleyways beneath the hospital. On one occasion, she brought her sister-in-law Jan with her, who remembers: "I only went to the hospital with her once, and that was the day she lunged at a photographer and smashed his camera on the floor for taking pictures of us. Barbara always tried to shield her family from being hurt by her bad publicity, and she would gladly take a person 'out' if she had to."

Finally unable to avoid the press any longer, Barbara issued an oddly disjointed statement on September 15 that was nothing short of amazing in its incongruity: "We (Franchot and I) are going to be married. I love him deeply. Neal is simply a beast—a vicious man who I, at first, thought was a nice guy. Franchot doesn't want a honeymoon until his face is well. And, well, I leave everything up to him. We had some spats before, and that's why Franchot and I broke up—but that was before I began dating Tom."

That same day, Tom Neal, sporting little more than bruised knuckles and a battered ego, issued the first of many public statements that revealed a man of almost painful simplicity. "I'm sorry to hear the guy's in the hospital. I hope he's not hurt bad," he told the *L.A. Times*. "I feel awful [about what happened]. I liked him even if we were in love with the same girl. I'll do anything I can to help, even give him a blood transfusion if he needs it."

Though possibly genuine in its intent, Tom's noble gesture died in its delivery. He went on to deny that he had hit Franchot over thirty times. "It was only three or four times," he insisted. "Hell, if I had hit him thirty times, he wouldn't have any face or head left!"

One of Tom's more understated (and ludicrous) quotes to the press during this time alluded to his and Barbara's wedding plans, now canceled. "I'm not paying for her Wassermann if she's going to continue to see Tone," he declared with an almost laughable sincerity. With very little effort, Tom's artless offerings became fodder for a ravenous press intent on crucifying him.

A few days after the attack, Barbara held court in the hospital parking lot, giving an interview to the *L.A. Examiner* while sitting in her new Ford convertible: "I didn't have a date with Tom that night (Thursday), but he was at my place when Franchot and I arrived. And he was in an ugly mood. He struck the first blow and it knocked Doc [Franchot] out cold. Then he pounced on him and just beat and beat."

In her extremely facile explanation, Barbara had left out two very pertinent details: the first being that she and Tom had been living together for weeks, and the second, that she had been out with another man on the eve of her wedding.

When questioned about her current feelings for Tom, Barbara replied, "Oh, I couldn't possibly even begin to talk about him. I just want to have nothing to do with him." In keeping with her ambiguous and evasive nature, Barbara did an about-face and cut the interview short when she announced she had an appointment to keep with studio executives to discuss a new motion picture. "But I'll be back at 9:30 in the morning," Barbara promised the newsmen.

With one eye blackened, and the other eye—as always—looking to keep her name out front, Barbara drove off, confident that she was defusing the prevailing belief that she alone had brought on the entire mess.

Barbara's ex-boyfriend Jerry Bialac was among those questioned about the brawl between Tom and Franchot. Courtesy of USC Library/Dept. of Special Collections/ L.A. Examiner Collection

Incredibly, on September 20, just five days after the fight—while Franchot lay recuperating in his hospital bed—Barbara and Tom were photographed slow-dancing at Ciro's, and were later seen the same night at a party at actor Jackie Coogan's home. This, despite Barbara's statement in the newspapers that "I am marrying Franchot Tone as soon as he's well. I haven't seen Tom Neal and I don't want to see him."

The *L.A. Daily News*, however, reported things differently. On September 21, it wrote: "Barbara Payton was seen by a *Daily News* reporter entering her home at 1803 Courtney Terrace with a man also definitely identified as Tom Neal. That was Wednesday night. Barbara and

Neal went into the kitchen to prepare a late night snack (after 12:30 in the morning). Later, with their meal completed, the couple went upstairs. It was nearly 2:00 a.m. when Barbara and Neal finally emerged from the front door and went to her convertible, laughing and giggling together. She slid under the driver's wheel and Neal climbed in beside her. She stepped on the starter (and off they went). Hours dragged on and by 4:30 a.m., they had not returned."

Uncensored magazine also reported on the renewed coupling of Barbara and Tom, stating: "Each morning before she sets out for the hospital, the beauty and the beast have breakfast in bed together. A fine romance, with home cookin'!"

Obviously, both Tom and Barbara were again satisfying their free-flowing appetites—this time, though, with a particularly reckless abandon. With a ravenous public hanging on every salacious word, the newspapers continued to recount details of the duo's affair for weeks afterward.

In an era notorious for its belief that social propriety was, at all times, paramount, the unsavory antics of Barbara Payton, Franchot Tone and Tom Neal tainted not only its three unlucky participants but also the entire movie industry as a whole. In rapid fashion, each member of the trio was summarily chastised in print, with Tom and Barbara, in particular, receiving almost unanimous vilification from the press. *Barbara Payton: The Cause of It All*, said one newspaper's headline, and it was an assertion shared by many. Tom was blasted in print as "The Pride of Muscle Beach," and "a none-too-bright, ne'er do well," while Barbara was similarly dismissed as "that tricky little vixen" and "a conniving, two-timing bombshell."

One of Barbara's so-called "close friends," in an anonymous interview with gossip columnist Sheilah Graham, showed little loyalty for the actress: "Nothing's wrong with Barbara, except that she's got a loose-leaf book for a heart. That girl needs to have her head examined." Bitchy Hollywood journalist Florabel Muir chimed in with her own observations, writing that she was puzzled, "...at how Franchot Tone, who has a very well-trained mind, could play around in a league of daffy dillies and muscle developers."

But perhaps the nastiest stab of all came from *Los Angeles Mirror* columnist Edith Gwynn, who wrote in her *Hollywood* column of September 18: "The cheap and disgusting didoes of the Payton-Neal-Tone 'triangle' is one more case where 95% of decent Hollywoodites suffer smears for the few who are continually degrading the town. And have you noticed that for years it's usually been 'the same few'? Since all contracts contain morals clauses, how come they're almost never invoked? B. Payton has figgered [sic] in shady, tawdry 'testimony' long before the current debacle, but if any studio disciplining was done, we've yet to hear of it! Why do they foster male or female types that obviously will sooner or later discredit Hollywood, when so many talented, clean, hard-working newcomers are starving for a chance?"

The people who knew Barbara best are quick to come to her defense today when asked about the possible reasons for her actions during this time. Was she truly playing Tom and Franchot against each other, for the thrill and ensuant ego boost, or had Barbara simply gotten in way over her head with both men and didn't know how to get herself out of the mess that she had created? Was it that she loved both men and didn't want to let either of them down, or did she love neither of them and was simply using them for different reasons? Barbara's son, John Lee, has his own theories, borne from not only knowing her, but also from the many years he's devoted to analyzing the (best and worst) events of his mother's life:

"I can't begin to guess what went on the day of the brawl, or why. But I must admit I've thought a lot about this part of Mom's life. To tell you the truth, I don't think my mother understood the concept of love, really, especially when it came to a man and a woman. I don't think she knew how to recognize it or to accept it, to appreciate it, or to give it. I personally believe it's the result of whatever terrible thing happened to her when she was a child. It seems reasonable to assume that when it came to men my mother would have wanted to be in control, because she had not been able to control the situation—or situations—that led her to being abused (as I believe she was), and could not have the love and acceptance of her father. I think she confused love with sex and power. I think it was a confusion so profound that it wholly altered her perception of reality, so profound that she must have, on occasion, found herself desperately clueless. Perhaps this was just such an occasion.

"As for the brawl itself, the questions, obviously, are many. Was it all about a jealous younger man with a short fuse and an overblown ego attacking a man symbolic of all that Hollywood seemed to believe Tom Neal never would be? Was it about an older man trying to impress a young and beautiful woman, and grossly underestimating the jealous rage and recklessness of a younger man? Was it about two men being manipulated by a calculating woman who wanted the sexual excitement of a classic bad guy but at the same time craved the approval and love of an older man who may have reminded her of her father? Was it about a woman trying to get rid of a boyfriend with nothing to offer but sex, and replacing him with a famous, wealthy older man who could make all of her Hollywood dreams come true? Was Tom Neal just a vicious bully? Was Franchot Tone arrogant and demeaning toward Tom? Was my mother just a conniving actress willing to do whatever might help her have everything she wanted, from sex to stardom? Or was she just unable to choose between two good but very different men?

"Or was it, perhaps, a little of all the above? When one lacks first-hand experience, and has only the memories of a small child, speculation is risky business. But here is what I know: She knew how to love her son. That's one thing about my mother I'm certain of. Perhaps the *only* thing I'm certain of."

Jan Redfield believes that Barbara loved both men; if not equally, then as fully as she could. "In her mind, I know that Barbara honestly thought she had done nothing wrong. She had given both Tom and Franchot everything she had—her heart, and yes, her body, too—so I could see her wondering what the heck had happened. You have to understand, that was how Barbara's mind worked. She didn't seem to have the foresight to know that if she kept carrying on that way, everything was eventually going to blow up in her face. She knew she was going to have to get around to letting one of them go, but she thought she still had some time to decide which one it would be. I've never known anyone else like Barbara."

Barbara's friend Tina Ballard offers, "I think she wished she could combine Franchot's qualities of wealth, intelligence and class with Tom's down-and-dirty, raw sexuality, and make a whole other person out of them. Barbara loved and admired both men, but for completely different reasons. The physical pull to Tom, though, was way stronger. Definitely."

Jan says, "It was like Barbara thought she was acting out a script on film, and she was standing on separate stages. Even back then, I'm not so sure Barbara had the tightest grip on reality. I mean, her behavior was so outrageous at times. She loved Franchot because he always took good care of her. And I know she felt the need for a father in her life since Lee was always so unavailable to her. With Franchot, that need for a father figure was fulfilled.

"On the other side of the coin, Tom Neal was the Wild Weed that she seemed to crave, and she just couldn't stay away from him. It's true, by the way, that she was hung on him. We're talking goo-goo eyes and dry lips, the whole bit. By the time Tom met Barbara, his career was definitely on the skids, and as much as I liked him, I felt that he did very little to help keep her career on track. He was wild and wooly, and so was she. What a combination.

"I've always felt that Tom came along at the wrong time in her life. Looking back now, it was like some colossally bad twist of fate that she even met him. Up until then, Barbara was doing so well in Hollywood, and I believe she could have gone on just fine if she hadn't met Tom."

District Attorney Ernest Roll, Franchot and an unidentified man during the investigation of the Tone/Neal brawl. Courtesy of USC Library/Dept. of Special Collections/L.A. Examiner Collection

Barbara swears to tell the whole truth to District Attorney Roll during her meeting with him on September 23, 1951. Courtesy of USC Library/Dept. of Special Collections/L.A. Examiner Collection

Finally, Tina Ballard surmises: "Sometimes a person is so damaged and so screwed-up, they can't help but screw-up other people's lives. They don't mean to, but down deep they're so hellbent on destroying themselves, they wind up bringing all the people around them down, too. I swear that was Barbara. She didn't intend to make a mess out of things, but she sure did, didn't she?"

Despite all the bad press she was getting following the brawl, and knowing full well that she was being perceived as a disloyal and shallow individual, Barbara seemed unconcerned with what was—and was not—deemed appropriate behavior for females in the McCarthy era of mass conformity. Unencumbered by internal restraints, and with what appeared to be a total lack of fear, Barbara continued doing exactly as she pleased. The incisive scrutiny being given to her personal life, a life now under almost constant surveillance by the press, was resulting in a fairly scathing expose of an indiscreet woman indulging in a socially forbidden, highly sexual lifestyle. That was pretty hot stuff for the staid societal climate of the 1950s—not to mention, extremely destructive to a fledgling career that was rapidly losing its promise.

If Franchot Tone's facial profile had been seriously damaged in the fight, Tom Neal's public profile fared much worse. According to writer David Houston, in a July 1988 *Filmfax* article, "While Neal stated that he regretted the incident, he had the misfortune to be quoted as also saying that the incident, which remained on the front pages for days, had probably helped his career." ("After all, I didn't do anything wrong like being named a Communist. I just fought for the woman I loved," Neal told the *L.A. Daily News*. "Regardless of the notoriety of this thing, it does get your name in front of the people.")

"He was wrong," observed David Houston. "His career stopped in its fast-paced tracks. Producers had lost confidence in the box-office appeal of 'a brute.'"

Just days after the fight, an all-too-earnest (and presumably straight-faced) Tom Neal told *Time* magazine, "I'm truly sorry. I hated to hit Tone, but Barbara kept egging us on. She really digs that blood and guts stuff."

Chapter Fourteen:
Damage Control, Hollywood Style

Whatever career momentum Barbara had previously generated, suddenly plummeted on September 19 when it was announced that she was being dropped from the title role in the 20th Century-Fox film *Lady in the Iron Mask* (1952) and would be replaced by British actress Patricia Medina. The medium-budgeted costume drama, which co-starred actor Louis Hayward, would have given Barbara's film career a much-needed shot in the arm as it was considered a fairly prestigious production at the time. But while the press reported that Barbara was "too emotionally upset to begin work at [producer] Walter Wanger's studio," the truth was that she had been fired. Wanger, who would soon be embroiled in his own *cause celebre* by shooting and nearly killing his wife Joan Bennett's lover, agent Jennings Lang, in an L.A. parking lot, evidently knew bad news when he saw it and privately admitted that he wanted no part of the troubled actress.

While Tom and Barbara continued to see each other on the sly, Franchot Tone was trying to decide on whether to file a felony assault action against his attacker, or a misdemeanor action on assault and battery charges. The beating he had endured had adversely affected his speech as well as his countenance, and Franchot feared that both were going to have a negative impact on his career.

"Although he physically recovered," Barbara later wrote, "Franchot, bless his heart, never talked the same way again." After being released from the hospital, he and Barbara, with whom he had reunited—again—were called before District Attorney S. Ernest Roll to give their own versions of what happened at her home on September 14.

On the morning of September 23, the couple marched downtown to Roll's office, both of them conspicuous in sunglasses designed to hide their battle wounds. A hint of Barbara's bawdy nature surfaced when one of the ever-present newsmen trailing after her commented on the large size of her glasses. "Yeah, the biggest I could find, honey," she quipped in a slick voice, playing the tough-as-nails broad with expert rigor. Once seated before D.A. Roll, Barbara offered an initial confession, of sorts, to him regarding her recent meetings with Tom. She admitted to keeping a date with him in Malibu, "…but just to discuss the publicity. Honestly, that was all."

Barbara went on to give Roll a fairly voluble account of what happened on the night Franchot's face was rearranged:

> "I'd been to dinner and to Ciro's with Franchot, and when we got home, Neal was there with another couple of characters and two strange women. I said to Neal: 'Out.' But he wouldn't go, and so Franchot invited him out to talk it over quiet like. Well, while they were out there, I thought I felt like I'd like to go swimming, so I went upstairs to change clothes. Then I thought they were out there a long time, and I came down and looked out of a window and they were arguing and I thought I ought to do something about it. I wasn't exactly dressed for going outside, so I went back upstairs to put on some clothes and I came down dressed and I went outside. I embraced Franchot and I invited him in. Then I turned away, and I heard something. And I turned around again, just in time to see Franchot flying right through the air…."

Barbara's statements to the D.A. had her playing the part of the wide-eyed innocent (and selfless mediator), but it seemed more than a bit contrived. In fact, knowing the events that led up to the fight, her account now reads more like a sugarcoated fantasy she had filtered through a smoke screen of monumental self-denial. She concluded her statement to Roll with the somewhat vapid comment, "Franchot's head was bouncing up and down on the pavement. I tried to separate them, and something hit me, and bop, I went out cold."

It is interesting to note that in her first set of interviews after the altercation, Barbara had unequivocally named Tom as the aggressor. Now, however, after spending some quality time with him, Barbara was making statements that were rife with omissions. It was clear she was now measuring her observations very carefully in order to protect Tom Neal—the man she truly loved—from a charge of felonious assault. Behind a wall of vague and guarded words, Barbara was straddling the proverbial fence and showing herself to be a woman whose sense of loyalty seemed as variable as the weather.

When talking to the D.A., Franchot Tone's memories of the brawl were understandably foggy. "Neal's first blow rendered me unconscious," he told Roll. "I regained consciousness two or three seconds subsequently, to find Mr. Neal sitting on top of me, beating me about the head and face. I raised my hand to protect my face, but lost consciousness again immediately." The D.A. noted in his report that Franchot appeared weak, with "…a puffed nose, a bloodshot left eyeball, and a ghostly pallor." Luckily for him, pancake makeup and his ever-present sunglasses kept the damage hidden from most photographers' cameras.

Upon completion of their depositions, Roll assured the pair he would be continuing his investigation of the matter, and then excused them. While Roll made plans to interview Tom and to examine the police and hospital reports, Barbara made plans to fly to her hometown of

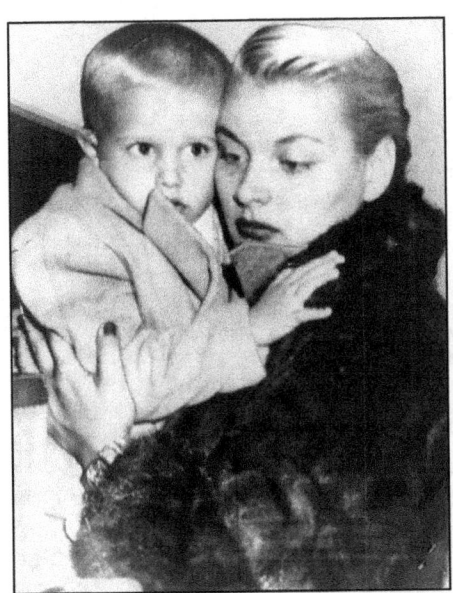 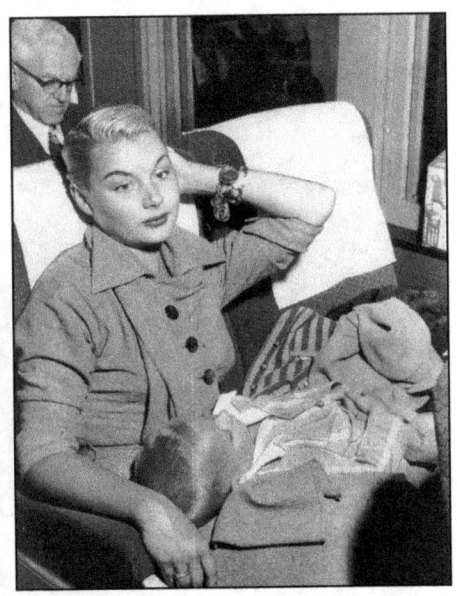

LEFT: *An intimate moment between a pensive Barbara and her four-year old son, John Lee, as they arrive at Duluth Municipal Airport on September 26, 1951. Courtesy of L.A. Public Library/Herald Examiner Collection / RIGHT: Barbara and a sleeping John Lee en route by train to her former home in Cloquet, MN. Courtesy of Star Tribune*

Cloquet. Two days later, she did just that, arriving at Duluth Municipal Airport on Wednesday, September 26 with her four-year-old son John Lee. At the terminal, Barbara was met by the usual coterie of newsmen and photographers, and by her aunts, Murel and Fay, who brought her to the family home in preparation for an impending celebration.

The following day, a sheepish Franchot appeared downtown before District Attorney Roll and delivered an unexpected bombshell to him, saying: "I have reconsidered this matter thoroughly and I feel the best interests of my family, my friends and my profession dictate my discontinuing any prosecution of my application for a complaint resulting from this regrettable occurrence." Roll, irate at the actor's turnabout, stared him down for several moments and then dismissed him with a curt response: "I'm through! This ends it!" Knowing that he had completely wasted Roll's time with what was essentially a farce, Franchot could do little but slink away with his credibility (and pride) barely intact.

Barbara's aunts, Fay (left), and Murel (right) accompany Barbara and John Lee to the airport to welcome Franchot in preparation of the Tone/Payton wedding. Courtesy of USC Library/Dept. of Special Collections/Associated Press

In retrospect, it seems strange that Franchot decided not to pursue a legal course of action against Tom, especially considering the extent of the injuries he had suffered, however his change of heart was certainly due to Barbara's influence. Evidently, Franchot would do anything—even exonerate the man who had rearranged his face—in order to appease his sweetheart's whims. This streak of masochism would surface time and again throughout their relationship, with Barbara later stating in her memoir, "I was his mania, his phobia; one half of his own split personality. He concentrated on me as if I were a script that he must learn overnight." Still, Barbara did little, if anything, to deter her suitor's obsessive preoccupation with her. Instead, it seemed she rather enjoyed it.

Following his debacle with the D.A., a still-convalescing Franchot made a quick exile out of Los Angeles on September 27, first boarding a United Airlines plane to Denver, where he made a connecting flight to Minneapolis, and then another to Duluth, where his excited bride-to-be awaited him at the airport (with reporters and photographers, naturally, on hand). With her arms outstretched and a handkerchief in hand, Barbara ran toward him and cried, "Darling!," as Franchot made a frantic beeline to her side. The couple's wildly theatrical embraces in the center of the terminal ignited a phalanx of crowding, clamoring newsmen. The combination of an electrical storm of flashbulbs and a nearly swooning Barbara made the scene not so much a private reunion, as it did a garish, public spectacle of particularly dubious taste.

The following day, on the afternoon of September 28, Franchot and Barbara were married in a civil ceremony in the living room of her childhood home at 405 Chestnut Street in Cloquet. Barbara's first cousin, Air Force Captain Robert Redfield, served as Tone's best man, while another first cousin, Cloquet resident Marjorie Melby, acted as her sole bridesmaid. The local newspapers reported that Lee and Mabel Redfield were conspicuously absent from the slapped-together ceremony, which lasted all of five minutes. Due to Lee's absence, Barbara was given in marriage by her father's brother, Tim, one of the few relatives that actually showed up for the event.

News stories gave a typical, 1950s airbrushed account of the nuptials, reporting on it as if it were a celebrity fashion show at one of Rodeo Drive's toniest dress shops. Gushed one paper:

Barbara's cousins Bob Redfield (left) and Marjorie Melby (right) stood up for Franchot and Barbara at their wedding, officiated here by Probate Judge Ed J. Johnson. Courtesy of Star Tribune

"Barbara was radiant in a Paris dress, one she had bought in Hollywood but had never worn before. The navy blue, two-piece outfit of tissue wool was trimmed with a stand-up taffeta collar and taffeta bustle. Her shoes were plain high-heeled pumps matching her dress. Gardenias and white and purple orchids formed her corsage. The bridegroom, still handsome despite his recent beating from Tom Neal, was neatly attired in a dark grey suit with subdued red stripe, white shirt and navy blue silk tie. He wore a white rose on his lapel. The two Hollywood stars exchanged 'I Do' before a beautiful, rose-banked fireplace."

Longtime *Minneapolis Star Tribune* reporter Barbara Flanagan, now in her 80s, was one of a handful of local journalists allowed inside the Redfields home to view the ceremony. "Both my photographer and I were

Barbara snuggles up to her new husband outside the Redfield's former home at 405 Chestnut Street in Cloquet, MN. Courtesy of Billy Rose Theatre Collection/ N.Y. Public Library For The Performing Arts

very surprised to be invited inside to attend the wedding," Flanagan recalls, "but Barbara's family was very cordial. Very Minnesotan, as I remember, and they seemed thrilled about her choice for a husband. Tone's face was still scratched up some (from the fight), but he was charming as ever.

"Barbara was absolutely sober and she looked good. Her small son sat under the grand piano and very quietly watched the wedding. He looked a bit overwhelmed by it all but he was cute as a button. The service was very brief, and I must say, I loved every minute of it."

For publicity purposes, husband and wife were photographed telephoning Barbara's parents in Odessa to share the good news, but in reality this was a staged gesture that was strictly for show. The truth is that Lee and Mabel, though no strangers to outrageous behavior themselves, were aghast at their daughter's antics and wanted no part of what had become an embarrassing chain of events.

"Even after our parents moved to San Diego in 1952, Dad only visited Barbara a few times in Hollywood," remembers Frank Redfield. "He was pretty disgusted by what was going on in her life at the time, and he said he didn't want to see her." As for the youngest Redfield, he, too, was absent from the wedding, as he was serving in the U.S. Navy at the time and was stationed at the base in Long Beach.

"I saw no need to attend that particular function," Frank says tersely. "Even back then, it didn't seem to me like it was going to last. My sister was a flighty thing at times."

"Other than Fay, Murel and two or three others, none of Barbara's relatives were at the wedding," says Frank's former wife, Jan. "And it was in the newspapers before the rest of us even knew about it."

Most of the citizens of Barbara's hometown seemed to share the Redfields decidedly unfavorable opinion of the event. Despite news reports of "screaming squad cars and teenagers banging on pails and ringing fireballs," Cloquet's Mayor, Roy Ranum, told the papers, "The type of publicity Barbara Payton is getting, has not been what Cloquet, in general, appreciates." In the same article, Joe Medley, the secretary of the town's Chamber of Commerce, concurred. "[The people in town] know who she is, but they aren't impressed," he said, while Ed J. Johnson, the Probate Judge who performed the nuptials, admitted, "I have married 400 couples in the last 13 years, but I have never seen a shivaree like this before!"

Feigning the innocence of a blushing young bride making her first trip to the altar, Barbara breathlessly declared, "I'm so happy I could cry." Remaining dry-eyed nonetheless, she and Franchot (who remained patently oblivious, it seemed, to everything but his new wife) overlooked the pall that surrounded the proceedings, and happily posed for photographs on the front steps of her childhood home. The foolishness of their hasty wedding seemed lost to them, if not to everyone else. Upon hearing the news of their union, Tom Neal told *Newsweek*, "I feel pretty badly [about it]. I thought I still had a chance until now. I hope they'll be happy. [As for me] marriage is the furthest thing from my mind. Frankly, there are so many beautiful women, and so little time." In true Hollywood fashion, Tom went on to say that he would be wiring his congratulations to the couple, as well as "shopping for a wedding gift." It is not known if he did either.

Following their reception at The Flame Supper Club in nearby Duluth (and their overnight stay at the Hotel Duluth overlooking Lake Superior), Barbara and Franchot returned to her family homestead the following morning to telephone several Hollywood columnists with the news of their wedding. Later, as the furor settled, one senses that the level-headed citizens of Cloquet breathed a collective sigh of relief when the couple hustled out of town on September 30 as abruptly as they had invaded it, heading to the Tones' family lodge on Muskoka Lake in Canada for a brief honeymoon before returning to Hollywood.

While the exact location of where Franchot and Barbara lived following their wedding remains open to question today, it appears they went back and forth between his leased house at 502 N. Foothill Drive in Beverly Hills and her apartment on Courtney Terrace, as neither home was relinquished after they wed.

To add to the puzzle, Franchot was said to have leased yet another house during this period. "According to Franchot's FBI files," reveals Lisa Burks, his biographer, "he lived at 8743 Shoreham Drive in West Los Angeles in August 1951." Whether Barbara ever lived there with him, however, is unclear.

Lisa says that Franchot's sons, Pascal (a.k.a. Pat) and the late Thomas Jefferson (a.k.a. Jeff) did have vague recollections of the house on Foothill Drive, and of seeing Barbara there, but she adds that it was difficult for them to be sure, as they were both very young at the time and were officially living with their mother, Jean Wallace, and her new husband, Cornel Wilde, at their home on Hillcrest Drive.

While John Lee Payton has very few memories of Franchot Tone, he says he seems to remember spending some time with his mother at Franchot's house, though he doubts they ever lived there. Jan Redfield claims that Barbara continued to live at her Courtney apartment following the wedding. "I know she was living there because that's where I visited her. I was never at any of Franchot's homes and I don't remember Barbara living anywhere else until later on, when she got the big house in Beverly Hills. Franchot may have spent time with Barbara at the Courtney apartment, but I really can't say. Honestly, I don't remember. But I do know that Barbara lived on Courtney Terrace from 1951 to about 1953."

Regardless of their somewhat baffling living arrangements, Barbara and Franchot were back from their honeymoon for just a few days when she was once again subpoenaed to appear before the Federal Grand Jury in its ongoing investigation of the Abe Davidian murder.

On October 5, the front page of the *L.A. Herald* announced, *Barbara Payton Called in Dope Slaying Quiz*, giving the besieged starlet another sensational headline she could have easily done without. Barbara's earlier testimony in October 1950 was unsatisfactory to Assistant U.S. Attorney Norman W. Newkom and his constituents, and the federal authorities were now intent on pinning her down under oath to a specific, unalterable story on the whereabouts of Stanley Adams on the date Abe Davidian was slain. A court date on the matter was scheduled for October 31.

Despite her impending appearance in court, in mid-October a seemingly unworried Barbara and Franchot ducked out of town for a whirlwind promotional tour of various southern cities (including New Orleans, Atlanta, Memphis, Greensboro, Birmingham and Miami) on behalf of her film *Drums in the Deep South*. Although their personal appearances were booked solid for the next two weeks, the tour received a mixed reaction from the public.

In Atlanta, the beleaguered couple donned their most glamorous duds and officiated at a "Miss Southern Belle" beauty contest (handing the winner, Betty Bracewell of Memphis, Tennessee, "...a seven-year contract, and a ticket to spend Christmas in London, and New Year's Day in Paris!"). Although it was reported that they were greeted warmly in Atlanta, things seemed to go steadily downhill after that. In Birmingham, for instance, the city's mayor firmly declined an invitation to attend a soiree given in honor of the newlyweds. Then, in Memphis, where there had been very little pre-advance publicity heralding her appearance, Barbara was booed by some at Loew's State Theater, appearing on stage before a small, disinterested crowd. In Miami, it was more of the same. *Variety* reported, "The personal appearances of Barbara Payton was taken in stride here [sic]. Reaction was on the tongue-in-cheek side. Payton and Tone were greeted at the airport in Miami by two locals dressed in Yankee and Confederate uniforms. This, a satirical take off on the Tom Neal-Franchot Tone battle for beautiful Barbara."

The excessive amount of bad publicity that the pair had generated over the previous weeks was looming heavily over what was intended to be (as stated in the promotional material), "a goodwill tour representing Hollywood's finest."

Barbara and Franchot couldn't see that the supposedly carefree facade of their relationship wasn't fooling anyone. If anything, they weren't being taken seriously; people were laughing at them. As a couple, the Tones had become little more than a tacky, industry joke, and sadly, everyone seemed to know it but them.

"She was embarrassing herself left and right," says Jan Redfield, "and it was like she didn't even know it. Barbara was moving so fast through life and you just couldn't keep up with her. People everywhere were making terrible comments about her and it was very hurtful for those of us who loved Barbara. But she kept right on going, with not a care in the world."

Chapter Fifteen:
A Nightclub Spit-Spat

Shortly after the end of his publicity tour with Barbara, Franchot landed in a particularly humiliating spot of trouble back in Hollywood when he had a run-in at a Sunset Strip nightclub with catty syndicated gossip columnist Florabel Muir. A portly, middle-aged shrew with scarlet hair (and a serpent's tongue), Muir—whose writing style, like her more celebrated contemporaries Hedda Hopper and Louella Parsons, consisted of one part pious self-righteousness with two parts venom—had been especially critical of Franchot, Barbara and Tom in her newspaper column, announcing in one edition that she was "...sick and tired of their juvenile and rather perverse antics." On the evening of October 29, Franchot had taken Barbara and his mother, Gertrude, to dinner at his favorite haunt, Ciro's, when he saw Muir dining with her husband, writer Denny Morrison, and her assistant, Betty Voight.

Greatly emboldened by the warm wash of alcohol coursing through his system, Franchot left Barbara and his mother, and approached Muir's table to confront her. Incensed with her for her repeated attacks on his character, and, in particular, for the obvious disdain she had shown Barbara, Franchot grabbed Muir's hand and asked her, "Florabel, darling, is Morrison your doctor or your psychiatrist?" When assured by the stunned woman that she and Morrison were wed, Franchot asked, "Have you got your wedding certificate with you?" Muir responded that she didn't normally carry the document with her, but that she would send him a copy of it if he was that interested in seeing it. "I couldn't be more uninterested," Franchot answered.

Sensing his annoyance with her, Muir provoked him with a coy dig: "Why, Franchot, you talk as though you're mad at me." The actor admitted, "Yes, I am. So mad, in fact, that I could just spit in your face."

Without missing a beat, he added, "In fact, that's just what I'm going to do." Then, while holding Muir's hand, Franchot leaned across the table and made good on his promise, hitting the wicked old crone squarely in the eye in the process.

In her published rehash of the incident, the newswoman groused, "He then grabbed me by my three-strand pearl necklace and tried to choke me by making a tourniquet of the pearls, at the same time tromping on my right instep and kicking me viciously about the feet, ankles and shins. At first I thought he was just stumbling, then noticed he was deliberately kicking. So I lifted my foot and gave him my right heel."

Veteran *Herald-Examiner* reporter James Bacon was among the industry people at Ciro's that night and claimed to have witnessed the altercation. He said, "Tone walked over and bent down in a gesture which looked to me, at first, as if he were going to kiss Florabel. In a moment, all hell broke loose."

That's putting it mildly. As the nightclub's orchestra filled the room with soothing music to dine by, the incident quickly escalated with Muir flailing away at Franchot, while Denny Morrison, in an attempt to strike his wife's attacker, somehow missed his target and landed on his derriere.

Barbara (who was, for once, exempt from the fisticuffs) and the dignified Gertrude Tone, not to mention an entire roomful of studio big shots, surely looked on in awe at a confrontation that had all the earmarks of your average barroom brawl, the only difference being in its unlikely opponents: the erudite movie star and the corpulent matron, carrying on in a bizarre, slapstick scene that played like an outtake from a Marx Brothers film. A jarring blend of horrified gasps and wicked peals of laughter were said to have reverberated through the room, followed by far less dignified, "grunting noises" from a panting Florabel Muir.

The row was ended within minutes when Ciro's dinner captain, Don Avilier, interceded and grabbed Franchot around the waist. Foaming and pasty-mouthed from the booze, Franchot was led back to his table, where a sympathetic Barbara and his mother embraced him. Muir, with her public embarrassment surpassed only by her righteous indignation, took advantage of her position as Police Reporter for the L.A.P.D.'s West Hollywood Sheriff's Office, and immediately called the department to file a citizen's arrest against her assailant on charges of assault and battery. Upon the officers' arrival, Muir demanded they body search Franchot, adding, in a conspiratorial stage whisper: "Quick, before he hides the marijuana cigarettes under the table." James Bacon wrote that when Muir's assistant, Betty Voight, suggested that her boss charge Franchot with spitting in a public place, Muir bellowed, "Since when in hell has my face become a 'public place'?"

In her subsequent statement to the police, Muir explained the reason for her suspicions regarding Franchot's level of sobriety. "He came over to our table with a great show of cordiality," she began, "but then he began talking wildly and aimlessly. All the time he was holding on to my hand and glaring at me with a strange glazed look in his eyes. The pupils of his eyes were distended and they didn't seem to be focusing. He didn't appear to be under the influence of liquor, but he certainly wasn't acting like a man in possession of his normal senses. His conversation was rambling; his eyes, beady, bloodshot and baggy. At no time did he tell me what he was mad about."

Immediately following his nightclub altercation with Florabel Muir, Franchot discusses the matter with Barbara. From the Author's Collection

SPITTING FRANCHOT 'TONE-D' DOWN BY MIRRORGAL
Mirror Columnist Florabel Muir (right) signs assault and battery charge against Franchot Tone (left) after he kicked and spit at her in Ciro's.

Franchot's October 29, 1951 "spit fest" with Florabel Muir once again brought him a barrage of bad publicity. From the Author's Collection

Irate at Muir's assumption that he was under the influence of illegal narcotics, Franchot insisted that he be taken to Los Angeles Emergency Hospital and tested for drugs. After it was determined, through a full examination, that there were no drugs in his system, Franchot was booked and spent the night in the county jail.

The next morning's newspapers seemed to derive great joy in reporting the melee, crisply referred to in various articles as "a salivary tussle," "a spittle-tiff," "an unsanitary shower-bath," "an unexpected expectoration" and "a nightclub spit-spat." In fact, Muir made haste to dispense the news herself, in her column: "Battling Franchot Tone, who was kayoed a few weeks ago by actor Tom Neal, apparently is looking for softer adversaries since that experience. He took me on last night at Ciro's. Going about spitting in people's faces could be a dangerous pastime. He just might meet up with another Neal."

Later that day, looking haggard and weary after his night behind bars, Franchot was regaled by reporters chanting, "For He's a Jolly Good Fellow" as he entered Beverly Hills Justice Court with his lawyer, Stanley Gleis. Once inside the courtroom, Franchot pled not guilty to Muir's charges of assault and battery and was later freed on $500 bail by Judge Henry H. Draeger, who set a misdemeanor trial date for December 11.

The viperous Florabel Muir often utilized her *L.A. Mirror* newspaper column, *Florabel Muir Reporting*, to sanctimoniously dispense her anal-retentive homilies to her loyal readers, and was certainly not going to deny herself the opportunity to discuss this latest incident in print.

"She was the bitch queen of them all," remembers Barbara's future acquaintance, RKO contract player Bill Ramage. "Of the three 'hag' columnists of the day (Louella Parsons, Hedda Hopper and Muir), Florabel was easily the nastiest. Hedda, at least, had a sense of humor. With a little care—and some ass-kissing—she could be defanged. The very Catholic Louella Parsons, on the other hand, was a sot. Always drunk, often 'out of it', and incontinent, to boot. In fact, she was known to leave her tiny little puddles behind in restaurants and offices all over Hollywood. Florabel Muir wasn't as powerful as the other two bitches, but she walked the police beat and she knew how to get her boys to swat a pretty mean nightstick. Quite simply, she was a vulture."

In her October 31 column, Muir wrote: "I deeply regret becoming involved in the unsavory affairs of Tone and his bride, Barbara Payton. I have no stomach for mixing it in the gutter with anyone, but I believe I have a right to go about my newspaper business without being required to wear a waterproof veil over my face when encountering persons about whom I have written.

"When I first knew Tone in Hollywood, he was a handsome, upstanding fellow displaying at all times a brilliant mind and charming manners. What has happened to him in the last few months is as big a mystery to me as to all his friends and acquaintances. It all began when I refused to treat his love battle with Tom Neal seriously. To me, it was a silly exhibition that reflected no glory on either him or that girl he married. I was prepared to drop my complaint had he exhibited the slightest regret for his guttersnipe behavior. He admitted spitting at me, but he denied kicking me in the shins. If he is unaware of his rough-foot play, he shouldn't be at large. He might inflict other painful injuries on me or someone else without knowing what he is doing."

The biddy's noble and unctuous platitudes—though cringe-inducing now—were, at the time, followed as closely as those of her acid-tongued peers, and brought Franchot (and Barbara, too, through association) only further public disgrace.

The Florabel Muir fiasco finally ended on December 11 when Franchot was fined $400 and given a suspended jail sentence of 45 days after pleading guilty to the charge of battery. Municipal Court Judge Henry Draeger dismissed the assault count against the actor after Franchot mustered up all his decorum and insisted, "Your honor, I did not kick the complainant and I did not use any vile language. However, I do admit I may have lost my sense of proportion and my sense of good

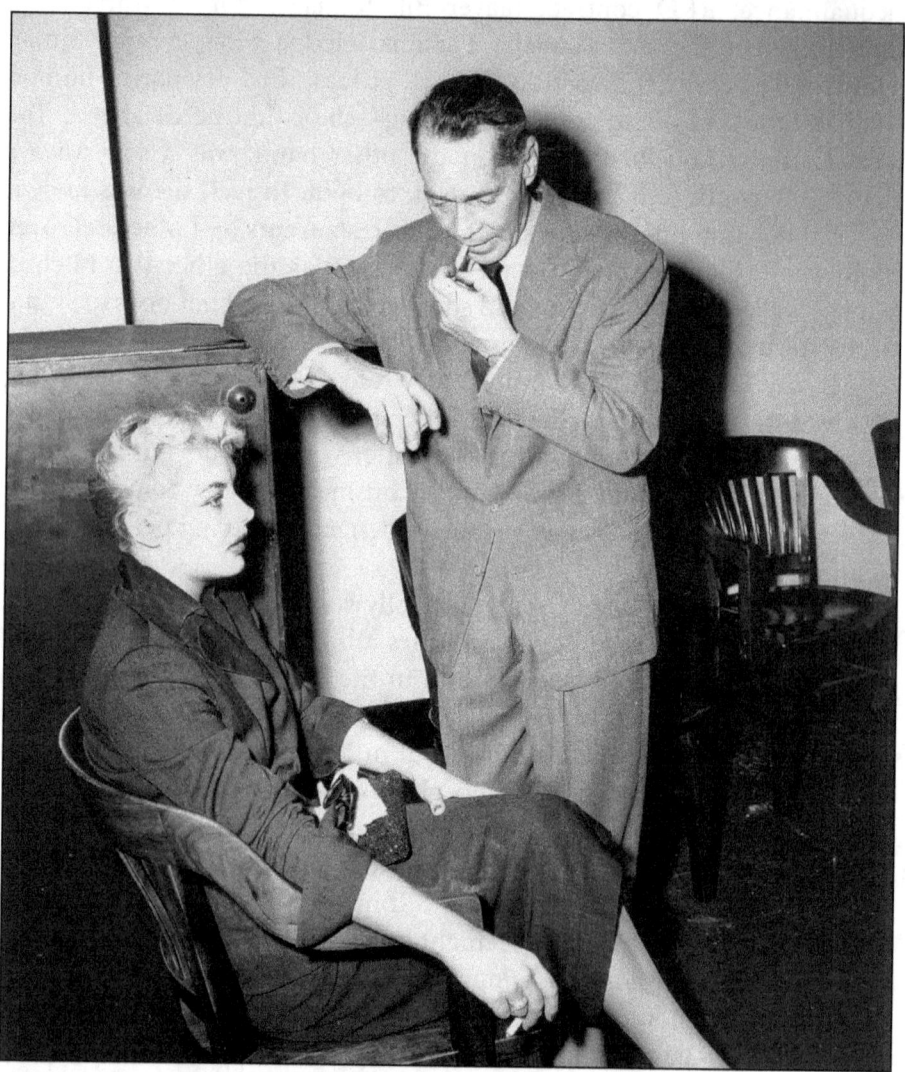

Franchot accompanies Barbara to her second appearance before the Federal Grand Jury in the Stanley Adams perjury trial. Courtesy of USC Library/Dept. of Special Collections/L.A. Examiner Collection

News article of Barbara's being excused from appearing before the Federal Grand Jury in the Stanley Adams perjury trial. From the Author's Collection

Tone's bride excused from appearing in dope inquiry

Blond Barbara Payton was excused yesterday from appearing before a special Federal Grand Jury investigation of the shotgun death of Abe Davidian, Fresno narcotic ring squealer.

Miss Payton, currently honeymooning with Franchot Tone in the east, had been expected to shed what light she could on a dinner party reputedly held in her apartment Feb. 28, 1950, the evening Davidian was gunned.

The party provided an alibi for convict Stanley Adams, Hollywood self-styled jewelry salesman indicted on a narcotics charge in a wholesale roundup of suspects believed to be members of the multimillion dollar dope ring of which Davidian reportedly was a member.

But another dinner guest was on hand to appear before the Grand Jury—Don Cougar, actor, now serving out a year's sentence in the county jail on a marijuana possession rap.

Cougar, one-time roommate of Adams, was with Barbara, Adams and actress Marie Allison when Adams got a phone call reporting Davidian's death, he testified earlier.

Heading up the renewed checkup in the Davidian case is Assistant U. S. Attorney Norman W. Newsom.

Six secret witnesses from the Fresno area also have been subpoenaed to appear and tell what they know of the slaying.

Davidian turned state's evidence after state police shot the tires off his sedan while he was allegedly transporting heroin to Fresno from the Los Angeles area.

—Daily News photo.
BARBARA PAYTON
No need to hurry home, Babs

After he was picked up and questioned by the FBI, 16 men were indicted on narcotic charges, including the Sica brothers, Fred and Joe.

Davidian's death left the government without a case and the charges were dropped.

Since then the FBI has been working steadily to rebuild its case against suspected dope ring members.

The best deals in town on household appliances may be found in the concise, up-to-the-hour Daily News classified ads.

conduct." As the *L.A. Daily News* reported, "The recipient of Tone's spittle and ultimate apology was not in court, but was duly represented by her attorney S.S. Hahn."

In the weeks that followed, Florabel Muir openly declared war on both Franchot and (especially) Barbara, whom she had long despised. Muir had the backing of both Hopper and Parsons, and the trio took every available opportunity thereafter to crucify Franchot and Barbara in print.

"Only Walter Winchell and the blonde columnist Sheilah Graham seemed to have any sympathy for Barbara," says Bill Ramage. "The rest of the Hollywood gossip scribes loathed her. Walter Winchell was a good friend of mine. He was a kind man and I know that he adored Barbara. As for Sheilah Graham, she lived openly with F. Scott Fitzgerald for years and loved sex herself, so she definitely understood Barbara."

When all was said and done, the entire incident with Florabel Muir proved a humiliation to all involved and was a conspicuous blight on Franchot Tone's already marred reputation. To make matters even worse, by the time the suit was resolved in December, his troubled wife had collected yet another round of negative headlines and was back in court again.

"With Barbara, it was always just one thing after the next," admits Jan Redfield. "Things had to be jumping all the time. There was never any rest for her, no peace and quiet. She was hooked on making these scenes. It was very exhausting."

The circus ride Barbara was on continued to spin at a breakneck pace, and though she didn't know it, her film career at Warner Bros. was spinning, too… right into oblivion.

Chapter Sixteen:
All the Wrong Moves

While Franchot and Florabel Muir were busy jousting in court, Barbara had her own courtroom issues to contend with when she was ordered to give a command performance before the Federal Grand Jury on October 31 in its ongoing investigation of the Stanley Adams matter. It was duly noted in all the newspapers that Barbara's demeanor in court was much more composed than it had been one year earlier. This time, her alibi passed muster with the hard-nosed Norman W. Newkom and the other government attorneys, and she was dismissed after 45 minutes. Stanley Adams remained in McNeal Island Prison under his perjury sentence, and the investigations of the Davidian murder ground to a halt.

The publicity, however, proved once again that Barbara just couldn't stay out of trouble. Rarely a week went by now where Barbara's name wasn't mentioned in the press in some negative way, either directly, as in this matter, or peripherally, as in the Tone/Muir disturbance—yet amazingly, she remained unconcerned with the damage being done to her career. It had gotten to the point where it seemed that nearly every move Barbara made was an almost calculated misstep, played out in an embarrassing irreverence for all to see.

Although Franchot and Barbara had barely begun their married life, the troubles continued landing before them, one after another, as if dropped like bombs from the sky. Hot on the heels of her latest court appearance came a widely-circulated news item in which her ex-boyfriend Don Cougar announced that he had often, in the past, paid the rent on Barbara's apartment, as well as given her money, "…when she was in pretty bad shape, financially."

Taken to Superior Court while in custody, Cougar gave the testimony as part of his explanation on why he hadn't paid off a judgment returned against him in the Anna Johnson assault case. The small-time hood, then serving a brief sentence in L.A. county jail for possession of marijuana, admitted to having no assets, but offered the information about Barbara's monetary gifts to evidently illustrate his altruistic bent.

The implied message in Cougar's account—that Barbara had been (using the vernacular of the day) a "kept woman"—was resoundingly obvious to everyone, including Franchot, and only served as yet another reminder of his enigmatic wife's lack of integrity. (One can almost envision Florabel Muir's delight over *this* piece of business.) With any sense of normalcy being kept at bay by the unending turmoil in Barbara's life, Franchot may have already begun to feel that his marriage was hanging by a very tenuous thread.

Barbara's career, meantime, took a major hit on November 19 when it was announced in the trade papers that William Cagney would not be exercising his option on her acting services. Jack L. Warner, who never had much of an interest in developing Barbara's career at the studio, immediately followed suit and dropped her from the Warner Bros. roster. In the end, Barbara's original, seven-year contract with Cagney Productions and WB Studios had lasted a scant 22 months.

The ruthless Jack Warner, known for years in Hollywood to be deadly when crossed, was equally known for often commissioning his executive assistant (and head of the studio's Casting Department) Steve Trilling to place phone calls to the other studio heads about not hiring certain stars. The practice had proved effective in the past as several other WB actors had been punished in this manner. Former leading lady Joan Leslie was one. So was 1940s "Oomph Girl" Ann Sheridan. In 1946, Leslie had balked at taking billing below the title of *Two Guys from Milwaukee*, a film she did with actors Dennis Morgan and Jack Carson, when Warner wanted to make the men a comedy team in the "Two Guys From..." series. As a result, Leslie was not only dropped from the studio after her next film, *Cinderella Jones*, but Trilling's efforts on behalf of his boss succeeded in weakening her subsequent film career. In the '50s, she wound up in several "B" Westerns at Republic Pictures before retiring at 31. Ann Sheridan, a huge star for WB in the 1940s, had also tangled with her employer, only to see a similar telephone campaign throw her own film career off-course.

Barbara, far less of an industry heavyweight than either Joan Leslie or Ann Sheridan, made Warner's smear tactics much easier to execute.

Her prominence in the Stanley Adams murder trial, the Tone/Neal fracas, her involvement in the Florabel Muir "spitfest," her almost daily presence in the news, and, especially, the widespread notion that she was, in the words of one of the tabloids of the day, "Glitterville's Top Tramp," were all perfectly legitimate reasons why WB would no longer support her career objectives (confused as they were). With all the notoriety Barbara had engendered, the feeling in the studio's front office was that she was simply too hot to handle, and far too dangerous and unimportant for them to protect.

Jack Warner allegedly loathed Barbara from her earliest days on the lot, and was said to have viewed her as little more than a loose broad with no morals and a big mouth. In the nearly two years that she had been under contract to WB, Barbara's motion picture career hadn't really amounted to much: Three films (two of which had featured her in small parts), a pair of loan-outs, a suspension for turning down work, and a ton of bad publicity. An unforgiving Warner felt that she was an embarrassment and more trouble than she was worth; a dime-a-dozen chippie who watched everything she touched turn to dust. She had been a major headache to him and he was glad to be rid of her.

Barbara is besieged by reporters following her firing from WB Studios in November, 1951. Courtesy of Harry Ransom Humanities Research Center/ Journal-American Collection

"I felt bad for Barbara," Virginia Mayo told Laura Wagner in recent years. "You always heard whispers about her around the studio. She wasn't untalented, it's just that her private life did her in."

With WB's firing of her, Barbara became a free agent, but was likely far more concerned about it now than she was when Universal cut her loose in 1949. The overall climate in town had changed toward her, and no amount of avoidance or denial on her part could hide that fact.

In an example of Hollywood's growing vendetta against Barbara for the humiliation she had brought to the well-liked (and long respected) Franchot Tone, as well as to the film community in general, Dore Schary,

Following their reconciliation, Barbara and Franchot are seen leaving Romanoff's Restaurant in Hollywood. Courtesy of USC Library/Dept. of Special Collections/ L.A. Examiner Collection

Barbara and Tom Neal looking both surprised and irritated at being photographed in this November 1951 candid. Courtesy of Jan Redfield

Metro-Goldwyn-Mayer's Chief of Production, and Darryl F. Zanuck, Vice President of 20th Century-Fox, both of whom had once publicly expressed an interest in buying Barbara's contract from WB, quickly changed their minds.

The day after Barbara's firing from WB, and after only seven weeks of marriage, the Tone/Payton union collapsed after a drunken quarrel that culminated at three a.m. when Barbara walked out on Franchot. Barbara's release from her film contract, and her relentless pondering on whether she ought to consider making a film with Tom Neal, instigated a raging argument of finger-pointing and recrimination in a relationship already buckling under a ton of excess baggage. After 53 days of marriage, Franchot filed suit for divorce on the grounds of extreme mental cruelty.

Exactly two days later, however, he and Barbara reconciled, with Franchot telling the press that he had dismissed his divorce action, and that he wanted "nothing in life without her." That evening, the couple dined at Romanoff's and partied at Ciro's in a mind-boggling display that left all but the most jaded Hollywood observers aghast.

In the frenetic footwork of their co-dependent dance, Barbara and Franchot neglected to see the sheer idiocy of their behavior and, in the days that followed, proceeded to reaffirm their undying love for each other in what seemed like daily public pronouncements. It had reached the point now where the press could almost predict to the minute when their next act of lunacy would occur. Once again, Barbara, clearly the star performer of this very sad comedy, did not disappoint them.

As she prepared to leave on another promotional tour for *Drums in the Deep South*, word had begun filtering through the grapevine that Barbara and Tom were indeed seeing each other again. Through clenched teeth and white knuckles, Franchot saw his wife off on her publicity junket, perhaps knowing with his keen intellect, if not his captive heart, that she had resumed sleeping with the man who had nearly killed him.

Chapter Seventeen:
Boozin' and Brawlin'

By early December it was obvious that Barbara and Tom had indeed drifted back into each other's arms, with *Exposed* magazine sleazily insisting that "although she had fought her desires, she had been unable to resist his bulges." Barbara herself would later concede, "I admit it, I was hung on him. He rocked my haunches every time I looked at him. When we made love, buds sprouted flowers and cupid got a medal. Those were toe-tingling days and nights." The macho Tom offered a more tired, eye-rolling response to her return by declaring, "Oh well, women come and go like trolley cars."

Realizing that Tom had joined Barbara on her publicity tour, and with his pride and his ego shattered, a humiliated Franchot prepared to reinstate his divorce action against her. Meantime, Tom and Barbara, with a kind of blind bravado, thumbed their noses at the fourth estate by allowing joint-interviews in which they brazenly flaunted their unconventional, openly-cohabiting relationship. In these same interviews, Barbara frequently proved a sullen, rude, and reportedly, confrontational subject—obviously a radical demeanor for a sweet-faced starlet in 1950s' Hollywood.

Jan Redfield admits that Barbara definitely had a surly side to her character. "She always acted like she didn't care what people thought about what she did, or how she acted. I know for a fact that she did care, but her tough attitude always implied the opposite. I don't deny she had a mouth on her. Barbara was always very outspoken, and some of the interviews she gave during that time made me wince when I read them. She came across so rude.

"When she was drinking a lot—which she was, during this time—her language could get pretty coarse. You have to understand, Barbara

A candid of Barbara talking to reporters outside her West Hollywood home in late 1951. Courtesy of USC Library/Dept. of Special Collections/L.A. Examiner Collection

was always striving to be an individual, not just a carbon copy of what women were supposed to be back then. She was very progressive in her thinking. Most people in those days weren't ready for that, especially from a woman."

As they made their way across the country on her publicity tour, Barbara and Tom's frequent public grandstanding and irreverent behavior garnered them reams of bad press. Veteran industry observer Skip E.

Barbara enjoyed shocking people and was often outspoken and irreverent in her interviews. Courtesy of Harry Ransom Humanities Research Center/Journal-American Collection

Lowe recalls their many embarrassing spectacles at popular nightspots like Ciro's and Mocambo. "Barbara and Tom were rowdy and a hell of a lot of fun, but they sure carried on a lot. Even back then, Barbara was a raging alcoholic, and when she was drunk, she would egg Tom on something terrible. She would start hanging all over some guy at the bar and before you knew it, Tom would end up having to drag her out of the place.

Barbara appears inebriated in this rare candid from late 1951. Courtesy of USC Library/Dept. of Special Collections/L.A. Examiner Collection

"Barbara herself once told me they were into rough sex, and that she liked to be beat up by Tom; she actually enjoyed it. It's almost like they were hooked on each other."

According to author John Gilmore, who knew the couple, "They were sort of bound together in a real seamy, rough-and-tumble addiction to one another; a relationship that one with any sensitivity would perish quickly in."

Following her publicity tour for *Drums in the Deep South*, Barbara and Tom returned to California and were met with a hostility that was fiercely palpable. Hollywood gossip columnists, then still the premier arbiters and watchdogs of good taste, were shocked at the shameless relationship of Tom Neal and Barbara Payton and were disgusted with their crude public behavior.

During this time, A.C. Lyles remembers Barbara telling him, "I know I'm getting bad publicity, A.C., but I couldn't care less. I'm having so much fun!" Mercifully, she and Tom were in town for just a few days when it was decided that it would be best for Barbara to cool off on another press tour. Despite dire warnings from both her friends and business associates that

Barbara looking wholesome during her rip-roaring tour of Chicago and NYC with Tom Neal. Courtesy of Harry Ransom Humanities Research Center/Journal-American Collection

her continuing alliance with Tom was placing her acting career in serious jeopardy, Barbara once again threw caution to the winds and took him along for company.

The duo hit Chicago first, in December 1951, where Barbara made several personal appearances on the seedy, strip-show circuit, this time to promote the equally seedy *Bride of the Gorilla*. Standing in the wings at Minsky's Burlesque House while a flabby stripper trolled the stage in front of a backdrop of tacky, satin bunting, a mercurial Barbara ignored Tom's presence and cruelly sang the praises of Franchot Tone. "I can't say enough about him," she gushed to a handful of newsmen. "Franchot really can't be compared to anyone else. He's simply the finest man I've ever known." It was reported that during Barbara's announcement, a puzzled Tom stood on the sidelines and "glowered" at her.

To help publicize her horror film, Barbara positioned herself outside the theater that night, in the bitter cold of a Chicago winter, and posed for pictures with a man dressed in a gorilla suit. The Associated Press sent out one of these campy shots to the wire services and it wound up running in many of the nation's most prestigious newspapers. Clad in a mink coat and with a comical look on her face, Barbara seemed totally oblivious to the possibility that her career could be heading in the wrong direction. To

Barbara poses with a man in a gorilla suit outside a Chicago burlesque house in December 1951. Courtesy of Jan Redfield.

everyone else, however, it seemed pretty clear that her days skirting the big time were through.

In less than two years, Barbara had gone from co-starring with the likes of James Cagney, Gregory Peck and Gary Cooper at Warner Bros., to appearing in a second-rate strip club with a phony ape man and an over-the-hill showgirl doing a tired bump and grind. Barbara's ditsy smile and clueless behavior clearly suggest that she lacked the foresight to know that she had climbed aboard a career track that was fast heading south.

As the Christmas holiday approached, Barbara and Tom left Chicago and continued her promotional tour for *Bride of the Gorilla* in New York City. During their stay at Manhattan's Carlyle Hotel, they attended several Upper West Side cocktail parties, where they were photographed schmoozing with the likes of gossip columnists Earl Wilson and Cholly Knickerbocker. With Barbara's low threshold for boredom, however, the good times couldn't possibly last. Her barely controlled need for excitement finally reached the breaking point one night when she allegedly ditched Tom—and promptly landed in a hotel brawl with six drunken cowboys who were in town for a rodeo.

"I met them in the crowd," she later wrote. "I became one of the group and we went to the automat. [Then] we all rode the subway down to their hotel in Greenwich Village." Once there, they continued partying as Barbara kicked off her shoes and, in her words, "...led some dances with the boys rooting for me."

Immersed in all this male attention, Barbara began playing her usual head games with the men and soon had them fist-fighting each other to see who would win her for the night. The end result was a demolished hotel room, a few arrests, and a triumphant Barbara, who had once again left a chaotic mess in her wake. She later wrote that the cowboys got their revenge for the trouble she had caused them by forming a protest line outside a local theater that was showing *Bride of the Gorilla*. They allegedly picketed the film with oversized placards that read, "Don't see Barbara Payton in this picture," which, of course, got her even more negative press.

"That whole mess Barbara got into with those cowboys really boggled my mind," admits Jan Redfield. "When I heard about it, I remember thinking, 'Barbara, what are you doing'? But knowing her, she probably just laughed it off."

As this off-the-wall incident shows, Barbara's apparent addiction to notoriety and her need to whip men into a frenzy over her had reached chronic proportions and showed no signs of abating. Like Jayne Mansfield in the 1960s, and tabloid darlings Anna Nicole Smith and Lindsay Lohan in later years, Barbara seemed to be on a frantic search for attention, be it good, or bad. But the payoff—though momentarily satisfying—was still never enough for her. Each mini-victory not only fed Barbara's rampant narcissism, it stoked her growing defiance, as well.

In June 2003, noted television pop psychologist Dr. Joyce Brothers explained the narcissistic personality thus:

> Narcissism and lack of self-esteem are frequently linked, surprising as this might seem. The constant need for praise and applause is usually an indication that in early childhood there was a distinct shortage of attention given to the child, and perhaps even of the affection that every child needs to build self-esteem.
>
> Because this self-esteem is so fragile, if this person does succeed and gain attention, she might feel unworthy and undeserving. She might then begin to sabotage her own success, destroying it because of her feeling that she's a fraud and worthless. The seeds of the defeat were probably planted long ago in her early childhood.

Barbara, of course, could be a case study for the type of person Dr. Brothers describes here. The early abandonment that Barbara had felt from her father had played a profound role in making her the outrageous and reckless hell raiser she had become. In many ways, she was still the little girl whose father was emotionally unavailable to her—the little girl who was also robbed of her innocence during that same period of time—and Barbara seemed to be on the prowl not so much for sex, but for some kind of personal validation. However, as Dr. Brothers suggests is so often the case, Barbara was going about it all wrong, and merely setting the stage for a lot of future heartache.

Following her donnybrook in Greenwich Village, Barbara's atrocious behavior continued when she was seen engaging in "shoving matches" with Tom at New York City's "21" and Billy Reed's Little Club. With fists and shot glasses flying, Barbara and Tom barrel-assed through Manhattan on a sea of liquor, and returned to Hollywood in late December with no new acting

LEFT: *By late 1951, Barbara was seen as a kind of pariah by much of the public. Courtesy of USC Library/Dept. of Special Collections/L.A. Examiner Collection /* RIGHT: *Barbara looking sad and exhausted after being questioned by reporters in Hollywood. Courtesy of USC Library/Dept. of Special Collections/ L.A. Examiner Collection*

jobs forthcoming. Soon afterward, Barbara dumped Tom for the umpteenth time, this time citing his "mean and uncontrollable temper" as the reason.

Barbara was then served with a summons and divorce complaint from Franchot on December 28, only to reconcile with him a few days later after he promised to dismiss the action. Their highly publicized reunion bewildered Franchot's supporters, who thought, perhaps, that he had finally gone over the edge in pursuit of his addiction. To everyone's shock, the couple resumed living together in January 1952. *This* reconciliation, however, would be their last.

On March 11, the front page headline of the *L.A. Herald Express* read, "*Babs, Tone in Violent N.Y. Battle*," proving that the bad times for Barbara were far from being over. The accompanying story revealed that she and Franchot had been staying in a suite on the 21st floor of Manhattan's plush Warwick New York Hotel, when a guilt-ridden and emotionally exhausted Barbara attempted suicide with an overdose of sleeping pills. This display of high-drama had followed a tremendous row in which Franchot had caught Barbara on the telephone with Tom, at which point he rushed over to her dressing table, picked up her jewelry box and then tossed it from the open window of their room. The article stated that Barbara reacted furiously to this by swinging the telephone at Franchot's head, nearly hitting him in the process.

A rare, never before published candid of Barbara outside NYC's Warwick Hotel shortly before her March 10, 1952 suicide attempt. Courtesy of Julie Sanges

After barricading herself in the bedroom, Barbara swallowed a handful of Seconal and flung herself across the bed. Upon forcing his way into the room and finding Barbara sprawled across the bed in a semiconscious state, Franchot forced her to drink several cups of black coffee while awaiting medical help.

It was later reported that Barbara's bungled attempt at suicide was resolved in an extremely messy fashion with an emetic administered by the hotel doctor. [17] Feeling unable to endure any more of this carnival-like atmosphere, Tone bailed out of the relationship on March 15.

Franchot Tone's biographer, Lisa Burks, believes it was at this point that the actor knew he had had enough. "I think Franchot ran into a unique problem with Barbara when he tried to change her into his definition of what a lady should be, particularly as his fiancée and wife, because she was ultimately un-moldable. Barbara's emotional issues were far too deep, and he either didn't see, or wouldn't accept, until it was much too late, that he was not qualified to help her.

"Franchot was extremely altruistic and I think he tried to give the relationship every chance, but he could not endure the humiliation of Tom's constant presence in Barbara's life. Her continued infidelity with Tom

An angry looking Franchot glares at Barbara following her suicide attempt in NYC in 1952. Courtesy of USC Library/Dept. of Special Collections/ L.A. Examiner Collection

Neal aside, I think Franchot finally gave up on Barbara when she, in a way, began to give up on herself. He liked to help people he cared about, but he wouldn't carry them if they weren't willing to do their share. And I think that he did so with much regret because Franchot was no quitter."

Immediately following Barbara's overdose, Franchot moved out of the Warwick Hotel, staying in New York, while she flew back to Los Angeles.

What Barbara learned next sent her through the roof. In a duplicitous move that rivaled the best of her own maneuvers, Franchot had tricked Barbara into thinking that he had dismissed his divorce action against her in January, when in fact, it was still on file. Barbara claimed that "in full faith and trust," she had neglected to file an answer to his suit, and, as a result, she had forfeited her right to contest it. Barbara was irate that she had been one-upped and manipulated into thinking their relationship was back on course, when all the while Franchot very cleverly had his irons warming in the fire. As her attorney, Milton Golden, explained, "He had tricked her into living with him again; to have her and not have her at

News headlines announcing Franchot's plans to divorce Barbara. From the Author's Collection

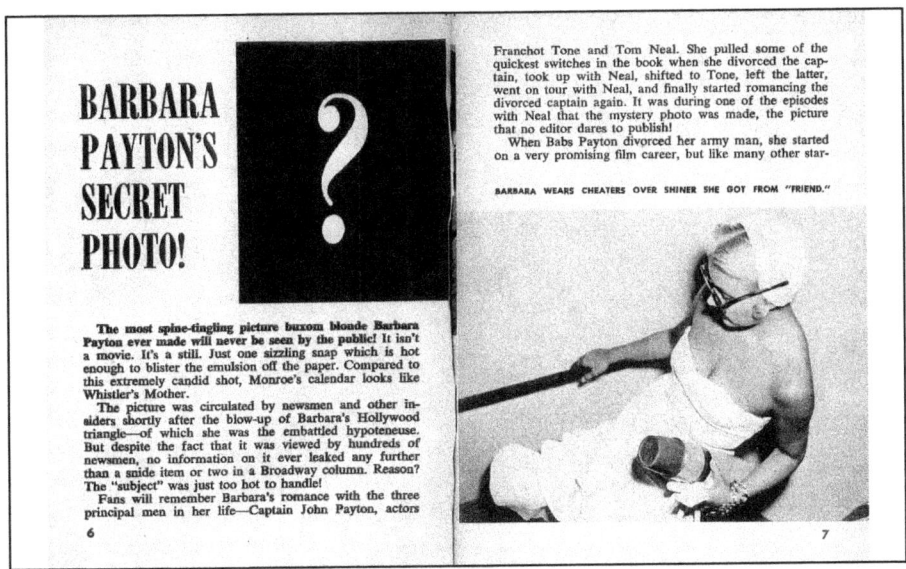

Tabloid article on Barbara's infamous "Secret Photo" with Tom Neal. From the Author's Collection

the same time, to suit his mood and convenience. The underlying motive seemed to be clear: a free ride, emotionally and financially." On March 21, Golden instituted an action to set aside the default and filed a cross-complaint on Barbara's behalf.

One week later, the deeply tanned, but nonetheless, exhausted-looking actress appeared in Superior Court, where she received permission to contest Franchot's suit. Incensed and depicting herself as a victim of "fraud and surprise," Barbara accused her estranged husband of remaining in New York in order to "starve her out" and defraud her of her property rights. "That's just like Tone," she told United Press. "I won't permit myself to be blackmailed and I will certainly stand up and fight for my rights."

Estimating Franchot's assets at $1,000,000, Barbara was asking for $1,500 per month in alimony, as well as $100,000 she described as community property. "I am anxious to get this divorce and to get on with my career," a phlegmatic Barbara announced.

Soon afterward, however, Barbara made a huge tactical error when she allowed Tom Neal to move back into her home. As she later wrote, in her typically dreamy fashion, "It was inevitable. His muscles rippled under my hands and we settled down to days of continuous love."

EIGHTEEN:
Over-Exposed

Unbeknownst to Tom and Barbara, on March 27, a trio of Hollywood detectives hired by Franchot had begun a stakeout of her home, photographing the couple through a first-floor window. Equipped with such cutting-edge technology of the day as high-powered telephoto lenses and infrared film, the detectives (James Callaghan, Robert Guthrie and Frank Sullivan) had obtained a few rolls of mildly incriminating evidence, mostly shots of a scantily clad Tom and Barbara embracing, and for want of a better phrase, playing house.

But it was the series of blistering photos they managed to shoot over a motel transom in early-to mid-April that provided Franchot with all the ammunition he needed to file an amendment on April 24 to his original divorce complaint. Though newspapers of the day cleaned up the results of the detectives' stakeout at an unnamed Hollywood motel, numerous reports through the years have verified that the photos the investigators had delivered to Franchot showed Barbara, naked but for a black garter belt and beads, performing oral sex on Tom Neal. (The legal profession at the time referred to it as "an unnatural act", while newspaper accounts, in a similarly vague manner, alluded to the couple "…taking other liberties in love.")

There is also an unsubstantiated report that the same intrepid detectives had managed to snap some incriminating photographs of a topless Barbara engaging in the same unnatural act in yet another Hollywood motel, this time with black actor and ex-*L.A. Rams* football star Woody Strode, who had a minor role in *Bride of the Gorilla*. Though this claim has never been confirmed, it is certain that the steamy photos of Tom and Barbara were introduced at her divorce trial as proof of her infidelity. Later, a hurting and uncharacteristically vindictive Franchot made several copies of the X-rated prints and then distributed them around Hollywood in sealed, unmarked envelopes, hoping the sexually explicit images would destroy Barbara's chances of getting any future film work. [18] Unfortunately, Franchot saw to it that Barbara's brother, Frank, and her sister-in-law and best friend, Jan, received copies of the photos, as well. "You can imagine my shock when I opened our mailbox one afternoon and found those pictures," Jan says today. "There was no note, no explanation; just two terrible pictures of Barb and a big, naked

Barbara and her doting attorney take a cigarette break during her divorce trial. From the Author's Collection

Barbara looks surprisingly carefree in court during her divorce from Franchot Tone. Courtesy of USC Library/Dept. of Special Collections/L.A. Examiner Collection

man with a tattoo on his arm. The man's face was hidden so I couldn't tell for sure if it was really Tom, but I remember thinking at the time that it wasn't. The guy in the photo looked like he had a much bigger build.

"I never told Barbara, or Lee and Mabel—or anyone else, for that matter—about getting those photos, but Frank was disgusted when he saw them and he burned them right away. I mean, can you imagine Franchot sending photos like that to Barbara's own brother? I thought it was a very cruel thing to do, and not at all like Franchot. He must have been extremely upset with Barbara to do something that crazy."

Enraged seems more like it. According to Franchot's biographer, Lisa Burks, who has spent well over a decade researching both his career and his character: "Franchot was generally easygoing and nonjudgmental, but Barbara clearly pushed his limits with her never-ending betrayals and her tendency to talk to the press about highly personal matters.

"At this point in his life, when Franchot was observed acting out of character (as in this case), by all appearances those actions were directly motivated by the extreme emotional pain that Barbara's fickle disloyalty caused him. By the time of their divorce proceedings I'm certain that

Franchot felt cornered into a position where fighting fire with fire was completely justified."

Barely rebounding from this latest ambush, a desperate and spiteful Barbara went to the newspapers on May 3 with the preposterous story that Franchot had threatened to kill her and Tom, and that she had only allowed Neal to move in with her to act as her bodyguard. Franchot countered with an accusation of adultery, and, of course, he had those sizzling photos in his possession to prove it. Barbara, along with her attorney, Milton Golden, appeared in Superior Court with her cross-complaint that the actor was "suffering from delusions, hallucinations and mental aberrations." Quickly losing ground, she added that she believed Franchot had made up the infidelity charges for the purpose of blackmailing her into accepting his terms, and "...for plain old revenge."

Seeing the futility of her efforts, Barbara's final plea was inane, at best. "I've changed my mind," she told Judge Mildred L. Lillie. "I don't want any alimony, I just want Mr. Tone to pay for my new furniture. After all, we ordered it when we were together." When Franchot's lawyer, Stanley Gleis, introduced the photographic evidence that proved without question that she had been unfaithful, Barbara's cross-complaint was quickly withdrawn and Franchot was granted a divorce by default on May 17, 1952. [19]

"Franchot knew when to walk away from a toxic relationship," says Lisa Burks. "The day he divorced Barbara, I doubt if he ever looked back."

Immediately following her divorce from Franchot, Barbara stood outside the courtroom and offered a gem of self-revelation to the *L.A. Mirror*: "When I married Tone, I thought it would last forever," she said. "But forever is just a weekend, more or less."

Barbara went on to say that she had received a lump-sum "cash consideration that was satisfactory" in the divorce settlement, and then added, "I'm going back to Tom if he'll have me."

Predictably, Tom took Barbara back for yet another go-round. With a fatuous and almost pitiful optimism, he blathered, "She is the most wonderful woman—from alpha to omega. This is one fabulous woman. I hope to marry her and have five or six children."

When told of Tom's comments, Barbara was suddenly less enthusiastic. Barely missing a beat, she kept the publicity wheels turning with a somewhat caustic response to his quote. "Marry Tom? I don't know about that. My career is so important."

As Barbara's fiery personal life raged on, her parents remained detached from the drama and were instead planning a change of residence. After nearly fifteen years in Odessa, Lee and Mabel had grown tired of both the grind of running their motel, and of West Texas, in general, and were seeking a slower pace in California. In part, they wanted to be near Frank, who had received an honorable discharge from the Navy that year and was living with Jan and their infant son, Les, near Jan's parents in Compton. By May, Frank had gotten a job with a construction company, building houses with his father-in-law up near Big Bear. Mabel, whose emotional support of her daughter remained steadfast despite Barbara's many indiscretions through the years, also wanted to be near her and John Lee, who was now five years old and still going back and forth between Barbara and Al and Dorothy Zollinger. Unlike his wife, however, Lee still had a mostly negative opinion of Barbara and had mainly agreed to the move so he could be near the rest of their family.

Following their move that spring, Lee and Mabel temporarily rented a small, one-bedroom house in the upscale Mission Hills section of San Diego, while looking for a bigger home they could purchase. Soon afterward they found what Jan calls, "the house of their dreams," and moved into a two-story, Spanish-style abode on a hilltop overlooking Mission Bay and the San Diego Airport; a beautiful and ornate place they would call home for the next 18 years.

"The house was neat as a pin," remembers John Lee Payton. "The goings-on inside, what with my grandparents heavy drinking and all, may have been crazy, but the house itself was always clean. The same goes for all of my mother's homes. They were always spotless, from the earliest apartment in Hollywood through Courtney Terrace and our later home on North Beverly Drive. I have always been a neat freak myself, and I suppose it's because I was raised that way from the very beginning."

Despite the interference of his frequent drinking, Lee Redfield immediately set out to make the outside of the new property at 1901 Titus Street into a landscaper's showplace. In a project that would remain a work-in-progress over the next ten years, Lee constructed a wrought-iron spiral staircase outside that led to a long balcony on the second story, as well as a backyard patio and a long stairway of stones that ran along the side property.

"Then, in the front of the house, Lee built a beautiful brick patio draped in bougainvillea and wisteria," recalls Jan. "He even built a little fishpond out there, too, which he stocked with koi and surrounded with tiny orange flowers. It was lovely. What can I say? The man was an architectural genius."

Most impressively, perhaps, is that in response to Mabel's desire for an in-ground swimming pool, Lee built one for her, from scratch. Working alone, and with only a shovel, a pick and a wheelbarrow for tools, he dug the hole for it by hand, even though the hillside was a mass of solid boulders. He managed to save the rocks he unearthed from the yard and eventually built a four-foot-high wall with them.

Ever the master builder, Lee had even found a use for his collection of "dead soldiers." "Lee never threw away an empty beer can," laughs Jan. "Instead, he set them in concrete and built a big wall with them."

He had built a wall between himself and his daughter, too—this one, also, of "dead soldiers."

Things had quieted down a lot in Tom and Barbara's lives by the time his nephew, Walter Burr, paid a visit to them that June. The 23-year-old had recently served as a paratrooper in the 82nd Airborne Division of the United States Army until his discharge in August 1951, after which he had returned to Illinois to attend Northwestern University. Admittedly fond of his uncle (and impressed with his and Barbara's fame), Walter decided to take in the sights of Hollywood during his summer break in 1952 and headed west in his green Pontiac convertible. He remembers being greeted warmly by Barbara and Tom, whom he insists were at a happy place in their relationship. "I got the sense that they were totally enamored with each other. You could actually feel the sexual vibes bounce off them when they were together. It was that intense."

One of the first things Walter did upon his arrival was to accompany Tom to the 20th Century-Fox lot where they had lunch with movie star Richard Widmark, who was an acquaintance of Tom's. "It was amazing," recalls Walter. "We hung out there for a while and then later Tom introduced me to actors Hugh Krampe [O'Brian] and Rita Moreno, who were both just starting out at the time. For a young college kid from Illinois, meeting all these attractive movie people was pretty damn exciting."

The next morning, Tom took Walter clothes shopping in Hollywood. "We went down to Vine Street, to Sy Devore's store, which was the most popular haberdasher in town. As soon as we entered the place, Tom pulled out a big money clip from his pants pocket and took out several one-hundred-dollar bills. He told the salesman, 'This is my nephew and I want

Tom Neal's nephew Walter Burr, during his vacation stay with Tom and Barbara in 1952. Courtesy of Walter Burr

you to get him all spruced up.' He wanted me to look more 'West Coast,' or more 'Hollywood,' I guess. Tom bought me several expensive shirts and ties and a beautiful sports coat that day. He was extremely good to me."

Walter's first impression of Barbara was that of "a very gregarious and down-to-earth girl. She was extremely animated in her body movements, like she was fueled by some powerful inner energy. Barbara had the look of a hot Hollywood sexpot, but she was also very real and accessible. I must say, the pheromones she gave off were devastating. The girl just exuded sex. Barbara was bold, but not in a temperamental way. I don't recall her using any profanity. She wasn't coarse in her language, at least not while I was around. She was, however, very self-confident; a real boisterous babe who loved to laugh and joke and bust people's chops. She had an enormous laugh: loud and gutsy, and just full of mischief. I had the feeling that Barbara would talk to anybody, regardless of who they were, or what they had, or didn't have. She was very impartial, and extremely avant-garde. I liked her a lot, right off the bat."

Soon after his arrival, Walter remembers Barbara's mother bringing John Lee to visit for a few days. During much of the Franchot Tone fiasco, the youngster had spent most of his time with Al and Dorothy Zollinger at their home in Compton. At five years old, John Lee was developing into a very quiet and well-mannered child. "Dorothy and Al Zollinger had a tremendously positive influence on me," he says today. "They were decent, hard-working people and they always made me feel like I was one of their own. In fact, my Aunt Janice, their daughter, was more like a big sister to me than an aunt."

A sedate and almost ethereal portrait of the gregarious and fun-loving Barbara Payton. Courtesy of L.A. Public Library/Herald Examiner Collection

Although Mabel had delivered him to Barbara's house that day, the youngster normally spent very little time with her and Lee, due to their heavy drinking. Jan says, "When he wasn't with Barbara, Johnny always stayed with my parents. Barbara never left him with Lee and Mabel for very long because she knew the environment in their home was not the best place in which to raise a little boy.

"Johnny, as well as my own four children, never stayed with my in-laws for more than a day or two at a time. As kind and generous as Lee and Mabel were, sooner or later they would both hit the bottle, and when they did, it wasn't a pretty sight. Believe me, when they got really tanked up I just wanted to hit the freeway and go home.

"I loved my in-laws very much but you could never disagree with Lee as he always made it clear that he (and no one else) ran the show."

John Lee says, "You know, I have absolutely no bad memories of my grandparents, just that although they were always friendly, they were almost always drunk, too."

Perhaps it was for the same reason that John Lee's visits with Barbara were so sporadic. Whenever her personal life got too complicated, John Lee was usually shipped off to the Zollingers until Barbara could get things under control again. Though his life with his mother was frequently interrupted, John Lee insists today, "My mother bore me, raised me and formed me forever. Please don't take that away from her. It is, in fact, all we have left."

Walter Burr remembers John Lee's incredible handsomeness and good manners. "Johnny was a gorgeous, sandy-haired little kid with a great personality. During my visit there, I remember we brought him with us to a couple of pool parties in Beverly Hills, and all the women just went bonkers over him. They all oohed and aahed and generally just made a big fuss over him. Johnny had a lot of poise and charisma for a child of five. You might say he looked and behaved more like a miniature grown-up."

Today, John Lee credits a lot of the good manners he exhibited as a child to both Barbara and the Zollingers' influence. "My mother taught me early on to behave, particularly around adults, as she always wanted me to make a good impression. I spent a lot of time with her at various parties and on different movie sets, especially at WB. When I stayed with her, which was often, at the Courtney apartment, Mom always liked to dress me up in little wool suits with short pants and a white shirt. That was fine with me as it often involved a night out with her at a Hollywood restaurant, which was always fun."

With John Lee's latest visit, Walter noticed that whatever time Barbara and her son had spent apart evidently hadn't diminished their love for each other. "Barbara doted on Johnny the entire time he was there. She read him bedtime stories every night and she was constantly hugging him and kissing him, too. Barbara appeared to be a marvelous mother. And Tom was very good with Johnny, too. He spent a lot of time with him and they got along great."

Barbara had tears in her eyes and John Lee bawled when the Zollingers came to retrieve him, but Barbara quickly shook off her sadness and later told Walter that her son's leaving was for the best, as she was far too busy at the time "chasing down a career," and thus felt she couldn't devote herself to his raising as fully as Al and Dorothy Zollinger could. Walter says that he was under the impression that the separation was only meant to be temporary and that Barbara would arrange for the boy's return, "soon, once she had her feet planted more firmly on the ground."

According to Walter, both Barbara and Tom kept themselves busy that summer with various professional pursuits. "They were up early every day, and then went off separately to their business appointments. Every morning, Barbara cooked breakfast for Tom and me, although it was rare for her to sit down with us. She said she preferred to skip breakfast and lunch because she was watching her weight for the movie cameras. Barbara was a wonderful cook. She whipped up some fabulous meals for us while I was there, from scratch. This woman didn't even have to look at a recipe. She was amazing."

Walter says this was further validated by his parents, who had met Barbara a few weeks earlier, when Tom brought her home to Evanston to meet his family. "I was still away at college so I didn't see her, but my folks told me she was a delight—real 'high-energy' and warm and always asking if she could help out in the kitchen. They said she prepared several meals for them (all of which were delicious), and that she even threw a party or two while she was there. My parents said that all their friends just raved about her."

In addition to practicing her domestic skills, Barbara had dipped her toe back into fashion modeling that summer. In May and June, she did several photo shoots on the beach at Malibu, and in Palm Springs, with renowned Romanian photographer Andre de Dienes, best known today for his extensive body of work with Marilyn Monroe. As was a common practice at the time, the photos that de Dienes shot were paid for by the model (in this case, Barbara) and were taken on "spec," for possible distribution to such 1950s men's magazines as *Pageant*, *Eye* and *Brief*. Most of the Malibu Beach images show Barbara surfside in a modest, one-piece bathing suit, while the Palm Springs photos were predominantly action shots of Barbara in a white outfit, taken on a tennis court at the Palm Springs Racquet Club. Although the majority of her modeling portfolio with de Dienes lacks the special magic he attained in his work with

Barbara lounges in the Malibu, CA surf in this rare shot by renowned photographer Andre de Dienes (May, 1952). Courtesy of Shirley de Dienes/ de Dienes Photographic Arts

Another superb de Dienes shot of Barbara from May, 1952. Courtesy of Shirley de Dienes/de Dienes Photographic Arts

A series of rare photos of Barbara by renowned photographer Andre de Dienes, from their Malibu Beach shoot in May 1952. Courtesy of Shirley de Dienes/ de Dienes Photographic Arts

Monroe, Barbara's beauty was nonetheless shown to good advantage in several photos now stored for posterity in the de Dienes Archive.

"Barbara introduced me to Andre one day at his photography studio in West Hollywood," Walter remembers. "She brought me down there to see some examples of their recent work together in Malibu. As soon as I walked into his studio, I noticed that Andre had several black-and-white shots of her hanging on the wall that he had blown up to about three feet-by-four feet. They were absolutely gorgeous pictures of Barbara, totally nude (except for a pair of sheer, flesh-colored panties) and riding a white horse, bareback, on a deserted, windswept beach. Needless to say, the photos were phenomenal. Andre and Barbara were both very proud of those pictures, and with good reason: they were incredibly hot. However, I don't recall ever seeing them published anywhere. I wonder whatever happened to them?"

Although the nude pictures of Barbara were said to have been part of a de Dienes photo exhibition at Santa Monica's G. Ray Hawkins Art Gallery in the 1980s, they apparently haven't surfaced anywhere since.

A de Dienes candid of Barbara swimming in the pool at the Palm Springs Racquet Club. Courtesy of Shirley de Dienes/de Dienes Photographic Arts

A publicity still of Barbara playing tennis at the Palm Springs Racquet Club. Courtesy of Shirley de Dienes/de Dienes Photographic Arts

Like most people in show business, Barbara and Tom took a great interest in their bodies and devoted a lot of time that summer to staying in shape, says Walter. "Tom spent most afternoons on Barbara's front patio working out with dumbbells, while she went to the Beverly Hills Hotel a lot, to swim and play tennis. I remember both of them going out on several job interviews, and although none had brought them any new film work, neither of them seemed to be hurting financially. Barbara owned a new Cadillac convertible, which they both drove, and she also had in her employ a lovely black maid named Mamie who was actually a very well-spoken and elegant woman."

Walter learned that Barbara had decorated the entire inside of her West Hollywood house herself, and he says that it was truly a sight to behold. "The house was impeccably furnished and I was very impressed with all the work she had done. Barbara's bedroom was an ice-blue color and the carpets and draperies were coordinated to match. She told me that she was extremely proud of all the material items she had amassed."

He would later find out why.

A self-professed authority on alluring feminine pulchritude, Walter was equally bowled over by the sheer perfection of Barbara's beauty. "If I had to equate her physicality with any other actress, I would say that Marilyn Monroe, obviously, comes closest—although I think Barbara had better legs. She also had dynamite skin. It was tanned and flawless and offset beautifully by her gorgeous blue eyes.

"As for the rest of her, Barbara was probably a perfect 35" on her mezzanine. When seminude, her boobs didn't bounce but were well-positioned on her chest. So, when in a bra and blouse, without a narrow waist, she looked incredibly sexy. Barbara wasn't thin, but she had just the right amount of weight to offset a great pair of boobs."

The college student saw a lot of Barbara's "boobs"—and everything else—that summer, for despite his presence there she had continued to indulge in her almost daily ritual of sunbathing completely nude in the building's front courtyard. While Walter admits to being taken aback the first time he glimpsed his hostess reclining naked on the low-walled patio, he soon learned that Barbara did it just as much for shock as for her own enjoyment.

"Barbara would lie there on her stomach, nude and covered in suntan lotion, and listen for any activity around her. Then, for instance, if she heard a car pull up on the side street next to her house, she'd flip over on her back just before the driver came up the sidewalk. Barbara would lie there spread-eagled and watch the person's eyes bug out of their head. Oh yeah, Barbara was a solid piece of work. She really got off on that.

"I'm not sure why none of her neighbors ever complained, or called the police. Unless, of course, they enjoyed the show, too."

And what about Tom? How did his notoriously jealous nature handle Barbara's desire to titillate her neighbors, as well as strangers who just happened to be passing by?

"It didn't bother him," says Walter. "Believe me, Tom had just as much moxie as Barbara. I'll never forget an incident that happened one afternoon while I was there. The three of us were sitting in the guest room when we heard this whirring sound coming from the apartment next to Barbara's. All the buildings in that little complex of apartments had adjoining walls so it was always very easy to hear what was going on next door. Barbara's neighbor was an unmarried, middle-aged woman who lived alone, and her bedroom faced the guest room. The buzzing sound continued for several minutes and then we heard this loud moaning. Tom stuck his head out of the window to get a better listen and said, 'I do believe our neighbor is pleasuring herself with a vibrator. Let's see if I can help her out.' Barbara and I just sat there, kind of dumbfounded, while Tom went downstairs and frantically rang the woman's doorbell. She let him in and within five minutes the moaning had resumed. Tom was over there, fucking this woman. I'll never forget it.

"When we realized what was going on, Barbara and I just looked at each other with our mouths wide open, and then she began laughing and slapping her knee. To say that I was surprised at her reaction is an immense understatement. Here, her boyfriend is fucking the daylights out of her next-door neighbor, and she's digging it. In fact, she's absolutely loving it. I learned that day that Barbara was confident enough in herself and in her power over Tom to let him have his fun, and he did."

Walter believes that Neal was a misogynist and that, like Barbara, he really got off on the seduction process. "I remember Tom telling me once: 'Show me a guy who doesn't go down on his girlfriend and I'll take her away from him.' Love it or leave it, that was his attitude.

"Looking back at Tom's life, I think he was always more interested in 'scoring' than in wanting to engage in, or develop, a meaningful relationship with a woman. But, I gotta hand it to Barbara. She pretty much always went toe to toe with him, and I don't think he ever pulled anything over on her."

Walter says that when Tom made his way back home from the female neighbor's bedroom, the first thing Barbara did was congratulate him on his stellar performance. "They both got a huge kick out of the whole situation and I was in total awe. The two of them were absolutely outrageous at times. A truly ballsy couple."

Barbara's appreciation of this unorthodox event was yet another example of her mischievous and freewheeling spirit. Totally devoid of any pretense or inhibitions, her manner was off-the-wall, but almost childlike, Walter thought. "The desire to shock people and to do as she pleased was actually kind of endearing. It seemed a form of innocent fun for Barbara."

As was her healthy sex-life with Tom. "They spent hours upon hours holed up in her bedroom—just laughing and giggling and having the time of their lives. It was never discussed by any of us, but they certainly didn't hide it. It wasn't really a big deal to them, I guess. In fact, they probably never even gave it a second thought. You know, if you're getting laid three times a day, you think that everyone else is, too.

"I think Barbara looked at sex as a recreational sport, I really do. I would hear them carrying on in there and think, 'Gee, what a great relationship.' It always made me smile."

But there was a dark side to all the frivolity, as Walter soon noticed. Within days of his arrival, it became obvious to him that Barbara had a very serious drinking problem. "Straight vodka was her drink of choice and on those days when she wasn't going on business appointments or modeling for Andre de Dienes, she would start hitting the bottle as early as ten o'clock in the morning. She would then continue drinking throughout the day and would consequently eat very little food. During the time I was there, I don't think I ever saw Barbara eat lunch, and she seldom ate dinner with us, either. She was always a bit buzzed. Not falling-down drunk, but definitely high. You know, in good spirits.

"Unlike Barbara, Tom did not drink excessively. I heard him get on her about the booze a couple of times, but they didn't really argue about it. He would tell her that she ought to lay off the sauce because she was starting to look fat. Barbara would listen very intently to his objections about the amount she was drinking, and she would agree to cut back. She would 'yes' him to death, and then drink just as much the next day. After a while, Tom dropped it and didn't bring it up again—at least not while I was there."

Barbara was continuing the family tradition started by her parents: early morning drinking that lasted the entire day, coupled with a total avoidance of the issue, and ending with a sincere apology and a vow to do better. Although no one realized it at the time, Lee and Mabel's influence on Barbara's behavior had left a lasting mark.

Barbara's excessive drinking was clearly behind an incident which validated the pride she had in both her home and in the power of her allure; an incident that Walter witnessed and seems especially amazed by, to this day.

Near the end of his visit with the couple, Walter attended a dinner party at Barbara's house; one of many that she threw, he says, "just for the hell of it." There were nearly 40 industry people in attendance, he remembers, including Andre de Dienes, a DuMont Television executive named John Klein, actors Kirby Grant and John Carroll ("who were good friends of Tom's") and their spouses, and several models and bit players.

Barbara prepared a veritable feast for her guests, and the food, libations and laughter flowed all night long.

Three-quarters of the way through the party, Walter claims that Barbara (who was, by then, deeply in her cups) climbed the stairs to a balcony overlooking the sunken living room, where most of her guests were gathered, and announced in an authoritative voice: "Attention, everybody. I hope you're all having a good time. I want everyone to notice how beautifully I've decorated this place. Look at all the gorgeous paintings on the walls, the expensive furniture, the fine china and crystal… all of it. Well, I just want you all to know that everything in this apartment was paid for on my back. And I'm damn proud of it, too."

According to Walter, Barbara's declaration was met with a discordant mix of titters and gasps (with a few gut-ripping belly laughs thrown in for good measure). "I had a mouthful of snails and I was so shocked, I almost choked on them," Walter remembers. He then looked at Tom, to see his reaction.

"He laughed," Walter says. "Tom stood there, holding his drink, and he laughed. I didn't know what to make of it, but I think a part of me cringed. Looking back on it now, I think Barbara showed a kind of disrespect for herself by saying that, I really do. And I'm not even sure she cared.

"At the time, though, I didn't go on thinking about it after it happened. I was an observer in Tom and Barbara's lives, not a participant, and I didn't judge them. I don't now, either."

After delivering her jaw-dropping admission, Barbara reeled across the balcony and then bounced almost sideways down the stairs to rejoin her guests. Her obvious drunkenness proved unsettling to Walter, who noticed a kind of black mood descend on her soon afterward. The playful and bawdy quality that he had seen in her up to that point had suddenly taken on an ugly and far more sinister twist. But perhaps it was just a more truthful example of Barbara's diminishing self-esteem.

When hearing this story, John Lee Payton's first thoughts are that his mother must have had, as he calls it, a "Jekyll and Hyde nature," and that she obviously put a lot of effort into protecting him from seeing the darker side of her psyche. "I don't remember that party," he says, "but Walter Burr's balcony anecdote pretty much makes me nauseous as it is so much like the sort of thing one might do if, for whatever reason, a tendency to humiliate oneself has become habit over the years.

"That apparent tendency of my mother's, reinforced by a wonderfully earthy wit and bold nature, isn't always pleasant to consider—either in the context of the moment or for her future. But I believe she had looked deeply into her interior mirror many years before and had found much there that was hateful to her."

Perhaps the incident was more telling than we know. The inner turmoil that had wrecked her past relationships, derailed her career and had already driven Barbara to attempt to take her own life with an overdose of sleeping pills was now finding her degrading herself blissfully before her friends and business associates. Barbara had become the butt of her own miserable joke and it was a clear sign that things were indeed turning sour in her "party girl" world.

Even with Barbara's increasingly outlandish behavior, Walter maintains that Tom kept his temper in check during the entire time he was there. "They never fought, at least not while I was with them. I don't recall ever hearing either of them speaking harshly to the other. Even when Tom got on Barbara's case over her drinking, he did it respectfully, and out of genuine concern for her. There were no harsh words; there was certainly no screaming. Barbara didn't seethe with anger; she was usually too upbeat and lighthearted for that."

Walter also insists that Barbara never once made any sexual overtures to him. "Even though I was her guest," he stresses, "she actually treated me more like her kid brother. She was gracious and sweet to me the whole time I was there but she certainly never propositioned me.

"Those two [Barbara and Tom] had their hands all over each other—morning, noon and night. She didn't need me, or anyone else.

"The most forward thing Barbara did was give me my first X-rated book. She said she had lifted it from Charles Laughton's bathroom (of all places) when she and Franchot Tone were at Laughton's house for a party. She gave me the book and told me to 'knock myself out,' or something like that. Barbara was a real trip."

As he prepared to head back east in mid-July, Walter remembers that Barbara was lining up some film work overseas. Although he didn't know it at the time, after he left he would never again see the woman he calls, "my beautiful friend."

"Things seemed to be improving a little for both Barbara and Tom, work-wise," says Walter. "And they were happy together. I was glad because I thought that maybe if their careers picked up, it would help Barbara slow down on her drinking. But that didn't happen, did it?"

Barbara en route to London to star in two films. Courtesy of Hulton Archive

CHAPTER NINETEEN:
Bad Blonde

Following her announcement in the L.A. papers that she was going to England "to do two films, and to study Shakespeare," Barbara left Hollywood (and Tom) for London on July 23. With their legendary affection for all things sordid, the British public had devoured every word of the Tone/Payton/Neal fracas and considered Barbara to be a hot property. "I've been greatly misunderstood in America," she told reporters, upon landing at London's Heathrow Airport. "The British, on the other hand, seem to understand me."

Hoping that her notoriety would transfer to big bucks at the box office, a British film company had rush-contracted Barbara to appear in two co-productions for Astor and Lippert Pictures, respectively: *Four Sided Triangle* (sometimes titled *The Monster and the Woman*) and *The Flanagan Boy* (a.k.a. *Bad Blonde*). Although star billing in both films might have sounded like a good thing to her at the time, Barbara must have known that being shipped overseas to work so soon after losing her contract with a major studio like Warner Bros. was a sure sign that her acting career was in serious trouble.

Barbara's new employer was Exclusive Films, a long-standing motion picture distributor in England that had revived its production division a few years earlier following a thirteen-year period of inactivity. In 1949, the production company was renamed Hammer Films and began concentrating on supplying British theaters with so-called, "quota quickies"—compact second features designed to play with larger, and usually American-made films, upon their release. Barbara went off to England to work for Hammer Films under The Eady Plan, a popular arrangement at the time between various American film companies and British Equity. Under this plan, American funds were kept in London

Barbara looks radiant at a London hotel party given in her honor in August 1952. Courtesy of Trinity Mirror

banks to be used specifically for film projects in which usually no more than two American stars would work with a British cast and crew on a motion picture to be produced entirely in England. Films made under The Eady Plan were mainly exported and distributed as programmers, and were rarely considered prestigious productions. Barbara's two films for Hammer were no exception and later played the bottom half of double bills when they were released in the U.S. in mid-1953.

A few days after Barbara's arrival in London, Hammer's Chairman and Managing Director, James Carreras, held a reception in her honor at the city's luxurious Dorchester Hotel. Carrerras (1909-1990) had assigned his son Michael, along with Hungarian-born Alexander Paal, to co-produce Barbara's first film for the company, *Four Sided Triangle*.

Several photographs of Barbara taken at the reception show her being treated like visiting royalty, with Alexander Paal toasting her with champagne as she stood smiling in the middle of a large circle of men. Although in some of the photos Paal appears to be quite smitten with her (he's even leaning on her in one of the shots, with her mink stole

Lobby card for the British Sci-Fi thriller, **Four Sided Triangle**.
From the Author's Collection

Director Terence Fisher (left), actor Stephen Murray and hair and makeup persons admire Barbara's beauty in this rare, on set candid from Four Sided Triangle. *Courtesy of George Douglas/Hulton Archive*

draped over his shoulders), by all accounts his relationship with Barbara was strictly professional.

With her warm welcome in London firmly in place, filming for Barbara's first British feature, *Four Sided Triangle,* commenced in early August at Hammer's Bray Studios, outside the town of Windsor (with location scenes filmed at the spectacular coastal village of Lulworth Cove, in the southwest part of England). Shot in five weeks with a budget of 25,000 pounds, the project was one of Hammer's first forays into the science-fiction and horror film arena. Unfortunately, it was not one of the company's best.

Although co-written and directed by the brilliant Terence Fisher, *Four Sided Triangle* was, alas, a rather drab and slow-moving affair that found Barbara top-billed and playing dual roles—one being a duplicate of a scientist's best friend's wife. As the forlorn Lena, an English-born but American-raised ne'er-do-well, Barbara returns to her hometown in the English countryside to inform her childhood physician, a kindly man named "Doc" Harvey (played by character actor James Hayter), that she plans to do away with herself after she finishes going through the inheritance her mother has left her. In a deep and sonorous voiceover in the film's opening scene, Doc explains that Lena had tried her hand at many things in America—art, music, writing—each one without success. "There are many scapegoats for our sins and failures," she tells him, "and the most popular is providence. I shan't blame anyone but myself."

Hoping to lift her fallen spirits, Doc reunites Lena with two local men who had been her childhood friends. It just so happens that the enterprising gents, Robin (played by John Van Eyssen, who would later gain fame as Jonathan Harker in Hammer's classic *Horror of Dracula*) and Bill (BBC Radio actor Stephen Murray), have invented a machine called "The Reproducer" that can copy anything by converting physical matter into energy. Soon, Lena's prior depression is replaced with an implausibly perky enthusiasm as she assists Robin and Bill in their experiments. When Lena and Robin announce their engagement, a jealous Bill, who also loves her, devises a plan to make a duplicate of her that he can keep for himself. While Robin is in London on business, Bill proposes the idea to Lena, who reluctantly allows the experiment to take place. The result is an exact clone of the original Lena, a woman that also loves Robin (an intriguing

Barbara being cloned in a scene from Four Sided Triangle.
Courtesy of The Borst Collection

plot twist that might have been riveting had it been handled more skillfully). The clone, named Helen, becomes terribly despondent over her conflicting feelings of loyalty and guilt, and while on her honeymoon with Bill at a coastal resort, attempts suicide by swimming out to sea.

Later, in a final effort to win his creation's love, Bill (with Lena's assistance) tries to eradicate Helen's memory via an experiment with electro-shock therapy, but in a climax reminiscent of *The Bride of Frankenstein*'s, a laboratory fire destroys the duplicating machine, killing both Bill and one of the women in the process. The fade-out finds Robin and the woman he managed to save from the fire, reunited in a London hospital, where he discovers, through a tiny scar on the back of her neck, that the woman he saved is his wife, the real Lena.

As the lone American in a provincial British setting, Barbara delivered a distracted and half-hearted performance, leading one to believe that she had seen the job as merely a temporary diversion from her nightclubbing activities in London. (So much for her aspirations to study the literary works of William Shakespeare.) In a prosaic bit of pap like this, Barbara must have felt she was under no obligation to extend any more than the most rudimentary effort, and it showed. Additionally hampered by a stagnant, creeping pace and its slapdash special effects (the latter aptly described by author Philip Strick in his book, *Science Fiction*

A provocative shot of Barbara and actor Stephen Murray from Four Sided Triangle. *Courtesy of BFI Stills, Posters and Designs*

Barbara and Tom Neal attend a theater function in London in the fall of 1952. Courtesy of Trinity Mirror

Movies, as "flashing lights and corkscrews"), *Four Sided Triangle* proved a crashing bore and did nothing for Barbara's career. The same could be said for one of its screenwriters, Paul Tabori, whose next effort, the Sci-Fi film *Spaceways*, was also roundly criticized. The director of *Four Sided Triangle*, however, did manage to move on to better things. In fact, near the end of the decade, Terence Fisher rebounded magnificently with *The*

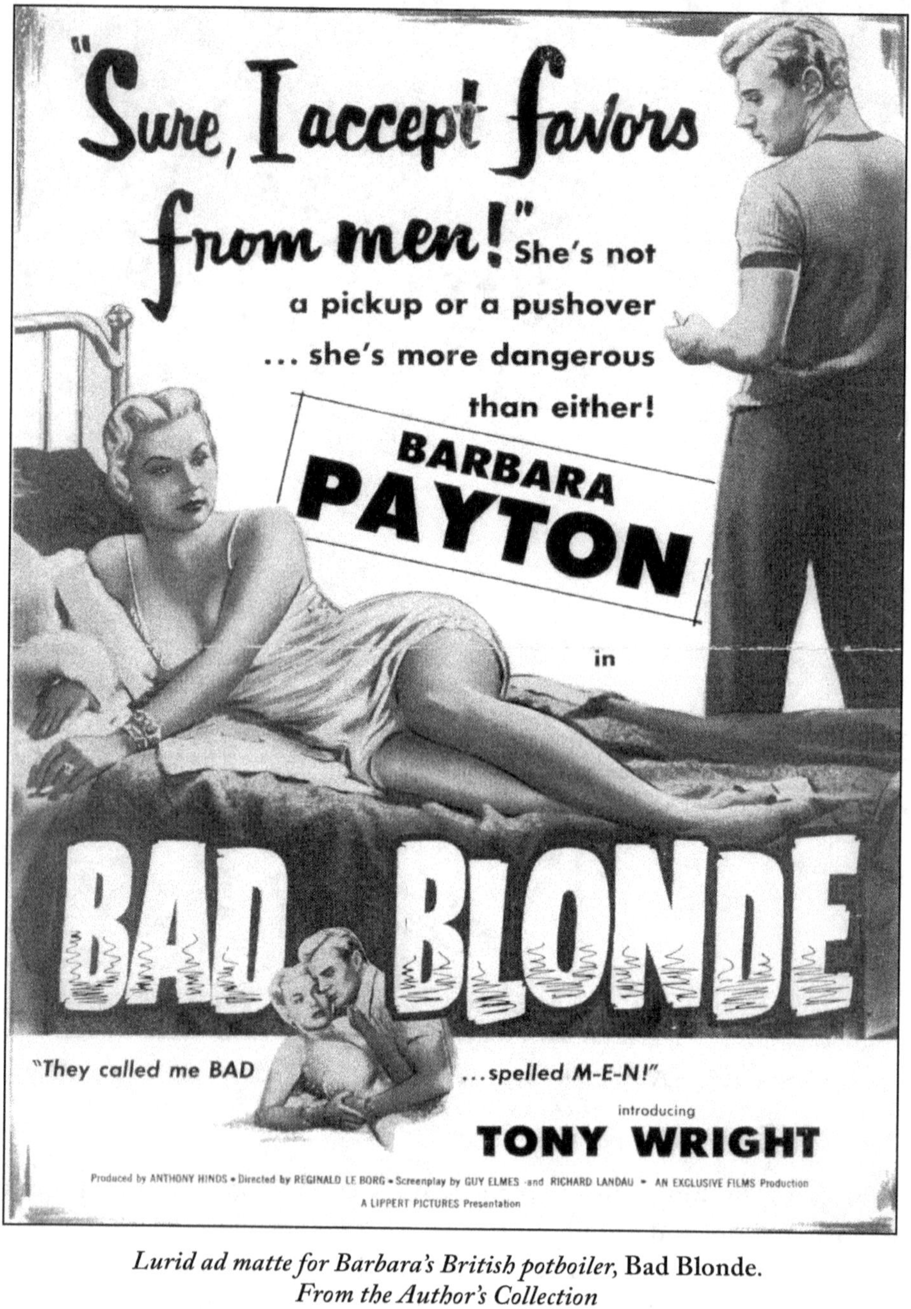

Lurid ad matte for Barbara's British potboiler, Bad Blonde. *From the Author's Collection*

Curse of Frankenstein and the previously mentioned *Horror of Dracula*, two much better genre films that became huge hits for Hammer Films.

Barbara's second Hammer feature, *The Flanagan Boy*, an equally flaccid piece directed by the usually dependable American director Reginald LeBorg (*Weird Woman*, *The Mummy's Ghost*), began its three-week shooting schedule on September 25, just a few days after she completed her work on *Four Sided Triangle*. By this time, Tom had followed Barbara overseas and the couple was staying together in her hotel room overlooking London's Hyde Park. It seemed that Barbara was initially none too happy about it either, for the *Hollywood Citizen-News* reported on September 13 that she had refused to pose for photos with Tom at a news conference that was held immediately after his arrival. "Neal seems to have some competition in male circles," alleged the newspaper; however, by the time Barbara began filming *The Flanagan Boy* two weeks later, whatever issues the pair had with each other appeared to be resolved.

Much like its predecessor, *The Flanagan Boy* was painfully weak in the entertainment department, with its sleazy poster art being one of its few redeeming factors. Blazoned above a sizzling photo of Barbara lounging on a bed in a white slip were the provocative words: "*She's Not a Pickup or a Pushover... She's More Dangerous Than Either. Made of Fire and Ice... They Called Me Bad... Spelled M-e-n!*" But despite the ad's campy and over-the-top wording, *The Flanagan Boy* was dull as dishwater.

In a screenplay that was loosely based on the sensational Snyder-Gray courtroom drama of 1927, a hard-looking Barbara was top-billed again, this time as Lorna Vecchi, an evil-hearted ex-taxi dancer who seduces a young boxer (Tony Wright) into murdering her aging, fight-manager husband, Giuseppe (Frederick Valk). At first, Wright's character, Johnny Flanagan, attempts to resist Barbara's less-than-subtle overtures (i.e., in one scene, they are in a nightclub, dancing, when she leans forward and first blows in his ear, and then kisses it; while in another, they meet at night in a darkened stable, where Barbara embraces her wavering prey, and in a low, husky voice, dripping with carnality, implores, "Just let it happen, Johnny. Let it happen"). Obviously, with all this heavy breathing and thrashing about, it's no surprise when Flanagan finally succumbs to the wily woman's charms.

At Lorna's urging, Flanagan drowns Giuseppe in a lake and makes his death appear to be the result of a boating accident, but his guilty conscience later makes him crumble under the pressure. After he informs

Frederick Valk and Barbara in a scene from **Bad Blonde.** *From the Author's Collection*

an enraged Barbara that he is leaving her to confess his crime to the authorities, the bad blonde kills him with a bowl of homemade soup that she's laced with poison. The film's finale has Johnny's trainer, who is savvy to Lorna Vecchi's wicked ways, planting some incriminating evidence in her bedroom, which leads to her arrest by the British authorities.

In a brilliant stroke of reality-based typecasting, the plot of *The Flanagan Boy* found the real-life femme fatale playing her cinematic counterpart—surely the film's main point of interest today. When, in a guttural tone of voice, she berates her weak-willed boyfriend for initially backing down on their murder plans, Barbara seems to be drawing on a familiar emotional scenario. "Get lost," she sneers, in a voice dripping with venom. "Oh, wake up, like me. You'll soon forget. I must've been crazy gettin' soft for you like that. Guess it must've been the body, but it won't happen again!"

As a sex-crazed woman seemingly consumed by passion, Barbara is all flaring nostrils, arched eyebrows and wet lips, with both her strident performance and turgid, unbecoming appearance bordering on the bizarre. One scene in the film has Barbara eyeing the boxer in the ring, slowly scanning the length of his muscular frame—and midsection—while licking her lips lasciviously. The resulting image was perhaps a tad self-revealing, and more than a bit perverse.

Though the overall plot of *The Flanagan Boy* sounds enticing, a la Marilyn Monroe's *Niagara*, the movie itself was a complete washout; cheaply made, poorly executed, and trashed by most film critics. To

Barbara as the evil Lorna Vecchi in **Bad Blonde.** *Courtesy of Wisconsin Center for Film and Theater Research*

make matters worse, Barbara's brittle, one-dimensional performance was devoid of any trace of nuance or skill, and was almost painful to watch.

If her British films lacked excitement, Barbara more than made up for it in her purported antics with Tom *off* the set. In late October, while staying at the Hertford Street flat they had moved into in the elegant Mayfair section of London, Barbara allegedly dumped Tom long enough to pick up a wealthy nightclub owner named Siegi Sessler.

A leading member of London's hard-partying, "café crowd", the German-born Sessler had a reputation as one of the U.K.'s most dedicated playboys and was said to put as much time into his womanizing as he did into running his nightclub. Years later, in several magazine articles, Barbara strangely insisted on referring to him as both a duke and an earl, as if upgrading his social status made their one-night stand much more intriguing.

Barbara's London liaison was said to have ended abruptly when Neal found his girlfriend making love to her new playmate on a bearskin rug in their apartment, and responded by throwing Sessler out of the place—sans trousers. Afterwards, Tom allegedly beat Barbara, who later admitted, "I didn't care. I enjoyed every minute of it."

Sporting a cut over her left eye, Barbara poured herself into a low-cut gown, telephoned reporters and posed for photos on her balcony. "This business of being beautiful just leads to trouble," she told the British weekly, *Film News*. "I don't know what it is that I've got that causes me so much trouble. Sometimes I wish I wasn't so lucky. Looking the way I do is a curse." Those words, of course, would prove all too prophetic.

Tom's beating of Barbara, the first on record—but possibly not the first to occur—obviously signaled a disturbing downward trend in their affair. The harmonious union that Neal's nephew Walter Burr had witnessed during his visit with them earlier that summer now seemed far more dissonant. The combination of Barbara's heavy drinking and wandering eye and Tom's highly combustible temper had unleashed a violent new dynamic in their relationship, and it hardly bode well for their future together.

Adding to Barbara's problems during this time was the fact that neither *Four Sided Triangle* nor *The Flanagan Boy* were hits at the box office (on either side of the Atlantic). When she and Tom left London to return to the States in the fall of 1952, Barbara had also left behind a decidedly mixed reaction to her among those with whom she had worked.

Sporting a cut over her right eye, Barbara talks to reporters following her hotel brawl with Tom Neal. Courtesy of Russell Westwood

While *Four Sided Triangle*'s co-producer, Michael Carreras, said at the time that he felt Barbara "had the goods to become a top international sex symbol," Terence Fisher was disturbed by the aura of doom that enveloped the beleaguered star, even then. "I thought she was an amazingly lovely girl who worked hard for us and certainly tried to do her best," a kind and diplomatic Fisher later said, "but Barbara seemed determined to surround herself with the most unsavory men. I remember there were always some surly types lurking around her on the set and Barbara was often seen arguing with them, and so on. She was an extremely beautiful person, but deeply troubled."

Chapter Twenty:
Riot on Sunset Strip

After several months abroad, Barbara returned to Hollywood with Tom in early November, with the actress sporting a faux British accent so thick, "...the Duke of Windsor might have envied it," as gossip maven Sheilah Graham—usually an advocate of Barbara's—wrote in her column. In her newly adopted British patois, Barbara formally announced that Tom had taken over the management of her career, and vowed that she would only be accepting, in her words, "really strong film roles." But by December, Barbara capitulated on that pledge when she donned a cave girl outfit and co-starred with Sonny Tufts, another scandal-plagued performer on a career slide, in an impoverished comedy titled *Run for the Hills*. It was Barbara's second and final effort for producer Jack Broder, who released the film through Realart Pictures and distributed it through his soon to be shuttered Jack Broder Productions.

Blond and husky Sonny Tufts, an embarrassingly inept performer whose professional memory has been sustained through the years by bad-film fanatics everywhere, was a former leading man at Paramount Pictures in the 1940s, where he starred in a series of failed comedies (*I Love a Soldier*, *The Well-Groomed Bride*, *Cross My Heart*, etc.) before being dropped by the studio in 1947 after 12 films. Born Bowen Charleston Tufts III in 1911 to a wealthy family of Boston bankers, he had graduated with honors from Yale and was a trained opera singer, but his conspicuous lack of acting talent and a fondness for the whiskey bottle had quickly laid his film career to waste.

By 1952, Sonny Tufts was known more for his frequent brushes with the law than for anything he had ever accomplished onscreen. In 1950 and '51 alone, he was arrested three times on charges of public drunkenness—once, after being found passed-out on a Sunset Strip sidewalk. Prior to his being cast in *Run for the Hills,* Tufts made outrageous headlines when he engaged in a brawl over a $4.65 dinner bill in a coffee shop while in the company of exotic Hollywood hula dancer Luuki-ana Kaeoloa. The following year, the 6'4" actor was in the news again, this time for biting buxom stripper Barbara Gray Atkins (a.k.a. "Melody Carol") on her upper left thigh. Atkins sued him for $25,000, accusing him of leaving one of her "key professional assets" permanently disfigured.

No sooner was that dispute settled out of court, when nightclub dancer Marjorie Von came forth to accuse Tufts of a similar offense—and

Ad for the 1953 comedy, Run For the Hills. *Courtesy of Wisconsin Center for Film and Theater Research*

upped the ante to $26,500. The ever-vigilant Los Angeles newspapers had a blast reporting on a trial rife with unintentional humor. "When all was said and done," wrote the *L.A. Times*, "the flame-haired Von settled for six hundred dollars and a bitten pin."

Evidently, Tufts' oral fixation continued unabated, and he was later arrested in 1955 when a woman named Adrienne Formarr charged him with "mauling, biting and pinching" her in a local restaurant.

These, and several other well-publicized events in Sonny Tufts' life, had made him a complete laughingstock in Hollywood, firmly cementing his status as a joke in the eyes of the entire industry. Perhaps then, it wasn't too surprising when someone had the brilliant idea of pairing one of Hollywood's leading Bad Boys with its reigning Bad Blonde for their next cinematic effort.[20]

Directed in broad, slapstick style by B-Movie war-horse Lew Landers (*The Raven*, *The Return of the Vampire*, etc.), *Run for the Hills*'s banal plot concerns an insurance actuary's paranoia over what he believes to be an impending nuclear holocaust, and his attempts to escape it by moving into a desert mine with his wife. When the local media turns the loincloth-

Cave dwellers Sonny Tufts and Barbara Payton in a scene from **Run For the Hills**. *From the Author's Collection*

clad duo into something of a sideshow act, they realize the error of their decision and seek to reunite with civilized society.

In the pantheon of truly stultifying performances by Sonny Tufts, *Run for the Hills* arguably contains one of his worst ever. Lumbering across a chintzy, papier-mâché set designed to look like a cave, Tufts appears flush-faced and glassy-eyed in several scenes, and looks to be plastered. When he pounds out a rollicking ragtime rendition of the classic song "Frankie and Johnny" on the piano, the actor rolls his eyes wildly and bleats off-key in a display that is so bad it has to be seen to be believed. In other scenes, he snaps out his dialogue with a discernible irritability, like he's itching for his next drink. All told, it is one abysmal performance.

Barbara, on the other hand, as Tufts' naive spouse, Jane Johnson, shows an endearingly flighty, almost Gracie Allen-like quality in her characterization, revealing a natural flair in her comic delivery that was unfortunately wasted on the screenplay's many unfunny lines.

Peppered with walk-ons from several lower-rung, if dependable, actors like Jean Willes, Richard Benedict and Byron Foulger, *Run for the Hills* had the look and ambiance of a Three Stooges short, minus the charm and energy. A musty, old vaudeville sketch in search of an audience, the new release went the way of Barbara's two previous films: straight to the bottom-half of double bills across the country.

With her high-pitched, Brooklyn accent, her 1950s-housewife attire, and her demure, dark hairstyle, a much more wholesome-looking Barbara had surfaced in *Run for the Hills*, and it was a refreshing change of pace. But while it was to Barbara's credit that she had taken on a different kind of role, the movie was a moth-eaten, bottom-of-the-barrel effort, and was not a success.

Unfortunately, under Tom Neal's management deal with producer Jack Broder, the actress had opted for a deferment in her regular weekly salary and instead asked for ten-percent of the film's profits. Barbara ultimately wound up with very little, however, as *Run for the Hills* proved to be a resounding flop.

The film's failure only added to the tension that seemed to be building on a daily basis between Barbara and Tom. Much to their detriment, rather than talking over their problems as two mature adults might do, they chose to ignore them instead, and lost themselves in all-night bacchanals on the Sunset Strip.

On the surface, liquor may have seemed the perfect salve to numb the resentment Barbara and Tom were feeling toward each other, but in reality it was only making their relationship more and more combative. By mid-1953, their days together as a couple were numbered.

During this time, Barbara's former boyfriend Steve Hayes was still pursuing his acting career, while working as the night manager of Hollywood's popular Googie's Coffee Shop, which was directly adjacent

Tom and Barbara in the lobby of Hollywood's Mocambo nightclub (1953). Courtesy of L.A. Public Library/Herald Examiner Collection

Barbara and Tom shortly before their breakup in 1953.
Courtesy of AP/Wide World Photos

to the legendary Schwab's Drugstore at the corner of Sunset and Crescent Heights Boulevards. A meeting place for a diverse group of Hollywood types—from its leading literary and thespian crowd, all the way down to its starving fringe set—Googie's is best known, perhaps, as a favorite haunt of actor James Dean, who was often spotted sitting in a back booth with an eccentric clique that included fellow actors Dennis Hopper and Maila "Vampira" Nurmi (a future neighbor of Barbara's).

Though his affair with Barbara had been brief, Steve had continued to run into her through the years at various bars and nightclubs in town, and they had remained friendly. Barbara and Tom usually made Googie's their last stop after a night out, and Steve recalls seeing them in there at least a dozen times during this period. More often than not, he says, they were drunk, as well as confrontational—not only to the restaurant's employees and to the other patrons, but to each other, as well.

"They were usually pretty stewed when they came in," says Steve. "Although Barbara was frequently laughing and carrying on, Neal would usually be scowling, and looking all pissed off at her. What can I say about Tom Neal? The guy was a mean-spirited bully, though I noticed he usually never bullied anyone bigger than himself. The trouble the two of them caused in the restaurant was always from them being too loud and boisterous. Both of them swore like sailors, and if anyone asked them to be quiet, Neal, more than Babs, would go off. For instance, if the waitresses were slow to get to their booth because of other customers, Neal would bang on the table and demand service. He was a real pain in the ass.

"I worked in a lot of coffee shops and parking lots during those years and I learned one thing: waitresses and parking lot attendants usually get a good handle on what type of person you are by the way you treat them. Waitresses, especially, are good when it comes to reading customers. Not one of my waitresses liked Neal. Most of them weren't too fond of Barbara, either."

Though he didn't really know Tom outside of Googie's, Steve admits to disliking him intensely. Apparently, Tom's browbeating nature was only made worse when he had a few drinks in him, and by all accounts, by this time both his and Barbara's drinking had reached an all-time high.

While Neal's nephew Walter Burr says, "Tom didn't do a lot of drinking when I stayed with him and Barbara that summer at her house," he adds, "that doesn't mean he couldn't knock them back if he wanted to. I don't find his [Hayes] description of Tom as being inaccurate or out-of-character at all. If things had gotten bad in his and Barbara's relationship, I could see him drinking more and getting a lot nastier with people.

"My uncle always treated me well, but he definitely was a bully. In fact, I'm sure it was his temperament that kept him from having a more successful acting career. In those days you had to kiss a lot of ass in Hollywood if you wanted to work, and Tom simply refused to do it. I think he'd sooner beat the crap out of a person than kiss their ass. My uncle had a massive ego, and a temper to match."

"I twice had run-ins with Neal," says Steve, "and but for Barbara interfering and telling him to knock it off, we probably would have gone outside. I was as big as him (and had been fighting guys for most of my 22 years because I was considered 'pretty' looking) and I was willing to fight him any time or place he wanted, but unfortunately he never took me up on it.

"The only reason Neal beat up Franchot Tone was that Franchot was older and a frail, elegant guy (at best). If she had wanted to, Babs herself could have probably kicked the hell out of Tone."

Steve recalls the second clash he had with Tom as being the worst of the two incidents at Googie's, and he says that it was brought on by Tom's manhandling of Barbara.

"It was the last time I saw them together," he says. "A Saturday night, I think, and they'd obviously had some sort of argument before arriving. When they walked in, Tom was gripping Barbara by the upper arm and although she wasn't struggling, she certainly didn't seem too happy about it."

At first, Steve says he resisted the urge to interfere. Though still fond of Barbara, he felt that she was at least partly responsible for the way Tom was treating her. "She was a big girl and could have dumped Neal anytime she wanted to. Staying with him for as long as she did led me to believe she actually enjoyed the rough stuff."

Steve stopped by their booth on one of his trips down the aisle, and said hello to Barbara. "She gave me a tight-lipped smile but didn't speak. Neal sat across from her and I didn't even bother to look at him. I went back to the front of the restaurant and after a few minutes I heard them arguing about something. Tom yelled at Barbara and when she yelled back, he reached across the table and grabbed her wrist and twisted it. I remember hearing their coffee cups being knocked over and seeing coffee spilling onto the floor."

The waitress who had been serving the couple came up to Steve and said that it looked to her like there was going to be trouble between them. She suggested to him that he should ask them to leave before things got any worse. But before Steve could attend to the matter, his then-wife Janet, who worked at Googie's on the weekends as a cashier, went over to speak to Tom, with whom she always had a fairly good rapport. She managed to calm him down, and both Tom and Barbara agreed to keep quiet.

Things appeared to be settled, but ten or fifteen minutes later, the couple was arguing and swearing at each other again.

By 1953, Barbara's hard-drinking and freewheeling lifestyle was beginning to take a toll on her looks. From the Author's Collection

"Everyone in the place turned to look," Steve remembers. "I went up to the table and said, as politely as I could (through gritted teeth, probably) that either they both cut it out, or they would have to leave. With that, Neal jumped up and got in my face, calling me the usual names one gets called in such situations. He told me to fuck off and then added, 'What the fuck are you going to do, asshole, throw us out of here?'

"I took off my wristwatch (it's a trick I learned early on that warns the other person that I'm not bluffing) and said, 'If I have to, yes.' Then I said, 'Actually, I'll just call the cops and have them throw the both of you out.'

"That's when Barbara got up and called Neal a fucking bastard, and then stormed out of the restaurant."

At that point, Rudy Diaz, a Hollywood vice cop who went on to become a character actor in films and TV, came into Googie's and joined Steve and Tom once he saw what was going on. After Steve explained the situation to him, Diaz told Tom to get lost or he would arrest him.

"Rudy was tough and very well known around The Corner," Steve says, "as was a guy named Big Bob Drummond, who never hesitated to jump in to stop fights before they got out of hand since he, too, had worked as a Hollywood cop. I'm sure Neal knew both of them and probably always tried to stay out of their way."

When Diaz threatened to lock him up, Tom immediately backed down. "I remember he told me that I was a lucky sonofabitch, and then he took off after Barbara. As far as I know, it was the last time either one of them came into Googie's.

"Truthfully, I wish I had gone outside with Tom that night and settled things with him, man to man. At two or three in the morning when most people had already headed home, and with Tom far from sober, the fight wouldn't have lasted very long. But maybe it's better I didn't. Tom was no pushover and even when you win a fight, you can still get hurt. And losing teeth or getting your nose broken isn't good for the old acting career, you know? But, God, I really wanted to smack him that night. What a prick he was."

Steve saw Barbara a few days later at Ah Fong's, a popular Chinese restaurant that was owned by Asian character actor Benson Fong (of *Charlie Chan* fame). Ah Fong's was located across from Schwab's Drugstore, in the same block as the Sunset Strip's famous Greenblat's Deli, the only one of the three businesses that is still standing today.

"Barbara was sitting in the restaurant alone and said she was waiting for some guy," says Steve. "I don't know whom, as she didn't say. Babs apologized for the ruckus that she and Tom had caused at Googie's and said she had dropped him for good. I was glad for her but frankly I didn't believe that their 'breakup' would last."

Steve Hayes' intuition was dead-on. A few days later, Barbara and Tom were back together and back in the gossip columns, too; this time,

Title lobby card for Barbara's slapdash 1953 western, **The Great Jesse James Raid.** *From the Author's Collection*

for causing a row at a party at an unnamed actor's house in Laurel Canyon. Apparently they were both inebriated and had been asked by the party's host to leave following a particularly unruly dispute that had turned physical.

"Barbara laughed about it and said that she and Tom had ransacked the joint," says Tina Ballard. "Throwing things around, and breaking stuff, and it wasn't even their house. It was like they had begun using each other as punching bags, and they didn't care who saw it. It was insane.

"Over time I saw Barbara's personality completely change. And it was absolutely all due to alcohol."

Chapter Twenty-One:
Hot Love Hits Tank Towns

Like two killer scorpions fighting in a cocktail glass, Barbara and Tom's relationship had become one long, bloody spectacle. Despite the fact that they were sinking fast in a mire of booze and violence, in early 1953 an undaunted Tom had a brainstorm. Why not seek out acting opportunities where the couple could capitalize on their notoriety—and rapidly withering fame—by offering themselves up as a package deal? Armed with what must have seemed like a brilliant idea to him at the time, Tom immediately went to his producer friend Robert Lippert at Lippert Pictures and pitched his and Barbara's acting services for a paltry sum.

A small-time movie studio that author Kirk Crivello, in his book *Fallen Angels: The Lives and Untimely Deaths of 14 Hollywood Beauties*, calls "the cemetery of burned-out stars," Lippert Pictures specialized in quick, inauspicious Westerns and lowbrow comedies featuring the likes of such lesser-known performers as Richard Travis, Sheila Ryan and Sid Melton. Having hired Tom in the past for the tepid programmers *Stop That Cab* and *Let's Go Navy!*, among others, studio chief Robert Lippert quickly accepted the actor's proposal. In March, 1953, he cast Barbara and Tom in a cheap, Grade-Z Western, *The Great Jesse James Raid*, which he had commissioned his son, Bob Lippert, Jr., to produce.

Shot partially on location in L.A.'s Bronson Canyon in just eight days, the film cast perennial B-actor Willard Parker in the role of the legendary title character, who reluctantly comes out of retirement to assist outlaw Bob Ford (Jim Bannon) and his ragtag gang of crooks in their attempt to steal $300,000 in gold.

Barbara, billed second in the minor role of Kate, a tough but tenderhearted saloon singer who is also involved in the heist, has a production number, "That's the Man for Me," which she delivers in a

James Anderson, Wallace Ford, Tom Neal, Willard Parker, Jim Bannon and Barbara in a scene from The Great Jesse James Raid. *From the Author's Collection*

suitably husky voice. Tightly corseted in a red velvet gown, Barbara shimmers on stage in her dance hall scenes, but elsewhere in the film she appears languid and bloated. (21)

An unshaven Tom, third-billed as a lecherous thug lusting after Barbara, also appears fatigued in a lifeless performance. The many nights the couple had spent drinking and bickering 'til dawn had obviously caught up with them, depleting their acting reserves and leaving them physically wiped out. In fact, the most energy either of them generates is when Tom wrestles with Barbara in a fight scene, during which she slaps his face and screams the immortal line, "You rotten, low-down, rummy piece of muck!" Later, in a bid to evoke some sympathy for her character, Barbara briefly shows a softer side to the most decent member of the gang, Johnny Jorette (played by James Anderson), to whom she whispers, in a world-weary voice: "Funny how you sometimes meet the nice ones at the wrong time." She delivers the line with a wistful and knowing quality, like it had been plucked from her own life. Despite the tender exchange between her bad girl character and Johnny, Barbara later suffers another on-camera death scene when the horse-drawn wagon she's riding in is dynamited, and crushes her under its wheels.

The Great Jesse James Raid, which reunited Barbara with *Bad Blonde* director Reginald LeBorg, was filmed using a grainy (and unremarkable) new photo process called Ansco-Color, and proved to be an overall dismal affair. According to its producer, though, it sold a respectable number of tickets upon its July 17, 1953 release, and was considered to be a minor hit for the studio.

"The film was well-received by theater exhibitors," claims Bob Lippert, Jr. "4,500 bookings in 1953 was exceptional for a 'B' or second feature. Considering that it had a budget of well under $100,000, *Jesse* made a nice profit. In fact, every film released through Lippert Pictures made a profit. Not one loss. That has to be a record."

Western film historian Boyd Magers agrees that the bush-league studio had its merits. "Lippert did produce some minor classics (*The Steel Helmet, Little Big Horn, Rocketship X-M*, etc.), so perhaps its somewhat bad reputation is undeserved. Robert Lippert definitely knew the market

Tom and Barbara before their fight scene in The Great Jesse James Raid. *Courtesy of Wisconsin Center for Film and Theater Research*

for his films, and knew how to make a buck stretch (and return), too. That said, however, *The Great Jesse James Raid* was not one of the studio's better efforts."

Bob Lippert, Jr. says that despite their noticeably worn-down countenance, Barbara and Tom did their best during the film's week-long shoot. "They were both competent and professional actors. Barbara and Tom always came to the set well-prepared, and they got along great with the crew. I thought that Barbara, in particular, really tried to do something with her part, even though it was quite small. I noticed that she attempted to convey a lot about her character, facially, because, you know, her dialogue in the film was rather limited. I had no problems at all with either her or Tom. They were good, all-around people; hard-working and very personable. After *Jesse*, I would have worked with them again if I had been given the chance."

A candid of a burnt-out looking Tom and Barbara on the set of The Great Jesse James Raid. *From the Author's Collection*

Rare, autographed ad for the summer stock play, The Postman Always Rings Twice. *Courtesy of Bill Baxter*

Commenting on Barbara's weathered appearance in the film, Lippert goes on to say, "To tell you the truth, I honestly don't think Barbara was all that irresistible or attractive; at least, not when we shot the film. She had gained an awful lot of weight. Whatever drinking she did was really sticking to her.

"Barbara wasn't a real looker, like Rita Hayworth was, for instance, but she was a nice person. Not a snob or anything like that, just a real down-to-earth, small-town kind of girl. But one, I might add, with a load of problems.

"Barbara blew it. She started out at Warner Bros. in 'A' pictures, had the whole world at her feet, and she blew it."

That realization, apparently, was not lost on Barbara. According to her pal Tina Ballard, Barbara hated nearly everything about the film: "She said the sets were dusty and hot and that she felt miserable the whole time. Barbara thought the finished film was a piece of trash and she said, 'Can you believe I had to do that lousy movie for next to nothing after working with James Cagney? If this is what my acting career has come to, I better just hang it up.' Barbara was really, really depressed after making the film and I think she kind of took it out on Tom for getting them into it in the first place."

Although *The Great Jesse James Raid* may have sold an admirable number of tickets, it failed to create a flurry of film offers for the lackluster acting team of Barbara Payton and Tom Neal. Subsequent plans for them to star in a picture to be lensed in Mexico fell through, as did an action film titled *Prisoner of War*. As a result, Tom abandoned his duties as Barbara's personal manager, leaving her career once again floundering, and without direction. It was becoming increasingly apparent that professional opportunities for the pair were rapidly drying up.

In the spring of 1953, as she was preparing to leave for England for a purported new film assignment, Barbara called reporters from the *L.A. Examiner* and *L.A. Daily News* with the earthshaking report that she had (again) ended her romance with Tom. A nonchalant Barbara was quoted as saying, "We just came to the end of it. The finale was that dull." However, when the film job in London fell through, Barbara ambled back to Tom and announced to the press that they would be married in Ensenada on May 19. Soon afterward, an offer surfaced for the two of them to act in summer stock, and with no other jobs pending, the couple postponed their marriage plans to grab the opportunity before it slipped away.

That June, a newly revitalized Barbara and Tom packed their bags and hit the highway to tour in a tasteless and quickly slapped together road show production of James M. Cain's *The Postman Always Rings Twice*, taking on the roles made famous by Lana Turner and John Garfield in the classic 1946 Hollywood film.

Barbara and Tom at the beginning of their summer stock tour of The Postman Always Rings Twice. *Courtesy of Harry Ransom Humanities Research Center/ Journal-American Collection*

A teasingly worded advertisement for the play beckoned: "*See Barbara and Tom Enact Torrid Love Affair Nightly in a Powerful Blend of Homicide and Passion!*" The entertainment weekly *Variety* was evidently not impressed, however, and wrote in its review of the play: "Payton and Neal may look the parts, but their performances are indecisive and strictly summer stock. Late in the second act, she dons a tight white bathing suit, and he puts on brief swimming trunks in a beach scene that's pretty embarrassing."

A far more complimentary opinion of the couple was given by the late Leslie Snyder, who was the ex-wife of television writer Howard Snyder and a former assistant to Louella Parsons. Snyder attended one of the show's first performances and was mesmerized by Tom and Barbara's onstage chemistry. "Their performances were electric," she told her friend,

Barbara, as she appeared in the summer stock production of The Postman Always Rings Twice. *Courtesy of Jan Redfield*

actor Bill Ramage. "The sexual passion that Tom and Barbara felt for each other was so evident and so real, it just blazed over the footlights. It was an exciting thing to behold."

Early publicity photos used to promote the play showed a shirtless, muscular and well-oiled Tom strutting his stuff in satin boxing trunks, with Barbara, at her most seductive, opting for a Monroe-like pose in a sexy, black negligee. The sordid aura that surrounded the couple seemed deliberately played up for its maximum exploitive effect.

Hot Love Hits Tank Towns is how the June 1953 issue of *Sensation* magazine described the tour; however, a press photo of the pair taken after they arrived in Chicago on July 23 suggested that some of that "hot love" had cooled. The photo showed an uncomfortable-looking Tom with his arm around Barbara, whose tumid appearance and horn-rimmed glasses had rendered her almost unrecognizable. Clearly, whatever enthusiasm the couple had mustered up at the beginning of the engagement had vanished less than two months later.

A publicity still of Barbara and Tom used to promote their play, The Postman Always Rings Twice. *Courtesy of Jan Redfield*

That point was driven home just hours after the photo was taken when, during the play's packed, opening night performance at the Drury Lane Theater, Barbara collapsed twice while on stage. After the first incident, in which she fell to the floor during a scene with co-star Greg Robbins, Barbara stood up and ad-libbed to the audience, "I must be

Hours before her drunken collapse on stage at The Drury Lane Summer Theatre, Barbara arrives at Chicago airport with her boyfriend and co-star, Tom Neal (July 23, 1953). Courtesy of Archive Photos

riding a charley horse," only to immediately collapse again, this time, in a dead faint. Moments later, Tom rushed in and with Robbins' help, carried her off to the wings. Soon afterward, it was announced that Barbara would be unable to continue working, and the rest of the evening's performance was canceled.

Following her collapse, Barbara was brought to the emergency room at nearby Evanston Hospital, where a muscle spasm in her left leg was given as the published reason for the incident. However, it was later rumored that for several hours prior to the show, she had been partying in the couple's room at the Blackstone Hotel, and had instead, passed out from too much vodka. Whatever the reason, Barbara made a complete recovery, following a few hours of rest at the hospital. The trade papers reported that "admission was promptly refunded to an angry audience of 650 persons who had come to see 'the Tempestuous Hollywood Lovers' emote."

As the summer-stock run of *Postman* limped along from Detroit, Pittsburgh and Chicago to several dead-end, backwater towns in the Southwest for its final performances, new rumors surfaced that Barbara and Tom were once again (as Tina Ballard had alleged) "using each other as punching bags." Naturally, the story hit many of the nation's newspapers, with syndicated columnist Dorothy Kilgallen writing, "Those explosions from way down in Texas are just Barbara Payton and Tom Neal staging battles—the likes of which haven't been seen in the Lone Star State since the Alamo."

The Postman Always Rings Twice ended its decidedly non-record-breaking run in September 1953, after which the bickering couple headed back to Hollywood to count their $1,500-a-week haul—along with their ever-diminishing prospects.

By 1953, Barbara's participation in these threadbare films and stage shows was a clear indication that her once red-hot acting career was sputtering to its inevitable end. In seemingly record time, her name had become absolute poison in Hollywood, especially to those who fancied themselves part of the town's elitist faction. The mischievous and fast-living hoyden from the tiny Minnesota town was now Hollywood's premier scarlet woman. A sex-behind-the-scenery, back lot honey with no morals; a female Tom Neal, if you will. Studio and stage doors alike were slamming shut to Barbara at an alarming pace, and the hollow echo they made could be heard all across town.

Between their frequent trips to the unemployment office, Barbara and Tom finally realized they had had enough of each other. By now, it was apparent that Tom was the victim of an unofficial, but very real, blacklisting, for his film work in Hollywood had completely dried up following *The Great Jesse James Raid*. As one report noted, "Barbara had been so hooked on Neal, she refused offers of better things to stay with him. In time, the offers stopped, and when no money came in, their love went out the window."

Tina Ballard says, "Barbara and Tom had the type of relationship where none of us ever knew what to expect next. After the fight with Franchot, no matter what Barbara or Tom did, or where they were seen, the newspapers just ate them up. Barbara started drinking more heavily, I think, because of all the stress she was feeling over her difficulties with Tom.

"When I first heard about her being drunk and fainting on stage in Chicago, I thought, 'Oh well, I may hate what she's doing to herself, but I still love her.' But you couldn't tell Barbara a thing. Even Tom couldn't. Barbara always listened—with her eyes wide open—and then she would turn around and do exactly what she wanted."

"In those years, Tom was on a supreme ego trip," offers his nephew, Walter Burr. "That, to me, was his biggest problem. He thought nothing of using people, particularly if he thought they could do him some good. That included Barbara, I'm sure. She took care of most of his bills when they were together, no doubt about it.

"My time in Hollywood with Barbara and Tom was a real mind-blowing adventure. It was a different world from what I knew, and I didn't like a lot of the people I met there. There was no honesty. Everyone, including my uncle, was talking about this movie deal, or that movie deal, and what their agent was up to. Barbara wasn't like that, though; she didn't seem to have the sickening ego that Tom had. She was always just 'regular folks' around me. I felt bad that their relationship didn't work out because I really liked Barbara. She had a hell of a lot going for her; probably a lot more than my uncle did, in fact."

"Barbara really was spellbound by that bum," says her future acquaintance, Bill Ramage. "According to Leslie Snyder (who often incurred her boss Louella Parsons' wrath by speaking up for Barbara), it was common knowledge in town that Tom Neal smoked a lot of pot, boozed and swore like a truck driver. By the time I met Barbara in 1958, word went way back that Neal was a total lowlife and a complete waste. I personally believe he helped destroy Barbara's career, as well as his own."

Barbara's son John Lee has a completely different take on Tom Neal: "I know they were a disaster for each other, but when I look at the photos I have of the two of them together, smiling and looking happy, I'm reminded of how they always seemed to be that same way when I was around them. Though I was obviously very young when my mother lived with Tom—I was only six years old when they split up—I remember him to be a fun guy who was never angry or abusive to me or my mother when I was with them.

"Tom was at home with us, and he was like a father to me. He taught me how to take a shower and other guy things; you know, like how to pee standing up. Tom wasn't one of the 'here tonight, gone tomorrow' guys in Mom's life. He was a nice man to me, never treating me like a burden or a nuisance, even though I've got to believe I probably was one, at times.

"I know nothing about Tom ever hitting my mother. I never even saw them argue. As far as I'm concerned, he won the fight (with Franchot Tone), and lost the war."

Tom hadn't only lost the war with Barbara; both of them clearly had lost the war with Hollywood, as well. Although they still had a small share of supporters among their fellow actors, by late 1953 Barbara and Tom were regarded by most of the industry to be Hollywood bottom fish; two failed opportunists on the fringes. "They were Hollywood 'white trash,'" says Skip E. Lowe. "Trouble with a capital T. People steered clear of them."

Tom and Barbara's professional problems, along with her incessant drinking, had created an atmosphere of unrelenting animosity, and word continued to spread through town that they were, according to Lowe, "beating the shit out of each other."

In the end, their relationship simply buckled under its own massive weight, and then collapsed in a dark cloud of dust. After two raucous years, Tom got off the roller coaster and moved out of Barbara's apartment right before Thanksgiving of 1953. He hung around town for a while hoping for another film, but when it didn't come, Tom split for Palm Springs, and a new life, in 1955.

The popular '50s tabloid *Inside Story* may have best summed up the news of their breakup. "Neal went back to his barbells," it wrote. "Barbara went back to the bars."

Bill Ramage says, "Barbara made her first big mistake by reacting to those 'hot peppers' that she said she felt when she first met Neal. A cold shower instead might have saved her a lifetime of Hell."

Barbara's final words on the subject of Tom Neal were characteristically flippant. With a cigarette dangling from her mouth and both hands on her hips, Barbara shrugged her shoulders and told reporters, "Yes, it's over. But he sure was great while he lasted."

Chapter Twenty-Two:
Back in the Arms of Trouble

Despite her blasé attitude, Barbara's split with Tom left her shattered. She had seemed to transfer her need for approval from her father to Franchot, and then to Tom, whose abandonment of her only reinforced her increasing lack of self-worth. "She really loved Tom," says Tina Ballard. "In fact, she idolized him, in a way. Even when there were problems between them—and there were many—Barbara would always look at Tom with such adoration (and awe). She was attracted to him physically, but I believe there was a lot more to it than that. I think she really admired his cocky attitude, and of course, deep down she believed she would be the one who would finally break through that tough-guy exterior of his. It was that challenge of getting the bad boy to reform and behave, you know? Though I'm not entirely sure she would have liked that, either.

"When Barbara and Tom broke up for good I don't think she was expecting it, and she was devastated. Barbara really seemed to go wild after that."

In an attempt to dispel the sadness and disappointment that surrounded her after Tom left, Barbara arranged for John Lee to come live with her on a more permanent basis. The six-year-old, though living very happily with Al and Dorothy Zollinger at their trailer home in Compton, jumped at the chance to be with his mother again.

For the first time since his infancy, John Lee got to spend an extended period of time with Barbara, and his recollections of their reunion in late 1953, he says, "are like memories in beige; kind of dusty, and frozen in time."

"When I lived with my mother on Courtney Terrace," he says, "a typical night out for us was dressing up and going to Chinatown for dinner. Ah, yes, Tiki dining and sugar cane in Chinatown. Drinks for

Mom, and Shirley Temples (or, in my case, Hopalong Cassidys) for me. That's a wonderful memory of just the two of us, together. Another is buying live lobster with Mom and watching her cook them alive. On those nights when we stayed home, we ate meals together in the dining room, just like other families do. Mom was a great cook and I loved everything she made, with the exception of rutabagas (truly a nasty vegetable). In those years, of course, the refrigerator was an icebox, and I remember the big blocks of ice it held and how Mom would chip at it for ice for our drinks.

"I also remember the many cocktail parties Mom threw at the house, the Hopalong Cassidy bicycle she bought for me, and playing alone in the alleyway and carports behind the building. It was at the Courtney Terrace house that I first started to read (*Dick and Jane* books, I believe). In fact, I spent many hours reading (and being read to by my mother) on the couch that faced the fireplace in the living room. She was absolutely 'hands-on' and patient with me, and I hung on every moment we had together."

John Lee recalls a memorable Christmas that year. "I remember hiding on the stairway landing one evening, waiting for Santa Claus to arrive. I could see the glow of the Christmas tree lights from there and

Barbara's son John Lee Payton on Christmas Day, 1953. Courtesy of John Lee Payton

I figured I would put cookies and milk out and just wait there for him. Well—and I am not making this up—I swear I heard sleigh bells on the roof that night. To this day, I wonder how my mother accomplished that. It was a child's fantasy come true, courtesy of Mom, no doubt. She had given me an exciting and unforgettable Christmas, and I remember how happy it made her, as well."

John also remembers a far less delicate episode involving his mother. "One afternoon I was sitting on the toilet and Mom had to *go* really bad. She said she couldn't wait, so she barged into the bathroom and climbed up on the sink and then peed in it, right in front of me. Afterwards, we both laughed about it like a couple of maniacs. Yes, I admit the incident was a bit off-kilter, but that's just the way it always was with Mom.

"Scattered memories of my mother, and of our home life together, some sharper than others, have kept her close to me through the years. The times I spent alone with her were always good."

Despite Barbara's rediscovery of her son and of the happiness he brought her, something inside her saw fit to undermine her efforts, just as it always had. Naturally, this involved a new man in her life, and yet another disastrous relationship.

Shortly after John Lee's return, Barbara began seeing a black man known only as "Budo" to her friends. He was a young Bohemian artist who built and sold intricately crafted mobiles for a living, and John Lee remembers him to be "a wonderful man", but one not without serious problems of his own.

Jan Redfield says, "None of us, other than Johnny, ever met Budo, and Barbara never offered much information about him, either. I do remember we cautioned her never to let Lee or Mabel know about him, though, as they both would have been very upset. There were two black people who worked for Lee back in Odessa—one, in the motel, cleaning and repairing things, and the other, a lady, helping Mabel in the house—and Frank said that Lee had always treated them pretty badly. In all honesty, Lee was very prejudiced toward people of color. If he and Mabel had known that Budo was involved with Barbara and Johnny they would have gone ballistic. I don't think the relationship (between Barbara and Budo) lasted more than a few months—if that."

"I idolized the man," says John Lee today. "Only he and Tom Neal remain in my memory as men who actually seemed to want me to be a part of their relationship with my mother. (Sadly, I barely remember

Franchot Tone at all, so I can't really say how he treated me.) Budo was the one who gave me my nickname of 'John-O.' I liked that because it sounded a lot like Budo to me, and I was crazy about him.

"Although I recall him being at our house on Courtney, I think Mom and I usually went to his apartment, somewhere in downtown Hollywood. They may have gone out in public together, but I don't think we three ever did. I remember his place was small and painted all white with beautiful wood floors. The front was divided off from the back by a kind of curtain, so it may have been an efficiency apartment.

"Budo was a very talented artist. Those mobiles he made were real contemporary-looking and beautifully designed. He and I even built some wooden airplanes together. They were gliders, made of balsa wood skinned with tissue paper, and we flew them on the big lawn in front of Mom's apartment. Of course, I mostly watched him build them, but he was always very patient with me. The last airplane we flew, a kind of Piper-looking aircraft, crashed badly, breaking the wings, but it didn't faze Budo. Really, not very much did. He was a pretty mellow guy."

But the truth is, Budo had a barely contained dark side, and one day, without warning, the demon inside him overtook the peaceful artist, and turned on John Lee.

One evening at Barbara's house, Budo, for reasons still unknown to John Lee, flew into a rage and came after the boy with a butcher knife. Fifty years later it is difficult for John to recall the exact scenario of what happened that night, but he suspects the attack may have followed an argument, or possibly even a breakup, between Barbara and Budo. He is also unsure of Barbara's whereabouts at the time of the attack. "She may have been chased upstairs by Budo and locked herself in her room, or she may have been trying to stop him from attacking me. Or, she might not have even been home. I just can't remember—maybe I've blocked that part out. All I know is that he came after me with that freakin' knife, and I thought I was going to die."

Frightened beyond words as Budo screamed and chased him through the house, the youngster crawled under a table on the landing leading down to Barbara's living room, and cowered there while the enraged man repeatedly tried to slash him with the knife. Luckily for John Lee, Budo couldn't quite reach him, but nonetheless continued screaming and jabbing at the air, hoping to wound the child in the process. After several nightmarish minutes that to a six-year-old must have seemed like an eternity, Budo gave up and bolted for the attic where he hid for the next two days.

While John Lee recalled Barbara being concerned by what had happened, she made no effort to notify the police (or at least, not right away). Perhaps she felt sorry for Budo, whose self-imprisonment in the attic seemed to convey his feelings of remorse for what he had done. Or perhaps she feared the negative publicity that would come if the story hit the papers. Or, and this is just as likely, perhaps she simply enjoyed the drama.

Barbara's constant need for danger and excitement in her life often found her orchestrating events that would then quickly spin out of control. Whether that was the case in this particular incident is not known, however it's clear that the turmoil she had helped create had now engulfed her son as well, whose only crime was his innocent trust in the adults responsible for his safety. That he would be subjected to an episode of such terror and violence was unconscionable of Barbara (whether intentional, or not) and proved that her maternal instincts were, at times, almost shockingly nonexistent.

For nearly two full days following the attack, Budo stayed cloistered in the attic, where, John Lee says, he and Barbara could hear him moving around and, at times, "Scratching at something. He wouldn't talk to us and he wouldn't come down. Finally, on the second day, my mother phoned the police. Two officers drove out to the house and somehow got him to come down and as soon as he did, they handcuffed him."

As the police officers dragged Budo past Barbara and John Lee, the little boy noticed that Budo had used the knife he had wielded on him to carve a big, bloody heart in his chest, along with Barbara's initials. It was a desperate act, for sure, but Budo's carved-up torso seemed to fascinate John Lee much more than Barbara, who seemed more perturbed than impressed. As far as she was concerned, the overture (outrageous as it was) was a complete waste of time. Once Barbara lost her respect for someone, it was gone, and no amount of self-mutilation, or anything else, could bring it back. And with Budo now turning on her son, well, it was clear that he had more than worn out his welcome.

In spite of the trauma that he had suffered, John Lee recalls how painful it was to know that his friend was going to jail. "As the policemen walked him across the lawn, Budo tried to hide the cuffs from me, all the while apologizing over and over again for coming after me with the knife.

We were both crying like babies and I kept telling him that I loved him. Even though I was scared out of my mind during the entire ordeal, I still cared a lot for Budo. Underneath all his problems, he was a wonderful person. But after he left that day with the police, I never saw him again. Neither did Mom, I guess. He was gone, out of our lives forever, and that was that."

Unfortunately, the kind of emotionally charged and violent scene that Budo had caused had become all too commonplace to Barbara, who by now saw an overly forceful nature to be a kind of mandatory requirement in her boyfriends. It no longer seemed important to her whether the drama was about two actors duking it out to win her favor, or a jilted (and possibly drug-addled) artist carving her initials in his chest. What was important was the feeling that she still had that kind of immense power and influence over men; Barbara needed that, it seemed, far and above anything else.

It is almost inconceivable today to think that no one in Barbara's family or circle of friends confronted her about her lifestyle following Budo's attack on her son, yet it appears that nothing was ever said about it. In fact, says Jan Redfield, neither Lee nor Mabel was ever told of the incident, and before long it was simply swept under the rug and no longer discussed, along with all the rest of Barbara's problems.

"Avoidance was the only way to keep peace in that family," says Jan. "Looking back now, it was a big mistake for everyone to turn a blind eye to the people Barbara was associating with, and to the things she was doing, but we always tried to make sure Lee didn't have a reason to go after her. Because, believe me, when he did, it always turned ugly.

"I guess we were all hoping that Barbara would just snap out of that crazy behavior once and for all and, I don't know, maybe grow up a little."

While Lee and Mabel rarely saw Barbara during this tumultuous period, they were spending a lot of time with Frank and Jan (who had recently given birth to their second son, Gary). Lee's objection to Barbara's lifestyle was in direct contrast to his unflagging support of his son and daughter-in-law, who were living in a modest home in North Long Beach following Frank's discharge from the Navy.

As Jan explains, "After Frank came home from the service he decided to go back to school. He wound up taking two years of flying lessons, funded by the GI Bill. Lee and Mabel came to visit us right after Gary was born, on August 22, and when Lee saw where we were living he

A 1953 candid of Barbara and her mother Mabel during one of Barbara's infrequent (and often troubled) visits to her parents house in San Diego. Courtesy of Arlene Shaner

immediately made Frank go out and look for another place for us to live. Less than one month later, Frank found a nice house for us in Los Altos, and Lee insisted on covering the down payment. In the early 1950s, three hundred and fifty dollars down and the rest on the GI Bill was a great deal, and we really appreciated Lee's help.

"Lee was always generous with Frank and me. In fact, he never denied anyone in our family, anything."

Jan's son, Les Redfield, now a successful businessman in L.A., agrees. "Grandpa Lee thought nothing of spoiling us kids. I was often asked to ride along with him to the market or liquor store or wherever he had

Barbara's last nice residence, at 1534 North Beverly Drive in West Los Angeles. Courtesy of Tim Choate

errands to run. One time I asked for a comic book while at the liquor store and he told me to buy all the ones I wanted so that we wouldn't have to make any more trips.

"Another time he saw a display of Cracker Jacks behind the counter of a little store near the house. He asked my brother and me if we liked Cracker Jacks, and when we said we did, he bought the entire display on the spot (maybe 25 to 30 boxes). Later, he ignored the objections of my parents and grandmother and insisted we could open every box. We went home that day with a large grocery bag full of loose Cracker Jacks.

"As a kid, I accepted my grandparents as they were and never really thought there was anything wrong with them. I know they drank a lot, and there were often visits that ended prematurely because of arguments, but no one seemed to take it personally, and life just went on without any apparent hard feelings."

That is, except for Barbara. As Jan says, "Lee always found fault with Barbara and with everything she did, and unfortunately that never changed."

CHAPTER TWENTY-THREE:
High Times and Heartaches

As her parents helped Frank and his family settle into a comfortable new home in suburban Los Altos, Barbara struggled to regain some order in her life in Hollywood. Humbled by her latest troubling liaison, the 26-year-old made a determined effort to cut down on her drinking and get herself back on track. Though still at liberty professionally, Barbara thought the best way to pick herself up would be to make a change of residence. In early 1954, she left her Courtney Terrace apartment and rented a bigger house at 1534 North Beverly Drive, near The Beverly Hills Hotel. Seven-year-old John Lee, faithful and devoted to his mother, as always, came with her.

A beautiful, ranch-style home with a small, second-story at the rear of the house and a built-in swimming pool, Barbara's new domicile sat on a nice piece of property that backed up to a steep cliff fifty feet high. With several spacious rooms, the house was a definite step up from the much smaller apartment on Courtney that Barbara had lived in, at separate times, with both Franchot and Tom.

Tina Ballard remembers the incredible amount of work Barbara put into the new house and how she had spent many hours and thousands of dollars making it the type of home that others would envy. "Barbara did most of the painting and wallpapering herself. Her bedroom, in particular, was beautiful. The walls were a light color of purple, or violet, with white trim, and there were wooden shutters on all the windows. That girl had an eye for style and color like you wouldn't believe. She had absolutely marvelous taste.

"Barbara's bed was huge, and the wall behind the headboard was done with a smoky gray and black marbled mirror as wide as the bed. The bedspread that Barbara had specially made at a store in Beverly Hills had a soft touch of lavender to it, her dressers were all white, and all the doorknobs had a sprig of violets on them. Everything on her dressers carried out the theme of violets. The carpets were white, all the way into the big, walk-in closet where her best clothes were hung, and even her dressing area and bathroom were fully carpeted in white. She really did a magnificent and very professional job. If she had wanted to pursue it, Barbara could have easily been an interior decorator. She was that talented."

John Lee remembers the house vividly, as well. "I loved living on Beverly Drive and I especially remember all the colors in the house. I recall the living room was painted a kind of orange/red color. The outer hallway was bright yellow with a charcoal carpet and the family room at the back was gray with an orange carpet that I spilled black model airplane paint on one day while working on a model and watching TV. There was a whale pelvis in that room that Mom had gotten in Mexico, which I used as a moon setting for my spaceman set. There was also an upright piano there where Mom and I would play chopsticks and stuff. When my mother was home, it was always fun whether company was around or we were alone, practicing ballroom dancing together, or watching her do some ballet-type moves in the living room. I recall one afternoon when she posed nude for an artist who did a life-sized mural of her, and that was kind of fun to watch. I remember we goofed around and laughed like crazy over some of the poses she struck. The mural later went up in the hallway, and it was beautiful.

"The inner hallway at the house ran between the front bedroom and the library to the kitchen and the stairs that led up to Mom's bedroom. There was a wide room with Mexican tile flooring and a high ceiling that ran between the main house and the pool house. It later became my bedroom and it had louvered jalousie windows in it, which I loved. My first bedroom, however, was just off the living room at the front of the house. It was a rich green color that Mom decorated with a Roy Rogers bedspread and a matching rug. Like every other kid back then, Roy Rogers, Howdy Doody and Hopalong Cassidy were my heroes. I also had a good radio in my room and I was hooked on all the radio shows of the time, from *The Lone Ranger* to *The Shadow*. I guess you could say I was a true child of the 1950s.

"My mother's bedroom was exactly as her friend Tina described. The walk-in closet was full of hundreds and hundreds of shoes, and about a

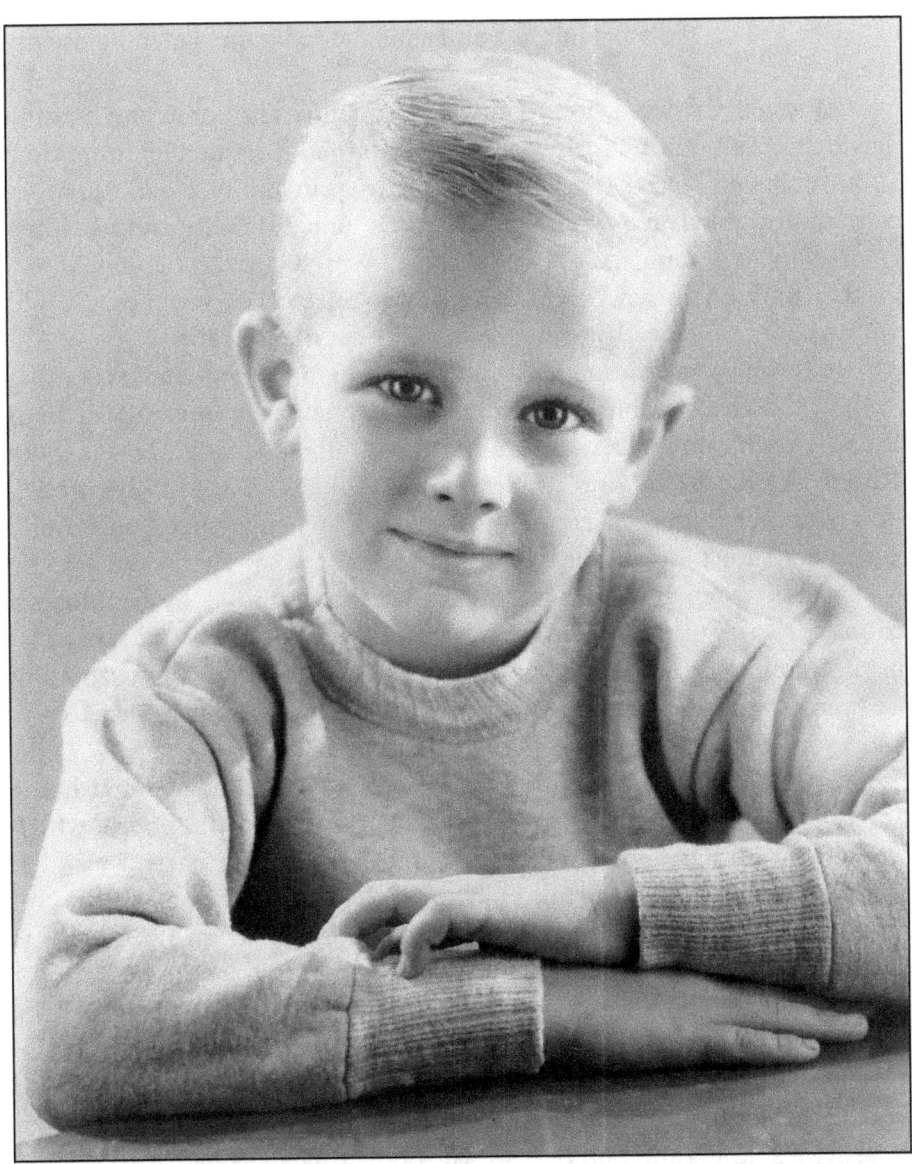

Barbara's son John Lee was her devoted companion at her new home on North Beverly Drive. Courtesy of John Lee Payton

dozen fur coats, and it was a wonderful place to go. I cherish the memories of being wrapped in my mom's furry hug before she'd go out for the night, or the laughter we shared when rolling around on her bed and playing toss with one of her 'falsies'. A goodbye hug from my mother when she was all dolled up and wearing one of her fur coats was an unforgettable experience. I can still feel her hug and smell her perfume when I close my eyes."

At seven years old, John Lee was frequently left home alone at the new house; sometimes, for several days at a time. "I spent a lot more time alone on Beverly Drive than I had at Courtney, including evenings. Mom was comfortable leaving me alone by then, and I didn't mind it, either. Even at a very young age I got along fine by myself, but, of course, if my mother took off somewhere and I ran low on food or supplies, I could always count on Dorothy or Janice to come get me if I called."

In those years, school for John Lee was an infrequent and, according to him, "barely tolerable experience." In fact, he has no memory at all of attending school regularly before the age of nine. "Mostly, I didn't go to school, as I recall," he says. "I have no idea where I was even registered. I do remember riding a school bus sometimes when we lived on Beverly Drive, but I can't remember the school itself.

"Later, when I lived with my father, I was tested by a guidance counselor to figure out where to put me. I was placed a year ahead of my age group and I attended both elementary and junior high school in Germany. Except for math, most school subjects came fairly easy to me, and I was generally happiest when buried in a book."

With so little time spent in school and a lot of time spent at home alone, John Lee loved to explore the property behind the house, which was almost rural in appearance. "I remember there was a narrow wooden staircase in the hill right behind the house that wound its way up the cliff to a small structure where I used to play. The view from up there was amazing. There were also huge avocado trees behind the house at the foot of the cliff which bore prodigiously large fruit. That entire area of Beverly Hills was gorgeous back then; it was like living out in the country.

"The swimming pool at the Beverly Drive house was very nice, too, both as a place to swim and for the grass around it where I played with my British tin soldiers and Dinky Toys. The pool also had a big flagstone patio next to it that felt great when hot from the California sun. You know that wet stone smell and warm feeling you get when you lie down dripping wet, beside the pool? It was wonderful.

"Although Mom often left me home by myself, there were regular times for us, too. Birthday parties with lots of toys, swimming, dancing and music, and I was always free to enjoy the many adult parties she threw at the house, too. By day, I continued to play alone for the most part, and was quite content to do so. It was at that house that I first began to enjoy observing human nature, and to enjoy my quiet, solitary times. I still do.

"Today, when I think of the house on Beverly Drive, I think of crystal-clear views from the hillside, bright colors in all the rooms, nonstop parties with loud music and laughter, and a beautiful swimming pool with thick green grass around it. It was an incredibly happy place and time for Mom and me. For a while, anyway."

Barbara's housekeeper, Mamie, had followed her from the Courtney Terrace apartment to her new home, and Jan Redfield remembers her continued loyalty to both Barbara and John Lee. "Mamie had a bedroom at the new house and she adored Barbara. She always took good care of her and Johnny. Mamie was a lovely woman who would have stayed with them forever if Barb didn't hit hard times."

John Lee agrees: "Mamie is a wonderful memory, going all the way back to those years at Mom's apartment on Courtney Terrace. She was a kind and loving person to us, always. I missed her when she was gone, believe me. A lot of the time, I think Mamie was the only real grownup around."

Once ensconced in her new home, and with her profile in town rebounding a bit following her breakup with Tom (and the end of her brief, and thankfully, unreported, interlude with Budo), Barbara attempted to restore some semblance of normalcy in her life. Part of her plan was to resume hosting the weekend dinner parties that had proved so popular at her previous home. Nearly every Saturday afternoon, she held an open house for her guests, which included a real cross-section of Hollywood show folk, from singer Eartha Kitt and fledgling actor John Saxon, to fellow platinum-blonde film starlet Peggy Maley and L.A. socialite (and alleged hardcore party animal) Diane Garrett. While her company mingled and caroused by the pool, Barbara could usually be found in the kitchen making a huge kettle of Buffalo Chili and one of her famous tossed salads, while sipping from her ever-present glass of vodka and orange juice. Though she had genuinely tried to cut down on her alcohol intake after her move to the new house, Barbara was soon imbibing as much as ever.

Jan attended many of these gatherings at Barbara's home and recalls how hard her sister-in-law worked to be the perfect hostess. "Barb always did all the cooking herself," she says, "and the food she prepared was just phenomenal. Barbara could put anything in a pot and turn it into a gourmet meal. The things she could do with shrimp, for instance, were amazing. I remember one party when she even had a bunch of fresh lobster flown in from Maine. In those days, Barbara invited a lot of starving young actors to her house, and, believe me, they all ate (and drank) very well."

Other guests during this time were Franchot Tone's friends Kent and June Modglin, who had remained friends with Barbara following her divorce from Tone. "Whenever they visited Barb they always brought her a case of Wente Brothers wine," says Jan, "which was pretty expensive. Barbara had the Modglins over a lot when she lived in Beverly Hills. We had dinner out by the pool and always had a great time; they were awfully nice people. One night they even had us over to their house. I'll never forget it; they lived in a beautiful glass house on top of a mountain that overlooked all of Los Angeles. We grilled steaks and drank grasshoppers, and Barbara and I got so tipsy we wound up having to stay overnight. I never drank very much after that."

One day at Barbara's, Jan remembered meeting the very sultry Eartha Kitt, "whom everyone called 'Kitten.' Barbara had taken me to see her perform a couple of times at the Mocambo nightclub, so I was really excited to finally meet her.

"Barbara loved to cook for people she liked. In fact, I think that was one of the ways she showed a person how much she cared about them. The more elaborate the meal, the more she liked you. She literally threw dozens of dinner parties at the new house, and she spent a mint on them, too. Her generosity was endless."

Raucous laughter and dancing were de rigueur at Barbara's parties, and to encourage the latter, she usually had a stack of 78s blaring on the record player in the living room. Her taste in music, as in people, was eclectic, with her collection including everything from Big Band (Artie Shaw, Tommy Dorsey and Glenn Miller) and swing (Woody Herman and Cab Calloway) to jazz (Duke Ellington) and even some raunchy, R&B (L.A. baritone saxophonist Joe Houston). [22]

"Her parties were always bi-racial," says Jan. "There were no color barriers in Barbara's world, and she wasn't status conscious, either. Her family and non-show business friends from Compton were always invited to her house right along with the movie stars. Everyone drank and danced and always had a good time. A lot of the guys at her parties were just starting out. There were lots of male models and bit players; people like that. These weren't men she was sleeping with. They were friends. Barbara opened her home to all of them."

Though still no more than a tyke, Barbara's son attended many of these gatherings, and remembered circulating and kibitzing like one of the adults. "The people and the pool parties were part of our regular routine back then," says John Lee. "I recall lots of drinking and carrying on, but I was certainly never mistreated by anyone, nor did I ever feel frightened by what I saw. It was just a bunch of rowdy, Hollywood people letting their hair down, and actually, it was very exciting for me to be part of it."

With Tom Neal and Budo out of her life for good, and with both her drinking and her feelings of loneliness gradually returning, as a result, Barbara started hitting the town again, soon after her move to Beverly Drive; this time, with an urgency she could barely contain. In one fell swoop, she dyed the front half of her platinum blonde hair a flaming red, resumed painting bizarre-looking tattoos of snakes and leprechauns on her face, and became an almost nightly barstool fixture at such local hot spots as Chasen's, LaRue's, and The Cock n' Bull. Bedecked in her finest jewelry and furs, Barbara was always friendly, often drunk, and reportedly seldom, if ever, went home alone.

"By then, she was doing some pretty off-the-wall things," claims Skip E. Lowe. "I remember hearing that Barbara had gotten into really wild behavior, like picking up strange guys in gas stations and in two-bit lounges up and down the Pacific Coast Highway. She was partying a lot at the Garden of Allah, and there were rumors that she was propositioning all the young bellboys at the hotel and taking them back to her bungalow."

Barbara's former boyfriend Steve Hayes concurs with Lowe that she was frequently seen carrying on at the Garden of Allah. "I saw her there myself," he says. "Because her reputation by the early '50s was quite sullied, the dates or wives I was with whenever I saw Babs were always put off by her. To them, she was nothing but a slut and a whore, and I think she knew they felt that way about her, too. She always acted like she didn't care, but deep down she had to feel bad about it."

"Barbara had a lot of internal conflicts," suggests Tina Ballard, in defense of her friend. "She seemed to have this dual nature, and most of us who knew the open-hearted and generous girl never saw the other Barbara, who was very—oh, how can I put it—damaged. You might say she kept that side of herself well hidden. I can see now that the other Barbara, the one who went out alone, and picked up strangers… the one

I didn't know… was very confused, and more than a bit desperate. But knowing Barbara, she probably told herself that all those hit-and-miss guys were 'boyfriends.' She could gussy up the hardest truth and make it smell like a rose, you know?"

Tina makes a strong point. By now it seemed that Barbara, like all sex addicts, had the self-deceptive part of her persona down to a fine art. Thinking of her many rendezvous as "relationships" was a way for Barbara to protect herself from the cold hard reality of what she was doing. She had become hooked on the typical high of the sex addict—the rush that comes with seeking out potential partners and then seducing them—and in this hyper-aroused state, Barbara may have felt a sense of empowerment that was impossible to resist.

"When I think about how Barbara was running wild during that time," says Jan Redfield, "I recall an incident that happened at one of her dinner parties that I think will explain a lot."

One evening in 1953 or '54, Jan says, Barbara had invited a few of her friends over for dinner, but during the party she suddenly felt ill and went upstairs to her bedroom to rest. Minutes passed and she still hadn't come down so Tina Ballard went to see if she was all right. What Tina found instead sent her running downstairs, screaming.

"I nearly jumped through my skin when I heard those screams," recounts Jan. "Tina had gone into the bedroom and found Barbara unconscious, lying on the floor in a big puddle of blood."

"Yeah, I screamed. It scared the hell out of me," says Tina. "I honestly thought Barbara was dead. I thought she had been stabbed by someone, and had bled to death, right there on her bedroom floor. I ran downstairs yelling, 'Something terrible has happened to Barbara. Somebody do something!'"

One of the other guests had the wherewithal to call for an ambulance, and within minutes Barbara was rushed to Doctors Hospital in L.A. "Barbara's fallopian tubes had burst due to an ectopic pregnancy," explains Jan, "and she had to undergo emergency surgery to have her right ovary removed. Barb had lost a lot of blood at the house, and she was quite ill."

Following the surgery, Barbara remained in the hospital for several days. "Mabel and I visited her every morning," says Jan. "During her hospitalization, Johnny and my two boys were shipped off to my parents in Compton while Mabel and I stayed at Barb's house so we could be near the hospital.

"For a while, everything was fine. Barbara was healing nicely, but then one day Mabel smuggled in a pint of vodka for her. She must have slipped it to her when I wasn't looking as I didn't know a thing about it. After a while, Mabel and I left the hospital and went back to Barbara's. That's when all hell broke loose."

The mixture of vodka and her pain medication evidently hit Barbara like a ton of bricks, and sent her into a mind-blowing frenzy. Despite her wobbly condition, she leapt out of her hospital bed, donned her mink coat and her slippers, and ran down the hallway. "Barbara was bent on leaving the hospital and coming home," claims Jan. "She even clocked a nurse who tried to restrain her. Hit her right in the chin, and decked her. Barb was always headstrong, and when she was on a roll, there was no stopping her."

Barbara managed to hail a cab outside the hospital, and the next thing Jan and Mabel knew, she was staggering through the front door of her house ("With her stitches and her hospital gown all askew underneath her fur coat," says Jan). "Even though she was usually fun to be around when she was a little high, at least in those days, Barbara was a real pain in the butt that night, due to all the medication and cheap booze in her system. She was laughing and swearing and just causing a total uproar. Believe me, it took every ounce of strength we had just to keep her down on the couch. She was so high she was almost out of her head."

The next morning, Barbara's longtime personal physician, a "Dr. Roberts," came out to the house to see her. "Barbara was so apologetic and so sincere, all Dr. Roberts did was scold her a little," remembers Jan. "Barb always had a way of grabbing at your heartstrings and even when she did something totally outrageous, you couldn't help but forgive her."

After examining Barbara and deciding that it would be all right for her to stay home for the duration of her convalescence, Dr. Roberts took Jan aside and dropped a bombshell on her. "I'll never forget it," she says. "Barbara's doctor looked me straight in the eye and told me that he was very concerned for her, not only because of her drinking, but because he believed Barbara was a nymphomaniac. He said he had spent a lot of time observing her actions over the years and that what he had seen and heard had convinced him she was emotionally ill. He told me that most women who have that problem [nymphomania] usually had a lack of affection in their childhood, and he asked me if I knew anything about her upbringing. Of course, I immediately thought of Lee and of how he was always so critical of Barbara, but for whatever reason, I kept it to myself. I didn't even tell Mabel about it. I'm sure I didn't want to create more problems between Lee and Barbara, because they were always at each other's throats as it was.

"Dr. Roberts was certain that Barbara's heavy drinking worsened this sexual problem of hers because it made her even more uninhibited. Naturally, I was shocked and didn't know what to say to him, so I don't think I said anything. Dr. Roberts felt that Barbara needed psychiatric help, but I'm not sure if he ever talked to her about it. I know I never did.

"What he said makes sense to me now—why didn't it make sense to me then?"

While Barbara's physician had obviously identified a possible cause for her chronic promiscuity, one wonders now if she may have suffered from an undiagnosed bipolar disorder, as well. Her son, John Lee, for one, thinks so. "In fact, I believe that my mother may have suffered from it for a long time and that she often used alcohol to medicate herself as her manic-depressive episodes grew more frequent and severe over the years."

According to the online encyclopedia website, Wikipedia, "Hypersexuality can be a symptom of bipolar disorder, which is part of the wider disease spectrum known as manic depression, and is generally associated with the manic phase of the disease. It can result in behavior that the manic person later regrets."

Validating this theory is author Kay Redfield Jamison, Ph.D, who wrote in her 1995 book, *An Unquiet Mind*: "Manic-depression distorts moods and thoughts, incites dreadful behaviors, destroys the basis of rational thought, and too often erodes the desire and will to live."

Barbara, of course, had frequently visited each one of these scenarios, which makes the argument of her having an undiagnosed bipolar disorder even more convincing.

Indeed, when looking at Barbara's lifestyle and at the often disastrous choices she made, it seems that an undiagnosed manic-depressive condition may very well have been lurking inside her ever since her adolescence. While there are medications today to control the condition, as John Lee points out, "In her time, the treatment for socially unacceptable and even irrational behavior resulting from manic-depression often was condemnation and ostracism—the very things my mother came to experience."

Despite this, it appears that Barbara tried, in her own way and at various times, to reach out for help; or at least, for some understanding.

"Barbara was always very explicit in her conversations with me, and she was always willing to talk about her sex life, too," says Jan, "but she and I had totally different opinions about that sort of thing. I was much more conservative, and when she would start talking about that stuff I always got very embarrassed. I remember she once told me that she never felt totally satisfied after her sexual relations, even if she thought she loved the man. I can look at all those conversations now and see that Barbara was probably trying to tell me who she really was, and maybe, in a way, she was even asking me for help. But I didn't take the hint, I guess, and of course, I regret that now.

"As for her excessive drinking, I saw it, but she was still functioning. It's not like she was drinking nonstop for days and then having to sleep it off, or anything like that. She was still out and about, and still taking care of Johnny fairly well. He always had clean clothes to wear, and he wasn't going around unfed, or anything. Of course, Mamie helped out a lot, too. She shielded Johnny from a lot that was going on. Regarding the other stuff Barbara was doing with all those men she hardly knew, she was aware that her family wouldn't accept any of that, so she was real good at keeping it from us. But I think her father always knew what she was doing; in fact, I'm sure of it. Lee always knew what Barbara was up to, and that's why he was so disgusted with her."

Of course, a strong argument can be made today that Barbara's strategy of using sex to compensate for her feelings of childhood neglect was directly tied to her father's emotional abandonment of her. Indeed, the rejection she felt by him may have played a profound role in making her the very damaged person she had become. If Lee Redfield did, in fact, know the cause of his daughter's increasingly frequent promiscuity, maybe the disgust he had always felt was not only for Barbara, but for himself, too—as well as for whatever may have occurred in their past that had breached their relationship so irreparably.

During this period of great chaos in Barbara's life, her libertine lifestyle remained press worthy; so much, in fact, that gossip columnists Hedda Hopper and Louella Parsons, the town's most scathing scandal mongers, as well as such lesser-known dirt peddlers as *L.A. Mirror* reporter Dick Williams and New York journalist Lee Mortimer, were mentioning Barbara's name now on an almost daily basis; that is, when not running blind items on her more lurid romps. In one of Hopper's syndicated columns, she christened Barbara "Hollywood's Hippest Hussy", a description that likely amused Barbara, rather than hurt her.

A circa-1970's photo of rugged, B-film actor Mickey Knox, who dated Barbara for a time in 1954. Courtesy of Mickey Knox

Though her film career had slowed down considerably, Barbara was still maintaining a high profile on the L.A. to N.Y. party circuit, and was dating a multitude of celebrities—married and unmarried, openly and secretly—in a frantic display of activity. While vacationing in Las Vegas at the Sahara Hotel (ca. 1953-54), she bedded the hotel pool's lifeguard (and soon-to-be movie Tarzan) Gordon Scott. A six foot, three inch Adonis with 19" biceps and curly hair, Scott was ripe for the picking. He later told underground filmmaker Nick Bougas that he and Barbara had "…an exciting roll-in-the-hay. Barbara hadn't gone completely around the bend yet. She still had it. She was hot."

Tough guy actor Mickey Knox also dated Barbara during this time, and remembers what he calls, "her wild innocence." Born in Brooklyn in 1922, Knox began his career on the New York stage and after serving in WWII, he had made a promising start in Hollywood as a contract player for producer Hal Wallis. His handsome looks and hard-bitten persona were shown to good advantage in a handful of late 1940s' film noirs (*I Walk Alone*, *The Accused*) and B-films (*City Across the River*), but by the early '50s, Mickey Knox's film career had noticeably stalled; due, in part, to his left-wing political leanings that had many in the industry believing he was a Communist. His subsequent blacklisting saw Knox abandoning the U.S. for many years afterward to live and work in Europe.

Barbara and Mickey Knox met at an Italian restaurant in Hollywood called Villa Frascati, which was located at the corner of Sunset and Crescent Heights Boulevard, and was frequented by many of the industry's top celebrities. As with all her past boyfriends, Barbara's exceptional beauty caught Mickey's eye immediately. He recalls, "I walked into the restaurant with my buddy Anthony Quinn, and right away I made eye contact with Barbara, who was sitting in a booth with a girlfriend. Tony and I agreed that both girls were gorgeous so we went over to introduce ourselves. We all hit it off right away so Tony and I joined them for dinner and drinks. Tony gravitated more to the girlfriend, which was all well and good, because the sparks were already flying between Barbara and me. Let me tell you, she was one hot number."

Besides her undeniable beauty, Mickey was most impressed by Barbara's candor, which he says cut through the group's surface chatter like a razor. "I noticed almost immediately that Barbara wasn't into bullshitting. She was a very straight-shooting, tell-it-like-it-is type person. And the conversation wasn't all about her. I found that to be refreshing, as well as a real turn-on."

Following dinner and a few rounds of drinks, the quartet left the restaurant, and Mickey and Barbara went back to her house in Beverly Hills. "She had a real nice place," he says. "Beautifully furnished, and with a big swimming pool out back. Right away, it was obvious to me that Barbara had done very well for herself."

Without further pretense, Mickey and Barbara made love that night, and it was the prelude, he says, to an exciting—and almost unbelievable—three-day marathon.

In an interview with author Patrick McGillan for the 1999 book, *Tender Comrades: A Backstory of The Hollywood Blacklist* (co-authored by Paul Buhle), Mickey Knox described Barbara as a compulsive and passionate lover who "…really enjoyed sex. She kept me in bed once for three days and nights, even feeding me [there]. She wouldn't let me get out of bed. I had to crawl out on my hands and knees. A helluva girl."

Today, Mickey adds a qualifying postscript to that account. "Barbara was extremely sexual," he says, "but not out-of-control. She was just interested in living in the moment and having a rip-roaring time. I must say, she was a fantastic lover—raring and uninhibited, and totally interested in my wishes and in giving me what I wanted.

"Barbara was terrific looking; a very vivacious girl, not to mention, lip-smacking sexy. She had a kind of native intelligence that was very intriguing. Not particularly book smart, but extremely intuitive."

Following their steamy, three-day encounter, Mickey and Barbara headed down to Tijuana, to continue their tryst in a locale legendary for its no-holds-barred abandon. "Over the next couple of months, we actually went down to Tijuana several times, to party. Barbara was both wild and innocent, which, of course, is a dynamite combination. She was an adventurous girl who was always ready for a good time."

One night during their affair, Barbara made a few postcoital confessions to Mickey, some of which surprised him. "Barbara told me that while she had liked and respected Franchot Tone, she was never in love with him. She did say, however, that she had loved Tom Neal, desperately. I had no reason to doubt her.

"Barbara also confided in me that she had only married Franchot to save Tom's ass from being arrested after the fight. I definitely detected some regret in her that she and Neal had split up. I think it tore her apart, actually."

Barbara's brief amour with Mickey Knox was a bit like a phosphorous flare—it flashed, red-hot, and shed a brilliant light, and then just as quickly, burned out. "There was no dramatic conclusion to it," Mickey says today. "It was just one of those Hollywood things that actors do. Soon after our affair ended, I left the country to work in Italy and I never saw her again.

"Barbara Payton was a very lovely and enigmatic woman and I greatly enjoyed our time together. Looking back, though, I have to say I saw an emptiness in her, almost like she confused being united with someone in the physical sense with being close to them emotionally. I think she was trying to fill that huge void inside her with anything she could find.

"It was as if Barbara was on the run from herself, and she never completely got away."

Following the end of her relationship with Mickey Knox, Barbara was delighted when her next suitor, a wealthy film star (whose identity is not known), bought her a $6,000 red Cadillac convertible for services rendered. "The second time he came back, I asked him what he was going to give me this time," she later wrote. "He got mad at me and I never spoke to him again. Enough of memories. They hurt."

One dubious rumor that floated around for years alleged that Barbara was also carrying on in the mid-'50s with former bandleader-turned-studio mogul Desi Arnaz, who was then enjoying tremendous success with his wife Lucille Ball on television's classic *I Love Lucy* show. A known womanizer whose penchant for flashy showgirls and hookers had long tormented his control-freak wife, Arnaz was said to have found Barbara to be completely irresistible. Sometime during this period, Ball reportedly learned of their affair and sought to humiliate Barbara, along with several other past and current flames of her husband's, at a private luncheon she held for them.

In a quote credited to singer Gordon MacRae's ex-wife Sheila, who was a close friend of Lucille Ball's: "[Lucy] once gave a luncheon for all the ladies in Hollywood who had slept with Desi—Ginger Rogers, actress Marie McDonald, Constance Moore, tennis star Gertrude 'Gussie' Moran, actress Gale Robbins and Franchot Tone's ex-wife Barbara Payton. After they were all seated, Lucy stood up, raised a glass to toast her guests, and announced, 'I want you to know there's only one person in this room who hasn't slept with my husband, and it's Sheila MacRae.'"

Today, Barbara's friend Tina Ballard laughs at the mere suggestion that such an incident ever took place. "Oh, that's a good one. I'm sure if Barbara knew Desi that well he would have helped her break into television. I mean, after all, he was one of the 'Kings of TV'.

"That story is total nonsense. Believe me, Barbara would have told me if she had gone out with him. I would bet that she never even met Lucy or Desi. Besides, do you really think Lucille Ball would have ever done such an outrageous thing as hold a luncheon for all her husband's mistresses? No way."

While Barbara's former boyfriend, Steve Hayes, agrees with Tina that the luncheon tale seems pretty farfetched, he is less inclined to discount the rumor that Barbara and Arnaz had an affair. "I never heard a thing about

Lucy hosting the luncheon but I would bet that if she had, *Confidential*, or one of the other L.A. rags, would have been all over it. A crazy scheme like that would have made a great article and even the legitimate newspapers in town would have jumped on it. No. Lucille Ball had too much class for that sort of nonsense. Besides, there is an unspoken code in the movie industry (back then, anyway), and that is: be careful whom you shit on, as one day they might be your boss.

"That said, however, I do believe that Desi would have slept with Barbara if he had a chance. Being a typical Latino, he was very macho and a bit of a Don Juan. And let's face it, like it or not, by that time practically the entire industry thought of Babs as an easy lay. In fact, with her blonde hair, blue eyes and hot body, she was probably just the type of chick Desi liked.

"But he wouldn't have given Barbara work in exchange for sex; that would have been far too risky. Desi loved money and success even more than women, and he would never have fed the press that kind of ammunition to use against him."

While the Arnaz/Payton affair remains open to question, one person Barbara did see for a time was Russian-born financier Serge Rubenstein, widely known in those years as a high-class bum and masher whose list of romantic conquests included many Hollywood actresses. Barbara and Rubinstein were seen together at various NYC clubs and she was also said to have been his houseguest for several weeks at his posh Manhattan apartment. But like most of Barbara's other past relationships, their liaison was short-lived. Several months after their affair ended, Serge Rubenstein was found beaten and strangled in that same NY apartment; a homicide that remains unsolved, more than fifty years later.

John Lee Payton admits that, as time wore on, the harmless and carefree parties his mother once threw at their Beverly Hills home, quickly became something else entirely. "By 1954 or so, the parties had gotten a lot rowdier and would often stretch late into the night or well into the next morning.

"In that house, I eventually came to see individual and group sex of every kind, lots of drunkenness and drug use, and all sorts of outlandish behavior. I didn't view it as anything out of the ordinary, however; it was just the way our little world worked."

The "sex regulars," John Lee says, were many and notable, and recognizable—even to a seven-year-old. "I saw many big stars at those parties," he says. "For a bunch of fine, upstanding celebrities, I'm amazed

By 1954, Barbara's wild behavior was attracting every drug dealer, punk and gigolo in Hollywood. Courtesy of Shirley de Dienes/de Dienes Photographic Arts

at how quick a lot of them were to later condemn my mother after she had given them such an easy venue to practice their hobby.

"By seven years old, I had come to know everything about sex, I suppose—except that it was also useful in making babies."

With her home now resembling a landing strip for every freeloader and satyr in L.A., Barbara no longer seemed very particular in her choice of companions and bounced from drug dealers to bit players to gigolos, generously bestowing her favors on all. Carrying on with punks and riffraff as often as she was with the classiest and most successful of Hollywood celebrities, Barbara was cutting a mile-wide swath through a town that was using her up even quicker than she was using it.

Sickeningly, life was going haywire again for Barbara, and this time her son was witnessing every degrading moment of it.

It was a tragic error in judgment for which she would eventually pay dearly.

Chapter Twenty-Four:
Fur Coats and... Heroin?

With the onset of the Korean War, in October 1951 Barbara's former husband, Captain John Payton, had been recalled to active duty with the Army Air Force, and was sent overseas. On Memorial Day, 1952, while navigating a B-26 bomber over Pyongyang, Korea, Payton's airplane was shot down and he was captured and held in a Communist camp for sixteen months. His son, John Lee, recounts what his father has related to him about the experience: "Dad said his plane was shot down while flying the last mission of his tour. Before their capture, he and the other crew members who had survived the crash had made their way to the coast, within view of an island that was supposed to be a rescue point for downed aircrews. They couldn't reach the island, however, and hoped somebody on our side would spot them. After three days, a local man saw them. They asked him to help and he said he would. Instead, he turned them in to the enemy."

While in captivity at the prison camp in Pyongyang, John Payton and his fellow crew members did whatever they could to make the best of an ominous situation. "My father told me that they made cigarettes by frying grass and rolling it in strips of wallpaper," John Lee says. "They were being held in an area of Korea where U.S. aircraft bombed frequently and when the planes would get too close my father and the guys would light up all their cigarettes because, as Dad put it, 'We were damned sure not going to leave any behind if we were going to get killed.'"

After nearly a year and a half behind enemy lines, John Payton and his crew were finally released in late 1953. Upon his return to the States, he telephoned Barbara, who immediately expressed an interest in reviving their long-dormant relationship. On March 27, 1954, in one of her many attempts to remain hot news, the out-of-work actress called the press to announce her plans to remarry her ex-husband, "within the next two weeks." Obviously, John was unaware of just how bad Barbara's lifestyle had gotten, and probably hoped she was still the same girl he had loved in Compton.

Still in a revved-up, publicity-crazed mode of operation, Barbara told the *L.A. Examiner*, "The other day I asked John if he would like to come to Hollywood and see me and our son, Johnny. He said, 'I'd like to come back to you both forever.'"

Barbara, the capricious, if somewhat cynical, romantic, loved to hear a declaration like that—at least for the short time it took to deliver it. She went on to tell the *Examiner* that she was retiring from acting and moving to Kansas City to be with John and their son.

Upon reading Barbara's announcement, a more levelheaded John Payton made haste to issue his own statement, in an interview from his new post at the Central Defense Air Force Base in Kansas City. "This is all a little premature," he told *The Journal-American* newspaper. "I've talked to Barbara, yes, and I'm going to talk to her again tomorrow night by telephone. But I don't have anything else to say about it right now."

Or ever, apparently. Just days after the media blitz, the couple's remarriage plans just as quickly bit the dust, sending a seemingly unfazed Barbara barreling back to the bars. It was her tried-and-true way of blurring the hurt of yet another failed relationship; this one, lost for the second—and last—time.

"As much as I loved Barbara," says Tina Ballard, "she had very little regard for John's feelings when she walked out on him in the late 1940s. They got together again a few years later, but after he had a chance to think about it for a while, he decided he really didn't want to pick up where they had left off.

"John was a solid, straight-arrow kind of guy and he had his military career to protect. Barbara was always a real handful, and I guess once John got an idea of what kind of life she had immersed herself in, he felt he couldn't deal with it anymore. It was around this time, too, I remember, that John first began building a case against Barbara for her lack of proper parenting skills. He started making noises to the Zollingers and to some others in the family about the caliber of people Barbara was associating with, and about taking Johnny away from her, for good. Of course, she really ran wild once she got wind of that, but that was the rebel in her.

"As hard as she tried (and I believe she did), Barbara just couldn't stay out of trouble."

Fur Coats and... Heroin? • 347

Sure enough, Barbara was in "trouble" again on May 23 when two fur coats bearing her name tags were found among a cache of stolen goods in an Inglewood, California cocktail lounge called the Trade Winds. Jailed on suspicion of receiving stolen property were the owner and operator of the bar, Jack Winger, 27, and Thomas Madray, a 42-year-old laborer who was an acquaintance of Barbara's.

When questioned by police, Barbara claimed she hadn't reported the missing furs (a $10,000 mink coat and a $2,500 ermine stole) because,

Barbara flirts with Supreme Court Judge Elmer Doyle (as her attorney Milton Golden looks on) after being questioned about her participation in the theft of her two fur coats. Courtesy of L.A. Public Library/Herald Examiner Collection

in her words, "I wasn't sure whether they'd been stolen or borrowed by a friend." Winger stood by his story—that he took the furs as payment for a $200 bar bill run up by an unidentified patron—and admitted that he had tried to sell them for $1,200.

Although there was strong suspicion on all fronts that Barbara was the unidentified patron Winger had alluded to, it was (curiously) never fully determined just how involved she was in the incident. Three days later, and up against an extremely skeptical media, Barbara opted not to sign a complaint against the two men and they were released.

With a naiveté both disarming, and maddening, Barbara told Deputy District Attorney Harry Johnstone, "I just want to forget the whole thing. I'm not mad at them, and I don't want to be tied up in court. The publicity would hurt me."

Barbara had reached this undeniable conclusion rather late in the game. The only publicity Barbara was getting—the only kind she had ever gotten, in fact—was bad publicity, but it seemed the reality of that continued to escape her.

The late cinematic bad-girl and genre film icon Yvette Vickers (*Attack of the 50 Foot Woman*, who passed away tragically in 2010) recalled meeting Barbara in the summer of 1954, following her trouble at the Trade Winds bar, and was deeply saddened by what she learned about Barbara's current lifestyle. Yvette said, "I was 18 at the time and dating Norman Levin, who was then the CEO of Thrifty Drugs [the well-known drugstore chain at whose Sunset Boulevard address Barbara's unconscious body would later be found]. He and I were dining at this nice restaurant on the Strip when Barbara came in alone and sat at the bar. Norman knew Barbara, and he introduced me to her. I can't begin to tell you just how stunning she looked that night. Barbara Payton was, without question, one of the most gorgeous women I've ever seen. She seemed like a very warm and friendly person, but also sort of preoccupied, and sad.

"Soon after Barbara arrived, a man came in and sat down next to her, and after about five minutes, they left together. I remember Norman telling me that the man was a well-known drug dealer and that he had heard from quite a few people in town that Barbara was sniffing heroin and that this guy was her supplier. I was absolutely shocked."

While it is unclear today whether Barbara was truly using heroin during this period, enough evidence points to her use of other illegal drugs, starting as early as the late 1940s, when she was often seen around

Legendary cult film actress Yvette Vickers, who had a memorable, if disturbing, meeting with Barbara in the mid 1950's. Courtesy of Yvette Vickers

town in the company of drug dealers Don Cougar and Stanley Adams. In addition to her use of amphetamines while at WB, those who knew Barbara said that she had also often turned to sleeping pills and marijuana in the years that followed.

"Barbara told me once that she sometimes smoked pot and that she really thought it no worse than drinking booze," recalls Steve Hayes. "I never drank or used drugs myself, so I wasn't privy to that side of Barbara's life.

"As for her possibly using heroin, or any other kind of opiate, all I can say is this: I knew her very well at the time and I never saw Barbara use heroin or even look like she'd been using it (as indicated by a user's leaden eyes and sluggish body movements). I saw that look in many beatniks and hippies in the '50s and '60s, so I knew it pretty well."

Steve also saw "the look" in Bela Lugosi, his downstairs neighbor at the Sunset Colonial Hotel. "As everyone knows, dear old Bela used opiates for years, and after he shot up, he always had that same far away, glazed look in his eyes. I never saw that in Babs. Ever."

Jan Redfield says, "In those years, I know that Barbara took diet pills during the day to give her energy and nerve pills at night to conk her out, but I never saw her do any other drugs (that is, other than alcohol). And I was around her a lot, too."

Barbara's future husband, Tony Provas, confirms her casual use of marijuana—if not her use of hard drugs—during the years they were married. "Barbara did, on occasion, smoke pot, but then so did most of the Hollywood crowd (and still do, to this day). While she sometimes smoked grass at parties or at get-togethers with friends, it was never a 'must do' sort of thing for her, and I think she mainly did it to be part of the gang.

"As for other drugs—no way. Barbara was always averse to ingesting or injecting any chemical substances in her body, and that most definitely includes heroin. I don't believe that Barb would have ever tried that stuff while there was still some sanity left in her life. But, alcohol, oh, yes. It was always alcohol for Barbara. And lots of it, too."

Despite her friends' and family's doubts that she had graduated to using heroin, by 1954 Barbara had tried just about every other illegal drug that Hollywood offered in those days. From smoking pot to popping speed (which she used almost daily to keep her weight down), to her constant use of sleeping pills and booze, Barbara was already on that long, winding road to addiction many postwar junkies called, "the route." Whether it had led her into the arms of Lady Heroin, however (as Yvette Vickers suggested), remains unclear.

Her acute alcoholism, pill-taking and possible use of heroin notwithstanding, Barbara's stunning looks had yet to be permanently damaged by her bad habits, said Yvette. "I can't understand it; Barbara was still very beautiful. It's just mind-boggling to me that despite looking so gorgeous and healthy, she may have actually been using heroin. But,

Title lobby card for Barbara's final film, the 1955 crime drama, **Murder Is My Beat**. *From the Author's Collection*

in a way, I suppose it makes perfect sense. Although she had a very good start in films, the town had completely turned its back on her by then, and that had to have made her very depressed. At that point, Barbara probably should have just picked herself up and gone somewhere else to live. *Why did she stay?*"

Yvette Vickers added that she never saw Barbara again after their one brief meeting that summer. "We didn't travel in the same circles. If we had, and if I had known her better, I would have tried to get her some help.

"The night I met her, she seemed like such a kind and lovely person. What happened to Barbara is just so sad. And to know it didn't have to happen only makes it sadder."

Chapter Twenty-Five:
The End of a Career

In June 1954, German-born director Edgar G. Ulmer began work on his latest Hollywood film, a tough, Grade-B crime drama titled *Murder Is My Beat* (Allied Artists), in which Barbara was given the female lead. [23] If Ulmer's best films deal with the plight of the misguided loser who strays from a righteous path to find comfort in the shadowy fringes, he found just the right actress for the role of *Murder's* troubled and ambiguous femme fatale—a character Barbara may have seen as a kindred spirit to her own jaded soul.

Considered by many today to be a genius, Edgar G. Ulmer was a true master of the expressionistic style of filmmaking, where his talent for design and visual experimentation spotlighted society's disenfranchised in such riveting works as the Boris Karloff and Bela Lugosi 1934 horror classic *The Black Cat*, John Carradine's lesser, but still noteworthy *Bluebeard* (PRC, 1944), and Tom Neal's magnum opus, *Detour*.

Underutilized by Hollywood due to his eccentric and iconoclastic nature, Ulmer refused to conform to the mainstream industry's demands, but eventually found his professional niche in several low-budget films of the 1930s and '40s. While the majority of his work was overlooked during his lifetime, it has won him widespread critical acclaim in the years since his death.

Though perfectly respectable in its own small way, *Murder Is My Beat* remains one of the lesser known entries in the Ulmer canon. Written by the prolific B-film producer and director Aubrey Wisberg, the movie's plot owes a lot to the film noir genre, even though the picture itself is completely devoid of noir's dark visuals and far more stylized ambiance.

The film's story finds blonde and buxom nightclub singer, Eden Lane (Barbara), engaging in a clandestine affair with a much older, married

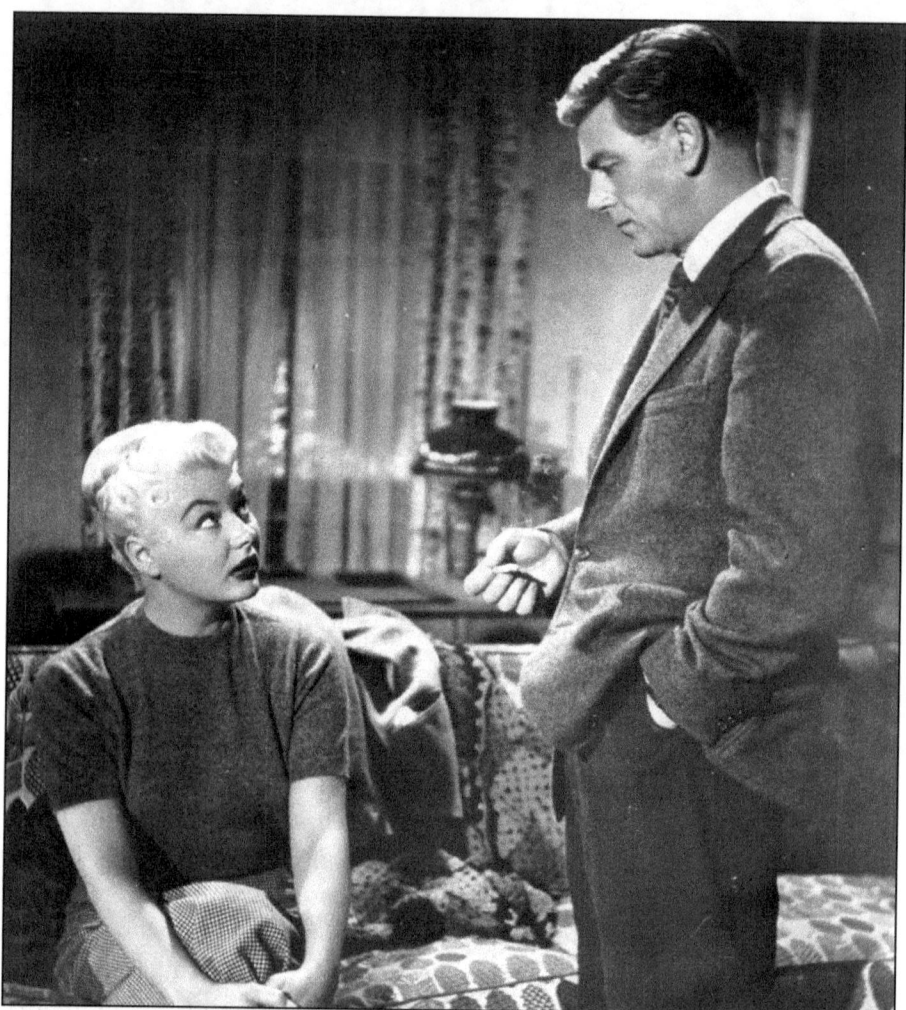

Barbara as nightclub singer "Eden Lane" and co-star Paul Langton in a scene from Murder is My Beat. *From the Author's Collection*

man, Frank Deane (played by Roy Gordon), the wealthy owner of a small-town ceramics factory. When the man's corpse is found in a fireplace (burned so badly it cannot be identified), Eden immediately becomes the police department's prime suspect. Before they can question her, however, she disappears, and is later tracked down to a secluded mountain cabin where she has taken refuge in a blizzard. The hard-boiled detective who has followed her there, Lt. Ray Patrick, played in suitably gruff fashion by actor Paul Langton, places her under arrest, but soon afterward he begins to question her culpability. Eden, however, is ultimately found guilty of murder and is sentenced to a jail term. While en route to prison by train, the woman sees Frank Deane standing on a railroad platform, and manages to convince Patrick (who has become enamored of her) that Deane is still alive. Hoping to catch up with the only man who can prove her innocence, the couple leap from the train and commence a search that leads them through a tangled maze of blackmail and murder. The end result is a tight little mystery featuring many of the crime film genre's most familiar denizens, including a world-weary femme fatale, the requisite tough-guy cops, a blackmailing dame, a wealthy, cheating husband, and his emasculating (and, as the film's climax reveals, maniacally homicidal) wife.

Barbara's wonderfully subtle performance in *Murder Is My Beat*, though unheralded at the time of the film's release over fifty years ago, is well-regarded today by a myriad of film critics. Even though her second-billed part is relatively small, Barbara's character is the axis on which the plot's crucial elements revolve, and her underplaying of the role, whether intentional or not, proved effective in creating an interesting character whose guilt is questioned throughout much of the film.

Barbara and Paul Langton are on the run in this scene from Murder is My Beat.
Courtesy of Wisconsin Center for Film and Theater Research

Barbara, Paul Langton and Tracy Roberts in a promotional still for **Murder is My Beat**. *Courtesy of Wisconsin Center for Film and Theater Research*

Authors Alain Silver and Robert Porfirio, two highly respected experts of film noir, applaud the careful nuance and skill in Barbara's performance, and write in *Film Noir: An Encyclopedic Reference to The American Style*, that "…Payton's portrayal of Eden in a neutral manner permits the suggestion of instability beneath the surface calm of her character's visage."

The strength of her performance was later echoed by author Robert Polito, in the 2000 book *O.K. You Mugs: Writers on Movie Actors*. In his essay, *Barbara Payton: A Memoir*, Polito writes, "Only Edgar Ulmer understood how to spin her anxiety into an advantage. Payton's tension [in the film] plays as suspense, her hesitations as possible instability, the intimation that she might indeed be a murderess."

While Barbara's performance in the film easily stands beside her powerful effort in *Kiss Tomorrow Goodbye* as among her very best moments onscreen, it would come too late to salvage a career that was, for all intents and purposes, already dead. Like so many of the B movies cranked out by Hollywood during this period, *Murder Is My Beat* was released quietly (on February 27, 1955), and passed through theaters largely unnoticed, leaving Barbara's truncated film career in ashes.

There may be several reasons why *Murder Is My Beat* proved to be the last acting vehicle for Barbara, perhaps the most obvious being that Hollywood's Bad Girl was clearly showing the physical signs of her drinking and drug use. The countless evenings she had spent abusing her body in various ways were beginning to take a tremendous toll on Barbara's appearance, and the film cameras (unforgiving as they are) had all too accurately documented her decline.

Murder Is My Beat shows Barbara looking visibly bloated; even more so, in fact, than she had appeared in *The Great Jesse James Raid*. Garbed throughout most of the film in a tight sweater and frumpy, checkered skirt, Barbara's heavily lacquered face had taken on a noticeably coarse look, and the unbecoming hairpiece the producers had slapped on her head had only made things worse. Though not yet 28, there was a hard-edged weariness now in Barbara's eyes, and it seemed a telling barometer of all her personal and professional failures. By 1955, Barbara's exquisite Nordic beauty—nearly unparalleled, just four years earlier—looked far less youthful and appealing on film.

Another possible reason for the abrupt end of Barbara's movie career is that her ambition to act—never the world's strongest—had simply yielded to her love of a good party.

Most likely, however, is that the trashy, ill-conceived reputation Barbara had so tirelessly created since she first appeared on the scene, had finally caught up with her. Her flagrant promiscuity, for years a well-known fact in Hollywood, had brought her nothing but disdain from the industry, and it was clear that the self-righteous moralists in town had finally seen (and heard) enough.

When you add into the mix her unapologetic nature, her refusal to curry favor with both the press and studio heads alike, and her overall

Barbara's jet-setting, hard partying ways are reflected here in her tired appearance. Courtesy of Jan Redfield

irreverence, it's obvious that Barbara had been deemed expendable by the industry-at-large, and no longer worthy of professional redemption.

As the sun set forever on her once-promising film career, Barbara was left with little more than a very troubled personal life, and an even more uncertain future.

Chapter Twenty-Six:
Wild Nights, Wasted Days

With her acting career now dead-in-the-water, Barbara fell back on what she knew how to do best: mask her unhappiness with lots of parties, alcohol, and men.

Her son remembers one of her suitors at the time, an older man of obvious wealth who came to the house one day to take John Lee shopping at the famous F.A.O. Schwarz toy store in Hollywood: "He bought me a cabin cruiser for the swimming pool that used a ton of batteries and was nearly as big as I was. It didn't do him any good, though, as far as scoring points with me. I didn't like him at all. Apparently, neither did Mom, as I don't recall seeing him around after that."

In his book, *Bud: The Brando I Knew*, author Carlo Fiore mentions an affiliation with Barbara that took place in the months following the demise of her acting career. Fiore, a failed actor-turned-struggling screenwriter, was a longtime pal of Marlon Brando—and a raging heroin addict. His drug abuse had destroyed both his acting and writing careers, and by the mid-'50s, he was on the periphery of the business, serving mostly as a dialogue coach (and glorified gofer) for his movie-star friend.

Fiore claims to have rented a room from Barbara during a time when he was trying to shake drugs, and she was living with John Lee on North Beverly Drive. A reed-thin and swarthy Italian of average looks, Fiore had been introduced to her by a mutual friend, and after passing what he refers to as Barbara's "careful inspection" of him, he took up residence in the pool house behind her home.

Although John Lee isn't certain if he remembers Carlo Fiore, per se, he does recall the many other transients who sometimes stayed at the pool house. "People have often referred to it as a studio apartment, but it was actually just a big room with a very high ceiling. The individuals who rented that room from my mother were struggling artists, writers and actors, mostly. There was one guy—a sculptor, I think—who was very odd. I remember he didn't talk much, if at all. Even as a kid, I thought that was really strange.

"Many of these fellows were just passing through and never amounted to more than intimate acquaintances of Mom's. I do remember hearing her and her friends sometimes, in her bedroom, or out by the pool. I was never treated badly by any of them, rather just ignored for the most part."

Apparently, Barbara also rented out the pool house to people other than her male friends. According to Jan Redfield, "A young, married couple lived there once for a couple of months, too. They were struggling financially, and I guess Barbara felt sorry for them as she charged them practically nothing to stay there. I think the guy was an actor friend of John Saxon's, or one of those other male starlets at the time who used to hang out at Barbara's pool. The wife, I remember, was a nice girl, but her husband struck as me as being a bit of a prude. At any rate, they didn't live there for very long."

Carlo Fiore's book mentions his happy memories riding down Sunset Boulevard in Barbara's red Cadillac convertible with her and her showgirl friend Mickey, whom he describes as "two gorgeous-lookin' broads." While he never mentions Barbara's own alleged drug use during this time, Fiore writes that her current lover was an unnamed black man who would arrive at her house on a motorcycle, and that he [Fiore] wandered over to the main house a few times and inadvertently saw her performing fellatio on her boyfriend on the living room floor. He also writes of Barbara's sexually compulsive nature and how she propositioned him, appearing in his apartment one morning at two a.m. with an invitation for what he calls "her specialty."

"Apparently she was interested only in oral sex," says Fiore. "There was something off-center about this girl—not sexually, but in some strange fashion she seemed to drive men insane. Maybe they just couldn't understand or keep up with her mostly compulsive behavior."

Barbara's preference for oral sex is corroborated by Walter Burr, who recalls an intimate conversation she had with him when he visited her and Tom in July 1952. "After she handed me that X-rated book she stole from Charles Laughton's bathroom, we talked about different sexual positions, and Barbara told me that she never felt more turned-on and contented than when she was giving a man [oral sex]. She also said she knew that most men wanted it almost more than regular sex, and she told me that she, in fact, preferred it, as well. I had to remind myself that day that she was my uncle's girl. Wow!"

Steve Hayes says, "Babs liked to do it, all right. And I was always willing to let her have her way with me, as they say."

On closer inspection, perhaps Barbara's sexual preference had its roots in the alleged abuse of her early childhood, which found her clearly disempowered, and often at an older person's mercy. Later on, by engaging in a sexual practice that saw her as the dominating force, Barbara could call the shots (so to speak), and in doing so, experience a feeling of being in complete control—something she surely never felt in the sexual situations of her youth. If indeed the act eventually became compulsive for her, as Carlo Fiore suggests, it may be that as Barbara's sense of personal empowerment lessened (due, in great part, to her escalating use of alcohol and drugs), her need to exert this kind of subtle mind control over the men she encountered, increased. While it's possible that Barbara's sexual preference made her feel far less exploited, her worst years of exploitation, ironically, still lay ahead.

Steve Hayes saw a distinct neediness behind Barbara's overtures. "Truthfully, I think she was willing to do anything, sexually, that put her in a position of being wanted or needed by a man. I'm also convinced sex was her way of proving to herself that men desired her. They say nymphomania is based on the desire to be loved. And no one wanted to be loved (or desired) more than Babs."

In *Bud: The Brando I Knew*, Carlo Fiore writes that the two a.m. visit from Barbara was the only time they ever deviated from their standard, landlady-and-tenant relationship. He goes on to reminisce how Marlon Brando often visited him at Barbara's home during the time he lived there. Apparently, Brando came to see Barbara, too. It was later said that Fiore had orchestrated the pairing after Brando told him that he was interested in having a sexual relationship with Barbara.

Tina Ballard contends that Brando not only stopped by during the day, via the front door, but that he also often made unannounced, "midnight visits" to Barbara's upstairs bedroom, as well. "To protect their privacy, he would climb in through the shutters of her upstairs window," Tina says. "I know that sounds a bit strange, but that's exactly what Barbara told me. There was a tremendous hill right behind Barbara's house (part of the Santa Monica Mountains National Recreation Area), and a section of it came so close to touching the second floor of the house, it made her bedroom window very accessible. According to Barbara, Marlon would climb the hill and sometimes surprise her by calling on her, late at night. She was amused by it, I guess, but I wouldn't say they dated. It was more of a fling.

"I never actually saw Marlon at Barbara's, though; she only told me about his visits. The only time I ever saw him in person was several years earlier, when Barbara lived in that small apartment building on Sunset Boulevard. Apparently, Marlon also lived there, in a room at the end of the hall, and I saw him one day going to get his mail. I remember he was dressed in a sleeveless, white undershirt and black pants. I asked Barbara who he was, and she said, 'Marlon Brando. Isn't he cute?' I must admit, though, that I wasn't impressed with him, as at the time I had never seen any of his films. Come to think of it, I wasn't impressed with most of the celebrities I met through Barbara. To me, none of them were really anything to brag about. They were ordinary people, with a lot of flaws, just like everyone else."

Carlo Fiore recalled in his book how he and Barbara watched the Academy Awards on her television the night Brando won the Oscar for his performance in *On the Waterfront*. Sadly, the days of Barbara attending such a prestigious event, as a guest, seemed behind her now.

Barbara's girlfriend Mickey and her husband Sandor were also frequent guests of hers during this time. Mickey was a former dancer in Las Vegas, and she looked strikingly similar to Barbara—platinum blonde, blue-eyed, and sexy. "I only met Mickey a few times," says Tina, "but I know that she and Barbara were close pals for a while. Mickey and Sandor were partyers, like Barbara, and the three of them had a blast together. They hung out a lot at the pool, spending the afternoons lying on chaise lounges, working on their tans, and drinking.

"Barbara's friends were all separate entities in her life. Apart from Jan and me, and June Bright, Barbara's girlfriend from her days as a Rita La Roy model, very few of us really knew each other (outside of saying hello to one another at Barbara's parties)."

Barbara was said to have comforted her friends, Mickey and Sandor, when their toddler daughter rode her tricycle off the edge of the family's fishpond, and drowned. "That happened just before Barbara left the North Beverly Drive house," recalls Tina. "It was a terrible tragedy, and Mickey and Sandor were devastated by the loss. But Barbara was there for them. Contrary to her reputation of being totally self-centered, this was a woman who really cared about people.

"Barbara and Mickey were fairly good friends, but I don't remember seeing her and her husband at Barbara's house following their little girl's funeral. They just fell out of her life one day, and never came back, as so many of Barbara's friends did."

In terms of her love life, no sooner had Barbara's black, motorcycle-riding beau (and Marlon Brando) disappeared from view, when trouble showed up in the form of a man named Don Metz. A tough guy on the fringes of both the L.A. underworld and the motion picture industry, Metz seemed to appear one day out of the blue, and just as suddenly, moved into Barbara's house. "Oh, he was bad news," says Jan Redfield. "Very rude, and uncouth. I didn't like the guy from the first time I met him."

Barbara's former flame Steve Hayes had met Don Metz a few years earlier, at gangster Mickey Cohen's house in Santa Monica. Steve knew Cohen through his acquaintance with the latter's right-hand man, Johnny Stompanato, a professional gigolo who in just a few years would meet his fate at the end of a knife wielded by Lana Turner's daughter, Cheryl Crane.

Of Don Metz, Steve says, "He was a real low-level hood and not in the same league as, say, Mickey Cohen or Bugsy Siegel. If I remember correctly, Metz was stocky and kind of Italian-looking in a flashy suit. Hollywood detective Fred Otash, I think, knew him; as did Rudy Diaz, the L.A. vice cop I knew from Googie's who became famous around town for his many celebrity drug busts. Don Metz was a tough, if minor, presence in Hollywood; definitely trouble, but nowhere near at the head of the pack."

Beyond Steve and Jan's negative memories of him, little else is known about this sinister character who briefly entered Barbara's life in the winter of 1955. "All I know is that he came in and took over for a while," recalls Jan. "There were always some rough-looking guys around him, and I could tell that Don was involved in something illegal. He was married—that much, I know—but Barbara never told me anything else about him."

Apparently, Metz lived with Barbara for just a short period of time. "He used her," adds Jan. "Who knows, he may have even beaten her, too. He took her right down the river, and then he threw her away. Don dropped Barbara just before she left for Mexico that spring."

A few years later, Jan remembers reading in the L.A. newspapers that Don Metz had been found splattered across Hollywood Boulevard after taking a flying leap off the roof of a hotel. "He should have taken that leap before he met Barbara," she says. "He was a bad, bad man."

People were passing through Barbara's life quickly now and by mid-October 1955, Carlo Fiore's sojourn at her house would reach its end, as well. In *Bud: The Brando I Knew*, Carlo laments the day when he was forced to leave the premises unexpectedly, "...when Barbara's finances suddenly collapsed and she lost the house and everything else." He adds that he stayed with other friends in Beverly Hills for a while, "before winding up with a French hooker." In 1978, Fiore died in Los Angeles at 59.

As for Marlon Brando's split with Barbara, author Darwin Porter, in his highly controversial 2006 biography of the actor, *Brando Unzipped*, alleges that their affair had ended abruptly when she attempted to blackmail him for money. According to Porter's book, Carlo Fiore once told him: "Payton was a known blackmailer [and] through some guise that I don't know about, she managed to get compromising pictures taken of her male victims. Don't ask me how, but she managed to get pictures of herself performing [oral sex] on Marlon."

Although Fiore's allegation is unverified and remains open to question, it obviously cannot be discounted entirely. In *Brando Unzipped*, Fiore explains Brando's retreat from Barbara's life, thus: "All that I know is that one day Marlon called me to his dressing room (on the *Guys and Dolls* set). 'Thanks but no thanks for fixing me up with our fellatio artist, Miss Payton,' he told me. 'Getting away from that bitch has cost me fifty thousand dollars, and you're to blame.'"

In defense of her sister-in-law, Jan Redfield says, "I don't know anything about Barbara blackmailing Marlon Brando, but I personally doubt that it ever happened. I saw her a lot during that time, and despite what anyone else says, she was far from being broke. That was before Barbara left for Mexico and she still had plenty of money in the bank. And as for the claim that she took 'compromising pictures of her male victims,' that is utter garbage. Barbara was wild and promiscuous, yes, but, trust me, she wasn't clever enough to set up a scam like that. This was a very unsophisticated girl. That information is so ridiculous and so disgusting, I feel ashamed for the person who wrote it."

Sometime after her liasions with Marlon Brando and Don Metz, and prior to the collapse of her finances, Barbara took off to vacation in Mexico with John Lee. She had made periodic visits to the country since her first time there in the summer of 1952, when she and Tom Neal went to La Paz on the Baja Peninsula, to fish for marlin.

Barbara loved everything about Mexico—from its most raucous hotbed of hedonistic pleasures, Tijuana, to the tiny, desert villages tucked away in its secluded coves on the Gulf of California. She would later say, however, that she loved the Mexican people most of all. "They were simple and their lives were so uncomplicated," she wrote in her 1963 memoir. "It's not like in America where they kiss you on the cheek as a greeting. There they buss you on the lips so hard that your teeth rattle. The people are sincere. A man will say, 'Will you go to bed with me?' He won't beat around the bush for a couple of evenings."

Many of the people Barbara would meet in Mexico seemed more interested in having a good time than in working—a concept that she had sadly come to adopt, as well.

"My sister went down to Mexico to party," says Frank Redfield. "It was a real swingin' place in those days, and by then, Barbara was all about having fun. At that point, she had been kicked out of films, and I don't believe she cared, either. She had been through a lot in Hollywood, and I guess she finally said, 'The hell with all of them, I wanna party.'"

A rare candid of Barbara on vacation in La Paz, Mexico, standing beside a marlin she caught. Courtesy of Jan Redfield

One of Barbara's favorite places in Mexico was the relatively undeveloped coastal port of Guaymas, on the Sea of Cortez. Located in northwest Mexico's Sonora state, Guaymas sits on a scenic inlet beneath the Sierra Madre Mountains, and has a population today of nearly 90,000. In the 1950s, however, it was far less inhabited and something of a well-kept secret, visited mostly by wealthy Arizonians (the border town of Nogales, Arizona is only a few hours drive from Guaymas), as well as celebrities seeking a vacation spot that was inconspicuous, yet elegant.

The port's most luxurious hotel in those days was The Playa de Cortez, a sprawling beachfront resort that was so beautiful, it quickly became a favorite getaway of some of Hollywood's most renowned stars. Nestled among lush tropical gardens of elephant trees and Saguaro Cactus, its owner, a middle-aged woman from Texas named Eldred Tanner, had built a business that had attracted some of the biggest names in the industry. From Clark Gable, Lana Turner and John Wayne, to Fred Astaire, Orson Welles, Bing Crosby and hundreds of others, the list of its celebrated guests in those days was endless.

John Lee remembers both Guaymas, and The Playa de Cortez, with great fondness: "Back then, Guaymas was a small place, a little town of narrow streets and very friendly people, and it had a nice, quiet beach. The Playa de Cortez was very open, kind of U-shaped with stucco walls and a tile roof, I believe. There was a fountain in the front with lots of greenery around a paved courtyard. The hotel was directly across from the beach with a little road between them.

"The beach was clean and white and usually deserted, except for me. There was no surf to speak of, and the water was warm and shallow; so shallow, in fact, that Mom and I would often wade way out from shore, shuffling our feet along the ocean floor, rooting around for abalone. I really enjoyed doing fun stuff like that with her; you know, just the two of us.

"My mother loved to fish for marlin and sometimes she took me along on her fishing trips. When we got back, she would often pose for photographs with the fish she caught hanging behind her on these big hooks. I remember seeing pictures of Mom standing there smiling in front of all these upside down fish with their stomachs falling out of their mouths. Totally gross."

As much as she loved her son, Barbara's parenting skills, alas, remained as lacking in Mexico as they were back in Hollywood. Without a trace of anger—or blame—John Lee recalls being left alone a lot by his mother, who would often, at a moment's notice, take off for parts unknown, leaving the eight-year-old to fend for himself.

"I spent a lot of time by myself at the hotel," says John Lee. "I also distinctly remember getting ringworm on that trip. Mom, God bless her, met a local, so-called faith healer on the beach, and she had him come to the hotel room, heat a coin and put it on a spot on my arm. He put a glass over the coin and—shazam—made the spot disappear."

Jan Redfield remembers the incident somewhat differently: "When Barbara came back from that trip to Mexico with Johnny, she immediately dropped him off at my parents' house in La Puente. Well, that poor little boy was a mess from head to toe. He had huge welts all over his body, and he was covered with ringworm—in fact, it was all through his scalp. I wound up having to take him to the doctor, who prescribed some medication for him.

"[Barbara's ex-husband] John was very upset that she had been so negligent down there with Johnny, and he told my mother that he was going to do something about it. He eventually did, too."

After delivering her son to the Zollingers, Barbara immediately took off for Mexico again; this time, with an unknown male friend with whom she returned to The Playa de Cortez. It was during this trip that she would meet the man who would eventually become her fourth husband. Tony Provas says, "Barbara would turn my life upside down, and back up again. Ours was a wild, wild ride, and I don't regret a minute of it."

The "ride," fueled by equal parts of booze and sex, would swerve down the same winding road as all of Barbara's other past affairs, and would end just as badly.

Chapter Twenty-Seven:
Down Mexico Way

Jorge Antonio (a.k.a. "Tony") Provas-Dominguez was born on November 27, 1933, the son of Greek immigrant Constantino "Gus" Provartakis, and Guaymas native Maria Monreal. Maria's lineage, in particular, was impressive: her father, Adolfo Dominguez, had been educated in Spain, France and England, and upon moving to Guaymas, was commissioned a Captain in the Mexican Army. As a young man, Adolfo served as a military aide to Mexican president Porfirio Diaz, and was later appointed to the post of Mexican Consul in Deming, New Mexico.

Tony's father, Gus Provartakis, had immigrated to America from Tripolis, Greece, where he was born in 1884. His parents, Vasilios and Vasiliki, owned a silk factory and tannery, but Gus had little interest in continuing in the family business and opted instead to seek his fortune in the U.S. In his early 20s, he settled in Nogales, Arizona, where he shortened his surname to "Provas" and met the beautiful Maria Monreal, whom he married in 1920. Gus became a pioneer in the film exchange business, and, with his cousin, later operated a successful chain of movie theaters in California and Arizona. In the early 1950s, the Provas family started a sportfishing business which eventually grew to become the largest fleet of sportfishing and party cruisers in Latin America.

Tony enjoyed a privileged childhood; one that he says was filled with "the typical joys and sorrows that most kids experience as they're growing up." On the plus side, there were more joys than sorrows, and some of his clearest memories are of the many sportfishing trips he took with his father. To this day, it remains his favorite sport.

"Sportfishing has been both my business and my life's greatest hobby," he explains. "It has taken me all over the world—from fishing for pike in lakes in the French Alps, and sailfish off the West African coast, to angling for trout in streams in Spain and Denmark, and steel head trout and salmon in the Pacific Northwest." Along with sportfishing, Tony has enjoyed wild game hunting as well, and remembers the time he and his father took actor Clark Gable duck hunting in Ciudad Obregon, Mexico. "My Dad went on his last deer hunt at 80, so you might say it was a lifelong love of his. It is also a great love of mine, and I hope to still be hunting (and fishing) in my 80s, too."

As a youngster, Tony spent the winters in Arizona attending school (kindergarten through twelfth grade), and the summers in Guaymas working as a mate on the family's boats. By the time he was an adolescent, he was also enjoying an active social life. He says, "I discovered girls at 11 or 12, and began falling head over heels in love every other week." At 21, he met the woman he calls, "the absolute love of my life, my Barbara (or 'Pate'—as in Payton—which I quickly nicknamed her). Quite simply, I saw her, and she completely took my breath away."

When Tony met Barbara, he was working full-time in the family business in Guaymas. By the mid-1950s, the business had grown to a fleet of 28 sportfishing and party cruisers with chartering offices in The Hotel Playa de Cortez and The Hotel Miramar, as well as in the Mexican ports of Mazatlan and La Paz. Coupled with the family's charter boat business was a 500-acre farm they owned in the Guaymas Valley, where they raised cucurbits: namely, watermelons, cantaloupe, cucumbers and squash, all for export to fruit and vegetable markets in the U.S. and Canada. The farm's export sales were handled by their U.S. brokers, Peerless Produce Company, out of Los Angeles. The Provas family had done well for themselves, both in Mexico and Arizona, and by this time Tony, with his Latin good looks (and attendant machismo), was living the footloose life of a swinging bachelor.

Barbara and her aforementioned male companion were nearing the end of their vacation at The Playa de Cortez when she met Tony, he estimates, sometime in April or May 1955. "My family rented a boat chartering office in the lobby of the hotel, and I was there one afternoon picking up the prior day's receipts when I happened to look up and saw a young woman talking to the desk clerk. She was with an older-looking man and they both had their backs to me. She had strikingly beautiful, platinum blonde hair—it was almost white—and a gorgeous, womanly figure. Even before I saw her face, I just knew she had to be good looking and very special, and I remember turning to our man in the office and saying something like, 'Now that's the kind of girl I'd like to marry someday.' He told me she was the Hollywood actress, Barbara Payton, and then I remembered that I had seen some of her films. Needless to say, I was very impressed."

Barbara and her friend turned around to leave, Tony says, when, "She paused for a moment, looked straight at me and smiled, and then walked away with her friend. Well, I must say—I melted. I was smitten like I'd never been smitten in my life, and there was no doubt in my mind that I had just seen the most beautiful girl in the world. Unlike other actresses whom I dated later on in my life, Barbara was more beautiful in person—*much* more beautiful, in fact—than she was on film."

Much to his delight, Tony managed to meet Barbara later that day at the hotel's pool. "She was by herself, sunbathing, so I went up to her and introduced myself. Barbara was extremely warm and engaging, and we hit it off right away. Over the next two or three days, we'd talk every time we had the chance, and when her friend decided it was time to go back home, Barbara told him that she loved the hotel so much she wanted to stay on a few more days to work on her tan. He left without her, and that was the beginning of our love affair. A love affair that was intense, blazing, and, at times, even a bit crazy, but at all times, at least for me, was one of pure joy and happiness."

Following her friend's departure, Barbara and Tony spent the next several days together—walking on the beach, fishing for marlin and sailfish, and partying at night. "And, of course, making love," he says. "Barbara was the most passionate woman that ever lived, and the best lover."

The Playa de Cortez's owner, Eldred Tanner, was especially fond of Barbara, says Tony. "Eldred loved movie stars, and she really loved Barbara. She knew that Pate liked to sing, so one night she asked her to get up in front of the guests at the hotel to sing a few songs with the band. Pate was thrilled. Of the three or four tunes she sang that night, the one I remember most is The Flamingos hit, 'I Only Have Eyes for You,' mainly because it was our favorite song. Barbara did a fine job singing it and received a standing ovation from the crowd. She was so proud, as was I, of this beautiful and talented specimen who said she wanted to be with me. Just like the words of that song, once I met Pate, I had no eyes for anyone else. The weeks we spent together at The Playa de Cortez were probably among the very best weeks of my life—and possibly, of Barbara's, too.[24]

"There with me in Guaymas, Barbara was happy for a time. After a while, I took her up to Nogales to meet some of my family and friends. Eventually, she even grew to learn the Spanish language so she could communicate more easily with all of them. She worked very hard at that."

Tony's parents, Gus and Maria, liked Barbara right away, and doted on her as if she were their own daughter. "Happiness aside," Tony says, "it soon became obvious to me that Barbara had a serious drinking problem. Not as serious as it would become later on, but bad, nonetheless. Unfortunately, it was a problem that would soon plague me, as well."

A few weeks into their affair, Barbara went back to Hollywood, Tony says, "to take care of some unfinished business." While she was there, he continued working but admits to missing her terribly. "We talked on the phone all the time while she was gone," he says. "Sometimes, two or three times a day. I was miserable without her."

While Barbara was back in L.A., she made two purchases at Hollywood's Sun-Fax Supermarket that would be the catalyst for a world of trouble afterwards. On September 21 and again on the 24th, Barbara bought several bottles of liquor at the market and paid for them with three personal checks. She had done this many times before without any problems so she hadn't thought anything of it. It was true that she had recently become a lot more careless with her money, but Barbara thought she still had things pretty much under control when it came to keeping track of the amount of cash she had in the bank. Sadly, this time she was terribly wrong.

Barbara did just as much drinking back in Hollywood as she had done in Mexico, and Jan Redfield remembers seeing her during her visit and being taken aback by her appearance. "Barbara was so bloated," Jan recalls. "She had chopped her hair real short by then and it made her face look even heavier. Barbara was very tan and very overweight, and she just looked hard. She looked like an entirely different person to me, and I was quite concerned for her.

"But Barbara just laughed like she always did, and said that she was all right. She was 'taking it easy' and 'having fun', she said. She went on and on about this new guy she met in Mexico (Tony), and how she was so in love with him. By then, I was used to hearing Barbara talk like that, so I didn't take it very seriously."

A few days after purchasing the liquor at the Sun-Fax Supermarket, Barbara returned to Mexico and Tony, where for the next three weeks they resumed their love affair and even discussed marriage.

Barbara laughs following her October 1955 arrest for passing bad checks at Hollywood's Liquor Locker. With her is her attorney Milton Golden. Courtesy of UCLA Special Collections/L.A. Times Photo

"We were madly in love," he says, "and I just knew we were going to have a long and wonderful life together. I was happy beyond words and so was Pate. I'm sure of it."

Barbara returned to L.A. again in mid-October, this time to pack up her belongings in preparation for her planned move to Guaymas, and to retrieve John Lee from the Zollingers so she could take him with her when she left town. She seemed to be riding a newfound wave of good fortune, and she told Jan that for the first time in a long time, things felt comfortable and right.

But within days of her return, Barbara's good fortune fizzled out as quickly as it had appeared, when the piper came calling, in the guise of a hard-nosed, L.A. cop.

Chapter Twenty-Eight:
Busted!

Barbara was arrested on October 14, 1955 after the three checks she had written in September at the Sun-Fax Supermarket were returned to the bank due to insufficient funds. The checks had totaled a measly $129.54, which was apparently a lot more than Barbara's bank account held at the time. Police detective Bert Young picked her up at her home, where she told him that although she had written the checks, "There's been a huge mistake."

John Lee was with his mother that day, and recalls the fear and confusion he felt when the police came to the house to arrest her. "One of my very last memories of our house on Beverly Drive is standing on the roof, of all places, looking over the front door and down to the driveway. I can still see the police officer placing handcuffs on my mother and putting her in the back seat of the patrol car, and then driving away. I didn't think I would ever see her again. For me, her arrest that day really marks the beginning of the end of her good days—though I suppose all the earlier mistakes Mom had made in her life were the true beginning. But I remember feeling very frightened and alone when it [her arrest] happened, as any eight-year-old would."

Later described in the newspapers as being "at least forty pounds overweight, and dressed in skintight black toreador pants and a bulging blouse," Barbara was hauled away that morning to the Beverly Hills police station to be fingerprinted and booked. In her initial statement to Detective Young, she admitted that she was broke, but added, "I'm waiting for a $200 advance on a big film deal to come through." Barbara said that someone, in the meantime, had promised to deposit money in her account to cover the checks, although she never identified who that someone was. Following an hour-long

Barbara smiled and mugged for the cameras after her 1955 arrest in Hollywood. From the Author's Collection

confinement behind bars, Barbara's lawyer, Milton Golden, paid her $1,500 bond, and she was released. A preliminary hearing on the charges was set for November 2.

To signify how quickly her life was unraveling, newspaper photos of Barbara taken at the time of her arrest revealed a frowzy, dissipated woman in a startling state of disarray. One photo, in particular, shows her mugging for the cameras with a noticeably wide-eyed and absurd look on her face, almost as if she didn't quite understand what was happening to her. Quite possibly, she didn't.

William "Bill" Ramage, a young actor and model who worked in Hollywood from the mid 1950s to the mid 80s, and a close friend of Milton Golden's, recalls the series of unflattering photos of Barbara that ran in the papers over the next few days. A fan of Barbara's from her Warner Bros. films, Bill was shocked by the drastic change in her appearance.

"While I would meet Barbara three years later at a party at the Goldens' house," he says, "at that point, I only knew her from her films. I had always admired her incredible beauty, but she looked really bad in those news photos. I can tell you, the expression in Barbara's eyes gives it all away. I would bet anything that she was popping speed at the time. In the photos taken right after her arrest, where she and Milton are seated at the police station, the pupils of her eyes are extremely dilated and wild looking. She looked as though she hadn't slept in days. Barbara was very heavy and she was probably taking a lot of that crap to help her reduce. You can see in those newspaper photos after her arrest that the toll of her lifestyle was already beginning to show in her looks, even as early as 1955."

"Barbara always struggled with her weight," says Jan Redfield, "and, of course, when she was drinking a lot, the extra pounds just piled on. I don't know how she ever got away with mixing diet pills with booze for all those years, but it definitely caught up with her."

For the record, Tony Provas claims to have no knowledge of Barbara's use of any other chemical substance besides alcohol. "I don't know anything about Barbara's using diet pills or any other drugs in those years," he says. "I didn't see any of that in Mexico. Her drug of choice (or necessity) was *always* alcohol."

Feeling confident that the bad check charges would be dismissed, but disgusted at the endless stream of difficulties in her life, Barbara threw in the proverbial towel. No longer able to pay her bills, she gave up her rented home and bitterly announced, "I'm fed up with the phonies in this town and I've had it with Hollywood!" She informed the press that she was moving to Guaymas for good, where, she said, "A producer friend of mine will put me under personal contract as soon as I get there. A blonde Hollywood movie star like me goes over big in Mexico." (25)

Hoping to bring her back down to earth following her fanciful rants to the press, Milton Golden gently reminded Barbara that she had been charged with a felony and would have to remain in Los Angeles long enough to stand trial. In a dizzy and almost amazing display of self-denial, Barbara apparently thought that she could just breeze on out of town and the charges against her would miraculously disappear.

Her name continued to stay in print as newspapers reported that the November 2 hearing was postponed to November 30 when Barbara fell ill with a severe cold. Just days later, however, she ignored Golden's objections and took off for Arizona, this time taking John Lee with her. "She woke me up in the middle of the night and we quickly caught a late flight out of L.A.," he remembers. "With Mom in her mink coat and her big, black sunglasses, it was all very secretive and intriguing." Barbara seemed to be tempting the fates now at every turn, with very little fear of the consequences.

Today, John Lee's memories of that trip are mostly unpleasant, as was his initial introduction, he says, to Tony Provas.

"I recall I spent a lot of time by myself at the hotel that Mom and I were staying at," he says, "while she was off somewhere, I guess, with Tony. It was very hot in Arizona, so when I wasn't swimming in the pool, I was in the room ordering up room service (which was usually strawberry ice cream), from the hotel restaurant downstairs.

"I had been left alone at the hotel for several days when I woke up one morning to find Mom and Tony together in the bed next to mine. For some reason, I loathed him from the start.

"In all fairness, I have to say that Tony was not rude or obnoxious to me, except for one instance, later on, when he actually became violent and pulled a knife on me. But at the time that I met him, I just took an instant disliking to him. By then, I had learned to spot users, and that's exactly what he seemed to be.

"Soon after meeting him, I recall Tony taking Mom and me deer hunting with some of his friends. Apparently none of them had any luck catching anything, and at the end of a long, fruitless afternoon, as we all trooped back to the hotel, a deer finally ran past us. Well, Tony and his friends shot at it, but they all missed it, and they were furious. So, they decided to take it out on a rabbit that had the misfortune to appear at the same time as the deer. They shot and shot at that poor rabbit like a bunch of madmen. It kept crawling up a little gully trying to get away from them, but it was no use. They shot it to bits.

"An awful memory of an awful man."

With the strong arm of the law—not to mention, an angry John Payton—bearing down on her, Barbara may have felt the need for a protector who could help mitigate the troubles facing her now that she was back in L.A. And what better protector than a love-struck young man, six years her junior, who was already at her beck and call? The solution to Barbara seemed obvious.

In a highly impulsive, split-second decision that Jan Redfield says, "stunned the family," Barbara took Tony as her fourth husband on

November 28 in Nogales, Arizona. A local Justice of the Peace, Fred U. Allen, officiated at the impromptu, two a.m. ceremony that, in retrospect, seemed like yet another of Barbara's brainstorms. Whatever sense of comfort it may have given her, however, would be short-lived.

Barbara's marital bliss was interrupted when she returned to California with Tony on November 30 and was promptly socked with a triple whammy. In rapid succession, she was ordered to go before the Superior Court for her bad checks arrest, hit with a default court judgment of $750 from her former landlord—for "doors, French window blinds, shutters, two built-in beds and a toilet seat" that Barbara had apparently absconded with when she moved out of the house on North Beverly Drive—and served with a show cause order, initiated by John Payton, to prevent her from taking eight-year-old John Lee out of state. Feeling blindsided once again, Barbara "freaked out," says Jan Redfield, and tried to suppress her anxiety with boatloads of liquor.

Deeply distressed by the court order, Barbara returned to Nogales with Tony, leaving John Lee with Al and Dorothy Zollinger in La Puente. "We went back to Nogales where I have family," says Tony, "and we did our best to carry on a normal life despite Barbara's serious personal problems back in California."

They spent time with Tony's friends, mostly young married couples like themselves. "In spite of her depression, Barbara hit it off with them right away," he says. "My friends loved Pate, and she was charming and warm to all of them, in return. Even at her most frightened or distressed, Barbara was always good at putting up a happy front if she had to."

Away now from his sportfishing business, Tony took a job as an assistant manager at a friend's furniture store in Nogales. "He needed someone to motivate his sales force, which handled both retail sales in the U.S. and wholesale sales across the border in Mexico," says Tony. Although he and Barbara would remain in Nogales for only a short time, Tony claims that he was successful in accomplishing this goal for his friend, although he says he was "much happier sportfishing."

Barbara and Tony left Nogales right after Christmas 1955, so she could be back in L.A. in time to face the music on the bad check matter. "Barbara was a nervous wreck," says Jan Redfield. "All that legal business and bouncing around from Hollywood to Mexico was starting to affect her health. She was very wired and rundown."

Barbara and her lawyer Milton Golden in court on the bad check charges. Courtesy of AP/Wide World Photos

At the December 27 hearing in Los Angeles, with her lawyer, Milton Golden, representing her pro bono, Barbara pleaded guilty to one of three counts of issuing three worthless checks. In the end, Superior Court Judge David Coleman handed her a 60-day county jail sentence, which he agreed to suspend on the condition she pay a $100 fine. Barbara, unable to pay the fine due to her complete lack of funds--and with Tony apparently unable to help her, either--sought relief not from her family or friends, but from Herman Hover, of all people, the owner of Ciro's nightclub. A benevolent Hover apparently sympathized with her plight and gave Barbara the $100 she needed, feeling that since she had spent so much money in his club over the years, he owed it to her. The *L.A. Herald Express*, referring to her as "*ex-actress Barbara Payton*," reported that her "automobile has been repossessed, and her furniture and clothing are in storage and under attachment."

Things had gotten tough for Barbara, and from that point on, they would only get worse.

Shortly after her arrest, all of Barbara's personal belongings had been put in a storage facility in Hollywood owned by the national moving chain, Bekins. "Since she was broke, she couldn't pay the storage fees," says Jan, "so the company eventually sold all her stuff in a private auction. Neither Lee and Mabel, nor Frank and I, had offered to help her out because we didn't know anything about it. Believe me, we would have given her the money to pay the storage fees if she had only told us that she needed it. But for some reason (probably due to her pride, because she was a proud person), she didn't ask for our help. Poor Barbara wound up losing nearly everything she owned."

Obviously, the $1,000,000 that Barbara would later claim she made from her divorce settlement from Franchot Tone, as well as from her seven-year film career and from favors to men in the business, was gone. Save for two mink coats that she left with her friend Tina Ballard ("for safekeeping," Tina said), Barbara, literally, had little more now than the clothes on her back. As she told *Confidential* magazine in 1963: "At the time, it seemed unbelievable to me that I couldn't put my hands on big chunks of cash like I used to, but face it, I couldn't. I was a real sap with money. One day I was rich, and the next I was poor. It was as if a devil of a magician waved a lousy, stinking wand and, poof, the money just disappeared."

Tony Provas insists that the entire bad check fiasco was due to a complete oversight on Barbara's part. "When those checks bounced, Pate had already left L.A. and was staying with me in Mexico, and that was the reason the market's efforts to get in touch with her before going to the police, had failed. Remember, those were the days before cell phones and answering machines.

"There's no question in my mind, now or then, that Pate believed there was enough money in her bank account to cover those checks. I remember her telling me that she felt the business that had brought the

John Lee and John Payton in 1956. Courtesy of John Lee Payton

charges against her was being grossly unfair for not waiting a bit longer before filing the charges.

"In the past, Barbara had spent thousands of dollars at that particular market, and she felt she deserved some consideration for an amount that totaled just a little over one hundred dollars. It was, and still is today, blatantly obvious to me that considering all of her past purchases from this establishment, that their rush to file charges based on such a minuscule amount was nothing less than a self-serving maneuver on their part to garner personal publicity and generate business at the expense of a famous, and formerly very good, customer."

That said, Tony concedes that Barbara's total inability to manage her finances was the real reason why she had landed in so much trouble. "Pate was always very careless with her money. It just wasn't that important to her. Half the time, she didn't know whether she had $10 or $10,000 in the bank; certainly not the most intelligent way to handle one's assets, but that was Barbara."

Her brother Frank offers a somewhat different opinion. "Regardless of what happened to her with those checks, in those years Barbara always seemed to have this real strong need to be a good provider to her family and friends. And trust me, when she was making a lot of money at Warner Bros., and really raking in the big bucks, she would have given you the shirt off her back if you needed it. I can't tell you all the users who flocked around her in those days. My sister was a very generous person, but she had a lot of questionable associates who were always ready to help her spend her money. That includes boyfriends and husbands, by the way."

Chapter Twenty-Nine:
The Greatest Loss of All

During the time of her various legal problems, Barbara's lack of finances forced her and Tony to rent a sparsely furnished flat at 615 North Rossmore Avenue in Hollywood. Their next-door neighbor was eccentric, Finnish-born actress Maila Nurmi, who at the time was enjoying cult stardom on L.A.'s late-night television, as the horror film hostess Vampira. In those days, Maila and Barbara often spoke to each other at Googie's Coffee Shop, but they were no more than acquaintances.

John Lee lived with his mother and Tony at the Rossmore apartment, and remembers his famous neighbor—as well as the decrepit condition of their new home. "I called it the 'Vampira Courts' because back then Maila's TV character was a big favorite of mine, and I remember staying up late every Saturday night to watch her television show with my Aunt Janice. Just knowing that Vampira actually lived next door to us was fabulous to me, even though I never saw her in person.

"The building itself, though, was a real dump. As I recall, one entered the apartment into a small living room, which had a tacky, purple wall with a single clef note painted on it—the only thing about the place that I liked. To the right of the living room was a kitchenette that was tiny and very drab. I remember the bedroom was at the back, opposite the kitchenette and a small dining area, and I think the bathroom was behind the bedroom. There was a closet that opened to the front room and the bedroom, and I often hid in that closet and spied on Mom's and Tony's intimate moments.

"I remember having chicken pox, or measles, when we lived there—the former, I believe. Somehow, Mom managed to scrounge up the bucks that Christmas [1955] to get me a big bicycle with white tires, and she kept promising to buy me a Marlin rifle, too. Even though times were tough, my mother always did her best to make me think we were still living 'the good life.'

"The biggest memory I have of Vampira Courts, though, is that the building was infested with cockroaches. I distinctly remember pouring out my breakfast cereal one morning and finding as many cockroaches in it as cereal.

"The place may have been a shit hole, but I didn't care; I was with Mom, and that was good enough for me. In all honesty, I cannot remember a single time when my mother spoke meanly to me, or treated me badly. That was not who she was. I was always happy to be in her presence and nothing else ever mattered to me."

"The apartment on Rossmore Avenue was a total nightmare," confirms Jan. "And it's true, it was *full* of cockroaches. I remember Frank and I going over there one day to pick up Johnny for a visit, and when we got back to our house, Frank had me take what few clothes Johnny was wearing and shake them out because he didn't want any roaches in the house. Then Frank sprayed all of Johnny's clothes with bug spray before I threw everything in the washer. Later, I had to take Johnny shopping for some sandals, socks and underwear because at the time he had very little in the way of clothing. The following week, when I brought him up to see my mother, she bought him some other things. I think all of us were very concerned for that little boy's welfare when he and Barbara were living in that place, because it really was filthy."

While Tony and Barbara rarely mingled with their exotic neighbor, Vampira, they did spend a lot of time at their apartment entertaining studio hairdresser Fritzy La Bar and her husband, Jack Merrick, who were longtime friends of Barbara's. "Fritzy was the hair stylist for Barbara on *Drums in the Deep South*," says Tony, "and they were drinking buddies from way back." At the time, La Bar was working with about 150 other makeup artists and hair stylists on the Mike Todd blockbuster, *Around the World in Eighty Days*, and she would often bring Barbara a lot of hot, studio gossip from the set. As Fritzy rattled off several amusing anecdotes about the film's stars, David Niven and Cantinflas, Barbara sat there transfixed, with a glass of vodka in hand, and hung on her friend's every word. The scuttlebutt Fritzy shared with her made Barbara feel like she was still a part of the industry.

Says Tony, "Like Barbara and me, Fritzy and her husband Jack both loved to cook, and the four of us spent many hours at our apartment and at their house on Crescent Heights, laughing and cooking up some fabulous meals, but also drinking a lot."

Amidst the laughter and libations—and spurred on by Fritzy's movie star tales from the studio—Barbara often talked about resuming her film career. "We all thought it would come about in due time," says Tony. "It was never a pressing issue." It was just taken for granted by everyone who knew her that Barbara would straighten up and that the movie studios would welcome her back.

Their many nights drinking and carrying on notwithstanding, Tony and Barbara found that they both shared a love of life's simpler pleasures, as well. Amazingly, beyond all the revelry, Tony insists, there were quiet times, too. "Due to our lack of money at the time, we often stayed in at night and read a lot of books. I also began to write quite a bit. In those days I was young and naive enough to think that I had a chance of writing the Great American novel, and Barbara would read and critique my various efforts. She never once failed to encourage me; she always told me to keep at it and to not give up. I don't think most people realize just how nurturing Barbara was. Despite her many problems, she was incredibly loving and always supported my dreams. Please make sure that people know that."

During their stay in Hollywood, Barbara and Tony also spent several weekends hanging out at the home of screenwriter and producer Earl Fenton, who was an old friend of Barbara's from the late 1940s. Crippled from a childhood bout with polio, and dependent on the use of a crutch and a cane to walk, Fenton had penned Barbara's film *Trapped* as well as the film noir classic *The Narrow Margin*, and was renowned in the '50s for the many wild pool parties he threw at his hilltop estate. [26]

"Earl lived way up in the mountains of Benedict Canyon and it was just one drunken bash after another up there," remembers Tony. "There was always a big crowd of movie people at Earl's, including Bob Mitchum, Brad Dexter and Barbara's old pal, Lila Leeds (who had returned to Hollywood after being banished out of the state for several years by the courts). We all drank up a storm around Earl's swimming pool, and had a rip-roaring time."

With all this partying and daydreaming of her lost career, Barbara wasn't allowing herself to see how trivial her life had become. In mingling with other show folk—most of whom were still actively working in the business—she was keeping the memories of her past fame alive, but doing very little to get herself back on track.

Strangely, Barbara loved all the negative attention she had gotten in the media following her arrest, and milked it for all it was worth. "When I'm in the headlines," she wisecracked to one reporter, "the price of newspapers goes up from seven to ten cents." Angry with Barbara for her increasingly foolish deportment, her attorney, Milton Golden, later admitted that he called her into his office after reading the quote, and gave her, "a real tongue-lashing." In his 1960 memoir, *Hollywood Lawyer*, Golden wrote, "Barbara was her own worst enemy. [But] the way she concurred in every charge I tossed at her soon disarmed me. If there's anything more futile than hitting your fist against a brick wall, it is pounding it into a feather pillow."

Barbara's wide-eyed amenity, which was a part of her persona as genuine as her willfulness, and her stubborn defiance of authority, was a source of great frustration to the people in her life, as Golden's comment suggests. Ever the charming chameleon, the frequently rebellious Barbara may have believed that her current legal problems were all retractable, and that by simply shifting gears and appeasing her barrister, she would be reinstated into Hollywood's upper hierarchy. How could she know that would never be?

Barbara's greatest and most crushing personal defeat occurred on March 12, 1956, when she lost custody of the person she loved more than any other: her nine-year-old son, Johnny. According to documents filed in Superior Court, Barbara's recently remarried ex-husband, with whom she had always been on good terms, had suddenly filed an affidavit on February 29 for both a restraining order against Barbara and an order providing for temporary custody of John Lee.

Shortly before doing this, John Payton had written a letter from his military post at Mather Air Force Base to Frank's mother-in-law Dorothy Zollinger, with whom John Lee was staying at the time, in which he had expressed his deep concern over his son's safety:

> Dear Dorothy,
> Just a note to keep you posted on the action I'm taking as regards to Johnny. I have hired an attorney in Los Angeles and he will present a request to the court to change my divorce decree so that Barbara cannot continue to take Johnny out of California without mine [sic] or the court's permission. If approved by the court I will have to appear for a hearing

someday this month. Other than that, I have no information to report and am just waiting now to see what happens.

I want to thank you again for telling me of what's going on. It's a shame everything is still as bad or worse with Barbara but I guess she just won't change. She's always talking about

Barbara, 28, with her ex-husband, Air Force Captain John Payton, during their custody battle for John Lee. Courtesy of UCLA Special Collections/L.A. Times Photo

going to Europe or someplace else, but [she] never does, so maybe she won't this time, either. If she does, however, leave Johnny with the people you mentioned, I'll have to step in and change her plans.

Your friend always,
Jack

In the February 29 affidavit, John had accused Barbara of exposing their son to "profane language, immoral conduct, notoriety, unwholesome activities and no moral education," and claimed that she was an unfit mother. Despite the gravity of these allegations, and the restraining order John had filed against Barbara on March 12 (the day Barbara lost custody of Johnny), the couple agreed to pose outside the courtroom for a series of incredible photos that showed them gazing affectionately at each other. Barbara's charm, evidently, died hard.

In the many newspaper accounts of the trial that were later filed, Barbara was pilloried as a dissolute Medea, with the malicious Hedda Hopper and UPI correspondent Virginia MacPherson leading the savage journalistic attack. Not surprisingly, the editorial flogging Barbara received from them, as well as from several others in the press, was harsh, swift, and all-too-effective. Superior Judge Elmer D. Doyle, who had exercised leniency with Barbara two years earlier, during her embarrassing "stolen furs" farce, this time determined that she had neglected John Lee, and ruled that she was to relinquish custody of him with rights of supervised visitations only.

Sadly, this consisted of but one single visit, held a few weeks later. John Lee was staying with Al and Dorothy Zollinger at their home in La Puente and remembers the day when Barbara showed up to say goodbye.

"It was late afternoon and Mom was driven there by some man I didn't recognize who stayed in the car. She came in wearing a mink coat and I was brought into the living room to see her. I remember that Mom knelt down and embraced me. She kissed me and we both cried, and she apologized over and over, saying that she was sorry she had been a bad mother, that she had tried so hard to be good, but was so sorry that she had been bad. It broke my heart because I felt, and I told her so, that she hadn't been a bad mother to me at all. I kept telling her over and over that I loved her, and when she finally had to leave, we were both devastated to have to say goodbye."

Milton Golden and Barbara look over court papers during the custody battle. Courtesy of USC Library//Dept. of Special Collections/L.A. Examiner Collection

From the Zollingers living room window, John Lee watched Barbara get into her friend's car and drive away. It was the last time he would see his mother alive.

For a brief time after the custody trial, John Lee stayed with the Zollingers, until he joined his father and his new wife—also named Barbara, ironically—along with her two children from a previous marriage, at their home in Sacramento.

In 1957, John Payton, Sr. was transferred from Mather Air Force Base, first to Bitburg Air Force Base, and then to Ramstein Air Force Base (both in Germany), where he and his family lived for the next four years. They

Milton Golden and a clearly devastated Barbara being escorted from the courtroom after she lost custody of her son. Courtesy of USC Library//Dept. of Special Collections/L.A. Examiner Collection

moved to Texas in 1961, when Major Payton was stationed at Randolph Air Force Base in San Antonio. John Lee attended the city's Robert E. Lee High School for nearly four years, but at his stepmother's insistence, he was sent to live with the Zollingers in Los Altos to complete the last half of his senior year.

"It was clear from the start that unlike my own mother, my stepmother Barbara didn't like me," John Lee recalls, "and she got rid of me as soon as she had an opportunity to do so. Still, she was a wonderful mother to her own children, all of whom adored her and felt she was the perfect mother. Although she and I were not close, I do admire her for that."

As for his father, it would be almost 20 years before John Lee could establish an amicable relationship with him, though he says that for many years up until the elder Payton's 2006 death, they were "as close as any father and son could be."

Following their final meeting at the Zollingers in 1956, John Lee had no further contact with Barbara—save for one drunken phone call she made to him, late one night, while he was living in Germany. "Mom was under the weather, and she was crying very hard," he says. "In fact, I could barely understand anything she was saying. Mostly she was just trying to tell me how sorry she was, and how much she loved me and missed me. I was in the fifth or sixth grade at the time, and I began crying as well. I was very, very confused by it all as I was half-asleep, and stunned to hear her voice. It was not a long conversation. Within a few minutes, we said goodbye, and our relationship, as we knew it, was over."

The final words between them—words of immense regret filtered through a wall of tears—are part of the bittersweet memories John Lee continues to live with today, nearly fifty years after his mother's death.

Barbara's former co-worker, Donna Martell, believes that the woman she once knew would never have gotten over losing custody of her son. Although she hadn't seen or spoken to her friend since the early part of the decade, Donna recalls her being a devoted and attentive mother to John Lee when the women worked together at Universal. "Johnny was such a sweet and beautiful child, and when I knew Barbara, she was always so loving toward him. I mean, she just idolized that little boy. I was absolutely shocked when I read the story in the papers that she had lost custody of him. I don't know what could have happened, but I'm sure that losing Johnny destroyed Barbara."

"She loved John-O beyond words," says Tony. "And John-O clearly worshiped his mother. He had spent some time with us (both in Guaymas and in L.A.). Not a long time; probably no more than two months, all told. But Barbara adored him.

"John-O was a very bright, very proper, well-behaved little boy. Barbara's relationship with him was that of a loving, doting mother, and a loving son. Losing him broke Barbara's heart."

It broke John Lee's heart, as well. Today, he mournfully recalls the agony he felt when forced to leave Barbara, and their beautiful home in Beverly Hills: "I did not want to leave my mother. It was as conscious and strong and painful a certainty for me as it was for her. The day I went to Sacramento to live with my father and his new wife, it was as if a knife had fallen between my past and the present, and what was past, was done, and never revisited.

"However things may appear to anyone else, I had the better part of nine wonderful years with my mother. She was a wonderful mother to me. I was so loved, so encouraged and supported, so wrapped in the full and wonderful complexity of life, that I feel it remains a gift as fresh this very minute, as the first day I opened it at birth.

"The dark part of my mother's personality that everyone else seemed to know about but me was so different from the kind and happy person I knew. I think she must have worked very hard at that. She seemed to be one person with all the other people in her life, and an entirely different person with me. Whatever haunted her so terribly never interfered with our relationship. Never.

"To this day, I don't believe Mom let me go willingly. In fact, I think she fought it with all she had, and I know from our later phone conversation (drunk as she was) that she had felt angry, frightened and helpless knowing the odds were against her in court—even in California.

"I think my father took me away from my mother (and my grandparents) for several simple reasons, and one that is much more complex: first, he was almost certainly afraid that she would take me off to Mexico with her if she had the chance to do so. Second, he felt that her

A 1956 photo of a wasted looking Barbara with her lawyer Milton Golden during the time of her various legal and personal problems in Hollywood. Courtesy of Los Angeles Times Photo

Barbara mugs for the cameras while a clearly uncomfortable Milton Golden looks on. Courtesy of L.A. Public Library/Herald Examiner Collection

life, and that of my grandparents, was just wrong. Third, I believe he felt I would not settle into the new life he had planned for me if my ties to the old were not severed.

"At a deeper level, however, I also feel that my father was punishing my mother by cutting her off from me so completely. As soon as he had custody, Dad was able to get a transfer to Germany, and he extended our time over there, to boot. To this day, I believe we moved to Germany mainly to get me away from Mom, and that although the court gave her monitored visitation rights, Dad made sure she was never able to exercise them even if she had tried. My father later admitted this to me.

"There is no doubt in my mind that my father loved my mother, and that he continued to love her till his dying day. But he didn't take the loss of their marriage very well, no matter how much he insisted that they remained close friends after their divorce.

"Taking me away from my mother was the most awful thing that ever happened to me in my life, even though living with my father was probably the best choice ever made for me. But at nine years old, it wasn't *my* choice, obviously.

"I don't think anyone realizes how close Mom and I were. If you look at the family pictures of the two of us together, it seems to me that you should be able to see it, but maybe that's only because seeing those pictures makes that closeness so immediate and so real again for me. My mother loved me, with all the love a mother can give, and I loved her with as great a devotion and trust, in return. It didn't matter what she did, who came and went in her life (and what they did), or if she was around a lot, or not. I loved her; I always knew she loved me. No words can convey how much I miss her."

Although she seldom spoke of John Lee in the years that followed, the loss of her son caused an open wound in Barbara that would never heal.

Cut off now from the one person who had loved her completely (and unconditionally), Barbara entered the final decade of her life unaware of all the misery that was still to come.

Chapter Thirty:
Battle-Scarred

Bare magazine, subtitled "The Confidential Keyhole," was an exploitative, true-crime tabloid of the mid-1950s that featured photos of scantily clad models and starlets alongside articles with such racy titles as "*I Toured the Passion Circuit,*" "*Inside a Hollywood Bordello*" and "*Mistresses Deluxe.*" The cover of the magazine's April 1956 issue brought Barbara's past and current troubles to light with the headline: *Babs Payton: Is She Through*?

Inside the piece, bylined by Emmett Sullivan, Barbara was described as a "pudgy blonde de-fused bombshell, considerably weightier in bosom and hips, but much lighter in the pocketbook." Sullivan pulled no punches in his discourse, and ripped into Barbara with a fierce hand. "The career of voluptuous Babs has been so intimately wrapped up with the twisted warp and woof of life in the sex-cinema capital, that she has become a symbol of the shoddier aspects of its glamour," he wrote, before proceeding to rehash Barbara's most embarrassing public blunders.

Along with Sullivan's verbal trashing of her, the *Bare* article ran a five-year-old photo of Barbara with Franchot Tone, in which she appeared noticeably fresh-faced and demure. It is particularly sad to note that in 1956, the wide-eyed young actress depicted in that photo no longer existed. She had been replaced by a woman caught in a firestorm of industry derision and public ridicule, and there was a look of wounded bitterness now in Barbara's eyes that was impossible to ignore. The *Bare* article was the first in a series of similar pieces over the next several months that validated the fact that both Barbara's professional and personal reputations in Hollywood had been seriously damaged and were now pretty much beyond repair.

LEFT: *Cover of the July, 1956 issue of* Confidential, *featuring a story Barbara sold to the magazine in which she exposed her 1949 affair with Bob Hope. Courtesy of Alan Betrock* / RIGHT: *Another issue of* Confidential *from 1956, in which Barbara's past affair with actor Guy Madison was revealed. Courtesy of Alan Betrock*

Extremely angry at being forcibly pushed out of the film industry—not to mention, with the literary gutting she had received in the *Bare* expose—Barbara saw an opportunity to get some profitable revenge that spring when *Confidential* magazine publisher Robert Harrison offered her $1,000 to blow the whistle on her 1949 romance with covert lady killer Bob Hope. Evidently still bitter over Hope ending their affair so abruptly, and now at a place in her life where she was truly hurting financially, Barbara spilled the beans in a biting and unflattering cover story for the magazine, titled *Have Tux, Will Travel… What Bob Hope Did With That Blonde*.

"Bob Hope is always zooming around the country," wrote *Confidential* staff writer Horton Streete, "but the liveliest tour of his life began when saucy Barbara Payton came for cocktails—and stayed for capers!" With an air of uncharacteristic bitchiness, Barbara told Streete of her first meeting with Hope in Dallas and then went on to reveal the affair that had previously never been publicly discussed. The comedian was allegedly enraged by her betrayal, according to author Lawrence J.

Quirk, who writes in his biography of Bob Hope, *The Road Well-Traveled*: "Hope reportedly came nearer to a heart attack than he ever had before or since, when Payton's tell-all hit the stands. He made haste to argue that Barbara Payton was a vindictive tramp who had dreamed it all up; a no-good slut who couldn't be trusted and shouldn't be hired."

Quirk goes on to say that Bob Hope believed Barbara wrote the article because she was "peeved that he had never cast her in one of his pictures or put her on his TV show."

In his lifetime, an icon of right-wing conservatism, and to many, the epitome of a true American humanitarian, Bob Hope was also a complex, and at times, mean-spirited individual with the ability to respond with a ruthless vengeance when sufficiently provoked. And Barbara's steamy prose in *Confidential* provided sufficient provocation for Hope to entertain, for a moment or two, the thought of leveling a lawsuit against her and Robert Harrison. That is, until his lawyers reasoned him out of it with the reminder that the resulting publicity would likely only make matters worse.

Hope's advisors never doubted that the charges were true—his endless extramarital flings had been an open-secret in Hollywood for years—but diluting the impact of Barbara's confessional was the most important matter at hand, and by publicly ignoring the issue, Hope could successfully do that.

If Barbara thought the Bob Hope expose would engender a career resurgence for her, she was sadly mistaken. In fact, it was obvious that in a battle between a beloved, box-office superstar and a desperate, ex-starlet-turned-total pariah, there would be only one victor—and it wouldn't be her.

Barbara's poison-pen revelations caused a minor ripple, perhaps some ribbing and a catty remark or two, and then quickly sank without causing any appreciable damage to Bob Hope's legendary career. Deafened by the abject silence that followed the *Bare* and *Confidential* articles, a defeated Barbara threw what few belongings she still owned into a cardboard box, and hightailed it out of town.

Following this latest travesty, Barbara and Tony returned to Guaymas, where he resumed working in the family business while she lost herself in a kind of stunned quiescence. The many personal hits she had taken over the past several months—not the least of which was losing her son—had left Barbara more than a bit battle-scarred, and she prayed for some serenity in her life.

Hoping to lift her out of her despair, and, as he says, "to find us a little slice of domestic peace," Tony began bringing home various animals with the hopes that Barbara might want to keep some of them as pets. As it turned out, she ended up keeping all of them.

"Before long," he says, "we came to own two dogs, Squirt and Maude, a blue-eyed black cat named Circe, a pet raccoon that Pate named Ricky, and two nameless angora rabbits that took their naps resting on Circe's stomach. Pate loved the animals, as did I, and after a while, she seemed to come out of her funk. Barbara always had a tremendous capacity for bouncing back—even during those times when she was so downtrodden and overwhelmed and drinking a lot. If you showed her a little kindness, Pate usually always bounced back. She just wanted to be loved, you know?"

Tony stresses that, "Barbara was so much more than your typical Hollywood glamour girl. During our time together, she enjoyed hunting and fishing, and the outdoors, in general. Sonora is a state in Mexico that is rich in fauna, and we spent a good deal of time studying the abundant wildlife in our area. Pate was always eager to learn more about the things I enjoyed. Now, does that sound like a selfish person to you, the type of person she has always been made out to be?

"When I think of Barbara's massive problems with alcohol, I almost get sick to my stomach because underneath it all she was a very creative and talented girl. Once when we were living in Guaymas, we bought an old, iron-framed bed at a small antique shop. The bed frame was very rusty and beat up, but Barbara took on the difficult and time-consuming task of completely restoring and refinishing it. The job took her several weeks to complete but she eventually did, and it looked fabulous. Barbara had done a superb job and received a lot of compliments on the bed by everyone who saw it."

Although she temporarily regained her balance in Guaymas, Tony says Barbara's drinking eventually resumed, which made their life together very difficult. "When she drank, we would fight like dogs," he says. "Pate's drinking often unleashed some terrible demons inside her. And although I always drank less than she did, when I did join in, it made things even worse between us. But at that point in our lives I still believed I had some control of my drinking and that I could take it or leave it. Barbara's drinking, on the other hand, was destined to pose the biggest threat to our relationship."

Thinking that a change in scenery might improve things for them, Barbara and Tony moved again in 1957; this time, to tiny Kino Bay (a.k.a.

Bahio Kino), a Mexican coastal town a few miles north of Guaymas on the Gulf of California. A pristine, six-mile stretch of sand framed by desert fields teeming with bighorn sheep and mule deer, it was a highly desolate spot in those years—a wild and beautiful commune of under 50 people (most of them, hard-drinking dropouts and fugitives that had burned their bridges elsewhere). An emotionally-bankrupt Barbara, still hurting over both the loss of John Lee and Hollywood's latest rejection of her, huddled beside this motley group of partyers, and welcomed their unique camaraderie. "By this time, Pate had a good conversational capacity of Spanish," says Tony, "so she was able to communicate fairly well with the people there."

While the majority of the dwellings in Kino Bay were little more than flimsy, tar paper huts, the house Tony and Barbara rented from Provas family friend, Victor Estrella, was a large, four-room structure with three-foot thick walls made of stone and concrete. Directly behind the house stood a smaller, three-room building made of cement blocks, which held two local women who served as Barbara and Tony's housekeepers (though how much "house" there was to "keep" remains suspect).

"Except for those two buildings, there was no electricity at all in the village," says Tony. "We had our own gasoline generator which provided all the power we needed for lights and appliances in both houses. With our half-dozen pets (and each other), Barbara and I had all we needed there, and she began to pull herself together a bit."

To make ends meet, Tony brought up one of his family's boats from Guaymas, and chartered it out for sportfishing. "The boat was a sleek 30-foot cruiser we christened *Pride,* and it was skippered by a wonderful guy named Joe Ortiz, who was one of our very best boat captains in Guaymas."

Tony eventually built a kind of makeshift airstrip nearby, and many of his customers who arrived in Guaymas were then flown to Kino Bay to fish in what was considered in those years to be virgin waters. The boat charters were handled through radio contact with the business office in Guaymas, which Tony maintained on a daily basis.

While Tony attempted to relaunch his sportfishing business in the bay, Barbara continued to languish in a state of self-imposed inactivity. A barefoot Bohemian in a bikini top and blue jeans, she spent hours wandering aimlessly along the deserted beaches, and tried to put all her memories of Hollywood—and of losing her son—far behind her. She would later write about her experiences there, in her autobiography: "I took to hanging around the bay. I let my hand droop over the side of our rowboat, letting the water lap at my knuckles. I did nothing all day but relax on the boat, in the hot sun and gentle breezes."

Although Barbara described her time in Kino Bay as if it were a kind of workman's holiday, the truth was far from the picture perfect idyll she painted. In fact, despite its gorgeous location, the village was an isolated and lonely place with conditions that were far more primitive than plush. It was a difficult situation for a woman, who was clearly battling not only a substantial depression, but her raging alcoholism, as well.

"The way Barbara was living down there was actually pretty horrible," Jan Redfield says. "Dirt floors, bed sheets slung over a rope to separate the rooms, and an old wood-burning stove for cooking. For Barbara to go from that beautiful, 15-room house in Beverly Hills to that awful apartment in Hollywood, and then, to that… that… hut, was unreal."

When told of his ex-sister-in-law's remarks, Tony was quick to counter them with a rebuttal. "For reasons of our own, Barbara and I chose to live in a poor fishing village, but we weren't poor. Thank God, and knock on wood, I've never been poor in my life. We went there to expand my business and to be left alone. Period."

Nonetheless, Tony's boat charter service never really took off in Kino Bay and he eventually abandoned it. Frank Redfield blames Tony's bad business sense at the time for its failure. "In those days, that whole area of Mexico where my sister was living was nothing but a haven for winos and beach bums. Kino Bay was little more than an old fishing camp and you had to travel about 30 miles down a dirt road just to get to it. There were some trashy adobe huts there, and a broken-down dock—and not a hell of a lot else."

According to Frank, and contrary to what had been reported in the newspapers, Barbara still had a few thousand dollars in the bank when she left Hollywood, but it eventually all went into setting up the business for Tony. "She paid for the dock to be fixed for the fishing boats, and for a lot more, too. Then Tony hired a bunch of lowlifes as boat operators, and they went out drunk and wrecked all the motor launches. The only people who went to Kino Bay in those days were derelicts that Tony found in the local cantinas. Tony talked Barbara into helping him set up that business and she wound up losing the rest of her money when it went under. In my opinion, Tony Provas is, and always has been, a total flake."

In response to Frank's comments, Tony will only say, "Frank and Janice weren't there, nor were Barbara's parents, although they did visit us, briefly, later on. None of them wanted to have anything to do with Barbara at the time, so there's no way they could have known what really happened down there, could they? I do know, however, and I stand by what I've said."

Randal Barrack was a 14-year-old student at Southwestern Military Academy in San Marino, California, when he and his best friend, Steve Jamison, spent the summer of 1957 vacationing with Steve's family at their home in Miramar, Mexico. Tom Jamison was married to Tony's sister, and he helped manage the family's fleet of sportfishing boats that operated out of The Hotel Playa de Cortez. Jamison and his family lived at The Kilsko, a beautiful waterfront home that was originally a popular dance hall in Miramar. "There was only one sidewalk in Miramar and it started at The Kilsko and ended at The Playa in Guaymas," says Randal. "Potential sportfishing customers at The Playa didn't have too far to go to find Tom, as his unofficial office was the hotel bar. Back then, Guaymas was like Cuba before Castro took over; wild and fun. It was some place."

In what he calls, "the best summer of my life," Randal met Barbara and Tony when he and Steve got into trouble by sinking a fishing boat in the Gulf, and were dispatched to Kino Bay by Steve's father as their punishment. "At first, we didn't know quite what to expect, since at the time Kino Bay was considered to be the end of the world," Randal recalls. "Just ocean, sand and some wooden huts. But to Steve and me it would prove to be one of the greatest places on earth. As soon as we got there, we felt like we were castaways on a desert island."

As a favor to Tom, Tony and Barbara became the boys' unofficial guardians and took them under their wing. While the teenagers were initially impressed by Barbara's blue-eyed and sun-bronzed beauty, Randal, in time, was even more taken by the incredible warmth she exuded. "Barbara had a characteristic that few women even know about, much less possess," he says. "She was, what the British call, *belting*. She was extremely appealing and made everyone around her feel really confident and good about themselves."

Although Barbara and Tony were living in conditions that were, at the very best, extremely lacking, they seemed to be at a happy place in their marriage. "From a 14-year-old's perspective, they seemed crazy about each other," says Barrack. "They got along great, and there were certainly no outward signs of any trouble between them that I could see."

That summer, Tony had brought two of Tom Jamison's 40-foot sportfishing boats down to Kino Bay with the hopes of stirring up some business, but Randal remembers there seemed to be very little work for him. "I can't recall Tony ever taking a client out fishing the whole time we were there. He was definitely at liberty, and spent most of his time with Steve and me. Tony was a smart and friendly guy, and Steve and I both thought he was neat."

At 23, Tony became a kind of surrogate older brother to the boys and kept them busy with fishing jaunts, and some clever storytelling. Randal recalls one such tale that occurred one afternoon when the boys and Barbara were sitting around inside and Tony came in to say that a Seri Indian chief from nearby Shark Island had arrived. "Tony told us that he was the leader of a tribe of practicing cannibals on the island, but that the Mexican government had stepped in to try to get them to stop. Anyway, Steve and I, being young kids, thought we might be the next course on this guy's menu. We were scared, yet fascinated by him: a real, honest-to-goodness cannibal. He came in and we tried to talk to him, but he chased us around like he wanted to have us for dinner! It turned out that he was a friend of Tony's and he was just on a beer run, or something. In the end, Barbara and Tony had a good laugh, and Steve and I had a bit of a thrill. Man, did I have some stories to tell when I got back to military school."

In addition to Tony's good-natured ribbing, the boys received a lot of nurturing and TLC from Barbara. Perhaps she welcomed the opportunity to lavish the kind of affection on them that she could no longer give John Lee. Randal remembers the night she set up a firebox oven on a wall outside the shack and cooked a turkey dinner for them. "It was delicious. Barbara did everything for Steve and me. She pampered us as if we were her own. She was just a stunning human being, in every way."

Randal also recalls Barbara showing them several photo albums full of pictures of her and her Hollywood friends, and how she told them stories about her years in the industry and about all the famous celebrities she had known. "She did talk a little about her wild life in Hollywood, and she was pretty honest about it, too. I didn't get the feeling that she was particularly embarrassed about all the scandals that she had been involved in. On the contrary, I thought she was kind of proud of how crazy and exciting her life had been.

"Barbara was a lot of fun, and she had an enormous amount of confidence. She was also a very intelligent person—how else could she have accomplished so much in Hollywood in such a short period of time? I think Barbara knew how to get people to do exactly what she wanted them to do, and that takes a lot of intelligence."

At least for the months the boys were there, Barbara and Tony's drinking habits had slowed down considerably. "I don't think they were drinking at all," says Randal. "Or, if so, certainly very little. It wasn't an issue for either one of them, as I recall."

After spending a perfect summer at Kino Bay, Steve Jamison moved with his family to Palm Springs, and Randal returned to military school in San Marino. Regrettably, Randal says he never saw Barbara or Tony again.

Nor, for that matter, has he ever returned to Kino Bay. "That was probably the best summer I ever had, and I think I would be disappointed if I went back there now, as an adult, and saw that the place had changed. No matter how beautiful it is, it could never compete with all the good memories I have of Barbara and Tony.

"Spending time with them at Kino Bay was the greatest experience of my early adolescence. Tony was terrific with us, and Barbara wasn't only gorgeous, she was also a wonderful person. I will never forget her."

Chapter Thirty-One:
Going for Broke

With the departure of her young friends, autumn of 1957 once again found Barbara as restless as the low cumulus clouds that drifted over her Mexican village. Although she had remained at odds with her father, Barbara missed seeing Mabel and wrote to her that November to ask if she and Lee would drive down to Kino Bay to spend Thanksgiving with her and Tony. Lee, who had met Tony briefly in Los Angeles, during Barbara's trial for passing bad checks, allegedly hated him on sight, and at first, refused the invitation. However, Mabel finally persuaded him that it might be a good idea for them to see for themselves if Barbara's life had indeed gotten better in Mexico, as she had insisted it had.

In November 1957, the Redfields made the trek from San Diego to Kino Bay, and were summarily appalled when they saw the miserable conditions in which their daughter was now living. It was a labored and uncomfortable reunion, according to Jan Redfield, who later heard about it from Mabel after she and Lee returned to California.

"Poor Mabel was so distraught when she saw that horrible shack Barbara was living in," recalls Jan. "Here she had cold-packed a turkey to cook on Thanksgiving, along with all the fixings, thinking that Barbara had a regular kitchen, and she ended up having to cook it on an old wood-burning stove. Lee was just as shocked with Barbara's living conditions as Mabel, but apparently he didn't have too much to say about it. Knowing how quiet and brooding he was, and how he felt about Barbara, I'm sure he just wanted to get out of there as fast as he could."

In keeping with the surreal turn of events, Jan contends that Barbara and Tony had even invited a Catholic priest from the village to join them for Thanksgiving dinner. "He was apparently a friend of theirs, and Mabel told me how Barbara and the priest got into this deep, philosophical conversation at the dinner table about religion, and God. I imagine Lee was confused by the whole thing (and probably not very impressed by it, either), but Mabel later told me that she was relieved to see that Barbara actually had a priest as a friend."

Says Tony: "While Barbara's parents were civil to me, I always had the feeling they would have been happier seeing her married to someone else. Still, I can't help but feel sorry for them. Seeing the way Barbara's life had declined—in terms of material possessions—must have caused them tremendous pain. But I was doing my best for the both of us, I really was. Her family may never believe that, but I know it's true."

Following a strained few days, during which the entire group's drinking reportedly resumed, Lee and Mabel decided they'd had enough of Kino Bay and returned to San Diego. "I remember Mabel saying afterwards that during their visit, Lee and Barbara had barely managed to keep their anger with each other in check," says Jan. "Mabel also told me that she thought Barbara had totally ruined her life. Barbara had confided in her mother while she was down there that she was very unhappy with Tony, and that she felt trapped by both him, and their marriage. Mabel was extremely upset when she told me about it, and just cried and cried. I think that's when the family decided to try to get Barbara out of there. They got hold of a male friend of Barb's from high school (whose name, for the life of me, I can't remember), who was living in Riverside, California at the time, and he arranged to have Barbara flown out of Mexico without Tony's knowledge. I don't know how they got word to Barbara about it, but they did, and she agreed to do it. I guess Tony came home one day and found a note saying that she had left him and had gone back to California. Talk about dramatic. But, then again, Barbara always made sure there was drama in her life."

"Her friend's last name was Enoch," remembers Frank Redfield. "I can't recall his first name either, but he was a nice guy, and his father owned the Enoch Chevrolet dealership in Riverside. Though I don't know for sure, I got the feeling that Barbara was going with this fellow."

Considering how disgusted Lee was with Barbara, her moving in with him and Mabel was obviously not an option, so instead she got an apartment in Riverside with Enoch. "They rented a cute little place," recalls Jan. "Or, should I say, her friend rented it, and Barbara moved in with him. I was there only once, but it really was nice."

Barbara wasted no time in setting up her next venture, which had her and Enoch opening a combination restaurant/bar in Riverside called The

Boar's Head, complete with an in-house jazz band. Where the financing came for the business remains unknown. "I have no idea where they got the money for it," says Jan, "but it had to be her friend's money because Barbara literally had nothing at the time.

"I remember they worked on the place together, and Barbara decorated it herself. They opened it pretty quickly, too; like, within a couple of weeks. Frank and I went down to the restaurant for dinner a few days after it opened, and I remember Barbara leaving her hostess position and sitting with us and ordering Chateaubriand. She told me she was testing the waiter to see if he knew how to serve it."

"Oh, I remember that meal," says Frank. "It was a French beefsteak dinner for three, served by an entourage of three waiters and the maitre d'. They all spoke with Persian accents. [It was all] very swanky. The meal was served to us with such pomp and circumstance, you would have thought we were royalty. As I recall, Barbara loved all the attention these guys were giving her, and she just ate it up."

"The small jazz combo Barbara hired for the downstairs bar was really, really good," adds Jan. "I forgot their name but we enjoyed them and even bought one of their LPs."

Despite all this, Frank maintains that his sister's new business seemed doomed from the start. "I knew something was wrong right away when I saw how few people were in the place the night my wife and I went there for dinner. That part of town where the restaurant was located was not a good area for traffic, and I don't think she and this Enoch fellow put enough money into advertising."

"I don't know what happened," says Jan, "but Barbara and her friend didn't have the restaurant for very long, when one night Frank and I got a call from him. He was so upset with Barbara, he was almost spitting nails. He asked us if we knew where she was, and, of course, we didn't. But apparently they'd had a big fight and he said the next thing he knew, Barbara had disappeared with all the beautiful, black leather bar stools she had him buy when she decorated the place. They were fantastic-looking (and expensive), and the next we heard from Barbara, she was in Chicago. She called us and said she had sold the stools to get money for an airplane ticket and that she'd flown to Chicago to stay with her friend, Lila Leeds. That whole episode was so totally off-the-wall, I still don't know what Barbara was thinking at the time. It was like her head was in the clouds, or something. I mean, she didn't even try to make a go of that restaurant. Frank and I were both very upset. And her friend, well, he was just disgusted with her, as you can imagine."

After investing a lot of his own money in the restaurant, Enoch was indeed angry with Barbara and exacted his revenge by telling Frank that his sister had been prostituting herself in Mexico, and that Tony was her pimp. "That's exactly what he told us," asserts Jan. "He said that Tony was setting up men to go on dates with Barbara, both in Guaymas and in Kino Bay, and that she didn't mind it, either. We were shocked to hear this and didn't know what to believe, but considering the way Barbara took off for Chicago to be with Lila Leeds—and knowing the trouble Lila would get into up there—I suppose it could have been true." [27]

As Jan has implied, Barbara's girlfriend Lila was indeed up to no good in Illinois. Following her 1948 marijuana arrest with Robert Mitchum, and her subsequent anti-drug cult movie, *She Shoulda Said No*, Lila Leeds' film career in Hollywood was over. After being drummed out of town due to several legal problems, she moved to Chicago in 1950, where she got a job singing torch songs in various nightclubs on the city's north side. That same year, Bud Arvey, the son of Chicago politician Jack Arvey, became her manager and fiancé, but Lila later ditched him for jazz musician Dean McCollom, whom she married in April, and with whom she later had a son, Shawn. Lila and McCollom toured Chicago's jazz clubs with a small band, but neither the band nor the marriage clicked, and by 1951, Lila was again using drugs.

Although she had been banned from California in 1949, following an arrest for reckless driving, in 1952 the California courts rescinded the order and allowed Lila to return to Hollywood. Once there, she looked up her old agent with the hope she could reactivate her film career, but he immediately told her it was a lost cause.

Back in Chicago by 1953, Lila's narcotics use continued to worsen, and she married her fourth husband, jazz pianist and fellow drug user, Irv Rochlin, with whom she had another son, Ivan. In April 1954, while Lila and Rochlin were separated, police smashed in the door of her shabby apartment and found Lila with two men who were known heroin addicts. Also wandering around the place were her two sons, now three and 15 months old, respectively. Lila was arrested for being under the influence of drugs and for neglecting her children, who were reportedly later put in a foster home. According to the 1950s tabloid, *PIX*, her drug addiction was so serious at the time of her arrest, she was placed in "the psychopathic ward" at Chicago's

Failure in Hollywood frequently destroys a girl's moral fiber. Lila Leeds was driven into drug addiction, Barbara Peyton drifted to the borderline of sordid sin.

1950's Nightbeat *tabloid photos of Barbara and Lila Leeds, which accompanied an article titled "The Queens of Sunset Strip: Inside Hollywood's Bedroom Jungle".*
From the Author's Collection

Cook County Hospital, where she was put through a six-day detox. Rather than cleaning up her act, however, Lila was soon back on drugs.

By 1957, Lila had hooked up with a man in Chicago who got work for her as a call girl for very wealthy, out-of-town men. Although she and Barbara had lost track of each other for a time in the early '50s, the women had become reacquainted at some point during Barbara's relationship with Tom Neal. When Barbara decided to split from her restaurant venture in Riverside, she called Lila in Chicago, knowing full well what her friend was doing now for a living.

Disenchanted with Tony and their marriage, bored with her brief try at making it in a straight business environment, and feeling a lot of guilt and self-hatred over the loss of her son, a defiant Barbara rushed boldly into her next profound misstep: joining Lila in her call-girl racket.

For failed starlets of the 1950s with a dearth of career options, especially sexy ones like Barbara Payton and Lila Leeds, trading on their physical attributes for money might have seemed like a perfectly natural and appropriate alternative to working in films, but it was a lifestyle choice that had disaster written all over it. In fact, of all the poor choices Barbara had made in her life up to this point, this was by far the worst. That she even saw it as a viable solution to her problems speaks volumes about her state of mind at the time.

By crossing over the line from sleeping around indiscriminately into outright, organized prostitution, Barbara had found yet another reason to subconsciously punish herself. It was a bad and bitter choice, made even more so because she did have other options. As Jan Redfield says, "The right way to live was always open to Barbara, and help was always there

Barbara's girlfriend, former actress Lila Leeds, shared a similarly wild lifestyle when she and Barbara hooked up for a time in the late 1950's. From the Author's Collection

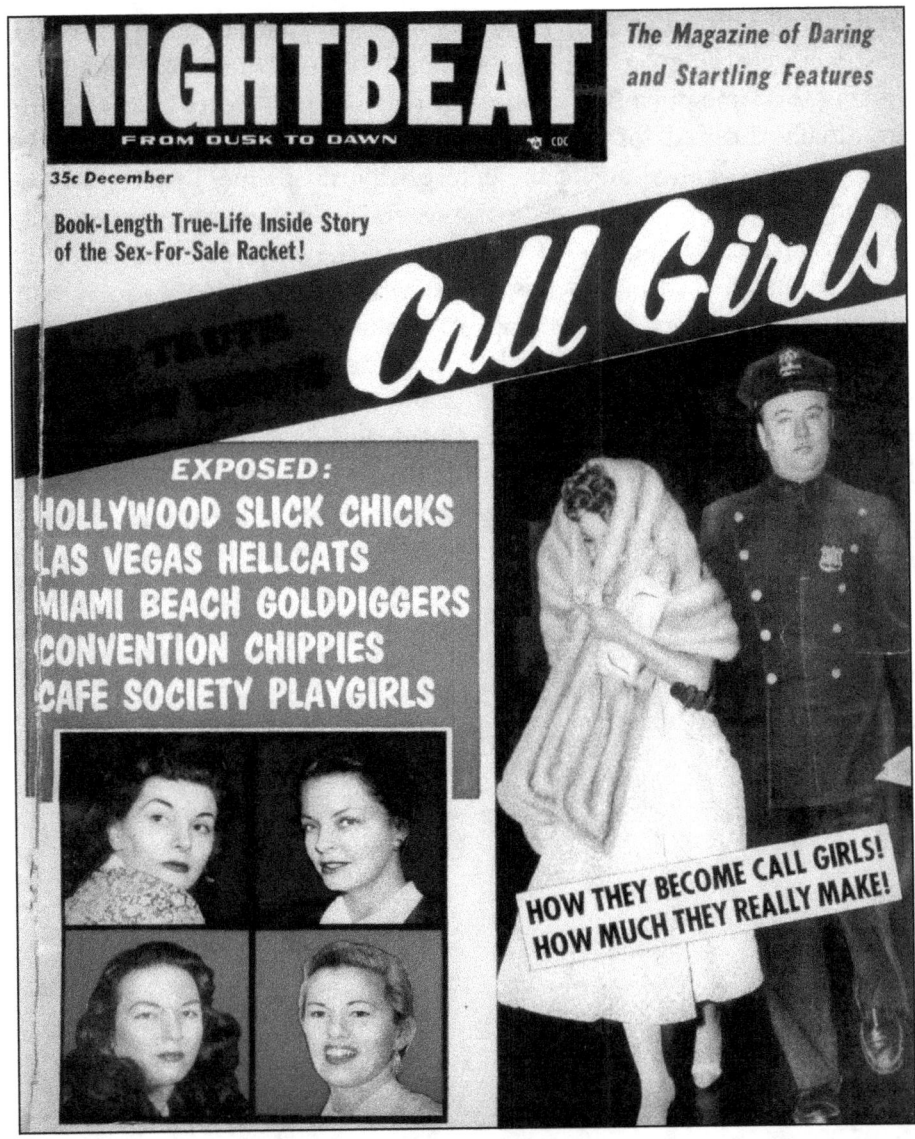

As word continued to spread through Hollywood about Barbara's tawdry and reckless lifestyle, she became a regular topic in such late 1950's tabloids as **Nightbeat: From Dusk to Dawn.** *From the Author's Collection*

for her, too. But she didn't seem to ever want to do the right thing. She only ever did what she wanted to do—no matter how much it wound up hurting her in the end."

Barbara's family had no idea why she had fled to Chicago and they wouldn't hear from her again for several months. In the meantime, she and Lila were holed up in an elegantly furnished suite at The Drake Hotel, and were carrying on to beat the band. Though their exact activities during this time obviously cannot be traced over 50 years later, Lila was eventually arrested for soliciting, while Barbara, for whatever reason, seems to have pulled out of the enterprise just in time. In fact, she was already back living on the west coast when Lila was caught, according to *PIX* magazine, "selling her wares on the street." An undercover detective named Russell Burton had busted her when she showed up for a date with him at the corner of Michigan Avenue and Walton Street, directly opposite The Drake Hotel. Lila later appeared in court and was sent to prison in 1958 for prostitution.

Following her release, Lila Leeds' drug use continued until 1966, after which she embraced a religious lifestyle, eventually becoming an ordained minister in 1973. All evidence suggests that her friendship with Barbara likely faded out by the late '50s. "They looked and acted so much alike, they could have been twin sisters," says Tina Ballard. "Not only that, but for years they both seemed hell bent on ruining their lives. It sounds like Lila eventually wised up. Too bad Barbara didn't."

Chapter Thirty-Two:
Drifting

Upon her return to Hollywood, little is known about Barbara's activities other than she moved in with a B-movie actor named Bobby Hall for a time. A background extra and bit-part player in TV Westerns, and a sometime bodyguard for several Hollywood celebrities, Robert "Bobby" Hall was a six-foot-four-inch, 250-pound rogue with massive shoulders, a thick neck, and squinty, deep-set eyes; sort of a taller and tougher version of Tom Neal. Like Barbara, Hall had a problem with alcohol, and like Tom, he had a violent temper to go along with it.

Barbara's friend and former lover Steve Hayes was a good friend of Hall's and confirms his Bad Boy reputation. "When I first started working in films, Bobby was already somewhat of a legend in town," says Hayes. "With his pushed-in face and whiskey voice, he was extremely memorable, and tough as they come. But tough as he was, he was also inclined to be more of a bully to those he perceived to be weak. If you pushed back, verbally or physically, he generally always backed down.

"Like Barbara, Bobby was also much more belligerent when he was drunk. I remember he caused a spectacle one night by pissing in the fountain on the patio of Villa Frascati on the Strip. The fountain had a statue of a little naked cherub urinating, and Bobby tried to emulate him by climbing into the fountain and dropping his drawers. Then he struck a pose like the cherub and started pissing in front of everyone. An ex-Hollywood cop named Big Bob Drummond and I had to practically beg the L.A. sheriff's department that night not to arrest him. Bobby was a total nut, and a real character."

When Barbara took refuge with Hall, he was living in a rear single room on the ground floor of the Sunset Colonial Hotel. Steve had lived in the building a few years earlier, rooming for a while with Hollywood house painter Dick Morris. "Whenever Bobby couldn't pay his rent," Steve says, "the hotel manager would kick him out. Bobby would always return when he worked on a film or did some bodyguard work and had some money, and the manager would give him back his room. Bobby hung out with tons of celebrities—everybody from Clark Gable to Jack Kerouac. He really got around."

In 1957, Barbara and Bobby Hall had already known each other for several years, going back to when she had starred in her 1951 film, *Drums in the Deep South*, for former slot machine thugs-turned-movie producers Frank and Maurice King. "It was during that time that I first saw them together," says Steve. "I remember going to an audition one day at the King Bros. office, which was located on the Strip next to the Sunset Colonial and across from the Sunset Towers Apartments. As I walked past the outdoor patio of the hotel, I saw Barbara and Bobby eating breakfast together. They both looked a little worn out like they'd had a rough night. I later kidded him about it, and he snarled that he wasn't fucking Barbara, he was helping her. I could tell that Bobby wasn't kidding, so I let it drop.

"Why was Babs with Bobby (both in '51 and again in '57)? It could have been that he took her home because she was falling-down drunk and he took pity on her. Or, it could be that both of them were drunk and ended up at his place. When she was really drunk, I don't think it mattered to Babs *where* she went. Half the time, she probably didn't even remember. Believe me, with people like Barbara and Bobby, they literally just followed the night to wherever it took them.

"I don't mean to imply that Bobby and Barbara were lovers. I don't know for a fact that they were. Bobby was a guy who had a strange place in his heart for people down on their luck, mainly because he was generally in the very same position. I think he and Barbara were soul mates in that they both realized that their mental states were somewhat fucked up.

"Bobby was a loner who didn't want to be a loner. Everyone liked him when he wasn't drunk because that's when he was a bully. But if he had money and was sober, Bobby was a pussycat to be around, and generous to a fault."

Bobby Hall once told Steve's then-wife Janet that he felt sorry for Barbara. "He said, 'Even though she's a fucking round heels, Barbara's a good person.' He added that Hollywood was a shit hole for abusing people on the down side (like Barbara). I'll have to agree with him on that."

Though Steve Hayes is not certain how long Barbara and Bobby were together—Hall died many years ago—it appears they stayed together for as long as they needed to, and then simply drifted apart. By early 1958, Barbara had gone back to Mexico, and Tony, while Bobby waited for his next acting job, which wouldn't come until the following year: a bit-part in a long-forgotten drive-in flick called *High School Big Shot*. After that, Hall had a few more film credits, both in the States and in Italy, before disappearing completely in the 1960s. "I heard that Bobby died of a massive heart attack," says Hayes. "The big lug had packed a lot of living into that ornery old heart, and I guess it finally just gave out."

It remains unknown today how Barbara obtained the money to return to Guaymas, but she did, and Tony welcomed her back. Despite her walking out on him and their troubled life together, Tony was still very much in love with Barbara—and she knew it. "Our separations were always due to Barbara's drinking," he says, "and to a lesser degree, by my own. A lesser degree, because I always drank less than Barbara. Except for the 13 months we spent in Kino Bay, where we actually drank very little, our heavy drinking always hovered over our relationship. It hovered over Barbara more than me, but I always seemed to try my damnedest to catch up to her."

After some months, Barbara and Tony eventually made their way back to the States, and showed up one day at her parents' house in San Diego. For some reason, they arrived without a vehicle, and Barbara told Mabel that they had hitchhiked from Guaymas and were on their way back to L.A. Apparently, they also looked pretty worse for the wear, although Barbara tried hard to keep up the pretense of success by waltzing through the Redfields front door in a full-length mink coat.

"Lee took one look at Tony and refused to let him in the house," recalls Jan Redfield. "After that whole fiasco at Thanksgiving, and with Barbara running away from Tony, only to return to him later on, Lee really hated him, so Tony had to wait for Barbara outside, at the curb."

While Mabel always welcomed her daughter back, no matter what condition she was in, Lee treated her with his usual tight-lipped indifference. The two avoided each other until Lee finally telephoned Frank and Jan in La Puente to come get Barbara and Tony and drive them to Hollywood.

"That was the first and only time I ever saw Tony," says Jan. "When Frank and I pulled up to the house, Barbara was bringing his lunch tray out to him at the curb, in her mink coat. It was pretty bizarre. They had been hitchhiking for a few days, so they both looked a bit rough around the edges, but, my God, she still had her mink."

Inside the house, Jan noticed that Lee was so perturbed with Barbara, he was almost seething. Upon Frank and Jan's arrival, and with not another word spoken to Lee, Barbara hugged Mabel and flounced out of the house, climbing into the backseat of Frank's car, with Tony sitting beside her. Jan was pregnant with her daughter Doreen at the time, and sat in the front seat with Frank.

Once the group hit the freeway, Barbara reached into the pocket of her mink coat and pulled out a pint of vodka, which she started chugging straight out of the bottle. Within seconds, Frank was being directed by a state policeman to pull over. The officer had been riding behind the car and he had spotted Barbara tipping her flask.

"The policeman made all of us get out of the car and stand on the side of the road," remembers Jan. "Here, I stood there like some criminal, with my big, pregnant stomach out to there. It was so embarrassing. Frank was really upset, too. Well, Barbara blew up and lit into that cop with both barrels. I'm surprised she wasn't arrested on the spot, because she went on to call him every foul name in the book.

"Frank finally explained to him where we were going, and he also convinced him that he didn't know that Barbara was back there drinking. Amazingly, the officer believed him, and let us go. But, believe me, the ride back to Hollywood, with a lot of hollering and cursing going on in the car, was not pleasant."

For the record, Tony Provas denies most of this ever happening. While he confirms that he and Barbara had visited Lee and Mabel in San Diego, he contends that his sister Mary had driven them up from Mexico and insists that they never hitchhiked to San Diego, "...or anywhere else, for that matter. And I most definitely did not sit on the curb outside the Redfields' house. I went inside with Barbara. Erwin [Lee] and Mabel never liked me, that's true, but they did allow me into their home." Tony also claims that the entire episode with the policeman never happened. "That whole scenario described by Janice Redfield simply is not true." Despite her ex-brother-in-law's comments to the contrary, Jan stands by her memories of the incident, and remains puzzled ("but not surprised," she says) by Tony's denial of it.

After Frank and Jan dropped them off in L.A., Barbara and Tony immediately looked up his friends, Guy and Ruth Simmons, at their beautiful home in Covina Hills, an exclusive section of suburban West Covina. Guy Simmons was a tough-minded Mormon in his late 40s who owned a poultry slaughterhouse called Simmons Poultry in nearby Baldwin Park, and he knew Tony from his many stays at the Hotel Playa de Cortez. "Guy was an ex-missionary and he was a wonderful, 'family man' who was devoted to Ruth and their little daughter," says Tony. "He and Ruth fell in love with Barbara, and she with them."

"Guy Simmons was big bucks," explains Frank. "His slaughterhouse in Baldwin Park was a very successful operation, and he wanted to build a similar business in Hermosillo, Mexico. When Barbara and Tony got wind of this, they did their best to convince Guy into letting them go into partnership with him."

Barbara, in the poultry slaughterhouse business? Apparently so, according to Tony, who confirms Frank's story, at least partly. "Guy approached me about getting involved in the business," he says. "We visited Guy and Ruth because Barbara and I thought that it sounded like a promising opportunity. My friend Jay de Zaracho, who was a successful politician, was going to be in on it with us, and we planned to build the slaughterhouse and run it from one of Jay's ranches in northern Mexico. However, for reasons I don't wish to discuss, the business never got off the ground."

Frank has his own opinion of what happened, and not surprisingly, he places the blame for the business's failure squarely on Tony's shoulders. "I met Guy through Barbara and I even went to work for him for a while. It was Tony's wanting in on the deal, and nothing else, that ruined it for Barb.

"I remember Guy telling me, 'I can sell poultry meat to the Mexicans for fifty cents a pound, and turn a huge profit down there. I'm willing to

Frank Redfield (right), seen here with his father Lee in the late 1950's, admits to not liking Barbara's fourth husband Tony Provas. Courtesy of Jan Redfield

set up the ranch and processing plant in Hermosillo with Barbara as a silent partner, but Tony's an idiot and I don't want him involved.'"

"As I said, I went to work for Simmons for a while," adds Frank. "I took an apprenticeship at his slaughterhouse in Baldwin Park, gutting and packing the turkeys and then driving the trucks to the market. I hated it. The factory was old and smelly, and Guy was a real slave driver. I quit after six months when he made me responsible for the other employees' safety."

"Guy liked Barbara," says Jan, "but he told Frank and me that he felt total contempt for Tony. He said he didn't trust him. Well, neither did we. The family never accepted Tony, mostly because we all believed he was using Barbara. I think Guy knew a lot more about what was really happening in Mexico between Barbara and Tony than he ever let on to us. After he declined to go into business with them, that was the end of their friendship (or whatever you want to call it)."

"If Tony had not insisted to be in on the deal, Guy Simmons would have done a lot for Barbara," claims Frank. "He said he was more than willing to have Barbara come on board as a business partner, and he had even hired a couple of Mexican attorneys to set it up. If it had worked out, it would have gone a long way in getting Barbara back on her feet. Tony's interference completely ruined that for her.

"My sister had rotten luck with men."

Again, Tony will only say, "That is absolutely not what happened, and once I write my own book on Barbara's life, the full story of Guy Simmons will be told."

With this latest disappointment, Tony and Barbara went back to Mexico and once again tried to find some stability in their lives, but for Barbara, by now it must have seemed like flogging a dead horse. Before long, she was making noises again about going back to Hollywood, for good. Apparently, none of this seemed too surprising to anyone.

With her inability to get any of the business endeavors she had tried off the ground since her arrest, it was inevitable that Barbara would always eventually make her way back to Hollywood, and to her very own Boulevard of Broken Dreams. She would later try to explain the irresistible pull the town had on her, in her 1963 memoir. "I think if I had remained in Mexico for the rest of my life I would have been happy as anyone could be," she supposedly told the book's ghost writer, Leo Guild. "But the career virus is virulent. Like TB [tuberculosis], you can arrest it

In August, 1958, 31-year old Barbara resurfaces in Hollywood in an attempt to restart her film career. Courtesy of USC Library/Dept. of Special Collections/ L.A. Examiner Collection

but you can never cure it. When you're an actress, you're an actress. It's a disease. You just rebel against doing anything else."

As Tony pointed out, it was always somewhere in the back of Barbara's mind that she would one day return to acting, but in her many attempts in the late '50s to do so, Barbara never even came close. With the industry's blacklisting of her locked firmly in place, the former movie star registered with a few local talent agencies like Central Casting, but was unable to get even bit-parts, or day work as an extra. "Bountiful Babs has bounced back to Flickerville," wrote *Inside Story*, of one of her more concerted efforts. "She's making the rounds of the cinema hiring halls and is getting plenty of offers, but no jobs." With each new rejection, Barbara wandered back to Tony and to their isolated and alcohol-ravaged existence on the Gulf of California.

Following an extended period of time where Barbara's name was out of the headlines, she resurfaced in February 1958 with a minor blurb in the papers when she was sued for nonpayment of back rent on the house on North Beverly Drive—a residence that she had long since relinquished. According to her former landlord, E.W. Frederick, Barbara had not only made off with many of the home's household fixtures, she had also skipped town while still owing several months on the rent. Frederick eventually obtained a decision in his favor, and although Barbara was ordered to cough-up a grand total of $854.44 to cover the amount that she owed, the monetary judgment remained unpaid at the time of her death.

Predictably, it wasn't long before Barbara's boredom and restlessness found her lashing out again at her husband. Stifled by a suffocating and joyless marriage that had, in her mind, far outrun its course, Barbara continued to drown her frustrations in booze. Meandering aimlessly between Mexico and California, she drifted, as if pushed along by the winds; never settling in one place for very long but, like a homing pigeon with a built-in magnet for pain, always returning to Hollywood.

Chapter Thirty-Three:
With the Best of Intentions

Barbara's marriage to Tony Provas, which, like all of her other past romances, she had shaken, stirred—and then tossed on the rocks—temporarily ran aground in August 1958. A group of wire-service photos from a press conference she held on August 12 show a surprisingly fit-looking and conservatively dressed Barbara back in Hollywood to publicly announce—to anyone who cared—that she was seeking an annulment from Tony and planning "a major show business comeback." Barbara had charged her husband with extreme mental cruelty and claimed he had refused to allow her to continue her film career. "The marriage was a total mistake," Barbara told reporters, "but I'm not giving up on love. Not by a long shot."

Tony remembers hearing about Barbara's press conference, and says he was surprised by her announcement that she wanted their marriage annulled. "I was back living in Guaymas at the time and I hadn't been in touch with Barbara for a couple of months. I was disappointed by the news, but I felt there was nothing I could do about it. We'd been through so many ups and downs together."

Today, John Lee Payton is quick to add a postscript to his previous stated opinion of Tony Provas, and it is just as negative. "I disliked Tony immediately after I met him, and the feeling intensified right up until I went to live with my father in 1956.

"A lot of men passed through my mother's life and I learned to evaluate them pretty early on. In my opinion, Tony Provas was utterly useless, and clearly one of the biggest losers. In fact, he was the only loser who stayed with my mother and me for any length of time. Lots of men have claimed to have had a lot stronger relationship with my mother than they actually had. But Provas was definitely the worst of the ones who were around for any time at all.

"He caught a ride on Mom's back when she was on her way down, accelerating the fall and glorifying himself for as long as she had anything left to take. Quite simply, he was a parasite."

Tony Provas was deeply distressed to hear his former stepson's comments about him, and in 2005, he attacked those claims with a vengeance: "What John Lee has said about me is light years away from the truth. As for 'disliking me immediately,' never—not once—did he manifest any ill feelings toward me. In fact, it was just the opposite. During the time I knew him, I did everything I could to win him over to my side. I loved his mother very much and my fondness for John was an easy extension of that love. Therefore, I am shocked by what he has to say now.

"All told, John Lee was with Barbara and me for no more than two months, and probably for a lot less time than that. A marriage is supposed to be a 50/50 type situation. For all practical purposes, Barbara was broke when I met her, so our marriage was more like 90/10 (with 90 percent being in my favor). Trust me, at that point in her life there was nothing left to take."

Perhaps the most damning and troubling claim of John Lee's is one that puts Tony in the worst light ever. It concerns an incident that John Lee maintains took place when he was living with Barbara and Tony at their apartment on Rossmore Avenue. Things were tough financially, and John Lee recalls his mother suggesting a possible way out of the situation, which apparently, enraged Tony.

"We were broke at 'Vampira Courts,'" John Lee says today, "the worst I remember in all my years with Mom. She wanted to do something about it (and had an opportunity), but when she told Provas that she could get us out of that mess by having sex with a man she knew who had a lot of money, Tony became furious. He said he was going to kill us both and pulled a knife on us, which I saw, but my mother didn't. When I yelled out to her that Tony had a knife, she stepped between us, and, backing me to the door, told me to run across the hallway to the neighbor's apartment. I did, and Mom later managed to calm him down. After her boyfriend Budo's knife attack on me a few years earlier, I never thought I would have to go through that again—especially from a man who was married to my mother—but I did, and it was terrifying.

"Tony Provas was a mean man, a man who did absolutely nothing for us, a man who apparently was content to do nothing. I wouldn't believe a word he says."

When told of John Lee's claim that this incident had occurred, Tony went to great lengths to refute the allegation, with a driving wrath that was keenly felt. "This is the most blatant lie of all and certainly the cruelest and most damaging to the memory of a mother who may have been 'a bad little girl' and 'naughty' for a great part of the time, but who, at all times, was the most loving and protective mother of a little boy whom she quite simply adored to her dying day.

"What does an eight- or a nine-year-old boy know about 'sex with a man who had the money'? Pure and simple bullshit from the mouth of the worst kind of liar. Barbara never said that. Never, never, never. She might, in a fit of anger—and to hurt me—say it to me, but again, never in front of John-O. She felt such a love for him, and such a need for him to love her, as well, that a statement like that would have been impossible for her to utter in his presence, or even within earshot of him. Barbara never even used profanity in front of her son.

"As for his claim ["he said he was going to kill us both, and pulled a knife"], how can I defend myself against this horrible statement? It's a lie; a horrendous lie. A dirty, blatant lie, uttered by a man who, as he did as a little boy, is probably still watching horror-filled television shows. Suffice it to say that I am incapable of carrying a knife on my person, except on my hunting trips. I am also incapable of 'pulling a knife,' as John says. I am incapable of even thinking about hurting another human being with a knife or any other weapon (let alone someone I love).

"When we were living at the Rossmore apartment, we weren't living on skid row. Our neighbor Vampira had a hit TV show at the time, and she wasn't living on skid row, either. There were no roaches in the apartment, or in the building, or in John-O's cereal, for that matter.

"I can't say for sure why he has said the things he's said about me, but I do know for sure that they are not true. I also know for sure that he is knowingly making these malicious and damaging statements against me, of whom he knows almost nothing, and of his mother, whose memory he should be protecting, not vilifying. Why would a son say these things about a mother he knows loved him more than anyone else on this earth? It's bullshit. It's all bullshit."

Whether one chooses to believe a man's vivid childhood memories, or the equally convincing testimony of another who insists he was nothing but devoted to both mother and son, it appears that Barbara and Tony's relationship was far more complex than anyone, outside of them, will ever fully understand. The one thing that is certain, however, is that there was an inexplicable bond between the pair that was strong enough to see them reunite, amazingly, in matrimony, only a few months after their annulment.

In Barbara's world, it seemed, nothing was impossible.

Barbara looks gorgeous in this rare photo from her August, 1958 press conference. Courtesy of USC Library/Dept. of Special Collections/L.A. Examiner Collection

With her announcement in August 1958 that she was leaving Tony and reactivating her acting career, Barbara had seemingly returned to Hollywood with the best of intentions. Her press conference photos certainly showed her looking in fine fettle. Although she was dressed in a tight, tailored suit that was about five years out of style at the time, the photos showed Barbara looking tanned, trim and, actually, quite lovely. It was almost as if her return to town—this time, to an admittedly small group of waiting reporters—had somehow magically transformed the actress in Barbara, restoring her fighting spirit, and endearing sense of humor, in the process. Clutching a pair of stock company, movie-star sunglasses, Barbara sat cross-legged on a tiny table and proclaimed, "The ants in my pants are crawlin' again!" Unfortunately, the statement was greeted by a round of derisive laughter, courtesy of the acerbic group of newsmen that had most likely gathered there to ridicule her. Barbara saw the rib-poking, and heard their sniggers, and she later told her friend Tina Ballard that it had hurt her deeply.

Today, when viewing the 1958 press conference photos of his mother, John Lee sees an unmistakable look of determination on her face that he finds extremely touching. When the photos were shot, it had been nearly two years since he had been taken away from her, and knowing now the many difficulties she had endured in the interim, only reinforces his respect for her. "The wide-eyed optimism in Mom's eyes is heartrending to me, made more so by the noticeable run in her stockings. She may have been down and her hands may have coarsened, and the news guys may have only been there to put her down, but my God, she was still a beauty, and she was gonna show them."

John Lee's observations about his mother are right; Barbara did look good (very good, in fact), and perhaps she had a reason to believe it wasn't too late to reclaim her career. The caption accompanying her press conference photos noted, "Miss Payton has been away from movie and TV work since 1955 but hopes to return to the Hollywood scene soon."

Despite the two years she had spent floundering—in every way—an optimistic Barbara had whipped herself back into shape and had indeed returned to the Hollywood scene, though it would prove to be far different from the one she had once known.

Eager to get moving with her comeback plans, Barbara borrowed some money from her mother and rented a tidy, first-floor studio apartment in a large house on the corner of Sunset Boulevard and Ogden Drive, right

Actor William Ramage met Barbara at a Hollywood dinner party in 1958. Courtesy of William Ramage

in the heart of Hollywood. Hoping to "start fresh, and with a clean slate," as she told her friend Tina, Barbara telephoned Milton Golden to see if he would handle her annulment from Tony. Both Golden and his wife Charlene were delighted to hear from the woman they had long considered to be a surrogate daughter and a younger sister, respectively, and planned a small get-together for her at their luxurious home on Sunset Plaza Drive.

Actor and model William Ramage was a good friend of Milton and Charlene Golden's, and was among the guests invited that summer evening to Barbara's party. A one-time contract player at RKO, the Texas-born Ramage was then working for Blue Book Models in Los Angeles, an agency whose founder, Emmeline Snively, was responsible for discovering Marilyn Monroe in the mid-1940s. He would later sign a personal management contract with former cover girl Anita Colby in New York, where he was, for a time, the highest paid male fashion model in the country.

Active in stage and television work, Bill's film career was topped off in 1966 with the lead role in a British spy thriller, *A Taste of Fear*, co-starring Anne Baxter. Following a stint producing several films with his business partner, actor Mark Damon, he became a Senior Vice President of a 12-branch bank with executive offices on Wilshire Boulevard in Beverly Hills, and has since retired.

Bill Ramage attended the Goldens' welcome-back party for Barbara with his date, former Paramount Pictures actress Joan Caulfield. Also in attendance were Charlene's close friend Evelyn Stebbins, the socially prominent wife of Arthur Stebbins, a wealthy, Los Angeles land developer, and her escort, a young actor named Leonard Fruhman.

An individual who admits to being blessed with a mind that has total recall, Bill says that Barbara prepared the entire meal herself that night, and recounts the superb quality of the evening's culinary fare: a sumptuous dinner of pasta and sausages, accompanied by a tossed salad with homemade garlic dressing, a hearty red wine, and a rich pudding for dessert.

Bill even remembers Barbara's outfit and her overall appearance that night: "Her dress was simple, almost dowdy, in fact. Not unattractive, just plain. The blouse was rather Mexican looking, pale blue with white lace around the shoulders and sleeves. The skirt she wore was full. No petticoat, just full. It was the same color blue, with a wide tan leather belt. She had on low-heel sandals of tan leather, no stockings. Very 'housewife.' Gorgeous hair, shiny, dark blonde (not platinum blonde) and simply combed, with bangs. She wore no make-up, but believe me, Barbara was lovely.

"It was a wonderful meal and a gorgeous starlit night," Bill continues. "Barbara drank very little with dinner, perhaps two glasses of wine. She seemed a very charming young lady; bright, clever, and a person of wit, and, as I recall, a terrific listener. I was only in my early twenties with little to show—the words 'callow youth' come to mind—but when I talked to her, Barbara looked straight at me with those beautiful and sexy blue eyes of hers and listened to my inane chatter as though I knew the secrets of the ages. Her eyes were spellbinding; almost hypnotic, in fact. It's a real turn-on when a woman looks at a man like that. I think men were fascinated by Barbara, and she knew she had them under her spell.

"God, she was unbelievably gorgeous that night. She had a dazzling tan, and seemed much more slender than she appeared on film. There was no sign whatsoever of any alcoholism and certainly no bad behavior on her part. Barbara was, in fact, as gracious as a duchess. And the laugh. Oh boy, the laugh. The tilt of her head, the laughing eyes, [and] that dynamite smile. She was almost ethereal, I thought.

"I met a charming and classy lady that night at the Goldens' home, and I was very impressed."

With her chameleon-like nature in top form, Barbara had shed her sometimes hard-boiled persona and moved among her fellow guests as though she was to the manor born.

Barbara had not only prepared the entire dinner that evening but had also spent the previous few days reupholstering Milton Golden's favorite chair and ottoman in his home office. In addition to cutting and sewing the fabric for the pieces, Barbara had wallpapered the entire room herself, and had painted all the woodwork and bookcases, too. Apparently the years she had spent slumming in two-bit dives in Hollywood and Mexico hadn't diminished Barbara's domestic skills, and Bill Ramage remembers not only the excellence of her handiwork, but also how it had impressed everyone in attendance.

"Evelyn Stebbins was a good friend of Irving Longinotti, who was the dean of interior designers in L.A. at the time, and her escort, Leonard Fruhman, worked part-time as Irving's assistant. They both saw how skillful Barbara was with fabric, color and design, and I think they were kind of hoping she would express an interest in going to work for Irving—but she never did."

That night after dinner, Bill recalls overhearing Milton and Barbara discussing her wish to have her marriage to Tony annulled, and how Milton had told her that this would require a lot of work from his office—by the hour—and that as it was, Barbara hadn't paid any of her prior legal fees to him in several years. Milton, exasperated by Barbara's insistence that the marriage be annulled, fought to keep his temper in check. "He had one, too," says Bill.

Ramage also remembers how Milton had insisted that Barbara find steady, full-time work, "a regular job outside the entertainment industry," and how quickly Barbara had changed the subject. In fact, she was clearly insulted by the suggestion. After all, she said, she had come back to Hollywood to regain her stardom, not to work in some mundane, nothing position where she wouldn't be noticed. The very thought of it was loathsome to her.

"Barbara owed Milton thousands of dollars by then that he had basically written off," says Bill. "He was a decent man, but a tough son-of-a-bitch in court. I mean this is a guy you wanted on your side. I watched Barbara that night on the terrace play 'kitty cat' with him. She could do it to any man. As I said, her gaze was almost hypnotic. Just moments before she had mesmerized me. It was a gift. No one else in my life has ever looked at me, when I am speaking to them, as Barbara did."

Later that evening, Charlene Golden took Barbara aside and gave her some clothes, including several new cashmere sweaters and one of her used mink coats. She knew Barbara was trying to get reestablished in town and she thought it was the least she could do for all the work Barbara had done at the house.

The clothes, however, weren't the only gifts Barbara received that night. A kindhearted Evelyn Stebbins, upon leaving the party, handed Barbara a sizable roll of cash, "for the delicious dinner" she had prepared for them. Barbara thanked her with a hug and a kiss on the cheek and laughed, "Why, Evelyn, I haven't gotten tipped like that since 1948, when I carhopped at Stan's Drive-In."

Barbara gratefully accepted the women's gifts and Bill remembers looking at Milton, who was by now, grimacing. "I don't think he was angry, per se, just somewhat frustrated and dismayed that everyone was pampering Barbara. He had seen her get that kind of preferential treatment too many times in the past, and he knew it did her absolutely no good."

Bill was the escort that night of the lovely Joan Caulfield, whose motion picture career predated Barbara's by a few years. Joan, also a business client of Milton's, and one of Charlene's best friends, had just completed work on a short-lived TV series for NBC titled *Sally* (in which she had the lead role). Through the years, she and Barbara had seen each other around town pretty regularly, and they were always friendly to one another. They had first met in the early 1950s, at the shop of one of Beverly Hills most exclusive milliners, Rex on Rodeo Drive, and Bill says they were happy to see each other again. "Contrary to the commonly held belief that Barbara was this evil Lorelei whom all women despised, she always got along fabulously with Charlene, and I know that Joan and Evelyn Stebbins were quite fond of her, as well."

Joan, then separated from her spouse, producer Frank Ross (the ex-husband of actress Jean Arthur), seemed especially sympathetic to all that Barbara had gone through in Hollywood. They spoke of some mutual friends, Bill said, and Barbara complimented Joan on her new hairstyle. At the end of the evening, Bill and Joan gave Barbara a lift back to her apartment in Bill's new Cadillac convertible. "With these two lovely ladies sitting beside me in the front seat," Bill says, "I was truly in my glory. Barbara sat next to me and she just exuded sex appeal."

Once at Barbara's apartment, Bill walked her to the door and she kissed him on the cheek. "When she kissed me—very sweetly, very innocently—on my left cheek with her right hand softly touching the other cheek, I truly felt the power of Barbara's magnetism," he admits. "It was electric. Whatever Barbara had, she had it in spades. And she knew it."

As he and Joan drove off, Bill remembers her expressing some concern that Barbara would likely have a great deal of difficulty finding any new acting work in Hollywood. "I recall Joan saying that the publicity Barbara had gotten over the years was 'damning' (especially during the custody fight for her son) and that Hollywood, for all its sins, was rarely a forgiving town.

"Joan said that although Barbara had quite a notorious reputation, she thought she was actually very sweet and so different from the cheap little hussy the papers had always made her out to be. She felt, though, that it was going to be very tough sledding for her and I remember Joan saying that she believed Barbara had made a tremendous mistake in coming back to town."

Several weeks later, Bill heard from Charlene Golden that Barbara's marriage to Tony Provas had indeed been annulled and that she had signed a contract with a talent agent named Leon Lance, an elderly man who had once represented, among others, actresses Terry Moore and Ruth Roman. Lance had been an active agent in Hollywood for many years, but by the late 1950s his business was winding down, and jobs for his roster of artists were scarce. Leon Lance rented a small, cluttered office on the Sunset Strip, but since he no longer drove, he would often have Barbara or one of his other clients drive him around town in search of work.

"Poor Leon Lance was really the bottom of the barrel," says Bill. "He was a nice little guy, but kind of daffy. In fact, the Yiddish word meshugina was often used to describe him. I think Leon's heart was in the right place and he probably tried his best to find work for Barbara, but by then he had lost whatever influence he previously had, and was actually kind of down-and-out. Charlene said that Barbara went out on a few job interviews when she was with him, but I'm sure it was a lost cause, right from the start."

Barbara stayed under Lance's dubious wing for a short time before deciding she might have better luck finding acting work on her own.

Actor Raymond Burr, Barbara's former co-star in *Bride of the Gorilla*, was enjoying tremendous success in the late '50s as TV's *Perry Mason*, and was concerned when he heard of Barbara's current problems. Remembering how she had helped him land the part in *Bride*, Burr tried several times to obtain a guest-star role for her on his television show, but all his efforts proved futile.

"Raymond Burr was a kind and wonderfully generous guy, and he liked Barbara very much," claims Bill. "Charlene said she heard that he went to both the show's producer, Gail Patrick-Jackson, and to Harvey Clermont, the casting director, on Barbara's behalf, to help plead her case. Ray knew she had talent, and Barbara still looked good, but no one at CBS wanted to hear it. Everyone in town knew all about her past problems—and her reputation—and the show's casting and production departments refused to insure her. Unfortunately, it's sad, but true: once a person is down in Hollywood, they're out."

Distressed with Barbara's inability to find work, Milton and Charlene Golden reportedly sat her down once again, as worried family members might do, and tried to persuade her to seek employment in another field. For the second time, they brought up her impressive interior decorating skills and suggested she use them to obtain full-time work outside the entertainment industry, with the Goldens even offering to help her get financial backing to open a business of some kind.

But Barbara balked at the suggestion, says Bill. "She claimed she wasn't expert enough to do that kind of work for a living, and she told them never to bring it up to her again."

Hard as it is to believe, Barbara still considered herself to be an actress, and was appalled by the suggestion that she should do something else with her life; this, despite the fact that she was now practically pinching pennies just to survive. Barbara's inability to handle her finances beyond the most elementary fashion had drained all her resources and had left her indebted to the Goldens, who were, understandably, beginning to lose their patience with her.

"Barbara's continual defiance drove Milt and Charlene to distraction," adds Bill. "That maddening, inflexible focus she had on trying to rekindle a dead film career. And dead, it was. It was as though Barbara had a mental block to heeding good advice. And these were two people who really cared about her, too. Barbara wasn't afraid of hard work; they knew that from all the redecorating she had done for them at their house. But she was insistent that the only thing she knew how to do was act and she absolutely was not going to do anything else. After a while, Milt and Charlene simply gave up on trying to counsel her, and I really can't blame them. Milton once told Charlene and me that the chances for the kind of film career Barbara wanted, 'ended with the first blow Tom Neal struck at Franchot Tone.' And I believe that, too.

"Milt had been very helpful to Barbara and she hadn't paid him for his services in a long, long time. He carried her on the books for many years, and his accountants were always on his back about it because Barbara's bill ran into many thousands of dollars. Both Milton and Charlene had gone above and beyond the call of duty to support Barbara, and they finally had to walk away. But believe me, in the years that followed, Charlene shed many tears over Barbara Payton and the terrible choices she made in her life."

In spite of her adamance, and as hard as she tried, Barbara couldn't get most casting agents or producers to even see her now, much less take her phone calls. Clearly, the days of her securing acting jobs by promising sexual reciprocation, were past.

"When Barbara went back to Hollywood in 1958, the studios wouldn't touch her with a ten-foot pole," says Tony Provas. "Barbara had been a blatantly bad girl, and in those years, that didn't fly with the public, or the industry. This, coupled with Barbara's never being able to say 'I'm sorry,' really sealed her professional fate.

"Earlier in our marriage, when she would mouth off to a gossip reporter or to one of those shrewish female journalists in L.A. who hated her so much, I used to take her aside afterwards and say to her, 'Damn it, Barbara! You have to watch what you say to these people. Tone it down, for God's sake, will you?' And she would look at me with her eyes blazing and say, 'Why? Why should I watch what I say? They don't! They say whatever they damn well want to and drop their nasty little innuendoes about me every chance they get. So I'm gonna sling it right back.'

"Barbara was an outspoken and controversial person and people had come to hate her for it. You see, in their eyes, she hadn't earned the right to be that way. She wasn't a mega-star like Bette Davis or Joan Crawford, who were both allowed to run roughshod over people. Barbara was just a washed-up little starlet to a lot of them, and they were going to enjoy stomping her into the ground."

Now finding herself far outside the parameters of the Hollywood mainstream, by 1958 Barbara saw that she had been almost completely forgotten. To some in the industry, Barbara Payton was a has-been; to others, perhaps, a never-was. It was a realization for her that was no doubt humbling, and extremely painful.

"She complained and cried about it a lot," says her friend Tina Ballard. "For a long time, Barbara really thought that Hollywood would give her another chance. By then, she had suffered a lot of pain in her life and she felt it had given her a depth to her personality that she didn't

Barbara's ex-husband Tony Provas (seen here in a 1970's photo) reunited with her briefly in the late 1950's. Courtesy of Tony Provas

have before. She was just itching to get back on the screen and prove to Hollywood that she could really act, you know? She thought she could do the kind of classy roles that Kim Novak was doing; maybe even act for Alfred Hitchcock. She even dressed conservatively in tailored suits and wore her hair up like Kim did so that people could see her in the same light. In fact, if you take a look at those press conference photos of Barbara from that time, you'll see that she kind of resembles Kim Novak. But in the end, it all added up to a big fat nothing.

"Unfortunately, Barbara's personal life always took precedence over her career. Then, when she decided to really zero in on it [her career], it was already too late and there was nothing left of it. And yet Barbara would always say, 'I'm gonna star in more movies, Tina. You'll see.' She always thought that, right up to the end."

One can envision Barbara's drinking habits shifting into overdrive as she came to see that rather than being given another chance, she had been kicked out of the filmmaking industry for good.

Chapter Thirty-Four:
Hanging on to Nothing

Having cut her marital ties to Tony just months before, and with seemingly very little remorse, Barbara was probably the last to imagine that the two of them would ever get back together again, but in late 1958, that is exactly what happened. Then again, considering her past track record of often returning to both her ex-husbands and former lovers numerous times after leaving them "for good," perhaps Barbara's reunion with Tony was not that surprising, after all.

The couple met again, not in Mexico, but at a hotel in Beverly Hills. By that time Tony had gotten back into dating and was playing the field with a host of lovelies on both sides of the border. "I had been seeing several different ladies and then I took up with a very wealthy woman I knew named Helen who hailed from Hubbards Woods, Illinois," he explains. "She and I were staying in a suite at The Beverly Hilton Hotel on Wilshire Boulevard and somehow, Barbara found out about it. To this day I'm still not sure how she knew I was there, but she did, and decided to pay me a surprise visit.

"Barbara had met Helen a few years before, in Guaymas, and they got along fine. Anyway, Pate came up to the suite, and I answered the door. With just one look, I knew I was still in love with her. She was still gorgeous. She was still Pate."

Tony invited his ex-wife in and claims that he, Barbara and Helen engaged in some small talk and even shared a few drinks together. He maintains there was no rivalry between the two women, and that they were friendly and pleasant to each other. "Then, when Helen stepped out of the room for a minute, Pate asked me if I was happy," he says. "Without a second thought, I said no. Pate said something like, 'Tony, let's get out of here' and I answered, 'Give me five minutes to pack my bags.' And that was it. We said our goodbyes to Helen when she returned (she understood), and we left."

Amazingly, those few words were all it took to restart the couple's relationship—at least, according to Tony. While he insists that he had never stopped loving Barbara, one wonders what her true intent was for seeking him out. Did she miss his companionship and the wild times they had together, and was she still in love with him, or did she already know she wasn't going to survive in Hollywood this time without his—or someone's—help? It's an intriguing question but one, unfortunately, that Barbara's family and friends cannot shed much light on.

"When Barbara went back to Tony," her sister-in-law Jan says, "it was like, 'Well, here she is on that damn merry-go-round again.' That's exactly what it was like. She'd get on it and she'd go way up and then she went around the bend and you wouldn't see her for a while. Then when she came around again she was all upset and she would want to get off the ride. It was pretty ridiculous."

After their reunion at The Beverly Hilton Hotel, Barbara and Tony moved into a small motel in the Valley for a week, so that they could make up for lost time, and see if the magic was still there. "It was," he reveals. "We were in love again—maybe more in love."

Following their week-long rendezvous at the motel, the couple went to Monterey Park for several days, where Tony says they housesat for friends of theirs who were on vacation in Guaymas. Thereafter, they drove to Nogales where they were married for a second time. "Afterward, Pate and I settled in a cinder-block house on my family's farm outside Guaymas," says Tony. "I resumed raising cucurbits, as well as overseeing their harvest and shipping to the States, and Pate helped me in the fields."

On the surface, it is just as hard to imagine Barbara Payton, the former glamorous film star and one-time habitué of Beverly Hills, living in a cinder-block house on a Mexican vegetable farm, as it is picturing her inhabiting a dirt floor shack in Kino Bay, but it actually makes perfect sense, considering the bizarre track the rest of her life had taken.

When contacted in 2006 to describe his life with Barbara in Mexico—the second time around—Tony Provas said he preferred to save that information for the book on Barbara's life that he has been working on "for several years." What is known, however, is that their reunion was short-lived, according to Jan Redfield and Tina Ballard.

"I don't know what possessed Barbara to marry Tony again," says Jan, "but I do know that she didn't stay with him for very long. In the late '50s, she still made frequent trips back up to San Diego and Hollywood to see her family and friends, and when she did, she never even mentioned Tony.

"I do think that Barbara's alcoholism worsened while she was living in Mexico. Each time she came back home she seemed to be in a lot worse shape than she was when she left. Barbara never talked about Tony or about what they were up to down there, but it's always been my opinion that whatever she was into was not healthy. She must have thought so, too, because after a while, she finally left him, and Mexico, for good."

Tina Ballard says, "I always had the feeling that Barbara's marrying Tony again was just another display of her doing things on the spur of the moment, without any thought or regard of the possible consequences. That's why I will always contend that Barbara was manic depressive, or bipolar. She had these 'flights of fancy' and did whatever felt good to her, but when things soured—and they usually always did—she just wanted out. I'm certain that applies to her second marriage to Tony, as well."

When pressed for information on their life together in Mexico in the late 1950s, Tony will only say: "Our second marriage lasted just a couple years, but we weren't together all of that time. [28] Barbara and I had already been separated for quite a while when we got our second divorce [sic]. After we separated, Barbara did return to Hollywood, that's true. She was drinking a great deal more by then, and she didn't seem to care."

At some point in 1959, Barbara apparently left her husband behind on his family farm and once again made her way back to California. Financially strapped, yet always seeming to have enough money for booze, Barbara crash-landed in a rundown apartment building near the corner of Sunset Boulevard and Fairfax Avenue, in a decidedly second-class area of Hollywood. The five-story Valencia Apartments had been built in the early 1920s as a respectable haven for some of the film capital's busiest character actors, but by the late '50s it had lost its grandeur, and was home to a somewhat hapless group of out-of-work extras, strippers and winos. Although it stood in an advanced state of disrepair, The Valencia, like some faded, southern belle, had managed to retain a shred of its former glory. Of course, the same could be said for a heavier, but still-beautiful Barbara, who seemed to have found, in this old tomb, a temporary refuge for her memories.

While sequestered at The Valencia, and with her fragile pride barely intact, Barbara once again put her acting aspirations aside and took two consecutive jobs in 1959 and 1960—working first as a hostess at The Saratoga Restaurant, and then as a counter girl at The Sunset Plaza Dry Cleaning and Laundry Shop. Every evening, Barbara would walk the three blocks from her room at The Valencia to The Saratoga, as she no longer had her prized Cadillac convertible to get her around town. Times were tough, and she had sold it some time earlier for a few hundred bucks.

Barbara later told Charlene Golden that her hostess job at The Saratoga was "all right," except for the humiliation she felt when seating the celebrities at whose opulent Beverly Hills homes she had once dined. It was a particularly demeaning experience for her to see people she had known socially, now pointing and whispering about her behind her back, or, worse yet, making sarcastic cracks, within earshot, about her obvious fall from grace.

Barbara eventually felt the need to blot out the malevolent stares and outright insults with frequent shots of liquid comfort. Before long, she was hanging out at the restaurant's bar long after closing, trying hard to numb the disgust she felt over her descent into common servitude. Barbara had learned all too well that Hollywood after hours can indeed be a very lonely place.

An actor friend of Bill Ramage's moonlighted as a waiter at The Saratoga during the same time Barbara worked there, and he claimed that she was a problematic employee who was not well liked by her co-workers. "I remember him telling me that Barbara was always 'buzzed up' and that when she wasn't walking around depressed or high, that she had a really bad temper and snapped at everyone," says Bill. "He also said she was beginning to lose her looks. I didn't see Barbara in 1959 or 1960 so I can't say how accurate that is. When I did see her again, in 1963, she was a completely different person."

Milton and Charlene Golden came into The Saratoga a few times for dinner as they were curious to see how Barbara was making out in her first real job in several years. They were no longer seeing her socially, which saddened Charlene, in particular.

"By now, Charlene was very worried about Barbara," adds Bill. "Her drinking was increasing, and she was withdrawing from all her old friends, including Sally Fiske and Leslie Snyder. Charlene said that when she saw Barbara, she acted very distant with her and Milton. That broke

Charlene's heart because she had always felt so close to Barbara. But she acted like she didn't want to know Charlene anymore."

Barbara's job at The Saratoga lasted just a few months before she was let go (allegedly, for coming to work stoned). Her time at the dry cleaners was similarly short-lived, and as her drinking habits worsened over the next several months, Barbara took a series of low-paying jobs—working as a cocktail waitress in a seedy strip joint, then as a shampoo girl at The Brush Wave beauty shop, even pumping gas for a while on Hollywood Boulevard.

"My life's been so messed up, it's hard to know *what* I want to do," she told her few remaining friends. As she disappeared further into the Hollywood background, Barbara's ever-loosening ties to the motion picture business grew more and more tenuous. She was well off the industry's radar now, and sliding further into obscurity.

Tina Ballard met Barbara for lunch a few times during this period and recalls how hard her friend was struggling just to stay afloat.

"For the first couple of years after she returned from Mexico, Barbara seemed very serious about wanting to return to show business," says Tina. "But deep down I think she knew that all the doors in Hollywood were closed to her for good. For a long time she seemed to believe that she could overcome almost anything the industry and the press threw at her, but then almost overnight I saw her whole attitude change. Barbara finally said she was willing to try other things [besides acting] to make ends meet, but she could never decide what those other things should be. It certainly wasn't hostessing.

"After she hit thirty, Barbara seemed to want to reclaim that feeling of still being young and desirable and wanted by every man who saw her," stresses Tina. "On one hand, she thought she still had a chance [in Hollywood], but on the other, she knew it was gone forever.

"I mean, how much of a chance did she really have when she was down to washing old ladies' hair, or waiting on bums in a strip bar? And, of course, by then she was drinking so much. She had gotten hard."

With the pickings nonexistent in Hollywood, Barbara may have felt she needed an escape from the frustrations of her failed movie career, part-time marriage, and general lack of options. In 1960, she left her apartment at The Valencia and returned to her parents' house in San Diego, to try to decompress and figure out what to do next.

It is important to note that Barbara showed up at her parents' home countless times in the 1960s, especially when there was no place else for her to go. Even more significant, perhaps, is that her desperation was such that she would go back to the source of much of her inner pain and emptiness—her father—for solace. It was as if Barbara was hoping each time she returned home that Lee would show her the love and support he never had, and that everything would finally be right between them.

It never took Barbara very long to see, however, that the hostility her father had always felt toward her, clearly hadn't dimmed in her absence, but was, in fact, renewed each time he saw her.

During her latest stay in San Diego, Barbara spent the afternoons vegetating by the pool with Mabel, and the evenings in the kitchen, preparing dinner for her parents. Far from being the benign family portrait this suggests, however, the trio's daily activities always included plenty of drinking, as well. "Sooner or later Barb and Mabel would always get into trouble together with the booze, which really angered Lee," recalls Jan Redfield. "I think he blamed Barbara for a lot of Mabel's drinking, but, in all fairness to Barb, Lee and Mabel always did pretty well in that area without anyone else's help." The truth is, Barbara and her parents were tied to each other in an alcoholic dependency that went back many, many years, and at this point in their lives, it was perhaps the strongest link they had.

As a child, Cheryl Perry lived across the street from the Redfields, and she recalls them being a friendly couple, but one whose personal problems were obvious to everyone around them. "Lee and Mabel were wonderful people," she says. "Their swimming pool was always open to all the kids in the neighborhood, and I was over there all the time. But it was common knowledge on our street that Lee and Mabel drank. They drank a lot.

"From what I have gathered, for many years Lee and Mabel drank more on the weekends, than they did every day. Unfortunately, though, liquor definitely became their worst enemy. In the early '60s, I remember seeing Barbara at her parents' house quite a lot. I was in junior high at the time, and I recall her sitting on the diving board and telling us kids about all the big movie stars she knew back in Hollywood. I don't remember too much of our actual conversations, but I do recall thinking at the time that her life sounded very glamorous. I mean, we were always so in awe of who she was, and who she knew. During this time, Barbara still looked good. Heavier, but still pretty.

"Sometimes Barbara, Lee and Mabel would sit around the pool and drink together, and when they did, they always drank to excess. And then, the hollering would begin. I could never make out what they were fighting about, but it happened a lot. There was obviously a lot of anger there. Such an unfortunate situation, because when Mabel, in particular, was sober, she became a completely different person; very soft-spoken and proper, [and] a real lady. When my family first moved to the neighborhood, Mabel was quite heavy, but over the years she lost a lot of weight due to her drinking. Unfortunately, when she drank, she didn't eat.

"We all loved Mabel. She was a sweet person with a big heart. Too bad the drinking eventually got the best of her, as it did Barbara."

Whenever she came home, Barbara always slept in a small guest bedroom next to Lee and Mabel's room. One day during this latest visit, Barbara showed a particular contempt for her father's despotic manner when she waited for him to go to work and then painted all the walls and furniture in her bedroom a defiant shade of black. When he learned what Barbara had done, Lee, naturally, was furious.

"He gave her one week to repaint it," says Jan, "but Barbara refused, saying that she loved the way the room looked as it reminded her of midnight—her favorite time of day. After a lot of arguing between them, Lee dropped it, but he later replaced all the furniture, and painted the room back to its original color."

Juvenile antics like this only heightened the already strained relationship between the 33-year-old Barbara and her father, and within days, they had both had enough.

As she always did whenever Lee reacted badly to her actions, Barbara took off into the night like a runaway teenager, and returned to Hollywood.

Sometime during this period, Barbara threw some clothes into a suitcase and scraped together the money for a bus ticket to Palm Springs, where her former producer Bob Lippert remembers seeing her one afternoon in a cocktail lounge at The Riviera Hotel.

"I walked up to the bar and sat down, and my God, I'm sitting next to Barbara Payton," he recalls. "I didn't introduce myself to her because it was obvious that she wasn't there to socialize. Barbara looked terrible. She was heavily made up and she looked very jaded and worn out. I remember glancing down at her hands and they were filthy. Dirt under the fingernails and everything."

Lippert later found out from the bartender that Barbara had taken a room at the hotel and was working out of the bar as "a $100 a night hooker."

At the time, Barbara tried hard to justify it to herself: "There are men who can't get love unless they buy it. I sell it. What's wrong with that? I admit I'm a little heavy, but for the act of love I have the perfect body. Men like to go to bed with a movie star."

But Barbara wasn't a movie star anymore. She was a confused and aimless child, trading on a once-glamorous reputation that she had long since destroyed. With her inability to see past the next drink—much less, the next man—Barbara seemed to be in a constant state of disarray and confusion. So numb was her spirit now, and her clarity of mind, impaired, that Barbara didn't even *know* how lost she was.

With her coarse and puffy appearance preventing her from getting much business in a town literally overflowing with beautiful women, Barbara's stay at the Riviera was obviously short-lived. When the manager of the hotel heard about her tax-free enterprise, she was promptly ordered to vacate the premises. By now accustomed to a life lived in exile, a world-weary Barbara packed her bags and left.

Much like the proverbial phoenix, Barbara rose from the ashes of her latest disaster and hitched a ride out of town on the hot, desert winds. A modern-day prairie harlot wandering the Wild West, she touched down next in Nevada, seeking solace for a while in the dusty gambling town of Searchlight, located several miles outside Las Vegas near the California border. While there, Barbara dated a gambler with mob ties (a man she coyly refers to in her autobiography as "Dick Fortune"). She later admitted that she also resumed turning tricks—though this time not in the lush environment of The Palm Springs Riviera, but in a tiny studio apartment behind a casino. For Barbara, it was a long way from Beverly Hills to what surely seemed the loneliest spot on earth.

Searchlight and "Dick Fortune" ultimately proved to be little more than momentary blurs on Barbara's twisted road map of memories. Within months, she was back on the road—with Hollywood, again, her destination.

Jan Redfield remembers seeing Barbara following her disastrous stopovers in Palm Springs and Searchlight. "She showed up one day at our house in West Covina in very bad shape. Barbara practically crawled out of a car driven by some sleazy-looking guy we never saw before. When I let her in the house, it was very apparent to me that she had gone some time without bathing. She was covered from head-to-toe in bug bites, and she looked like she had been off rolling around in the mud somewhere.

Barbara was wearing a dirty, one-piece playsuit of red and white polka dots, with some white trim around the collar and cuffs, no belt, and a red bandana on top of her head that covered most of her hair. She had really ratty-looking moccasins on her feet, which, by the way, were filthy. I just shoved her in the bathroom and fixed the shower for her, and I told her to strip off her clothes and toss them on the floor.

"I threw Barbara's clothes in the washing machine (with lots of soap and bleach) and gave her one of my outfits to wear when she was done showering.

"Barbara claimed she had been up in the Nevada mountains camping with whoever it was that dropped her off, but I had my doubts about that."

Jan recalls that Barbara left that day, as quickly as she had arrived. "Without Frank's knowledge, I slipped her some money because she said she was broke. After the one guy left, another man came and got her, and off she went. I felt so sorry for her. Barbara seemed to have lost interest in accomplishing anything with her life—except for bumming around—and there was just no talking to her."

Back in Hollywood by 1961, Barbara returned to The Valencia Apartments and managed to patch herself up enough to make another halfhearted assault on the industry. Tony Provas claims that it was during this period that he saw Barbara for the last time. Although the couple was still legally married, it seemed a mere formality as they hadn't lived together, much less seen each other, in many months. Tony was staying in L.A. by that time—he had taken a job in a pipe and tobacco store in Westwood Village, and he had bumped into Barbara, he says, at The Cock 'n Bull Restaurant on Sunset Boulevard.

"I ran into her unexpectedly, and I was quite stunned by how different Barbara looked. At the time she mentioned that she was living at The Valencia Apartments on Sunset and that she was trying to get back into the business. She was friendly enough, but you would never have known we were married. Barbara was drinking a great deal more by then, and she had gained a tremendous amount of weight. Pate was fast losing her looks, and it didn't seem to bother her. Seeing her like that was extremely upsetting to me."

It was so upsetting that Tony decided to end their charade of a marriage soon afterward. "We were legally divorced," he says, succinctly. "I had tried to make a go of it with her a second time, but it was no use. By that point, Pate was more of a stranger to me, than a wife. I walked away and so did she, and I'm not even sure she cared."

Barbara, as she appeared in the early 1960's. From the Author's Collection

In a similarly evasive (and rather ominous-sounding) passage from her memoir, Barbara later said, "It was a short marriage that I don't even want to talk about. It didn't last long. There are good things and bad things I want to forget. That's my privilege. So I prefer not to dig up certain things."

Perhaps it will take Tony Provas's future book on his relationship with Barbara to finally address the many questions that continue to surround their time together in Mexico. At the very least, one hopes that the book will explain, as he promises it will, the complete story of their life together.

With her fifth marriage (to her fourth husband) now over, Barbara resumed her efforts to jump-start a career that had long since derailed. By 1961, she was again sleeping with producers and casting agents in town, in an attempt to get work. Desperate to re-enter show business, Barbara had put herself on the market, with few, if any, pretensions.

A telling incident occurred when Barbara slept with one well-known producer and then looked for the envelope containing the three hundred dollars that he usually left for her afterwards. This time, she was angered to find only one hundred dollars in the envelope. When she questioned him about the amount, he explained to her, "Three hundred was a long time ago. I don't want to hurt you, Barbara, but you've lost a little since then. To me, right now, you're worth about a hundred dollars."

The illusions in Barbara's life seemed to be fading as quickly as her dreams.

Although no offers for acting had come her way since her initial return to Hollywood in 1958, by 1961 the 33-year-old former starlet had been tracked down by an unidentified freelance photographer who wanted to take some nude photos of her. "He supposedly told Barbara that he would shoot them on 'spec,' and then submit them to a few men's magazines until he got a bite," recalls Tina Ballard. "I told her that she was crazy to even consider the offer, but she went ahead and agreed to it anyway. Over the course of a few weeks, Barbara met with the guy at a couple different locations in Hollywood, and she later raved about what a fantastic experience it was. When she told me that, I felt sick to my stomach, as I knew what it meant. It was obvious to me that Barbara didn't have a clue as to what she was doing. Thank God I never saw those photos."

Deluding herself into thinking that this opportunity would revive her long dormant modeling career, a now redheaded Barbara soon found herself lounging on cheap vinyl couches in low-rent studios hidden high above the Sunset Strip. The studios were little more than dingy back offices with see-through wardrobe screens and busted ceiling fans; forgotten little hovels where Hollywood's washed-up fringe set played out the misplaced fantasies of their youth. In this sordid setting, Barbara shed her clothes and writhed dutifully for booze and rent money. Sadly, it was a long way from 1946, when she was posing in pinafores and modeling the Junior Miss line for Saba of California.

An ex-stripper from coastal Oregon named Norma "Knockers" Dodson allegedly befriended Barbara in the early '60s when they both lived at The Valencia Apartments, and in 2001 she resurfaced after seeing a TV special on Barbara's life on E! Entertainment Television's now-defunct *Mysteries & Scandals* show. Then in her mid-70s and, in her own words, "still the gum chewin', finger snappin' fox I always was," Norma claimed to have seen Barbara's contact sheets from her modeling sessions, and admits to being taken aback at how badly her friend had photographed.

"Those pictures were horrific," recalled Dodson. "Barbara had dyed her hair a carrot red for the occasion, and she had these bushy, jet-black eyebrows that made her look old and horrible. Not to mention, she had really 'ballooned up' from the booze. Barbara was way too heavy to be posing that way—you know, stretchin' and rollin' around; puckering her lips and blowin' kisses. Striking poses she thought were sexy. Trust me, nothing about those shots was sexy.

"I met the guy who took the pictures when he was in Barbara's room, talking to her about doing them, and I was not impressed. I mean, here I was, with a knockout shape, and this guy wants to shoot *her* naked? It didn't make any sense. He struck me as being very bookish and odd, and he also stunk to high heavens. You know, like he had crawled out from under a rock somewhere. Let me tell you, Hugh Hefner he wasn't. That's why I contend that this so-called professional photographer was really some kind of nut who just wanted to bed down with her. He did, too. Barbara said that she was so happy he had given her a chance at getting back into the business, that sleeping with him was the perfect way to repay him. She had a delusional way of thinking that was just very, very sad.

"Barbara was a little lost babe in the woods. She came on all piss and vinegar, like a real tough number, but she was a little lamb inside. An easy mark for every Tom, Dick and Harry that came down the pike. Barbara wrote the most beautiful poems about her life and she was really a very sensitive girl. She cried if you were hurtin', you know? At the time I tried to counsel her a little bit, but in those years I was fighting a bad drinking problem myself, so who was I to tell her what to do? I remember looking at her modeling photos, though, and thinking, 'Oh, boy, this little thing has really lost it.'

"You know, she disappeared from my room that day with those damn contact sheets tucked under her arm, and I didn't see her again for weeks afterward."

Luckily for Barbara, nothing from her 1961 modeling sessions was deemed marketable, and the resulting prints were never published—disappearing one day, along with the mysterious photographer who took them.

Soon afterward, when it became clear to her that the film and modeling industries had closed their doors to her forever, Barbara gave up the fight and descended on the streets of Hollywood.

Unemployable and near destitute—and with her alcoholism skyrocketing out of control—Barbara turned to hooking full-time. As she would later write, in her autobiography, "It's when you start to slip that one night you say to yourself, 'What's a whore?' Because when the big money stops coming in, but you're still living the same way, money becomes something real instead of figures on a business manager's pad. Now, money means paying the rent, food, clothes and drink. And that last item is the most important. If not for that, you'd be thinking twenty-four hours a day about paying the first three."

While living at The Valencia Apartments, a lonely and morose Barbara would often accept visits from a few old-timers she had known from her days at Universal and Warner Bros.—a craggy and booze-sodden lot of third-rate cowboy actors and failed bit-part players, who were, in Barbara's words, "…mad for my big bosom and womanly form."

Barbara, in turn, welcomed the companionship of other out-of-work show folk, and appreciated whatever modest favors they offered her. Swapping war stories in her grungy dustbin over shots of rotgut whiskey, she and her guests would gaze out the window at the sunlit streets below, and recall their long-lost glory days.

But all the hazy memories and forced laughter in the world couldn't keep Barbara's plummeting morale afloat. Each night, as the shadows of dusk turned to darkness over Hollywood, Barbara tilted the Venetian blinds on the windows of her room, and with her profile harshly lit in flashing neon from the street lights below, Barbara did whatever she could, to forget.

Frustrated that she had been barred from making the show business comeback she had hoped for, Barbara upped her alcohol intake and watched her movie-star looks disintegrate under its liquid assault. Tailored suits and bikinis soon gave way to tent-like caftans and dressing gowns she left on for days. Barbara's acting career, which once held real promise, now faded into a dim and distant memory.

"She lost herself at the bottom of the bottle," said Norma Dodson. "Me, I had just been shakin' my can in two-bit bars up in the Pacific Northwest. By the time I rolled into town and wound up at The Valencia (due to my own battle with booze), I hadn't really lost that much. But, my God, Barbara had lost that big house in Hollywood, as well as all her jewelry and her expensive clothes, and cars. And all those high-toned, movie star friends of hers; every one of them had left her high and dry.

She was down to nothing, you know? Getting by on wit and grit. She was hurting so bad, and she just wanted it to stop. You know, 'Go away'!"

During this extremely dark period of her life, Barbara was involved in an incident that is heartrending in its poignancy, and revealed her seldom seen tender side. One morning while sitting outside The Valencia, she found a small, starving dog that had been abandoned by its owners, and despite the building's strict "No Pets" policy, Barbara brought the animal into her apartment to care for it. An adorable male cocker spaniel with a black coat, white chest and long ears, the dog was given the name "Tux" by Barbara, who quickly grew attached to her new friend.

Barbara understood this dog, living on the streets; cold, hungry, and alone. She looked into his sad eyes, and knew exactly how he felt. When the building's landlord heard that she was hiding Tux in her room, and warned her that the animal would have to go, Barbara refused to get rid of him. As a result, she was promptly evicted, and landed homeless on Sunset Boulevard.

Surrounded by a pair of scuffed-up suitcases, a tattered old mink coat, and with her dirty-blonde hair pulled back in a ponytail, an obviously distraught Barbara was sitting with Tux on a bus stop bench at the corner of Sunset and Fairfax, ruminating about her next course of action, when two local men recognized her and approached her to ask if she needed help.

The late Hollywood actress Marian Miller, who lived at the time in an apartment on Fairfax Avenue, knew these men only by their nicknames of "Chip" and "Dale." They were well known in the neighborhood as a colorful gay couple in their mid-20s who were employed as window dressers at a downtown L.A. department store.

Marian recalled that one of the men had told her that they were so touched by Barbara's story of being thrown out of her apartment for not getting rid of Tux that they invited her and the dog to stay with them. Barbara and Tux moved into their apartment on Fairfax and Fountain, where for the next several weeks the men provided them with a safe and loving home.

Barbara did all the cooking and cleaning for this makeshift family, and apparently tried very hard to keep her inner demons at bay. Chip and Dale were often seen walking Tux down Fairfax Avenue on a gaudy, gold leash, and were said to be ecstatic that they had been given the chance to take care of someone who had once been, "...a real, honest-to-

God, Hollywood movie star." Barbara's unexpected stroke of good luck, however, would end within a matter of weeks.

In a scenario similar to what had happened at The Valencia, Barbara soon became the target of an irate and unyielding landlord who demanded that she vacate the premises immediately. Marian Miller recalled that the landlord's problem was not with the dog's presence in the building, but with Barbara's. "He told her that everyone in the building knew she was a filthy rotten slut and that no one, including him, wanted her living there," said Marian. "Imagine how that made Barbara feel?"

Not wanting to cause any trouble for Chip and Dale, who had been so kind to her, Barbara moved out, leaving her beloved Tux in their care. Marian remembered Chip telling her that Barbara refused his offer to help her relocate some place else and that while it broke Barbara's heart to leave Tux behind, she did it to protect the dog from the terrible life she knew was awaiting her on the streets.

Following this incident, Barbara's self-hatred resurfaced and she resumed her desperate lifestyle. Marian said that she often saw Barbara wandering around Hollywood during the next several months, usually walking alone and almost always looking unwashed and disheveled. In those days, Marian patronized a small hair salon called The Brush Wave, located next to an A&P supermarket on Sunset Boulevard, and she said she was surprised one afternoon to see Barbara in there, getting her hair done. Barbara had briefly worked at the salon a year or two earlier, and later admitted that she was so impractical with money that she had often forgotten to pick up her paycheck. Marian's hairdresser told her that the female owner of the shop would sometimes see Barbara walking past the place, heading for a Shell gas station on the west side of Sunset. She said that Barbara would often use the sink in the gas station's restroom to clean up and wash her hair. The owner of the salon had known Barbara from better days, and would sometimes call her into the shop for a cup of coffee. Then, if one of the operators wasn't busy, she would have them shampoo and bleach Barbara's hair, free of charge.

"Make her platinum blonde again, on the house," the owner said. "For a moment, let's have Barbara think she's back at Warner Bros., getting the royal treatment from the studio hairdresser."

Barbara's first cousin, Mary Kuitu Nunley, says that although she and most of their other relatives no longer had any contact with Barbara, Jan Redfield saw the troubled woman occasionally, and always tried to help her.

"Barbara would call Janice out of the blue and ask her to pick her up somewhere," says Mary. "When Janice went out to get her, she said that Barbara would look like death warmed over, just terrible. Jan would get her cleaned up and then she would bring her to the beauty shop to get Barbara's hair washed and set. Janice would call me and say, 'Oh, Mary, you should see Barbara now. She looks like a million bucks.'

"Barbara had a very resilient nature. But, I guess a person can bounce back just so many times."

Jan agrees. "Sometimes a person is down so low, and for so long, they just forget how to help themselves. I know that's what finally happened to Barbara. Helping herself was no longer an option because she no longer thought it was possible, or that she even deserved it. She believed she had drawn her lot in life, and that unless someone was going to come along and save her, she was just going to live out the rest of her days, drinking and punishing herself. The self-hatred she felt must have been enormous."

During this period, small expressions of kindness, like some strangers putting a roof over her head for a few days, or even her sister-in-law bringing her to the beauty shop to get her hair done—while certainly not the kind of help Barbara truly needed—nonetheless helped boost her spirits, if only for a moment.

Unfortunately, though, there was no denying that Barbara's life was growing increasingly more desolate. Desperate for some sort of validation that she still had something to offer the world, and buoyed by the endless surge of alcohol in her body, Barbara continued to seek comfort wherever she could. It was this very search, however, that led her straight to her next disaster.

On February 7, 1962, Barbara was arrested for prostitution when she approached an undercover cop in a bar on Sunset Boulevard and offered to have sex with him for $40. Reporters from the *L.A. Times* were waiting to photograph her arrival at the police station, and the startling images they caught that day reveal a life completely out of control. Clad in a mink coat that had seen better days, and with her sad doe-eyes resembling those of a hunted animal that had been cornered, Barbara looked drawn, distraught and totally spaced-out.

As Andrew Dowdy writes in his book, *The Films of The Fifties: The American State of Mind*, the photos of Barbara at the police station show "a plump blonde, eyes red from crying, her puffy face a reminder that the body treats alcohol as a fat. Nobody could believe she was the starlet who once

Barbara at a Hollywood police station after her arrest for soliciting sex from an undercover cop (February 1962). Courtesy of Los Angeles Times Photo

looked like Lana Turner." As someone who had experienced, firsthand, the horrors of an embattled life, Barbara's physical appearance resembled that of a heavyset European hausfrau imprisoned in her own personal Holocaust.

With one look at her haunted eyes, it's clear that Barbara Payton's life had become a tawdry and wretched affair. The B-film actress of the 1950s

An abandoned swimming pool at the Jet Inn, an inner-city motel that Barbara sometimes took refuge at in the early 1960's. Courtesy of Tim Choate

had morphed into a real-life version of the bad girl characters she had once played, but now all her troubles—and tears—were real.

Following her arrest, Barbara was processed and released in her own recognizance, with a court appearance scheduled for a future, if unstated, time. Nothing is known about Barbara's whereabouts or activities in the following months, however her next appearance in the news proved that the horrors of the night were far from finished with her.

Chapter Thirty-Five:
Drowning in Memories

On Saturday, July 21, just five months after her arrest for prostitution, Barbara, wearing nothing but a tight, one-piece bathing suit, a white sweater and a pair of gold slippers, and with her legs blotted with bruises, staggered into a Hollywood police station to report an attempted rape at the hands of a teenage gang. Earlier that day, Barbara and a male companion, middle-aged diaper distributor Robert Sherry, had phoned the 77th St. police station from their motel room at the Jet Inn, located at 4542 W. Slauson Avenue, near Los Angeles International Airport, to report an entirely different incident.

A hazardous, high-crime corridor of the city that is dotted with ugly, industrial properties and cheap motels, Slauson Avenue is also near Hollywood Park, the racetrack where Barbara had once dropped thousands of dollars in the early 1950s. Now, deep into her losing streak and down on her luck, Barbara was one step away from being homeless again, and was back living among a desperate lot of troubled, L.A. outcasts.

"The area around the Jet Inn, especially in the early 1960s, was deadly," says Bill Ramage. "Whites were foolish even to drive down that part of Slauson. And no sane, white woman (blonde at that) would have been found in such a dangerous place, no matter what dire straits she was in. What in the name of Hell was Barbara doing there?"

At first, Barbara and Robert Sherry claimed their motel room had been broken into, and that Barbara had been beaten, but soon afterwards they changed their story to one which had her being sexually assaulted in a nearby lot by a teenage street gang. Officer J.E. Newman drove a banged-up Barbara and her companion to the station to report the incident.

When Barbara reeled into the police station to file the complaint, the building's fluorescent lights revealed a block of red and white human bite

The Jet Inn Motel, the place where Barbara was staying when she was allegedly beaten by a teenage gang. Courtesy of Tim Choate

marks on her arms and upper torso, as well as several missing teeth. She also stank of cheap booze. For his part, her cohort Robert Sherry, bleary-eyed in a bolo tie and with his pants hiked up tight over a bloated belly, looked more like an extra in a B-western bar scene than a big-city, diaper salesman. Once again, photographers from the *L.A. Times* were waiting at the police station with their cameras poised, eager to capture the human wreckage standing before them.

One of the images the news photographers snapped that night is riveting, and to this day, reverberates with a chilling sadness. It shows Barbara, boozed-up and stupefied, posing in a hallway at the precinct, her head tilted on an angle, her hands pulling at her bathing suit like a timid and contrite schoolgirl. Though far away and glazed over, her eyes that night held the reflection of a million faded dreams.

During her filing of the assault incident, Barbara appeared disoriented, confused, and in another one of the news photos where she is giving her statement to the desk sergeant, almost repentant. She showed the officers the many angry kick-marks on her legs, and then told them

Drowning in Memories

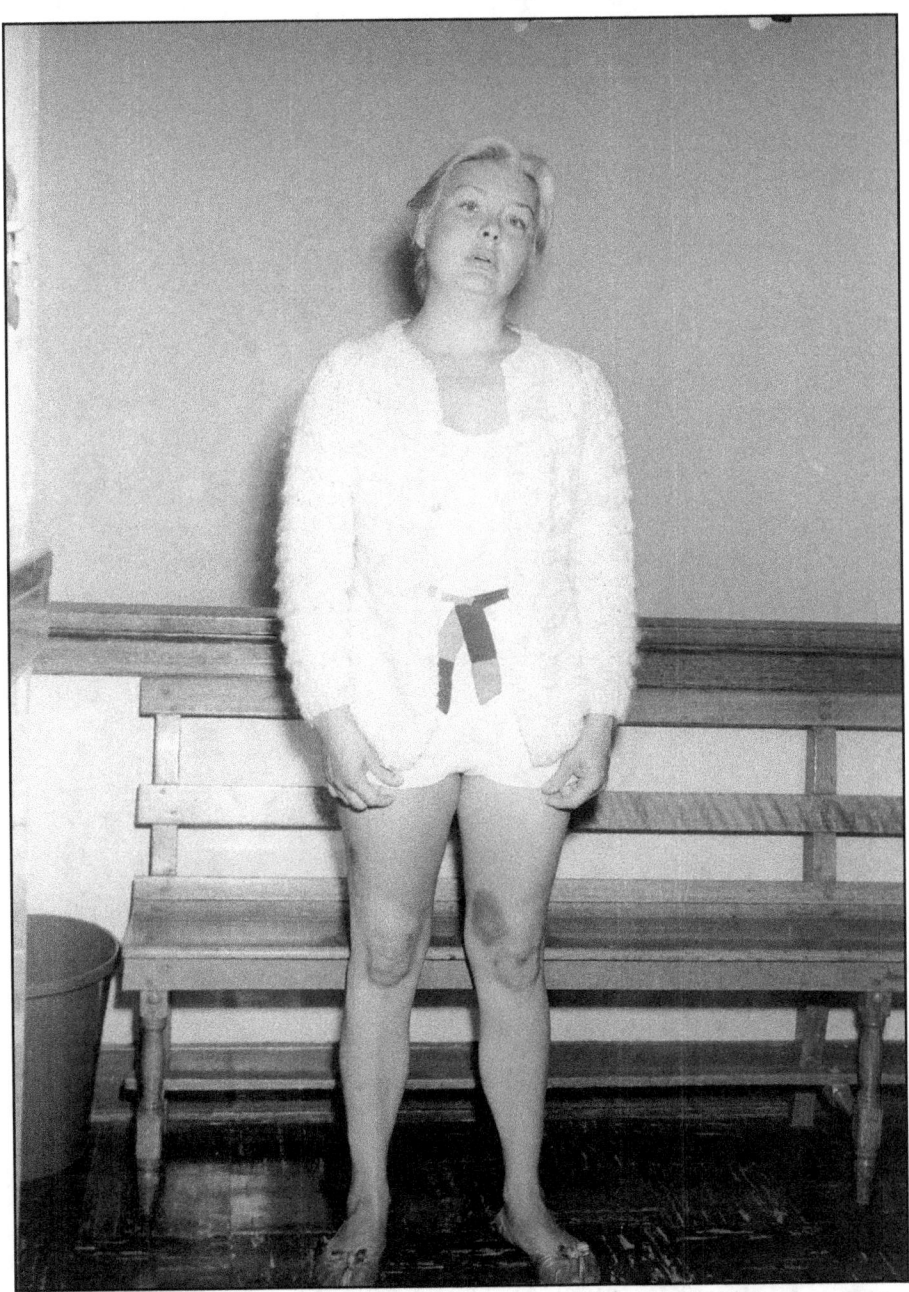

35-year old Barbara in a Hollywood police station after her July 21, 1962 beating and attempted rape at the hands of a teenage gang. Courtesy of UCLA Special Collections/L.A. Times Photo

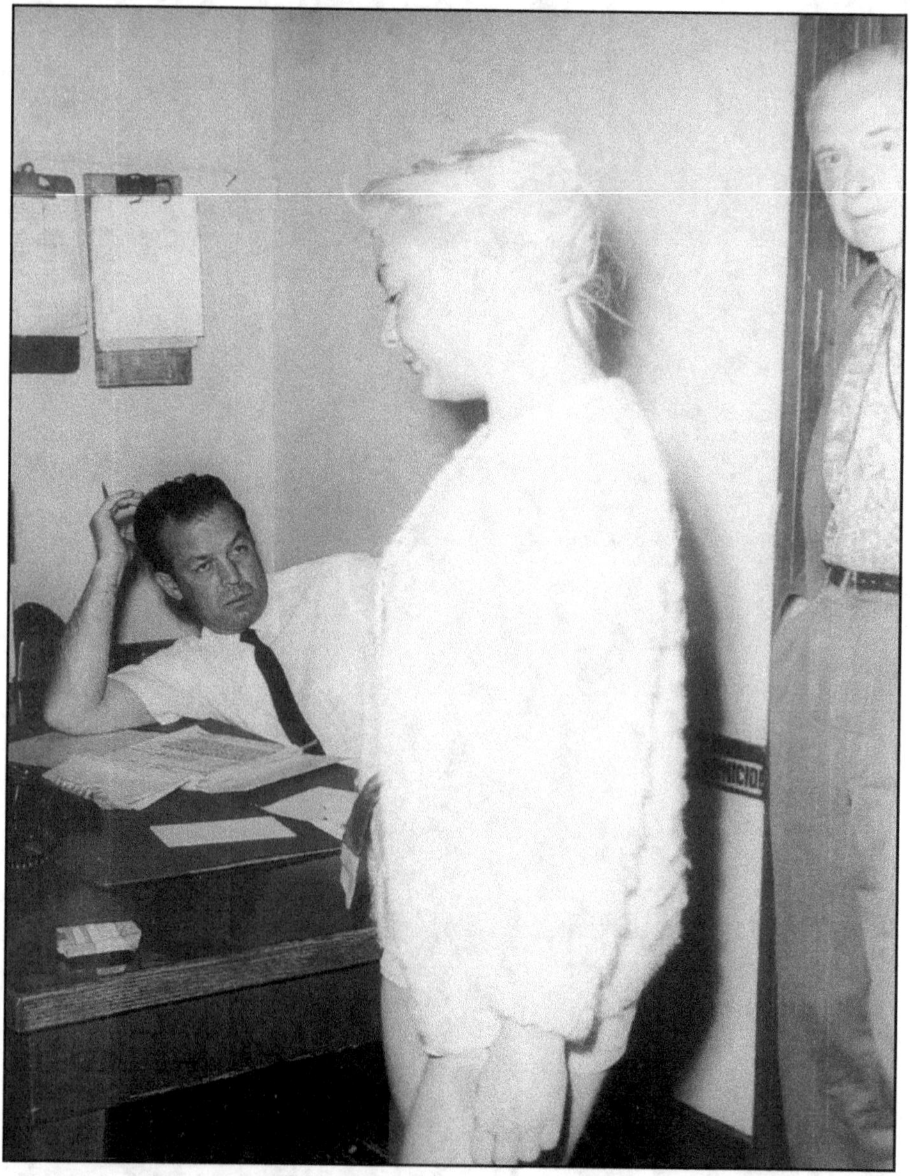

Barbara with a disgruntled desk sergeant (left), and her companion, diaper salesman Robert Sherry (right), at the time of Barbara's beating. Courtesy of UCLA Special Collections/L.A. Times Photo

that she had been forced into a car by the teenage hoods and driven to a vacant lot in nearby Windsor Hills, where the youths pummeled her with their fists and feet, and then attempted to rape her. Barbara claimed they had eventually dumped her out of the car, and then sped off. Detectives at the precinct apparently didn't take her accusations seriously, though, as Barbara had dramatically changed her original complaint (and none too convincingly, either). She had also obviously been drinking, and was unable to give an accurate description of her attackers. Apparently, neither could her witness, Robert Sherry, who ungallantly bounded from the premises soon thereafter. The police officers, willing to cut Barbara a break due to her past life as a celebrity, placated her by promising to investigate the matter, and then paid for a cab to take her home.

The next morning—while countless people across the country attended Sunday church or joined their families for breakfast—a barefoot Barbara was discovered passed out on a bus stop bench on the corner of Stanley Avenue and Sunset Boulevard, while still clad in the bathing suit and sweater she had on the day before. Police officer R.W. Smith said he observed Barbara "stagger up to the bus bench and collapse. Her feet were filthy, and she was fast asleep by the time I got to her to investigate." Barbara was said to be incoherent and in an agitated state when awakened, and was immediately charged with public drunkenness. She was arrested and later released on $21 bail.

Amazingly, Barbara was arrested again the following Saturday, July 28; this time, at a female friend's Hollywood apartment. Neighbors had phoned the police to complain of a rowdy afternoon party in which she was seen "cavorting naked in front of two men and an open window." When the officers arrived, they found a nude and highly inebriated Barbara in the company of the woman who rented the apartment, Ruth Kellett, 29, and the aforementioned two men (who were not identified in the papers). Strangely, Barbara was the only member of the group who was unclothed. A news article of the incident reported that upon their arrival, the officers witnessed her "laughing nervously while clumsily attempting to get into a dirty, terry cloth robe."

Barbara told the policemen that she had no permanent home address and owned no other clothes besides the bathrobe, and that she had been staying with Ruth Kellett for "a couple of days." She and Kellett admitted they had been entertaining the two men in question, and then, according to the article, "...Barbara got sassy with the bluecoats and had to be restrained."

Although the two men at the apartment were not held, Ruth Kellett was arrested that day on some unpaid traffic warrants, while a befogged and strung-out Barbara was hauled in for drunk and disorderly conduct. She was detained at L.A.'s Lincoln Heights Jail for several hours until some of her drinking buddies from Hollywood arrived that night with her bail.

In the florid, self-righteous and over-the-top reporting style of the scandal rags of the day, Barbara was once again raked over the coals following her July 1962 arrests. *Vice Squad* magazine described her appearance on the night of her July 21 beating, in a mean-spirited article unflatteringly titled *How Franchot Tone's Ex-Wife Became a Common Prostitute*: "The woman looked worn. Haggard. Spent. Her overweight, uncorseted body was a grim reminder of a life of self-abuse—too much, too often, over too long a period of time. She was bruised and battered. Purple welts stained her large, sausage-like arms, and a big shiner stretched out from her eye until it covered half her face. Her stockingless legs were discolored. Her champagne-blonde hair, heaped in a precariously-unbalanced array on top of her head, looked like a wig she had put on without the aid of a mirror. She was in short, a mess...."

Twelve years earlier, writers fell all over themselves reaching for the right adjectives to accurately describe Barbara's stunning looks. Now, at the lowest ebb of her life, the onetime model and actress was hearing an entirely different set of adjectives being used to describe her current appearance—ugly words that wounded her deeply and reminded everyone, including Barbara, that she had fallen a long, long way.

Chapter Thirty-Six:
The Road to Hell

"I feel the deepest sympathy for her and retain the most lovely memories of the time we spent together." With his characteristic formality intact, Franchot Tone issued this statement upon hearing of the dreadful circumstances that had led to Barbara's re-emergence in the news. As always, a man of impeccable civility (whose sense of recall was no doubt obscured by time-aided sentiment), Franchot had spoken these words from the luxurious surroundings of his current home in New York City.

The odyssey that he had begun eleven years earlier, an odyssey that had taken him far away from Barbara and the hell they knew together, had eventually brought him back to the altar of his first love, the theatre, and in 1962, Franchot was in rehearsals for his next Broadway play, Eugene O'Neill's *Strange Interlude*.

Just as Franchot's journey had delivered him back to the well-heeled world of New York high-society—the world of fine arts, debutantes and literary scholars—so had Barbara's journey taken her down into the dark Hollywood underground, from which it seemed, for her, there was no escape.

While their daughter wandered lost in this netherworld of almost unfathomable horror, Lee and Mabel Redfield were living comfortably (if not quite carefully) in their attractive, Spanish-styled home in San Diego. Although their own alcohol abuse had continued to worsen over the years, the couple had somehow managed to hold onto their secure, middle-class lifestyle.

For the most part, Lee had remained estranged from Barbara, although Jan Redfield claims that Barbara and Mabel sometimes kept in touch through letters.

"Mabel wrote to Barbara whenever she had a mailing address for her, which wasn't very often," says Jan. "And Barbara wrote when she could, I guess (or when she thought of it). Mabel kept all of Barbara's letters in an old, wooden box that sat on top of the coffee table in the living room. Sometimes late at night, especially if she had been drinking all day, Mabel would sit there and reread those letters, over and over again, and just cry her eyes out. I don't know what Barbara had said in those letters, but whatever it was made Mabel so sad."

"I don't think my parents fully understood the depth of Barbara's problems," says Frank Redfield, "nor did they know about all the trouble she was in at the time. I know I didn't. I was married with four small children to raise, and Barbara and I had grown apart. Unfortunately, I was also drinking a lot in those days, so there were problems in my life, too.

"You have to understand, my sister didn't contact us much in those years, and a lot of times we didn't even know where she was living. Then again, she didn't want us to know. I'm sure it was because she felt bad about herself, and she thought that if we knew about what was going on in her life, we would think badly of her, too. But my mother, especially, would have always helped Barbara—if she had only reached out for it, that is."

In 1962, Lee Redfield was working as a maintenance man at The Convair Garden Club in Balboa Park, near The San Diego Zoo, while Mabel stayed home for the most part, and drank. Their former neighbor Cheryl Perry says, "As a child, I would often help Mabel clean up around the house, and later on, when I was older, I would sometimes go next door to wash and set her hair. She was usually drinking beer when I was there, but I was never afraid of her or Lee, nor did I ever fear they would hurt me in any way. They were both very kind to me—even when they were both drunk, which was often."

Mabel's behavior, always pretty eccentric, had seemed to grow stranger through the years. There was a noticeably dizzy quality in her thinking that her former neighbor in Odessa, Berniece Johnson, still finds amusing today.

"I remember when my mother-in-law, Lottie Johnson, laughed so hard after receiving a phone call from Mabel," says Berniece. "The conversation from Mabel went something like this: 'Lottie, we just bought a new Thunderbird convertible and I want you and Oscar to come out to California to visit us. Lee will drive us up the west coast to Canada, then all the way across to the east coast, and then back across the country to San Diego. I'll pack us a nice lunch.'

"I'm sure Mabel was drinking that day," adds Berniece. "Everyone knew she had a real problem with alcohol. She always did."

Cheryl Perry recalls another odd incident: "When Lee's sister Fay died in 1964, he and Mabel inherited a lot of money and were given many of her antiques, too. I remember an expensive Persian rug that Fay left for Mabel. The Redfields put it down in their dining room and then noticed that parts of the rug were faded. One day Mabel called me over to the house and asked me to bring my crayons. She wanted me to color in the parts of the rug that had faded. I'm sure the rug was worth several thousand dollars, and there I was sitting on the floor, using crayons to color it in. Even as a child, I thought that was so funny. And Mabel, she just laughed and laughed."

Another time Mabel wrapped herself in her sister-in-law Fay's old squirrel coat, which had been in storage for over 30 years, and pranced around the house like a flapper while Jan captured the antics with her camera. "Barbara was also there that day," says Jan, "and I took several pictures of her helping Mabel model the coat. It was during one of those many times in the '60s when Barbara had cleaned herself up a little and had come home for a while. Well, she got right in there with Mabel, Lee and Frank, camping it up with that coat, and carrying on, and just having a grand old time. Mabel had such a happy and joyful spirit when we were all together, and we all loved her very much."

Jan and Frank's oldest son, Les, remembers how highly emotional his grandmother could be, and how quickly alcohol could take her from the

A family photo of Barbara with her mother Mabel, brother Frank and father Lee during one of her many stays at the Redfield's home in San Diego. Courtesy of Jan Redfield

most blissful state to the saddest of tears. "I recall a visit from Mabel when we were living in West Covina. Dad and Lee had gone to Minnesota to visit some of our relatives after Aunt Fay died, so Mabel came alone. One evening during her visit, we all went out for dinner, down to Shakey's Pizza Parlor, where there was live entertainment. I remember Mabel downing several bottles of beer and then asking the musicians if they would play 'The Yellow Rose of Texas' for her. Well, they did, and as they were playing it, Mabel was so overcome with emotion, she jumped up and danced a jig around the restaurant. Mabel waved her arms around and kicked her legs way up in the air and just had a blast. I don't think that anyone who saw that performance has ever forgotten it. It was great.

"Even though Mom and us kids thought Mabel's jig was hilarious, she broke down and cried on the walk home because she thought she had embarrassed us. My grandmother was a loving and outgoing woman, but she drank way too much. So did my grandfather."

Given the ever-present flow of alcohol in their home, it is little wonder that Lee and Mabel never stopped drinking long enough to consider just how far their daughter's world had fallen.

And fallen, it had. While attending a movie memorabilia show at the New Yorker Hotel in NYC recently, a former Hollywood photographer who knew Barbara, shared a particularly disturbing tale from this period. The two had first met in the early 1950s on the set of one of her Lippert pictures, and through the years they had seen each other frequently around town. Now in his late 70s, and not wanting any trouble, "Ray" only agreed to speak about his former friend with the stipulation that his identity remain anonymous.

He recalls Barbara's wildly out-of-control drinking, and how it had wrecked, in his words, "a decent and beautiful girl." Like industry observer Skip E. Lowe, Ray said that nearly all of Hollywood despised Barbara by this time, and thought of her as "a bad joke that just wouldn't go away." He remembers an incident that occurred in late 1962, when a drunken Barbara telephoned him and begged him for a loan of $35. She slurred something to him about leaving her husband in Mexico and about being broke, and said she was house-sitting for a producer friend in the Hollywood Hills. She told him that she "had gone through her old address book" and that when she saw his name she had hoped he would be willing to help her. Ray agreed to lend Barbara the money, and drove out to meet her at the remote location she gave him.

"It was way up in the hills on a dirt road," he remembers. "A flat-roof house all by itself, with the back part of it perched on stilts. Barbara was waiting for me in front of the house and, my God, she was so plastered she could barely stand. I was really taken aback when I noticed the rundown condition of the place. The yard was overgrown with weeds and vines and all the windows in the house were smashed. I remember there was a bird, like a bald eagle, circling over the house, squawking, but other than that, it was very quiet and desolate up there."

Ray goes on to describe the scene as a kind of "mid-century modern" version of the Norma Desmond estate in *Sunset Blvd.* ("a decrepit piece of Southern California Gothic," as he put it) and remembers thinking that it was possible that Barbara wasn't really house-sitting, but had—much like a homeless squatter—taken occupancy of an abandoned piece of property. Set back off the road on the edge of a cliff, the house-on-stilts was trashed; the in-ground swimming pool, a rancid mix of rotting leaves and foul-smelling water.

Barbara, badly bloated in a stained halter-blouse, moccasins and tiny, bikini bottoms, was so out of it, she not only offered to perform oral sex on her friend, but asked him if he would like her to strip so he could photograph her swimming naked in the pool. Ray said that although he refused to take advantage of either of her proposals ("I didn't even have a camera with me," he says), he did give her $100, "to help her out of the obvious fix she was in." Visibly uncomfortable with the still-vivid memory of seeing his friend in such a desperate and miserable condition, Ray remembers feeling at the time that "Barbara was somehow comfortable in this garbage dump, like she thought she belonged there.

"I begged her to let me help her. I told her I would take her anywhere she wanted to go, to a family member's house, or to a friend's, but she said no. All she wanted was a lift down to Sunset Boulevard, so against my better judgment, I did as she asked. Once down there, Barbara jumped out of the car (with the hundred bucks I'd given her still in her hand) and bounded down the street in her halter-top and briefs. People were staring at her like she was some kind of nut. Barbara looked like hell on earth."

The elderly gentleman recounted this story with a discernible sense of pity, and blamed Barbara's downslide entirely on Tom Neal. Shaking his head emphatically, he said, "Barbara Payton deteriorated faster than anyone I've ever seen, in every way. She was a sweet, fun-loving person when I first met her, and then over time, she became this raunchy, foulmouthed pig.

"The kid just couldn't keep her legs closed, you know? I mean, it got to the point where any bum with a couple of bucks on him could sweet talk her right out of her pants, no problem. Directors, producers, the guy in the next car. It didn't matter *who* asked her. They would hand her a line, and off she went, just like a child. She took crumbs. It was a sickness, like a sick kind of Russian roulette. It was pathetic.

"I believe Barbara was of the opinion that she had to go to bed with anyone who asked her. I don't think it ever even occurred to her that she could say no.

"In my opinion, Tom Neal was total scum, and he ruined that girl. He took her right down the toilet with him. She was fine before she got involved with that bastard."

What seems lost to this man is that a part of Barbara had been tough—and even cunning—long before Tom Neal had entered her life, as countless men, including Bob Hope and Franchot Tone, had all-too painfully discovered.

And, of course, she was emotionally scarred, as well. Every day for Barbara had become a battle against a deep and relentless self-loathing, and it was a battle that was getting harder and harder to bear.

Barbara made one of her periodic visits to her brother and sister-in-law's house in late 1962 or early '63, looking even worse than she had a few years earlier, when she had turned up filthy and had told Jan that she had been camping in the mountains.

"By then, Frank and I had moved from Los Altos, and we were living in West Covina," says Jan. "Well, one day Barbara appeared out of nowhere, looking as bad as she ever looked. Again, she showed up a mess, but this time, she was wearing blue jeans and a nasty old flannel shirt. Barbara had put on a ton of weight, especially in her face and belly. Her chin was sagging so far down, it was almost hitting the top of her chest. She looked awful. I threw her in the shower and had to toss her jeans and shirt in the trash can, they were so dirty.

"I found Barbara a cute, pink-and white-checked-shorts ensemble that I had bought when I worked at the May Company, and I told her to put it on. At the time Frank was working the night shift at Aero-Jet General and she said she didn't want to see him, so before he got home she made a phone call and some fellow came and picked her up. I never saw the person, only the car at the curb. Barbara didn't give me any information on who the guy was—or where she had been—but before she left the house, I gave her a good, strong lecture. I asked her how could she let herself go like that, and told her that she just had to straighten herself out or something terrible was going to happen to her. I was quite stern, but she didn't want to listen to me. I remember her saying something like she had nothing left, and couldn't remember where she had lost it.

"She had lost it all right. I was very sad by that visit. I really think something inside Barbara had snapped. Her eyes were so cold, almost like a wild animal's. I had the feeling that she was on a lot more than just booze. I told Frank about it when he got home from work the next morning and he alerted Lee and Mabel, but they said that they hadn't seen her in a while. I think Barb said she was heading for Mexico again, or somewhere.

"It was a long time before we even heard from her again."

Away from her family's critical eye—and counsel—Barbara's nauseating excursion continued its slow-motion spin through a twilight and shadow world of fleabag motels, dingy barrooms, and fly-by-night encounters with other lost souls. In early 1963, she moved into a $40 a month apartment in a rat-infested building (now a gas station) at 7655 Sunset Boulevard, rooming for a while with Russell Avist, a 34-year-old African-American bootblack who doubled as her pimp. There have been printed reports over the years that state that Barbara, under Avist's urging and tutelage, appeared in a hard-core stag reel in the early 1960s, however no real evidence of the film exists. Therefore, the claim remains questionable, and is considered unsubstantiated.

Hollywood veteran Skip E. Lowe, who saw Barbara several times around town during this period, remembers a woman on a whirling carousel of doom and completely at her wit's end. "Poor Barbara looked absolutely horrible," he says. "Her skin was like leather. Her hair was still platinum blonde, but ratted and uncombed. She was running around in a panic, panhandling on Sunset Boulevard and selling off everything she had in order to get money for booze and drugs—her jewelry, her furniture, even a transistor radio. She had no money for anything, not even to fix her teeth. They were so bad, her mouth smelled like crazy. She looked like a bag lady in her fifties." At 36, Barbara was sinking fast.

Municipal Judge Mario L. Clinico issued a bench warrant for Barbara's arrest on March 8, 1963 when she failed to appear for her trial on the earlier soliciting charge. Soon afterward, things got even worse when Barbara was knifed by a trick and received thirty-eight stitches for the stab wound. "Thirty-eight stitches from my fleshy belly down," is how she put it.

Her observations about the knifing were downright chilling in their apathy. She later remarked, "It isn't very clear to me, but I think it happened in a cinder block shanty, somewhere in the Valley. Some filthy drunk got mad at me when I wouldn't do what he wanted. Guess I gotta be more careful in the future."

"I saw the scar from that stabbing, a few months later," says Jan. "It was during one of those times when Barbara had crawled back to San Diego, and I saw the scar one day when she was outside at the pool. It was an angry-looking thing, and I was speechless. Barbara didn't say where she got it, and so as not to rock the boat, I didn't ask. I remember having the feeling, though, and I don't know why, that she had gotten it in Mexico. I'm sure she probably showed it to Mabel, but I doubt if Mabel ever told Lee about it. There was an unspoken rule in that family that we were never to discuss any of Barbara's problems, with Lee. That goes for her arrests and what she was doing in L.A; none of it.

"Mabel loved Barbara so much and she was always willing to do, say (or *not* say) anything to cover for her. She sure did her best, anyway. But, yeah, I saw the scar, and it was very upsetting. The thought that someone had actually stabbed Barbara in the stomach sickened me. My God, they could have killed her."

At the time of her stabbing, it was said that Barbara's live-in pimp, Russell Avist, the black shoe shiner from Cosmo Sardo's Barbershop, somehow scrounged up the money to pay for her medical treatment. In less than a year's time, Barbara's asking price for her sexual services had slid downhill fast, from $40 to $5 a trick. As her addictions worsened, so did her feelings of worthlessness, and Barbara responded by becoming even less discriminating in her choice of sex partners.

During this period, Barbara became a willing—some say, eager—participant of the five-minute, five-dollar date; quick encounters on Sunset Boulevard for five bucks a throw, in cars parked with their motors running. The woman, who once earned $10,000 a week as a bona fide Hollywood movie star, was still in Hollywood, dispensing crude, curbside sex—where the names of her partners were neither discussed, nor required. Barbara would frequently have sex with these men, and in her confused and heavy-lidded haze, forget to collect any money from them afterward. She had entered the Devil's Lair and stood helpless as the darkness of that world swallowed her.

Clinging to the barest remnants of her deep spiritual beliefs, Barbara sometimes kept a small statue of St. Jude with her, and when really drunk, she would take it out of her purse and talk to it. Barbara was often seen walking around town, sobbing—railing loudly in a guttural voice against God and the cruel fate that had left her so hopelessly adrift. A fate that had sadistically plucked her from an opulent lifestyle in Beverly Hills, and had dropped her, kicking and screaming, into the darkest bowels of L.A.'s back streets and alleyways.

On Monday, September 23, 1963, officers from the Hollywood Vice Squad raided Barbara's Sunset Boulevard apartment and arrested her again for prostitution. She was thrown in jail, where she remained for the next 22 days.

Whether Barbara was able to fully comprehend what was happening to her is uncertain today. At this point in her life, the assault on both her mind and her spirit was so relentless, a part of her may have simply disconnected, just to survive. The desolation of a cold Los Angeles jail cell was nothing compared to the inner desolation she felt outside, on the streets, and Barbara may have even felt a strange sense of relief during her confinement. If so, it was short-lived.

Three weeks after her arrest, on October 17, Barbara stood before Los Angeles County Court's Municipal Judge Bernard S. Seiber, and pleaded innocent to the charge of prostitution. Seiber pointed out to her that despite her plea, Barbara had submitted her case to the court without testimony of her own to contradict the arresting officers. He explained that unless she defended herself, he would be forced to arrive at his decision solely on the basis of the evidence provided to him by the authorities.

It was reported in the papers that Barbara, speaking in a "low, weak voice," asked Seiber if he would read the police report to himself. She was obviously embarrassed by its contents and didn't want the rest of the courtroom to know the exact details of her arrest. Judge Seiber complied with her request and, after reading the report, admonished Barbara with all the bombast he could muster.

"I find it wholly regrettable that a person of the obvious talents and capabilities of you, Miss Payton, has sunk to such low depths," he bellowed. "I do hope, however, that there is still a germ of respectability somewhere within you that will enable you to be rehabilitated."

An October, 1963 photo of Barbara at her municipal court hearing on prostitution charges in Los Angeles. Courtesy of UPI Photo

In a trial that lasted all of eight minutes, Seiber ruled that Barbara was guilty of prostitution and sentenced her to pay a $150 fine or spend another fifteen days in jail. Barbara somehow paid the fine, although how she raised the money for it remains unknown.

A UPI wire photo of Barbara, taken in a hallway outside the courtroom that day, subsequently appeared in many of the nation's newspapers. It showed her clothed in a shapeless sack dress and sitting in a roundup of hookers—looking vacant-eyed, and totally defeated.

While the L.A. newspapers largely avoided reporting on Barbara's current way of life beyond small, back-section blurbs, the more widely distributed exploitation tabloids jumped on the story with a series of prominent articles that absolutely trashed her character.

Vice Squad magazine led the pack, detailing "a tale of vice and corruption, whoring and perversion," while unkindly describing Barbara as "a convicted prostitute who will maul a mattress with any unwashed beatnik—or any creep of any kind, color or character—who has a buck to burn in the flaming embraces of her ever-loving arms." *Uncensored* climbed aboard the bandwagon with its article titled *Did Too Many*

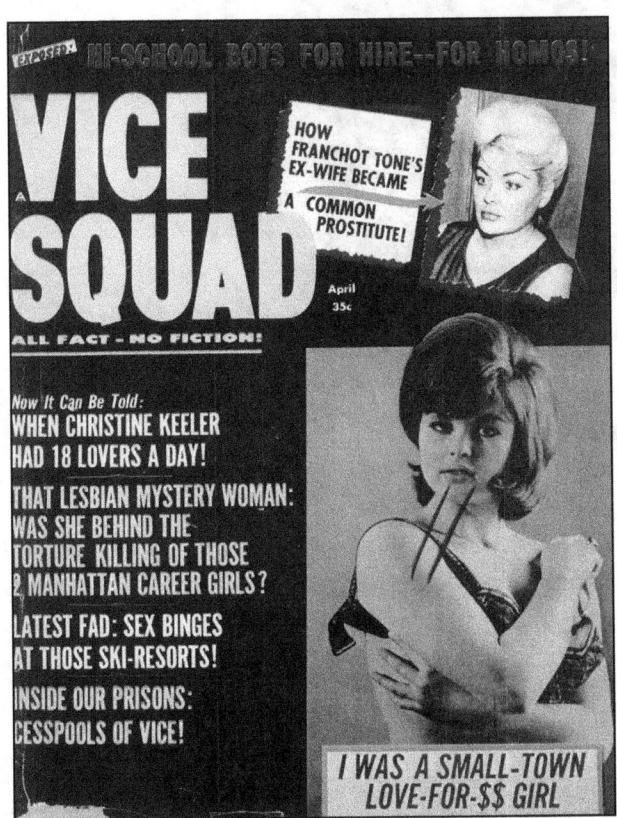

April, 1963 issue of Vice Squad *magazine, with an article on Barbara's heartbreaking fall from grace. From the Author's Collection*

Barbara looking downtrodden in 1963. From the Author's Collection

Boudoirs Ruin Barbara Payton?, stating: "A toboggan ride few, if any, stars of her generation have taken. Here's Hollywood in the raw!" Not to be outdone, *Inside Story* followed with its cover article, *Barbara Payton: How She Went From a Plush Life to a Lush Life* ("You might say her decline was measured in fifths").

In *Modern Man's* story, *Barbara Payton: A Hollywood Tragedy*, the magazine declared, "Trying every trick to plow a path to stardom, this fast-rising actress also furrowed deep gutters, which inevitably became her trap." With an almost religious zeal, *Vice Squad* insisted, "It's a tale that MUST be told, because out of one woman's tragic life can come a realization of the tragedy awaiting all who walk the path of unbridled carnal appetites, untamed lascivious lusts, and uninhibited sensual sin!" In the paperback book category, Pyramid Books issued a raunchy little compilation of movie star scandals, titled *Hollywood Confidential*, coaxing its readers to "meet the buxom beauty whose kisses once brought her a palatial mansion with two dozen servants [sic]… and who now lives on strange men's $5 bills."

Barbara, maligned now by the masses, was receiving a public stoning that Hollywood had rarely ever seen before, and seldom with such a salivating and heavy-breathing fervor. It was obvious that *Uncensored Magazine* had already sealed her fate when it wrote: "For Barbara Payton, there *is* no tomorrow… not for the good-time girl whose story ended up on a Hollywood police blotter."

The media's denigration of Barbara, persistent and unrelenting, must have, in her more lucid moments, seared her very soul. In the glare of the tabloids attack, Barbara had become the newest member in a bizarre sideshow of fallen stars. She was Hollywood's very own Mary Magdalene, a wicked trollop whose only remaining value, it seemed, was as a target of intense scorn and ridicule.

Flying blind in a sea of darkness, wounded and alone, the midnight angel was spiraling downward; out of control and lost, and with her wings in flames.

Chapter Thirty-Seven:
Lost in the Fog

Bill Ramage remembers vividly the cold, windswept night in early November 1963 when he met Barbara for the second time. An autumn storm of uncommon ferocity was dropping bucket loads of water over Hollywood, rendering many of its side streets flooded and looking like a neon ghost town. Although just five years had passed since Bill and Barbara's initial encounter at the home of her former attorney, Milton Golden and his wife, Charlene, it might as well have been a lifetime.

"I owned a '63 Oldsmobile convertible back then, and I still remember how hard it was raining that night," Bill says. "In fact, if I close my eyes I can still hear the crisp, whip-like sound of the raindrops hitting the roof of the car. It was late in the evening and I was driving through an area in town commonly known as Gower Gulch, heading toward Sunset Boulevard. Because of the storm, it was even darker than usual. It was a miserable night."

The young actor had turned off Gower Street and onto Sunset (just around the corner from Columbia Pictures), when he saw a woman soaked to the skin, walking alone on the mostly empty street.

"The first thing I noticed was her unique carriage: head up, shoulders back, the long, deliberate strides. She looked very determined. Watching her from behind, I thought right away that she walked like a movie star. As soon as my headlights shone on her and she turned around, I caught a glimpse of her face and I saw that it was Barbara Payton. I immediately pulled over to the curb and rolled down the window to ask her if she needed a ride. I was shocked when she leaned into the car because her face looked terrible. She looked dazed."

Bill reminded Barbara of their meeting five years earlier at the Goldens' dinner party, and although it had appeared to him that what he said to her hadn't quite registered, she accepted his offer for a ride and got in the car.

"She asked me if I would take her to The Coach and Horses Bar on Sunset Boulevard," Bill recalls. "I tried very hard not to let it show, but I was horrified at how bad Barbara looked. She was wearing a thin, light-pink cotton blouse that was hanging out of a pair of pink Capri pants, and she had these cheap-looking, white plastic sandals on her feet. I remember noticing that she wasn't carrying a purse, and I later wondered if she even had any identification on her. She was far too heavy for the Capris and they were almost splitting at the seams. I could also see that her arms were bruised.

"Even though she was wringing wet, Barbara looked dirty. I know that sounds unkind, but it's true. I just couldn't believe that this battered and beaten-up woman sitting next to me was Barbara Payton."

Certain that her walk in the storm had left her, as he says, "chilled to the marrow," Bill turned up the heat in the car and noticed that Barbara seemed disoriented and mentally lost. "She kept forgetting my name. She must have asked me what it was at least half a dozen times. Barbara didn't appear to be intoxicated, per se, but she acted vague and distracted."

It was an awkward few minutes, says Bill, and he felt uncomfortable because Barbara looked so defeated and worn out. He remembers that her blonde hair was hanging in her face, and that she was also missing a few front teeth.

"Barbara kept putting her hand up in front of her mouth whenever she'd speak, which wasn't too often. I knew she must have been self-conscious about her missing teeth, but I had noticed them right away, when she first came over to the car. It was hard for me to accept the fact that this bedraggled person was the same lovely girl I had met in 1958 at Milton and Charlene Golden's elegant dinner party. But, then again, she *wasn't* the same person anymore, was she?"

As the rainstorm continued its liquid symphony above the barren streets of Hollywood, Bill noticed that the car's wipers almost resembled a metronome as they squeaked across the windshield. The combination of their steady, synchronized movement and Barbara's slow-motion demeanor was oddly haunting, and Bill remembers feeling the utter despair that surrounded her.

Bill told her that he had recently seen Charlene Golden and Barbara responded that she hadn't seen her, or Milton, "…in a long, long time."

Her speech, at all times, was extremely tentative, almost as if she found it difficult to string together more than two or three words at a time. Bill spoke of a few other mutual acquaintances: Leslie Snyder, who worked for many years as an assistant to Louella Parsons; fashion model Eloise Peacock, who knew Barbara through Rita La Roy and had always liked her; and actress Joan Caulfield, who was also fond of Barbara—but he could see from the flatness in his companion's eyes that she was "somewhere else."

"I had the feeling that something drastic had happened to Barbara, perhaps a head trauma or a psychological breakdown of some kind. Her eyes were frightening. At times when she looked up at me, I swear to God they were 'crossed.' I finally asked her if she was all right, or if she needed anything, and she assured me she was fine. Barbara appeared so beaten down by life, I felt like crying. It was as though all the spirit and light had been squeezed out of her and all that was left was a kind of zombie."

After several moments of silence, Barbara asked Bill to pull over and let her out of the car. They were only a block or two from The Coach and Horses, but she said she wanted to walk the rest of the way. Bill tried several times to talk her out of it as it was still raining heavily, but Barbara insisted that she would be all right. "I think she was afraid that I was trying to get too close to her, or something," he says. "I had been expressing concern for her, and it was as if she suddenly realized that and couldn't handle it. Barbara just wanted 'out,' so I did as she wished and I pulled over to the curb." Barbara thanked Bill for the ride and again asked him his name.

"I felt so sorry for her. The person I had met five years earlier at the Goldens' was classy, bright and very witty. A charming girl, and a very good listener. The person I spoke to in 1963, on the other hand, was an empty shell. It was the most terrible thing I've ever seen."

Somewhere on Sunset Boulevard, Bill says, he bid goodbye to Barbara, who, without answering, got out of the car. He recalls watching her walk into the downpour, and how her almost regal carriage again amazed him as she headed down the street. "Even in her sad condition, it was obvious that she hadn't forgotten her starlet's training. Barbara continued on toward The Coach and Horses with great presence, like she was rushing to make her 'evening performance', which, I guess, she was."

After she left, Bill Ramage sat in his parked car for several minutes, trying to shake off the bitter chill that had descended upon him. Once he was sufficiently recovered from the horror of seeing this once-beautiful woman in such a tortured and wasted state, Bill found himself wondering what had happened to Barbara, and—more importantly—what would become of her.

Feeling a profound sense of pity for this sad creature, wandering alone in the night, Bill sat there as Barbara walked into the fog and rain, and then disappeared.

It was the last time he would see her alive.

Chapter Thirty-Eight:
I Am Not Ashamed!

By the early 1960s, Barbara's life of late nights, bare bodies, cigarette smoke and hangovers was sliding downhill at a ghastly pace. The wayward juggernaut she had been riding non-stop for nearly ten years had crushed everything in its path, including most of her relationships—and *all* of her self-respect. One can only wonder what went through Barbara's mind now as she watched herself spin completely out of control.

Today, the skid-row nightmare Barbara was living in, is almost beyond comprehension. Still, the questions beg to be asked: Where were all her friends and contacts from her movie-star days? Had she burned all her bridges? Was she beyond help? Help, certainly, was not forthcoming for Barbara. At least not the kind she needed.

In 1963, Barbara received an offer from Holloway House, a North Hollywood paperback publisher, to recount her life story for them. At the time, the editor and owner of the company was a middle-aged man named Leo Guild, who was a well-known gossip columnist and a former television and radio critic for *Variety*.

Bentley Morriss was employed by Holloway House in those years as a marketing manager in charge of book sales, and he eventually became its president; a position he still held as of 2006. He recalls that it was Leo Guild himself who came up with the idea of doing a book on Barbara's life. "Leo thought the story of a girl who fell from stardom to total obscurity would make a dramatic story. I must say, Leo Guild was a delightful guy. Over the years, he loved the horses as much as he loved his wives, and, believe me, he had plenty (of both). Leo started his career working in the publicity department at Warner Bros., and apparently that's where he first met Barbara. A few years after he did Barbara's book, he ghost wrote Hedy Lamarr's memoir, *Ecstasy and Me*, but Miss Lamarr wasn't pleased with

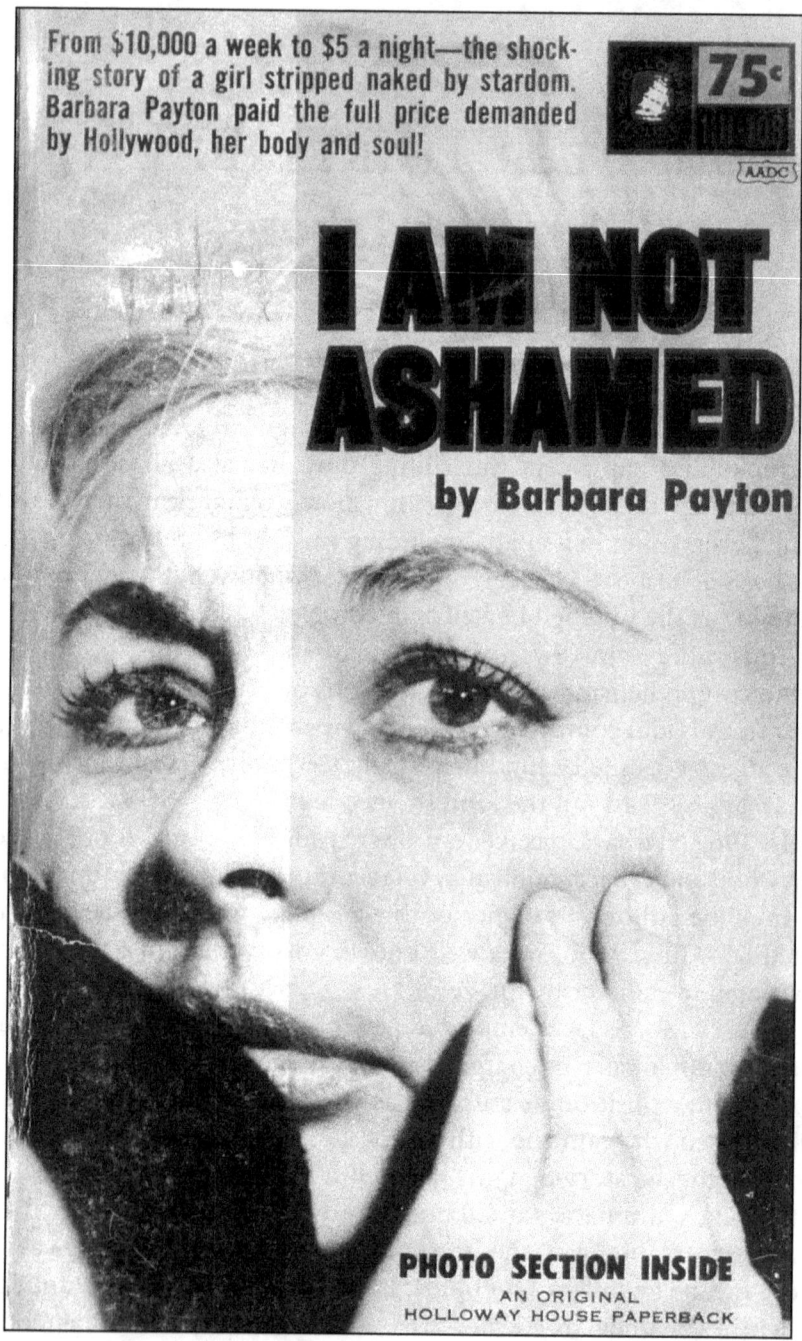

Barbara's infamous biography, I Am Not Ashamed, *was published in 1963 by Holloway House Books. Courtesy of Holloway House*

its steamy content, and later sued him for allegedly misrepresenting her story.

"I know that Leo believed that Barbara's saga was one the public would just devour. I can still remember the somewhat unique method he used to entice her to do the book. He had heard that she spent most of her time at The Coach and Horses Bar, so he sent a check over there one day with a note, and, do you know, she got in touch with him almost immediately? She bought a case of red wine with the check, and she told him that she couldn't wait to 'spill the beans.'"

Once she agreed to the project, Barbara and Guild set up a time to meet at the efficiency apartment she was living in on Sunset Boulevard. Sounding a lot like a hard-boiled dick in a gritty, 1940s film noir, Guild later wrote that as he entered her building for the first time, "…the smell in the hall was of cooking cabbage. Misery reigned in that hole, at least by the sounds I heard. Her apartment was #6." Guild had not seen Barbara in person since the early '50s, when they were both working at Warner Bros., and he later admitted to being startled by her appearance when she answered the door.

In a 1967 article he wrote about Barbara for the men's magazine *Pix*, Guild described their meeting in painfully graphic terms: "I knocked [on the door] and she yelled, 'Entre vous.' Barbara stood alone in the center of a room of unbelievable chaos. She was pig-fat and wore a man's shirt, and that's it. The shirt just made it past her crotch. There was a red, angry scar coming from under the shirt and running down her thigh. 'Of course, I remember you,' she smiled. I noticed she was unsteady on her feet."

Guild gave an earlier account of their meeting to *Pageant* magazine in January 1964: "When I met Barbara and started to do her life story, she lived almost entirely on red Dago wine and was reduced to prostitution. In spite of all this, she was cheerful and lived with her scrapbooks."

When he came out to her apartment, Guild claimed that Barbara had quickly admitted to him that she was trading her body for cash. "There are men who can't get love unless they buy it," she reasoned. "I sell it. What's wrong with that?"

The *Pix* article also alleged that Barbara had a new pimp at the time; a "big, husky Negro man" named "Broncho," who hovered in the background while she turned tricks during Guild's visit. "He said he was Barbara's 'manager,'" Guild wrote. Broncho allegedly told him, "All money comes to me, hear? I've kept her eating and drinking and happy, too. I get her all her customers so I got to get me some rewards. Just give me all the money."

In the magazine article, Guild wrote, "While Barbara and I talked, there were raps on the door. Barbara would scream, 'Go away! Come back later.' One young Negro pushed the door open and waved a bill. Barbara got up furiously and slammed the door shut, almost chopping off his arm."

The *Pix* article, if true, offered a chilling account of Barbara's current way of life, made more so by her matter-of-fact acceptance of her situation. "I'm not ashamed," she allegedly told Guild, on the night of their meeting. "I once made $5,000 a week, and now I'm a prostitute, but I'm not ashamed. I contribute more now to humanity than I ever did as an actress."

Over the next several days, Leo Guild conducted a series of taped interviews with Barbara amid the noise and clutter of her squalid den. He allegedly paid her a flat fee of $2,000 for the project—doled out to her in periodic installments—which, of course, quickly disappeared in booze and drugs. Says Bentley Morriss: "Leo would frequently send a check over to Barbara at the Coach and Horses, as part of her payment, knowing full well that she would use it to buy a case of wine. As down-and-out as she was at the time, that's the way Barbara wanted it (to be paid in booze). Incredible, isn't it?"

Unfortunately, the resulting collaboration of Barbara Payton and Leo Guild (which Guild, utilizing one of Barbara's quotes to him, titled *I Am Not Ashamed*), reflects the disjointed babbling of a woman whose thoughts were severely compromised by the copious amounts of alcohol she ingested in his presence. "She drank glass after glass of wine," said Guild, "her spirits greatly improving with each swallow."

"I always have a little too much wine in me," Barbara admitted, "but you can bet your tootsies that every word is true. I'm too old to bullshit the public."

Despite this claim of Barbara's, very little of the information she reveals in the book is accurate. Throughout its 190 pages, many individuals' true identities are withheld, and several of Barbara's recollections are often vague and nonsensical. Mystifying assertions bubble up out of nowhere, many of them as unintelligible as they are bizarre. "I'm clear crystal. You tap me gently, and I ring clear and cool. Nothing phony here," she promises in one breath, only to dish up muddled dross in the next. [29] Sadly, the 75-cent paperback seemed little more than stream-of-consciousness trash that Barbara and Guild tore off in quick fashion to keep her awash and drowning in old memories and alcohol.

Barbara's off-the-top-of-her-head dialogue contained such weird, booze-driven gems as, " If I could just wash my boyfriend's shirts, cook clams and do a skit with Art Carney, I'd be happy," and "It's hard for me to start at the beginning, and go in a straight line to the end," to "…but I'm getting away from my point. And I'm realistic, and must stick to my point."

With not a single thought to the possible repercussions, Barbara unleashed several candid announcements throughout the text—sensational disclosures that Leo Guild had obviously included solely for their shock value. These included surface discussions of her alleged dalliances with lesbian relationships: "They always happened after men shattered the few ideals or illusions I had left," to her affinity for Black lovers: "I love the Negro race because lately they're the only ones who appreciate my blonde beauty, or what I have left of it. White men don't seem to go for me anymore. I will only accept money from Negroes. In time, I believe the Negro will inherit the earth."

Barbara's highly inflammatory confessions—at least for the era in which they were written—unequivocally cemented her bad-girl status, but brought her little in the way of sympathy for a life many believed she had actively chosen. With a no-holds-barred abandon, powered by booze and drugs, Barbara dropped these blistering bombshells in an obvious attempt to shake everybody up, and to prove that she was not above using any method she could think of to push her way back into the Hollywood fold. But, as journalist Steve Richards so aptly wrote in his 1999 article for Canada's *Sockamagee* magazine, *Barbara Payton: No Tears, No Pity*, Barbara's attempt to restore her fame via the release of her vulgar memoir was a miserable failure. "This wasn't a stepping stone for reviving her career," said Richards. "This was simply one last chance for Barbara to play the part of 'movie starlet.' She was soon back to the Los Angeles streets and cheap wine."

By 1963, Barbara's ex-husband Tony Provas had moved back to Los Angeles from Guaymas, and was managing a pipe and tobacco store in Westwood Village, near the UCLA campus. Prior to his acquiring the job he had met and married a former actress by the name of Jorian Clair, who had given up that profession to pursue a freelance writing career. Tony had not seen Barbara since they had gone their separate ways in 1961, but

TOP: Barbara poses like the starlet she no longer was, in this photo from her autobiography, I Am Not Ashamed. Courtesy of Holloway House / LEFT: A rare outtake from the photo session Barbara, 36, did for her autobiography in 1963. Courtesy of Jan Redfield / RIGHT: A photo of Barbara at the Jet Inn which later appeared in her autobiography. Courtesy of Holloway House

he was certainly aware of her recent troubles. "It was hard to lose track of Barbara because she kept popping up in all those yellow tabloids," he says. "Naturally, I was concerned about her, but after our final separation, I never contacted her again." Tony picked up a copy of *I Am Not Ashamed* soon after it was published, and remembers how appalled he was with its content.

Today, like most other individuals who knew Barbara, he is quick to discount the book's veracity. "Although some of the incidents and characters described were factual," he says, "they were altered to a certain extent in order to depict the kind of sensationalistic fantasy its real author—Leo Guild—wanted to present. Because Barbara was in such a constant stupor at the time, I have no doubt that she was easily manipulated by Guild, and was thus unable to stay on top of what he was writing. He took whatever crumbs she was able to spit out and then he added his own ugly spin to them. Trust me, the majority of the book's content was highly fictional.

"For instance, Leo Guild wrote that I was an 'itinerant fisherman.' That is a gross and demeaning lie. There's nothing wrong with being an honest, hardworking, itinerant fisherman, it's just that I wasn't one, and never have been. I was in the sportfishing business—big difference. It's impossible to know if Barbara told him that, or if Guild took it upon himself to make it up, but it was completely inaccurate.

"By 1963, Barbara would have agreed to do or say anything for another bottle of wine or vodka. However, had she, in an unlikely sober moment, ever read the book herself, she would have indeed, 'been ashamed.' Unfortunately, though, after we separated for the last time, Barbara was never sober again."

Bill Ramage concurs with Tony Provas' assessment of the book, and has harsh words for Leo Guild, as well. "Everyone in the industry knew he was a lout. Guild was a drunk and a liar, and by then his reputation was in the toilet. And a few years after the book was published, he wound up in not much better shape than Barbara. Alcoholic, and broke. By the 1960s, Leo Guild was persona non grata everywhere. Believe me, Barbara did herself no favors aligning herself with that creep."

Jan Redfield remembers Barbara's flippant attitude about both the book, and Leo Guild. "She told me that 'some guy' paid her $2,000 to talk into a tape recorder, and to take some pictures of her at a motel, but she said he just went ahead and wrote whatever he wanted. Barbara wasn't

Probably the worst, and most shocking image of Barbara from her 1963 photo session for I Am Not Ashamed. *Courtesy of Holloway House*

angry about it. In fact, she treated it like one big joke. God only knows what she did with the money he gave her."

If the oblique text of *I Am Not Ashamed* proved a major disservice to its subject, the contemporary photographs that accompanied it were nothing short of grotesque. Shot in a seedy motel room at the Jet Inn by Los Angeles photographer Phil Jacobson, they showed a fat and wasted-looking Barbara inexplicably reclining in several provocative poses reminiscent of those from her youth. After her aborted attempt to get back into modeling a few years earlier, Barbara seemed determined to get her current countenance into print.

Out of the two rolls of film that were reportedly shot that day, only a handful of photos found their way into the book, with one, in particular, standing out as a true abomination. In a desperate attempt to come across as an alluring sex object, Barbara was seen lounging on a couch at the motel, with a stripper's fur boa slung over her shoulders. Either Jacobson or Barbara herself had allowed the top of her dress to be wrenched down to her waist, revealing a tiny, black bra on a torso that was frighteningly swollen. An ashen figure in a threadbare setting, Barbara appeared soft and pasty, and looked as though she had been pickled in a vat of booze. Her eyes, once so warm and appealing, had a tragic and almost desperate look to them, like she was daring her audience to resist her (that is, if they could). Barbara's gruesome attempt in the photo to capture a long-gone, come-hither look, was a graphic display of her decline quite unlike any other, and only succeeded in plunging her into overt self-parody. Anything but provocative, the image was shocking and demoralizing, and to this very day it resonates with a haunting and heartbreaking pathos.

Bill Ramage was repulsed when he picked up a copy of the book and saw the photo in question. "When the camera turns on you, it does so with the vengeance of Hell itself," says the former model. "To me, Barbara's allowing that awful 'aged starlet' photo of her to be shot is incomprehensible. How could a photographer degrade her like that? Once swathed in a $10,000 mink coat, she plopped down on that ratty couch and wrapped that moth-eaten, filthy-looking fox fur piece around her throat. It looked more like a noose. And that embarrassing look on her face. God rest her soul, I'm convinced she was out of her mind."

Author Stone Wallace shares Bill's aversion to Barbara's so-called, "aged starlet" photo. "In that shot, Barbara actually reminded me of a slightly slimmed-down version of that John Waters transvestite, Divine. I cannot think of any other Hollywood personality (let alone movie sexpot) who declined so dramatically in their appearance as Barbara."

In their discussion of the film *Sunset Blvd.*, and of its lead character, the demented and delusional former silent-screen star Norma Desmond, authors Jay Robert Nash and Stanley Ralph Ross write in their massive film encyclopedia, *The Motion Picture Guide*: "[Desmond] slips visually backward into the time of her heyday, into the very past she has yearned once more to embrace, magically escaping real life to live forever inside the illusion."

These were fitting words for Barbara as well, who, in a tangled kind of trance, had somehow slipped back into the starlet posturing of her youth. But where once the famous glamour icon Andre de Dienes had photographed a gorgeous and suntanned young girl luxuriating in the surf and climbing the cliffs at Malibu Beach, Barbara's current circumstances found a drab and weathered woman—her pale and tumescent form now harshly framed in flashing neon—posing, as Andrew Dowdy writes, "in motel studios with rolled-down blinds, playing her unscripted part entirely from memory."

Following a brief blast of noise upon its release, *I Am Not Ashamed* sputtered along for a few months—it was even serialized in a handful of tabloids and men's magazines of the day—before landing in the back-bin section of used book stores across the country. With its failure to resurrect her fame, Barbara retreated back into the shadows, and to her self-induced misery.

Retired L.A.P.D. Sheriff's Detective Joe Lesnick worked the beat on Hollywood's Sunset Strip from 1961-1967, and remembers crossing paths with Barbara some time after her book came out in 1963. Lesnick and his partner, Ben Lopez, were working narcotics at the time, and were attempting to develop a case on a heroin dealer who was living in a seedy hotel on Sunset Boulevard, just below Fairfax Avenue. He says, "We collected the evidence, went into the hotel, and arrested the guy who was dealing heroin. All of a sudden, this heavyset blonde that we had seen out front a few minutes earlier, came staggering down the hall, barefoot and clad only in a men's pajama top."

At first Lesnick didn't recognize this disheveled wreck as Barbara Payton, the former movie star. "Barbara couldn't have looked worse if she tried. She was dirty, her face was blotchy and puffy… she was just a mess. We went to her room to get her to put on some clothes, and we found an outfit of a blackened spoon, a hypodermic needle and an eyedropper sitting on the nightstand. We couldn't slow her down on the profanity. I mean, it was just wall-to-wall, crazy stuff. Really sick stuff that I had rarely heard before, much less from a woman.

"I didn't really know it was her until the guy we had arrested told us, because she looked so bad; worse than you could ever imagine. I said to him, you know, 'What's with her?' He said, 'Well, she's kind of dingy, but, believe it or not, she used to be a movie star. That's Barbara Payton.' And then I looked at her, and I could tell it was her, but she had slipped a long way." Joe Lesnick recalls busting Barbara that day for possession of a hypodermic syringe, and for being under the influence of narcotics. "We nabbed her with a load already under her skin," is how he put it.

At the time of her arrest, Barbara's medical condition was so poor she was immediately put into detox at L.A. County Hospital, where she was confined and treated in a locked ward. Jan and Frank visited her there, and recalled the distress they felt upon seeing Barbara for the first time in months.

"It was several months after her book came out," says Jan, "and it was right before Easter, so I brought Barbara a basket of colored eggs topped with orchids. She was in the jail section of the hospital, and we were passed through a security door to a big room where she was lying in bed."

"Somebody had obviously belted her in the mouth and knocked out some of her teeth," recalls Frank. "Either that, or they had rotted out due to her not keeping up on her hygiene. Barbara was an absolute wreck. I almost got sick to my stomach seeing her like that."

Jan says, "Barbara was so beaten down and sad at the time, and she looked terrible. I remember she was very grateful for the basket I brought her. In fact, you would have thought I'd brought her a bunch of diamonds instead of some orchids and Easter eggs. It was very, very sad. I remember we both cried."

After seeing her, Frank claims he tried to get Barbara committed to a mental hospital, but that his request was refused. "Believe it or not, the powers-that-be felt that Barbara wasn't truly mentally ill. Well, if she wasn't ill then I don't know what you'd call it. The girl was very, very sick—mentally *and* physically. She was shot. Gone. Anyone could see it.

"When she was released from the County Hospital, Barbara voluntarily went to a halfway house in Hollywood. That is, for one day. She later told us she left because they remembered her from her movies, and she was embarrassed. My sister was a very proud and private person and, in a way, she didn't want to be helped. She chose to bear the burden of her problems, alone. Like my father always said when we were kids: 'We don't cry over spilled milk, we just mop it up.' I guess that's just what Barbara did."

Incredibly, following her release from L.A. County Hospital, the charges against Barbara for heroin possession, and for being under the influence of narcotics, somehow disappeared in a morass of red tape. When private detective Robert Scott, of Inter-Agency Investigations in

Beverly Hills, researched Barbara's L.A.P.D. arrest records in 2003, he found no evidence that she was ever tried for either offense.

As Joe Lesnick explains, "Due to insufficient evidence and some quick legal juggling, the charges against Barbara were dropped, which was a crime in itself because it cut her loose and sent her right back onto the streets."

It is almost incomprehensible today to think that Barbara could keep slipping through the cracks of the L.A. legal system this way, but that's exactly what was happening to her. In the eyes of the law, much like to the industry in which she once worked, it was almost like Barbara no longer existed.

"It is criminal that she wasn't offered some kind of meaningful intervention," says Bill Ramage. "It's true that red tape and bureaucracy are endlessly boring, but this lady was addicted and desperately ill. The courts should have seen to it that she was kept off the streets so she could dry out and get the psychiatric and medical help she needed."

All true, but it wasn't meant to be. Several months after her heroin bust, Joe Lesnick arrested Barbara again; this time, he says, for being in possession of a stolen outfit. "I think the second arrest happened quite a while after her book came out. She had somehow gotten a job managing a hotel at Sunset and Ogden, three or four blocks from what's generally thought to be the beginning of the Sunset Strip. The area itself isn't bad, but that particular building she was living in and managing was an absolute hell hole, the worst in twenty miles. You know, shabby, like a flophouse. It was later torn down, and I believe the Screen Directors Guild stands there now."

Unlike her first arrest, Lesnick remembers Barbara being extremely passive when he picked her up on the shoplifting charge. "She seemed resigned to her fate and went into the station willingly. No swearing, no anger. She wasn't the least bit difficult." He recalls Barbara pleading guilty to the charge, and that she did some time at the county jail. [30] "I've seldom seen anyone sink as low as Barbara Payton," adds Joe Lesnick. "She really hit rock bottom."

In his book, *Laid Bare: A Memoir of Wrecked Lives and The Hollywood Death Trip*, writer John Gilmore recounts a meeting with Barbara in the mid-1960s. At the time, Gilmore was working on a manuscript about the death of Hollywood transient Elizabeth Short, which would later become the book *Severed: The True Story of The Black Dahlia Murder*. Exiled actor

During her most difficult years in the 1960's, Barbara lived in several modest apartment buildings like this one located over Wilcox Liquors in Hollywood. From the Author's Collection

and aspiring movie mogul Tom Neal, in his own attempt to muscle his way back into the business, had expressed an interest in making a motion picture of the Black Dahlia story, and had approached Gilmore to write the script. Word of this had somehow reached Barbara on the streets, and she contacted Gilmore to discuss an alleged encounter Franchot Tone had with Elizabeth Short prior to her 1947 murder. John Gilmore and Barbara were brought together through her former publisher Holloway House, which also churned out several paperback potboilers of Gilmore's in the early-to-mid '60s.

In *Laid Bare*, Gilmore divulges, "She'd hit the skids. She was turning cheap tricks to stay afloat—boulevard creeps and jokers on Main Street. [Barbara] was shooting smack but denied she was a junky. A talented beauty who turned into a fat, pathetic slob."

It is difficult to reconcile this description of Barbara Payton with the doting mother and lighthearted cutup that her son, John Lee, and sister-in-law, Jan Redfield, knew, but the sad truth is, Barbara had undergone a complete transformation, and was sinking to ever lower depths.

Gilmore writes that a producer (not identified), who had known Barbara in her heyday, spoke of her haughty, superior attitude: "She thought her shit didn't stink," said this man. "She was a pig's ear Cagney had the hots for, and everyone tried to turn her into silk. She was a pig with a pig's attitude about life."

However accurate this assessment may or may not be, it is important to remember that Barbara did not act alone in her downfall. In many ways, it was clear she was both the user and the used. First and foremost, Barbara had a chronic medical condition—a chemical dependency on alcohol and other drugs that clung to her with a fierce tenacity, for many years. Secondly, rehabilitation facilities for substance abuse were not as widely promoted or as readily available in the mid-1960s as they are today, even in a state as progressive as California. Back then, funding for any kind of mental health aid was extremely lacking, and quite difficult to obtain.

Still, as Bill Ramage points out, "Barbara, because of her years as an actress, could have been treated for her problems at the Motion Picture Home and Hospital in Woodland Hills. Although in those years not much was known and/or discussed about addictive behavior and mental disorders, Barbara's SAG insurance would have probably paid for her hospitalization. Regardless of her alcoholism, which is an illness, it seems that nothing was ever done to institutionalize Barbara for treatment when the courts do it as a matter of routine with other habitual offenders. That, to me, is a crime."

Bill adds, "Can you just imagine Barbara looking at herself in the mirror as she deteriorated, and saying: 'You stupid, silly girl. You had it. You had it all. How could you fuck up so? Look at yourself!' Then, grabbing a bottle. Replay that scene a thousand times, and I bet that's how she lived. That lost, little girl grew to hate herself; I'm sure of it. In addition to how Hollywood, and really all of society, came to reject her, Barbara was clearly her own victim."

Bill brings up a good point. Aside from Barbara's internal feelings about herself, in those days there was also the social stigma attached to being an addict. Like so many others, Barbara lived during a time when drug and alcohol addictions were thought to be manifestations of a personal weakness, and of a lack of character, rather than as symptoms of a valid medical illness. On so many levels, Barbara Payton was clearly a victim of the times in which she lived. As her son, John Lee, says, "Mom was about a decade or two ahead of her time. In the 1970's and 80's, there would have been help for her; I'm sure of it. Talk about a person being born too soon."

The aforementioned producer that John Gilmore quotes in his book, professes that Barbara's sex life was "more important to her than being an actress, than being a professional." It is sad to say, but a careful look at Barbara's life seems to verify this claim.

Since her first known intimate exposure to the opposite sex in that dark, Texas auditorium, and surely since her first arrival in Hollywood, Barbara's raison d'etre seemed to be solely as a purveyor of sexual favors. One must wonder just how many people in her childhood—and later, in the years that followed—encouraged this self-exploitation, as misguided and destructive as it was.

Truly, the burning question remains: at what point had Barbara crossed the line from sleeping with men in order to get acting jobs, to sleeping with men as her job—and whoever taught her that any of it was right?

Chapter Thirty-Nine:
Trapped in the House of the Rising Sun

At the time of his meeting with Barbara, John Gilmore was appalled by her horrendous physical condition. She was "fat and bleached-out," he says, "a walking mess with sores on her face and the backs of her hands, which she had tried to hide with pancake makeup that didn't match the color of her skin."

Gilmore later wrote that Barbara had recently lost her job managing the hotel on Sunset Boulevard, and was living in a falling-down, red brick apartment building located right on the edge of the Hollywood Freeway. Barbara told Gilmore that she was "writing poetry for beatnik journals" and that she was in such poor financial straits, she was about to be evicted again.

Sitting beside him at a lunch counter of a drugstore on the corner of Santa Monica Boulevard and Western Avenue, Barbara also told him that Franchot Tone had known Elizabeth Short, whose life and hideous death Gilmore was then researching, and that shortly before her murder, they had had a kinky sexual encounter after meeting at the Formosa Café in Hollywood. According to Gilmore, Barbara claimed that Franchot had once begged Elizabeth Short to defecate on him as a prelude to sex. That story, obviously, cannot be proven today.

While it's certain that many of Barbara's memories by this time were nothing more than delusional fantasies fueled by her rampant drug and alcohol abuse, John Gilmore feels the information Barbara gave him on this matter, and others, was entirely plausible, if only slightly "gilded." He later used the material Barbara shared with him in his *Severed*, *Laid Bare* and *L.A. Despair* book projects.

Gilmore, who knew actor Dennis Hopper in the 1960s, also recalls a sexual tryst between him and Barbara. "Dennis Hopper, then in his mid-

20s, said that he went downtown once and did a number with Barbara in a back booth on Hill Street. He told her he would try to get her a part in a picture. She was, according to Hopper, very eager."

Whether Dennis Hopper ever actually tried to get film work for Barbara is not known, though obviously, none would materialize. Although physically and mentally ravaged by her alcoholism, pill popping and frequent use of heroin, Barbara was still trying to reconnect with Hollywood, still trying to mean something to someone in the industry. She had long ago lost her grip on the brass ring, but hadn't given up her desire to grab it, just one more time.

In his book, *Fallen Angels: The Lives and Untimely Deaths of 14 Hollywood Beauties*, author Kirk Crivello details the tragic lives of several Hollywood actresses, including Barbara's. When interviewed for this project, Kirk said that he first saw Barbara on the Sunset Strip in 1949, when he was a star-struck teenager, and she was a sexy contract player, poised at the brink of stardom. Camped out on the sidewalk outside Ciro's nightclub early one evening with his autograph book in hand, he had spotted her leaving the club with a man he said he recognized through news photos as Stanley Adams, the dope dealer who would be arrested that year for the murder of FBI informant Abe Davidian.

"At the time, I didn't know who Barbara was," says Kirk, "but I thought she was probably an actress because she was so beautiful. I remember she and Adams kissing each other, and then getting into a white Jaguar convertible and speeding off. The image of her throwing back her head and laughing, and of her blonde hair blowing in the wind at dusk, is still very memorable to me. It was like a scene out of a movie. Barbara was gorgeous."

Many years later, in the early 1960s, Kirk and a friend, bit part actor Ray Foster (*Let's Make Love*), were driving through Hollywood when they saw a middle-aged woman sitting on a bench at the corner of Gardner Street and Sunset Boulevard. Kirk, a onetime film extra in Hollywood whose inside knowledge of the business is largely unrivaled, immediately recognized Barbara, and stopped the car to ask her if she needed a ride. She answered in the affirmative and asked him if he would take her to Western Avenue so she could visit a girlfriend. Barbara climbed into the car and sat between Kirk and his friend.

"Barbara said she had just been to the beauty shop," says Kirk. "Although she was quite heavy, Barbara looked well and didn't act like she was drunk—although I did notice there was an unmistakable trace of booze on her breath."

Within minutes, Barbara was regaling the pair with stories recounting her past glory days. Kirk recalls one anecdote about Bob Hope that was actually quite touching. It seems that while Barbara was under contract to Universal in 1949, and living at the apartment on Cheremoya Avenue that Hope had rented for her, they would frequently spend the night together, and then in the morning, Hope would drive her to work. During those commutes, they would often play a game where they would attempt to guess the professions of the people they passed en route to the studio. Unconcerned that they were engaged in an illicit affair, the couple behaved like any other man and woman that were infatuated with each other; cuddling close together in the front seat, the rubber-faced Hope mugging endlessly, and Barbara laughing at his cornball jokes; mooning and flirting.

"It was fun," Barbara told her companions. "Bob was such a nut."

The innocent way Barbara recalled the memory, Kirk says, was highly poignant to him, and almost reminiscent of a schoolgirl's breathless review of her very first date. The fact that she had been carrying on with a married man was truly insignificant to Barbara—now, as much as then. That part of her character, the heavily-guarded part that protected her from too much introspection and self-judgment, was, as always, blissfully and wholly intact. An integral part of Barbara's survival mechanism, it was a defense cast-in-stone that she would never discard.

Kirk Crivello says that another friend of his, actor Don Bastian, remembers seeing Barbara in a far less favorable situation in the mid-1960s. Bastian was walking down the Sunset Strip one afternoon when he saw a woman he positively identified as Barbara leaving a store called The Liquor Locker. "Don said that Barbara was weaving and that she was clearly soused," says Kirk. With her hair "looking like a straw broom and dressed in a torn, cloth jacket," Barbara reportedly downed an entire pint of booze, tossed the empty bottle in a trash can, and then staggered down the middle of Sunset Boulevard. "With all the traffic, and Barbara weaving in and out, Don said she could have been killed," says Kirk.

An equally unfortunate incident was witnessed by a woman named Lee Gold, who for years worked in town as a personal assistant to former MGM actor Tom Drake. Gold remembers getting off a bus one evening and seeing two men carrying Barbara out of the Sunset Strip nightclub,

Whisky a Go-Go. The men were on either side of her, holding her up by her elbows, and Barbara was, in Gold's words, "Babbling, and beyond plastered."

When Gold stopped her to ask for an autograph, Barbara brightened and somehow managed to straighten up and pull herself together long enough to honor the woman's request. But right afterwards, says Lee Gold, "Barbara crumbled, and fell to the sidewalk, in a heap." Her male friends picked her up and carried her to a nearby car, where they tossed her into the back seat, Gold says, "like an old bag of dirty laundry." Barbara had already passed out, and was leaning her head against the car window with her mouth open, when they drove off.

During this same period, Hollywood film historian Tony DeMartino remembers finding Barbara living at the Highland Apartments, a dark, crumbling fortress on the corner of North Highland Avenue and Franklin Boulevard. "A rough-looking black man in a stained T-shirt answered the door and let me in," says Tony. "Even though the place was unbelievably filthy, Barbara was very nice and happily obliged my request for an autograph. She looked quite bad, however, with horrible-looking sores on her face and both arms. I had the feeling she was trying to make the best of a very bad situation."

All these Barbara sightings of the mid-1960s confirm that her life had reached an all-time low. Yet, incredibly, things were about to get even worse.

While Barbara continued on her relentless quest to find new and imaginative ways to torture and degrade herself, her parents, Lee and Mabel, had their own catastrophe to deal with in early 1965 when their home nearly burned to the ground. "It happened in the middle of the night while they were asleep," remembers Jan Redfield, "and if it hadn't been for their dog, Dusty, I'm sure Lee and Mabel would have been killed."

Jan explains the events that night: "Mabel was asleep in the front bedroom and Lee was in the back room. Dusty must have smelled the smoke because he climbed on top of Lee's chest and barked real loud to wake him up. Then Dusty jumped down and started heading toward the front room where Mabel was sleeping, and when Lee saw all the smoke he crouched down real low and crawled right behind the dog.

"Dusty led Lee to Mabel, who was by then lying on the floor, unconscious, and Lee threw open the French doors in her bedroom and dragged Mabel by her arms out to the patio. It was like a scene out of an old *Lassie* episode. The neighbors must have heard all the racket and I guess that's when they called the fire department."

It was later determined that faulty wiring in the walls of the house was the cause of the blaze, which resulted in extensive damage to several rooms, including the dining room, living room and kitchen. Only the bedrooms were spared, says Jan, "Because Lee had enough sense to shut the hall door so the fire wouldn't spread. Afterwards, it looked like someone had dropped a big bomb on the roof over the dining room, and it went clear on through to the rooms downstairs. The floor actually fell through to the rooms below which were near the swimming pool, and all the beautiful beveled glass windows in the breakfast nook were blown into slivers. It was a frightening sight, and poor Lee and Mabel, though unhurt, were a mess."

Mabel was particularly distraught, Jan recalls, with the loss of several personal items, including one that had been given to her by her daughter. "All of Mabel's expensive silver, and her dining room furniture, were burned and destroyed in the fire. In fact, the silver had melted solid to the top of the table. But the thing that really saddened Mabel was the loss of the beautiful framed portrait of Barbara that was hanging on the living room wall. It was one of Barbara's early modeling shots when she still had her dark hair, and Barbara had given it to Mabel as a present. That portrait of Barbara was exquisite, but it burned up in the fire and there was nothing left of it but the frame. That just about killed Mabel."

Following this incident, the Redfields were forced to move into an apartment, Jan adds, "At the bottom of the hill, where they stayed until the Titus Street house was rebuilt. That took about a year, I think, but at least the apartment they were in was nice. Things eventually went back to normal, but that whole ordeal really took a toll on them. I mean, they already had a full plate as it was, worrying about Barbara."

It is a striking parallel, perhaps, that Barbara's portrait would be burned and destroyed in her parents' house fire at the very same time her own life seemed to be going down in flames. At some point between 1965 and 1966, while Lee and Mabel were living in their "nice apartment," Barbara had moved into what would be one of the worst of her latter-day Hollywood abodes. Her new home was the shabby Wilcox Hotel, a monument of ruined lives on the corner of Yucca Street and Wilcox Avenue, an area of town described cryptically by underground filmmaker Nick Bougas as "the seediest spot in the universe."

The Wilcox Apartments (formerly Hotel), on Wilcox Avenue and Yucca Street in Hollywood...Barbara's home for a time in the mid 1960's. From the Author's Collection

A foreboding and desolate block of burned-out and empty buildings, it was the same Skid Row section of town where the infamous, cross-dressing film director Ed Wood and former Little Rascal-turned junkie Matthew "Stymie" Beard lived at the end of their lives. Bougas, well known on the west coast for his series of graphic crime and scandal documentaries, describes the area as akin to the kind of wasteland left standing after an atomic war. The Wilcox Hotel made the Valencia Apartments, Barbara's ramshackle resting place in the early '60s, look like the Ritz, in comparison.

"That part of Hollywood is where elderly actor Victor Killian was chased down and beaten to death by a couple of junkies for his television set," recalls Nick Bougas. "And in that very same area, two hookers were found beheaded at the Motel 6. There was also a huge stone flophouse on Yucca where a particularly savage band of gay bikers was nailing young boys to homemade wooden torture beds in the basement. And that was the last place I saw local punk rock legend El Duce of The Mentors frolicking with a herd of homeless winos just prior to his being struck and killed by a train. That area of Hollywood [Wilcox and Yucca] is the absolute bottom of the barrel. YUCCA is right! Poor Barbara."

"The Wilcox Hotel was a true shit-hole," says Bill Ramage. "It was a U-shaped building with a courtyard out front, and there were often derelicts passed out all over the place. There was an old fountain in the courtyard that was always dry, and littered with beer bottles and empty bottles of cheap wine. Back then I had a maid who lived on Ivar Street, which was near the Wilcox, and when I drove her home she would always tell me to avoid that particular side street because it was 'too easy for good people to get hurt' there."

Former *Hollywood-Citizen News* adman Bill "Red" Hilser remembers the Wilcox Hotel, as it was located across the street from the newspaper where he worked for several years in the 1960s. He says, "In those days, I was part of a crew of ten printers that built ads for the paper from seven o'clock at night to three in the morning. We worked in the front of the building on the second floor, directly facing the Wilcox Hotel. Sometimes I parked my '62 Porsche in front of the hotel, and even when I'd get off work at three in the morning, there would often be quite a few characters milling around outside the hotel, and in the street. The famous (or is it infamous?) TV psychic, Criswell, from the Ed Wood films, had his compound on Yucca, and a lot of times I couldn't get to my car without one of his young, male friends trying to hustle me. I even remember Ed Wood himself, out there one night, in full drag, trying to talk to me. Ah, those were some wild and crazy times in Hollywood."

A man named Jerry Reeder owned a bar back then called The Gaslight, on the corner of Yucca Street and Cahuenga Boulevard, and in 2001 he spoke of Barbara's frequent visits to the bar. A former junior executive at Desilu Studios in the 1950s (he was hired by Desi Arnaz to handle Lucille Ball's personal finances), Reeder later resigned from that position after tangling with the imperious redhead, and went on to become a barman at The Gaslight. When one of the partners at the bar died, Reeder bought a half-interest in the business, but continued working behind the counter as well. For several months, Barbara was a regular at the bar, and Jerry got to know her pretty well.

The Gaslight was just around the corner from the Wilcox Hotel, and Barbara would often come in for a drink as soon as the place opened, which was at six a.m. "I liked Barbara," Reeder said, "but she was often sauced to the gills and somewhat incoherent as she had usually been up all night drinking. Barbara rarely had more than five or six dollars on her, so I would always set her up, on the house. She came in basically to continue her binge from the night before, but she never caused any trouble. Barbara was down and out, and so badly bloated by then, and I felt sorry for her."

Reeder was surprised one day when Barbara came into the bar ("stone cold sober," he said) and began touting the merits of the classic James Joyce novel *Ulysses*, a book neither easily read, nor understood. "She discussed the book at length with me, and I was astounded at her level of intelligence," he admitted. "All in all, I felt a lot of sorrow at the loss of what could have been, at one time, a great career because she did have so much talent and beauty; and yes, intelligence, too."

Jerry Reeder eventually went into the restaurant business, and later owned a half-interest in two very successful restaurants on The Sunset Strip called The Left Bank and The Best Sellers. They were near the opposite end of the Strip, far away from Cahuenga and Yucca, and served a much different clientele than those that patronized The Gaslight. After he sold the bar, Reeder said he never saw Barbara again. (31)

In 1966, while living at the Wilcox Hotel, Barbara met an out-of-work, bit-part actor named John Rayborn, with whom she quickly fell into an affair. An ex-Marine sergeant who earned a Purple Heart for injuries sustained while fighting the Japanese on the island of Saipan during World War II, Rayborn had amassed over 350 television credits during the fledgling medium's golden years in the '50s. Born Ira John Rayborn, Jr., in Chicago on January 13, 1926, he had worked a series of wildly diverse jobs in his youth—from being a fireman for a Chicago railroad and working as a fry cook in New Mexico, to baling hay in Nebraska and tending bar in Lake Tahoe—and had served his country overseas, before settling into an acting career in the late 1940s. With his rough-hewn looks and gravelly voice, he moved to Hollywood in 1949 and found steady television work over the next decade playing hoods and mobsters, but by the mid-1960s, John Rayborn had fallen on hard times. Shortly before his death from a heart attack on July 8, 2003, he spoke passionately about Barbara, and about the demons that had chased him all the way down to Skid Row.

"I was a drunk," he confessed. "In the 1950s I was still a functioning drunk, however, and was thus able to get a lot of TV work and bit parts in

A year 2002 photograph of ex-actor John Rayborn, a former lover of Barbara's at the Wilcox Hotel in the 1960's. Courtesy of San Diego Union Tribune

films like *Blood Alley*, with John Wayne, and *The Line-Up*. In those days, I hung out with all the big-leaguers: Mickey Rooney, Sammy Davis, Jr., John Carradine, Angie Dickinson. I was friends with all of them. John Carradine was probably my best friend—we got sloshed together a lot. I also dated some well-known ladies in town like Ella Raines and Bonita Granville, and for several years I enjoyed a great social life. But then it all came crashing down."

In between small, supporting roles in such popular television shows of the day as *Dragnet, The Rifleman, Bonanza* and *Bachelor Father*, John watched his escalating addiction to 151-rum deplete his bank account, and eventually decrease his work output to sporadic bits—hardly conditions where one can remain financially solvent. "So, I started stealing things to get money for booze," he admitted. "In fact, I quickly became a lying, deceiving, no-good son of a bitch. By the mid-1960s—I can't remember the exact year—I was sleeping in deserted cars and on piles of old trash bags in people's garages, and then I landed in that godforsaken Wilcox

Hotel. It was a disgusting place, and I remember it smelling like a sewer. I actually saw Barbara for the first time, though, at The Coach and Horses Bar. Once we started talking, we both had a good laugh when we found out we were living in the same dump."

Kindred spirits paddling in reverse against the forward tide of life, Barbara and John Rayborn shared Hollywood horror stories with each other and soon afterward decided to alter their living arrangements at the hotel. "Barbara was having trouble making her rent each month, so, in my drunken miasma, I gallantly offered her succor in my room—with carnality, of course, uppermost on my mind.

"At first it was just nonstop sex; two drunken slobs, inchoate and amoral, fooling ourselves into thinking we were having a good time. When it came to sex, Barbara had absolutely no boundaries. But it wasn't a joyous thing. It was more, oh, I don't know, more like an act of desperation. Like, 'I'll give you everything, and then some, and you'll like it (and me) so much, you won't ever want to leave.' I learned right away that it was no-holds-barred with Barbara. She was always willing to do whatever it took, you know?

"Once our paths crossed, Barbara and I holed-up in that stinking room for the next four or five months. And when I say stinking, I mean stinking. The best way to describe the room was that it smelled like dirty underarms, and even dirtier sex. Semen and sweat. It was very, very grim.

"There were always at least 15 empty bottles lying around, the ashtrays were full and overflowing with cigarette butts, and we kept the shades pulled down during the day to keep the sunlight out. Barbara and I basically flopped around all day, drank Ron Rico rum, and screwed. Nice life, huh?"

Despite the couple's inability to stay sober for very long—or perhaps, because of—they often engaged in marathon conversations about their lives and the various travails they had encountered in their plunge into Hell. John recalled many of these all-night, soul-baring sessions as well as the surprisingly articulate manner in which Barbara shared her thoughts with him.

Just like Jerry Reeder at The Gaslight, John Rayborn was impressed with how philosophical and introspective Barbara was. "She had a sharp mind and an excellent vocabulary: drunk, stoned or sober. When she pulled herself together a little, she even enjoyed reading books. No kidding.

"Barbara was also a very spiritual girl. I remember her carrying a crumpled piece of paper around with her that had a quote from the Bible written on it. Barbara read it a lot, so I assume it held some personal meaning for her. It was from the Book of Joshua, as I recall: *Be strong and courageous. Do not be terrified; do not be discouraged, for the Lord your God will be with you wherever you go.* Funny I should remember that, but she read it out loud all the time, and cried. Words she depended on, I guess.

"I know Barbara felt a lot of guilt about the way she was living, but she just wasn't able to help herself. We would sit around sometimes and write poems together, and I know that Barbara felt she deserved everything bad that had happened to her. She believed all those things the papers had always said about her—that she was this wicked, evil woman—and she wanted to punish herself. By then, it was all about her carrying on in a sleazy and demeaning way in order to reinforce her feelings of self-hatred. And she seemed desperate for attention; any kind of attention (good or bad), just as long as people noticed her.

"I can remember her sometimes standing at the window of our room and pulling off her top to flash her tits to all the people down on the street. And we would both laugh about it. Now, I ask you, is that pitiful, or what? We were both out of our ever-loving minds. Barbara once told me that Hollywood had used her all up, and then when it was all finished with her, it had tossed her to the curb, she said, 'just like yesterday's trash.' The biggest problem of Barbara's was that she was afraid to be successful."

As she herself had claimed when she left Hollywood in July 1952 to work in London, John insisted that "Barbara really wanted to perform Shakespeare. And I believe she could have, too. She had far more talent than Monroe, Mansfield or any of the other Hollywood blondes. Hell, you can't even put Barbara in the same category. If you really stop to think about it, she was always a little bit different from the pack. She never played the stereotypical, dumb blonde parts the others played, because she couldn't. It wouldn't have been believable, see, because Barbara was *anything* but dumb.

"You know, when she went to Warner Bros. in 1950, she finagled such a good deal out of Jack Warner and Bill Cagney that (for a short time, anyway) she was the highest paid actress in the country.[32] Granted, it might have been for just a couple of months or whatever, but hey, that's really saying something."

A supreme raconteur, John Rayborn displayed a high level of enthusiasm in his animated discussion of the woman he called, "the love of my life."

"She hated Franchot Tone," he said flatly. "She told me that sometimes when he got crazy drunk he would beat her up and tell her she was 'nothing but common trash.' And as for that bastard, Tom Neal. Let me tell you, I knew Tom Neal in the '50s. He was a complete jerk off, and one depraved son of a bitch.

"Neal was nothing but a sorry-ass little squirt with big arms and an even bigger attitude. He and Barbara fought like cats and dogs because Barbara never took any shit from him (or from anyone else, for that matter). Trust me, she was a very assertive woman. I called her 'Hell on wheels with an angel's face.'" John laughed and shook his head. "She was really something."

In the relatively short time he knew her, John said that he saw a woman whose inherent idealism was quickly—and completely—overtaken by apathy. "When I met Barbara, she still kind of gave a shit; not that much, mind you, but she could still get pissed off and fired-up over things that really mattered to her. I also know that she had an overwhelming desire to clean herself up after all those terrible years of drinking and drugging. She wasn't using heroin when I knew her, that much I know. But, then, over that brief period that we were together, she suddenly seemed to stop caring, about everything. Something inside her died. Looking back now, I can see that the poor little thing was (spiritually) all worn-out. Once she stopped giving a fuck about life, that was it.

"I think the worst thing I ever saw Barbara do was the time I walked into the room and saw her on her knees servicing one of her johns in front of that very same window she often flashed her tits in. It's like she wanted every stranger that passed by on the street to see what she was doing (like she got off on it). Well, when I walked in on that little scene, I just exploded. I kicked her trick's ass and—I'm ashamed to say—threw Barbara around, too. 'What the fuck are you doing?' I said to her. But she was so out of it, she couldn't even explain herself. Although I was completely psychotic from alcohol at the time, even I knew she must have lost it to pull a stunt like that. But now I can see, Barbara had shut down. She had just shut down. I really believe that was the beginning of the end for her."

"I saw Barbara's 'window performance', too," claims former *Hollywood Citizen-News* employee Bill Hilser. "As I said, I worked on the second floor at the newspaper. Barbara's room was also on the second floor of the hotel, just above the lobby and the courtyard. I never saw the guy she was shacked up with [John Rayborn] but at night when she used to bring customers to her room, she would keep the lights on, open the drapes and use a chair right behind the window. It was good advertising, I guess, because half the night crew at the paper wound up using her services. If you were on the second floor of the newspaper, as I was, you got quite a show."

In Barbara's mind, perhaps, her window performance was just a different kind of action scene in the surreal film noir her life had become— the ultimate 'money shot,' if you will. Though flickering street lamps had replaced the studio lights, and the crowd that had gathered to watch her emote was admittedly a bit more raw in their reactions, Barbara was still the Star giving the people what they wanted. No longer a movie star at Warner Bros., maybe; but a star, nonetheless.

As for her state of mind at the time, John Rayborn was right that Barbara had pretty much checked out by now. She was almost completely disconnected from life—she was certainly disconnected from sex—and it seemed the only way she could go on existing was to somehow find a place outside herself to crawl into and hide. Although now completely out of control, once away from her memories (and her conscience), Barbara could be a totally different person; one who felt in control, even if just for a moment. It was no longer about Barbara being 'an alleycat in heat', or her having the 'insatiable sex drive' that Hollywood had always gleefully whispered about. It was about the infinite emotional void inside her that she knew, even through the heavy haze of drugs and alcohol, would never be filled. Sex had long been Barbara's way of communicating with the world, but it had now become her punishment, as well. It numbed her temporarily from the real pain in her life—that deep, gnawing wound of being abandoned time and time again, by others, as well as herself. The pain had chipped away at her soul to the point where Barbara no longer felt sex, or shame, or really much of anything. How could she, when she was no longer even there?

Bill Hilser says, "One evening before work, I met Barbara on the corner outside her building and before I knew it, she was on her knees giving me head for five dollars in the alley behind the paper. I had fifteen minutes before my shift started, and the price was right. By that time her looks were totally gone, but what the hell. "

Amid all this chaos and degradation, Barbara and John Rayborn eventually parted ways, although by 2002 he couldn't recall the exact reasons why. "I don't think we formally split-up, per se, we just kind of drifted apart. I lost the room at The Wilcox and went back to sleeping in abandoned cars, alleyways and various crash pads around town. And I remember hearing that Barbara got a job working as a janitress at some fleabag motel on Sunset Boulevard. You have to remember here, I'm not talking about places that housed the crème de la crème of Hollywood. The Wilcox Hotel was a human garbage dump full of trash and kooks, and that included Barbara and me. After a while, Barbara felt totally trapped in that world and couldn't find her way out.

"As for me, I kept drinking from sunup to sundown and I really don't know how I survived. Then, in 1976, I somehow got a part as a bartender on an episode of *Police Woman*. I think my old pal Angie [Dickinson] arranged it for me, but I was so drunk the whole time I was on the set I didn't even remember doing the show until I saw it later on television. That was it for me, and right afterward I admitted myself to the Glendale Community Hospital Center for Alcoholics. I suppose you could say I was one of the lucky few back then who got help. I'm happy to say I had my last drink on July 18, 1976. I only wish Barbara had found somebody to help her."

For several years until his death in 2003, John Rayborn worked for the Marine Corps Recruit Depot in San Diego, where he was among dozens of combat veterans who volunteer their time to counsel and assist recruits preparing to graduate from boot camp. Understandably proud that he was able to pull his way out of the ashes, he also expressed a great deal of regret that Barbara was unable to survive the abysmal lifestyle that had already consumed her by the time they met.

"You know, at one point, we actually talked about marriage," John said, ruefully. "Looking back now, I can see that an extended pairing like that would have been a sure-fire way for both of us to self-destruct. When we finally went our separate ways, I had the feeling that it was only a matter of time before Barbara went down for the count.

"I can't tell you how much it hurts to know I was right."

Chapter Forty:
Down in Dreamtown

Following the end of her short-lived affair with John Rayborn, Barbara allegedly resumed her use of heroin and was soon evicted from the Wilcox Hotel. Lost, emotionally ill, and with nowhere to turn, she began living a hand-to-mouth existence in a vulture's nest of rundown, hot-sheet motels along Sunset and Wilcox Street, and Sunset and Highland Avenue.

The motels, many of them adorned with peeling, plastic palm trees and burned-out neon signs, had festive names like The Sunset Palms, The Hollywood Sunset Lanai, The Highland-Pacific Palms, The Hollywood Tropics, and The Sunset Sands, but they were far from being the benign rest stops their faux-tropic names implied. Dreadful places rife with shootings, gang brawls and rapes, they were a meeting ground for the weak—and the wicked—and no place for a broken heart like Barbara's.

In her one-way slide into Motel Hell, Barbara had gone from plush, well-appointed suites at The Beverly Hills Hotel, to filthy, flea-bitten rooms with shag carpeting and bolted-down lamps; the kind of joints where guests pay hourly rates, and fornicate to a street symphony of wailing police sirens and screams-in-the-night. In this sleazy setting, a wrecked and bloated Barbara rolled over sweat-stained mattresses and indulged in sexual encounters so base, they played like scenes lifted from the paintings of Hieronymus Bosch. Hollywood's dark angel had fallen, head over halo, into the underbelly of an inner-city slime pit, and straight into her own Hell on Earth.

Barbara bounced between these concrete deathtraps for a while before coming to rest for several months at one of the worst—The Hollywood Palms Motel, located on the north side of Sunset and LaBrea. A vile cesspit teeming with a particularly noxious band of drifters, dopers and thieves, the motel was a clutter of broken jalousie windows and boarded-up rooms, girded by a weed-strewn parking lot and a swimming pool so filthy, the L.A. Health Department later condemned it. Barbara had landed in a place devoid of the barest amenities, where even the most macho men were routinely killed for their pocket change.

"Talk around town was that there wasn't even a pay phone on the premises," says Bill Ramage. "Apparently Pacific Bell wouldn't replace the one that used to be there because it was constantly vandalized. Management of the place was said to be nonexistent. How did Barbara ever survive that hell hole? Poor baby, she must have been the optimist of all time."

Despite her extremely poor health, Barbara obtained a job on the motel's housekeeping staff, where she changed bed sheets and scoured toilets in exchange for a free room. Whatever memories of orchids and moonlight that Barbara had once found solace in, now completely disappeared behind the crumbling walls of an inner-city inferno.

Not surprisingly, Barbara's time toiling as a Skid Row chambermaid was extremely brief. Far greater than her desire to survive—in the conventional sense, by working—was her desire to debase herself, and Barbara continued down a path of total degradation. Propelled by a raging masochism fed by her self-loathing, low self-esteem and defeatism, she seemed hell bent on destroying her life. Finding herself firmly entrenched in a boneyard of lost and wasted souls, Barbara watched an endless flow of boulevard psychos and derelicts cross a path to her bedroom in a grey, faceless parade. A human receptacle for the worst kind of sexual acts imaginable, she handled it by drinking nonstop and fixing on smack until she was nearly comatose. She was no longer partying or getting high… she was doing these things to disappear.

Often, after she'd fix, and whenever she managed to scrape up a few extra bucks, Barbara would hitchhike or walk to her favorite hangout, The Coach and Horses Bar, and nestle into a corner nook. A solitary figure hunched over a shot glass, a strung-out Barbara sat in the shadows beneath the bar's blackout drapes, and drank herself into oblivion.

The bartender's son, author Robert Polito, recalls Barbara's sad appearance in *O.K. You Mugs: Writers on Movie Actors* [*Barbara Payton: A Memoir*]: "She oozed alcohol even before she ordered a drink. Her eyebrows didn't match her brassy hair. Her face displayed a perpetual sunburn, a map of veins by her nose. [Her feet were swollen], and she carried an old man's pot belly that sloshed faintly when she moved. She must have weighed 200 pounds."

Barbara would land at the bar every Friday night at eleven o'clock, and remain there until closing time. Then, in her gold slippers and stained, oversized dressing gown, she would stagger to the street to walk, or hitch a ride, home—usually alone, and always three sheets to the wind.

"She was seen often along Sunset Boulevard," says Kirk Crivello, "either waiting for a bus, or hitchhiking. 'I'm flat broke. Flat broke,' she would tell drivers who stopped to give her a ride. It was pathetic."

The Coach and Horses Bar on Sunset Boulevard in Hollywood--Barbara's favorite watering hole in the 1960's. From the Author's Collection

These days, The Coach and Horses Bar stands in slow-rotting seclusion at 7617 West Sunset Boulevard, surrounded now by an Indian restaurant and a used car lot packed with a bruised army of old Cadillacs left over from the Eisenhower era. It is a corner of town where the ghosts of all the dreamers who lost everything here, lay scattered along the Strip like so much trash. "The Dream Dump of Hollywood" is how author Nathanael West once described this battleground. For many of the industry's used and abused, it is the final stop on their Hollywood tour.

Although he didn't know Barbara, a longtime bartender at the Coach and Horses was nonetheless eager to reminisce about her now legendary patronage.

"People come in here all the time wanting to know about Barbara Payton. I've been told by several individuals who knew her that she was at the bar almost every night in the '60s. She'd sit right over there," he recounts, pointing to a stool that was somehow fittingly empty. "William Holden came in here a lot in those days, too, but I heard he always sat at the other end of the bar and never once talked to Barbara. Other than those two, though, it was pretty much 'street people' who frequented the place. That hasn't changed much. You know, this part of town isn't exactly Rodeo Drive. Everything I've ever heard about Barbara suggests that she basically just sat there, got drunk and bitched about how Hollywood had given her the shaft. I was told that she really looked like twenty miles of bad road by then. That's probably why Holden stayed away from her. But, you know, I heard he was always pretty wasted, too.

"Funny, isn't it? One rich movie star slumming, and another forgotten has-been, with not a pot to pee in, both sitting in here, getting loaded. Miles apart in some ways, but totally the same in others. Whoever said life's not fair?"

Skip E. Lowe says, "In those days, Barbara would attend Hollywood premieres as a spectator on the sidewalk, just another movie fan in the crowd." Her days in front of a motion picture camera now light-years behind her, Barbara stood among the crush of bodies—like some ghoulish, hollow-eyed specter—and angrily watched the few remaining ties to her past fame disappear. Barbara would stand there—fat, high, looking horrible—hoping to be recognized. Not surprisingly, she seldom was.

"That really pissed her off," says Lowe. "In her mind's eye, Barbara hadn't changed that much, so she couldn't understand why nobody knew it was her, or why they didn't care. She blamed Hollywood for everything that had happened to her."

In this melancholy state, all the bittersweet memories and faded dreams of Barbara's past would come flooding back to her. As she recalled, in *I Am Not Ashamed*: "Bathing in fame during the halcyon days in Hollywood was delicious. The whole beautiful scene seemed like it was for always. I remember the night I walked into the Presidential box at the opera with my mink coat dragging on the ground and me on the arm of the handsome Franchot Tone. And how everybody looked at me with admiration. I remember how at a premiere of my own movie during which I was paid one hundred thousand dollars, the press fought to talk to me. Man, I was really something.

"I could tell you stories of those wonderful years when the public address system at a premiere announced: 'Miss Barbara Payton's car... Miss Barbara Payton's car...' And there I stood with bleacher crowds cheering me, autograph hounds dogging me, and the world's most handsome men on my arm."

Barbara, like one of the sad, desperate creatures in Nathanael West's *The Day of The Locust*, stood alone at movie premieres now, staring past the velvet ropes at a life that once was, and could have been, and still hoping for the chance to be part of a Hollywood parade that had long since passed her by.

Clearly, Barbara never got over being exiled from the business. John Gilmore recalls her telling him, "First, Hollywood takes your body. Then, it takes your soul. Once it has both of those things, it has no use for you anymore." Indeed, as her friend and longtime counsel Milton Golden once noted, "To those who have basked in fame, anonymity must seem a form of slow death."

When not attending film premieres, Barbara frequently passed the time sitting in darkened movie theaters, losing herself in a celluloid fantasy that helped blot out the harsh realities of the world outside. Bill Ramage recalls: "There was a theater on Sunset Boulevard, just east of Gardner, called The Oriental, that I heard Barbara particularly liked to go to, especially during those times in the 1960s when she was homeless. The admission was cheap, something like 90 cents, and it was pretty third-rate. It usually opened around 6:30 in the evening and it ran a lot of old double features and B-films. Barbara would often get there early and stay until closing, around one a.m., and then she'd go to The Coach and Horses

Bar for last call. A young man I knew who worked at the theater would sometimes bring her shampoo and nail polish so that she could wash her hair and paint her fingernails in the ladies' room. The dear little thing. Even though she didn't have a nickel to her name, she still tried to look good, bless her heart.

"After a while, Barbara was allegedly barred from the place because she would often pass out in her seat, and the manager would have trouble rousting her and getting her to leave. She had been reduced to being a street person at this point, and it was very, very sad.

"The police harassed her. The rumors around town were wild: she had venereal disease, she was insane, she'd sleep with anyone for a cheap jug of wine. I know someone who approached her once—the kid who worked as a box boy at the A&P on Sunset. He told her that he had a dollar and some pocket change, and he asked her if she wanted 'to go somewhere and have a good time.' Barbara laughed at him and said, 'Don't worry about me, son. I am having a good time. Now, go back to the A&P and grow up!' I overheard the kid tell this story to some people in the market, and they all laughed. So many people were cruel to Barbara. Trust me, 'Dreamtown' can be, and often is, a cesspool."

Another place of refuge for Barbara during those years was, amazingly, the old Hollywood Public Library, on Ivar Street, between Selma Avenue and Hollywood Boulevard. A bit-part TV actor named Ken Carson worked there part-time in the 1960s, and claimed later on to have spoken to her on several occasions. "I was amazed at what a fine vocabulary she had," he said, echoing John Rayborn's memories of Barbara. "And I was equally amazed at how well read she was. At first, I had no idea who she was; in fact, when I found out, I had a hard time believing she had once been a beautiful movie star. No one there believed it. She looked so different.

"Barbara often came into the library on rainy days, and she always sat alone at one of the back tables. She rarely talked to anyone, although she did speak to me. The head librarian felt sorry for her and she always allowed her to read in the library, sometimes for hours at a time.

"Despite her often compromised condition, Barbara was a voracious reader. I remember she had a pair of dime-store reading glasses that she always kept tucked inside her bra. As I recall, she never carried a purse, and her clothes always looked like they had come straight from an old thrift store down on the bowery.

"Barbara had, what I would call, a hard personality—tough, cynical, a bit cagey, even. But she never caused any problems. She just sat there alone, and read."

Jan Redfield says, "Barbara was always an avid reader. Going back to when I first met her in Compton, there were always books lying around her various homes that she had just read, or was about to read. Barbara was a very intelligent girl and very well spoken; I can't stress that enough. How sad that she wound up having to go to the library to read. But you know, by then she rarely had enough money to buy a newspaper, much less a book."

During this time, Barbara also frequented a Denny's Restaurant on Sunset Boulevard, near The Coach and Horses. She knew the fry cook there from her early days as a carhop at Stan's Drive-In, where he had been the manager, and she also knew she could always count on him to feed her on those nights when she was hungry and without shelter.

Sometimes drunk, often filthy—but mostly just sad and lonesome—Barbara would wander into the restaurant in the middle of the night, and often caused a scene with her pitiful and shocking appearance.

One night, Bill Ramage claims, a patron asked the cook why "that old whore is always eating in here and never pays." Bill says that Barbara's friend exploded. "He ran around the counter, grabbed the guy by the neck and threw him out the front door, telling him that he'd smash his face in if he ever came back. That shows how people who really knew Barbara, felt about her. Even though she had become this sick joke in town—someone to laugh at and to push around—people who knew the real Barbara obviously still loved her.

"Why those people didn't get her the help she needed, though, is beyond me. As anyone who saw her wandering around Hollywood in those days can tell you, Barbara was being victimized and harassed on every level. But she never gave up. Year after year of that kind of life, and she never gave up. I don't know how she did it."

Chapter Forty-One:
Detour to Death

By the early 1960s, Barbara's former lover Tom Neal had come through a period of relative peace and quiet in his life only to once again see fate chase him down. After his movie career collapsed in the wake of the Franchot Tone fiasco, Tom moved to Palm Springs in 1955 in an attempt to get a fresh start. The ex-actor immediately found work as a bouncer at a rowdy cocktail lounge called The Doll House ("a pretty slick place and a real pick-up joint," according to Bob Lippert, who often saw him there), but he left the job after six months to become part-owner of an Italian restaurant called Dominick's. However, in keeping with Tom's propensity for bad luck, the restaurant went out of business soon afterward.

No stranger to a hardscrabble existence, Tom picked himself up by the bootstraps after his food business failed, and decided to learn the landscaping trade. According to author Art Lyons in his *Palm Springs Life* magazine article on Neal, titled *Killer Career*, Tom had first become interested in it "...by watching Japanese gardeners who trimmed the hedges of his former two-acre estate in Bel Air." Starting at the bottom as a day laborer, Tom worked for several local outfits in Palm Springs and soon gained enough knowledge to apply for his landscape architect's license. In 1957, he started his own business, Neal's Nursery, which in a short period of time became very successful.

That same year, Tom was interviewed by UPI journalist Vernon Scott, and sounded confident that his life was back on track. "I wouldn't go back to acting for anything," he told Scott in the syndicated article, *Tom Neal's Life Takes Amazing New Turn*. "[With my business] I'm outside all day long, I'm my own boss, and I don't have to worry about waiting for a call to work. No agent shoves me around, and there's no stretching the bank account between pictures."

Tom's nephew, Walter Burr, confirms that his uncle was experiencing a run of good luck at the time, the likes of which he hadn't seen in years. "At one point in the early '60s, my uncle employed fifteen people and owned three landscaping trucks. He had a nice little business there in Palm Springs."

1950s B-movie producer and studio head Bob Lippert, who, with his father Robert L. Lippert, had branched out from filmmaking into building apartment rental units in the Coachella Valley area near Palm Springs, remembers hiring Tom back then to handle the design of the property.

"No one can ever say that Tom was afraid of hard work," says Lippert. "He was a very talented landscaper who put in long hours and always did a very exceptional job for us. Even in his 40s, Tom maintained his muscular build and seemed to be in excellent physical condition. He worked out with weights all the time, and he was a strong son of a gun. But he was always a little bit testy. If you looked at him sideways, or caught him on an off day, you were asking for trouble."

In 1956, Tom married a local woman, an attractive, 33-year-old stewardess for Pan-Am named Patricia Fenton, with whom he had a son, Patrick Thomas (born March 14, 1957). The family lived in the heart of the desert oasis, in a modest, well-kept house on Potensio Road that had a tennis court and swimming pool.

Walter Burr remembers: "The house backed up to director Howard Hawks' home, and I recall them sort of sharing the tennis court and swimming pool. It was a real nice spread, and as far as I know, Tom and Pat were very happy there. I never met Pat, but my mother did, shortly after Tom married her. She said that Pat was quite beautiful."

Tragically, Patricia Fenton Neal succumbed to cancer in 1958, causing a grief-stricken Tom to ship his infant son off to his hometown in Illinois to live with his oldest sister, Mary. His landscaping business eventually suffered as the next few years saw an increasingly troubled Tom living a transient existence between Evanston and Palm Springs.

On June 7, 1961, Tom married for the third time. The former Gail Lee Kloke (born November 12, 1935) was a sexy-looking brunette who worked as a receptionist at the exclusive Palm Springs Racquet Club. The ex-wife of professional boxer Buddy Evett, she and Tom allegedly knew each other all of three days when they decided to tie the knot in Las Vegas.

Described by writer David Houston as "a dark-haired version of Barbara Payton," Gail was known in Palm Springs as a hard-drinking, loose-living party girl, and as a woman who supposedly took little interest in Tom's small son—preferring a night on the town to one spent at home with her new husband and stepchild. In a July 1988 interview with Houston for *Filmfax* magazine, Tom Neal, Jr. remembered, "I always had the feeling that Gail, well, she didn't hate me, but she just couldn't be bothered with children. She wanted to go out and have a good time. But I was part of the package, I guess."

Gail Neal was 21 years younger than Tom, and Walter Burr says the age difference was often a topic of conversation in Tom's family. "My parents and I met Gail when she and Tom visited us in Evanston at Christmas. I was personally stunned by this young woman—she was gorgeous. I remember some of us in the family wondering how Tom had attracted her and all the other beautiful young women he had dated after leaving Hollywood. I mean, he had been an actor, that's true, but only in B-level films. By 1961, Tom's motion picture career was long a thing of the past. He was 46 years old and graying, a middle-aged man, while Gail was young, sexy, and extremely hot."

Despite their considerable age difference, Tom and Gail seemed to get along well, at least for a while. Much like Barbara, Gail was a splendid cook, although it was a skill she rarely practiced due to her frantic social life.

"I saw her hard at work one Christmas in my parents' kitchen," says Walter. "She prepared a fabulous meal for us. She really seemed 'into' Tom, totally. Trust me, it wasn't an act."

Despite Walter's assertion that Tom and Gail were happy, the next few years saw their marriage deteriorate. As he neared 50, Tom had grown jealous of a much younger wife whose frequent flirting with other men was said to be anything but subtle. In an environment where Gail's boozing and Tom's anger commingled on a daily basis, things crumbled rapidly.

The couple had moved into a small apartment at 2481 Cardillo Road outside Palm Springs, and were barely speaking by the time Tom decided to close their joint bank accounts—an action his wife evidently found intolerable. "It was my understanding that by early 1965, Gail had finally decided to ask Tom for a divorce," says Walter. "She apparently had enough of his jealous rages and temper tantrums, and his closing of their joint bank accounts had really sealed the deal for her. I think that Gail just woke up one day and decided that Tom wasn't fun anymore, and she wanted out."

In January 1965, a deeply distressed Tom went back to the family home in Illinois, where his son was staying with Tom's sister Mary. Whether he did this simply to see Patrick again, or to restore some peace between Gail and himself, is not known. However, the events following his return to Palm Springs on the afternoon of March 31 suggest that Tom may have used that time in Illinois for a far more sinister purpose.

On Friday, April 2, 1965, less than 48 hours after his return home, Tom Neal's years of quiet anonymity ceased when he was arrested for murdering his wife during a lover's quarrel. It seemed the natural apex to a cycle of rage that had seen its true beginnings many years earlier.

The night before his arrest, Tom had walked into a local restaurant and told its two owners, with whom he was friendly, that Gail had been shot to death, and that he was responsible. Thinking it was an April Fool's joke, the two men did not believe him at first. However, when he insisted it was true, they notified his attorney, James Cantillon, in Beverly Hills, who immediately drove to Palm Springs and met with Tom. At 6:30 a.m. the Palm Springs Police received a call from Cantillon, asking to have

LEFT: New York Daily News *headline of 51-year old Tom Neal's arrest in the Palm Springs shooting death of his wife Gail, 29. Courtesy of Walter Burr /* RIGHT: *A 1965 photo of Tom Neal en route to jail. Courtesy of L.A. Public Library/Herald Examiner Collection*

officers come out to the Neals' house. It was then that Gail's semi-clothed body was discovered on the living room couch. It was reported that her green Capri pants had been "ripped and pulled below her waist" and that she was half-covered by a blanket.

Tom's initial story to the authorities was that he had confronted Gail with an accusation of infidelity, "...when she grabbed a pistol from the coffee table and began waving it around." He claimed that in the ensuing struggle the gun was discharged accidentally. Gail was killed instantly by a single .45-caliber bullet fired into the back of her head. Walter Burr says, "We were later told by a forensic analyst with the Palm Springs Police Department that the bullet passed through Gail's brain, came out the left side of her head and lodged itself in the sofa pillow." *The Palm Springs Desert Sun* reported that "one spent cartridge was found on the floor under the coffee table but the gun was nowhere to be found." It was like a crime scene out of one of Tom's cheapo, 1940's noir films—only this time, there was no director around to yell "Cut."

Following his arrest, Tom was held without bail for four days, and then was officially charged with Gail's murder. With the financial assistance of some of his former industry friends, he acquired the services of a new lawyer, prominent Palm Springs criminal attorney Leon Rosenberg, to replace James Cantillon, who withdrew from the case early on. From the outset, prosecutor Roland Wilson was asking for the death penalty, accusing Tom of shooting his wife in a cold-blooded ambush.

The murder trial began in Riverside County Superior Court on October 11 and lasted seven weeks, with Tom giving contradictory and confusing testimony throughout. Rescinding his earlier claim that his wife grabbed the gun from the coffee table, he later testified that Gail had drawn the automatic on him while the couple was engaged in sexual relations on the sofa. He admitted that he had accused her of sleeping with several other men just moments before she withdrew the gun from beneath a pillow and held it to his head. It was then, Tom said, that they began struggling on the couch for the weapon, when he accidentally struck her hand, and Gail was killed.

Though hampered by its inability to produce the murder weapon, the prosecution was intent on proving that Gail's death was no accident, and that Tom had murdered her due to his insane jealousy. A bombshell was dropped when Prosecutor Roland Wilson brought forth a key witness, a friend of Tom's by the name of Robert Lawrence Belzer, who testified that Tom had confessed to him that he had indeed shot his wife as she lay napping in their home.

Belzer, part owner of the Tyrol Restaurant in nearby Pine Grove, an establishment where the Neals had dined frequently, claimed that Tom had come to the restaurant only hours after the shooting, and that he was "punchy and rambling". According to Belzer, Tom told him that he had killed Gail because "she was my whole life and I couldn't live without her." In a bizarre side note, the newspapers mentioned that Belzer was a Buddhist monk from whom Tom had often sought spiritual advice.

Following Robert Belzer's testimony, other witnesses for the prosecution were called to the stand: Belzer's business partner, James Willett, who claimed that Neal had also admitted the killing to him; and David Garthwaite, a young waiter at a Palm Springs steak house, who said he knew the couple well, and testified that he had waited on them on the afternoon of the killing. Garthwaite opposed the defense team's assertion that Gail was emotionally unstable, and reported that both husband and wife seemed "calm and content" on the day of her death.

Evidently, the trio's testimonies were quite convincing. Six weeks into the trial, Tom's defense attorney, Leon Rosenberg, could see that his efforts to obtain a not-guilty verdict for his client had hit a brick wall. Though it had presented only eight of its thirty prospective witnesses, the prosecution rested its case on November 16, confident that the jury of nine women and three men had heard enough.

Although there is no known photographic evidence to prove it, it is alleged that Barbara appeared unexpectedly at Tom's sentencing hearing in November. Looking less like an ex-movie star—and more like a denizen of a backwoods trailer court—Barbara was described as "plump, blotchy, and missing several front teeth." Wrapped in an old fur coat, she reportedly watched the proceedings at the Indio Courthouse from her seat in the peanut gallery, staring intently at her former lover through thick black sunglasses. Though twelve years had passed since their affair fizzled out, the bond Barbara had always felt with Tom had somehow remained intact. Author Kirk Crivello claims that Barbara had often told her friends, "Tom Neal is the only man I ever really loved."

After the jury pondered the verdict for two days, Tom was convicted of involuntary manslaughter on November 18, 1965, and was sentenced to serve a prison term of one to fifteen years. Relieved that he hadn't been found guilty of murder, Tom reacted with a tired smile, and later told newsmen, "It's been a long, tough road."

Today, for the first time in more than 40 years, the Neal family (courtesy of Walter Burr) goes on record with what they were told had happened the night Gail Neal was murdered. Says Walter, "The information that was given to us from a forensic analyst with the Palm Springs Police Department is that Tom was lying in wait for Gail behind the drapes in their living room. At around five p.m. she returned home from work and plopped down on the couch when Tom stepped out from behind the drapes. After a brief stab at lovemaking, they started fighting and that's when Tom put a .45 caliber automatic to Gail's ear and fired it.

"After Tom killed Gail, he asked my parents for $10,000 so he could hire (famed attorney) F. Lee Bailey to represent him in court. They refused and Tom wound up having to liquidate his assets in order to pay for his legal defense. To this day, I believe that the animosity Tom's son Patrick has long felt toward much of the family was fostered by his father telling him that Gail's death was an accident, and that if he had been able to afford F. Lee Bailey to defend him, he wouldn't have gone to jail."

As in so many cases of homicide, the gun used to kill Gail Neal was never found. However, Walter offers the following explanation that, while unverified, certainly puts an interesting spin on what might have happened to the weapon. "Just prior to Gail's murder, my sister Betty came upon a .45 automatic one day that was stashed under a stack of towels in our parents' basement storeroom in Evanston. This was the same time that Tom came back to Illinois to see Patrick. After Gail's death, Betty had a hunch and went to the storeroom to see if the gun was still there. She lifted the towels, and it was gone.

"There was never any doubt in our family that Tom killed Gail—and not in self-defense, either. He was my uncle and I cared about him, but I have to be honest here. Tom was a loose cannon for many, many years and I think his intense jealousy of Gail just built up until it finally put him over the edge. Something went terribly wrong between Tom and Gail, and as a result, she lost her life."

As for Barbara, the renewed kinship she felt with Tom, and her apparent sensitivity for what he was going through, reportedly led to her writing to him a few times while he was in prison. However, little else would come of this unholy (re)alliance, as Barbara's time was rapidly running out.

A latter day photo of Franchot Tone, who passed away on September 18, 1968, at the age of 63. From the Author's Collection

Neal's friend John Gilmore believes that both Barbara and Tom exhibited sociopathic tendencies throughout their lives, which made their subsequent downfalls almost inevitable. "Barbara was absolutely a borderline sociopath," says Gilmore. "She was a manipulator and an operator from the very beginning, going back to when she tricked her first husband into bringing her to Hollywood. (33) Barbara admitted this to me in the mini-biography she gave me during the ill-fated Tom Neal/ Black Dahlia movie project. When talking to her, I noticed that Barbara showed very little remorse for her actions. She seemed to have that same sense of defiance and entitlement that all sociopaths have.

"Tom, I'm afraid, was a 14-karat psychotic. We had a number of long talks in Hollywood that I feel, looking back, were quite revealing—certainly showing a highly unstable nature (subdued by booze and pills), that when linked with Barbara, they were like a highballing, runaway train."

Finally, Gilmore says, "If Barbara had been able to play her cards right, she might have got up to bat. By playing her cards, I don't mean the casting-couch business, since Barbara did that most uninvitedly—and with people who did her little, if any, good."

Chapter Forty-Two:
Death of a Prince...
Death of a Pauper

Unlike his former nemesis, Franchot Tone had turned to the theatre and to television for work after his association with Barbara ended, and had made the transition successfully. His biographer Lisa Burks, says, "Whether Franchot ever forgave Barbara or not remains a mystery, because he rarely, if ever, spoke about her to anyone after their divorce. Because of this, I'm led to believe that he did forgive her, in his own quiet way. I do know from several people that he felt sorry for her problems and was saddened by the way her life turned out, but he also knew from experience that there was nothing he could do to help her, because Barbara seemed unwilling or unable to help herself. He chose to move on with his own life after the divorce, and neither perpetuated nor dwelled on the drama of their relationship as the years passed."

Like Barbara, it appears that Franchot also struggled with a longstanding addiction to alcohol, though he was far luckier in that it had never seriously impeded his overall standard of living—much less, delivered him to Skid Row. While it is widely believed that Franchot had become a serious alcoholic later in his life, it is nonetheless apparent that he was able to maintain his lavish way of living throughout the struggle, as well as forestall, at least for a while, whatever ill effects the disease would eventually have on his health.

Career-wise, Franchot starred in numerous stage plays in the years following his time with Barbara, including Edward Chodorov's *Oh Men! Oh Women!* and William Saroyan's *The Time of Your Life*, as well as in a highly-touted, off-Broadway production of *Uncle Vanya* in 1956. A film version of the latter was produced the following year. "Franchot not only starred in both the film and the stage production of *Uncle Vanya*," says Lisa, "he directed them, too. It was a project that was both his focus and his passion for several years." While the play was successful, the film (which he co-directed) apparently received limited distribution, and remains one of the actor's more obscure efforts.

Also in 1956, Franchot married his fourth wife, former Warner Bros. starlet Dolores Dorn (*Phantom of the Rue Morgue*), a beautiful, 22-year-old woman whose blonde and blue-eyed countenance was, not surprisingly, highly reminiscent of both Barbara Payton and Jean Wallace. Unfortunately, the Tone/Dorn marital relationship followed the same path of discord as Franchot's previous unions, and the marriage ended after three years.

In 1957, Franchot gave a brilliant performance on stage as the tormented alcoholic Jamie Tyrone in Eugene O'Neill's *A Moon for the Misbegotten*. Other stage roles followed, including a 1963 stint on Broadway in the Actors Studio revival of O'Neill's Pulitzer Prize-winning play, *Strange Interlude*. "Franchot had remained lifelong friends with Actors Studio founder Lee Strasberg, who directed the play," says Lisa. "Another good friend of his was Broadway producer Jean Dalrymple, with whom Franchot purchased The Fourth Street Theatre, in Manhattan. They intended to mount several experimental plays there, but Franchot later sold his shares when he became ill." In 1962, he returned to motion pictures in the highly acclaimed political drama, *Advise and Consent*, in which he briefly appeared as the President of the United States.

"That one was for Otto Preminger," says Lisa. "Franchot also did a cameo for Preminger a few years later in the film *In Harm's Way*. During this period, Franchot spent a good deal of time writing and developing ideas for television, theatre and film, working with writers, directors and producers of all levels, and from several different countries. He stayed very busy, always."

As Dr. Daniel Niles Freeland, Franchot briefly joined the cast of television's popular *Ben Casey*, starring Vince Edwards, in 1965, but soon afterwards fell ill with lung cancer. A lifelong smoker, Franchot was living at the time in a magnificent townhouse on Manhattan's East 62nd Street, where his ex-wife, Joan Crawford, frequently visited him during his illness. "They had remained close friends after their divorce," reveals Lisa. "Franchot and Joan saw each other often, especially in his final years, when both were living in New York. They were seen in public together and also kept in touch on the telephone. Franchot and Joan Crawford enjoyed an affectionate friendship until the day he died, and the same can be said for his relationships with his other ex-wives, Jean Wallace and Dolores Dorn."

Whatever personality clashes Franchot had experienced with these women seemed to disappear over time, and were replaced with an easygoing rapport, something he obviously had never been able to find with Barbara.

After a torturous three-year battle with cancer (during which one of his lungs was removed, in an attempt to avert the disease's progression), Franchot finally succumbed to the illness on September 18, 1968, at the age of 63. Lisa Burks reports that all three of his surviving ex-wives attended his funeral. This, of course, speaks volumes on the loyalty he engendered in the people who knew him well.

One obituary, alluding to his long film career, described Franchot's many roles as a dashing society sophisticate as being "only a pale echo of his wild and elegant private life." His biographer respectfully agrees: "After Franchot's relationship with Barbara ended, his life continued on with a sophisticated vengeance, although not in the glaring spotlight he had experienced previously.

"Franchot lived every day to the fullest, both professionally and personally. When he did occasionally stumble due to ill health or his drinking, he always got back on his feet again, driven by a creative desire to demonstrate his acting strengths and (especially) by his wish to be a good role model for his sons."

At the time of his death, news reports estimated Franchot's estate at $500,000 (approximately 2.8 million dollars in 2007 currency); a figure Lisa believes is pretty accurate. "Franchot left his family well provided for," she says, "in light of the fact that this was money he had earned over his lifetime and not reflective of any family wealth he had inherited. He left the bulk of his estate (cash, property and investments) in trust to his two sons, but he also bequeathed generous monetary gifts to several of his longtime employees.

"Contrary to what has been written in the past, Franchot died in the same comfortable fashion in which he had always lived."

It seemed a fitting end to a full and immensely privileged life.

Tom Neal, on the other hand, should have been so lucky. In stark contrast to his onetime rival, the washed-up actor and convicted wife-

A devout Christian Scientist, Tom Neal allegedly read the Bible every day during his incarceration at Soledad State Prison. Courtesy of L.A. Public Library/Herald Examiner Collection

killer spent the early part of his jail term in a steel cage at Soledad State Prison, near Salinas, California. Tom was later transferred to the State's Institution for Men at Chino, a medium-security facility, and placed in its work-furlough program, from which he was paroled in December 1971, after serving six years of his one-to-fifteen-years sentence. In 1988, his son told freelance writer David Houston: "When my Dad was in prison, I never lost my love for him. He wrote me one letter a week, and I wrote, not that often, but a lot. He really cared about me."

In their book *Hollywood Players: The Forties*, James Robert Parish and Lennard DeCarl write that upon his release from prison, Tom told reporters, "Women in my life brought me nothing but unhappiness." (The authors go on to question how much happiness he brought them.) They

Looking far older than his 58 years, Tom Neal is released from prison in December, 1971, after serving six years of his one-to-fifteen years sentence. Courtesy of L.A. Public Library/Herald Examiner Collection

mention that photos of Tom taken at the time of his parole show a man who "looked like a younger Tom Neal made up for a horror movie."

Writer John Gilmore claims that Tom's prison sentence had left the man a mere wisp of his former self. "I saw Tom a couple times around Hollywood after he got out of the joint; he was only a shadow. I took him to lunch once at a restaurant on Franklin Avenue called the Hollywood Hills Café. It was the same café Tom and I had coffee in a number of times back in '62-'63 when we were working on the Black Dahlia script. After

Tom Neal's death notice (August 7, 1972). Courtesy of Walter Burr

prison, he was mowing lawns to stay alive. Nobody knew who he was, or cared."

Echoing this assertion is Jay Robert Nash, who writes in his book, *Murder Among the Mighty*, "Neal returned to Hollywood (not as a forgotten actor), but as a forgotten gardener, looking for lawns to mow."

Tom Neal's fast and furious life ended with all the fanfare of a muffled whimper on August 7, 1972. Shortly after his release from prison, he and his 15-year-old son Patrick (who had lived with Walter Burr's sister, Nancy, during Tom's incarceration), moved into the low-rent, Gene-Ray Apartments, a Googie-styled architectural complex at 12020 Hoffman Street in Studio City. Reunited for the first time in years, the pair "ate hot dogs and donuts" (according to Patrick), watched television together, and tried to live a normal life as father and son. Shortly afterwards, Tom got a job co-producing an Encino-based TV show called *Apartment Hunters*, a program that was designed to assist Southern California's new residents in their search for affordable housing.

Tom's time behind bars had apparently quelled some of his rancor, for his son recalls a man who had meditated and read psychology books in prison, and had also, over time, found a degree of peace in his life. "Dad was a devout Christian Scientist and he spent years studying metaphysics and the philosophy of mind and science unity," says Patrick Neal. "These things totally changed him for the better. My father was a smart man who did some stupid things, but he was always a good and loving father to me."

Florence Brooks, their former neighbor at the Gene-Ray Apartments, also has fond memories of the newly-rehabilitated Tom, saying, "He was a very nice, older-looking man who was always exercising and doing laps in the pool. He and his son lived in Apt. Q and I was in Apt. S so in the six months or so that they lived here, I saw them a lot. They seemed very close."

Brooks, who has been a resident of the Gene-Ray Apartments for over forty years, reveals that on the day before his death, Tom had gone out to help a friend put up a fence around some property that the other man owned, and came back home feeling sore and looking extremely tired.

"He had complained to me, in passing, of having a bad case of heartburn," recalls Brooks, "but apparently he didn't think too much of it, and he went to bed. The next morning, Patrick found his dad's body. He was already gone."

"I called him and I noticed he wasn't stirring at all," the younger Neal told David Houston. "I picked up his hand to wake him. It was cold. I let go of it, and it dropped like lead."

At 58, Tom Neal's death was attributed to congestive heart failure. At his behest, his body was cremated and his ashes were scattered over the Pacific Ocean by some of his former industry friends, most of whom had not seen him in several years.

"My father faced his entire life as a film noir movie," says his son. "And I agree. It can be a real bitch, with more bad in it than good." [34]

Chapter Forty-Three:
The Darkest Hour

While the two men who played such pivotal roles in her life lived out their final years on the New York stage and in prison, respectively, Barbara's life continued to fall apart on the streets of Hollywood. Her former friend at the Valencia Apartments, Norma "Knockers" Dodson, remembers seeing Barbara for the last time in a bar at 5th and Main, which has long been considered the heart of downtown L.A.'s Skid Row. "I hadn't seen her in about five years," says Norma, "and at first, I wasn't quite sure it was her. I took a triple-take, and when it finally clicked, my mouth must have dropped down to the floor. Barbara looked like death warmed over. She was in some flop joint hanging on a couple of Filipino guys that she said were merchant marines. They were shoved into some booth eating shrimp with their dirty fingers, and drinking like there was no tomorrow, and all three of them looked filthy. Barbara had her hair piled up in a lousy lookin' bun with big blonde strands hanging down in her eyes, and she was wearing a light-colored shift that was stained and completely see-through. She barely remembered me, but when I reminded her about the Valencia, she whooped and hollered and acted like I was her long-lost cousin. Barbara wanted me to sit down with them but I couldn't as the guy I was with said he didn't want to have anything to do with her. She told me that she and her friends were staying at the King Edward Hotel over on 5th and Los Angeles Street, and she invited me to stop by sometime and party with her. But I knew that place and it was the dive of all dives, and there was no way I was going over there. I was still in a bad way at the time with my own drinking, but I think seeing her looking like that was a real revelation to me. I cleaned up after a while, and stayed clean, and I only wish Barbara could have done the same. The last time I saw her, I may have been down to just a few plug

A sad and shocking photo of 39-year old Barbara taken shortly before her death. From the Author's Collection

nickels and some buttons, but I think all she had left was whatever air was still in her lungs."

Norma remembers Barbara leaving the bar after a while, "with those two Filipino guys and a couple other sleazebags they had buddied up to, and I can just imagine what happened when they got back to the hotel. I felt bad at the time, but you know, it was hard to feel too bad about her because she had acted so crude and unfeeling. Her heart was as cold as ice, and when she laughed it reminded me of something that jumped out at you at a funhouse or a freak show. You know, kind of crazed, and hysterical. She always had those big, beautiful blue eyes, but the last time I saw her, in that bar, they were glassy and a lot less blue. I could see that the Barbara I used to know—the girl who wrote poems and cried for you—was gone.

"Why couldn't Barbara have held onto that sweet person? Why did she have to let her go?"

Norma Dodson was not the only former friend of Barbara's who saw her during her final days in Hollywood. Much like Bill Ramage, Barbara's old boyfriend Steve Hayes recalls a disturbing meeting with her when he picked her up hitchhiking one day in 1966. Nearly ten years had passed since Steve had last seen Barbara, and he wasn't prepared for the shocking deterioration in her appearance.

"I was married to my fifth wife, Constance, by then," he begins, "and I was driving my Oldsmobile convertible along the residential section of Hollywood Blvd. one evening, on my way home to our house in Laurel Canyon. Barbara was hitchhiking, but I didn't recognize her at first as her face and her body were so badly bloated. When I looked in my rearview mirror, though, and I saw that it was her, I stopped and gave her a lift to Stanley Avenue."

In a scenario that was almost identical to Bill Ramage's encounter with Barbara, Steve says that when he picked her up, Barbara appeared disheveled and was nearly incoherent. "She didn't remember me at all and kept asking me if I was sure she knew me. Barbara was a total mess. The best way I can describe it is that her body looked like a gooey lump of white wax. Her face was puffy and blotchy, and her hair was ratty-looking, like it hadn't been brushed—much less, washed—in weeks. She was missing some teeth, and her breath, unfortunately, smelled like a sewer full of stale whiskey bottles. I'm sorry to say that, but it's true. I remember that after letting her off, I had to put the top down on the car, because the stench was so bad. I also noticed that she had seemed embarrassed about not having all her front teeth. When she spoke to me, she kept her mouth partly covered with her hand, hoping probably that I wouldn't notice the gaps. But when I let her off at Stanley Avenue, she stumbled a little and her hand dropped, and that's when I noticed the missing teeth. I don't recall how many were gone, just that there was a gap big enough for a couple of teeth to fit in. Remembering how glamorous and well-groomed Barbara was in the 1940s and '50s, it was quite unsettling, to say the least.

"Just before I dropped her off, Barbara told me that she was living in San Diego, but that she had come to Hollywood 'to visit some friends.' Suddenly, she seemed to remember me and she started crying. I asked her what was wrong and she said that she had ruined her life, and that she was sorry she had not lived up to everyone's expectations. It was actually quite sad. I tried to comfort her, but I don't think Barbara heard a word I said. She gave me a hug, kind of half-kissed me on the cheek, and staggered up the driveway of a gray-fronted house. After that, I never saw her again."

Despite the less than lucid demeanor she had displayed, Barbara was correct when she told Steve that she was living in San Diego—although this time it wasn't with her parents. Instead, she was rooming with an elderly Native American man who lived in a tumble-down bungalow just a few blocks away from Lee and Mabel. How well Barbara knew this man remains unknown.

"That was a very strange situation," says Jan Redfield. "Not surprisingly, none of us knew anything about him other than he was a full-blooded Native American, and that he was a lot older than Barbara. I doubt whether she knew very much about him, either, when she moved in with him. That man had to be even older than Lee. We drove past his house once, to see where Barb was living, and the yard was very junky looking, with big piles of trash heaped up behind a busted chain-link fence. I'm sure Barbara saw, too, because as soon as we stopped the car in front of the house, to get a better look, the shade in the picture window went down. That Indian man must have been a heavy drinker, like Barbara, and I'm pretty certain that the two of them had latched on to each other so that neither one of them would have to drink alone.

"Being that this man lived so close to Lee and Mabel, who were back in their home by then (after the house fire), I have no idea why Barbara chose to live with him when she could have just as easily gone to stay with her parents, unless she and Lee were on the outs at the time.

"During those last couple of years of her life, Barbara bounced around between San Diego and Hollywood so much, it was almost impossible to keep track of her whereabouts. But one thing's for sure. Every time Barb came back to stay with her parents, it was always 'party time' for her and Mabel. They would both carry on and hit the bottle pretty hard together—usually while lying on chaise lounges out by the pool, but sometimes in the living room, too. Mabel was always so grateful whenever Barbara came home alive and in one piece, she'd cry tears of joy, and just wanted to celebrate with her, I guess. But Lee would always cut both of them off when things got too out of hand, and that's when Barbara would split again (usually, for Hollywood). Most of the time we wouldn't hear from her again for several months."

Following her stay with her Indian friend in San Diego, and her subsequent return to L.A., little else is known about the events in Barbara's life in late 1966 and early 1967. Like so many times before, she had simply slipped back into the shadows, and disappeared. Finally, when she did surface again, the news couldn't have been sadder, or more heartbreaking.

When Barbara was found unconscious in the parking lot of the Thrifty Drug Store in February 1967, she had been living on the streets for several weeks, languishing in the wreckage of her destroyed life. After the L.A.P.D. determined that there had been no foul play involved in the incident, and that Barbara had simply passed out in the parking lot after an all-night bout of drinking, she was admitted, as an indigent, to the charity ward at L.A. County General Hospital. Filthy and with her stomach badly distended from her rapidly failing liver, Barbara was diagnosed as suffering from "chronic alcoholism, malnutrition and over-exposure to the elements."

Though she had abused her body for years, with little lasting effect, Barbara's health was now in total ruin.

Bill Ramage remembers hearing about the dumpster incident the following day, when he and his girlfriend, Pat Unger, were shopping at the A&P market next door to Thrifty Drugs.

"I was horrified when I heard what had happened to Barbara," he says. "Everyone in town seemed to be talking about it. I absolutely remember standing there in the supermarket thinking that Barbara wouldn't be alive for much longer. I just knew, somehow, that she was on her way out.

"You know, I heard that when they found her in the parking lot, the sanitation workers thought her body was a bag of trash. To this day, when

I really stop to think about that poor beautiful girl, lying there like a piece of garbage, I almost lose it."

Curiously, despite the shocking nature of the incident, a conspicuous absence of printed information on it exists. The story also failed to make any of the local newspapers, and although it was rumored that a

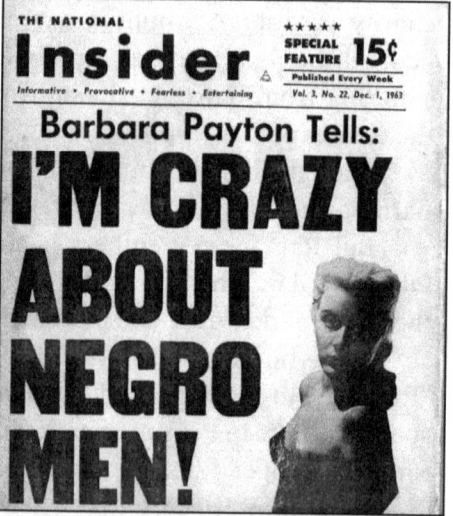

A montage of the many tabloid articles on Barbara's life that suddenly appeared in the four or five months preceding her death. From the Author's Collection

Los Angeles County social worker was assigned to Barbara's case, this information cannot be verified. All that is known is that Barbara was hospitalized at the County-USC facility for several weeks, at which time she rallied enough to realize that her days in the sewers and bars of Hollywood were—blessedly—nearing their end.

It is now believed that immediately following her hospitalization, Barbara—homeless and broke, her liver now irreversibly ravaged by cirrhosis, and in constant physical pain—was taken by the social worker to her parents' home in San Diego.

Though they couldn't possibly know it, Lee and Mabel's prodigal daughter had come home to them for the last time.

The dying end of a midnight cigarette, Barbara had crawled back to her parents' doorstep on a trail of guttering embers. While it was obvious that she had been committing a slow-suicide for years, Barbara now seemed to be in an accelerated tailspin that had, ironically, brought her back, full-circle, to her parents. "The head shrinkers always told me I had the compulsive urge to see myself destroyed," she once wrote. "That, in the end, it would be my final pleasure."

In retrospect, it is unlikely that the Redfields were in any position to help Barbara fight her demons when, at this point, they could no longer even fight their own. In fact, upon her return, Barbara's self-abuse would continue unabated in her parents care—helped, no doubt, by their unwillingness (or inability) to curb their own excessive drinking.

Family relative Richard Kuitu claims that Lee, at first, did not want Barbara to come home, but that he had finally relented when Mabel insisted that they help her. "I was told by the family that Lee thought of Barbara as a total embarrassment and a disgrace," says Kuitu. "He felt that Barbara had basically destroyed her life and he supposedly had little sympathy for how sick and depressed she was. And this was his own, flesh and blood daughter. It was sad."

"That's not an accurate statement," counters Jan Redfield. "Lee took Barbara in that last time, when she was so sick, without any hesitation. Now, that doesn't necessarily mean that all the arguing between them had stopped, but he did soften toward her at the end."

Although Lee had most recently worked as a maintenance man at the Convair Garden Club in nearby Balboa Park, he had lost that job—and several others, over the years—due to his alcoholism.

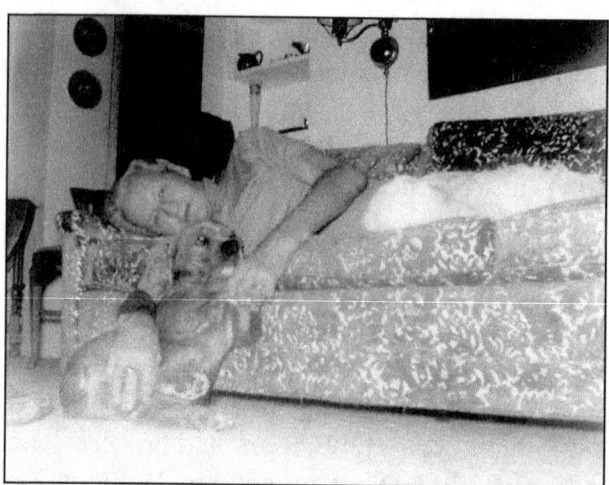

Lee Redfield with the family dog, Dusty, during a rare peaceful moment in a household ravaged by severe alcoholism. Courtesy of Jan Redfield

"After he left Convair, Dad really started to go wild with the drinking," says Frank. "It got pretty terrible, pretty fast."

Things had gotten so bad, in fact, that Lee had even stopped engaging in one of his favorite hobbies, which was building scale models of ships. According to his family, he had always derived a great deal of pleasure from the activity, going back to his earliest days in Cloquet. But now, more often than not, the models sat untouched in both big and little pieces throughout the house, unfinished and gathering dust. "The ships were sailing vessels complete with cannons and rigging," says his grandson, Les. "They were very detailed and everyone who saw them raved about how beautiful they were. They would have made wonderful museum pieces if they were still around, but they're not."

Like so many other things in the Redfields home—material, and otherwise—the model ships Lee created would one day be lost amid the constant drinking and cluttered minds of its trio of occupants.

Much like her husband, Mabel had only worked sporadically in San Diego, and by 1967, the 62-year-old woman had become something of a shut-in, passing the days away under a dark cloud of depression. "By this time, Mabel was putting whiskey in her coffee cup and taking tiny swigs from it all day long," says Jan. "Lee, on the other hand, gulped his whiskey straight out of the bottle." The couple, whose intermittent income was greatly enhanced three years earlier by an inheritance left by Lee's sister, Fay, were still close to Frank and Jan, and doted on their four children. "My kids evidently lit a spark in Lee and Mabel as they were always gentle and good to all of them," says Jan, "even when they were drinking. My in-laws were very generous with their love, and with the many wonderful gifts they gave us. If anything, they became even more generous after Aunt Fay died."

Over the years, Fay Redfield had invested most of the money she made from her boyfriend George Calvert's oil wells, in the stock market, and when she died on August 28, 1964, her will stipulated that her shares in Shell Oil and Mobil were to be split among Lee and their other two surviving siblings, Bob and Murel. Between the stock and the $250,000 in cash that Fay had left him, Lee had made out very well indeed.

"For a couple of years, Lee and Mabel lived quite well from the interest and dividends they made off Fay's stock," says Jan. "Then, all of a sudden, Lee started unloading all of the stock for cash. Believe it or not, he used the money to buy new cars for everyone. That is, for everyone but Barbara."

Lee's car-buying spree began in 1965 when he bought Fay's dark blue Cadillac from her estate. Next came a 1967, powder-blue Thunderbird for himself, and a fully loaded, Ford Station Wagon for Frank, followed by a Ford Fairlane for Jan ("With a big red bow wrapped around the roof," she says). "Lee actually offered the T-Bird to my mother on our first visit after he purchased it," says Jan's son, Les. "But my parents declined and said it was impractical as a family car."

"Lee even bought a new car for Barbara's first cousin, Shandra, who lived in Minnesota," adds Jan. "She was Aunt Dora's daughter and she and Barbara were very close friends. I'm not exaggerating when I say that Lee

Mabel Redfield, shown here holding her granddaughter Doreen, grew more reclusive and depressed in the 1960's as her alcoholism worsened. Courtesy of Jan Redfield

almost bought out the entire Ford dealership in San Diego. Every few months, it seemed, he would go out there and buy someone else a new car.

"The point is, Lee bought new cars for anyone in the family who wanted one, but he deliberately excluded Barbara. She was heartbroken over that (not that she was in any shape at that point to own a car)."

Shortly after Fay's death, Richard Kuitu visited his aunt and uncle and remembers being amazed by their flagrant overspending. "Even though he was out of work, Lee went through Fay's inheritance money like it was water. He and Mabel even hired a chauffeur to drive them around for a while. It was ludicrous. And then came the T-Bird. It was a real flashy car, and Lee was in his glory. All this time, he and Mabel were both spending money like it was going out of style, and still drinking up a storm.

"The worst part, though, was that after all those years, Lee was still beating Aunt Mabel. It was not a good environment that Barbara returned to; not at all. A beautiful home on the outside, maybe, but a House of Horrors inside."

Once again, Jan Redfield refutes Kuitu's comments about her father-in-law. "Richard Kuitu was very young when a lot of this was going on and a lot of what he claims to have heard from so-called 'family members' has influenced his way of thinking (apparently, for the worst).

"A lot of gossip traveled from San Diego to Odessa in those years and most of it was false. It's too bad that Richard was never around to know the truth, but he was only a teenager when all this stuff was supposedly going on and he rarely even saw Lee and Mabel. He wasn't there to see what was happening—only what he obviously heard when stories were carried back to the relatives in Texas.

"Lee Redfield never beat his wife. I was there; I would know. There was absolutely no physical abuse between them. For anyone in the family to even suggest this makes me very sad; not to mention, more than a little angry."

Her ex-husband agrees. In his typically pithy fashion, Frank Redfield says, "Richard Kuitu didn't know my folks at all, so I can't figure out why he's conjured up such a tale. My dad never beat my mother. Ever."

Lee Wiseman, a man whose mother lived next door to the Redfields' home at 1901 Titus Street, remembers meeting Barbara for the first time after she came back to live with her parents in April 1967. "The strongest memory of Barbara was being greatly surprised when Mrs. Redfield introduced her as her daughter," says Wiseman. "Sadly, Barbara looked just as old as her mother. The years, unfortunately, had not been kind to Barbara. Her alcoholism was quite apparent, as was that of both her parents."

Mr. Wiseman's mother, who had always avoided Barbara as she disapproved of her wild lifestyle, evidently changed her opinion of her once she got to know her better, during her final visit. "Much to my mother's surprise, she grew to like Barbara. In fact, when Barbara was both physically and mentally up to it, they would sometimes spend an afternoon together, discussing their lives. My mother felt that Barbara was basically a good person who had been used and abused by others." [35]

It has been reported that in the last months of her life, Barbara was estranged from her fifth husband; an antiques dealer named Jess Rawley, and was seeking a divorce from him. Little else, however, is known about Rawley (born May 3, 1930).

"Jan and I never met him," says Frank Redfield, "and I don't believe my parents ever did, either. In fact, none of us knew a thing about him. He was another mystery man in Barbara's life, plain and simple."

A 2003 check of credit bureau records by L.A. private detective Robert Scott showed only that Rawley lived in Long Beach and La Habra, CA., and that he died in L.A. County on April 14, 1998. Beyond that, Jess Rawley remains a shadowy figure in the murky puzzle of Barbara's last days.

The final weeks of Barbara's life saw her a tough-mouthed slattern who scuffed around the house all day in a shapeless shift and flip-flops, while grousing nonstop about the lousy cards she had been dealt. Totally spent in every way—mentally, physically and spiritually—she went through the various motions that each day required, but no longer cared about the outcome. Shambling from room to room in a drained and aimless fashion, it was almost as if Barbara knew she was only biding her time while waiting for the axe to fall.

"I saw Barbara when she first came back to San Diego," says Jan Redfield, "and she really looked bad. She was much heavier, especially in her lower stomach, and she had adopted a very bitter attitude. If Barbara felt like it, she had a great way of just tuning it all out, and that's exactly what she did when she came back home to Lee and Mabel. I noticed she was especially like that with a few of their neighbors. She didn't like some of them and Barbara was always snappish and rude if she saw them in the street; you know, like she was itching for a fight. That was very unusual for Barbara as she usually liked everyone she met.

"I remember there was an old lesbian couple who lived down the hill from Lee and Mabel, and Barbara was really bad with them. She hated them with a purple passion and also hated the fact that they would sometimes come up to visit Mabel. In fact, I was there one time when Barbara shouted them right out of the house and told them never to come back. So much for those awful rumors that Barbara had become a lesbian; I don't believe it for a minute. If you could have seen how mean and hateful she was with those two old ladies, you wouldn't believe it, either.

"Several times she tried to give me that same nasty attitude, but I always told her, 'Barbara, don't pull that tough girl act on me. I can see right through you, and I like the other Barbara better.' That usually put her in her place. Maybe that's why she and I were always so close—we never pulled any punches with each other. We were never afraid to say how we felt, and when she came home to stay with Lee and Mabel, that hadn't changed. But, my God, she was so depressed. There's no doubt in my mind that Barbara had given up. She had just given up."

Truly courting her own demolition by completely abandoning her will to live, Barbara was rushing headlong toward what seemed to be an inescapable and welcomed destiny. "The idea of her dying before she was 40 was something she had resigned herself to years earlier," says Tony Provas. "A sort of unconscious death wish, if you will. There is no doubt in my mind that Barbara knew what she was doing all along, and she chose alcohol and a horrendous lifestyle to accomplish the deed."

Her race was greatly hastened on April 25 when a drunken Barbara, with Mabel in tow, took Lee's Cadillac out without his knowledge and rammed it into a parked car at the corner of Fort Stockton Drive and Stephens Street, just a few blocks from the Redfields' home. When the smoke cleared, both the front grill and the headlights of Lee's prized Cadillac were smashed and in pieces on the street.

At the request of her family, San Diego historian Peter Steelquist has carefully researched the scene of the accident and says that apart from Barbara's inebriated state, he understands how easily she could have lost control of the car (especially if she had been speeding). "According to the April 25, 1967 edition of the *San Diego Union Tribune*," says Peter, "the weather on the 24th had been rainy, and on the 25th it was cloudy, but clearing. I am very familiar with the corner where the accident happened, and I know that there have been many other car accidents there. When you are approaching Stephens Street on Fort Stockton Drive, the road is very wide, but where it meets Stephens, the road narrows abruptly. Drunk or not, it would be easy for Barbara, or anyone else, to misjudge that particular convergence in the road, and to have an accident, as a result."

The San Diego Police Department traffic investigation report that was issued after the accident, stated that neither Barbara nor Mabel was hurt in the 3:15 p.m. crash, nor was Barbara charged with drunk driving.

"The police called Lee and told him that Barbara had wrecked his car at the bottom of the hill and that he should come down and get her and Mabel," recalls Jan. "They made sure to tell him that Mabel wasn't hurt, just dazed, but that Barbara seemed a bit under the weather. It's amazing to me that she didn't get busted for that."

Although on the surface, Barbara's beating a drunk-driving rap may have seemed like a tremendous stroke of luck, it was, in reality, an ominous prelude to what was to come.

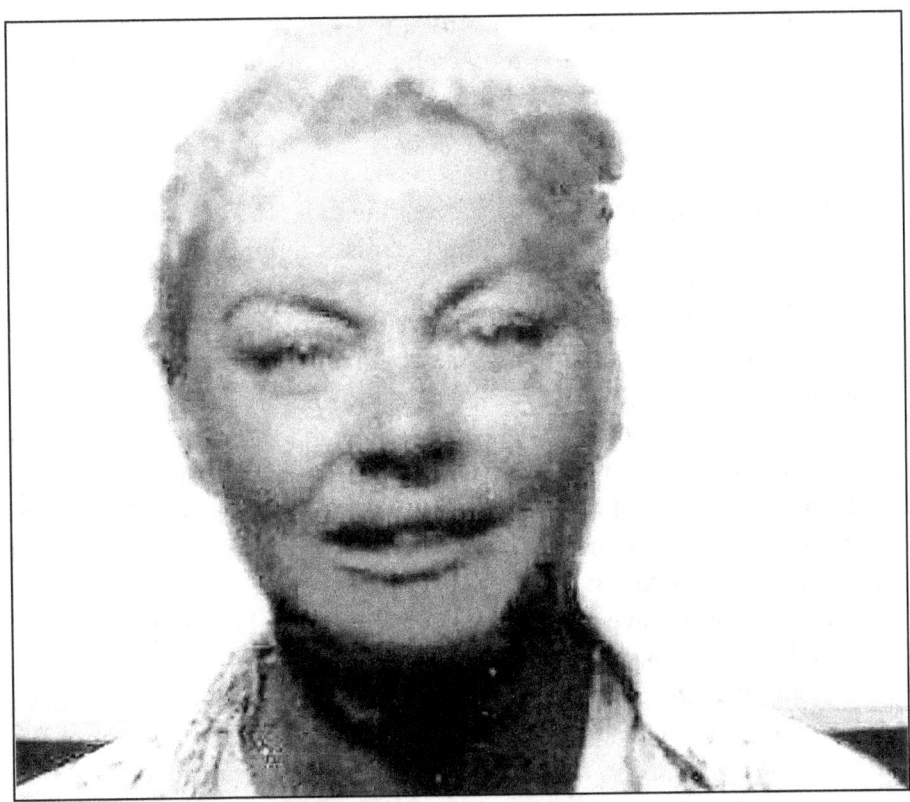

One of the last known photos of Barbara shows her managing a weak smile despite the incredible sadness in her life. Courtesy of Jan Redfield

The Redfields' neighbor, Cheryl Perry, remembers the car accident and says that, contrary to the information in the traffic investigation report, Barbara was indeed hurt in the crash.

"My parents and I went over to see Barbara right after the accident," says Cheryl. "She had hit her head on the inside of the windshield and the entire left side of her face was black and blue. However, she kept telling everyone that she was all right.

"Over the next few days, Mabel would yell across the street for my mother to come over with an aspirin for Barbara: 'Bring over an aspirin for Barb, willya?' Apparently, she hadn't been treated by a doctor so she hadn't been given anything for the pain. I found that extremely sad; not to mention, a little strange."

Jan Redfield says, "Whenever anyone in the family got hurt, Lee's favorite thing to do was to wash the wound out with Fels-Naptha (a strong, laundry bar soap). Lee would always say: 'Just let me clean the little bugger out with Fels-Naptha, and it will be all right.'

"Barbara was banged up pretty badly, but, apparently, Lee and Mabel thought they could doctor her bruises at home with just soap and some aspirin. Obviously, they were wrong."

Jan's theory aside, Barbara's not receiving adequate medical attention at the time of the accident may have been due more to Lee's anger with her for taking his Cadillac out without his permission (and then wrecking it), than in his wanting to "doctor" Barbara with Fels-Naptha soap.

To make matters worse, at the time of the crash, Barbara and Mabel were en route to the local liquor store, which enraged Lee when he found out about it.

As Jan explains, "For years, Lee and Mabel had a credit account with another liquor store in town, and that store used to make regular deliveries to the house a couple of times a week. But after Barbara came home that April, Lee cut off the family's credit with the liquor store's manager and made sure the guy knew not to deliver any more booze to the house. Barbara was not to have one more drop of booze in her body—not even one—and Lee was going to make sure of it.

"The only thing available to Barbara and Mabel by then would have been the cheap wine at the little corner store down at the bottom of the hill, and that's where they were going when Barbara wrecked Lee's car."

Undeterred by a total lack of legal restraints—and with no one in her insular world savvy enough to predict her impending doom, much less, protect her from it—Barbara continued her march toward disaster.

It is compelling to theorize what might have passed through Barbara's fragmented mind in her final days. Perhaps the terrible self-loathing she had felt for years had finally convinced her that she was now well beyond redemption. Or perhaps she had finally come to realize there wasn't very much of a future for a 39-year-old hooker whose pain-wracked and worn-out body was essentially shutting down from alcohol poisoning. Perhaps every last ounce of hope Barbara had that things could ever be better, was gone.

Barbara must have sensed she was coming to the end of the road, for the fighting spirit that had carried her through all her prior battles had vanished, leaving only the shell of a very sick and battered soul behind.

When told of Barbara's serious medical problems and increasingly bleak mental outlook, Jan and Frank brought their two youngest children, Diane and Doreen, to Jan's parents' home in La Puente, and then rushed with their sons to San Diego. By now, Barbara was spending a lot of time in bed, in a small room downstairs near the swimming pool that Lee had turned into a bedroom for her. The combination of her constant physical pain and her hideous depression now kept Barbara isolated and alone in that room for days.

Always a man of few words, Frank found it was no easier to talk to his sister now when she was so despondent, than it had been during her happier times. Beyond the utterance of a few weak, if well-meaning bromides, he mostly just stared at Barbara in disbelief and wondered how she had gotten to such a dismal place in her life. "I didn't know what to say, or do," Frank admits. "But I guess I somehow knew it was already too late for Barbara. One look at her could have told you that."

Unlike her husband, Jan saw Barbara's situation as desperate, but not hopeless. She carefully monitored Barbara's overall attitude and demeanor and purposely chose a time to talk to her when they would be alone, just the two of them. "On May 7, the last night of her life," Jan says, "after everyone else went to bed, Barbara and I stayed up in the living room and talked until the wee hours of the morning. We talked about lots of things; things we had never really discussed before. I remember Barbara saying that night that she wished she'd had more children, and she wished she still had Johnny, too. She missed him so much and it killed her that she hadn't seen him in so many years. She also said that she wished she hadn't wasted so much of her life 'trying to get to the top.' She said she knew she had made a real mess of things and yet she wasn't quite sure how it happened. Barbara said to me, 'Janice, why wasn't it ever enough for me? And how come after I lost it all, it didn't make everything better? Was my having too much, too soon, worse for me than if I had never accomplished anything at all?' She threw all these really tough questions at me and I didn't know how to answer them. I would say that at the end of her life, Barbara had many regrets.

"She told me that she never really knew how to communicate with men other than being a sex object to them. Barbara said that when they were attracted to her she didn't believe them, and that when they weren't attracted to her, she didn't know why. I think that the feeling of betrayal that Barbara always felt from Lee was the same feeling she got from all the men who used her.

"Because of everything she had done with all those men, I think Barbara felt very ugly inside. And it was almost like she wouldn't stop abusing herself until she made sure the outside matched the inside. Barbara admitted that she knew from the time she was a teenager that she was never the girl that men would respect, so she had just decided that she would do whatever she wanted to do. It broke my heart to hear her talk like that. I am convinced that it wasn't just about sex for Barbara; it was about being with somebody who cared about her—even if only for a few minutes.

"She was so depressed and found only negative sides to everything we talked about. No matter how hard I tried to cheer her up, she made it clear that she didn't want to be cheered up. She told me I would understand how she felt when I was 39. Well, I was 34, which wasn't that far off, but I think I knew what she meant.

"Barbara had seen a lot more of life than I ever had—too much of it, I think—and she was so tired."

A minute glimmer of Barbara's former playfulness momentarily surfaced when she told Jan that, "She always wished she had boobs as big as mine. We had a good laugh over that one. But it was the kind of laugh that would have gone straight into tears, if I had let it."

Seeing a brief flash of the old Barbara encouraged Jan to ask her friend to have some faith in the future. Much to Jan's dismay, Barbara's response was one of unbridled anger. "She raised her voice and growled, 'For God's sake, Janice, don't preach to me.' I wasn't preaching, though.

I was just trying to give her some hope. But Barbara didn't want to hear any of it."

Barbara told Jan that the years she had spent in Mexico had been her happiest. "But not with Tony," Jan is quick to add. "She made sure to tell me that. Barb said the people down there always treated her like she was special, and that they weren't phonies, like the people in Hollywood.

"Barbara also said that she wished Lee had loved her as much as he loved me and my kids. We talked about feeling like sisters, and how sad it was that we both had brothers whom we weren't close to. [36]

"I think it was almost the crack of dawn when Barbara and I finally went to bed. By then, we were both pretty exhausted. But, you know, it was sort of a beautiful visit we had together. Despite Barbara's pessimistic attitude, we ended our conversation with me feeling just a little bit more at peace about things. But when I hugged Barbara, well, it was like hugging a stone. There was no feeling there. She was cold. Looking back now, I believe she knew. She knew she was leaving.

"I didn't know it then, but when we hugged 'goodnight,' we were really saying goodbye. Well, here come the tears."

Jan Redfield says it is important for people to know that her sister-in-law was absolutely not drinking during the last week of her life. "Barbara had stopped drinking right after the car accident. Anything that has been said or written to the contrary is a lie. She did not drink right up to the end, nor did she 'drink herself to death.' She had made a firm commitment to herself to quit, and that's exactly what she did. I watched Barbara throw her life away with both hands, but she does deserve to have the truth told about her final days, and as God is my witness, that is the truth. Lee and Mabel may have still been drinking, but Barbara, God bless her, had stopped."

Though she is to be commended for this last act of courage, it was sadly a case of too little, too late. With the clock running down, there was no way that Barbara could have undone the terrible damage of the past 20 years. It wasn't only her health and her physical appearance that had taken a beating in all that time. Her spirit, and her soul, had been ravaged, as well. To be fair, Barbara may have quit drinking with the best of intentions—or she may have simply been too ill to continue. Loyal to the end, her sister-in-law Jan chooses to believe that Barbara had stopped drinking because she wanted to. And maybe that's exactly the way it should be.

Feeling unsure of what they had been able to accomplish with their visit, Jan and Frank returned to their home in West Covina on Sunday morning as he had to go back to work on Monday.

"The last time we saw Barbara," says Jan, "she was sitting on the floor in the living room, with a colored scarf around her head, watching some old, black-and-white cartoons on the TV. When we were leaving, Barbara refused to come out to the patio to say goodbye. She just sat there in a daze and watched her cartoons. That's the last image I have of her alive."

On the ride home, Jan tried to talk to Frank about Barbara's terrible physical health and depression, but he said he was tired and didn't want to talk about it. Jan dropped the subject, and instead just gazed out the car window, she said, and cried.

The following day at around three p.m., Jan and Frank's telephone rang, and their world fell apart.

CHAPTER FORTY-FOUR:
Crossing the Bridge of Sighs

Barbara's long and lonely ride slammed to a sudden stop on May 8, 1967 at 1:50 p.m. According to the San Diego County coroner's report, she had been resting on the living room couch for several hours that Monday when she suddenly arose and announced to Lee and Mabel that she wasn't feeling well. With her body rumbling in dreadful spasms that knifed through her chest and stomach, Barbara staggered into the bathroom and barely made it to the toilet, where Deputy Coroner R.W. Gillespie later noted, "She had a loose bowel movement and then slumped to the side." At that point, Mabel heard Barbara groan and rushed in to find her daughter fading fast in the throes of death. Barbara may have stirred a bit in her mother's presence, but it was already too late to save her. She was hanging by a thread, but it wasn't to a thread of life so much, as it was to that transitory stage between life and death when the soul has already started its next journey. It was later reported by the coroner that Mabel "...tried to hold the decedent's head up, when the decedent gasped a few times, and then completely stopped breathing." Jan reveals that Mabel got down on the floor and cradled Barbara in her arms and then cried out for Lee, who found his daughter dead in his wife's embrace. When the Deputy Coroner arrived at the Redfields' home, Barbara's lifeless body, barefoot and clad only in a turquoise-colored, terry cloth dress, was sprawled across the bathroom floor, with Mabel, in tears, sitting a few feet away from her.

In an ironic metaphor too obvious to miss, Barbara was found lying beside the toilet bowl; a bizarre and somehow fitting location for a life she had so willfully and senselessly trashed.

By the time the police got to the house, morbid lividity had already set in, discoloring much of Barbara's body in mottled blots. "My mother

*1901 Titus Street in San Diego...the place of Barbara's death on May 8, 1967.
From the Author's Collection*

told me that within minutes of her death, Barbara's skin turned black from her waist down to her feet," says Frank, almost incredulously. "She looked banged up, I guess. Everything inside her system must have just shut down at once."

Although the toxicology report from Barbara's autopsy showed that there was no blood alcohol in her body, which verifies Jan's claim that Barbara had stopped drinking several days earlier, there was little doubt that alcohol had not contributed to her death. In fact, the cause of

Hollywood Star

Barbara Payton, 39, Dies in Obscurity

The Los Angeles Times

SAN DIEGO — Barbara Payton, the stunning blonde whom Franchot Tone and Tom Neal fought for in Hollywood's most celebrated fistfight of the 1950s, died here in obscurity this week, authorities disclosed yesterday.

She was 39. Investigators learned she had been ill a week and apparently died of natural causes.

HER PARENTS found her dead Monday on the bathroom floor at their home. It was two days before detectives investigating the death realized who she was.

As Tone's fiance she went from bit parts to stardom in two big-budget films opposite James Cagney and Gregory Peck

Then, in September, 1951, when Neal defeated Tone in a bloody, one-sided fight which left Tone hospitalized two weeks, she suddenly became world famous.

THE FAME turned to notoriety in the weeks which followed. The film industry, anxious to forget the bad publicity, instead forgot her.

Her roles got worse and her career faded away — everywhere but in the headlines.

They told of her marriage to Tone, two weeks after the fight; their separation seven weeks later ("she couldn't forget Neal, Tone said"); legal disputes and spicy testimony, ending in a divorce three months later; a subsequent marriage and divorce; arrests for passing bad checks and drunkenness, and, finally, for

BARBARA PAYTON

prostitution.

WITH A Hollywood writer she wrote a paper-back book which told how her career plummeted from one Hollywood scene to another: From nightclubbing on the Sunset Strip, where she wore a $10,000 mink coat and drove a new cadillac convertible, to the seamy side street where she lived with a bootblack, working as a prostitute.

She was married four times: To William Hodge, a high school flame she married as a teenager in Texas; to World War II air force pilot John Payton, by whom she had a son, John Lee Payton, in 1947; to Tone, and, in 1955, to a furniture salesman in Nogales, Ariz., George Anthony Provas. It also ended in divorce.

Surviving are her parents, Mr. and Mrs. E. Lee Redfield, her son, now a serviceman in Vietnam; and a brother, Frank Redfield of West Covina, Calif.

Barbara's newspaper obituary. Courtesy of Jan Redfield

Barbara's passing was listed on her death certificate as "acute pulmonary congestion with focal pulmonary hemorrhage due to portal cirrhosis," or heart and liver failure, the culmination of twenty years of heavy drinking and hard living. Other details found on the death certificate are especially poignant; tactfully, if untruthfully, listing her last occupation as "actress," and her last place of employment as "Warner Bros. Studios." The truth, of course, was far less embellished.

It was two days before police authorities realized who the deceased was—or had once been—as Barbara's ghastly countenance prevented any easy recognition of her from her movie-star days. Although she died six months shy of her 40th birthday, one officer noted that, in death, "Barbara Payton looked like a woman twenty years older than her reported age."

For some reason, despite Barbara's wrecked appearance, the family decided to allow her body to be viewed in an open casket. "Barbara was laid out in a private room at the Benbough Mortuary in San Diego," says Jan, "but only after Lee sent me to a clothing store to buy a new outfit for her. He gave me the money for it and told me to 'buy something nice for Barbara.' The poor baby was so swollen none of her old clothes would fit her."

Due to the depressing circumstances surrounding her death, it was decided that Barbara's viewing and funeral would be combined in a single afternoon service. "Late that morning," says Jan, "I was called down to the mortuary by the funeral director to inspect Barbara's hair and makeup before he let the people in. Well, I was so upset when I saw what the mortician had done to her, I insisted that he do everything over."

As Frank noted, the bruised condition of Barbara's body at the time of her death was so bad, it looked like she had been physically beaten. "We were told that the lack of oxygen in her as she was dying caused her entire body to turn very dark," says Jan. "I guess the mortician tried to fix this by applying very heavy pancake makeup and bright red lipstick to Barbara's face and lips. Well, he must have plastered everything on with a trowel—he gave her a very harsh and grotesque look and it upset me terribly. She looked like a clown, or like some horrible freak from a sideshow. I made him take all of it off her and start over from scratch, as Barbara would never have allowed him to put that much junk on her face. She was a naturally beautiful girl and she looked so much better after he fixed what he had done to her.

"Still, by then, poor Barbara looked so old. *So old.*"

According to Jan, the family took turns that day going to the funeral home. There were very few people there: Frank and Jan, and their three oldest children; Lee and Mabel; Jan's parents, Dorothy and Al Zollinger; Dave and Tina Ballard; a few other neighbors and friends of the family, but not one person from Hollywood. "News of Barbara's death had hit all the newspapers, so I'm sure everyone up there knew about it," says Jan. "But not one of them came. Not one."

At one point during the day, Frank was standing in the back of the room talking to some of the Redfields' neighbors when a pair of strangers stormed the room and immediately walked up to the casket.

"No one there knew this man and woman," says Jan. "They just stood there and stared at Barbara for the longest time and then Frank saw the woman take a big pair of scissors out of her purse and try to cut off a piece of Barbara's hair. That was the last straw. Frank threw them out of the place and he also told the funeral director that no one was to be let into the room after that, except for family, or very close friends.

"We were all upset by what that woman had tried to do. I mean, can you imagine, trying to take a souvenir of hair off a dead person? In Barbara's lifetime, she had always attracted creeps and users, and even in death, the vultures were still out to get her."

Tina Ballard recalls the utter devastation of Barbara's parents. "Poor Lee and Mabel were heartsick at the funeral," she says. "Mabel must have been heavily medicated because she looked like a wobbly old rag doll. In fact, she was so out of it, she was almost incoherent. I was very surprised to see Lee, who was always such a strong man, reduced to a state I can only call semi-comatose. His whole attitude and physical bearing were that of someone who was totally defeated. There was a heaviness in the air, in that room; no nervous laughter (as you'll sometimes hear at those things), or small talk; just absolute sadness over how this girl's life had ended. I felt that way, too. I had lost one of the great loves of my life, my dear friend, Barbara. It took me a long time to get over it. In fact, if I am to be really honest, I never have."

Barbara's son, John Lee, then 20 years old, was serving in Vietnam when he received word of his mother's death. His military unit wasn't easy to track down, but his father had somehow managed to find him when nobody else could. Feeling a myriad of emotions ("a blur of pain, remorse, and even relief," he says), John made his way to Danang, eventually caught a troop plane for San Francisco, and arrived in Los Angeles on the day of Barbara's funeral. At the very last moment, Jan was dispatched by the family to retrieve him at the airport and take him to San Diego. His cousin, Leslie Redfield, remembers John being "freaked out by all the traffic and the speed in which my mother drove back to San Diego," but John himself only remembers what he describes as "the terrible funeral."

As he walked into the viewing room, the first thing John noticed, he says, was its size. "The room was quite small. There were a number of floral sprays, but I can't recall any of the senders. There weren't many people there, but the room, I remember, was very, very hot. Uncomfortably hot. My memories of the actual funeral, though, are kind of spotty."

Verifying what Tina Ballard said about Lee and Mabel's almost insentient demeanor that day, John Lee says, "They looked at me standing before them and I could tell from their blank faces that neither one of them had a clue who I was. My grandmother was absolutely beside herself and Lee seemed so utterly numbed by bewilderment and loss, he was almost mute. Quite frankly, I was very surprised, because I knew how he always felt about Mom. I don't know, maybe it was guilt over how he had treated her."

John was much more than surprised—horrified, in fact—at his mother's appearance. "Oh God, Mom looked terrible. Since I hadn't seen her in eleven years, I was expecting some change, of course, but nothing like that. Mom was so unrecognizable that I told Dorothy, who had dragged me up to the casket to see her: 'That's not my mother. It can't be.'

"At the time of her death she had lost most of her hair, which was kind of a yellowed gray color. She really didn't look fat or bloated to me; just very, very dead. All the structure seemed to have collapsed in her face so that it had completely lost its shape. She looked way older than 39."

Although Jan had gotten the mortician to redo Barbara's makeup, John Lee was appalled by the hasty, 'patch job' he had done. "The funeral director had made her face up so badly she looked more like Norman Bates' mother than Barbara Payton, and it was truly horrible to see her like that. It took some determination on several people's part to keep me off the guy who did that to her. I cannot tell you how much I wanted him dead."

Thinking of the many years that had passed since he had last seen his mother, John Lee says, "After my father and stepmother kicked me out of our house in San Antonio in 1964 and I went to live with the Zollingers (again), I realize now that I should have taken the time to try to find Mom.

It makes me ashamed and angry with myself that apparently I never made the effort or even asked about her, to my memory. I know it wouldn't have been pretty—I remember that body in the casket all too well—but I can't stress how deeply I regret now that I didn't at least attempt to find her, and see her again.

"The truth is I may never have even thought about her until the day I was inducted into the service and had to spend the night in a seedy hotel in downtown L.A. I walked the nearby streets that night, looking into every bar to see if she might be there. But, otherwise? I let her go and I let her down, which to me is just very, very shameful and sad."

Following her bare bones funeral service, Barbara's physical presence on earth quickly moved toward extinction. Many years before her death, Barbara had written the word "cremated" over and over in a journal that Jan had found. Whether it was an unconscious behest jotted down haphazardly, or an eerie prophesy of the final physical act upon her body, Barbara's remains were indeed cremated, with her ashes placed in a crypt at San Diego's Cypress View Cemetery. Because she was still legally married to Jess Rawley at the time of her death, the State of California insisted that the plaque on the crypt read "Barbara Lee Rawley." However, neither he, nor any of her other ex-husbands, paid their respects to Barbara, or to anyone in her family, following her death.

Barbara's life, tortured for far too many years, was finally over. Although it was reported in her tiny, back-page obituary that she died of natural causes, her death was more accurately a slow and arduous suicide that began the day she left her sleepy little suburban life in 1947 for the hallowed grounds of Hollywood Babylon.

In a town built on greed, fantasies and lies, Barbara gorged herself on its riches, only to watch each of her dreams disappear. But Barbara alone was not entirely responsible for her demise. Perhaps Hollywood, and the often futile dreams it offers to the weak, the misguided, and the lost, was also to blame. Like a cruel and unforgiving lover that had left her at dawn on some lonely back street corner, once the town was through with Barbara, it never looked back. Overwhelmed by a life of wretched excess, and surrounded by sadness, Barbara died alone, a crushed and broken woman.

Just four years earlier, she had tried to explain what had happened to her life to writer Leo Guild, when they were preparing her autobiography. "When you're on top, there isn't any way to go but down," she allegedly told him. "Men, pills, liquor, lesbians, pressures, and disappointments all had a hand in it.

"There were a lot of broken promises. I was from a small town; I believed everybody. But no one was telling the truth."

At one point, Guild said to her, "You're still a young girl, Barbara. Why have you let yourself go like this?" Her reply was both profound, and heartbreaking. "I didn't need to be pretty anymore," she answered.

Perhaps that said it all.

Chapter Forty-Five:
Memories of a Life Lost

Barbara's death likely elicited far more discussion within her family and the film community than among the general public, most of whom had forgotten about her years earlier. A film producer, who was acquainted with Barbara (and who wishes today to remain anonymous), remembers what some in the industry had to say about her passing. His comments, while crude and ungracious, are a powerful commentary on how badly she is still regarded by some, over 40 years after her death.

"To tell you the truth, I don't believe there were too many tears shed in town when she died," he said. "I, for one, was actually surprised that she had lasted as long as she did. With the terrible way she lived, Payton was lucky she hadn't been murdered years before. I have never seen anyone throw their life away as shamelessly, or as completely, as Barbara did. She took every opportunity that was ever handed to her and just cast them to the winds. It's like she got off on it [the pain and havoc she caused herself, and others]. That's why I don't feel sorry for her.

"Look, you want the truth? She was a hooker with a hooker's mentality—even when she first started out. Barbara was a sullen, haughty, stuck-up bitch. It was a sin the way she played both of them [Neal and Tone]. She literally ruined one man's career, and the other one's face. Honest to God, I can't find anything good to say about her. She was a greedy and conniving slut; a whore that would fuck your dog if it humped her leg. She got everything she deserved."

Also apparently unmoved by Barbara's suffering is author Darwin Porter, whose book *Howard Hughes: Hell's Angel*, cruelly refers to her "black, whoring heart," and describes her as "a nympho" who later became "a broken down and snaggle-toothed whore."

One strongly suspects that if asked for their opinions of the Hollywood bigwigs who wined, dined and bedded Barbara (many of whom were married), these "gentlemen's" responses would be infinitely less harsh and far more charitable.

Another author, John Gilmore, whose meetings with Barbara in the early '60s were few and fleeting (at best), has a similar lack of sympathy for a woman he all too easily calls "a monster." "Unlike nine million other girls (and guys), Barbara was given her chance big time," he contends. "Everybody rooting for her, everyone giving her all the help and care they could—again and again—until it was too late, until she had burned all her bridges.

"Adolf Hitler was also an innocent child at one time, and there is no real evidence of anyone abusing him. We are all innocent at one time, but then we grow up and make choices. Hitler made his choices, as did Barbara.

"I do not have any sympathy for Barbara; I was impressed and intrigued by an innate intensity she had that came across onscreen (sometimes). I knew her, as I know a whole battery of naysayers who, believe me, would not be inclined to join in any canonizing of Barbara Payton.

"This is a woman who never gave anything positive to the industry. She was a Hollywood loser, someone who threw her chances away. Which she did, time and time again, while her monster raged. The once-pretty face and lovely eyes only served as a mask to hide that monster. But then the monster died, too, and what you had was the walking dead woman.

"Barbara needs a monument to self-destruction," concludes Gilmore. "She is a guide book to all the other nine million girls who will not make it, will not survive, and will follow Payton's course, for many reasons, including being monsters."

Despite Gilmore's comments that Barbara was a "monster," an argument can be made that Barbara was more likely the monster's spawn. The true evildoers, it would seem, were those who snatched away a little girl's innocence—and with it, any chance of her emotional well-being—all those years ago.

Or those, perhaps, who continue to look at Barbara's life with a cruel and jaundiced eye, today.

Franchot Tone's biographer, Lisa Burks, has spent several years researching Barbara's life, along with Franchot's, and holds a much more sympathetic view of the actress than any of the previous critics.

"When I first started my research, I must admit, I did not like Barbara," says Lisa. "I thought she was a fickle, conniving troublemaker who used Franchot and other well-known men for publicity and to advance her career. But after looking at the entire scope of her life, I now feel a great deal of compassion for her, and I can see why, aside from her obvious sex appeal, Franchot fell for her.

"I think Barbara was a fun-loving and lovable person who, unfortunately, burned just about every bridge behind her along the way, due to her odd behavior; behavior that, in Barbara's world, probably seemed perfectly normal. Barbara had a good heart, and I think she wanted happiness for herself and for those she cared about, but she wasn't quite emotionally equipped to attain everything she dreamed of becoming. Through no fault of her own and being a natural-born beauty, she was damaged at an early age by the inappropriate sexual attention paid to her, and, apparently, by outright sexual abuse when she was a teenager. I really believe that these elements from her past set the stage for so many of her questionable actions later on. Barbara was a sexy woman who didn't understand healthy sexuality. Looking for love in all the wrong places, as it were.

"Barbara seemed to have many little girl personality traits, yet she was very much a woman physically. Given her background, that could not have been easy to live with, especially in Hollywood.

"I have to say that Barbara has carved a niche in my heart, something I never expected to happen. I feel very bad about the way her life ended up. I think she could have been a solid star, but more importantly, I think she could have found personal happiness no matter what she was doing, had she been treated for her problems."

Yvette Vickers, who shared similar "glamour girl" roots as Barbara (Yvette was a *Playboy* centerfold Playmate in July 1959), later developed into an accomplished actress in sixteen films, several stage plays, and over 200 television shows, and admitted that apart from her pleasant conversation with Barbara in 1954, she, too, had somewhat negative feelings about her for a long time. In the mid 2000s, Yvette said, "Although I liked Barbara when I met her, I later heard all those horrible stories about her character and I had a hard time understanding why she allowed her life to get so bad. My problem with her was knowing that she had been handed an awful lot, right from the start, and yet she seemed to deliberately throw it all away.

"I mean, here I was, in the 1950s, completely serious about my acting career—attending workshops, studying my craft, doing lots of stage plays and TV commercials, taking ballet classes several times a week, just generally working my ass off (for whatever job would come my way), and yet Barbara, with seemingly very little effort on her part, moved up the ladder so quickly. She got leading roles right off the bat, and I'm still not convinced she was ever really serious about her career. But, you know, I have come to see the absolute sadness and emptiness in Barbara and I have a lot more sympathy for her now.

"Looking back, I believe that Barbara probably felt she was undeserving of her early success in films and that's why she allowed it to slip away from her so easily. Hers is a tremendously sad tragedy—definitely one of the worst stories I've ever heard. Barbara was a gorgeous woman and a talented actress, and I thought she was really good in the Cagney film, in particular. She accomplished a lot in a very short period of time, and without any real training to speak of.

"Just imagine what Barbara could have done in the business, and in her life, if she had treated herself with a lot more dignity and 'tender loving care'? She was a worthwhile person, and I only wish *she* had believed that."

Other individuals who knew the fallen beauty in admittedly varying degrees have similar thoughts to share. Her friend and former co-worker at Universal Studios, Donna Martell, says, "When I heard about Barbara's death, I broke down and cried. It is so sad what happened to her, she had so much potential. I was touched by the girl because I felt this was someone who could have been somebody. And she was just going about it the wrong way. There's absolutely no doubt in my mind that she could have been as big in the industry as Marilyn Monroe, but it seems she just couldn't keep her personal life out of her business life.

"Despite the path she chose for herself later on, I have very fond memories of Barbara. She was so sweet when I knew her; she worked hard and she was truly interested in becoming a good actress. Barbara's death literally broke my heart, and I'll never forget her."

In March 2006, Robert Easton, who was in Barbara's film *Drums in the Deep South*, spoke of the sadness he felt when he heard the news of her death. "I felt very bad about it. I never saw her in person again after our film, but, of course, I had read about her various problems over the years. Barbara had an incredible warmth about her that was extremely endearing. She was a very sensitive girl with warm and expressive eyes that you could just lose yourself in.

"Barbara was very professional on the set of *Drums*. There were no displays of ego, no temper tantrums. She treated everyone well, and wasn't demanding or condescending to anyone. Even when one of the King Brothers, the obese one, insisted she always sit on top of his lap, Barbara did it without complaining. I thought she showed a lot of interest in acting and she definitely showed potential; not only in our film, but in several others, as well. What often happens, though, if you're a person who has very strong emotions (like Barbara), is that while that can be very helpful in an artistic sense, if you give full rein to those emotions, it can often destroy your personal life. I am convinced that's what happened to Barbara.

"Although she was far from being a predator herself, it does seem to me that Barbara got involved with a lot of predatory men who took advantage of her. She struck me as being an extremely loving woman who had an almost desperate need to be loved in return. A pity, isn't it, that she never found the kind of love she was looking for."

The late director Richard Fleischer, who in 2002 remembered how hard-working and high-spirited Barbara was on the set of *Trapped*, said, "I was very surprised [to hear how she died]. I never saw her again after we completed the film, and I apparently missed all the news of her troubles over the years as I had no idea her life had gotten so bad. I thought she was off to a nice start with our film, but then she fell right off the tracks, didn't she? Barbara had so much going for her. What a shame."

Although he shares his colleagues' affection for her, Mickey Knox disagrees with their belief that Barbara was serious about her acting career. "When I knew her, Barbara wasn't interested in acting, or in pursuing work; she just wanted to chase guys, and have a good time. By 1953, she had completely lost whatever ambition she previously had. Even during our affair, I often had the feeling that there was something dark in her past that was holding her back and keeping her from believing in herself. She hid it well, but I always sensed its presence, nonetheless.

"Barbara was tremendous looking and had a good deal of acting talent, but by the time I came to know her she was not interested in doing anything with her life. And I think that's a damn shame. Despite her irreverence, Barbara was a very decent woman. She wasn't a bitchy person, nor was she cruel. She was open and (at least on a surface level) had a real *joie de vivre*. I felt terrible—lousy—when I heard how she had died, and I still do. Barbara didn't deserve to go down that way."

Walter Burr says, "I was shocked, naturally, to read about Barbara's death. After she and Tom broke up, I don't think he ever mentioned her to me again. Just like he did before he met her, Tom moved on from one babe to another after they split. In fact, it wasn't until his marriage to Pat Fenton in 1958 that he really settled down.

"I didn't know anything about Barbara's life after 1952, so I was startled when I read in her obituary about all her personal problems, and especially, about her many arrests over the years. When I knew Barbara, she was not a raging drunk. She drank every day, that's true, and she was always pretty raucous at parties, but not so that you thought she was vying for everyone's attention. The Barbara I knew was a lively, upbeat and generally happy person.

"I thought Barbara was a really neat creature. She was just very, very hip, you know? Barbara was probably way too much for the 1950's, but I think she would have fit in now just fine. She and I had many amusing chats, and she was honest and intelligent and always had something worthwhile to say. Barbara wasn't self-centered. This wasn't a woman who was always off somewhere gazing at herself in a mirror. Barbara was more about making the other person feel good. She was great.

"She and Tom had plenty of friends in Hollywood, but in Tinseltown, friendship isn't the same as it is in Illinois. When I was out there, I saw that there was very little sincerity in those people; everything was a facade. Everyone in Hollywood always seemed to be competing with each other, so no one ever admits they've lost a part, or that they're out of work. My two and a half months in that town was certainly an illuminating experience, but, believe me, I was happy to return to Evanston.

"As for Barbara, she probably should never have left Minnesota."

Her small-town roots were also mentioned by her onetime lawyer, the late Milton Golden, a steadfast advocate of Barbara's even after his professional association with her ended. Golden once wrote: "What distinguished Barbara from other, more conventional Hollywood beauties, was a contradictory wholesomeness. I think she would have been happier had she lived as nature intended her to live, in the simple, uncomplicated existence of a country girl. If only she had not been beautiful."

Holloway House publisher Bentley Morriss also points out the "country girl" qualities in Barbara. In 2003, he said, "Barbara had what I call a suburban naiveté. In fact, I don't think she ever completely shed her provincial, Midwestern roots. When I met Barbara in the 1960s, she was

gone, God bless her, but she wasn't coarse like you would think a street person would be. She was rather unsophisticated, and, believe it or not, almost childlike in her demeanor. I still remember how awed she was when she stopped in at the company one day to discuss her autobiography with Leo. Barbara kind of shuffled in slowly and her eyes widened when she saw all of us in our suits and ties. I don't think she had been around a straight business environment for a long, long time.

"One must remember, when Barbara first hit town, every night was a huge party to her. She went to all the nightclubs and hung out with some of the town's biggest stars, and it got a real hold of her. She woke up every day and saw her name and picture in all the newspapers. You know, you come to Hollywood and then one morning you wake up and you realize you're a star. Barbara let it all go to her head, perhaps, but I challenge anyone not to have their mind screwed up at least a little by all that stuff. The only difference is, what happened to Barbara is far worse than what happens to most of them out here. And it went on for so long. Amazing. Just amazing."

Author Kirk Crivello recalls a woman whose sheer courage was nothing short of astounding to him: "Although I only spent time with Barbara on that one occasion when I gave her a lift, I got to know her a little and I thought she was very nice. A kind and upbeat lady, which is miraculous, really, considering all that she was going through at the time. Seeing a little bit of the person she was, I believe in the end Barbara was probably very sorry for the way her life turned out, especially for the people she hurt along the way, like her family and her son."

Bill Ramage, an individual who met Barbara just twice—five years apart—has nonetheless closely analyzed her life over the years, and feels tremendous compassion for "that sad, lonely woman in the rain." He states, "It's obvious to me now that Barbara was on a self-punishing, self-flagellation course. No one deserves the kind of life she had (later on), and she had ten years of it. Ten years of the toughest, roughest days a civilized soul could endure. A stabbing, mental illness, addiction to alcohol and drugs, vicious treatment by most of all mankind. Unbelievable. How did she stand it? Her body. Her mind. Why didn't anyone help her? Why didn't she get help?

"We are all responsible for ourselves, that's true. Even Barbara. But I believe she resisted all efforts at rehabilitation because of her libido. The unstableness she exhibited was a byproduct of her overt sexual compulsion.

It is as strong in a woman as it is in a man. Barbara's lusty appetite for all things, coupled with her artistic temperament and a probable bipolar disorder, was a surefire recipe for disaster. And yet, through it all, she never intentionally meant to hurt anyone; I am certain of that.

"What a sad story. It is more than a cautionary tale. It is a portrait painted in dark tones of a very ill lady. Not just a life out of control, it is Hell itself. A picture of mental aberration gone beyond help. I really believe Barbara's bizarre behavior and total self-destruction were caused by a severe mental illness. Her conduct in 1963 when I gave her a ride was not the conduct of a rational person. She couldn't remember my name for two minutes even though Bill is one of the most common names there is. Her eyes told the whole story; they were not the eyes of a well person. She definitely was deranged. Yet, the shell of the person, her innate kindness, was still evident to me. There was inside her no longer attractive face and body the essence of the likable person she had always been, and it broke my heart.

"You know, it isn't easy to get into the movies, and almost impossible to become a star. But, Barbara did. She made it, and, damn, is it ever hard to do. No one went as far as she did to fall with such utter horror and so sadly to the depths of a living Hell on earth. I would like to see 3/4 of our population see all their dreams, the things we all take for granted, blow up in their faces and remain pure. The people she turned to: a big, sympathetic black guy or two, a couple of gay kids, the street people down on Skid Row—why, even Jack the Ripper and the Hillside Strangler would have probably looked good to her after a while. Under those same conditions, little Mary Pickford herself might have turned whore. Yet, even in the direst of straits, Barbara always seemed to think she would get another shot at it [fame] and that the next time it came around for her, it would last.

"Barbara was not a throwaway, nor was she a bad person. For anyone to write or claim otherwise, is cruel and untrue. I am so tired of people hurling venom at her. Barbara was not an evil barracuda, despite what other writers have suggested. She was lovely, gracious and kind—not a predator. And, in my opinion, not a nymphomaniac, either. She was undoubtedly a sensualist; that was her power. She, perhaps, learned to use it indiscriminately, which over time engendered her immense guilt. It turned into a sexual torture for her. I think Barbara used her strong sexual drive the way she used alcohol, drugs, even degradation—to escape. She was a terribly frightened child inside. A nice girl, but for some inexplicable reason, she chose to debase herself.

"I still think Barbara had remarkable courage to live her life for so many years even though she was powerless over alcohol and was apparently so self-loathing she didn't seek help. Barbara did, however, face life and did not end it by her own hand. She may have become the crude, coarse dame so many people said she became, but I personally believe she was only acting the part of a tough broad. Too much is known about the other Barbara, the lost lady who wanted to be loved, popular, the center of adulation. All the ladies I knew who were friends with Barbara, adored her: Charlene Golden, Leslie Snyder, Sally Fiske, Eloise Peacock, Joan Caulfield, all of them. They saw the same girl I saw: a sweet, wounded person.

"Call her names. People will, but she was a lot stronger than most. Indomitable, really. Poor misguided angel, if only she had used the skills she had: her talent at interior decorating, her ability to reupholster. Her cooking—she made an exquisite marinara sauce. The barefoot and carefree 'earth mother' I met at the Goldens' home in 1958 was the real Barbara, I think. She was totally without artifice. The sad soul she became: it was the soul of an artist. Barbara was obviously her own worst enemy. Dreams die. So, sadly, do people. That said, I want it known that the Barbara Payton I choose to remember is the one I met at the Goldens' home. She was a bright and charming girl, with a big, wondrous laugh and unbelievably beautiful eyes.

"I'll remember her laughter and the way she looked that balmy, starlit night, always."

Incisive Hollywood observer Nick Bougas bemoans the waste of a talent that he believes was greater than most are willing to concede: "For whatever reason Barbara chose to toss off the stellar opportunities that abounded in her life, her greatest sin, I believe, was betraying a quite sizable acting gift. I think she was genuinely effective as a player and, had her work ethic been as strong as her libido, perhaps she would have enjoyed the kind of sedate, fulfilled existence and legitimate career that actresses like Virginia Mayo and Marie Windsor had. Unfortunately, Barbara had that rebellious, living on the edge, rock-star attitude long before it was fashionable. It's kind of ironic, but there's no doubt in my mind that if she were alive today, her behavior would probably raise very few eyebrows."

Author Stone Wallace, who has written biographies on George Raft and Ed Wood's ex-girlfriend Dolores Fuller, admits to being extremely moved by Barbara's story: "Barbara's life leaves a very disturbing impression. We see such self-abuse all the time, but Barbara was such a beautiful girl of such unlimited potential, that hers is the absolute saddest celebrity breakdown. In the past, I always thought that Bela Lugosi was the ultimate Hollywood tragedy. But not according to Dolores Fuller, and definitely not now, after learning what Barbara's life was like after her career ended.

"Barbara's descent into Motel Hell is a true 'punch in the gut.' Living in filth and squalor for years, while desperately trying to grasp onto a fleeting feather of her former glory, is just extremely sad to me. Barbara's saga makes Frances Farmer's life seem like a romp down the yellow brick road. It is a textbook example of the total self-destruction of a human being. I remain devastated by the knowledge of what happened to Barbara."

One of the most avid followers of Barbara's life and times is Carolyn W. from Texas, who works in an academic setting and admits to being "completely and utterly spellbound by Barbara's story." Beyond the psychological and spiritual aspects of what happened to her, Carolyn says she is fascinated most by Barbara's countless years of self-sabotage. "Her life is such a tragic example of how substance use in excess can make one have a skewed perception of themselves and the world. Needs and wants become muddled, [and] self-worth declines. I understand Barbara's alcohol and substance dependence began very early in her Hollywood years. Her almost sociopathic manipulations of men and trading her body for jewelry, movie roles, and any kind of attention prove that the value she felt as a human being for anything other than her looks, must have been nil.

"The thing that is so hard for me to accept is how she seemed to put her child way down on the totem pole while engaging in her promiscuous activities. However, I do realize that Barbara was very young and immature when she had her son. Her focus back then was on becoming a movie star, not on being a great mother. But knowing that others helped raise the boy and that alcoholism was always a big problem in her family, there's no telling what little John Lee saw and experienced in his formative years. I have no doubt that Barbara loved her son, but she seemed totally ill-equipped to provide him with healthy mothering.

"It is so sad that this woman did not have the strength to get herself out of the hell in which she lived. And very sad that neither her friends nor her family could help her, either."

Another ardent fan of Barbara's, an attorney named Millie Peterson, says she is mesmerized by every part of Barbara's story, including her final years, when "she absolutely abandoned her vanity—when that is the very thing that pushed her so far."

Millie adds, "Barbara's downfall was so tragic, but not unforeseeable. The mental illness that went undetected, her family problems, and Lord knows what else she suffered as a young girl, all signaled that there was trouble ahead. She was so driven, but by what? I don't know. I don't think she knew, either. There seemed to be a manic tendency in Barbara. Her childhood and pre-Hollywood life must hold some very dark secrets.

"Barbara's family seemed to fail her so completely. It was like they just stood there and watched her life go down the drain, and never even tried to do anything to stop her. That, to me, is the greatest tragedy of all. She seemed to have no support system. She was totally on her own."

Producer Herman Cohen told Tom Weaver, "It was horrible how she died, downtown, as a whore, selling herself for five bucks. That just made me ill when I heard about that. Look, like all whores that I ever met, she had a heart of gold. She was a whore who got lucky. Barbara Payton was a lovely person. I liked her."

Former actor-turned-writer Steve Hayes knew many of the top stars in Hollywood in the 1950s and '60s, and counts Barbara as being one of the town's most quixotic and affecting characters. "Barbara was gregarious and intelligent, but when she was drunk she was very, very difficult. A pain in the ass is more like it. However, when sober, Barbara didn't even know the meaning of the word 'malicious.' She wasn't a cruel or cunning person. I would say her best and worst asset was a basic and open honesty. It didn't seem to me that Barbara was ever on the hustle for her career; more that she slept with you because she wanted to.

"Barbara was a strange woman. One who was at once fun-loving to the extreme, guileless and friendly and likable, yet one who definitely had demons, or she wouldn't have set out to destroy herself; she would have realized what she was doing and pulled in the reins. But the whole problem was, she was having so much fun in the '50s, her attitude always was, 'Why stop?' Barbara had many strange sides, but one thing never varied: she just wanted people to love her.

"Many times during my conversations with her, Barbara would break off in the middle of a sentence and stare at me as if trying to read my mind. 'What?' I would ask her. 'Why are you looking at me like that?' She would smile, almost sadly, and say: 'I was just thinking, wondering if you really liked me.' I would always laugh and say, 'You nut, of course I do. If I didn't, you would be the first to know. Just ask Gloria (my former wife, an actress Barbara knew pretty well). She would tell you I've never been famous for tact.'

"Barbara would nod. 'I know,' she would say. 'I know you love me. But I just like to hear you say it.'

"Barbara was a fun-loving girl who just wanted to have a good time, and believe me, there were plenty of ways to have a good time back then. I would suggest that people not blame her for that. Blame her (if you must) for not being strong enough to quit drinking."

In an interview shortly before his death in July 2003, Barbara's former lover John Rayborn admitted that he still thought about her every day. "I miss her; she meant a lot to me. What a terrible waste. A waste of talent and beauty and kindness, and everything else she had to offer the world. Don't let anyone ever tell you that the girl wasn't talented. Barbara had talent—great talent—but she was terrified of success.

"You know, over the years there have been a lot of bad things that have been said and written about Barbara—and granted, she often showed a terrible lack of judgment—but I think it's important to let people know that she was an extremely intelligent person who just gave up. Barbara had a lot of problems and was quite cynical by the time she came into my life, but she had a good heart.

"There was genuine kindness and beauty in Barbara's soul and I sincerely believe I was the one she finally loved. Although we were both deep into our alcoholism during our affair, we were in love—arguably reinforcing the old adage, *in vino veritas*. God bless her."

Barbara's longtime friend Tina Ballard rues the fact that they grew apart just when Barbara seemed to need a friend the most. "In the late 1950s, and all through the '60s, Barbara kept disappearing, and when she would show up again she would go to either Jan or me for help. I would get hysterical with worry and try to lecture her, which would always cause her to run off again. I guess I handled it all wrong, but I didn't know what else to do. I was always concerned about what Barbara was doing to herself, but she just never seemed to want to listen to anyone's advice. Back then, we didn't know anything about 'tough love' or 'interventions.' We would just give advice and hope for the best, but with Barbara that was asking for a lot. She needed more. A lot more.

"Barbara had a very tough time in that jungle [Hollywood]. Her teeth weren't sharp enough and her claws weren't long enough to fight all the enemies she had there. Trust me, that town really is a big, bad place. It was, back then, and I'm sure it still is, now. People who are truly genuine are difficult to find, and when you do find them, they are usually not related to the film industry. All those men that were passing her around; I'm sure it was a damn big joke to them, but did any one of them ever stop to think that maybe what they were doing was cruel? They disrespected her, and she just accepted it, like she didn't deserve anything better. Take my word for it, there are a lot of creeps in L.A. What I learned from what happened to Barbara is that glamour is just an illusion, and that nothing but a lot of crud lies beneath the glitz. When Barbara's defenses were down, no one—including me, unfortunately—was there to protect her. I live every day with the thought that I could have done more [for her]. I should have; I just didn't know how.

"I've come to believe that when Barbara was sleeping around, what she was really saying was to all those men was, 'I'm here for you. I'll give you everything I have, just love me.' Wanting to be noticed. Wanting to be seen, you know, and—loved. I think that sex meant everything to her, and it meant nothing. It was a way to cover up that terrible wound inside her, which, I believe, was the sexual abuse in her childhood. I remember she once told me that she didn't much care for it [sex], and yet she said a lot of her dissatisfaction with Franchot Tone was caused by his alleged impotence. I believe now that she, in fact, didn't like sex, and that all those times later on when she went with strangers, she was just trying to feel like she belonged to someone—even if only for a couple of hours. She needed that intimacy. That feeling of being close to someone, of feeling needed. Someone—or something—did a real number on Barbara when she was a child, and she obviously never got past it. Whatever abuse she had encountered had caused a real sickness inside her that would eventually destroy her.

"In my opinion, three things killed Barbara. Booze, sex, and self-hatred. With each drink, and each stranger she slept with, she threw more and more of herself away, until there was nothing left. I want to cry my eyes out now when I think about it.

"She was my sad and lonely friend."

Over the years, Barbara's second husband, John Payton, refused to discuss his ex-wife in depth, and right up to the time of his passing, that never changed. During an exemplary military career that found him traveling all over the world, Payton married the former Barbara Smith in 1956 and adopted her two children from a previous marriage. While Barbara Smith Payton would pass away from cancer in the late 1990s, their daughter, Jana Payton Lackey, will only say that her father retired as a Colonel in the United States Air Force, and that he lived a life of quiet repose in a southern U.S. locale until he passed away on Memorial Day, May 29, 2006. Lackey is similarly disinclined to talk about Barbara, but did, however, offer the following: "Our family has always avoided talking about Barbara and about what happened to her, and we will very likely continue to do so. As my late mother was also named Barbara, my father didn't want her to feel like she had to compete with the first one, so he simply never brought her up. By the time I was born, John Lee was in the service, so I never met his mother.

"Dad told me that Barbara's downfall started while John Lee was just a small boy. He felt terrible that he was not there to stop it, but they were already divorced by then. My half-brother lived with Barbara during some of her worst times in Hollywood, and he still remembers a lot of them. That is the main reason why he and my father always denied interviews regarding her—and why my father continued to do so right up to the end. Dad was 'old school' and felt that 'something never mentioned, does not exist.' Thus, he didn't discuss Barbara with John Lee, or with anyone else in the family. Ever."

With Barbara's place in the family picture blurred by her ex-husband's longtime silence, it was surprising to receive a note from Jana Lackey several months later, where she modified her earlier comments, to show that her father had indeed never forgotten Barbara. "My Dad told me many wonderful stories about Barbara over the years, and I am just sorry that some of them cannot be told to the public. But I gave him my word that I would not discuss Barbara, and even though he's gone I must never break that promise to him. Just know that Barbara was not always what she became at the end. She was a decent human being. My father had a total love and respect for this woman, and no amount of scandal, or time, ever changed that for him."

Barbara's fourth husband, Tony Provas, does not share Lackey's reticence about discussing his ex-wife and he freely recalls the devastation he felt when hearing the news of Barbara's death. "Given her lifestyle, as reported in the media, I had been expecting it and thought I had steeled myself sufficiently to accept it when it came. I was wrong. I couldn't accept it. I was actually angry with her for having died—I think I was even angry with God. I had never in my adult life, had someone I loved so dearly, die, and I was shattered.

"Barbara's troubles began on the day she was born. Her unwavering, independent spirit and her indifference toward what people said, or thought of her, certainly helped to destroy her life in the end. In the good years, those traits were part of her charm. Later on, they would prove to be her downfall.

"Deep inside, Barbara was a person that was all love, warmth, kindness and generosity. What she projected, however, was an outward facade that was glaringly 'wow'; daring, riotous, wild, and even a bit smutty. Too many people believed the facade and never got to know the real Barbara. She was the most generous person I have ever known. She gave away thousands of dollars to people she thought were her friends who, when she finally hit rock bottom, wouldn't even acknowledge that they had ever even met her.

"At the very end, Barbara was a sad, frightened, and very sick girl, and I pray that God has surrounded her in heaven with peace and beauty and joy to make up for the cruel and terrible punishment she had to endure down here."

Jan Redfield spent nearly twenty years of her life selflessly offering her sister-in-law a helping hand and a shoulder to cry on, and Barbara's death left a formidable impact on her that she still feels today. "No matter how short her fame, and no matter how short her life, Barbara has had a long lasting effect on the people who really knew her. I was blessed to have her in my life. Barbara was the big sister I always wanted. One of my best friends, she always took time to listen to me, and she had the compassion to understand what I was feeling. It saddens me to think that I might have been able to help her more, when she needed something—anything—to cling to.

"People need to understand, though, that the right way was always open to Barbara. But for some reason she always chose her own way—and unfortunately, it was the wrong way, with no future.

"I really believe with all my heart that something bad happened to Barbara very early in her life that put her on that terrible road she went down. I know that some people in the family have wondered if Aunt Fay's boyfriend, George Calvert, acted inappropriately with Barbara when she visited them in Odessa as a child, but I will never believe that. Uncle George, as he was known to all of us, was a good man and he would have never done that to Barbara (or to Fay). I have personally always thought that whatever may have happened to Barbara, happened in Cloquet, rather than in Odessa. You know, when she was really young.

"But Barb, obviously, always had a lot of problems, and then when she lost Johnny, I think a part of her mind just went away and never came back. As far as I'm concerned, that was the beginning of the end for her. That, and never having her father's approval. She wanted that more than anything, and it just never happened.

"When she was in trouble, Lee would always let her know it was her own fault; if she did something outstanding, on the other hand, he wouldn't congratulate her, he wouldn't say a word. Mabel was always so loving and close to Barbara, but Lee never opened any doors for her—especially the one to his heart. I still see Barbara as that little girl who trusted someone she shouldn't have trusted; a little girl whose father, for whatever reason, chose to abandon her emotionally. I still don't know what happened first (or even if the two things are related), but I do believe that from the beginning, Barbara was always searching for some kind of security.

"Barbara had so much love to give—but she should have saved some of it for herself. She radiated self-confidence (and sometimes even arrogance), but within herself she was as insecure as a child. That little flame that Barbara set in my heart has never been extinguished, and it never will."

His half-sister Jana Payton Lackey's comments notwithstanding, John Lee Payton surfaced in 2005 to share strictly loving thoughts of his mother: "Mom was a warmhearted and loving person, and when she was around, my life was filled with laughter and fun and excitement. She loved to play, and she was able to be both a mother and a pal to me. She had a fabulous laugh, was always glad to give and get hugs and kisses, and could play like a child, though she most often treated me like a miniature adult. My mother was also very generous, not only with me, but with everyone around her. Many people stayed at our house (gratis); some, for long periods of time.

"I don't think Mom took herself too seriously. I also think she was stubborn because she never seemed to give up no matter how bad things got. Even at nine years old I knew what she meant when she told Tony Provas that she could get us out of the bind we were in, with her body. I also knew why she was willing to do it. Mom would always do whatever needed to be done. She was a survivor, but a survivor with terrible timing.

"Yes, she was definitely brash. Careening through countless relationships the way she did, proves that. Announcing a comeback in 1958, after all the trouble she had gotten into in Hollywood, was definitely brash, and naive. She didn't pretend to be anybody she was not (except on camera), so she didn't pay homage to the press or ever try to make herself over in their image.

"I think my mother's greatest quality was her willingness to take chances. It was also her worst. I don't think she ever believed she actually could lose—not me, not her career—so she only anticipated success. She had a lot of strength, but hadn't the strategy to back up the tactics she employed. When I think of her, I think of the expression: 'Old age and treachery will overcome youth and skill.' My mother was so young during her movie career and her only prior life experience was far, far away in the barrens of West Texas. She was, I think, emotionally unprepared for the major film studios, like Universal and Warner Bros., although I believe she was more than sufficiently talented to play at that level. That is to say, it's one thing to be on the roster, but another thing entirely to be the manager. Mom clearly saw herself as both, and maybe eventually she could have been, but her time ran out.

"I believe it's fair to describe her as a liberated woman. She lived in the here and now, and she lived fully. Was she a fatalist? A hedonist? I don't know. Maybe, like so many other people, she was just winging it.

"I've seen several of Mom's films and I think she did well. I have no idea what she herself thought of her acting skills, but it was obviously enough to keep her working at trying to reclaim her film career to the exclusion of everything else, long after all hope for a comeback was gone. I don't know if she ever wanted a sedate life, or even if she would have known what to do with one.

"You know, when we lived on North Beverly Drive, nonstop parties were part of the general routine of our life. For her funeral, though, only a handful of people sent flowers and nobody but family came. Many years later, during a TV tribute to James Cagney, I remember Frank Sinatra looking straight into the camera and saying something like, 'Oh Barbara, how we miss ya.' But that was long after Mom died. On the day of her funeral, none of her Hollywood friends were willing to be with her (or with us), to pay their respects. That made me sad then, and it makes me sad, now.

"After I was taken away from my mother, I never had a single letter or a visit from her, and in the seven or eight years I was with my father and my stepmother Barbara (before I went to La Puente to live with the Zollingers again), I only had that one drunken phone call from Mom. It may be that there were letters, but I never got them, or other phone calls that were refused. After I had been with my father for a few months, Mom did send me a huge, gift-wrapped box with a hook-and-ladder fire truck, a pumper truck, an ambulance or emergency van, and a working fire hydrant. I think they were all Tonkas, and very expensive. My stepmother was livid, and those were the last gifts I ever got from Mom.

"I think she would have wanted to stay in touch with me. God knows I wanted to see her. But it would have been hard for all of us, I guess. I think that taking me away from Mom was good for me, but very, very bad for her. Still, the terrible guilt I feel to this day for not being there somehow for my mother, for not somehow finding a way to help her, strikes deep in my heart.

"No matter how well things eventually turned out in my life, I cannot be certain they would not still have turned out as well had I been allowed to stay with her—or if she had me taken away from her for a probationary period where she would be forced to either get her life together, or lose me forever.

"I want to stress that while there were some hard moments with her, she was a great mother to me, and taught me to be a strong and free-spirited person—just like her. This often makes me a real pain-in-the-ass, I expect, but it is still a wonderful legacy. I know it may seem strange that a mother who could leave me alone for long stretches, with strangers for even longer stretches, and who exposed me to way more of 'the wild side of life' at a very early age than most people see in their entire lives, could be a great mother, but she was. I can't even begin to tell you how much I loved and continue to love her. I miss her so much. I've missed her so much for so many years that the hurt of it is indescribable.

"You have got to believe that whatever weaknesses she may have had, whatever failures and disasters she may have brought down on herself, she was still a wonderful mother and gave me a great start on the person I am, and the life I live today.

"There is no doubt in my mind that Mom was a woman born ahead of her time. She was full of life—strong, proud, generous and unselfish. That people believe and understand this is extremely important to me. Book, or no book."

Finally, Frank Redfield remembers, with both anger and regret, the woman Hollywood had completely forsaken, and the sister he wished he had saved. "In the early 1950s, when I was in the Navy, stationed in Long Beach, Jan and I went to see Barbara a few times in Hollywood, and I can still remember all those fantastic dinner parties she threw at her house on North Beverly Drive. Barbara would prepare a turkey and a ham and a roast beef and all the fixings to go along with them, and when she was done, her dining room table had enough food on it to feed half the town. Whenever Barbara cooked, it always looked like something you would see at a Roman feast. In those years, her house was filled with some of the town's biggest names and movie stars, and they all swam in her pool and helped themselves to her food and her booze. Sometimes, Barbara would have 'house painting parties' for her friends, and she would feed them then, too, and give them all the beer and wine they could drink. A few years later, when she was down and out on the streets of Hollywood, not one of those people helped her. They saw her, but they no longer knew her, if you know what I mean. It was a disgrace."

"I didn't see Barb much, after the '50s," Frank adds. "I was very occupied with my jobs and my marriage, and was busy helping raise our four children, and, unfortunately, I also had my own drinking problem to contend with. Consequently, Barbara and I often lost track of each other. Of course, I regret that now, more than you know.

"But one thing's for sure—I always loved my sister. I was proud of the person she was, and I still am. Barbara was good to me, and I have very fond memories of her looking after me, especially when we were kids, back in Odessa. We used to fight with each other, but she always let me win. We just had a lot of fun together. I want people to remember Barbara as a hardworking, hard-playing, but especially, as a very loving, person."

CHAPTER FORTY-SIX:
And Life Goes On

While the initial impact of Barbara's death sent shock waves through her family, very little would change in Lee and Mabel's world in the months and years that followed. "Mabel was kept sedated for a long time afterward," says Jan Redfield, "and Lee just spent all his time with her, taking care of her and helping her any way he could. They had so much love for each other, and they were truly united."

Unfortunately, the couple had remained united in their drinking, as well.

"Yes, they both kept drinking too much," Jan admits. "That's what alcoholics will do if they don't get help. Mabel tried her best to drown her sorrow over Barbara, but I guess she never really did. In fact, over time I think she just got more depressed. She would sit and drink and read Barbara's old letters and just wail. And other times she would sit there with Barbara's childhood photos scattered in front of her, and she would just throw her fist into the air, like she couldn't take it anymore. It was so sad. As for Lee, well, he drank as much as Mabel did, if not more. This went on for a couple of years after Barbara died."

Mabel's health was the next to give out, on September 25, 1971. "Mabel died at home, in bed," says Jan. "She had a bad case of the flu and it went straight into pneumonia. She just gave up, and passed away in her sleep."

Mabel Redfield was 66 when she died, which in itself is amazing, considering how long her alcoholism had lasted. "Mabel was laid out at Benbough's Mortuary, just like Barbara," Jan says. "And her funeral services were every bit as bland as Barbara's, too. Still, it was sad. I felt I had lost my own mother."

According to Jan, Lee fell into a tailspin following Mabel's death and quickly lost himself in misery and beer. "Then, right out of the blue, some dingy lady who claimed she had once been a friend of Barbara's moved in with Lee. She cooked and cleaned, and did God knows what else.

"By the time I heard about it and called Frank (we were divorced by then) to come and throw her out of the house, the dizzbox had already cleaned Lee out of a lot of his valuables. We found out later that she had 'stored' them with her daughter down in L.A., for 'safekeeping.' What a mess that was."

Among the many personal items the woman had made off with were family photo albums and memorabilia from Barbara's career, as well as a few original paintings, the antique Persian rug that Fay Redfield had bequeathed to Lee and Mabel, and some of Mabel's jewelry and her fine china. "Again, the vultures came," says Jan. "They didn't have Barbara around anymore to pick at and devour, so they came after her parents, even though one of them was already dead."

When told that his father had fallen prey to what was obviously a mother and daughter team of grifters, Frank drove down from his home in Glendora and told Lee's lady friend to leave the house or he would call the police. "After a big to-do, the woman's daughter came and got her," says Jan, "and they very reluctantly returned the beautiful silverware that she stole that was always Mabel's favorite. To this day, I have no idea what happened to all the other stuff they took, but I guess they pawned it somewhere for the cash."

By now, Lee was in extremely poor shape and was no longer able to care for himself, so Frank decided to place him in a nursing home near where he lived in Glendora. "He was only there for a few months, though, before his health really nosedived," says Jan. "Like Mabel, it didn't take long for Lee to just give up. He missed her so much."

Lee Redfield died alone in a nursing home, less than one year after burying his wife. Imbued with a constitution sturdy enough to keep the negative effects of his drinking at bay for most of his life, he had lived far longer than his daughter, but had finally called it a day at 74. "His heart gave out," says Jan. "Like everything else, I found out about his dying after the fact—from Frank. He phoned one day to let me know, very matter-of-factly, that he had taken Lee's body back to San Diego and had buried him next to Mabel. To complete the circle, Lee, too, was laid out at Benbough's, though my kids and I, obviously, missed the services. We were heartbroken that we hadn't been invited to them, as we really loved Lee. He was a private man, and not easy to know, but he was a good man.

"I went to the cemetery many times over the years to bring flowers to Lee and Mabel's graves. When I did, I always made sure to bring a single rose for Barbara, which I left at her crypt.

"Despite their problems, Lee and Mabel were a wonderful couple, and I loved them dearly. During the 1960s, things were difficult for all of us in the family (for many reasons), but for me, the good memories will always outweigh the bad. Of Lee and Mabel, and yes, of Barbara, too."

As for Frank and Jan Redfield, despite having serious marital problems by the late '60s, they did their best to help Lee and Mabel overcome their loss after Barbara died. "We went to their house every weekend till things quieted down a bit," recalls Jan. "It was peaceful for a while, but then, Lee and Mabel's drinking really picked up again and before long, so did Frank's.

"I learned a lot of things about life from Barbara and Frank, and their parents, that I didn't even know existed, and not all of them were good, either. During our marriage, Frank always drank too much and I was always the sober one who drove us home (and tried to keep our family solvent and intact). Believe me, I saw enough of what drinking did to all of them—from Lee and Mabel, right on down to Barbara and Frank—to decide early on that it wasn't for me."

It was immediately following Barbara's death, Jan says, that her marriage to Frank really began to deteriorate. "One thing led to another, and soon it was beyond the patching-up stage. Lee was extremely upset when Frank and I separated, and he told me that no one else would ever take my place with them. Several circumstances led to Frank and me divorcing in 1968—but that's not important now. We stayed in touch for a while because of our four children, and Frank got married a few more times (three, to be exact). I haven't heard from him in years, but he stopped drinking long ago, and I hear he's doing well."

"I have no regrets," adds Jan, who has never remarried. "I've lived a good life with all four of my children by my side, and I now have 12 grandchildren and five great-grandchildren. I wonder what Barbara would think of that. She was always an affectionate (and generous) aunt to my kids, and they loved her very much."

Forever taciturn, like his father, all Frank will say about his life before and after his parents' death is, "I worked at Douglas Aircraft for a couple years, and then I secured a job at Aero-Jet General in Azusa where I worked for many years in Classified Materials. I later lived in Glendora,

California for a while, then I moved to another place in the state called Dana Point, and then I bought a houseboat and lived at both the Long Beach and San Diego marinas for a while. Other than that, let's just say that I'm married to a great lady named Marilyn, that I stopped drinking years ago, and that I'm still kickin'."

Frank Redfield remains fiercely protective of his parents' memory, and of his sister's, but he says that it breaks his heart to dwell on what happened to all of them, and "at 75 years of age, I just can't do it anymore. Therefore, this closes the book on my publicly discussing them, forever."

By the early 1960s, Barbara's ex-husband, Tony Provas, had left Mexico and was living in California, where he had put both the "joy and madness" of their time together behind him, he says, "in order to regain my sanity." In 1961, he began working at a pipe, tobacco and men's gift store in Santa Monica and eventually became the manager of the very successful Tinder Box International, Ltd., an enterprise of 225 quality pipe and tobacco shops across the country. Later, when he and his partners sold the business to a Canadian conglomerate, Tony stayed on under a contractual agreement as vice-president in charge of wholesale sales, product acquisition and supplier relations.

"Wearing my product acquisition hat," he says, "I spent a good deal of time traveling all over the world—Europe, Asia (including Red China), Latin America, the Pacific Rim, you name it. I've actually lost count of how many times I've flown around the world on business."

After the Barbara chapter of his life was over, Tony attended both UCLA and Cornell University, and in the 1970s and '80s he was listed in the book *Who's Who in the West*, as a result of his many accomplishments in the industry. He proudly states that his current home, a beautiful hilltop villa overlooking the bay in Mexico, is filled to the brim with numerous awards he was given during his years as a top executive with Tinder Box International.

Obviously, the troubled times Tony had shared with Barbara were mercifully short-lived for him, and he was not only able to move on with his life, but prosper—spiritually and financially—as well. Following his divorce from writer Jorian Clair in 1974, Tony married Estrella Vasquez, who would later become a partner in a very successful art gallery in Beverly Hills. The couple was amicably divorced in 1986 after ten years of marriage. Tony's current wife is a beautiful woman named Cuqui, with whom he is enjoying a sedate retirement filled with lengthy sportfishing excursions and hunting trips. "We are very happy," he says. "I feel more at peace with myself and the world than I've ever felt before."

And yet, he admits: "Every now and then the pangs of guilt over what happened to Barbara still come back to haunt me. Had I persevered more, life might have turned out less tragically for Pate. But, I was young and unworldly, and I didn't understand her illness until many years later, years after her death, when I had to face up to my own alcoholism.

"I must say I am still an alcoholic. I will probably die an alcoholic, but, thanks to God, a wonderful woman, and a team of great doctors, I have finally managed to get my drinking under control. In fact, I haven't had a single drink in nearly fifteen years."

Following his final split with Barbara, Tony never saw any of her family again. "Nor did I make any effort to contact Barbara's parents after her death," he says. "I felt it would have only added to their sorrow. My cousin, Mary, though, stayed in touch with the Redfields. Mary had a summer home in La Jolla, just outside San Diego, and she and Pate were great friends during the time we were married. Mary was very fond of Pate and she faithfully brought flowers to her crypt on a regular basis until she too passed away several years ago.

"If there is one thing I want to make sure people know about Barbara it is that although she was incredibly wild and outrageous—and most definitely, a bad girl—she was not a bad person. Other writers have attributed all these disgustingly off-the-wall and decadent traits to her, but it's just not so. I hate to destroy people's beliefs because I know a lot of individuals want to think that Barbara was the ultimate in 'bad' and that there has never been anyone in Hollywood worse than her. But I knew this woman for nearly eight years and I know what I'm talking about. There was a strong thread of goodness in Barbara—a soulfulness and a deep sense of kindness in her that those other people could only hope to have. I have no bad memories of her. None."

Barbara's son, John Lee, with whom Jan Redfield has remained extremely close, has had the kind of life his mother would have wished for him. During his first year of military service he attended Yale University's Institute of Far Eastern Languages, and following his stint in Vietnam, he married the former Diane Robertson. After completing his enlistment, John enrolled in the University of Texas at Austin as a part-time student while working full-time as the chief of staff of a state senator's office in Austin, a position he held for seven years. Though he and his wife were

LEFT: A 1963 photo of John Lee Payton, unaware at the time of his mother's difficulties in Hollywood. Courtesy of John Lee Payton / RIGHT: John Lee was serving in the Vietnam War at the time of his mother's death. Courtesy of John Lee Payton

divorced during this time, John graduated from UT and attended Austin Presbyterian Seminary for a while. Later, he was editor of the University of Texas System's publication, *Texas Times*, during which time he met and married the former Karen Dinscore. In the 1980s the couple moved to the Texas Hill Country to raise horses, but eventually returned to Austin, he says dryly, "to escape medieval society."

Today, John is a Microsoft Certified Systems Engineer and operates his own business in the Midwest. He has been, as he describes it, "joyfully married for over 25 years to Karen, my soul mate, who works as a medical practice administrator." They have a dearly loved miniature Schnauzer, Bridget, and an eccentric cat named Shorty. Life is good for Barbara's only child, which her family and friends agree is something she always wanted.

"I think about her in some way, every day," John says. "Her light remains a permanent image to me, and rather than it fading, it grows brighter and sharper as the months and years go by. In my mind there is little notice today of the tortured movie star, or of the ruin visited upon her. There is only the simple love a child feels for his mother, a kind of awe and wonder, and a yearning to return once more to that sweet embrace, to feel her happy kiss, and the secure certainty of being held safe within her arms. These are the feelings I have for my mother, and nothing, or no one, can touch them."

It is difficult to think of any other Hollywood actress who went from leading-lady roles to the nightmarish depths to which Barbara ultimately descended. When watching her beauty and talent radiate across the screen in one of her early films, like *Trapped* or *Kiss Tomorrow Goodbye*, it is unsettling to know that you are seeing a young woman who would later experience so much agony in her life.

While certainly responsible for much of the chaos and trouble that surrounded her, perhaps Barbara's greatest sin was simply being born on the wrong side of society's double standard. Clearly, hers is a perfect example of what happened in that era to individuals—particularly women—who believed they could play the Hollywood game with their own set of rules, and win. In fact, no show business tragedy more than Barbara's illustrates the unforgiving wrath 'Old' Hollywood inflicted on those who challenged its cast-in-stone, unwritten code of behavior. Once she came up against the industry's top guns and revealed herself to be a ballsy and irreverent woman whose unconventional lifestyle held little regard for the social norms of the day, Barbara was summarily dismissed from the town's loving fold.

Hollywood can be a ruthless and unforgiving taskmaster, especially to a strong-willed nonconformist—and a female one, at that. One can almost imagine the town's collective pleasure at the thought of breaking Barbara, and its satisfaction when her subsequent troubles forced her permanent exile from the industry.

With a beauty that dazzled the eye, an unquenchable love of fun, drama and danger, a zestful libido, and a wild, rebellious spirit, Barbara was done in by the many weaknesses within her. Over time, her life became a cruel and desperate thing—her fate sealed by long-term drug and alcohol abuse, her undiagnosed mental illness and her lengthy, final descent into overwhelming despair. Her pursuit of sex soon overtook her real quest—to find genuine intimacy, and nurturing—and eventually brought her to the brink of madness. Spiraling down through a catastrophic loss of self-worth and self-esteem, from dizzying wealth into the desolate poverty she lived with for over ten years, Barbara sank into a maelstrom of misery created, in great part, by her own hand. She never learned to help herself, and perhaps just as importantly, her family seemed to suffer from a kind of paralysis, as well—knowing that something was terribly wrong with her but not knowing what it was, or what to do about it. In the end, with a mountain of obstacles stacked against her, Barbara didn't stand a chance.

Hers, it seems, was an incomparable feminine beauty destroyed by the fragilities of the human condition. Even more heartbreaking, however, was the self-destruction of her soul. In Barbara's world, rules were made for others. Early on in her life, she heard a different trumpet call, and she followed it to her doom.

During the audio taping of her memoir in 1963, Barbara allegedly told Leo Guild, "All through my life, even though I thought of myself as a fairly good human being, I was always attracted to evil."

John Gilmore, in his few meetings with Barbara, evidently saw this characteristic in her as well, and says, "Barbara was a fallen angel, but she prided herself on being a bad-girl."

Fallen Angel or Bad Girl? For all that she endured, perhaps it is not unreasonable to think of Barbara, rather, as something of a martyr. With her eyes wide open and her head held high, Barbara sacrificed everything she owned to chase her dreams in Hollywood. She lay down on its altar and willingly handed over all of it—her body, her mind, her very soul—only to be left morally bankrupt in the end. As Bill Ramage puts it, "The siren song of the Hollywood seas beguiled and hypnotized Barbara. But it is not a sea at all. It is a cesspool. And Barbara, poor thing, drowned in it."

The fact that all of Barbara's dreams dissolved after she had actually made most of them come true is one of the saddest and most ironic tragedies of all. That, and her turning her back on herself. Why she did this is anybody's guess, and remains the single most unanswered question about her brief life on earth.

Perhaps the answer to this mystery, and to so many others in Barbara's life, lies hidden in some dark childhood secrets; secrets buried, untold and lost forever, in some vast, intangible space between the Minnesota pines and Texas skies.

In recent years Barbara's story has come to symbolize the downside of sordid film noir glamour, the ultimate Hollywood dream gone ultimately wrong. Somewhere in her story of incredible sadness and pathos lies a strong cautionary tale for the countless young women and men who, to this day, continue to leave their hometowns for Hollywood, and for the lure of its spotlight. They might do well to learn the saga of the wild and beautiful Barbara Payton, taking careful notice of her missteps and, especially, of the tragic, final outcome of her life. Certainly, her story, though unpleasant,

*Barbara met her hapless destiny on L.A.'s Hollywood Boulevard.
From the Author's Collection*

has tremendous potential in preventing other aspiring actors from making similar mistakes. With that in mind, we might consider naming Barbara *Guardian Emeritus* of all Hollywood Starlets. In this way, it's assured she won't ever be forgotten again. And that, I think, would make her happy.

In the crumbling wasteland of this modern-day Babylon, the Santa Ana wind blows the remnants of a fallen angel's shattered dreams across the Sunset Strip. Somewhere in that wind are the haunting echoes of Barbara's memories, from *I Am Not Ashamed*: "If I get a wine with bubbles in it and I drink enough of it, I can look at my reflection in a store window and see myself as I was the first time I wore a mink. I don't go out much anymore, and when I do, it's just down to the Coach and Horses on Sunset Boulevard for a drink. It's just a short walk to the place and once in a while, I steal a look at a window. I try not to look, and I only see what I want to see."

Tonight, if there is any justice at all, this sad-eyed sentinel hovering somewhere over Hollywood, has finally won the peace—and understanding—she found so elusive in life.

Epilogue

The first weekend after Barbara's funeral, Frank and Jan Redfield drove up to San Diego from their home in West Covina to see how Lee and Mabel were faring. As they were coming up the long hill leading to the Redfields' house, Jan noticed that Lee was out in the street, leaning over to place a small box at the curb, next to some garbage cans. The box was open and Jan immediately recognized its contents as those once belonging to Barbara.

"That little box contained all the things Barbara had owned when she died," says Jan. "A couple of folded-up housecoats, a pair of blue jeans and a sweatshirt, the terry cloth dress she had died in, her flip-flops, and a pair of her old moccasins on top. It was garbage day and Lee had left the box for the trash man."

Lee later admitted that he wanted to remove all physical reminders of his daughter from the house. "I know Lee loved Barbara," says Jan, "but he just couldn't stand her lifestyle. In the end, it had killed her, and those few belongings of hers only reminded Lee of all that she had lost. For years he wanted her to get on the straight and narrow, and she just refused to do it.

"Later that day, the junk man came and took away all the garbage—including those final possessions of Barbara's. It was sad and it broke Mabel's heart, but Lee insisted it was for the best. 'They were just clothes,' Lee said. 'Not memories.' I remember him sitting on the patio and just quietly watching the garbage truck take away that last little bit of Barbara's stuff. Once the truck was out of sight, Lee put his head down for a minute and just shut his eyes. But he didn't cry. He was always too strong for that."

As Lee had always said to his family, "We don't cry over spilled milk, we just mop it up."

During his lifetime, Lee Redfield would never admit what Barbara had meant to him, not even in his final days at the nursing home. But one hopes today that whatever problems existed between them have now been resolved, wherever they are, and that they are at peace with one another, just as a father and his daughter should be.

More than forty years after her death, the star that fell to earth has somehow been restored and burns brighter than ever. Her legacy can be found in the loving memories of those who remember her: from her devoted son, who continues to feel her presence in his every heartbeat and breath; from her surviving family and friends, who remember her beautiful eyes, her kindness and all the laughter; to the many thousands of people across the world who continue to be moved, and mesmerized, by her story.

These people know that Barbara mattered. She mattered.

And she will never be forgotten.

A rare autograph of Barbara's from the 1960's.
Courtesy of John Lee Payton

Notes

1. This is not entirely accurate. Several newspaper articles from June 1949 state that Barbara had just been signed to co-star with former war hero Audie Murphy in the U-I western, *The Kid from Texas*. However, by the time the film was made, later that year, Barbara had already left the studio. When the picture was released in June 1950, actress Gale Storm played the role initially meant for Barbara; that of Irene Kain, Murphy's leading lady.

2. Barbara would have been fortunate to have fared as well in Hollywood as Donna Martell. The latter worked often, both in films and television, and as of 2007, she was still a popular guest at many movie memorabilia shows throughout the country.

3. The film *Mighty Joe Young*, of course, would be made later that year, with future Howard Hughes girlfriend (and alleged "secret wife") Terry Moore starring in the role that Frank Redfield claims was first offered to Barbara. Though not a huge box office hit upon its initial release, the heartwarming film, and its endearing title character, would eventually garner a huge legion of fans, making *Mighty Joe Young* a bona fide classic today.

4. It is thought that Barbara's son lived predominantly with Al and Dorothy Zollinger during this time.

5. Don Cougar was the former boyfriend of Barbara's pal, Lila Leeds (*She Shoulda Said No*), the sexy, blonde starlet who made national headlines on September 1, 1948, when she was arrested

in Hollywood with actor Robert Mitchum and two others, for possession of marijuana. In her own rapid descent into infamy, Leeds (born Lila Lee Wilkinson on January 28, 1928 in Dodge City, Kansas) served 50 days in the L.A. county jail, was barred from the state of California in 1949 after a reckless driving arrest, and was later arrested in the mid-1950s on drug and prostitution charges. She eventually turned her life around, however, and by 1973, Leeds was working as an ordained minister of a spiritualist church on Hollywood's Skid Row. She passed away on September 18, 1999.

6. Though not specified in the trades, the film Universal wanted Barbara for was most likely *Francis*, the first installment of the popular series that featured Donald O'Connor and the smart-mouthed title character, a talking mule. Actress Patricia Medina later won the role of O'Connor's love interest in the film.

7. Another legendary hotel in town, the Garden of Allah, occupied an entire city block on the corner of Sunset and Crescent Heights Boulevards, land that had once belonged to silent film actress Alla Nazimova. In the 1920s, Nazimova was advised by her business consultants to convert her palatial mansion on the property into a hotel with bungalows that would cater to some of the town's biggest stars. By the time the complex was finished, however, Nazimova was bankrupt and was forced to sell her shares of the business. In the end, the ailing, ex-movie star was reduced to renting a tiny room in a corner of her former home. For years, a classy getaway for the industry's most serious artists and hell raisers alike, the Garden of Allah eventually lost its luster, and in June 1959, it was torn down and replaced by a shopping center.

8. Barbara's divorce from husband John Payton, from whom she had separated in 1948, would be granted in September 1951 (exactly one year after the decree was issued).

9. In their book, *The Motion Picture Guide*, authors Jay Robert Nash and Stanley Ralph Ross suggest that Gregory Peck was "somewhat offended that he had to play opposite a no-name actress like Payton after having worked with the likes of Ingrid Bergman, Greer Garson

and Jennifer Jones." This, despite the fact the actor received a generous $210,000 from Warner Bros. to star in what was essentially a very average and nondescript film.

10. Marty Baumann's *The Astounding B Monster* website quite accurately calls Tom Neal, "a stereotypical struggling actor who trooped through any number of horse operas and cut-rate soaps."

11. The June 1964 issue of *Modern Man* magazine describes Tom Neal in 1951 as "…a real Hollywood glamour boy. Built like Tarzan, topped with dark, curly hair, and with a mouth so crammed with teeth it makes a Pepsodent ad look like a case of pyorrhea."

12. *Detour*'s strong constituency of admirers is such that, in 1993, it was the first Poverty Row movie chosen by the Library of Congress for celluloid preservation.

13. At one point in the early 1940s, Tom Neal shared a Malibu Beach house with Errol Flynn and actor Bruce Cabot (of *King Kong* fame). Tom Neal, Jr. claims that, "Dad told me once that during the time the three of them lived there, they would pass-around Hollywood starlets back and forth to one another, like they were candy."

14. In his book, *Women in Horror Films*, author Gregory Mank writes that Tom Conway "…would turn up decades later as an alcoholic derelict in a Venice Beach boarding house." After years of battling the bottle, liver disease would claim the actor's life in April 1967.

15. Barbara later told police she awakened to find herself lying on top of a comatose Franchot Tone. A tabloid article, written right after the incident occurred, reported, "When Neal socked her, Barbara's party dress tore clear up to there… revealing the sexy legs Tone and Neal both knew so well."

16. One of the oddest and most absurd allegations about the brawl comes from author Darwin Porter. In his 2005 book, *Howard Hughes: Hell's Angel*, Porter asserts that the eccentric billionaire had his aide, Johnny Meyer, pay Tom Neal many thousands of dollars

to stake out Franchot Tone and "beat the shit out of him." This was supposedly done as retribution, not only for Tone's alleged attack on Hughes a year earlier, in which the actor had reportedly found him in bed with Barbara and knocked out two of his front teeth, but also for a death threat that Tone was said to have later made to Hughes. According to Porter, after the Tone/Neal brawl, Barbara was also paid off by Hughes—to the tune of $300,000. While Darwin Porter's spin on the altercation is rather fanciful, both in its intrigue and its complexity, his various claims about it remain highly unlikely (and even downright laughable). Porter seems to be unfamiliar with the term 'crime of passion', which most would agree seems to more accurately describe the events surrounding the brawl.

17. Barbara later vehemently denied the story of her attempted suicide. "It's ridiculous," she told reporters. "I love life way too much to ever want to leave it voluntarily."

18. The pictures were evidently so sought after, they reportedly made their way across the country to the east coast, as well. Tom Neal's son, Patrick (a.k.a. Tom Neal, Jr.), claims that former 1930s child star Frankie Thomas once told him, "Every stockbroker on Wall Street in the 1950s owned copies of those photos." The younger Neal, however, has never seen them, nor can he recall his father ever mentioning them to him.

19. The final divorce decree was issued one year later, on May 21, 1953.

20. His appearance in the infamous, if popular, camp classic, *Cat-Women of the Moon* (1954) notwithstanding, Sonny Tufts' Hollywood film career pretty much faded out after *Run for the Hills*. Following a handful of disastrous TV talk show interviews in the mid-1960s, in which he appeared noticeably drunk on-camera, he made his final film appearance in 1967, in the dreadful junkyard feature, *Cottonpickin' Chickenpickers*. Two years later, he made news and tabloid headlines when he was hospitalized after falling off a bar stool at Hollywood's Cock 'n Bull Lounge, and, on June 4, 1970, Tufts died of pneumonia at Santa Monica's St. John's Hospital, at the age of 59.

21. In their book, *Hollywood Players: The Forties*, authors James Robert Parish and Lennard DeCarl assert that, "Barbara's acting [in the film] consists of trying to encase her voluptuous charms in a too-tight, too-small blouse."

22. Later on, Barbara followed her passion for jazz and R&B into the dim and smoky nightclubs on L.A.'s (mostly black-populated) Central Avenue, where, for a brief time, she openly dated African-American jazz trumpeter Bernard "Step-Buddy" Anderson. Unfortunately, however, nothing else about their alliance is known.

23. Barbara later claimed that her role in *Murder Is My Beat* was bankrolled by her affair with an affluent stockbroker she would only identify as "Mr. Shellout."

24. Strange as it seems, apparently there are no photos that remain of Barbara and Tony together. He claims that while there were once several photographs of the couple ("as well as home movies my family took of us") stored in a wareroom at his family's home in Nogales, Arizona, they are no longer there ("and I don't know what happened to them").

25. While Tony Provas says he cannot recall any film producers in Mexico ever offering to hire Barbara, he concedes that it could have happened, and that "Barbara may have simply forgotten to tell me about it."

26. Tragically, in 1972, at age 63, an emotionally spent and out-of-work Earl Fenton would commit suicide in Hollywood, by way of a gunshot wound to the head.

27. Tony Provas emphatically denies this allegation, and adds that he does not wish "to dignify it with a rebuttal."

28. The Redfields claim that Barbara and Tony were, in fact, barely together at all during their second marriage. "Barbara always spent a lot more time in California than she did in Mexico," says Jan Redfield. "Even when they were married, I believe her visits there were few and far between."

29. Barbara's claim in her autobiography that she was given a non-speaking, walk-on part in the Frank Sinatra/Dean Martin comedy-western, *Four for Texas* (Warner Bros., 1963) remains highly doubtful. A close inspection of the film shows no evidence of Barbara, not even in the most crowded of background scenes. She also falters when she states in the book that her birth name was Barbara Faye, and that she once appeared in a Dennis Morgan/Jack Carson film at Warners Bros. According to her family, neither statement is true. Finally—and perhaps, most outlandishly—Barbara states that while she was in England in 1952 she was given the part of a nun in a British film. Needless to say, this allegation, too, is totally false.

30. When he researched the L.A.P.D. Archives in 2003, private detective Robert Scott, of Inter-Agency Investigations in Beverly Hills, was unable to find any record of Barbara's incarceration following her 1960s' arrest for shoplifting.

31. Jerry Reeder died in Palm Springs on New Year's Day, 2002, at the age of 69.

32. This claim of John Rayborn's has never been proven, and with Warner Bros. having nothing in its employee file on Barbara except for several 8 x 10 glossies, the claim cannot be verified and remains doubtful.

33. Barbara's former husband, John Payton, adamantly denied this allegation. In 2005, the retired Air Force Colonel insisted, "That's not what happened at all. The Barbara I knew and loved was not deceptive and would never have 'tricked' me into doing anything, much less, moving to Hollywood. It is simply not true—like so many other things that have been said (and written) about Barbara."

34. Using the name Tom Neal, Jr., Patrick Neal worked at an acting career for a while and starred in producer Wade Williams' remake of *Detour* [1989], playing the same hapless character his father had played forty-four years earlier. When the picture failed to generate much interest from film noir fans, Patrick subsequently gave up acting and went to work as a building contractor in Kansas City, Missouri.

35. For the record, neither Lee Wiseman, nor Cheryl Perry (who was also a neighbor of the Redfields), claim to know of any physical abuse occurring between Lee and Mabel. To the majority of people who knew them, the couple's genuine devotion to each other precludes any chance of that ever happening.

36. Jan's brother, Ron Zollinger, also battled addictions to drugs and alcohol, and in 2002 he succumbed to a heart attack at age 59.

Selected Bibliography

Adams, Jerome. "How Lila Leeds Became a Dope Addict!" *Hush-Hush*, January 1957: 8-11, 46-49.

Andrews, Allen. "Miss Payton Goes Home to Cook." *Illustrated*, November 1, 1952: 16-17.

Benson, N.E. "The Girl Who Made Peck a Bad Boy." *Confidential*, May 1956: 37-39, 56-57.

Blottner, Gene. *Universal-International Westerns, 1947-1963: The Complete Biography.* Jefferson, N.C.: McFarland & Company, Inc., 2001: 321-324.

Buhle, Paul, and McGillan, Patrick. *Tender Comrades: A Backstory of the Hollywood Blacklist.* New York: Griffin Trade Paperback, 1999: 356, 362.

Cassa, Anthony. "Barbara Payton: No More Tomorrows." *Hollywood Studio Magazine*, Vol. 15, No. 9, 1982.

Corvell, Al. "Why the Boys Won't Ask Barbara Payton 'What's Cookin'?" *Uncensored*, March 1958: 24-26, 57.

Crivello, Kirk. *Fallen Angels: The Lives and Untimely Deaths of 14 Hollywood Beauties.* Secaucus, New Jersey: Citadel Press, 1988: 54-67.

Dowdy, Andrew. *The Films of the Fifties: The American State of Mind*. New York: William Morrow and Company, Inc., 1973: 200-202.

Eyewitness Detective. "The Rise and Fall of Barbara Payton," May 1956: 26-29.

Fiore, Carlo. *Bud: The Brando I Knew*. New York: Delacorte Press, 1974: 13-132.

Fishgall, Gary. *Gregory Peck: A Biography*. New York: Scribner, 2002: 156-159, 274.

Fowler, Will. *Reporters: Memoirs of a Young Newspaperman*. California: Roundtable Publishing Company, 1991: 282-286.

Gentry, Milt. "Barbara Payton: A Hollywood Tragedy." *Modern Man*, June 1964: 8-10, 51.

Gilmore, John. *Laid Bare: A Memoir of Wrecked Lives and the Hollywood Death Trip*. Los Angeles: Amok Books, 1997: 201-205.

Golden, Milton M. *Hollywood Lawyer*. New York: Signet Books, 1960: 169-192.

Grange, Kenneth. "Barbara Payton's Downbeat Diary." *Exposed*, April 1956: 54-56.

Guild, Leo. "She Wasn't Ashamed." *Pix*, Autumn 1967: 24-25, 32-33.

Healey, Richard J. "The Queens of Sunset Strip: Inside Hollywood's Bedroom Jungle," *Nightbeat*, December 1957: 20.

Hollywood Yearbook. "We Deplore Tone-Payton: Everybody Kissed the Bride!" Vol. 1, No. 3, 1952: 68-69.

James, Stephen. "Caught... Guy Madison in Barbara Payton's Boudoir!" *Confidential*, March 1956: 23-25, 56-58.

Johnson, Tom. "Fallen Star." *Los Angeles*, November 1987: 166-176.

Lamparski, Richard. *Lamparski's Hidden Hollywood*. New York: Simon & Schuster/Fireside, 1981: 114.

Lyons, Arthur. "Killer Career." *Palm Springs Life*, August 1989.

Mank, Gregory William. *Women in Horror Films, 1940s*. Jefferson, N.C. McFarland & Company, Inc., 1999.

Marlowe, David. "The Girl Who Fell Out With the Headlines." *Picturegoer*, September 20, 1952: 10.

Marx, Arthur *The Secret Life of Bob Hope: An Unauthorized Biography*. New York: Barricade Books, 1993: 249-257, 258, 259, 261, 299.

Nash, Jay Robert. *Murder Among the Rich and Famous: Celebrity Slayings That Shocked America*. New York: Arlington House, Inc., 1983: 165-170.

—— and Ross, Stanley Ralph. *The Motion Picture Guide*. Evanston, Illinois: Cinebooks, 1986.

On the Q.T. "How Call Girl Lila Leeds Became a Republican Plot," July 1956: 20-23, 48-50.

O'Sean, Donald. "Barbara Payton: How She Went from a Plush Life to a Lush Life." *Inside Story*, January 1963: 20-21, 54-56.

Parish, James Robert, and DeCarl, Lennard. *Hollywood Players: The Forties* New York: Arlington House Publishers, 1976: 398-403.

Payton, Barbara. "How I Went from a $10,000 a Week Movie Queen to a $5.00 Party Girl!" *Confidential*, June 1963: 13-19, 54-56.

Payton, Barbara. *I Am Not Ashamed*. Los Angeles: Holloway House, 1963.

Peary, Danny. *Cult Movie Stars* New York: Simon & Schuster/Fireside, 1991: 400-401, 427-428.

Police Dragnet Cases. "Dope—Vice and the Mobs: New Thrills for Jaded Passions." September 1955: 28-31, 49-52.

Polito, Robert. *O.K. You Mugs: Writers on Movie Actors* [*Barbara Payton: A Memoir*]. New York: Vintage Books, 2000. 23-24, 25-33.

Porter, Darwin. *Brando Unzipped.* New York: Blood Moon Productions, Ltd., 2006: 513-516.

Quirk, Lawrence J. *Bob Hope: The Road Well-Traveled.* New York: Applause Books, 1998: 187-188, 235-238.

Rains, Bob. *Beneath the Hollywood Tinsel: The Human Side of Hollywood Stars.* Prospect, Connecticut: Biographical Publishing Company, 2001: 70-72.

Richards, Steve. "Barbara Payton: No Tears, No Pity." *Sockamagee!* Winter, 1996: 2-3, 25.

Routh, Marianne. *Cruel City: The Dark Side of Hollywood's Rich and Famous.* Malibu, California: Roundtable Publishing Company, 1991: 163-165.

Rimoldi, Oscar. "Tom Neal: A Tormented Life Marked by Violence and Tragedy." *Hollywood Studio Magazine,* Vol. 17, No. 1, 1984: 22-24.

Screen Stars. "When Stardom Doesn't Come." June 1964: 24-25, 55-56.

Sensation. "Barbara Payton: Hot Love Hits Tank Towns," June 1954: 25-29.\

Sheilah Graham's Hollywood Yearbook. "Tone-Payton: A Great Show While It Lasted!" Vol. 1, No. 4, 1953: 34.

Shepler, Michael. *The Barbara Payton Story.* Berkeley, CA: Hit & Run Press, 1988.

Silver, Alain, and Porfirio, Robert. *Film Noir: An Encyclopedic Reference to the American Style.* Woodstock, New York: The Overlook Press, 1980: 191.

Sloan, Craig. "How Franchot Tone's Ex-Wife Became a Common Prostitute." *Vice Squad*, April 1964: 22-25, 47-53.

Smith, David H. *Midnight Marquee Actors Series: Lon Chaney, Jr.* Arlington, VA: Midnight Marquee Press, Inc., July 1997: 203-207.

Somers, Gene. "Did Too Many Boudoirs Ruin Barbara Payton?" *Uncensored*, February 1964: 32-33, 42-43.

Streete, Horton. "Have Tux, Will Travel… And That's What Bob Hope Did With That Blonde." *Confidential*, July 1956: 11-13, 48.

Strick, Philip. *Science Fiction Movies*. London, England: Octopus Books, 1976.

Sullivan, Emmett. "Babs Payton: Is She Through?" *Bare*, April 1956: 3-6.

Thomas, Bob. *Joan Crawford: A Biography*. New York: Bantam Books, 1979: 93-94, 101.

Warren, Bill. *Keep Watching the Skies!: American Science Fiction Movies of the Fifties, Volume I, 1950-1957*. Jefferson, N.C.: McFarland & Company, Inc., 1982: 113-114.

Weaver, Tom. "Remembering Lon Chaney, Jr." *Cult Movies*, No. 38, 2003: 49-51.

────── *Attack of the Monster Movie Makers: Interviews with 20 Genre Giants*. Jefferson, N.C.: McFarland & Company, Inc., 1994: 47-49.

Whitman, George V. "Sin, Sex and Death—Hollywood Unveiled." *Police Files*, August 1956: 14-19, 59-60.

Wroth, Bert. "Lila Leeds Nabbed As Chicago Call Girl." *Pix Annual*, Fall 1958: 18-21, 51-52.

INDEX

Adams, Stanley, 142-143, 226, 237, 239, 496
Allison, Marie, 50
Anderson, Bernard "Step-Buddy", 597
Arce, Hector, 110
Arnaz, Desi, 341-342, 501
Avist, Russell, 467-468

Bacon, James, 206, 230-231
Bad Blonde (a.k.a. *The Flanagan Boy*), 279, 287-290
Ball, Lucille, 70-71, 341-342, 501
Ballard, Tina, 40-42, 63, 111, 135-136, 155, 177-178, 181, 193, 203, 212, 214, 303, 315-316, 319, 327-328, 333-334, 341, 346, 361-362, 381, 414, 428, 435-436, 438-439, 441, 447, 557, 558, 572-573
Ballard, Dave, 41, 136, 557
Barrack, Randal, 403-405
Bastian, Don, 497
Baumann, Marty, 595
Bautzer, Greg, 62-63, 66-67
Best, James, 52
Bialac, Jerry, 61, 112-113, 198, 207
Blyth, Ann, 53-54
Bougas, Nick, 500-501, 569
Brando, Marlon, 359, 361-364
Bride of the Gorilla, 170-171, 173-174, 176, 178, 181, 195, 248-249
Bridges, Lloyd, 77-81
Bright, June, 47, 362
Briskin, Ted, 61
Broder, Jack, 170-173, 176, 178, 293
"Broncho", 481

Brooks, Florence, 533
Brothers, Dr. Joyce, 250
"Budo", 321-324
Burks, Lisa, 97, 133, 142, 225, 253-254, 259-260, 527-529, 562-563
Burr, Raymond, 173, 178, 433
Burr, Walter Delano, 182-183, 187, 193-194, 262-266, 270-276, 299, 316, 360-361, 518-519, 523, 566

Cagney, James, 37, 85-86, 92-93, 97-99, 249, 492, 577
Cagney, William, 86, 91, 93, 98-99, 105, 151, 238, 505
Calvert, George, 15-16, 18-19, 543, 576
Carreras, James, 281
Carreras, Michael, 281, 291
Carroll, Harrison, 102
Carson, Ken, 514-515
Castle, Peggie, 59
Caulfield, Joan, 429, 431-432, 477, 569
Chandler, Jeff, 52
Chaney, Lon, 152, 173-174
"Chip", 450-451
Clary, Patricia, 88
Close to My Heart, 167-168
Cochran, Steve, 103, 105-110
Cohen, Herman, 171, 173, 194-195, 571
Cohen, Mickey, 62, 563
Confidential, 69-70, 154, 167, 342, 381, 398-399
Conway, Tom, 173, 175, 195, 595
Cooper, Gary, x, 103, 107, 110, 249
Cougar, Don, 50-51, 60, 83, 106, 136, 142-144, 237-238, 593

607

Craig, James, 159
Crawford, Joan, 60, 117, 123, 129, 187, 190
Crivello, Kirk, 496-497, 511, 522, 567
Cross, Jimmy, 198, 200
Curtis, Tony, 52

"Dale", 450-451
Dallas, 103, 105-106, 110, 112, 153
Davidian, Abe, 142, 226, 237, 496
De Carl, Lennard, 531-532
de Dienes, Andre, x, 266-270, 274, 488
DeMartino, Tony, 498
Detour, 188-190, 353, 595, 598
Diaz, Rudy, 302
Dodson, Norma "Knockers", 447-450, 535, 537
Dorn, Dolores, 528
Douglas, Gordon, 154
Dow, Peggy, 52, 59
Dowdy, Andrew, 176, 452-453, 488
Doyle, Elmer D., 390
Drake, David, 81-82
Drums in the Deep South, 112, 159-166, 246, 386, 416, 564
Duff, Howard, 52
Duncan, John (a.k.a. Johnny), 62

Easton, Robert, 161-165, 201, 564-565
Evil Eyeful, The, 151

Felton, Earl, 81, 387, 597
Fiore, Carlo, 359-362, 364
Fisher, Terence, 282, 285, 291
Flanagan, Barbara, 222-224
Fleischer, Richard, 75-76, 79, 81, 565
Flynn, Errol, 68-69, 102, 106, 112, 114, 116, 192, 595
Foster, Ray, 496-497
Four for Texas, 598
Four-Sided Triangle (a.k.a. *The Monster and the Woman*), 279, 281-285
Fowler, Will, 204
Foy, Bryan, 68, 113
Francis, 594

Gable, Clark, 130-131, 370, 416
Garden of Allah, The, 116, 333, 594
Gardner, Ava, 102, 190

Gilmore, John, 63, 246, 490, 492-493, 495, 513, 524-525, 532-533, 562, 588
Goetz, William, 51, 100
Gold, Lee, 497-498
Golden, Charlene, 28, 428-429, 431-434, 440-441, 476, 569
Golden, Mildred, 12, 24
Golden, Milton, xi, 28, 254-255, 260, 376-377, 380, 388, 428-434, 440, 476, 566
Graham, Sheilah, 210, 235, 293
Great Jesse James Raid, The, 305-310, 357
Guild, Leo, 25, 110, 479, 481-483, 485, 559-560, 588
Gwynn, Edith, 210-211

Hahn, S.S., 145
Hall, Bobby, 415-417
Harrison, Robert, 398
Hayes, Steve (a.k.a. Ivan), 66-69, 105, 112-113, 115-117, 130-131, 168, 201, 297, 299-302, 333, 341-342, 349-350, 361, 363, 415-417, 537-538, 571-572
Heisler, Stuart, 103, 105
Hilser, Bill "Red", 501, 506-507
Hodge, William, 28-29
Hope, Bob, x, 69, 70-72, 75, 102, 398-399, 466, 497
Hopper, Dennis, 495-496
Hopper, Hedda, 201-204, 229, 233, 235, 337
Houston, David, 215, 518-519, 531, 534
Hudson, Rock, 52
Hughes, Howard, 62-63, 65, 561, 593, 595-596
Hughes, Mary Beth, 168

I Am Not Ashamed, 25, 480-488, 513
Ireland, John, 61, 63

Jacobson, Phil, 486-487
Jamison, Steve, 403-405
Jamison, Tom, 403
Johnson, Anna, 83, 238
Johnson, Berniece, 16, 19, 21-22, 29-30, 462-463
Johnson, Tom, 29
Jones, Ray, 52

Kellett, Ruth, 459-460
Kid From Texas, The, 593
Kilgallen, Dorothy, 315
King Brothers, The, 112, 159, 163, 416, 565
Kiss Tomorrow Goodbye, 85-86, 93, 97, 99, 102-103, 132, 152, 357
Kitt, Eartha, 331-332
Knox, Mickey, 338-341, 565
Kovisto, Aile, 11
Kuitu, Richard, 14-15, 24-25, 541, 544

La Bar, Fritzy, 386
Lackey, Jana Payton, 574, 576
Lady in the Iron Mask, 217
Lance, Leon, 432-433
Lane, Vicky, 191-192
La Roy, Rita, 47, 49, 362, 477
Laughton, Charles, 276
Laurie, Piper, 59
Le Borg, Reginald, 287, 307
Leeds, Lila, 387, 409-412, 414, 593-594
Leslie, Joan, 238
Lesnick, Joe, 488-490
Lippert, Bob, Jr., 305, 307-310, 443, 517-518
Lippert, Robert, 305
Lohan, Lindsay, 250
Lowe, Skip E., 195, 244-246, 333, 464, 467, 512-513
Lowery, Robert, 62
Lubin, Arthur, 100
Lugosi, Bela, 172, 350, 353
Luokkala, Barbara Lee, 8, 14
Lyles, A.C., 60, 63-64, 96-97, 246

MacRae, Sheila, 341
Madison, Guy, 159, 166-167
Madray, Thomas, 347
Magers, Boyd, 53, 307-308
Maley, Peggy, 331
"Mamie", 197, 271, 331, 337
Mank, Gregory, 595
Mansfield, Jayne, 250, 505
Martell, Donna, 52, 55-57, 59, 62, 70, 393, 564, 593
Martin, Inez, 183
Marx, Arthur, 69-70
Mayo, Virginia, 92, 99, 157, 240, 569
Mc Colloch, Beverly Moore, 26

Meeker, Ralph, 61
Menzies, William Cameron, 160, 162-163
Merrick, Jack, 386
Metz, Don, 363-364
Meyer, Johnny, 63, 595
"Mickey", 360, 362-363
Mighty Joe Young, 64, 593
Miller, Barbara Payton, 31, 36
Miller, Marian, 450-451
Mitchum, Robert, 387, 410, 594
Modglin, June, 131-132, 332
Modglin, Kent, 131-132, 332
Monroe, Marilyn, x, 85, 113, 289, 429, 505, 564
Montgomery, Robert, 53-54
Moore, Terry, 432, 593
Morriss, Bentley, 479, 481, 566-567
Muir, Florabel, 210, 229-237, 239
Murder is My Beat, 353-357, 597
Murphy, Audie, 593

Nazimova, 594
Neal, Gail Kloke, 518-523
Neal, Patrick (a.k.a. Tom Neal, Jr.), 194, 518-519, 530-531, 533-534, 595-596, 598
Neal, Tom, 181-195, 197-215, 217-227, 243-252, 257-260, 262-263, 265-266, 271-276, 287, 290, 293, 296-297, 299-303, 305-319, 353, 465-466, 492, 506, 517-525, 529-534, 566, 595-596
Nunley, Mary Kuitu, 14, 451-452
Nurmi, Maila (a.k.a. Vampira), 385-386, 425

O'Connor, Donald, 99-100, 594
O'Donnell, Judson, 200, 204
Once More, My Darling, 53, 55
Only the Valiant, 151, 153-157, 159, 165

Paal, Alexander, 281
Parish, James Robert, 531-532, 597
Parsons, Louella, 28, 201, 204, 229, 233, 235, 337, 477
Payton, Barbara Smith, 573-574
Payton, John (a.k.a. Jack), 31-38, 41-42, 44, 49, 345-346, 388-392, 394-396, 573-574, 594, 598

Payton, John Lee, x, 42-45, 49, 56, 211-212, 261, 263, 265, 275-276, 317, 319-324, 327-331, 336, 342-343, 345, 359-360, 366-367, 375, 378-379, 385-386, 388, 390-396, 423-425, 427, 493, 549, 557-559, 570, 574, 576-578, 585-587
Pearce, Ann, 59
Peck, Gregory, x, 151-152, 154-155, 157, 249, 594-595
Pecos Pistol, 53-54
Perry, Cheryl, 442-443, 462-463, 548, 599
Peterson, Millie, 571
Peterson, Nan, 80
Polito, Robert, 356, 510
Porter, Darwin, 63, 561, 595-596
Postman Always Rings Twice, The, 310-315
Provas, Tony (a.k.a. Jorge Antonio Provas-Dominguez), 62, 178-179, 350, 369-373, 377-383, 385-387, 393, 399-405, 407-408, 417-421, 423-427, 432, 434-435, 437-439, 445-446, 483, 485, 551, 574-575, 584-585, 597

Quirk, Lawrence J., 398-399

Raft, George, 57-60, 102
Rains, Bob, 69-70, 99
Ramage, William (a.k.a. Bill), 105-106, 110, 233, 235, 312, 316-317, 376-377, 429-434, 440-441, 455, 475-478, 485, 487, 490, 492-493, 501, 510, 513-515, 537, 539-540, 567-569, 588
Rawley, Jess, 545, 559
"Ray", 464-466
Rayborn, John, 502-509, 514, 572, 598
Redfield, Erwin Lee, 6-10, 13-17, 19-21, 24-25, 34, 138-139, 221, 261-262, 324-326, 337, 407-408, 417-418, 442-443, 461-464, 498-499, 538-539, 541-548, 553, 556-558, 576, 581-583, 591-592, 599
Redfield, Fay, 6, 9, 15-19, 220, 543-544, 575-576, 582
Redfield, Frank Jr. (a.k.a. Tim), 6, 17, 221
Redfield, Frank L., 6, 7, 10, 17
Redfield, Frank III, 8, 14-16, 18-21, 23-24, 26, 28-29, 33, 36-37, 39, 44-47, 63-64, 132, 135, 138-139, 224, 324-325, 365, 383, 402-403, 408-410, 417-420, 462-463, 466, 489, 542, 544, 549, 554, 557, 578-579, 582-584, 591, 593
Redfield, Jan Zollinger, 44-47, 49, 52, 58, 63, 68, 72, 75, 99-100, 106, 128-129, 132, 134-135, 138-139, 157, 168, 207, 212-213, 224, 226, 227, 243, 249, 258-259, 261-262, 264-265, 321, 324-325, 331-337, 350, 360, 363-364, 367, 372, 377-379, 381, 386, 402, 407-410, 412-413, 417-418, 420, 438-439, 444-445, 452, 461-463, 466-468, 485-486, 489, 498-499, 515, 538-539, 542-552, 556-558, 575-576, 579, 581-583, 591, 597, 599
Redfield, Leslie, 7, 261, 325-326, 463-464, 542, 558
Redfield, Mabel Todahl, 7, 9-10, 13-15, 20-22, 24-25, 31, 34, 75, 135, 138-139, 221, 261-262, 324, 334-335, 407-408, 417-418, 442-443, 461-464, 468, 498-499, 538-539, 541-548, 553, 557, 576, 581-583, 591, 599
Redfield, Murel, 6, 18, 220, 543
Redfield, Robert, 221
Reeder, Jerry, 501-502, 504, 598
Rich, Buddy, 50
Richards, Steve, 483
Rode, Alan K., 76
Roll, Ernest, 217-220
Roman, Ruth, 103, 105, 110-111, 432
Rosenstein, Sophie, 52, 57
Rubenstein, Serge, 342
Run for the Hills, 293-296, 596
Russell, Gail, 166
Russell, Marjorie Melby, 13, 15, 221

"Sandor", 362
Saxon, John, 360
Scott, Gordon, 338-339
Scott, Robert, 489, 545, 598
Seiber, Bernard J., 469-471
Sessler, Siegi, 290
Sheridan, Ann, 238
Sherry, Robert, 455, 459
Short, Elizabeth, 490, 492, 495

Silver Butte, 53
Simmons, Guy, 418-420
Sinatra, Frank, 102, 577, 598
Siodmak, Curt, 173
Siodmak, Robert, 173
Six, Bert, 90
Skolsky, Sidney, 113, 114
Smith, Anna Nicole, 250
Snyder, Leslie, 28, 311-312, 316, 440, 477, 569
Stebbins, Evelyn, 429-431
Steelquist, Peter, 546-547
Stevens, Craig, 159
Stompanato, Johnny, 126, 363
Strasberg, Lee, 120, 528
Streete, Horton, 398
Strode, Woody, 257
Sturges, Preston, 67-68
Sullivan, Emmett, 397

Tanner, Eldred, 366, 371
Thomas, Bob, 123
Thomas, Frankie, 596
Todahl, Dora, 7, 13, 543
Tone, Dr. Frank J., 119, 141
Tone, Franchot, 117, 119-135, 141-143, 145, 147, 150, 167, 181, 193, 195, 197-215, 217-227, 229-238, 248, 251-255, 257-260, 461, 466, 492, 495, 506, 517, 527-529, 562-563, 595-596
Tone, Gertrude, 119, 141, 229-230
Trapped, 75-83, 387, 565
Tufts, Sonny, 293-296, 596
Turner, Lana, 102, 126, 190, 310, 363, 366, 453

Ulmer, Edgar G., x, 188, 353
Universal-International, 51-53, 55, 59, 66, 69-70, 99-100, 125, 593, 594

Vickers, Yvette, 348-351, 563-564

"W", Carolyn, 570
Wagner, Laura, 92, 99, 157, 240
Wallace, Jean, 126-129, 145, 147, 225
Wallace, Stone, 86, 487, 570
Warner Bros. Studios, 85-86, 90, 102, 103, 105, 112, 128, 136-137, 149, 151, 159, 167, 176, 238, 240, 505, 595
Warner, Jack L., 105, 144, 167-168, 171, 238-239, 505
Weaver, Tom, 80, 171, 194-195, 571
White Heat, 85-86, 92
Wilde, Cornel, 128, 225
William Cagney Productions, 86, 91, 97, 99, 102-103, 151, 238
Williams, Tex, 53, 59
Williams, Wade, 188, 598
Winger, Jack, 347-348
Winters, Shelley, 52
Wiseman, Lee, 544-545, 599
Wood, Ed, 500-501, 570
Wyne, Brandy (a.k.a. Gloria Brower), 112-113

Young, Gig, 132-133, 151

Zollinger, Dorothy, 44, 49, 261, 263, 266, 319, 379, 388-392, 557, 558, 578, 593
Zollinger, John Allen, 44, 49, 261, 263, 266, 319, 379, 390-392, 557, 558, 578, 593
Zollinger, Ron, 44, 599

www.ingramcontent.com/pod-product-compliance
Lightning Source LLC
Chambersburg PA
CBHW060906300426
44112CB00011B/1363